THE PROPER ORDER OF THINGS

THE PROPER ORDER OF THINGS

Language, Power, and Law in Ottoman Administrative Discourses

HEATHER L. FERGUSON

Stanford University Press
Stanford, California

Stanford University Press
Stanford, California

Printed and bound by CPI Group (UK) Ltd, Croydon, CR0 4YY

Library of Congress Cataloging-in-Publication Data

Names: Ferguson, Heather L., author.
Title: The proper order of things : language, power, and law in Ottoman administrative discourses / Heather L. Ferguson.
Description: Stanford, California : Stanford University Press, 2018. | Includes bibliographical references and index.
Identifiers: LCCN 2017050465 (print) | LCCN 2017053018 (ebook) | ISBN 9781503605534 (electronic) | ISBN 9781503603561 (cloth : alk. paper)
Subjects: LCSH: Turkey—History—Ottoman Empire, 1288–1918. | Discourse analysis—Political aspects—Turkey—History. | Order—Political aspects—Turkey—History. | Administrative law—Turkey—History. | Turkey—Politics and government. | Imperialism.
Classification: LCC DR486 (ebook) | LCC DR486 .F48 2018 (print) | DDC 956/.015—dc23
LC record available at https://lccn.loc.gov/2017050465

Cover image: *'Ahdname* issued upon the accession of Mehmed III reaffirming the terms of Ottoman sovereignty within a genealogy of rule traced back to Selim I. Hungarian National Archives.
Cover design: Rob Ehle
Typeset by Bruce Lundquist in 10.25/15 Adobe Caslon Pro

CONTENTS

ACKNOWLEDGMENTS

All books contain within them an untold story—exactly what it took to transform a series of archival tours and piles of notes into a finished product. For most this is a tricky metamorphosis, and for me it required a community of supporters who believed the transformation was possible even when I could not. I owe a deep debt of gratitude to many who fulfilled this role throughout my academic journey and thus allowed me the opportunity to persevere. This book's story begins with Abraham Marcus, who, during my time at the University of Texas at Austin, unwittingly instilled in me a love for the Ottoman past. Perhaps it had something to do with his instrumental oud playing, but more likely it was his determination to transform meticulous archival research into a portrait of Aleppo's historical horizons, sadly now rent asunder by escalating crises. I may never forgive him for sending me on a journey that would take many years to complete, consuming eight consecutive summers with intensive Arabic, Turkish, and Ottoman language programs and involving archival tours without which I would never have experienced the beauty and the tragedy of being a historian.

My years in the history department at the University of California, Berkeley transformed my interdisciplinary background into a basis for historical inquiry. Leslie Peirce and Mary Elizabeth Berry, sometimes gently, sometimes urgently, forced me to look at what it meant to ask questions historically, and their voices lived on in my head as I labored over the sentences contained in these pages. It has certainly been a lesson in humility to recognize that my answers will perhaps never satisfy, but my ways of thinking and imagining have been expanded by their interventions. I often recused myself from history to the classrooms and offices of anthropologists, where William F. Hanks helped me tweak my understanding of the relationship between historical practices and linguistic forms. His creativity and indefatigable inquisitiveness continue to serve as models for me as I think through research problems and intellectual constructs. Undeniably, I would not still be among the academic fold were it not for the constancy and care of my mentor, Beshara Doumani. He took a chance on my idiosyncratic approach to history, instilled in me practical paleographic tools, and then sustained his passion for my potential as a scholar even when my own lapsed. With his own intellectual endeavors as a standard, I pushed to find my way through the administrative practices of the Ottoman Empire. Words will always fail to express my appreciation, for it was he who helped me across the divide.

Someone pessimistically told me early on that one had to choose between academia and life. I have now come to believe in the possibility of both, and for that I owe much to a community of supporters who believe in simplicity but act with passion. Joel Beinin acted as a mentor and guide from Stanford, sometimes in my darkest hours, and without him my transformation from student into scholar would never have happened. My community of supporters also includes Baki Tezcan, whose wide-ranging historical curiosity and generosity of spirit continues to inspire. The boundless historical curiosity of Linda Darling, her archival work ethic, and visionary approach to weaving the two together provide a model I can only hope to approximate. Guy Burak's voluminous knowledge of historical and contemporary scholarship and creative investigation of the past helped me to maintain an inquisitive approach to my own research even as the months slipped by. He often guided me to scholarship in wide-ranging regions and disciplines, and these threaded their way into the conceptual routes I adopted in this book. A onetime research project with Ira Lapidus turned into years of walks and talks in Berkeley gardens and Madrid museums, and his detailed comments on early drafts guided my approach to writing. Lena Salaymeh and Elyse Semerdjian frequently reminded me to stride forward with courage and commitment, and they also enabled me to see when it was time to finally let go. And this book would never have been written without almost daily contact with David Moshfegh, who is perhaps more grateful even than I to see this project finally materialize. He served as a sounding board, an intellectual interlocutor, and proved himself a master of turning tricky conceptual problems into witty prose.

Research for this book began in Istanbul in the summer of 2005 and has since taken me on many routes and sojourns through the city of Beirut and the coastal highlands of Lebanon, to fortress castles-turned-archives in Budapest and Simancas, and through paleographic conundrums and conceptual puzzles. I remain humbled by the rich and diverse resources that have often overwhelmed me in their immensity, and I would like to thank the staffs of Istanbul's Başbakanlık Archives; Süleymaniye Library; Istanbul University Library; Topkapı Palace Museum Archive and Library; the İslam Araştırmaları Merkezi (İSAM); and the Research Centre for Islamic History, Art and Culture (IRCICA). I am grateful for help from directors in the Tapu ve Kadastro Archives in Ankara and the National Library. While in Budapest, I used Turkish to communicate with Ottoman archivists in the National Archives of Hungary and pored over newly drafted catalogues of materials related to the Ottoman Empire. In Beirut I drank many cups of coffee with directors at the National Archives and was granted a personal tour of Charles V's regal insignia at the archives in Simancas. My tours of places and documents were supported by grants from the American Research Institute in Turkey and the American Council of Learned Societies, as well as by generous faculty research grants from Claremont McKenna College and the Gould Center for Humanistic Studies. In addition, under the directorship of Robert Faggen, the Gould Center generously provided the means necessary to transform ideas into a printed book.

My time as a member of Claremont McKenna College Department of History and general participation in the Claremont Consortium has fundamentally transformed my approach to teaching and scholarship. My colleagues are humbling in their brilliance and productivity one and all, and they possess varied and variegated approaches to historical inquiry that have informed my own. I would like to thank Diana Selig, Lisa Cody, Arthur Rosenbaum, and Nita Kumar for welcoming me into the department, supporting my evolution as a scholar, and helping me to set time lines amid hectic duties. Gary Hamburg has been incredibly generous with his time, and his sharp critical eye has guided me through the terrain of the campus and of the writing process itself. Jonathan Petropoulos and Wendy Lower are both prodigious scholars and thoughtful colleagues, and their ability to combine the two remain significant models for my own academic career.

Lily Geismer, Tamara Venit-Shelton, and Albert Park graciously extended their eyes to drafts and their hands to cheer me on, and Shane Bjornlie, Sarah Sarzynski, and Daniel Livesay demonstrated dedicated commitment to research and indefatigable good cheer that sustained me as I paced hallways and walked the neighborhoods of Claremont. Ken Wolf, at Pomona College, has seen me through these past years through caffeine-fueled weekly conversations that often lasted hours, and Carina Johnson modeled an extraordinary approach to comparative history. I am so grateful for the rich and vibrant intellectual community at the Claremont Colleges.

Finally, and profoundly, I want to thank my mother, who remained avidly involved from a distance through personal messaging and stimulating conversations; my father, who spent many weeks helping me when I might otherwise have been left alone with my thoughts; and Clio, my little canine muse, who kept me walking and so kept me from losing perspective. Most important, Jerry Coté, who probably now knows more than he ever cared to about the early modern Ottomans, has allowed the book to inhabit our lives for the entire time we have been married. I am eternally grateful to him for reminding me that there is a universe that exists in the present, outside our doors, and for waiting for me there until I could return from the archives, documents, and manuscripts of the past.

TRANSLITERATION AND PRONUNCIATION

Quoted passages from Ottoman Turkish, Arabic, and Persian source materials are fully transliterated using a simplified version of the *IJMES* system. Otherwise, the use of special characters is limited to titles of works or for terminology linked to the arguments presented in the text. Ottoman Turkish and Arabic words are provided in italics with modern orthography. The use of the Arabic definite article *al-* for personal names appears without signifying the elision with the following consonant (e.g. "al-Din" in "Fakhr al-Din" should properly be pronounced "ad-DEEN"). For Ottoman personal and geographical proper names, I have adopted Anglicized terms without diacritical marks. Thus, I use *Aleppo* rather than *Halep* and *Katip* rather than *Kātip*. For the provincial seat in Greater Syria, however, the transliterated form *Trablus* differentiates the region from Tripoli, Libya. Terminology employed in Ottoman Turkish but derived from Arabic intellectual traditions shifts in transliteration, depending on the circumstance. Hence *qanun* is used for "law" or "principle" when addressing its etymological derivation and meaning, yet *kanun* is used when exploring its formulation within Ottoman governing parlance. Ottoman Turkish and Arabic words that have migrated into English, such as *emir*, *ulema*, and *janissary*, retain their standard English spellings.

Equivalency Guide for Distinctive Turkish Letters

c j, as in *journey*

ç ch, as in *charity*

ğ unvocalized, lengthens preceding vowel

ı i, as in *bird* or e in *women*

ö ur, as in *hurt* or French *eu* as in *deux*

ş sh, as in *shimmer*

ü u, as in *mute*

Long Vowels in Arabic or Ottoman Turkish

ā a, as in *ah*

ī ee, as in *weed*

ū oo, as in *too*

Although the original sources presented here use the lunar *hijri* calendar, which commences with Muhammad's flight from Mecca to Medina in 622 CE, the dates are provided in Common Era format.

THE PROPER ORDER OF THINGS

INTRODUCTION

The Structure of Empire and a Grammar of Rule

> Gratitude for power is demonstrated by providing shelter and protection to the weak, and by redressing wrongs through the law of justice. . . . Gratitude for the paradisiacal gardens at your palace means to protect and shelter the subjects [*re'aya*] who seek refuge under the shadow of sovereignty. . . . As the prophetic *hadith* said: "You [rulers] are all shepherds and are all responsible for those under your rule."
>
> —Tursun Bey, *Tārīḫ-i ebū'l-fetḥ*[1]

In 1652–53 Tarhuncu Ahmed Paşa, grand vizier to Mehmed IV (r. 1648–87), organized a systematic review of the Ottoman Empire's account books. He gathered scribes of the finance office and head bureaucrats to identify indiscriminate spending and to work toward submitting an annual budget for the upcoming year.[2] There was nothing particularly innovative about this consultative body or its objectives, as reforms in the imperial council during the era of Sultan Süleyman's reign (1520–66) had moved toward interventionist accounting procedures. This effort, however, came amid a particularly discordant moment in the management of Ottoman imperial order and stability. Tarhuncu Ahmed Paşa's demand for a fiscal reevaluation of palace resources joined a series of ventures undertaken by early modern statesmen to address global challenges to centralized states in the late sixteenth and early seventeenth centuries. Price revolutions, climatic change, urbanization, internal rebellions, and demographic mobilization threatened to undermine the compartmentalized political and social order that had sustained composite empires and kingdoms. Vast increases in population across Eurasia beginning in the late 1400s had severely challenged agrarian institutions by the 1600s.[3] Unforeseen monetary fluctuations due to imperialist ventures across the Atlantic interrupted customary modes of revenue-raising and encouraged greater mobility among the empire's inhabitants.[4] This mobility was armed, often literally, by new techniques of recruitment and rebellion. Combined, these factors necessitated a reinvention of legitimacy on the part of the Ottoman establishment, as power shifted in both form and content.[5]

Between 1589 and 1648, finance ministers, grand viziers, religious officials, military commanders, and two sultans lost their lives in an ongoing battle to define the nature and extent of sultanic power in the face of these challenges. Responding to the turmoil, political and intellectual elites suggested new theories of governance and agendas for reform. Outspoken religious preachers rallied urban populations against perceived corruptions in state affairs and social practice. Provincial governors formed armed militias and fomented support for their own regional powerhouses, daring to openly challenge imperial forces. And the bureaucracy expanding behind the walls of the dynasty's Topkapı Palace engendered its own rival cohorts and interest groups capable of both selecting and strangling a sultan.

The outbreak of war with Venice over the island of Crete in 1645 further strained the dynasty's coffers and contributed to the radicalization of political protest across the imperial domain. The battle for the Aegean would last until 1669, but the Venetian capture of Tenedos in 1646 and blockade of the Dardanelles in the following year squeezed the fortunes of dynastic order.[6] Sultan İbrahim (r. 1640–48) had met a violent death when scarcities and heavy taxation aligned garrisoned soldiers in the capital, religious functionaries, and palace factions in yet another dramatic imperial shakeup. The sultan was first imprisoned and then, with a nod from his powerful mother and a religious edict from the head jurisconsult, strangled.[7] Yet his death did not replenish the treasury. Regents of İbrahim's son Mehmed IV, who was only six years old when he ascended to the sultanate, were unable to distribute the donative to the military defenders of the realm despite their necessary participation in the ongoing Cretan campaign. Nonsalaried cavalrymen, dependent on ritualized dispersions of funds and gifts to cement their livelihoods and their loyalty, led yet another uprising to secure more favorable financial reward. Like rebellions in the previous decades, agitants gathered in Istanbul's Atmeydanı (Hippodrome), the traditional center for the dispersion of sultanic largesse and the site where soldiers and elites of the realm swore oaths of allegiance to their sovereign.[8] Suppression of the revolt by garrisoned troops in the city highlighted escalating tensions between cavalry units (*sipahi*) supported by land grants and infantry soldiers (*yeniçeri* or janissaries) recompensed through salaries.

The cavalry units embodied an agrarian imperial ecology dependent on land as the nexus for social control, political alliance, and economic viability. As holders of land grants (*timar*), they administered taxation policies and were required to mobilize men and impedimenta for military campaigns. Janissaries, however, originally recruited through a human tax on non-Muslim populations (*devşirme*), had increasingly become part of a commercialized market economy, acting as real estate agents, coffee-shop owners, and investors. In administrative documents or in the various forms of history writing, commentaries, and reform manuals that proliferated along with the tempestuous movements of the day, neither cavalryman nor janissary adhered to the bounded social, political, and economic roles assigned to them by statesmen, bureaucrats, and intellectuals. But both administrative document and intellectual treatise constructed an idealized system of governance that assigned clear divisions between social groups and sought to remedy present concerns by reasserting foundational principles.

This book suggests that imperial efforts to create and shape a vision of provincial order were intimately linked to, and mutually defined by, the ability to wield influence through legal commands circulated in textual form. These commands were essential to extending centralized authority across vast distances. Thus, while military forces were obviously key to both regional control and expansionary campaigns, internal rebellions and external rivals were also managed through an elaborate reliance on textual edicts of sultanic authority. As such, circulating edicts created a web of textual authority that accompanied and legitimized the use of force. The web of sultanic edicts first created and then imposed a legal and social order, placed the diffuse inhabitants of the realm within intelligible categories used as the basis for both taxation and redress, and gradually articulated a claim to universal sovereignty aimed at subverting internal challengers and external rivals. The arguments contained here thus build on studies concerned with the relationship between empire and textuality and the mechanisms by which the circulation of documents characterized and, in the act of characterizing, produced a particular conception of sovereignty. This conceptual framework defined and supplemented imperial authority and was deployed in the midst of the varied crises Tarhuncu Ahmed Paşa sought to address.

Defining an Ideal Political Order

Tarhuncu's move toward fiscal reforms, and thus toward altering the status quo of palace factions, would cost him his head.[9] He joined the list of ten grand viziers who were appointed and summarily executed or dismissed between 1648 and 1656, when a new innovation of dynastic succession granted the Köprülü family sole jurisdiction over the vizierate until 1703. His death, however, was not in vain, as one probable participant in Tarhuncu's imperial workshop on fiscal reform produced a short pamphlet outlining the perceived financial and moral crises of the empire. This pamphlet, composed by a sometime chancery scribe, prolific writer, and bibliophile with the sobriquet Katip Çelebi, endured as a landmark diagnosis of the crises that ailed the empire. Significantly, it focused on tensions between ideals of administrative order and the realities of provincial management. Katip Çelebi crafted his *Düstūrü'l-ʿamel li ıṣlāḥı'l-ḫalel* (Guiding principles for the rectification of defects) in 1653 according to a vision of proper imperial order and prosperity that had long shaped administrative strategies and textual representations of the Ottoman dynasty.[10] His introduction indirectly references his participation in Tarhuncu's efforts to balance the budget, and in the text he humbly sketches the key problems facing the empire and proffers solutions. His narrative reveals several constituent features of an idealized Ottoman imperial order and introduces key intellectual interlocutors in the process.

First, he adopts a genre of writing that cloaks his criticisms within an acceptable tradition of advice-giving to rulers. Known as mirrors for princes (*speculum principis*) in Latin, this form of writing spanned Eurasian courtly contexts and appeared as *pandnameh* and *andarznameh* (book of advice) in Persian, *nasihat al-muluk* (counsel for kings) in Arabic, and *nasihatname* (book of counsel) in Ottoman Turkish.[11] This genre typically assumes the centrality of a ruler to the health of the state and addresses issues of personal comportment, education, moral probity, and the appointment of wise council and loyal administrators and invokes past exemplars of just rule for present guidance. In the hands of Katip Çelebi and other Ottoman authors of similar treatises during this period, however, the genre morphs from a standard treatment of the sultan's personhood into an analytic summary of political affairs.[12] Neither sultan nor vizier figures prominently in his pamphlet; instead, the state and its destiny stand as objectified units of analysis.

Second, Katip Çelebi builds the organizational features of the state from a composite intellectual tradition that folds philosophy, medical practice, historical analysis, and religious dictates into a set of guiding principles for proper governance. These all appear in summary form as the indices of a coherent political system in Katip Çelebi's text, and in this way they highlight key components of the seventeenth-century Ottoman intellectual world.[13] Medieval philosophers and polymaths such as ibn Farabi (d. 950) and ibn Sina (d. 1037) reshaped Aristotelian ethics and Platonic republican virtue into a lexicon of proper governance inflected by a commitment to the edicts of Islam.[14] These were further qualified by the adoption of two overlapping theories of the body politic: Galen of Pergamon's (d. circa 200–216) extension of anatomical medical practice to philosophies of the social body, and the notable historiographer ibn Khaldun's (d. 1406) assertion that states, like individuals, adhered to cyclical life stages from birth to death.[15] Katip Çelebi drew on these intellectual legacies to describe the Ottoman state as an imperial body composed of organs and humors mapped onto social strata, one that was now evincing signs of maturity and disease that must be diagnosed and treated: "The long-lived Ottoman state has reached its three hundred and sixty-fourth year in the year of the Hegira 1063 [1653]. In accordance with divine custom and human nature, signs of irregularities have emerged in the temper of the sublime state and it is faltering in its natural powers." For this reason, a decree was issued that elect personages and experienced members of the imperial council "gather and take the pulse of this patient and prescribe a cure for this disease so that it [the state] may not—God forbid—yield to a more difficult end."[16]

The body politic emerges in stark outline in the opening sections of the pamphlet. Katip Çelebi explicitly defines the term *devlet* (with its variant meanings of state, fortune, or the fortunate state of the sultan himself) as kingdom (*mülk*) or sultanic power (*saltanat*) that exists "by a form of custom" through the collectivity of individuals who come together in a sociopolitical order.[17] Katip Çelebi suggests that societies, like the human body, "are compounded of four basic fundamentals and ruled by means of state administrators," who are further "bound to the rule of the sublime sultan." He then argues that the symptoms of disease can only be cured if harmony and balance are restored.[18] The basic social strata of the state—men of the military, religious officials *cum* administrators, and the productive actions of merchants and agriculturalists—remain guarded by the spirit and soul of the ruler. Katip Çelebi places these groups in a schema of social order and distributive justice articulated in both linear and graphic forms as the "circle of equity."[19] According to this circle, no sovereign state can exist without a collectivity (*rical*), no collectivity without the sword of defense (*seyf*), no sword without monetary support (*mal*), no fisc without a productive agricultural strata (*ra'iyyet*), and no continued cultivation without justice (*'adl*). Katip Çelebi proposes that the stress on the treasury caused by burgeoning military ranks should be addressed not primarily by cutting the numbers but by securing the productivity of the realm and thereby a surplus for the treasury. Thus, the edicts of just rulers, administrators, and loyal men of the sword appear as his practical suggestions for how curative measures might be implemented and, through these measures, the imperial body's age of maturity prolonged.[20]

In what marks the third facet of his idealized narrative of the Ottoman state, Katip Çelebi asserts that the realm's durability depends on the reinstatement of a natural order. This order, embodied in the fundamental social divisions and interdependencies described earlier, is also configured as an ancient law or practice, the *kanun-ı kadim*. But Katip Çelebi invokes legal order in three ways. In the section devoted to the conditions of the cultivator, he emphasizes the need for a just law (*kanun-ı 'adl*), so that oppression does not diminish yield for the treasury. When prescribing a mechanism for a numerically balanced military, he explicitly invokes the *kanun-ı kadim*, here referencing the interdependency between monies for defense and an organized system of land tenure. Finally, in a concluding statement of warning and entreaty to the elite of the realm capable of reforming the state, he conjoins dynastic, religious, and rational principles (*kanun-ı şer'i ve 'akli*). This insertion of reasoned analysis disrupts a more typical effort to wed mechanisms of state policy with those enshrined in the official Hanafi school of Islamic legal interpretation.[21] It is also a reminder that, even as Katip Çelebi asserts an "ancient" legal code as the basis of a natural imperial order, this code was situationally configured and in this treatise contributed to a deliberate interpretive act: he constructed a vision of collective sovereignty, defined this sovereignty via a selective reading of a mixed intellectual legacy, and warned that the empire would fall to ruin if his prescription and dosage were not judiciously followed.

Katip Çelebi's diagnostic lens, though focused intently on the state of affairs in the Ottoman Empire, was far from myopic. It gestured toward comparisons within the arc of Ottoman history and, if extended to include Katip Çelebi's larger oeuvre, equivalencies with external rivals and competitors. The fourth component of imperial order, therefore, addresses the role of the sultan in securing the system as a whole, and it foregrounds the use of comparative measures to understand dynastic power.[22] He characterized the reign of Sultan Süleyman as a model for emulation, a nostalgic idealization common among seventeenth-century treatises. But he also tempered current crises by referencing past disruptions: "crisis in this sublime state is not new" as challenges emerged in each phase of its consolidation and expansion. He lists three key moments for comparative purposes: "power struggles within the sultanate," which accompanied initial efforts to define a hierarchical order; "the evil wrought by Timur," a reference to the self-stylized Chenggisid warrior's defeat of Bayezid I in 1402, which disrupted the early success of an Ottoman dynastic state; "and later the emergence of the *celālis*," the collective term used by chroniclers for a wave of rebellions that swept the Anatolian and Arab provinces of the empire from the 1590s to the first decade of the seventeenth century and highlighted the potential refusal of imperial inhabitants to heed dictates of social order.[23] For each disruptive moment, "appropriate measures" resolved the crisis and ensured the stability of the state, and, Katip Çelebi implies, so, too, would they resolve the current crisis if a deliberative set of diagnoses for the body politic were duly followed.

This book argues that the various rubrics and devices Katip Çelebi deployed in his manual for state reform emerged from an imperial discourse of proper order and stability. His *Düstūrü'l-'amel* represents both the culmination of efforts to define order and sovereignty in the Ottoman Empire and a new platform that shifted interpretive analysis from the mid-seventeenth century onward. His effort to document crises facing the state within both a specific genealogy of political analysis and a transregional apprehensiveness concerning shifting global dynamics provides the capstone for the arguments constructed here. The period explored in these pages thus encompasses the fifteenth-century consolidation of Ottoman dynastic authority in Istanbul, its regional extension and reformulation in the sixteenth century, and finally the global crises that provoked a period of reassessment in the late sixteenth and early seventeenth centuries. The combined chapters assert that the rubrics detectable in Katip Çelebi's treatise amount to a particular grammar of rule, or a set of discursive categories imposed through administrative edicts and idealized in interpretive treatises, intent on overcoming the challenges posed by a far-flung imperial space. This imperial space was partly managed by a discursive construct of proper order and social harmony, which served simultaneously as a means for creating categories of stabilization (genre), a set of administrative strategies (practice), and a standard for articulating history (objectification). Thus, each chapter introduces a discrete mechanism for assessing the interaction between categories, strategies, and analysis as they collectively constituted an Ottoman imperial system of rule. More pointedly, the book illustrates the way in which Ottomans themselves acted as political strategists and analysts, and the itinerary of their efforts to define the natural order of the state should not be suborned to our own.

Language, Order, and Power in Early Modern Eurasia

The "natural order of the state" was an early modern mania. Often, debates concerning how to identify the state, or where to locate it in the Ottoman past and in the early modern period more generally, miss the implications of this point.[24] As Michel de Certeau argued, the sixteenth century gave birth to historiographic praxis, when jurists, magistrates, and literati took to the pen to provide a sovereign with the familial, political, or moral genealogy necessary to legitimize his power.[25] Certeau posited, however, that their goal was not solely to justify or legitimize but rather to produce a technology of the state. Men like Katip Çelebi were tacticians of history who organized the representation of the past in order to substantiate the exertion of sovereign power in the present.[26] As tacticians they, too, focused on practices, analyzed successes and failures, and created a "typology of feasible relations" between a dynast and the "conjunctural variants" of his domains.[27] They constructed a "discourse," defined here as the strategic manipulation, and suppression, of the divide between a dynast's claim to power and the limits imposed by a particular imperial environment. Ultimately, they wrote of the past in order to construct a vision of order in the present and to deliver a lesson on the proper techniques of political management for the future.[28] Katip Çelebi's example thus illustrates the critical point that there is a difference between "the political," conceived as the "configuration of the power relations that organize a society as a legitimate entity," and "politics," which "refers to the strategies, practices, institutions, or discourses whose purpose is to construct and retain hegemony within a polity."[29] This book pushes this insight further, however, to argue that strategies and practices of the state also configured the state and together created a coherent rubric for imperial durability.

Coherence was key, as the early modern period contained a Eurasian theater of claimants to imperial universalism.[30] Mongol invasions of the thirteenth and fourteenth centuries connected disparate zones first through conquest and then through an exchange of goods, peoples, seeds, germs, and patterns of social and political organization.[31] Extending from the eastern Mediterranean, in the wake of the khanates' collapse, regional agrarian empires emulated the successful combination of taxation policies and warrior nomads and embraced a Mongol vision of world conquerors. The Ottomans dominated southeastern Europe, the eastern Mediterranean, and the Black Sea regions, along with Mesopotamia, Palestine, Egypt, coastal North Africa, and the Hijaz. Muscovite rulers shaped dynastic ambitions along the Volga and in Siberia; the Ming (1368–1644) and the Qing (1644–1912) dynasties maintained hegemony over China, Tibet, substantial regions of central Asia, and its tributary kingdom of Korea; the Safavids (1502–1736) encompassed the modern territories of Azerbaijan and Iran; and the Mughals (1526–1857) dominated northern India. Moving to the west of the Mediterranean, the Habsburgs turned Iberian expansion and warfare between papal and regional authorities into a Latin Christian imperial hegemony when Charles V was crowned Holy Roman emperor in Bologna in 1530. The Ottomans served as the pivot—geographically, structurally, and conceptually—between the eastern and western regions of the Eurasian landmass.

Within each of these contexts rulers and their agents managed large composite domains with distinct cultures and ecozones, organized internal diversity into elaborate hierarchical systems, cultivated a sense of suzerainty in which dependency was assumed, generated an elite literary culture that became the symbol of ceremonial and diplomatic grandeur, and possessed the "inclination to present universal imperial rule as an expression of cosmic order."[32] Thus, the postulate of world rule ironically accompanied the fragmentation of the globe and reinforced efforts by state tacticians to craft an image of imperial invincibility against both internal and external rivals. Naval expeditions sponsored by the Ming dynasty into the Indian Ocean between 1405 and 1433 magnified the glory of its rule and served to compel regional princes to accept the "son of heaven" as their overlord.[33] Safavid Shah Isma'il (r. 1501–24) and Ottoman Sultan Selim I (r. 1512–20) exchanged wittily composed, accusatory letters and vied for the title of the Muslim community's ultimate guardian.[34] Emperors in the Mughal dynasty in India assumed titles such as *Jahangir* (world seizer) or *Shahjahan* (king of the world) even as they battled with dissident regional elites and a resurgent Hindu imperialism in the south.[35] The reformation and the Thirty Years War challenged the Habsburg claim to universal empire under Charles V (r. 1519–56) and his son Philip II (r. 1556–98), yet expeditions and conquests in the "further beyond" across the ocean broke through the political boundaries of the old world into those of the new.[36] And Ottomans, Habsburgs, and Safavids engaged in protracted warfare and a politics of intimate rivalry for as long as each dynasty endured.[37]

The early modern mania with the state was thus born out of a competitive milieu in which multiple rivals laid claim to universalist rule. These claims further depended on a particular orientation to the text, and to the creation of textual authority, that was vulnerable even as it asserted triumphant narratives of power. This textual authority contained two fundamental components. First, it was premised on a written script and thus on the emergence of a courtly language and of a chancery system charged with managing the realm in the ruler's name. Süleyman and Mughal Emperor Akbar (r. 1556–

1605) turned respectively to Ottoman Turkish and Persian as canonical languages of imperial order and literary acumen, and similar moves toward a standardized language developed for French, Polish, and English in the mid-sixteenth century.[38] Chancery records shifted from linguistic hybridity to hegemonic supremacy under their rule. Translation projects, history writing, campaign manuals, and commemorative manuscripts quickened during their respective reigns. These combined to form textual technologies that also served as instruments of control used for recording expenses, distributing official appointments and land grants, regulating administrative protocols and taxation schemas, and noting decisions of the imperial council, contributing to the expansion of both textual and territorial sovereignty. Adopting a language of the court therefore fostered the development of three pillars of imperial order: an elite administrative class defined in part by linguistic competence; a preserved corpus of edicts that promulgated imperial supremacy via a specific idiom of power; and a dynastic linguistic medium that defined the shape, even if it did not control the content, of intellectual activity. The language of the state thus became a herald of its power.

The second fundamental facet of textual authority is that this script, or language of rule, was also a discourse, in the sense that it generated a particular textual habitus. Brinkley Messick argued that a "textual habitus," formed through the linkages among a polity, a social order, and a discursive formation, constituted a particular orientation to authoritative texts. His focus was on the Yemeni culture of jurisprudential manuals interposed with everyday legal practice in the *shari'a* courts. As such, he drew attention to how discourse analysis bridges the divide between conceptual or ideological frameworks and administrative practice. Combined with Certeau's observation that discourse also mediates the divide between ideals of imperial power and limits imposed by the realities of rule, this book focuses attention on an Ottoman paper trail. The Ottomans' obsession with paper and voluminous, document-generating activities is a noted feature of their imperial dominion, but it was also in itself a legitimizing practice. As mechanisms were developed to record and register petitions, survey human and material resources, and issue commands, territorial control became inextricably linked with an evolving textual corpus. This corpus sublimated anxieties of fragmented power to assertions of imperial universalism and became the means by which composite empires managed distance and organized diversity into an ordered system of state power. Textual edicts and preserved records thus inscribed a set of institutional expectations and serve as a record of sociopolitical practice. A state script thus became a script for the state. This book therefore recognizes that, as a composite empire, much of the state's authority depended on distributing shares to regional power brokers to co-opt them into an integrated system. Each of its chapters, however, highlights how the distribution of shares was also determined according to a principle of proper order and shows that this principle of order reinforced the Ottoman dynast as hegemon and hegemonic mouthpiece of imperial stability.[39]

Genre, Practice, and the Objectification of History

The Proper Order of Things traces how the production of specific record-keeping genres and administrative discourses served to shape and augment imperial authority as the Ottoman Empire rapidly expanded in the fifteenth and sixteenth centuries. It suggests that the Ottoman governing apparatus produced and managed a textual terrain that fit diversity into an actionable grammar of rule. This grammar of rule constituted a core administrative strategy comparable to other early modern empires ever more reliant on the circulation of documents to instantiate sovereign authority. Yet the particular legacies of the text, legal intervention on the part of the ruler, and overlapping rubrics for assessing just rule led to a unique vision of Ottoman imperial order. This vision of order was then used by literary elites in the seventeenth century as a means to analyze and evaluate both the history and the consequences of Ottoman conquest, expansion, and endurance. The new mapping of Ottoman imperial practice outlined in this book suggests that conceptual models came to serve as strategies for provincial governance and thus seeks to bridge a methodological divide between cultural and political history.[40] Lawmaking activities at the Ottoman court extended the jurisdiction of the sultan over provincial territory by enticing regional power brokers and official delegates into collaboration. This collaboration was defined as a relationship between a benevolent sovereign and a loyal servant, and revenue shares were distributed according to categories defined by justice, equity, and a proper sociopolitical ordering of relations. Scholars have explored this collaboration in part by assessing the way in which rebellious actions sought not to disrupt the ideological claims or legitimacy of the state but rather to influence its proportional dispersal of gifts, rewards, and resources. "The viability of the Ottoman state," as Tosun Arıcanlı and Mara Thomas suggested in the clearest articulation of this trend, "was due to the convergence of the interests of the participants of the distributive game at a locus demarcated by the state. There was a common interest in participating in the redistributive process as opposed to being excluded from it. Rebellions developed on arguments over shares and not principles."[41] Thus, cadastral surveys, fiscal budgetary reports, legal rescripts, copies of sultanic commands, registers of land grants, and petitions directed to the imperial council illustrate more than a political economy of land management and taxation. They also generated the very categories and principles of organization on which an Ottoman understanding of statecraft and sovereign authority came to rest.

The construction of an Ottoman body politic occurred gradually over time and emerges only as the sum of many otherwise distinct and seemingly unrelated legal records and registers. The earliest register (*defter*) of the imperial council (*divan-i hümayun*) dates to 1479, but now more than 300,000 registers and 150 million loose papers (*evrak*) are preserved in the Başbakanlık Osmanlı Arşivi (Prime Ministry's Archives) in Istanbul.[42] The massive data-gathering projects of the state therefore demonstrate shifts in imperial priorities. Detailed land-surveying systems, for example, were gradually abbreviated into summary form and then neglected in favor of records managed by a specialized financial department.[43] Bound legal regulations that assessed taxes and civil order by province gave way to a standardized code used as a normative guide for disputes and adjustments.[44] Registers that recorded in minute detail the granting of tax benefices reveal the networked ties and regional alignments deemed essential for stable agrarian administration.[45] Chronological copies of imperial edicts composed in response to reported incidents across the domain were formalized into bound registers during the reign of Süleyman. But the task of recording the voluminous information outgrew the scope of one administrative category, so a new register, intended specifically to address petitioner's complaints, appeared a century later. Furthermore, if the sultan and the grand vizier were on campaign, two (and sometimes three) simultaneous registers of these edicts were maintained: one with the military force and one with the vizier's delegate who remained in the capital.[46] These varied registers collectively embodied an Ottoman imperial practice and, more specifically, captured a power play, an attempt to define and sustain authority by manufacturing an archive of dispersed and collected paper that attested to that authority. Head chancellors of Süleyman's reformed bureaucratic system were fully cognizant of the links between document, sovereign authority, and proper imperial management, and they collected examples of documentary types of imperial correspondence, which were presumably circulated as guidance manuals.[47] The "problem" of history, or of historical analysis in this instance, is to determine not solely what the documents *say* but how *the saying* was organized to shape a particular understanding of imperial order. In other words, the historical labor of this book is to assess the tactics through which the Ottoman ruling elite sought to impose, via either sword or pen, the "legitimate" categories of order and intelligibility on both an internal and external audience.

It is thus important to keep in mind that the Ottoman governing apparatus during the fifteenth through the seventeenth centuries was only one claimant to power among many. What differentiated the state (seen here as the combination of sultanic personhood and those representatives who acted in his interest, or who embraced his interest as a vehicle to achieve their own), and endowed it with the authority necessary to maintain a ruling status, was precisely the ability to maintain order and thus to ratify the meaningfulness of the classificatory system it employed. Authority, then, was measured by social harmony (*asud u hal*). Rebellions or social disturbance (*fitne*) posed a direct challenge to the government's superiority over the claims of others. As a consequence, the legislation of the early modern state was almost exclusively negative. The prevalent notation of unsatisfactory conditions and violations of existing laws was explicitly used as the causative rationale for the promulgation of regulatory measures. *Fitne ü fesad* (disorder and sedition or corruption) played a persistent rhetorical function in regulatory edicts and in the diagnostic formulations of contemporary Ottoman observers.[48] Imperial correspondence attributed this disorder or general mischief (another interpretation of *fesad*) to those actors, both official and unofficial, who challenged the organizational categories employed by the state.[49] These categories were also conceived as the mechanism whereby the state maintained a just system and invoked homologies between the cosmos and the ruler; thus, the sultan stood as the guardian of justice and the guarantor of the realm. The link between justice and order was famously articulated by Idris Bitlisi (d. 1520): "The justice is in placing everything in its proper place."[50] Injustice, or *ẓulm*, was an act of misplacing, of putting a thing in a wrong or improper place.[51] Justice, then, was a hybrid and fluid category. It was a necessary virtue of the ruler, a yardstick against which imperial intervention was judged, a measure of social hierarchy and political balance, a rationale for complaint, and an index for comparison with past achievements or present corruptions. Wielded by administrators of the state, however, justice constituted a universalized language of stabilization that made a virtue out of public order and thus out of the social, political, and economic alignments necessary to ensure imperial continuity.

We can see this discourse of order enacted within three significant genres of Ottoman administrative documentation or literary production: *liva kanunnameleri*, or provincial legal regulations promulgated by the sultans during moments of conquest, reorganization, or succession; *mühimme* registers ("things of import"), comprising collections of sultanic edicts within the tradition of the *kanun* but addressed specifically to various state and extrastate actors and contexts; and *nasihatname* ("advice literature"), a collection of late sixteenth- and early seventeenth-century treatises concerning the best model for government in a period of profound change. The *kanunname* significantly forged an alignment (both literal and figural) of regional realities with the language and classification schemas contained in proclamations of administrative order. This genre of imperial documentary production thus framed relationships among the sultanate, representative surveying officials, recipients of grants or collection privileges in return for service, and the inhabitants who generated the wealth of the empire. The *kanunname* therefore embodied the Ottoman establishment's struggle to fulfill two potentially contradictory goals: first, to ensure the continuity of an imperial treasury large enough to finance its daily operations and campaigns; and, second, to protect the socioeconomic viability of the agrarian community from the abuse and usury of the persons or groups it relied on to collect taxes. To achieve these goals, the *kanunname* created a written record of transactional law. Legal regulations extended imperial authority, fitted provincial realities into actionable frameworks, and ensured that future edits, expressions of grievance, penalties, or appointments would all refer to this new framework. The promulgation of *kanunname*, therefore, served as one means to create an Ottoman law (*kavanin-i āli-i ʿOs̱mān*) and established a distinct mechanism through which the Ottoman establishment might monopolize and manage military expansion and territorial incorporation.

The copies of sultanic orders, along with council and chancery activities recorded in the *umur-ı mühimme* registers, vividly embody the imperial project of the Ottoman administrative apparatus.[52] They serve as a textual record of imperial time, arranged chronologically rather than geographically, and capture both the anxieties and the ambitions of the sultanate. Arguably, they also serve as an intermediary presence between legislation and correspondence promulgated from the imperial council and petitions addressed to the sultanate from the provinces.[53] These registers of important affairs constitute the basis for arguments presented in Chapters 4 and 5 concerning the elaboration of proper order as an imperial discourse, first in the conquest of Buda and the brokered occupation of territories in Hungary beginning in 1541 and then within the framework of the "reterritorialization" of rule in Greater Syria from 1585 to 1640.[54] Records of past efforts to organize the realm then became the focus of scholars *cum* bureaucrats who composed various *nasihatname* along the lines of Katip Çelebi's treatise.[55] Adopting the mirror tradition to camouflage critique with the jargon of counsel, scholar-bureaucrats transformed techniques of registration into a conceptual framework for analysis. In so doing, they also identified a reform-minded remapping of the Ottoman state apparatus.

The categories in the *kanunnameler*, the legal edicts of the *mühimmeler*, and the reformist sentiments of the *nasihatname* all worked incessantly to produce actionable links among land, population, justice, and governance. These depended on an explicit interweaving of sultanic authority with legal precedent. Governmental edicts and orders, "legal" because they were consented to, represented an administrative strategy manifesting both regulatory and productive features: regulatory because they imposed order on unwieldy patterns of land tenure and fixed the social landscape within a specific rubric of rule, but also productive because such laws created new grammars for social interaction, providing a vocabulary in which rights and obligations were countenanced and grievances stemming from their violation addressed. This book, then, traces the imprint of governing practices in the language deployed by these genres and argues (1) that they reveal a brokered terrain between multiple interest groups vying for resources; (2) that the Ottoman administrative apparatus, as one of these interest groups, legitimized its higher claim to resources via a notion of cosmic harmony and the proper order of things and sought to align disparate interests to imperial claims; and (3) that, as a discourse and a practice of alignment, proper order was thus a structure or grammar of rule both formed by historical processes and the frame by which these processes were interpreted within Ottoman bureaucratic and literary productions.[56] In other words, the language of power was not simply state-generated, or a rationalization of coercive means, but rather a way of structuring experience and rendering it intelligible that reflected the intergroup accommodations or "alignments" necessary to sustain an imperial universe.[57]

Certainly, the need to align state and regional interests was not in itself unique to the Ottoman Empire. Other composite empires and dynastic systems of rule such as those of the Habsburgs and the Russian Romanovs were also forced to negotiate with regional elites and willingly relinquish some degree of autonomy. Thus, the Ottoman conquest of the territories across southeastern Europe and into Arabic-speaking territories; the cleverly contrived Habsburg expansion via marriage alliances; and the Russian push into Ukraine, Poland, Belarus, the Baltic states, and later the Muslim communities of central Asia and the Caucasus were all based on particular, negotiated arrangements with varying levels of recognition and submission to authority. Much of the comparative literature explores this phenomenon in terms of how an imperial core related to provincial peripheries.[58] With this as the primary structural assumption, most scholarship assumes that no coherently strong "imperial society" existed but rather only a constantly reworked bricolage of state-domain compacts.[59] Yet the impressive durability of these empires (the Habsburgs ruled nearly four hundred years, the Romanovs from 1613–1917, and the Ottomans formally from c. 1299 to 1923) inhered largely within strategies aimed at incorporating multiple domains within a grand narrative of rule. This book contends that negotiation as a *strategy* of rule did not obviate the necessity for a *language* of rule and that the Ottoman example clearly demonstrates the connection between textual and territorial sovereignty.

An Analytic Itinerary

The book's six chapters integrate administrative practice with ideological norms and provide examples of how a discourse of sociopolitical order can serve as the means to assess the evolution of imperial sovereignty from the fifteenth to the seventeenth centuries. Conceived in three sections, these chapters shift from how documentary genres asserted and augmented imperial authority, to the way in which these genres formed a set of categories—what I have called a grammar of rule—that oriented Ottoman administrative practice, and finally to the means by which both genres and practices became objectified and idealized into an Ottoman vision of order in the early seventeenth century. Thus, in the first section, "Establishing Genres" (Chapters 1 and 2), the book moves from comparative spatial and textual tactics adopted by centralizing Eurasian courts, to the gradual evolution of legal frameworks for administrative control of conquered territories and of a bureaucratic staff that came to typify the state even if the sultan remained the ostensible head. The second section, "Genre in Practice" (Chapters 3 through 5), then identifies how these centralizing strategies, administrative practices, and bureaucratic cadres evolved within military campaigns and protracted occupations that redefined notions of Ottoman imperial frontiers. The final section, "Objectifying Generic Politics and Practices" (Chapter 6), revisits tensions between documentary genres intended to produce social order and discordant realities of provincial rule in order to resituate Ottoman responses to the global seventeenth-century crises. It argues that the literature of reform redirected medieval theories of governance into a new analytic mode. This literature activated a vision of proper order, objectified an "ancient" Ottoman law or way, and thus idealized a nostalgic version of imperial history. This nostalgic version became enshrined as the "classical" Ottoman state in early twentieth-century historiography, thus hampering any attempt to assess change in terms other than decline. By contrast, this book emphasizes the "classical" panoply not as a system or set of institutions but rather a strategic political category deployed by reformers as an analytic technique.

Implicit in this organizational structure are the four principles of analysis embodied within Katip Çelebi's treatise: attention to genre, to the relationship between conceptual models and administrative practice, to the role of sultanic authority as an anchor for imperial order, and to the significance of comparative historical analysis. As such, I use an Ottoman tactician as a guide to historiographic interpretation. Chapter 1 demonstrates that qualities once thought to be unique to the Ottoman confederation were of a piece with other imperial strategies to affirm the power of the court amid disparate territorial domains. The chapter builds a basis especially for thinking about the relationship between an expanding bureaucracy, a new set of spatial protocols within an established palatial seat, and the textual habits that extended authority outside the palace confines. It draws on comparisons with the Habsburg court in Spain, addresses the emergence of a hierarchical imperial chancery, and outlines features of a scribal culture that play a key role in the book as a whole. Chapter 2 shows how diverse practices of land management and competing regional legal traditions gradually cohered into an imperial program of revenue generation. I argue that the process of crafting and dispersing both general (*kanunnameler*) and provincial legal regulations (*liva* or *eyalet kanunnameleri*) was also a process of genre creation, whereby taxation schemas not only naturalized social relations but also became actionable frameworks for state and nonstate agents. Their form, as an expression of dynastic authority, and their content, as an assessment primarily of various tax obligations and privileges, serve to illustrate the mechanism whereby Ottoman dynasts asserted a new sovereign law amid competing legacies of land management and sought, ultimately, to generate a stable vocabulary for sultanic intervention. Chapter 3 analyzes the emergence of new cohorts of bureaucrats under Süleyman I (1520–66), who developed collaborative projects that expanded the jurisdiction of the sultan. His reign marked a shift from hybrid to hegemonic textual forms and demonstrates the coincident importance of military and textual campaigns. Anxieties over competition with rivals such as the Habsburgs and the Safavids contributed to an administrative reorganization and an obsessive focus on information gathering.[60] This led, as one example, to a new mechanism of registering imperial affairs, the *mühimme defteri*, which "captured" the varied activities of the administration. Collectively, the copies of daily transactions recorded in the *mühimme* illustrate the Ottoman establishment's effort to make regional realities conform to imperial order and to co-opt political factions capable of subverting dynastic authority.

Chapter 4 presents the northern "external frontier" of Buda and the occupied Hungarian territories as the fulcrum in which new strategies of governance and imperial display emerged. I argue that rival Ottoman and Habsburg imperial claims each relied increasingly on linguistic manipulations to assert jurisdictional power. The chapter further explores the way in which clear boundaries between sovereign powers were never certain but were rather constantly asserted through diplomatic letters and surveillance tactics ever more reliant on imperial translators. While typically assayed in terms of the "limits" of Ottoman expansion, here Buda and the Hungarian territories became the crucible for an emergent framework of imperial sovereignty. Chapter 5 moves to an "internal frontier" in Greater Syria and the province of Trablus-ı Şam and addresses a long military and administrative campaign beginning in 1585 to reinstate order in a rebellious territory. The chapter traces the imperial response to dissident rebels in the desert and coastal highlands by focusing on the Sayfa family, whose activity as regional governors shows the tenuous nature of Ottoman authority and its reliance on intermediary networks to police the boundaries between rebel and official. It traces the Ottoman establishment's efforts to "reterritorialize" previously conquered regions, examines gestures toward the uneven nature of imperial control, and highlights how imperial claims to revenue remained contested despite military ventures into the territory. Chapter 6 focuses on the link between medieval political theories and a flourishing Ottoman intellectual engagement with ideas concerning a perfect order of governance from within a sense of crisis. It traces examples of a mode of political analysis, distinct from advice-giving, that linked justice to proper governance rather than to religion or the sultan. The chapter demonstrates that Ottoman literary producers of the seventeenth century, although apprehensive of change, became innovators themselves and revived rational modes of political critique in the process. They further focused on the textual apparatus of the state, such as methods of registration and surveying, as the key to its power and sought to restore a commitment to textual transparency. The conclusion suggests that in the seventeenth century scholars and bureaucrats came to focus on the archival past of the state itself. Preserved registers became a means through which to trace lawful and unlawful claimants to the human and material resources of the realm. These registers of the past then served as models for state practice and thus became part of a new means of ordering the realm. Together, the chapters illuminate the intersections between sovereign claims, bureaucratic organization, administrative practice, and the textual habits that produced both a documentary record and the baseline for analytic reflection by Ottomans and Ottomanists alike.

A Durable Structure

The story told here is both diachronic and discursive. It is the story of an empire, at once familiar and strange—as all historical constructions are—told through the shifting vocabularies of power deployed by the Ottomans in their quest to thrive within a competitive, early modern state environment. The durability of this dynasty and political configuration does not cease to amaze. The initial followers of Osman gradually created a confederation of interests able to successfully outmaneuver competitors in the fourteenth century and established characteristics of statecraft that framed, even as they also evolved, an imperial venture that persisted into the twentieth. The empire comprised lands that crossed emergent metageographical divisions between Europe and Asia; administered a settlement pattern that linked triumphant urban milieus with rich agricultural hinterlands; managed a polity defined by monuments to the Muslim faith, yet composed of immense demographic and confessional diversity; and produced rulers absolutist in their representations of political authority yet particularistic in their strategies of incorporation. The sheer extent, both geographic and chronological, of the Ottoman Empire's history confounds scholars and modern-day visitors marveling at its architectural remnants alike. Once spurned by the "father" of the modern republic of Turkey, Mustafa Kemal (Atatürk), as the misguided dark ages of an irrational past, this imperial heritage is now resurrected as the defining ethos of contemporary presidents and consumed in elite popular shopping districts where both Turks and tourists purchase trinkets and T-shirts modeled on old Ottoman coins and ornamentalized representations of sultanic patronyms. These phenomena constitute an "Ottomania" in which scholarly agendas, political trajectories, and popular culture collide.[61] Eighteenth- and nineteenth-century popular conceptions of inner-palace life, replete with the intrigue of harems, eunuchs, viziers, and bathhouses, generated the powerful literary and figural images that a now renowned twentieth-century critic, Edward Said, used as the basis for his own popularization of representational politics in *Orientalism*.[62] While *orientalism* is now a commonplace term in the halls of academe, the scenes of exoticism and despotism Said characterized as Western projections are once again glorified in various media. A soap opera dedicated to the "classical age" crisscrosses former Ottoman dominions, as television viewers in cities such as Istanbul, Amman, and Cairo once again share a theatrical stage of imperial wonder despite nationalist aversions to an imperial past.[63] Nostalgia for an Ottoman past also informs radical political agendas such as those of Raja Shehadeh, who criticizes the dismembered geography of Israel/Palestine and yearns for a prenational integrated zone.[64] Yet it also shapes neoliberal policies of the current Turkish state, as myths of past unity underlie exclusionary policies in the present.[65] Nostalgia thus threatens to reassert static and idealized orientations of the Ottoman Empire that historians have wrestled with for decades. Resilience, however, is distinct from stasis, and it was the Ottoman Empire's resilience in the face of new constellations of power that originally inspired and intrigued the early modern traveler, the contemporary tourist, and the careworn historian alike. Recognizing that this resilience, and the unbroken continuity of the dynasty itself, was achieved through ceaseless acts of recalibration in the face of both historical and natural ruptures and transformations, this book proposes that forms of textual authority inscribed a discourse of order. This discourse, produced to overcome distance and manage the empire, evolved into a unique conceptual model *and* administrative strategy that sustained the empire and embodied its legitimacy within the framework of a proper order of things.

PART I

Establishing Genres

CHAPTER ONE

THE SOVEREIGN STATE

Spatial and Textual Politics in Early Modern Eurasian Courts

> And it is the way of the viziers, the military judges (*ḳażī'askers*), the keepers of the registers (*defterdārs*) and the chancellor (*nişancı*) to sit in my imperial council (*dīvān-ı hümāyūn*). The viziers should be seated first, on the one side should be seated the military judges, under them the keepers of the registers, and on the other side the chancellor should be seated.
>
> —Abdülkadir Özcan, "Fatih'in teşkilat kanunnamesi"[1]

At some point between 1477 and 1480, a year before the death of Sultan Mehmed II, a chief member of the emerging Ottoman chancery made the first attempt to codify courtly protocol and state administrative practices. Attributed to Leyszade Mehmed Efendi, these organizational regulations (*teşkilat kanunu*) gradually coalesced into a circulated rescript of laws, and, by 1620, bureaucrats and historians referred to them as the "*kanunname* of Mehmed II."[2] These regulations enshrined principles of imperial seclusion and definitively set the Ottoman dynast apart from former rivals, visiting dignitaries, and from his expanding cadre of palace and provincial servants. In it Mehmed II purportedly abolished earlier practices of eating communal meals with his courtiers and military retinue and delimited his public presence in the imperial council to two major religious holidays.[3] It further removed him from the daily operations of the council and thus dealt mostly with intricate administrative details and hierarchies. It laid out the protocols for scribal, religious, and provincial officials, procedures for submitting petitions to the imperial council, appropriate salaries and benefices attached to each official position, and the decorum incumbent on all servants of the realm. It further outlined court ceremonial, carefully explaining who sits where, who may approach the sultan, and who was required to pay homage by kissing the hand of the sovereign (*el öpmek*).[4] This *kanun* gradually formed the basis of an "Ottoman way," or *kanun-i Osmani*, that would preoccupy later commentators intent on both describing and prescribing the proper order of things. Obsession with court protocol further distinguished the Ottoman dynast from his contemporaries; even the ceremonial courts of the Habsburgs and the French did not adhere to a written digest of procedures and ranks.[5]

While the general effort to locate the Ottomans within a broader Eurasian context continues to challenge Ottoman exceptionalism, much of this literature focuses on the dynamics of the frontier and intermediary figures, on military ventures, or on diplomatic exchanges between rulers or their representative court elites.[6] "The Sovereign State" addresses, instead, the spatial and textual strategies adopted by newly established courts during the fifteenth and sixteenth centuries and argues that the constitutive features of these centers situate the Ottoman ruling establishment and its various tactics for control within a shared landscape.[7] This chapter traces the circulation of documents and insignia of power that sought to render the dynasty durable by promulgating an imperial vision outside the palace walls. It further argues that these efforts created specific textual habits, which in turn shaped the record-keeping practices on which the empire relied to disperse a particular vision of order. It thereby suggests that both the established center and the circulated imperial command reveal vulnerabilities, as attempts to dictate administrative affairs depended on textual edicts that could proclaim, but only haphazardly implement, dynastic authority. I begin by describing shared characteristics of early modern courts and then outline both the physical and symbolic thresholds that distinguish claims to sovereign authority from efforts to control provincial affairs. Finally, I examine the varied forms of written scripts and imperial edicts within the early Ottoman establishment and demonstrate how they transcend the threshold between palatial power and daily governance.

Commensurate Courts: The Space of Imperial Power

Like many of its early modern competitors, the Ottoman ruling establishment forged a bureaucratic system built on subordinate patronage networks and ever-expanding surveillance tactics intended to secure power amid increasingly unstable regional and global dynamics.[8] Developments formerly considered singular to Ottoman imperial trajectories were in fact widely shared by centralizing states in the early modern period. These include the proliferation of the household and the military, the assertive power of regional elites, the gradual sacralization of both law and imperial identity in the mid-sixteenth century, the architectural features of palace life with its attendant politics of access and intimacy, the expansion of the palace household itself, and the imitation of the household model by various vizierial and governorial establishments. Although a rhetoric of absolute power dominated the textual productions of these ruling establishments, their regimes were far more ambiguous and attenuated than absolute. In fact, claims to absolutism and to universalism often concealed a deep-seated anxiety over the limits of influence in dispersed and composite imperial settings. This anxiety pervades the documentary productions of early modern chanceries, where new forms of textual authority were elaborated in order to manage far-flung imperial space.[9]

The imperatives of first achieving, then expanding and maintaining, imperial power led to elaborate mechanisms used to confirm the superiority of the Ottoman dynast over former rivals. Allegiance, and rituals of submission, required from intermediary figures in newly conquered or incorporated territories, as well as from supplicants and diplomatic envoys, consolidated the nature and range of sultanic authority. The early example of textual protocols attributed to Leyszade and Mehmed II's reign embodied the syncretic mechanisms adopted by the Ottoman dynasts to assert sovereignty. They folded into their courtly protocols many of the regulatory tactics of their predecessors: existing regulations of former Byzantine provinces, traditions circumscribed by the legal dictates of Islam, and the models of the Oghuz Turks, from whom the Ottomans now claimed their descent.[10] The *Book of Dede Korkut*, an epic story cycle of Turkic customs and conventions adopted by early Ottoman elites as an "origin tale," indicates the delicate balancing of these influences.[11] The assertion and preservation of hierarchy was the strongest import of these tales, which designated "the proper warrior" as someone who "is ultimately led to submit to his lord, thus mitigating violence, securing group loyalty, and allowing the ruler to demonstrate his magnanimity and generosity."[12] Kissing the hand of the sovereign, and adhering to courtly protocol, came to embody the means by which the Ottoman dynast asserted superiority and overlordship. Rituals of submission enfolded potential rebels back into the order of things and reinforced balance through the performance of custom. Replication of the ritual encounter between ruler and supplicant became in itself an iconography of power.[13] When Mustafa 'Ali (d. 1600) remarked on the sultan's palace household in his famous *Book of Counsel for Kings*, he identified obedience and submission as the hallmarks of the courtly establishment: "they are so used to serving him [the sultan] and to carry[ing] out his noble orders in perfect obedience and are in their hearts so much attached to him with complete submission and affection that only the demons that served at Süleyman's court—peace be upon him! can have been command-obeying to such an extent."[14]

Composed only decades after Istanbul's conquest, Mehmed II's *kanunname* framed rituals of submission within the context of new dynastic genealogies that shaped the Ottomans as inheritors of universalism.[15] The city of Istanbul itself served as a palimpsest for this bid to universalism, and its past imperial layers shaped later characterizations of Ottoman victory.[16] The Greek chronicler of Mehmed II's reign Kritoboulos (*Historia*, c. 1467) conscientiously placed the sultan within the Alexandrine line of sovereignty.[17] Kritoboulos emphasized Mehmed II's knowledge of Greek and Latin and insisted that he had Arian's life of Alexander (the *Anabasis*) read to him on a daily basis because he desired to "be proclaimed sovereign of all the world and all the people; that is, a second Alexander." The earliest chronicle written in Ottoman Turkish of the sultan's reign by Tursun Bey (c. 1490–95) cites in its opening line a Qur'anic reference to Alexander and inserts him as the primary role model for the divinely sanctioned Ottoman "world emperor" (*pādişāh-ı cihān*).[18] Mehmed II's "new palace," built between 1559 and the mid- to late 1560s, redefined the triangular isthmus between the Golden Horn and the Bosphorus Straits as the space of Ottoman power. Kritoboulos characterized Mehmed II's mosque complex and the Topkapı Palace, his first major monumental architectural projects, as part of a "plan to make the city in every way the best supplied and strongest city, as it used to be long ago, in power and wealth, glory, learning, and trades, and in all the professions."[19] The palace would have dominated the view of the city's inhabitants or that of new arrivals, diplomatic envoys, and merchants as they approached the capital of the Ottoman Empire.[20] As recorded by a Jewish court physician to Murad III, the suggested extent of the palace walls exceeded five thousand meters, encircling an expanse of seven hundred thousand square meters, with built structures occupying perhaps seventy-eight thousand of those meters. An astounding presence in a highly symbolic locale, the palace, its city, and its dynasty of rulers came to form a clear collective insignia of imperial power.

The coincident emergence of a palace and its administrative protocols illustrates the way in which the power of the dynast depended increasingly on his embodiment in both spatial and textual forms. The Ottoman conquest of the Byzantine capital of Constantinople stands out as such a well-known date that it is perhaps a cliché to employ it as a benchmark in any historical analysis. For textbook audiences 1453 is either an end or a beginning: the end of the medieval period or the beginning of the early modern; the end of Byzantium or the beginning of a world-renowned Ottoman era; the end of eastern Christianity or the beginning of Muslim global dominance. Scholars have worked to unpack this simplicity, often by showing continuity across these presumed divides, and by presenting evidence of heterogeneous institutional, religious, and sociocultural forms. Some examples of this effort include the Ottoman adoption of certain Byzantine provincial divisions and tax categories;[21] the role of "Christian" regional leaders in early military campaigns, serving on advisory councils and posted to key administrative positions;[22] syncretic spiritual forms that continued to shape authoritative action;[23] the adaptation rather than destruction of cultural artifacts and monumental architecture,[24] even of the structure that once enshrined the coronation of Byzantine emperors—the Hagia Sophia turned Aya Sofya;[25] and the various strategies to incorporate non-Muslim populations into the revenue base.[26] There is less consensus, however, concerning what actual import the conquest had for the Ottoman establishment itself. Some have argued that Mehmed II consciously manipulated the success of 1453 to reconstitute the Ottoman confederacy within the framework of universal empire,[27] whereas others have suggested that no true imperial consciousness fully existed *throughout* the duration of the empire.[28] This chapter argues, however, that the conquest should be understood as a spatial assertion of centralized rule. The establishment of a recognized seat of power further linked the Ottomans to a transregional awareness that triumphant spatial claims were necessary for a secure bid to universalist imperial authority. But grand palatial designs and lavish court ceremonials performed an imperial coherence that the actual governance of the realm lacked. Thus, court ceremony masked anxieties concerning the efficient administration of far-flung domains. The following sections illustrate how these anxieties, transparently displayed in the daily tableaux of the Ottoman establishment, are also more opaquely present in its textual productions.

Distant Anxieties and Courtly Dynamics

Distance, both spatial and temporal, constituted a singular challenge for composite early modern empires, and the strategies adopted to manage this distance reveal principles of order and organization imposed on the landscape. The expansion of a courtly household, and the emergence of increasingly specialized administrative positions, accompanied efforts both to produce the textual authority of the state and to manage the record-keeping practices that sustained its reach. The establishment of permanent courtly seats thus also depended on the creation of protocols for the production of official imperial correspondence intended to disperse and sustain the sovereignty of rulers outside their palace walls. Protocols for correspondence and sultanic edicts generated in turn ever more elaborate bureaucratic systems. Established seats of power thus precipitated the need for knowledge circuits, textual routes capable of extending, canvassing, and displaying power across imperial domains.[29] Paradoxically, while both the palace and the written edict attempted to fix, stabilize, and reconcile these domains to centralized power, they also opened up new forms of vulnerability. Regional opposition, such as social rebellions, political intrigue, or the assertion of alternative written forms, destabilized the position of the state as a dispenser of rules and order.[30] Still, rebellions of both the sword and the pen mimicked the forms and ceremonials of the court and so ironically served to strengthen and extend its power. Even challengers evoked the language of absolutism, and the dynamic between the assertion of imperial power and its manipulation created a particular textual habitus within which both the sovereign and the populace operated.[31]

Positing a "textual habitus" focuses attention on the personages that constitute the Ottoman establishment, the protocols that affix them to the sultan, and the record-keeping practices that enunciate the supremacy of imperial claims over rivals. This textual habitus recrafts notions of "center" and "court" such that they can no longer be viewed as monolithic institutions disconnected from their provinces but rather as forces constituted precisely by the scripted codes produced to manage imperial domains. The space of the empire is thus defined by an assemblage of relationships that ensure "continuity and some degree of cohesion" across domains through a dispersed set of encoded expectations. Protocols such as those inscribed in Mehmed II's *kanunname* therefore indicate how imperial power partially inhered in the ability to determine the norms of acceptable behavior and to represent those norms in both textual and material form.[32] Here, the term *court* is metonymically used to represent not just the ornate architectural palaces of rulers but also the site of convergence for the political, fiscal, artisanal, sacral, and discursive relationships that together constitute a ruling household.[33] The court is thus neither a single entity nor even a unitary household because competitive groupings associated with consorts, wives, or heirs often possessed their own patronage networks capable of challenging the ruler's. Instead, the early modern court should be seen as an unsteady fusion of interests and practices, dependent on the networks that it also sustains and limited in turn by the necessity to craft and maintain an administrative and ideological interdependency between regional and imperial elites.[34] More pointedly, although conquest extended Ottoman territorial claims, true dominance emerged only as the government established itself as the chief medium for written representation of the Ottoman world.[35]

Significantly, attention to the space of the empire and the textual codes that manage it reinforces the point that the "realms" of early modern polities were far from unified bundles. They themselves contained "multiple cores and variegated edges."[36] Efforts to control territory therefore often devolved on mechanisms to ensure oaths of submission or threats of punishment. Thus, despite absolutist claims, the durability of centralizing states required an unceasing recalibration of interpersonal relationships, and the court became a marketplace where favor was traded and power brokered.[37] It was at once a marriage market, where internal and external alliances were carefully managed;[38] a labor market, compelling the in-house presence of craftsmen, artisans, cooks, engineers, scribes, and bureaucrats commanding the movement of messengers, translators, soldiers, mercenaries, surveyors, and tax collectors outside its walls;[39] a real estate market, defining the status of, or granting and seizing land, as well as usufruct rights to taxes accruing from villages, institutions, tariffs, or customs;[40] and a cultural broker, setting the standards for taste and style in commodities and ideas, and blending palace and populace through ceremonial displays and the founding of charitable institutions and monumental architecture throughout the empire. Collectively, these practices yielded a fairly standard vision of courtly prominence shared across otherwise distinct ruling bodies. As John Adamson has persuasively argued, this "standardization of expectations" about what a "properly constituted court" should possess came to typify courtly politics during the early modern period.[41] His list includes the magnificence of the palace household itself; its hierarchical organization and administration through distinguished departments responsible for provisioning, parading, and entertaining; the emergence of a bureaucratic cadre of elites; the protocol established to regulate these elites and their interactions with the ruling household; an expression of piety and a calendrical observance of religious rituals; and an extensive apparatus devoted to the hunt.

Adamson acknowledges that these aspects of court dynamics may indeed have existed earlier and may also develop as common (and thus without historical weight for the early modern period) characteristics of settled, centralized rule. He maintains, however, that the true import of the list derives from its combination of features and thus from the mutual assumption carried across imperial boundaries that they *must* be present for "any sovereign court that aspired to be taken seriously by its peers."[42] The audience of the court, although differently assayed and addressed, consisted of both external and internal competitors. In Adamson's formulation this audience was not, for the most part, "the public" in the sense of the populace at large. Instead, it was selective and intentional—other sovereigns and their diplomatic representatives combined with the emerging officialdom of the empire itself. Hence, the ambassadorial visit became the centerpiece for this new court politics, wherein the grandeur of the festivities, the pomp and circumstance associated with garnering access to the sovereign (or being denied this right), and the exchange of gifts that marked mutual recognition of status and honor held captive both sets of eyes: the visiting dignitary and his retinue, and the members of the ruler's household and officials in attendance.[43] And the sovereign, ensconced in magnificence and signifying central power, was as much a part of the scripted system as its creator. Yet this scripted scene of courtly pomp and circumstance, with its "public" of peers and rivals, overlooks the role that written edicts played in generating at least a semblance of territorial coherence. The public of these edicts was indeed the populace, and their circulation fostered a specialized language with a set of discursive rules that bound together both the ruling apparatus and the subjects it sought to manage.

Fixed Abodes and Mobile Paradigms

These new spatial and textual notions of order can be identified in the process whereby confederacy around the house of Osmanlı remade itself into an image of imperialist world conquerors, with Istanbul serving as its triumph and its proof. The Ottoman shift toward residential court life occurred rather early in a new normative landscape that linked sovereignty to an established seat of power. Apprehensiveness concerning the ability to assert territorial control from a restricted courtly sphere served as an important countermodel, where an urban capital was understood as more of a liability than an asset. Emperor Charles V definitively embraced peripateticism as a necessary strategy for rule. He dismissed courtly establishments and reputedly insisted that "kings do not need palaces."[44] Even Versailles was a latecomer to the cabal of palace grandeur, and the court of France itself only acquired permanency in Paris after the accession of Henri IV (r. 1589–1610) and the conclusion of disabling interreligious continental warfare. But despite concerns over the limits of centralized power, established courts and their cities came increasingly to dominate the early modern political sphere. By the 1520s the dukes of Bavaria claimed Munich as their urban center; the Tudor kings of England became ensconced in Whitehall, at Westminster, in 1529; Florence housed the Medici upstarts in the 1530s; and the Austrian Habsburgs established Vienna as the prime location from which to maneuver across their various imperial frontiers in the 1540s, although, as they briefly wrested lands from the Ottomans, they spatially proclaimed this triumph by moving the court to Prague between 1583 and 1615. The late sixteenth century bore witness to

Madrid as the new stronghold of the Spanish Habsburgs and the relocation of the Savoyard court from Chambéry to Turin in 1563; and the kings of Poland, under Sigismund III Vasa, claimed Warsaw as their capital in 1597. Even the Dutch Republic, a mobile power if ever there was one, established a resident court at Delft in 1583 and later at The Hague.[45]

Although the Ottomans forged an early commitment to "capital-building," shifting from Bursa (1326) to Edirne (1361) and finally to Istanbul (1453), tensions between horse-driven conquest and throne-issued proclamations continued to place primacy on mobility as a tactic of governance. Even with the dynasty's assertion of permanency in Istanbul after 1453, much of the palace personnel and financial overhead was devoted to mobility, either in terms of campaign mobilization or the elaborate rituals of the royal hunt.[46] The sultanate as an institution, defined as a set of structural constraints and habituated actions despite the idiosyncrasies of individual sultans, tended to observe seasonal residence patterns that approximated the nomadic alternation between summer pasture (*yaylak*) and winter quarters (*kışlak*). Significantly, the court in its entirety often moved to hunting grounds either within the environs of the capital city or farther out, toward the territories of Thrace. Several sultans, primary among them Mehmed IV (r. 1648–87), spent a considerable amount of time in the alternative palatial grounds at Edirne, and many retreated there when disturbances in the capital became too taxing or distressing.

Furthermore, the continued emphasis on tents and garden pavilions, even within permanent monuments, blurs a rigid contrast between established monumental residences and more mobile structures.[47] Gülru Necipoğlu suggested that even the courtyard architecture of the Topkapı Palace reproduces the plan of approach to the sultan's military pavilion while on campaign.[48] Head falconers (*şahinci başı* and *çakırcıbaşi*), dedicated to the technologies of the hunt, were not only part of the *enderun*, or inner service, of the sultan but also part of a clear hierarchical movement from these positions to top levels in government, including that of the grand vizierate.[49] So, too, the masters of the stables were recognized as intimates to the sultan and, correspondingly, to the goals of display and conquest that equestrianism and the hunt continued to represent across Eurasian courts. Accordingly, the powerful Rüstem Pasha, the longest-serving vizier of Sultan Süleyman and perhaps the vizier most linked to schemes and stratagems for mobile centralization, once served, according to the 1527 payroll accounts, for 150 *akçes* as the sultan's stable master.[50]

The Ottoman dynasty's triumph over the other sixteen successor principalities that the Seljuk sultanate of Rum had once, albeit loosely, folded into their ambit of rule testifies to the early leaders' savvy manipulation of an ethos of the frontier with that of enduring permanency.[51] These strategies were adapted in part from the Seljuks. As a semiunified dynasty with an increasingly centralized base in Konya during the first half of the thirteenth century, the Seljuks forged new authoritative ground amid a crumbling Byzantium. Its composite notions of statecraft, proficient combination of nomadic and settled life patterns within a coherent administrative structure, and itinerant patronage networks dedicated to creating institutions of trade (*khan*), pilgrimage (*zawiye*), and education (*medrese*) enabled first the Mongol Ilkhanids and then the Ottomans to follow in their wake.[52] Thus, until the Mongols conquered the Seljuks in 1243, Seljuk rule created a real, if porous, frontier-minded (*uc*) unity. The mix of Greek, Syriac, Armenian, Turkic, Kurdish, Arabic, and Persian-speaking populations that assembled under the Seljuks generated a polyglot system of rule that was heavily Persianized. Yet the Seljuk state also deployed Greek forms and Turkic titles in literary and documentary productions, and Arabic was utilized in institutional practices sanctioned by Islam, such as the charitable endowments of the *waqf* and other transactions concerning property and family.[53] These would all form the basis of early Ottoman consolidation efforts.

Mixed heritage, syncretic cultural practices, heterogeneous troop contingents, and conflicting ambitions characterized thirteenth-century Anatolia. This was a dense, competitive milieu, and the Ottoman following was quite small. But the extreme political fragmentation enabled even this small contingent to capitalize on the polymorphous landscape for its own advantage. Beginning in the 1230s, in the wake of Mongol incursions into Armenia and then Anatolia, a small tribal contingent moved from the territory between Erzincan and Erzurum, via Karaca Dağ in the vicinity of Ankara, to the Byzantine-Seljuk border: Sultan-öyügü and Sögüt.[54] According to early historical tales, their *beylik* (principality) was established by an assemblage consisting of only four hundred tents, and the founder of the dynasty, Ertoğrıl/Ertoğrul (d. c. 1280), father of Osman I (1281–1324), initially had only 340 fighting men (*nefer kişisi*). Ottoman chroniclers, in a later effort to "restore" an imperial origin story, "remembered" that their first territory stretched as far as Bilecik and İne Göl, which were the Byzantine frontier fortresses named respectively Belokomis and Angelokomis.[55] A clear Ottoman conquest movement was born in direct victorious confrontation with Byzantine forces, first at Karaca Hisar in 1288, then at Bapheus (near Nikomedeia) in 1302. These conquests quickly pivoted from defeating armies to seizing fortresses, the beginnings of a wise assessment that the fortress constituted the basis of administrative control. Thus, according to early Ottoman historians, Osman seized Bilecik (Belokomis), Yar-hisar, İnegöl (Angelokomis), and Yenişehir (Melangeia) by 1304, and these became the foundational sites of an emergent Ottoman state.[56]

Although this was a state on the move, the urban-mindedness of the emergent Ottoman confederation can be traced throughout the period of early consolidation. Thus, the dynasty's claim to be "kings of the territorial divisions (*mulūk al-ṭawa'if*)" of medieval Anatolia also illustrates a certain primacy given to architectural permanency prior to the conquest of Constantinople. Raiding and absorption of Thracian cities and the establishment of new urban monuments and structures went hand in hand with prowess in battle, especially until the definitive defeat of the Akkoyunlu ruler Uzun Hasan in the mountainous terrain of eastern Anatolia in 1473.[57] No matter how fleeting or seemingly insecure their presence in a newly conquered province, the Ottomans consistently marked their passage and their intent to endure while also stimulating further investment in urban development primarily through the use of charitable endowment (*vakıf* in Turkish; *waqf* in Arabic). The most common forms of endowment were the mosque, *medrese*, and associated *imaret* complexes (including rooms for study, lodging for functionaries and students, and often soup kitchens, bakeries, and other social services). Even when Bayezid I (r. 1389–1402) spent only a winter in Veria (1393–94), he dedicated time to constructing an *imaret* that would bear his name.[58] These construction projects marked the gradual conquest of Thrace and movement into southeastern Europe, as well as the incremental gains made within the Anatolian peninsula. One prime example within the Thracian context is Murad II's (r. 1421–44, 1446–51) city foundation in northern Thrace at Ergene (modern Uzunköprü). As Rhoads

Murphey notes, "his bridge over the Ergene is said to have taken 18 years to complete (1426–44) and when completed it spanned a distance of 392 metres supported on 174 columns."[59] From its inception, and certainly by the late fourteenth century, the Ottoman confederacy seemed invested in the built environment even as their own control over territories remained fragmented and dependent on physically traversing the landscape.

The mixed governing strategies of the early confederacy—part horizontally shared power structures, part emergent centralizing institutions—were formidably redirected by Mehmed II's post-1453 strong-armed policies. These intentionally undermined the power of marcher lords, of early advisory cohorts, and of rival interest groups and institutions with claims to the productive capacity of the land. He refashioned both the population and cityscape of Istanbul to proclaim the legitimacy and permanency of these reforms. Thus, the conquest of the city set in motion a new courtly protocol and, along with it, dynastic designations of the state. The *devlet*, or virtue, honor, and fortune once associated directly with the person of the ruler, came increasingly to stand for the order of the dynasty and, gradually, of the state itself.[60] Phrases such as *āl-i ʿOs̱man* and *devlet-i āl-i ʿOs̱man* shaped the confederacy into a coherent dynastic system. This dynasty ruled over the well-protected dominions of the state (*memleket/memālik-i mahrūse-i ʿOsmanī*). The majesty and exalted status of this dynasty (*memālik-i devlet-i āliye-i ʿOs̱māniye*) was also then deemed eternal (*devlet-i ebed-müdded*) and provided a clear imperial claim of a reconstituted Ottoman polity.[61] This imperial claim came with a script, one that possessed both spatial and written forms.[62] Both scripts managed, in their distinct ways, the thresholds among the sultan, the expanding courtly household, and the protected dominions outside the palace walls.

Threshold Scripts and Practice in Ottoman and Habsburg Court Settings

The ideological and spatial practice of threshold architecture, as discussed within Ottoman or Islamic studies more generally, is all too often characterized as something unique to an Islamicate civilizational forum. Bernard Lewis provides a rather typical example of this approach: "This contrast between Islamic and Western usage illustrates very clearly the Muslim perception of power relationships in horizontal rather than, as in Christendom, in vertical terms. This is a society which always in principle, and often, at least to some extent, in practice, rejects hierarchy and privilege, a society in which power and status depend primarily on nearness to the ruler and the enjoyment of his favor, rather than on birth or rank. . . . In this as in much else, Muslim political language reflects the Muslim ideal of social mobility."[63] In contrast, keen attention to hierarchy and social status emerged in tandem with the ceremonial of established early modern courts. And, while the Ottoman officers of the "in-between," the *mabeyinci*, quite vividly map this spatialization of power, orientations to space defined according to inside, outside, and in-between are arguably part of the larger semiological corpus of early modern Eurasian court systems.[64] This orientation to space imposed new spatial divisions between public and private areas within the palace complex and, perhaps ironically, contributed to the abstraction of the state from the personhood of the ruler.[65] Here, two trends in the careful management of access to the sultan illustrate the process whereby palace-centric protocols came to define dynastic power more generally: the increased emphasis on a "hidden" ruler and the various strategies deployed to "enact" the presence of that ruler despite, or as a result of, his distance from the daily workings of power.[66] The association of distance, threshold access, and a hidden ruler—all designed to accentuate or sacralize power—captured instead a shift toward bureaucratization and thus toward an administrative apparatus that functioned distinct from the presence of the ruler. These transregional strategies thus highlight quite dramatic transformations in the built environment of the court, in the visibility of its sovereign, and thus in the link between the personhood of the ruler and the state.

This is vividly apparent in the Habsburg Spanish court, especially after Philip II (r. 1556–98) enacted rigid threshold policies for attendance on the ruler. Four public spaces with strictly policed access granted only by rank preceded the monarch's private quarters. The last of these, the royal study, "was reserved for papal nuncios, cardinals, viceroys and the president of the Council of Castile. Meetings were carefully choreographed, and only the arrival of a papal emissary triggered any royal concession to the statuesque immobility of the king, as in this instance the monarch would advance a few steps to greet him."[67] The "hidden" ruler within the Habsburg domain is perhaps best exemplified in the San Lorenzo de El Escorial monastery, built by Philip II to commemorate his victory over the French at the Battle of St. Quentin in August of 1557. Scholars' emphasis on access and occlusion, all too often characterized as harbingers of a declining Ottoman state, hinges on the argument that the palace increasingly replaced the campaign as the central space of sovereign action toward the end of the sixteenth century and that sultans and princes were held as virtual captives of court intrigue.[68] Here, however, we can note the ways in which occlusion highlights the emergence of an alternative structure of power, one dependent on bureaucratic intercession and a tightly scripted narrative of access to the sovereign. With shared strategies for maneuvering between conquest and settled rule, the Habsburg dynamic serves to illuminate the Ottoman.

Philip II decidedly broke from his father's (Charles V) peripatetic court and almost immediately commenced on a quest for an ideal court space, establishing a residence first in Toledo, then Madrid, and finally a reimagined royal identity within the walls of El Escorial. Each shift illustrates an assertion of power and sovereign will, as Philip II eschewed both Toledo, as a space dominated by the archbishop, and Madrid, which came to represent courtly delights of the hunt and entertainment, for the hallowed sanctity and commemorative space of El Escorial, where the pantheon of interred Spanish Habsburgs still rests. Like the establishment of the "new palace" of Topkapı commissioned by Mehmed II and completed by 1468 at a slight remove from the commercial heart of Istanbul, and the decision beginning with Süleyman and continuing with Murad III to expand the interior regions and incorporate the households of concubines, wives, and mothers, Philip II's shift to Madrid was also a clear indication of the dramatic increase in the royal household's size.[69] Due in part to the incorporation of Burgundian court protocol into a Castilian royal tradition and the resulting "doubling" of positions, this expansion also corresponded to the "in-gathering" of potential rivals and foci of power.[70] Hence, the royal apartments in Madrid housed not only the queen but also Crown Prince Don Carlos, the king's sister Juana, and the household of their half-brother Don Juan of Austria. Moreover, visiting ambassadors and attending members and officials of the Councils of State representing Castile, Aragon, and the Indies, along with a surfeit of military orders, were all assigned quarters in the royal court in Madrid, as were the staff of the Chapel's Royal and the leaders of the Inquisition.

These dynamics were also at work within the threshold construction of the Topkapı Palace. In Ottoman Turkish, the *ṭopḳapu sarāyı*, "cannon-gate palace," also known as the *sarāy-ı cedīd-i ʿāmire*, "new imperial palace," was originally built by Mehmed II between 1463 and 1478 on the grounds of the Byzantine Acropolis and was organized around three consecutive courtyards. Its outer, open "court of processions," or *alay meydānı*, with the attendant bustle of trade and market, ensured both the provisioning of the palace and its ability to redistribute wealth through acts of largesse. A second court, separated from the first by the "middle gate," or *orta ḳapu*, shifted these activities into the more limited domain of the *dīvān*, reserved for servants of the realm and for visitors deemed worthy of a vizierial or sultanic reception in front of the third "gate of felicity," or *bābü's-saʿāde*. This gate separated the inner court, the *enderūn meydānı* enclosing the sultan's private domain, from the operations of governance. The imperial kitchen (*maṭbāḫ-ı ʿāmire*) occupied the entire right side of this courtyard, and the imperial stables (*isṭabl-i ḫāṣa*) lined the left.[71] This courtyard was also known as the "court of justice," or *ʿadālet meydānı*, since it served as the site of the council hall, adjacent to the gate of felicity. It further included the public treasury (*dārü'l-ḫazīne* or *ḫazīne birūnī*) and, by the mid-sixteenth century, the architectural symbol of Ottomanized notions of proper rule, the tower of justice (*ḳaṣr-ı ʿadālet*). Activities of reception and governance were all staged before the exalted gate, the *bāb-i ʿālī* (an alternative term for the gate of felicity), which marked the threshold between the apparatus of the court and the living quarters of the sultan. Through this gate, the spatialized dictates of access moved servants of the realm or the esteemed visitor from external apparatus toward internal might.[72]

The "seat" of government associated with this threshold was variously represented by terms for the third gate, the Ottoman imperial court, such as the *asitāne-i salṭanat-aṣiyān* (threshold of the abode of the sultanate) or the *ʿatebe-i seniye* (the exalted threshold), *dergāh-ı muʿallā* (exalted Porte), and *südde-i saʿādet* (threshold of felicity). Thus, the quotidian activities of the empire took place within a scripted protocol that proffered the "sublime threshold" as the synecdoche of power. Yet the practice of governance itself occurred in the second court within the chambers of the council hall, where the members of the *divan* met four times a week—Saturday, Sunday, Monday, and Tuesday—to render decisions concerning petitions, requests, and reports from across the imperial domains. The members of the council included, in declining rank,[73] the grand vizier; the two supreme judges of the realm (*kadı'asker*, lit. "military judges"), separated in 1481 into the territorial divisions of Rumelia and Anatolia;[74] two *defterdar*s, or "keepers of the register," the chief financial ministers also divided between Rumelia and Anatolia;[75] the *nişancı*, or the head chancellor;[76] various officials adorned with the rank of vizier; and, after 1536, the governor, or *beylerbey* of Rumelia. The grand admiral of the Mediterranean fleet; the master of military standards, tents, and bands; the head diplomatic envoy; and the commander of the imperial gatekeepers, guarding the consecutive gates of the palace, were in attendance but were not "seated" members of the council. As this chapter's epigraph indicates, Mehmed II's *kanunname* outlined a precise seating chart for the jurists, finance ministers, and head chancellor, who together constituted the key administrators of imperial order.

The main chamber hall of the council then opened into the chancery, where between fifty and one hundred scribes sat taking notes, and a third domed pavilion where the records of the council were held and sealed after the meetings; at the end of the lunar calendar year the records were enclosed in leather bags for preservation and future reference. Sultans could listen to the deliberations of the imperial council through a latticed window positioned between the main three-domed pavilion of the imperial *divan* and the tower of justice, since the tower was connected by a narrow corridor to the inner court and also availed the rulers of a belvedere from which to view processions in the second court unseen. Rather than the sultan himself, it was the grand vizier who came to sit as head of council and deliberated in the name of the sovereign.

The council and the scribe, then, positioned at the threshold of Ottoman dynastic power, became conduits for the nexus between a fixed abode and the textual authority that enunciated the power of the sultanate across imperial domains. Sultanic commands dispatched from these environs, or from horseback during campaign seasons, depended on the authority of a script and on the allegiance of intermediaries across the domain. These commands were crafted to overcome distance, with imperial edicts flowing outward from Istanbul and reports by investigators, governors, judges, and surveyors flowing into a knowledge database that informed the sultan and his agents of regional affairs. Yet this knowledge database also depended on the employ of royal servants and thus precipitated the expansion of the dynastic household itself.

From Sultan to Household: Protocols of Authority

While serving as a polysemic marketplace—acting as a focus for taste and a showcase for competitive imperial display—a settled court represented a strikingly dramatic shift in both the meaning and practice of imperial power. The establishment of a permanent seat set in motion a process of abstraction that ultimately led to a new form of political analysis and commentary. Although the distinction between "household" (attending the ruler) and "bureaucracy" (attending to the governance of the empire) remained somewhat "blurred" and often shared proximate locations within palace designs, a gradual disentangling of the two became one of the most significant transformations of the early modern period.[77] Within the Ottoman context the expansion of the palace household after the capture of Constantinople and co-option of regional rivals into administrative positions gradually shifted power from sultan to the sultanic apparatus.

Bureaucratic organization, salaried officers, new ministerial ranks and functions, along with new fiscal and documentary policies, all served to reinforce a wedge between the personhood of the ruler and the court. The Habsburg court commentator Alonso Nuñez de Castro, for example, answered his own question of "what exactly was the court?" by "enumerating each of the king's many councils found in Madrid."[78] Likewise in Germany the official lists of court personnel came to be known as *Hofstaaten*. The expansion of the early modern ruling household and gradual designation as the armature of the state is quite noticeable in other court traditions as well. The dukes of Bavaria's Munich-based court increased from 162 bureaucrats in 1508 to 866 in 1571 and to more than a thousand by the end of the seventeenth century. Florence's Medici household evolved from 168 salaried officers in 1564 to 792 in 1695. Perhaps the greatest increases occurred in the French and Ottoman courts. The French royal household's servants swelled from approximately a thousand under François I (r. 1515–47) to between eight and ten thousand under Louis XIV.[79]

The expansion of the Ottoman dynastic household was also accompanied by increasingly rigid structures with clear definitions of court hierarchy. It is telling that the first recorded compilation of salary lists appears only in 1478, after the establishment of Istanbul as center and capital of the newly realized empire and more than ten years after the completion of the palace grounds, whose transactions and inhabitants these records would tally for centuries.[80] Mehmed II, as the primary overseer of this expansion, warned against changing the basic organizational design for this household structure in the future.[81] Thus, the original register, with its three chambers—high chamber (*has* or *oda*), treasury chamber (*hazine*), and pantry chamber (*kiler*)—its cooks (*tabahhin*) and food tasters (*zevakkin*), gardeners (*bağbanan*), gatekeepers (*bevabbin*), falconers, keepers of hounds and mastiffs (*sekbanan* and *zagirciyan*), along with tailors (*hayyatin*) and armorers (*cebeciyan*), included the basic outlines retained by successive sultans until at least the major reorganizations at the end of the seventeenth century.[82] These participants in the daily reproduction of dynastic power remained a fixture of the Ottoman Empire until eighteenth-century shifts toward the Bosphorus, the construction of shoreline palaces, and a diffusion of court life across the waters and landscape of an expanding city altered the status of Topkapı Palace.[83]

Thus, from 1478 onward the Ottoman household became inexorably linked to palace culture, to the *kanun*s regulating interdependency, and thus to the enumeration of dependents and their salaries in expense registers. From a core administrative staff of 530 and elite cavalry corps of 222 members (*hünkar kulu/kapı kulu*) registered in palace salary lists from 1478, the immediate household staff reached its highest point of 10,714 in 1609, whereas the numbers of elite corps (as distinct from the janissaries) rose to 5,008 in 1528 and reached 11,044 in 1568.[84] These salary lists, and documents recording the extended dynastic household's daily activities, institutionalized clientage networks (*intisab*). They also brought the deeply politicized nature of bending regional elites to the sovereign will into the domain of an established court. The grant of distinguished status (*müteferrika*) marked the interdependent relationship between sovereign power and elite allies.[85]

The lists of these personages were included in various collected documents beginning with Mehmed II's efforts to establish institutional standards.[86] From bids for a unified Anatolian presence in the late fifteenth century, to subsuming the heirs of conquered or incorporated dynasties in the sixteenth, this conferred status was pronounced through specified salaries and the bestowal of gifts. It was also dispensed to sons of governors (*evlad-i ümera'*) and to the descendants of former regional and grand viziers, thereby belying the sense that the Ottoman system was entirely meritocratic, even if it never approximated the entrenched aristocratic forms of its Eurasian rivals.

The circulation of rewards that marked the reciprocal nature of elite status also indicates the interdependent nature of sovereign authority. Gifts for the establishment and maintenance of these relationships included grants for accoutrements associated with appointment to office, including cloth, vestments, cash, and food-ration allowances as well as stipends to support the procurement of clothing, dress, and uniforms for court attendants. Gifts were also exchanged with foreign diplomats or tribute payers when received at court. These were considered part of a custom (*'ādet*) of reciprocity, and gifts placed the participants in an exchange that also reified and sanctioned an organized hierarchy.[87] In recognition of symbolic or actual tribute and homage paid to the sultan, these gifts circulated either within the confines of the palace itself or as dispatches to regional officials to initiate terms of service or to supplement their continued activity within the orbit of sultanic administration. This circulation of gifts required constant diligence and maintenance by the sultan and his record keepers. Daily records of the council, certificates of office, salary books for grant recipients, and court chronicles of diplomatic embassies and treaty negotiations all noted the primacy of gifts as a mark of imperial sanction. Yet gifts also indicated that the sultan's power depended on the incorporation of regional elites and on the proliferation of duties and functions required of them. Court ceremony and the exchange of service for reward thus retained order even as the numbers of Ottoman officialdom expanded.

As the sultan's household and his domain grew larger than either he or his immediate advisers could manage, new staffing strategies were adopted. The incorporation of "new men" into the administrative apparatus was a significant feature of early modern courts. These royal favorites (*valido/*

privado), who, in deed even if not in name, guided the administrative affairs of the realm, served to centralize and consolidate power and usurp landed aristocracies.[88] Dependent on the sovereign and thereby held hostage by service to his name and person, the figure of the royal favorite came to mediate between the sovereign and the vested interests of regional elites. The sovereign relied on this *arriviste* to counter resistance to centralizing aims, and the "new man" became the symbol of absolutist tyranny for those marginalized by the institutional protocols of a settled court. For the aristocratic grandees of the Habsburg, Bavarian, Burgundian, French, English, Sabaudian, Prussian, and Muscovite domains, the dismay expressed toward an *arriviste* was the dismay of those with hereditary rights replaced by favored men newly charged to serve, counsel, and protect the realm from enemies without and tyranny within. For the Ottomans, critics of centralizing tactics came primarily from the mixed cohorts of men who had participated in the early expansionary ethos of the Ottoman confederation or from the independent Türkmen principalities of Anatolia that gradually submitted to its suzerainty. These men, the marcher lords (*uç beyleri*) as Cemal Kafadar labels them, depended on the syncretic religious and managerial policies of the nascent state to maintain a degree of independence.[89] But centralization tactics, beginning with Murad I's (r. 1363–89) appointment of regional governors and reliance on captive recruits, undermined the authority of these early cohorts. Mehmed II further institutionalized the *devşirme*, a process for manufacturing consent and loyalty among officials of the realm adapted from early 'Abbasid strategies.[90] This system of recruitment, whereby a tax on the young men of conquered provinces populated the various administrative and military posts of the empire, testified to the combination of coercion and social mobility inherent in the Ottoman system: the humble page, janissary soldier, scribal attendee, and even grand vizier were all products of this early system.[91] These became the sultans' servants (*kul*) and thus members of his own household, whether posted in private chambers, garrisoned cities, or at the head of armies.

Hostility to this system of recruitment and to other trappings of centralization, such as a treasury and systematic taxes that diminished the grants and financial rewards of the marcher lords, emerged in tandem with assertions of dynastic sovereignty. An anonymous chronicler that clearly reflected the viewpoint of the marcher lords asserted that the ideal ruler should live a simple life, provide his men with raiding opportunities, and share his wealth.[92] He reproached the introduction of a state treasury and yearned for an earlier period when rulers were "not yet greedy," as "whatever came into their hands they gave away again, and they did not know what a treasury was." The chronicler associates the development of "greed" with a centralized treasury and attributed this to Persian court traditions, other Türkmen beyliks in Anatolia, and the Çandarlı dynasty of high-ranking religious scholars and viziers who served under Murad I:[93] "When the Persians and Karamanids became the companions of the princes of the house of Osman, these princes committed all kinds of sins," and, the chronicler goes on to say, "when [Çandarlı] 'Ali Paşa came to the Ottoman lords, sin and wickedness increased. Until then nothing was known of account books. The practice of accumulating money and storing it in a treasury comes from them. The house of Osman was a solid people, but these outsiders came to them and introduced all kinds of tricks."[94] He also criticized the organization of the *devşirme* and the process whereby "in just a few years" an inner page might become part of the elite janissary guard of the sultan and replace the established privileges of the marcher lords.[95] Sultan Bayezid I was also accused of accumulating wealth and power and, thus, of aiding in the turmoil that led to his defeat by the forces of Timur at the Battle of Ankara in 1402. Aşıkpaşazade's dynastic chronicle (c. 1490) suggested that Bayezid had kept riches to himself, succumbed to the temptation of greed, and was thus forced to watch as Timur took it and consumed it all. He further noted that the antidote to greed is charity and that "the sultan needed many friends who had full bellies and were not pre-occupied by the concerns of hunger."[96]

By associating account books and centralized fiscal policies with dynastic rule, even oppositional rhetoric assumed a link between the empire's textual record and a dynast's bid for universal power. This opposition to dynastic hierarchies accelerated with the pomp and grandeur that was architecturally realized in the Topkapı Palace. Critics correlated palace life with greed, injustice, and wickedness, and they decried the reification of sovereign power. Mehmed II further exacerbated this opposition by confiscating the wealth of former allies, establishing the normative career paths for both religious and administrative officiates, and implementing more standardized procedures for tax collection and the surveying of imperial resources.[97] Chroniclers who attempted to temper criticism of settled palace life and the Ottoman dynast's bid for universal sovereignty focused on the just distribution of resources, charitable acts, and the role of the sultan in assuring balanced and harmonious relations. Tursun Bey, for example, emphasized a general attitude of humility and willingness to dispense charity and justice as key attributes of this newly positioned ruler: he "should show gratitude for his sovereignty [*salṭanat*] by dispensing justice to all men, by acting benevolently, and by supporting people." A ruler's exalted status and fortunate acquisition of a vast realm should engender "empathy with the fate of the downtrodden." Possessing a rich treasury should engender actions of charity "without expectations of return." And, as noted in the epigraph to my introduction, he continued with a definitive statement that linked the power of the dynast to justice and protection.

Laws of justice and largesse were architecturally realized in the chamber of petitions and in the massive real estate of the palace's second court, devoted to the kitchens and to the dispensation of food for salaried employees, visiting dignitaries, and the poor during major religious holidays. The new chamber of petitions (*'arż odāsı*), referenced in Mehmed II's *kanun* and presumably built in the last years of his reign, illustrates the tension between an elevated sovereign and expectations for access to his judgment by petitioners. The *kanun* called for the construction of a chamber of petitions in the third court and directed that "my sacred majesty" will listen to the petitions brought forward by viziers, army judges, and finance officers four times a week.[98] He then only listened to deliberations of the imperial council in the second court through a latticed window (*kafes*) and increasingly restricted access to his personhood. Furthermore, although the connection between food, banquets, and allegiance shaped within a Seljuk ruling ethos and adopted by early leaders of the Ottoman confederation continued to demonstrate sultanic largesse, Mehmed II gradually removed himself from displays of public eating.[99] While later sultans, including his son Bayezid II, rolled back policies implemented in the name of centralization and briefly restored the habit of sharing a meal with his janissaries, the *kanun* ultimately came to structure the basic protocol and practices of administrative oversight within the palace walls.[100] Moreover, once the imposing wall that continues to surround the Topkapı Palace was completed in the final years of Mehmed II's life, the power of the Ottoman dynast was indelibly linked to his separation from the city, his distinct position at the head of a courtly and administrative hierarchy, and his reliance on rituals of respect and subordination rather than familiarity and comradeship.

But while these symbols and scripts for courtly power were postured as a bid for absolute power, the actual mechanisms of governance were far more accommodationist than absolutist. The personal retinue of the sultan, the guards of the palace doors, the proliferating service industries of the palace, and the appointed head officiates of the realm suggest that bureaucratic management rather than absolutist rule dominated palace life, if not its ceremonial expression. Thus, the early modern politics of granting access to the dynast, uniquely realized in the Topkapı Palace, also revealed the fragility of absolutist claims. The sultan may have been the pivot in this dynastic system, but he was far from an absolute ruler. Entrenched expectations of sultanic favor and charity, his careful cultivation of patronage relationships, and his required diligence in an ever-expanding territorial bureaucracy circumscribed his power, even if these actions were meant to augment central control. True, Gülru Necipoğlu's widely circulated argument that "the architectural, institutional and ceremonial organization of the Topkapı Palace perfectly reflected the system of absolute monarchy and helped to perpetuate it" continues to profoundly shape assumptions of Ottoman absolutism. But, like its rival courts, this absolutism was more performance than fact.

Scripted Courts: Scribal Traditions and Imperial Proclamations

The performance of absolutism, then, depended simultaneously on the monumental architecture of a palatial court, the protocols designed to impose a hierarchy of control on servitors of the realm, and the imperial edicts dispersed to sustain the Ottoman dynast's claim to universal sovereignty. The sections that follow turn from the spatial to the textual forms of these claims and suggest that what on the surface might seem fairly basic practices of writing and recording the affairs of state in fact contained within them a scripted universe of power. Yet even as various records of imperial acts carried the insignia of imperial authority and reinforced the singular presence and voice of the sultan, they were in actuality collective acts that point toward the replacement of the ruler by his bureaucracy.

There are many terms for *writing* within Ottoman imperial documents, and the diverse epistolography of the realm itself demonstrates a complex, multilayered bureaucracy that enfolded disparate practices into a new imperial order.[101] The terms for writing were often used interchangeably and within the same text, although over time they came to be more formalized and could indicate distinct documentary genres. Thus, Persian *name* and Arabic *kataba*, respectively meaning writing or to write, give us *mektub* (letter) and compound words designating types of documents such as *kanunname* (legal regulation or script), *'adaletname* (rescripts of justice), or *'ahdname* (treaty or agreement). The most common term for writing within Ottoman documents, however, was *yazı*, referencing both an epistle and the act of writing itself. Terms specifically designating a ceremonial imperial script became increasingly commonplace to indicate the "sign" of sovereign authority and the dynast's power invoked by the document itself: *hatt-ı hümayun* (imperial script, writing) and *tevki'* (sign, signature, note). The use of the term *hümā* is particularly significant, as it indicates a blend of Persian, Turkic, and Islamicate principles of fortune and sovereignty reshaped within the early Ottoman polity.[102] The mythical *hümā*-bird's shadow represented divine election "alighting" on a candidate spiritually qualified to receive it. Its shadow thus indicated the good fortune of being selected as a leader and implied unique qualities of wisdom and illumination.[103] The adjective *hümayun* was consistently used not only for sultanic decrees but also for the imperial council, the army, and even the tent occupied by the sultan while hunting or during seasons of military campaign.

Other common forms for *order* or *decree* also existed within Ottoman administrative documents; thus, *emr* (to order), *hükm* (rule, mandate, injunction), and *buyrultu* (from Turkic *buyurmak* "to command") indicate the authoritative statement of the sultan, even if they did not always rely on his direct intervention.[104] *Ferman-ı hümayun* (imperial order) designated edicts issued with the sultan's cypher, or *tuğra*, emblazoned as the opening to the command.[105] The diplomas (*berat*) that also carried the *tuğra*'s imprint and granted privileges or affirmed the appointments of various dignitaries and specified incumbent duties were further differentiated according to the type

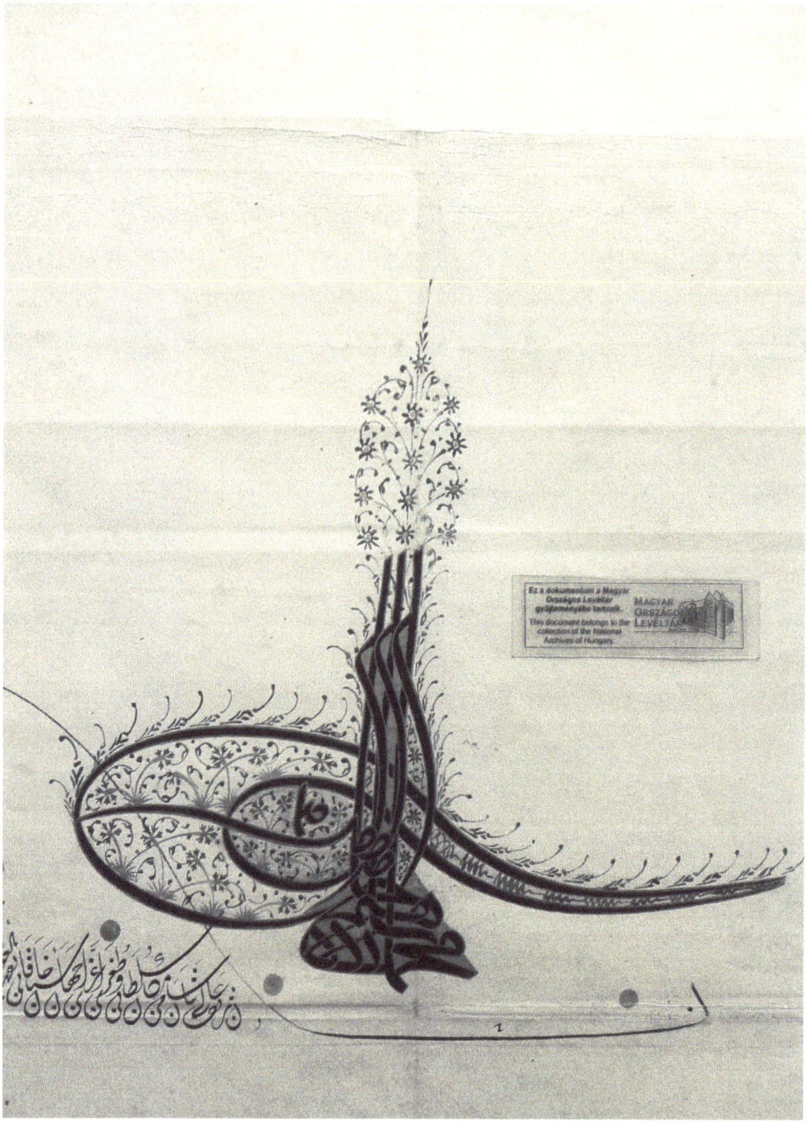

Figure 1. *ʿAhdname* issued on the accession of Mehmed III (r. 1595–1603) that reaffirms the terms of Ottoman sovereignty within a genealogy of rule traced back to Selim I (r. 1512–20). *Source*: Hungarian National Archives, P1286.

of award: examples include the *tımar beratı* (for grants of usufruct), *iltizam beratı* (recognition of a tax-farming status), and *serdarlık beratı* (recognition of a field commander). These diplomas were issued in the name of the sultan or by named dignitaries with the power to distribute resources and direct services, although even a high official rarely acted without reference to the sultanic voice of command. There were also records that, depending on their import, may or may not have included a sultanic seal (*mühr-i hümayun*). These were labeled reports or digests (*telhis*) and compiled in the vizier's chancery from drafts (*tahvil*), dispatches or dictations (*tahrir*), and general reportage from across the empire (*takrir*). The ubiquitous certificate, or "passport" (*tezkere*), used for safe passage, customs, or other permissions requiring the movement of persons or properties, also made up a huge percentage of the daily activities of the various divisions of the Ottoman chancery.[106] The organization and circulation of imperial records, from a sultanic writ bearing the sovereign seal to a draft copy used for internal reference, embodied the administrative apparatus of the empire in action. The need for scripted records led to increasingly specialized offices devoted to legal, fiscal, diplomatic, civil, and military regulations and to divisions between internal imperial administrative affairs and relations with external rivals. Records produced by these specialized offices, such as certificates of officeholders, tax registers, and treaties, gradually generated an archival history from within which the Ottoman establishment acted, and they demonstrate rather vividly how accurate knowledge of the realm's affairs was essential to the continued assertion of power. Without the map of the realm inscribed in these records, and without the power of written correspondence to convey and implement the authority of the dynastic court, the empire's order could not be ensured.

Even with this accumulated archive of recorded acts, however, the scripted universe of Ottoman imperial power was also tenuous and vulnerable. While imperial judgments emanated from the chancery, it would still be a mistake to refer to the Ottoman chancery as one, monolithic institution or to assume that "communication" entailed a direct link between the sultan (or even the imperial council) and the intended audience. Even the increased specialization of the council reveals the fragile nature of imperial commands. The high dignitaries of the state (grand vizier, treasurers elected for each major subordinated unit, military judge, admiral of the navy, army chief, head secretary) who also constituted the imperial council (*divan-i erkan-i devlet*) each had his own chanceries. These, in turn, were often further subdivided into multiple sections, as was the case of the financial institutions of the *defterdar* (chief fiscal administrator of the realm). Certainly, the administrative headquarters of the sultanate retained oversight through its own imperial chancery (*divan-i hümayun kalemi*), but this, too, was subdivided into offices devoted to the records of general governance, the preparation of edicts, decrees, and international correspondence (*beylik*), management of appointments and the renewal of *berat*s (*tahvil kalemi*), and the other miscellaneous allocations to Ottoman officialdom (*ru'us kalemi*).[107]

Evrak (ad hoc assertions or commands) and *vesika* (formalized imperial rescripts) asserted sultanic authority, but they were generated by a detailed hierarchy of palace-centered officiates. Even sultanic rescripts imprinted with the dynast's "signature," or *tuğra*, which directly invoked the personhood of the ruler, indicate instead the dependent nature of dynastic authority. When and by whom these signatures were deployed, where they were placed on the document, and what substitutes, if any, were allowed on the sheets of paper issued from the threshold of sultanic power illuminate the vulnerable relationship between text and power.[108] As the embodiment of the sultan, the *tuğra* was also referenced by terms meaning imperial cypher, sign, or banner (*nişan-i hümayun*, *tevki'*, *'alamet* respectively) and is the subject of much controversy concerning its origins and adoption by leaders in the early Ottoman confederacy.[109] Its features were striking: reaching a height of anywhere between ten and thirty centimeters; composed in gold, red, and blue inks; and inscribed by trained scribes specially assigned to this duty, their physical presence on a document transformed the paper into a richly ornamented imprint of the sultan himself. Some have argued that the three dramatic lines around which the monogram of each individual sultan was fashioned demonstrated a direct association with the "horsetail" (*tugh*) and thereby evoked an association among horses, horsetails, and sovereign authority that harks back to the central Asian steppe. Others simply link it to Murad I, the first known Ottoman dynast to employ the *tuğra*, and argue that it preserves the trace remnants of his actual handprint. Regardless of origin, the design remained fairly consistent, as did the practice of appending the phrase *khan al-muẓaffar da'iman* (the khan, always victorious) to it. This insistence on employing a title and a genealogy notably connected to central Asian nomadic ventures, even if they were manufactured rather than actual, stands as an able reminder of the continued evocation of mobility within the apparatus of centralized, established rule.

While the *tuğra* embodied the sultan and inscribed his authority on the scripted products of the imperial administrative offices, the actual mark was affixed by another, the *nişancı* or *tevki'ī* (the one who inscribes the imperial cypher). Initially, the *nişancı*'s role and office entailed the meticulous preparation and assessment of imperial acts that would be committed to paper and thus, by bearing the sultan's *tuğra*, disperse his authority throughout the empire. He scrutinized their contents for legal veracity and technical virtuosity and ensured that each record containing the sign (and the seal) of the sultan was worthy of his mark. He was thus also called the *müftü-ü kanun*, or the expounder of imperial law, and thus the counterpart to the scholar of divine law (*müftü-ü şeri'a*). But he was not alone in handling these records and ensuring their validity. A corps of officiates variously ensured that sultanic writs were properly maneuvered through the chancery and ultimately safeguarded for future reference. Thus, there were *kesedar*s who carefully secured and preserved documents prepared for the eyes of the high council and for the seal of the grand vizier *cum* sultan in special bags (*kese*); an inspector (*mümeyyiz*) who maintained the standards of the texts and cosigned them; a legal clerk (*kanuncu*) who verified the lawfulness of any declared act; and a department (*mukabeleci kalemi*) that compared final, pristine versions of original drafts for ultimate circulation. Finally, the *tuğrakeş* painted and affixed the *tuğra* itself. Furthermore, as outlined in Mehmed II's *kanunname*, three officials could lawfully use the imperial signature and seal on decrees related to their specific jurisdictions: the grand vizier for "affairs of the world" (*umur-i alem*), the *defterdar*s for affairs of the treasury (*mal*), and the *kadı'asker* for affairs concerning canon law (*şer'-i şerif*).[110]

Thus, even prior to the mid-sixteenth-century expansion and reorganization of bureaucratic offices, the triumphant declaration of sultanic writ emblazoned at the top of imperial correspondence was a collective act, not a singular assertion of the sovereign.[111] Still, the sultanic *tuğra* transformed Ottoman dynastic pronouncements into recognizable talismans of the empire. Its production required artistic and technical knowledge, and it serves as a reminder of the increasingly specialized nature of the administrative apparatus that formed it. The "sign" of the sultan invoked his presence and traversed diffuse territories even when he remained within palace grounds or was engaged in campaigns elsewhere in the empire. Furthermore, the practice of inserting signatures (called *pençe* or *imẓa*), stylized after the *tuğra* even if they were less complex and less ornately drawn, also became quite common across the bureaucratic spectrum.[112] A textual technique thereby served as a formalized tactic to implement administrative order within the context of a large composite empire.

Titular Trends: Canvassing Power and Displaying Humility

In addition to formal characteristics of administrative records such as the *tuğra*, textual products of the Ottoman establishment also conscientiously crafted a vocabulary of power and a grammar of rule through the terms drafted to identify and assign attributes to the sultan. This accumulated vocabulary illustrates the evolution of an Ottoman conception of sovereignty and calls attention to the significance of historical context in the careful use of titles and adjectives conferring authority. Significantly, the common referent for Ottoman rulers, *sultan*, was used only warily, and with a certain reserve, by Ottoman dynasts at least until the reign of Mehmed II, and even then it was primarily employed within correspondence circulated abroad: to rivals, challengers, subordinates, and tribute payers. It was thus a term used to broadcast the image of dynastic power to rival figures outside the realm. Within the empire's rather indefinite borders prior to the conquest of Constantinople, the preferred terms remained *khan* or *bey*, harking back to Turkic, if not Türkmen, traditions of linguistic preference and thus directly to leadership by consensus, by ability, and by demonstration rather than by membership within a particular family.[113] The use of *sultan* by rulers emanating from the Trans-Caspian region, termed in the late medieval period *Khwarezm* or *Khwarazmshahid*, did at one point appear on a coin Orhan minted ("*al-sulṭān al-ʿāẓam*"),[114] but Bayezid I reportedly asked the symbolic leader of the *umma* in Cairo, Caliph al-Mutawakkil (served 1389–1406) for permission to use it as a designation of his authority within the territories of Rum. It remained suggestive of regional, rather than universal, authority at this point.[115] But Bayezid *did* use the title *sahib-i kiran* (lord of the auspicious conjunction of the planets) and struck coins with a cluster of three dots to represent major planetary bodies in alignment as a reference to cosmological homologies between earthly rule and heavenly order.[116] This title and symbolic gesture foreshadowed the transregional articulation of power the Ottoman dynasts would initially adopt after the conquest of Constantinople and then reassert during the reign of Süleyman (1520–66). The exclusivity of power denoted by *sultan* became more commonly referenced only after the 1444 victory over a reignited crusading force at Varna by Murad II and then, in more declamatory fashion, after Mehmed II assumed his post-1453 Ottoman imperial garb.[117]

Yet, just as exclusivity was cemented in Anatolian and European provinces, new ideological challengers appeared in the East with the establishment of a Safavid dynastic structure (1501–1722, 1729–1736). Although this new contest forced a reassessment of Ottoman religious identity, and arguably contributed to the gradual Sunnization of Ottoman orthodoxy, literary stratagems deploying the designation of caliph (*ḫalīfe*) did not become the sole, or even primary, basis for claims to power. Instead, "lord of the two continents and of the two seas," a soubriquet acquired by Mehmed as his due after Constantinople became an Ottoman city, stood as the most recognizable identifying phrase in imperial records. Likewise, inclusive rhetoric continued to play a prominent role both as an acknowledgment of a majority non-Muslim population until the conquest of Mamluk territories under Selim I from 1516 to 1520 and as a result of mixed legal traditions and religious loyalties among the inhabitants of these lands even after their conquest. While scholars have emphasized the expression *ghazi sultan* both as a sufficient explanation for early Ottoman conquest and as an indication of the religiosity of the dynast, this title tended to be used only in particular circumstances and by a group of authors who were later sublimated by the centralizing statesmen of the sixteenth century.[118]

Just as titles varied depending on whether the intended audience was internal or external, so, too, did the tone of the text itself. The modes of address and formulaic invocations utilized within edicts, proclamations, diplomatic exchanges, nomination letters, or responses to various petitions issued from the sultan's administrative apparatus (*bab-ı ali*) thus also contributed in fashioning a vocabulary of power.[119] Correspondence sent to recipients outside the boundaries of the realm generally adopted titles and tones that underscored dominance, military might, and political superiority, whereas those for an internal audience employed adjectives indicating care, compassion, and protection for the inhabitants of the empire. Thus, the sultan jockeyed for position within a dense competitive field of external rivals with phrasings emphasizing his power, force, fearsomeness, and courage.[120] Adjectives deployed in external correspondence also foregrounded his superior status, employing descriptors such as *august*, *of great renown*, and *esteemed*, along with *fortunate* (*devletlu*) or *felicitous* (*sa'adetlu*). From the latter term the designations for the sultan's residence and extended household were also derived: *babü' sa'ade* (gate of felicity) or *darü' sa'ade* (abode of felicity).[121]

Internal correspondence deployed techniques that emphasized surveillance and constant oversight, even as the use of paternalistic tropes "softened" this oversight. The standard conclusion of most chancery records that contain sultanic writs, *baki ferman sultanımındır/padişahındır* (it remains the sultan's sole prerogative to issue commands), indicates an insistence on sultanic oversight for even the most trivial matters, even if that oversight was often only formulaic in nature. This phrase, with adornment, also appears in petitions *to* the sultan and thereby mirrors the sultanic emphasis on protective compassion in internal correspondence. Petitionary records also employ several key literary devices for adopting a posture of humility and supplication before the sovereign. Elaborate phrasing and literary forms appear even in the most modest requests. Many emphasize the auspicious and honorable rule of the sultan and characterize him as tender and solicitous of even the neediest of his subjects.[122] The accretion of four or five honorifics that highlighted the just, benevolent, and compassionate nature of the sultan, along with his mercy and generosity, typically appeared as the petitions' opening. Adjectives emphasizing protection, distribution, and order were followed by a rhyming compound for the title, most often using *sultan* or *padışah*: one such common phrasing was *padışah-i 'alem-penah*, meaning ruler or protecting lord in whom all the world takes refuge. The formula for closing (*hatime*) in petitions also adopted the forms of sultanic edicts but added adjectives that once again underscored finding favor in the eyes of a merciful sovereign: "for the rest, the remainder of the decision/order and decree belongs exclusively to our most merciful sovereign" (*bāḳi emr ü fermān merḥametlu pādişāhımızındır*).

Sultanic posturing for internal and external audiences, and the adoption of this vocabulary by the petitioners themselves to fit within formulaic expectations for the adjudication of grievances, paralleled shifts in diplomatic correspondence. Thus in both internal and external correspondence formulaic norms gradually inscribed a vocabulary of imperial absolutism and control. The shift from regional to imperial designations accompanied the expansionary conquests of Selim I (r. 1512–20) and his son Süleyman. Chancery developments also accompanied these conquests, as diplomatic exchanges increasingly deployed a standardized Ottoman imperial script, thus requiring a massive reordering of foreign diplomatic networks.[123] This linguistic transition is easily visible in shifts in letters that negotiated treaties, proclaimed victory, or addressed conflicts of interests between sovereign powers. Mehmed II's letters proclaiming victory over the Mamluks were composed in Arabic, and he used Persian when communicating with Turko-Persian rulers in Anatolia and beyond.[124] Ottoman-Venetian transactions prior to 1482 appeared in Greek or Italian. Bayezid II's (r. 1481–1512) exchanges with Venice concerning commercial and political treaties were in both Ottoman and Turkish. Under Selim one document relies on Ottoman Turkish, and another includes both Ottoman and Italian. Süleyman's treaties, however, were issued in Ottoman, as was all correspondence with the Venetians thereafter.[125]

Although hybrid forms and multilingualism continued to percolate through the realm, especially in relation to Arab or central European provinces, written correspondence increasingly proclaimed a vision of imperial unification and solidity. The relationship between script and authority represented a form of linguistic colonialism as centralizing dynasts sought to standardize governance in composite territories. French became the primary language of administration by royal ordinance in 1539, and a similar measure was passed in the same year in Poland. In 1536 English was proclaimed the singular language for record keeping and oath taking, thereby co-opting Welsh territories by an Act of Union.[126] And by the mid-sixteenth century, Persian had become the dominant administrative language of the Mughal and Safavid courts.[127] The formalization of linguistic boundaries accompanied the intensification of diplomatic exchange across frontiers of authority. Renaissance diplomatic circles dealt with unwieldy combinations of Ottoman, Venetian, Genoese, Catalan, Serbian, Hungarian, and Wallachian, yet these hybrid forms also ironically reinforced a turn toward scripted orthodoxies.[128] Within the Ottoman context Habsburg and Safavid rivalries intensified declarative assertions of dynastic exceptionalism and imperial universalism. Ottoman naval movements in the Mediterranean and Indian Ocean further contributed to creating a pen-dependent geopolitics, and letters bearing imperial insignia of power circulated to Buda, Vienna, Isfahan, North Africa, the Persian Gulf, Paris, Brussels, and Gujarat.

At this point titles formerly adapted from Greco-Roman or eastern European contexts such as *Tsar*, *Basileus*, and *Imperator* were dropped as designations for the Ottoman dynast and then were easily conscripted as *intitulatio* for foreign rulers.[129] Even this boundary is difficult to maintain, however; a title from Alexander the Great (*İskender du'l karneyn*, lit. "Alexander, lord of two horns"), for example, translated into Ottoman garb continued to play a strong role in imperial correspondence: *sultan-i selatin-i şark ve garb* became rather standard fare throughout Ottoman diplomatic letters. Furthermore, Ebu's-su'ud Efendi, chief jurisconsult and active participant in the administrative reforms of the sixteenth century, referred to Sultan Süleyman as "Khusros of Khusroses" and "Kayser of Kaysers" and even "the breaker of Kaysers" and "the one who casts dust in the faces of Khusros and Kayser," uniting in the figure of Süleyman both Mediterranean and Persian imperial traditions of titulature.[130] He further invoked these titles in the midst of efforts to define an Ottoman Sunni orthodoxy, demonstrating that the elasticity of titles, their transcendence of particular religions, remained a key strategy for displaying sultanic might and that circumstance as much as ideology shaped their use within imperial correspondence. Süleyman, on the conquest of the Moldavian fortress of Tighina, issued a proclamation that emphasized the triple identificatory heritages of the Ottoman sovereign: "the shah of Baghdad and Iraq, the Caesar of Rome and the sultan of Egypt."[131] In slightly adapted form this tripartite assessment of Ottoman dominions appeared in later formulations, as well, although here it is noteworthy that the persistence of Persianate philosophical ruminations concerning fortune and felicity are also referenced in the readoption of the title *sahib-i kiran* under Ahmed I (1603–17): "the lord of the fortunate conjunction of [i.e., ruling over] the Roman, Persian and Arab kingdoms" (*sāḥib-ḳirān-i memālik-i Rūm ve'l-'Acem ve'l-'Arab*). Ottoman, Safavid, and Mughal dynastic rulers adopted this designation especially in moments of crisis and apocalyptic events. It positioned the ruler at the conjunction of astronomical and temporal movements and thereby suggested an ordering of both divine and territorial realms under his auspices.[132]

Formulaic Ambiguity: Creating Consensus amid Fragmentation

While competition for territorial authority contributed to a hardening of linguistic borders, internal commands sought to impose hierarchical order on inhabitants of the realm as well. The formulaic features of imperial command, however, reveal the tenuous thread of textual authority even as they asserted sultanic suzerainty over lands and peoples. These formulae were designed to draw the attention of readers or the audience who listened to the oral enunciation of imperial edicts to the necessity of obeying the requirements outlined in the text.[133] Commands that were drawn up in bound registers by Süleyman's courtiers were more elaborately stylized than those found in the earliest records. Both, however, are merely copies of orders composed by the vizier or various officials in the chancery and thus begin with phrases referencing a record composed "after the fact."[134] The early imperial commands open by referencing the state of affairs represented in the petitions they address. They quote the details of the original petition precisely and note that these conditions have been made known to the sultan from the reported request for redress.[135] The command itself (*buyurdum ki*) then carefully inscribed the measures to be adopted, often referencing the outcome of an investigation into previous legal decisions or surveys, and then generally insisted that the sultanic command reasserts an order dictated by both divine and dynastic tradition (*şer' ü kanun*). These edicts then generally conclude with the phrase "thus you should know" and assert that the recipient should recognize the trustworthy nature of the physical text as a sign of imperial authority.[136]

Later registers inserted repetition, threat, and references to punctual conformity into the dictates of the command. More often than not, these insertions also took the place, of a full recitation of the petitions' content. On the one hand this seems to suggest a more efficient process of copying; on the other hand it is possible to argue that the emphasis shifts from the nature of regional affairs to the textual structure of the command itself.[137] The copy of the sultanic order, then, was intended to preserve the decision and the injunction of the sultan rather than the affairs of the petition that prompted it. Later imperial edicts emphasized the timely fulfillment of demands and reinforced the texts' imperial authority with the adjective *exalted*: "as soon as this exalted imperial letter reaches [your hands], it should be known that . . ."[138] These commands also often included a warning that "after this you will not act by any other means" (than those described in the document).[139] As if this decisive statement were not enough, addressees might also be threatened with punishment: "a great misfortune will befall you" if the recipient failed to act in immediate accordance with imperial dictates.[140] The closing, like the opening, contained a kind of entreaty; here, a phrase verified the credentials of the document: "you should recognize and trust that this text is true" (*bitti taḥkīk bilip 'itimād ḳılā'sız*). Such formulaic constructions indicate that documents intended to command more often entreated and relied on threats and repetition to ensure that the imperial voice was "heard" by the diffuse recipients throughout the realm.

Significantly, records attributed to the direct intervention and penmanship of the sultan, the *hatt-ı hümayun*, insert *more*, rather than less, ambiguity and distressed authority in both the formulae and the narrative content of the sultanic writ. Most assessments of sultanic decision making or governance rely primarily on diplomatic correspondence (*name-i hümayun*) and thus on collected volumes whose primary purpose was scribal training.[141] These collected texts included representative types, employed an ornate literary script (*inşa'*), and focused primarily on conquest and victory, thereby eulogizing the sultan by way of listed examples. Designated scribes also composed "sultanic letters" of congratulation or condolence to ministers and officials of the realm. Sultanic writs composed "on the surface of" incoming reports, dispatches, or summaries of chancery decisions did insert the pen of the ruler into matters of state.[142] But the most direct records of sultanic locution and intervention can be found in the *beyaz üzerine hatt-ı hümayun*.[143] This latter corpus serves as the Ottoman version of a "white paper," here indicating that the sultan composed a directive on a "blank" sheet of paper, thus acting on his own inclination and for his own purpose rather than merely appending a note to an already-constructed order. The prevalence of the latter—notes that contained the formulation "it remains the sultan's sole prerogative to issue commands" (*baki ferman sultanımındır*)—designates a scripted response to petitions or brackets very brief additions. The "white papers," however, exist as rare records of sultanic compositions. As Murphey notes, "since they were produced ex-chancery and designed to fill a momentary and often transient need, their preservation is largely accidental or the product of peculiar historical circumstances."[144] They were "accidental" because they were not part of the organized preservation of imperial records and thus failed to find their way into the emerging textual terrain of the Ottoman state as a distinct category. This in and of itself should give us pause: the direct compositions of the sultans were not, in themselves, deemed "normative" enough to the continued reproduction of Ottoman power to warrant methodical conservation and publication. Even the collections of sultanic correspondence did not include the sultan's direct notations. Their idiosyncratic nature, perhaps, did not render them "useful" for pedagogical purposes within the secretariat, nor were they systematically collected in the preserved registers of the Ottoman establishment. Even the heading for these directions, "*hatt*s written [by the sultan himself] based on sudden inspiration (*karihe*) and on the spur of the moment," suggest their existence outside the bureaucratic system of document production.[145]

Preserved within the University of Istanbul's library collections, a rare copybook containing 326 directives from the reign of Murad IV (1623–40) illuminates the role these sultanic insertions played in establishing sultanic authority through textual forms. Eighty of this corpus of *hutut-ı hümayun* appear to have been written by Murad himself, with the remaining examples dictated to governors of Egypt and Buda, the grand vizier, and the commander of the janissaries. These personal directives of Murad IV seemingly circulated among a small elite, exerted often-microscopic control over everyday events, and disparaged examples among his appointed officials and servants of fiscal abuse, falsification of records, and immoral behavior. The writs vividly demonstrate the vulnerability of sovereign authority, alternating between pleas for obedience and condemnations of infractions. Indeed, the language in these orders was strikingly more threatening than the formulaic warnings (*la'net*) that typically concluded official documents and thereby call attention to the likelihood that even a direct sultanic command might be ignored or disobeyed.

Furthermore, these preserved orders highlight the way in which imperial authority depended on the co-option and consensus of elites who often pursued their own fantasies of power and control. The sultan had to *convince* his *kul* that they were, indeed, dedicated and loyal servants. To achieve this end, he relied on three interdependent factors: access to information, control over official appointments, and mechanisms to elicit cooperation and maintain loyalty. Court messengers, garrisoned janissaries, and regional district and provincial governors contributed alike to formalized reports sent to the sultan from surrounding provinces or from the throes of a military campaign and thereby created a surveillance network that sustained the reach of the sultan. Surveillance thus relied on the "gathering in" of documents from various administrative postings, from campaign commanders, and from *kul*s scattered across the empire. Murad IV mentions several times the need for "papers" to arrive, for a coherent collection of noteworthy news of events and traditions, for administrative records and reports from transimperial locales, and for due diligence on the part of his officials in delivering all of this information: "You wrote to me saying: 'I promise to send the register of vacant cavalry posts with the regimental commandant,' but as yet there is no sign of him. Whatever you have managed to complete to date send it on, however little it may be. Later on I will compare your records with the main register kept here. Be assured if I find the slightest evidence of dereliction on your part I will not hesitate to punish you accordingly."[146]

In fact, pleas for information, updates, news reports, and supervision of past petitions and the implementation of law were sprinkled throughout the directives: *elçi gelip* (the envoy arrived [and made oral representations]); *kağıdlar gelip* (written reports were received . . .).[147] The constant cross-checking with preserved registers and requests for "submission of financial reports" illustrates the exhaustive and consuming effort necessary for the oversight and administration of daily affairs. The sultan depended on these threads of information, and the Ottoman establishment as a whole became ever more reliant on a preserved archive containing a history of negotiation, strategies employed by previous sultans, and possible avenues for the future. The sultanate relied on the information in this archival database to distribute land grants, positions, and rights to tax collection, as well as to assess the loyalty of servants and to make reapportionments accordingly. Information gathered and recorded became the basis for both reward and punishment. In such a far-flung imperial context, however, the sultans were also forced to rely on various intermediaries to send the dispatches gradually accumulated in the archive and for the implementation of any new directives. Dependencies therefore abounded, and only when the sultan was proximate to the situation at hand could direct intervention be made. The sultanic writ, then, stood in for this intervention. Yet frustration over distance and the networks of dependencies suffuse these sultanic writs even as they form a miniarchive of administrative acts.

Locating the Sovereign in Composite Empires

As evidenced in both spatial and textual forms, claims to absolute power and universal authority accompanied the establishment of the court and courtly politics in the Ottoman context and in the early modern period more generally. Yet this authority was a fragmented construct—reliant on textual, political, and diplomatic feints to secure a semblance of mastery and control. Yet while the commensurable historical trends and dynastic strategies that took root in the fifteenth century and expanded into the sixteenth may challenge easy conceptions of absolute power, they by no means suggest that the sovereign was removed from the center of his domain. Even when physically distant, say at El Escorial rather than within the adjudicating passageways of the Real Alcázar, or witnessing the affairs of the *divan* (council) from behind the screen that separated the sultan's quarters from the daily affairs of governance, the sovereign was still the primary source of authority, his seal still rendered edicts and declarations licit, and he still enacted edicts that bound officials to him, to the realm, and to the land or its products.[148] As the ultimate source of authority, the ruler could make or break the careers of his administrators, and he, or his imperial council, served as the arbiter of justice and order within the realm. At issue was not the "centrality" of the ruler, either physically or ideologically, nor even the constraints such centrality imposed on his person and on the system of rule his personage embodied. But the place of the sovereign was less a matter of the sultan's *personhood* and the standards and protocols that defined his position as ruler. It was instead the sovereignty of a *text* capable of enacting the command of the sultan across the territorial expanse of empire that reproduced and sustained the dynasty and the state.

The Ottoman dynasty's investment in textual knowledge production and consumption was so pronounced precisely because it depended in large part on textual command and preserved registers for securing and displaying its power. Daily record keeping of council meetings, copying of incoming reports and petitions, and the issuing of imperial edicts, certificates, diplomas, and rewards constituted much of what the government and its officials *did* and was thus inseparable from what that government *was*. There was a basic presumption of textual competence not only among appointed Ottoman officials but also among elites across the empire. This presumption also entailed compositional dexterity across a variety of genres, including an emergent canon of official chronicling and commentary.[149] The Ottoman establishment depended on textual production in order to "see" and thus to "know" its imperial domains.[150] The sultanate thus acted on the assumption that demands for information would be acknowledged, and duly provided, by designates of the state or confirmed regional intermediaries. While cartographic representations formed one essential facet of this process of knowledge construction, the empire was also daily reconstructed through textual commands, which became the primary medium for imperial control.[151] This medium generated a "papereality," or a tendency to rely on "official written documents to represent the world."[152] This world, presented or "represented" in imperial writ, was part of the state's effort to fabricate textual authority and thus to render knowledge sovereign—complete mastery rather than fragmentary control. It was thus a world defined by a vision of imperial order dependent on the sultan yet resorting to the inscription of his personhood in a textual habitus of power and control. These preserved registers thus seek to constrain far-flung domains and multifarious confederacies of regional and interimperial intermediaries, yet in the end they stand only as an empire of paper, or an empire *on* paper. While this empire of paper may indeed have been commanded by the sultanate, and its durability constitutes the only knowable archive of its actions, it is a limited order—an order constrained by the view of bureaucratic officialdom and intended to transform a diverse realm into a legible order.

The textual productions of the expanding Ottoman bureaucracy thus formed a readable textual map of the empire. Preserved remnants of these efforts canvassed the realm, displayed the sultanate's power, and masked the vulnerabilities of the Ottoman establishment under the supremacy of an imperial sign and cipher. As the promulgation of both general and provincial legal regulations, the *kanunname*s vividly illustrate this process of rendering the empire legible to inform administrative practice. These legal regulations extended the legislative arm of the sultanate and asserted territorial sovereignty against rival claimants and potential dissidents. Chapter 2 moves to the mechanisms of the *kanunname*s, whereby a vision of universal order and imperial command served as the sieve through which information was assembled and dispersed. By joining together disparate sources of knowledge and land administration strategies, these regulations served as an index of imperial domains, a set of categories for assigning revenues and policing sociopolitical boundaries, and thus a new grammar from which administrative action constructed a readable landscape.

CHAPTER TWO

THE STATE OF STABILITY

The Kanunname *as a Genre of Administrative Governance*

> For in that time [the rule of Sultan Selim I], within the ways of the Sultanate a soundly-established rule, and in the affairs of the Caliphate a firmly-constructed system was observed and accepted; the *dirhems* and *dinārs* of the good order of the state were coined with the abundance-marked dye of the laws (*ḳavānīn*).
>
> —Mustafa Celalzade, *Selimnāme*[1]

As the massive engine of military campaigns consolidated the Ottoman hold on Anatolia and extended the boundaries of the empire across peninsulas, seas, and mountain ranges, two tangible objects accompanied the sultan or his commanders in battle: the "purse," or treasury, and the "register," or preserved record of past edicts, cadastral surveys, copies of treaties, and regional petitions that measured and accounted for the resources of the realm.[2] Wagonloads of single-leaf edicts and key registers physically accompanied military ventures up through the eighteenth century. In 1638 they were assigned considerable space in the caravan outfitted for Murad IV's (r. 1623–40) successful attempt to recapture Baghdad. An edict that mandated the number of pack animals requisitioned for the campaign itemized "54 pack horses for the use of the Office of the Registry, 3 pack horses for the Keeper of the Registers, 10 pack horses for the Chief Keeper of the Daily Accounts."[3] Registers such as those pertaining to land grantees obligated to participate in military campaigns (*sipahi*), regional administrative appointments, surveys of human and material resources, salaried officials, and copies of sultanic ordinances were placed in tents and guarded as part of the army's treasury (*ordu hazinesi*). Supplementary records covering transactions up to thirty years old were also dispersed to key provincial locations along the campaign route, housed within reach for necessary consultation.[4] This chapter extends the connection between spatial and textual protocols presented in Chapter 1 and demonstrates how military achievement was inextricably linked to the development of systematic record-keeping practices. These practices produced an "active archive" capable of enumerating the resources of the realm and assimilating new conquests into a workable administrative order. More pointedly, the sections that follow show how registers and notebooks (*defter*s) that recorded land-distribution rights, regional administrators, and local practices *implemented* and *managed* the conquest after the army's return to the capital. In Halil İnalcık's words, "the *defter* was the basic tool of the Ottoman government."[5] As a primary example of this practice, *kanunname* emerged as a genre of governance during the reigns of Bayezid II (1481–1512), Selim I (1512–20), and Süleyman I (1520–66). It also examines regulations limited to particular provinces newly conquered by the Ottoman state, such as the *kanunname* of Trablus-ı Şam in Greater Syria formalized in 1517, as well as the *kanunname*s issued to Erzurum and Buda in 1540. In combination these legal regulations gradually asserted the supremacy of Ottoman law over previous legislation, articulated principles for administrative action in a given region, and balanced revenue extraction against prescriptions for just rule and the relief of the downtrodden.

The Importance of Record-Keeping Practices in the Ottoman Domains

Doubtless, the primary purpose of archiving activities both on campaign and after was to assess the tax base of conquered populations in order to assign revenue sources either to the cavaliers in the Ottoman army or to regional leaders, who were in this way enfolded into an Ottoman-defined governing structure. Grants of small or moderate size (*timar* and *ziamet*),[6] along with larger assignments (*has*)[7] generally allocated to the sultan himself as sultanic domains (*has-ı hümayun*) or to members of the court and higher administrative personnel such as viziers and provincial governors, depended on a surveying mechanism of potential revenue sources.[8] State authority turned on the ability to assign rights to resources, and the successful recipients represented members of groups with the social and material power necessary to enter into negotiation with the state. Therefore, it was a major administrative priority to register taxes through cadastral surveys (*tapu-tahrir defterleri*), as these records were crucial to the empire's fiscal and symbolic reproduction.[9] Thus, the impulse to survey and register territories did not cease with conquest or with the transformation of land-tenure patterns that shifted emphasis from cadastral surveys to tracking monetized flows of resources.[10] In the correspondence of the imperial council, pervasive refrains to "look over" or "review" (*nazar olunmak*) claims to state revenues or granted privileges suggest that Ottoman administrators fully understood the relationship between information and the power necessary to assert the primacy of the state's claims over those of other interest groups.

Yet there was also a grander process at work in the production of an "active archive." Early modern sovereignty, as noted in Chapter 1, depended on the ability to establish a new spatial and textual habitus that organized in turn the politics of the court, imperial correspondence, and the insignia of sultanic authority. Rapid military gains necessitated the extension of this textual habitus outward to new provinces. This expansion, and administrative efforts to organize or contain the resulting geographic and social heterogeneity, has led to an oft-repeated commonplace among scholars of Ottoman empire-building: flexible and particular responses to newly conquered territories and to the demographic variations of their inhabitants. Flexibility, however, was less the goal than the seeming result of an attempt to fit diversity within a hierarchy of control enumerated through imperial record-keeping practices. The goal was legislative oversight, and the appearance of diversity belies a consciously fabricated rubric for order and administrative coherence as the Ottomans sought to align provincial realities with imperial agendas. This legislative oversight was achieved through two forms of registers that gradually overlapped with each other and constituted a "defterization" of Ottoman governing practices: the cadastral surveys that mapped regional resources, and the legal regulations (*kanunname*) that transformed these maps into a forum for transactional law.[11]

Cadastral surveys organized human and material resources, guarded against potential clashes among interest groups over dues and privileges, and asserted an established practice against which potential innovations (*bida'at*) were forestalled.[12] Although the ordering of domains shifted considerably over the course of the sixteenth and seventeenth centuries, comprehensive (*defter-i mufassal*) registers covered either a whole province (*vilayet*) or subprovince (*sancak*) in which villages were grouped by district (*kaza*) and subdistrict (*nahiye*).[13] Towns and large villages were further subdivided into quarters or wards (*mahalle*) and sometimes even into streets (*zuqaq*). Within each town quarter, village, and—depending on their primacy in a given region—tribal unit, taxpayers were listed by householder and divided into a married (*hane*) or unmarried (*mücerred*) fiscal unit. Reference was made to nontaxpaying members of the population—prayer leaders, scribes, descendants of the prophet, and the mad, blind, and disabled. A further division between Muslims and "the rest" was indicated by a separate listing of Christians, Jews, Kurds, Türkmen, nomads, and—in the case of Greater Syria—Jundi Mamluks, gesturing toward the continued significance of this Egyptian-based ruling establishment. That "the rest" was not solely based on confession but also included nonsettled or nonaligned elements of the population should be noted because they often garnered the most attention in summary (*hulasa-i ijmal*) registers, which aimed to fix an otherwise mobile tax base into a synoptic view for the sultan.[14]

While the cadastral surveys in effect "gathered in" the human and material resources of the expanding Ottoman territories, the ordinances of the *kanunname* "dispersed outward" via sultanic edicts (*ferman*) a particular vision of imperial order and sought to render that order and its categories legible to the inhabitants of its domain. The *kanunname* combined sultanic edicts with passages describing regional conditions and thus enfolded diversity into an imperial regulation that asserted the rights of the sovereign to define public order and to ensure a mechanism for the extraction of resources. Empire-wide regulations (so-called "general" *kanunname*) and those issued to particular provinces (*liva kanunname*s) created archived registers that transformed diverse categories of land, population, dues, privileges, and crimes into revenue streams.[15] Issued at the accession of a sultan, after conquest, or in response to exigent circumstances, these legal proclamations proliferated throughout the Ottoman provinces. As surveyors worked to tabulate regional practices, fit them into an imperial model of fiscal discipline, and then transform them into a legal ordinance, these practices gradually enfolded otherwise scattered regions and diverse lifestyles into an actionable grammar of rule. This was especially true after bureaucratic reforms early in Süleyman's reign reconstituted these legal regulations as preambles to cadastral surveys, thereby structurally indicating that they would serve as the prism through which regional variations might be interpreted and legislated.[16] The production and circulation of bound registers therefore facilitated the emergence of textual and legislative authority within the Ottoman Empire. By defining a particular logic for ruling conquered territories, this textual authority served political ends. Yet it was also not wholly commensurate with the agendas of the imperial governing apparatus, as the circulation of *kanunname* gradually created a discursive terrain that exceeded dynastic control.[17] In an illustration of the critical interplay between territorial and textual authority, however, it was through these legal regulations that provincial realities came to be *written into* Ottoman strategies of governance. They thus provide the clearest record of the dynasty's efforts to articulate, both for themselves and for the inhabitants of their domains, a framework within which administrative actions might be conducted. The following sections demonstrate how dynastic sovereignty came to be configured through the production and circulation of both general and provincial *kanunname*. They seek to distinguish between the registers in which sultanic edits were recorded and the *kanun* of a state that came to both embody principles of order and govern according to them. As both conceptual and physical "regulations," sultanic edicts inscribed principles of administrative practice and thus a grammar of rule that first defined and then enabled the imposition of sovereign authority. To elucidate the process whereby circulated legal regulations came to inscribe dynastic sovereignty, the next section explores the varied meanings of law and statecraft inherited by Ottoman administrators and focuses on how the *kanunname* gradually evolved into a system of dynastic law. The chapter then moves on to address how these regulations, whether formalized into a general *kanunname* by a specific sultan or distributed to restive provinces, created specific organizational principles for administrative action and how these principles amounted to a grammar, or legal vocabulary, that was variable yet resilient. The chapter concludes with a reassessment of the meaning of "custom" (*örf* in Turkish; *'urf* in Arabic) so as to present the deft legal mechanisms that folded customary laws of predecessors or rivals into a rebranded system of Ottoman governance. The chapter thus tracks the intersections among record-keeping practices, the formation of legal statutes, and the extension of dynastic sovereignty through the armature of textual authority.

Legacies of Lawgiving and Strategies of Imperial Governance

Confronted by the intricacies of regional power structures and systems of land tenure, the Ottoman establishment asserted the right of the sovereign to regulate the productive surplus of its agrarian base and to prescribe norms for criminal and public law.[18] However, this extension of legislative authority faced limits both social and structural.[19] Social limits occurred insofar as inhabitants of the realm were liable to evade, disrupt, or challenge the assertion of imperial law, and imperial agents weren't always properly trained or deployed to assess regional differences. The structural limits, however, illuminate an enduring tension at the heart of the *kanunname* enterprise: the tension between a dynast's right to issue *kanun* and legislate social and political order, and the dictates of the *shari'a*, the Islamicate tradition of divine law that defined the basis of the Muslim community (*umma*) and also adjudicated matters of personal status, inheritance rights, property transfers, and a large range of commercial transactions.[20] Internal to theological and jurisprudential interpretations of the *shari'a* was a long debate concerning the relationship between sovereign power and divine principle, and this was particularly assessed in terms of what legislative role might be accorded to the ruler of a Muslim polity. The evolution of a politics of statecraft (*siyasa*) in early Muslim ruling establishments accompanied the more volatile question of rightful leadership, as the prophet Muhammad's death in 632 catalyzed an enduring theological, philosophical, and political debate concerning succession and the proper role of a leader.[21] While the evolution of *kanun* as a mechanism for dynastic legal intervention is connected to questions of statecraft, or *siyasa*, it also became a distinct method of governance, as the following sections illustrate.

In the ninth through the eleventh centuries the coincident emergence of a cohort of religious scholars (*'ulema*) and cultural encounters with Greco-Hellenic and Persianate philosophical traditions reenergized debates concerning the relationship between divine ideals and temporal power.[22]

Classical manuals of jurisprudence within the Islamicate tradition also addressed the main tenets of government (*imara*) and administration (*wilaya*) and suggested that sovereign authority was necessary for both the well-being of the community and the rational order of society.[23] Al-Mawardi's (d. 1058) "ordinances of government" articulated some of the main tenets of this evolving sense of governance in a text, *al-Aḥkām al-sulṭāniyya w'al-wilāyāt al-dīniyya*, that became an instant classic and remained influential for Muslim polities in later periods.[24] In this treatise al-Mawardi reversed the customary modifiers for religious (*diniyya*) and political (*sultaniyya*) norms and suggested instead that his manual would address the divine nature of sovereignty and the administrative practices of religious structures.[25] Within this framework a ruler was entitled to obedience if he adhered to the principles of Islam and governed with justice and wisdom.[26] He then possessed authority over the entire community and territories of the *umma* and was allotted jurisdiction over legislation in cases where there was no clear ruling from the Qur'an, *hadith*, or the prior consensus of legal interpreters (*fuqaha'*). The ruler adjudicated affairs of the realm and addressed petitioners' complaints in courts designated for this purpose (*mazalim*) distinct from *shari'a* courts presided over by the *'ulema*.[27] Governance thus demanded the careful navigation of rulers (*ulu al-'amr*), or those who command, between the norms of the *shari'a* and the everyday techniques developed to maintain social and political order.[28] These in combination yielded a system known as *siyasa shar'iyya*, which yoked together *shari'a* norms with the practice of governing and then significantly shaped shared religious and political principles of administration even within diverse historical contexts.[29]

Qanun (Arabic) was therefore initially adopted as a means to address aspects of public life (criminal and fiscal) not fully elaborated on in the *shari'a* or, more radically, as a way of bending regional customs (*'urf*) to the purposes of the state.[30] It could thus be used to indicate the propriety of a ruler and courtly elites and as a moral standard against which actions were judged. These disparate usages are especially clear within the Mamluk sultanate of Egypt (c. 1250–1517). Here, as Guy Burak has illustrated, compilers of biographical dictionaries and encyclopedias relied on an understanding reminiscent of the original Greek meaning of the term *kanon* and used it as a yardstick for measuring the appropriateness of a principle or standard.[31]

In this guise ibn Manzur (d. 1311–12) stated that "the *qānūn* of any thing is its manner and its scale." Ahmad al-Nuwayri (d. 1332?) used *qanun* to assert that ignorance is worse than evil "because the principle of evil [*qānūn al-sharr*] is known, whereas the principle of ignorance [*qānūn al-jahl*] is not."[32] Parallel to this use of *qanun* as a principle of measure, however, was also a focus on social and political practice and thus on the tradition of issuing manuals that guided the proper behavior of the administrative elites. Al-Qalqashandi's (d. 1418) manual for scribes includes the phrase "standards of chancery" (*qawānīn dīwān al-inshā'*) as a reference to proper comportment.[33] This association between *qanun* and court protocol played a role in the Ottoman context as well. The *kanunname* of Mehmed II inscribed the first set of guidelines for administrators of the realm and outlined the daily practice of governance. The introduction to the influential chancery manual of Feridun Ahmed Bey (d. 1583), which he composed as a scribe in the service of grand vizier Sokullu Mehmed Paşa (d. 1579), pays close attention to protocol and gives an itemization of the administrative elite.[34] Even Arab elites who in the eighteenth century began writing themselves into Ottoman elite literary culture did so partly by producing their own lists enumerating the dynasty's courtly household and extensive bureaucracy. The Damascene chronicler ibn Kannan's (d. 1740) *Gardens of Jasmine in Recounting the Qanuns of the Caliphs and Sultans* serves as an explicit guide to the privileges, obligations, salaries, insignia, and ceremonial of the military units, administrative bodies, and religious posts under the discretionary authority of the sultan.[35] Furthermore, legal regulations promulgated by the imperial council for specific groupings, such as *kanun* for the *yeniçeri* (janissaries), also illustrate the continued significance of the relationship between *kanun* and protocol incumbent on various segments of society.[36]

But this understanding of *qanun* tended to locate principles of judgment and standards of measure outside the personhood of the ruler and thus potentially served to restrict his authority rather than extend it. Notably, in the introductions to their works, ibn Kannan and Feridun Bey sought to legitimize the dynasty by invoking imperial genealogy, a practice that became a fixture of *kanunname*s and treatises in fields as diverse as political geography, advice manuals, biographical dictionaries, and encyclopedias. This explicitly *dynastic* character of Ottoman *kanun*-making drew from yet another tradition: that of the Mongols and of various Anatolian principalities that challenged the early consolidation of the Ottoman state. The legacy of regional actors is particularly important for its role in driving a wedge in the debate over the legality of Ottoman *kanun*, especially as the dynamics of conquest extended dynastic authority over taxation policies and public order. Consequently, an imperial order co-opted the canonic principles of the *shari'a* and displaced local agents in the process.[37] The tradition of the *yasa* refers to the Chinggisid legal system established in the empires of central Asia and carried into southwestern Asian regimes such as the Ilkhanid or, as *törü*, the Timurid.[38] The law, *törü* or *yasa*, was presumed to be the foundation of the state and the primary assurance for the sanctity and stability of the regime. This foundation was centered in the dynastic legitimacy of the founders, Chinggis Khan and Timur. Thus, the collection of laws, customs, and edicts that circulated as *yasa* (Chinggisid) or *törü* (Timurid), despite fluctuating over time, remained fixed in their lineage of origin.[39] Unlike the Indo-Persian emphasis on absolute authority, with *'adl*, or justice, its only limit, or the *shari'a* as a limit to sovereign authority, the *yasa* provided the very basis of orderliness in a realm.[40] This legal order was defined genealogically and contributed to the emergence of two variant meanings for *örf* within Ottoman descriptions and practices of lawmaking: a classical sense of *örf* as *'adet*, or custom, designating diverse regional conditions and their incorporation into the *kanunname*; or, linked also to the legacy of *yasa* and *törü*, *örf* indicated the "custom" of sovereign legislative power, or *örf-i saltanat*.[41] Both meanings indicate the extension of the sultan's legislative power over territories and regional practices enfolded into the ambit of his rule. The import of these combined meanings can also be inferred from the title given to imperial agents who registered provinces and actively composed general and provincial *kanunname*. These men were designated the *ehl-i örf*, or the people of "imperial custom," who were products of the hierarchies of education and service imposed by Mehmed II and had attained elite chancery or religious positions within the council. As graduates of the *medreses* he founded, and having followed a career path of appointment he designated in the *kanunname*, these men were products of a newly crafted imperial system and agents of its "custom."[42] The title of Bayezid II's general *kanunname*, *Kitāb-ı ḳavānīn-i örfiyye-i 'Os̱mānī*, also potentially played on the double meanings of *örf* as it could be translated as "the Ottoman book of customary *or* imperial regulations."[43] However, the interpenetration of regional and imperial practice through designations of *örf* vividly illustrates yet again the relationship between registering territorial difference and promulgating laws to manage this difference.

The practice of lawmaking was thus specifically tied to a register and to the act of recording the basic features of land administration. This association also had a long legacy, as al-Mawardi linked the act of issuing *qanun* with a specific designation of a tax register, thereby moving *qanun* outside of theological interpretation, courtly protocol, or dynastic right.[44] Each of the major Muslim-based ruling establishments across the region shared an understanding of *qanun* as "register." When Rashid al-Din (d. 1318), the author of a newly imagined universal history that placed his patrons, the Ilkhans, within a cosmic genealogy shaped by Islam, sent a letter of guidance to a Shirazi governor, he invoked both the principle of justice and the notion of the *qanun* as an imperial tax register. He explicitly cautioned the governor against taxing the populace beyond the regulations (*qanun*) of the sultan's council.[45] *Qanun* thus stood as both an act of registration and a limit on oppression by setting a standard measurement for the extraction of human and material resources. This carried over into the Ottoman context, as *kanunname* and the cadastral survey were increasingly bound together to manage revenue streams and assert the right of the sovereign to do so.

Composed during Mehmed II's initial attempt to define the spatial and textual rubrics of imperial power, Tursun Bey's formative history directly referenced the *yasa* traditions of Chinggis Khan and captured an early sense of the multiple valences of law and state in the Ottoman context. He navigated a rising concern over how to sanction new legislative claims while maintaining the legitimizing rhetoric of the *shari'a*. Tursun Bey also argued for a dynastic genealogy, yet, following earlier writers of ethical treatises such as Nasir al-Din Tusi (d. 1274), he suggested that lineage alone could not accredit a candidate for governance. Instead, a ruler should possess the qualities of virtue (wisdom, courage, gentleness, and justice) that harkened back to Plato's philosopher king and al-Farabi's adaptation of this king into a reasoned lawmaker: "No one [ruler] can be worthy of praise or be truly proud unless it is by reason of possessing all or some of these four virtues. Those who take pride in their descent and lineage can only do so because they have fathers and ancestors who were [also] known for these virtues."[46] Virtue thus defined the Ottoman lineage, as the dynasts could not claim a direct line either to the prophet or even, as Timur had claimed, to Chinggisid world conquerors. In his introduction Tursun Bey thus directly invoked the sultan's legislative function as the legitimating practice of the Ottoman dynasty and positioned *örf* and imperial law as the means to maintain world order:

> The laws based on principles that ensure felicity in this world and the next are called divine government, or *şerī'at* and determined by the *ehl-i şerī'at*. There are [also] laws based on reason that enable the proper order of the world (*niẓām-ı 'ālem*) such as those composed by Chinggis Khan. In these laws, events are connected to their causality [historical conditions], and they are called sultanic governance (*siyāset-i sulṭānī*) and imperial law (*yasağ-ı pādişāhī*) and named *örf* within our tradition (*örfümüzce*). The continued maintenance of [this system] requires the existence of a ruler (*pādişāh*). There is no need for a prophetic lawgiver in every age . . . ; however, in every period, there is a need for a ruler who possesses the authority to establish laws and to implement measures for the sake of public welfare. If his authority is lost, no law can be enforced and people cannot live together. They would destroy both each other and the order of the world.[47]

Tursun Bey suggests that the order of the world depends not just on an established sovereign authority but also on his ability to unite the legal principles of the *shari'a* with the practice of imperial governance exemplified in *yasa* and *örf*. Here, too, there is a double innuendo between *örf* as both imperial lawmaking and a designation specifying Ottoman traditions and practices. Most important, perhaps, is the direct link he ascribes between law and order.

The multiple valences of *qanun* and sovereign authority became even clearer during the era of Süleyman. When his chief chancellor, Celalzade Mustafa, composed the preamble to the *kanunname* of Egypt in 1525, he framed its legal contents in the following manner: "Some of the just and compassionate *qanuns*, which [were initially issued] in ancient times and [came down] from my [Süleyman's] noble fathers and great grandfathers, are linked

[to] an old principle and in a straight link, and should be followed."[48] Several tactics are of note here and appear in various formulations in both general and regional *kanunnames* addressed below. First, this passage contains an assertion of historicity and thus the suggestion that a reference to "ancient times" provided its own authority and referenced a continuous legacy of lawmaking by the Ottoman sultans. Although the Ottoman military had conquered Mamluk Egypt only seven years prior, the laws of the Ottoman dynasts, this formulation suggests, carried a veritable and august legacy. Second, the "straight link" to genealogical forebears locates the force of the laws within a chain of virtuous legislative authority. Celalzade Mustafa then further characterized the historicity and genealogical weight of these laws as a "principle" that "should be followed." This principle, a carefully fashioned rubric of Ottoman custom, suggests that *örf* (custom) and the *ehl-i örf* (term designating state agents) abrogate all previous traditions, authorities, and legal rubrics.

Örf as a legal precedent with a double valence in the *kanunname* both affirmed the emergence of an "Ottoman way" and constituted a clear acknowledgment that long-standing regional practices, if not accommodated, led to social disorder. Such upheavals threatened to destabilize an imperial authority predicated on the maintenance of a just order and so prompted conciliatory rather than coercive governing practices. As compiled in the various *kanunname*, Sultanic proclamations, then, both ratified previous customs and established a new one by codifying and stabilizing them into a circulated, written text.[49] The legitimizing discourses of *kanun*, *shari'a*, and *örf* together reinforced an idealized vision of proper order amid the chaos of expansion, attempting to squeeze new territories into stable categories of governance. These efforts entailed a distinctly expanded definition of sovereignty, one that laid claim both to a genealogy of past exemplars of territorial rule and to the legal domain of the *shari'a*. Celalzade Mustafa's encomium for Süleyman in the introduction to his treatise dedicated to the accomplishments of his former ruler, Selim I, calls on all of these various markers of sovereignty.[50] The "Ottoman throne of sovereignty and prosperity-destined imperial seat" is now blessed by the presence of Sultan Süleyman, a ruler "who has Darius as his slave and Alexander as his servant" and with "Cyrus as his page" is also "as fortunate as Bahrām and has Chosroes attending him."[51] This itinerary leading back to early Persianate traditions is then complemented by explicit references to territorial domains, extending from the holy cities of Mecca, Medina, and Jerusalem, to the territories of Rum and Egypt, to conquests in Iraq, Belgrade, Buda, and Rhodes. He then draws a direct equation linking law, textual authority, and order. He identifies Süleyman as "the protector of the heartland of piety and of Islam, the one who sits on the throne and couch of the *şerīʿat* and of the guardianship, the pearl of the crown of territorial conquest . . . the index to the royal book, the preface and heading of the treatise on world-government, the one who sets up in order the signs of world-subjugation . . . the strong rope of the religion . . . the result of the great sovereigns of the dynasty of Osman."[52]

Celalzade Mustafa then references God's blessings, for "Thou hast made him king over the world; thou hast made his court a refuge for monarchs. Thou has made him custodian of the kingdom of the *şerīʿat*. . . . The banner of his power has reached the sky; it has risen to the sun and attained the heavens."[53] Celalzade Mustafa's sovereign was an all-encompassing sovereign, the alpha and omega of world order, supported by both religious and political power, and thus the epitome of a universal ruler. Yet this conception of sovereignty was forged from within a protracted negotiation between territorial realities and administrative categories.

The Quest for an Imperial Law: Genre and Practice in the General Kanunname

The variant understandings of *qanun* as a principle, a legal practice, a tax register, and a typology of imperial order are all bundled into the textual terrain occupied by the *kanunname* and rendered them a robust genre for managing territorial diversity. Mehmed II's general *kanunname* explicitly linked the preservation of political and social order to a continued legacy of lawgiving. The section devoted to court hierarchy concludes with an injunction: "So many affairs of the 'state' [saltanat] have been put into order. Hereafter, let my sons also continue to promulgate laws."[54] Mehmed II further referenced ancestral provenance by claiming that "his *kanun*" is also the "*kanun* of my father and grandfather" and ordered that this organization of the state should be followed through the generations.[55] Moreover, although presumably sultanic ordinances were not binding on successors, Mehmed II demanded obedience from his descendants and thus planted the seeds for a general *kanun-i Osmani* that would transcend succession crises and dynastic upheavals. Three of his immediate successors, Bayezid II, Selim I, and Süleyman I, each issued a series of provincial *kanunname* and, more significantly, composed general *kanunname*s that built on the legacy of their predecessors and embodied imperial projects of territorial and ideological expansion particular to their reigns.[56] Whereas early iterations of sultanic ordinances tended to address specific issues, territories, or social groups, these *kanunname* inscribed the organizational agendas of Ottoman dynastic authority.[57] They enfolded new territories into textual registers that, in their declarative assertion of sultanic legitimacy, also promised to curtail the regional power of former and current rivals, such as the Akkoyunlu and Dulkadır principalities in Anatolia; the Mamluk dynasty across the Hijaz, Greater Syria, and Egypt; the emergent messianic Shi'i Safavid foes to the east; and the Habsburgs to the north.

Each of these rulers would play a formidable role in the evolution of a legal written corpus, and they would do so in the face of particular challenges and distinct achievements that defined their *devlet*, or their personal bid to the Ottoman sultanate.[58] Bayezid II was initially confronted by a coalition of anticentralization supporters united behind his brother Cem and later by disenchanted groups in Anatolia and southeast of the Taurus Mountains. Shah Isma'il mobilized these groups and capitalized on popular messianic preaching in these regions to found a Shi'i-inflected Safavid state in 1501. Bayezid, in order to consolidate his own position of power, thus carefully emphasized the religious basis of his authority and stemmed the tide of his father's more radical policies of property confiscation, forced repopulation, and cultural hybridity.[59] He also spent much of his reign, outside of conquests in the Morea, attending to the expanding Ottoman administrative apparatus. As a result, his *kanunname* managed the increasing complexity of the empire through a massive physical and conceptual expansion from the more skeletal form of Mehmed II's regulations.[60] It was organized in three major sections with distinct subheadings, contained more than 250 statutes, and outlined a clear role for the adjudication of *siyaset* measures, or the political laws of the state.[61] This organizational pattern, and many of the specific formulations, would continue to circulate in the regulations composed by his successors. Selim I's acquisition of the sultanate was also troubled by a brother, Ahmed, and a rebellion, the Şahkulu, in eastern Anatolia, that ultimately brought Safavid supporters into a by now typical Ottoman succession crisis.[62] Selim's success in this struggle then propelled him, for the remainder of his reign, to quite aggressively face down both the empowered Safavids and the more established and bureaucratically centralized Mamluk sultanate.[63] From a triumphant entry into Tabriz in 1514 after a major victory against the Safavid Shah İsma'il at the Battle of Chaldiran, he pivoted to a series of battles between 1516 and 1517 that ultimately yielded him the territories of the Muslim heartlands from the Hijaz to Cairo and earned him the title that designated him the new legitimate representative of the Muslim *umma* writ large. These conquests marked the first moment in which the Ottoman sultan governed a Muslim-majority empire, and his rule was now qualified by the title of caliph (*halife*), which sacralized his power as the protector of Islam and the two holy cities of Mecca and Medina. Yet, despite the increased weight of Islam numerically and symbolically in the empire, Selim's *kanunname* would extend and fine-tune the *siyaset* power of the state, and even clarified juridical points typically left to the discriminating scholars of the *shari'a*.[64] Furthermore, the fact that multiple, even if some falsely attributed, copies of his *kanunname* were preserved across the realm attests to the increasing complexity of the governed population, to the sophistication of scholars and statesmen emerging from imperial *medreses*, and to the heightened focus on the legal apparatus of the sultanate's attempt to staff and adjudicate the realm.[65]

Posterity granted Süleyman "the lawgiver," or *kanuni*, as an epithet, yet quite clearly his reign marked a consolidation of trends long under way. He governed an empire with the amassed tools of an advanced military and naval fleet—a hierarchically structured system of imperial administrators, judges, and bureaucrats—and record-keeping practices that ensured the unhindered flow of revenue to support cultural endowments and continued territorial expansion. Under his lengthy reign the empire pushed its borders to their furthest extent, maintained battle lines against the Safavids and the Habsburgs, and simultaneously monopolized the Mediterranean Sea while challenging the Portuguese in the Indian Ocean. The general *kanunname* of his court also amassed the accumulated tactics and provisions of his forebears in order to expand the role of the state in legislating political, social, and fiscal order.[66] Various lawmakers of Süleyman's court also consulted multiple regional and general *kanunname* to generate a more comprehensive summation of *kanun* practices.[67]

There were clear innovations as well. Whereas previous regional *kanunname* had simply incorporated the legal customs of rulers such as the Mamluk sultan Qaytbay or the Akkoyunlu leader Uzun Hasan, by 1540 these had been firmly replaced by Süleyman's ambitious lawmakers. They now most notably included a redefined role for the head chancellor (*nişancı*) and for the leading jurisconsult (*şeyhülislam*) who together would dramatically reform the relationship between religious and state law in order to manage the increasing complexity of governance. Although later sultans, such as Murad III (r. 1575–95), Mehmed III, and Ahmed I also issued significant *kanun* regulations, these tended to reflect regional *kanunname* and focus particularly on issues of land transfers. Their *kanun* were less significant than the *'adaletname*s (rescripts of justice) these sultans relied on to adjudicate pressing concerns and disturbances between the population and the shifting coterie of state agents.[68] Süleyman's *kanunname* thus established the foundations of the Ottoman legal system (*kanun-ı kadim*) that arose out of the legal ordinances and intellectual commentary of the late sixteenth and early seventeenth centuries.[69] It also served as the primary basis for a new systematized *kanunname-i cedid* (new *kanunname*) formulated more than a century later, in the early 1670s.[70] This latter *kanunname* was organized by clearly categorized entries and extracted texts from the earlier circulars and stood as the standard legal framework until a new period of reforms with radically different agendas and stakes began in the late eighteenth century and ultimately resulted in the reorganization (*tanzimat*) of the civil (1830s) and land (1858) codes.[71] Thus, beginning in the 1480s and then fully realized by the 1540s, the Ottoman *kanun* traditions elaborated a textual habitus that extended the legal and territorial sovereignty of the Ottoman dynast.

Bayezid I: Organizational Rubrics

Bayezid's *kanunname* dramatically extended imperial intervention into domains of public law, especially in relation to criminal punishments, sociosexual norms, taxation related to landed property, and social hierarchies imposed on inhabitants of the realm and its various servants. His *kanun* also served as a key source for the version of Süleyman's *kanunname* composed by Celalzade Mustafa and introduced the basic organizational and discursive grammar adopted by each major *kanun* compilation. It thus provides an organizational guide for claims concerning the links among law, text, and sociopolitical order asserted in this chapter. The *kanunname* opens with a preamble (*mukaddime*) that includes praise for the sultan, the reasons for legislating, and the basic structure of the text that follows. The *mukaddime* begins by stating that God rendered the sultan the very cause and reason of order and that this order also necessitates comprehensive obedience to his ordinances.[72] For this reason, it continues, the *kavanin-i örfiyye-i Osmani* compiles preexisting independent *kanun* issued as *hüküm*s or *ferman* and presents them in three primary sections (*bab*): criminal law (*cinayat*), taxes (*rüsum*) collected by regional or imperial agents, and the general conditions and administrative patterns of the population at large (*re'aya muhtass ahval*).[73] The criminal measures proceed first with the intricate vagaries of sexual crimes, ranging from adultery to abduction to house invasions that were also associated with sexual transgression. Then detailed provisions are listed for assault and battery, as well as murder, followed by procedures for theft, robbery, and various property transgressions, along with immoral behavior such as the drinking of alcoholic beverages, loitering, and fleeing the scene of a crime. Significantly, the use of fines (*cürm*) and discretionary punishments (*ta'zir*) throughout this section of the *kanunname* indicates a combination of *shari'a* guidelines and state policies for adjudicating social order.[74] For instance, the first statute requires that a Muslim male who was proven according to the standards of the shar'ia (*şer' ile sabit*) to have committed adultery (*zina'*) must pay a monetary fine based on his social status (well-off, middling, poor, and destitute); this statute was then also applied to adolescents and women.[75] Canonical proof required the presence of four adult male witnesses and entailed punishments outlined in the Qur'an for transgressions of God's order (*hadd*). Because producing four witnesses was notoriously difficult, customary law and the judge's discretionary use of beatings became standard. Here, however, even though the crime was proven and punished according to the *shari'a*, a monetary punishment was also assigned. Monetary fines became the trump card of state power.[76] Bayezid's *kanunname* also carved a discretionary role for the sultan to administer punishments for major infractions; these punishments included death, bastinado, shaving the beard, scorching the forehead, and exile, among others. Titled "On Siyaset Punishment Only" (*mücerred siyāseti beyān ider*), this stands as the clearest indication of the sultan's expanded role in relation to procedures formerly adjudicated solely by the *shari'a* and were also rather "spectacular" in their performance of state power.[77]

Both the second and third sections contain seven chapters (*fasıl*) and bear the title "On *sipahi*, on *beytü'l-mal*, and on the taxes collected from the *re'āya* by the *sipāhī*." The *kanunname* here inscribes the basic principles of agrarian governance and the various expectations assigned to administrators, cultivators, and urban as well as nomadic populations. It first outlines the obligations of military service for land-grant recipients (*ahval-i sahib-i timar*), along with provisions due and problems that may arise in efforts to administer villages and collect revenue (*tasarruf*) from them. The third chapter addresses market taxes, customs, and other revenues intended for the state treasury. Here, the incorporation of three brief statements of regional *kanun* measures for Semendire, Morava, and Rudnik, as well as complaints from Konya concerning burdensome yearly obligations, indicates the hybrid nature of the general *kanunname*: they both inscribed categories of measure and attended to ongoing regional processes of negotiation and potential conflict that were then used as the basis for future regulations.[78] This becomes even more apparent in the remaining three chapters, where standard measures and local variations together indicate a living, active assembly of legal traditions. The fourth chapter delineates taxes due on imperial domain lands (*miri*), as well as on animals, and various commercial and manufacturing taxes such as from mills or dye houses. Critically, this chapter first attends to the intricacies of the *çift* tax, defined as a plot of land capable of being plowed by two oxen under the continuous labor of a household (*hane*). Halil İnalcık identified this as both a head tax and a land tax and the single most significant fiscal measurement of the Ottoman regime, given that possession of a tract of arable land rendered the cultivator both taxable by the state and obligated to the local administrator of the region.[79] The *çift* tax took into account the productivity of the land (high, medium, or low) and of the labor associated with it. A "complete" (*temam*) *çift* thus assumed the presence of a household, while a half (*nim*) *çift* indicated variables of daily or partial labor; there were also different amounts due from married (*bennak*), unmarried (*mücerred*), and poor (*kara*) members of the *re'aya*. Although the *kanunname* sets the *çift* tax at thirty-six *akçe*s and the half *çift* at eighteen, the same section then immediately itemizes fifteen provincial variations in the tax fixed for individual provinces and thus assumes regional differences.[80] Furthermore, it required twenty *akçe* from non-Muslim agriculturalists and so, as in other sections of the *kanunname*, explicitly attended to the empire's confessional diversity.[81] Different regional measures were also recorded for taxes on sheep (*resm-i ağnam*), one *akçe* for two sheep is listed as standard, but in Vidin only one *akçe* was collected for three. And in the case of commercial taxes on mills, the *kanunname* simply includes a collection of regional regulations.[82]

These regional variations continue into the fifth chapter, which addresses rates incorporated into the imperial revenue stream according to the categories inscribed as a "tithe" of one tenth or one eighth as prescribed in the *shari'a*. Tithes were assessed on agricultural products from lands that were not directly incorporated as part of the sultanic domain (*miri*).[83] The sixth *fasıl* describes variable conditions in rural territories and attempts to police potential irregularities. This is particularly clear in regulations described as *bad-i hava*, literally, "wind in the air," which formally recognized the irregular income (*tekalif-i örfiyye*) that trustees of the land might assess on its occupants.[84] These might include a bride tax, taxes on the registration or loss of property, its transfer and division, or other assorted measures, but the list also arbitrarily excluded other local customs. The *kanunname* attempted to forestall various delegates of the state from simply inventing new levies or exploiting the population for their own purposes. Thus, the text commands that these "irregular" conditions be inscribed in the *defter* as a check against future variation.[85] The section on military campaigns defines the relationship of land-grant recipients, the cultivator, and the defense of the realm. It creates a clear division (*kismet*) between those who work the land and pay taxes (*re'aya* or *halk*) and those who collect the taxes and participate in military campaigns (*'askeri*). The privileged status of the latter seems clear, but it was also slippery, since during intensive campaign seasons, cultivators might be commissioned as soldiers (*müsellem*), irregular cavalrymen or infantry troops (*yaya*) and exempted from taxes as well. Moreover, these privileges might also be extended to nomadic groups (*yörük* and *tatar*) or regional paramilitary groups (*eflak*, *voynuk*, or *canbaz*) when necessary.[86] The passages devoted to taxes assessed on fishing, grazing land, and winter pasturage, as well as those devoted specifically to cultivators-turned-soldiers, attend primarily to the dangers of tax evasion inherent in either physical movement or the symbolic passage from one social category to another. Registering mobile populations, and ascertaining when a cultivator should be relieved of tax burdens when on campaign, how his burdens might be assessed on others, and how long his newly acquired status might endure were diligently specified and tracked across the *defter*s. Such statutes indicated that even as the *kanunname* imposed clear categories and social divisions, the borders between were porous, potentially disruptive, and thus necessarily inscribed into a permanent text of imperial affairs.[87]

The third and final section of the *kanunname* specifically addressed the conditions of the *re'aya* in seven chapters, touching on questions of inheritance, general rights and obligations of Ottoman subjects, the status of non-Muslim inhabitants of the realm, and the status of unmarried or mobile elements of the population. Of particular importance here were the problems that might arise when a cultivator has abandoned land, as this prevented the orderly registration of material and human resources and diminished the amount of arable land that sustained an agrarian taxation system. Property transfers were also minutely managed, for similar reasons, especially in the case of death or when non-Muslims were incorporated into imperial domains. The statutes specified that only a son could inherit the father's right to the disposition of the land, and that he must pay a tax (*tapu*) for this right to be granted and recorded in the appropriate registers. Concerns over the status of non-Muslim rural populations were addressed in the second chapter of this section. The inheritance of a deceased non-Muslim, for example, required an investigation by both the local judge (*kadı*) and a delegate commissioned by the imperial council.[88] Only when the relationship between the deceased person and an heir was documented through these channels would a *hükm-i şerif* (imperial command) acknowledge the claim. This imperial intervention into inheritance rights and property transfers typically defined by the *shari'a* was an important assertion of sovereign legal rights. These sovereign rights were also configured territorially, as the fifth chapter of the *kanunname* distinctively includes the provincial statutes for the paramilitary *eflak*s from the region of Wallachia and, as in previous chapters that referenced Semendire and Vidin, provides notations for how to assess taxes and fines between the two monetary units of *filori* and *akçe*, as well as how to bind irregular units to the land in a relatively fluid border zone.[89] The final two chapters address unlawful encroachments or innovations on the part of the *'askeri* such as fines on commercial shops and properties or excessive taxes. These sections also included regional complaints of oppressive measures and lists of obligations owed by the rural population to the palace proper, such as the storage of wood for the maintenance of kitchens. This latter point indicates the way in which provincial resources were essential for the continued circulation of sultanic munificence.

In combination, the statutes of Bayezid II's *kanunname* provided an organizational rubric for the regulations compiled during the reigns of his son and grandson. Furthermore, although *kanunname*s fluctuated in form, more comprehensive regulations tended to follow the structure outlined in Bayezid's reign. As provincial *kanunname*s became more prominent over the century, they, too, incorporated categories defined in Bayezid's *kanunname*, even as they added increased specification based on regional concerns. A sharp divide between provincial and general *kanunname*s, therefore, misses the way in which both forms addressed particular concerns even as they elaborated general categories. These general categories sought to define sociopolitical boundaries, assess and distribute shares to imperial resources, and ensure the proper registration of the realm. They regularized differences, and rendered them part of an actionable vocabulary of administrative governance.

Selim I: Defining Shares and Policing Categories

The *kanunname* attributed to the reign of Selim I did not contain the same intricately structured divisions of Bayezid's, nor did it begin with a *mukaddime* introducing the plan or import of the *kanun*. The progression of topics remained fairly similar, however: criminal fines and punishments; agrarian relations and standard taxation on markets and commercial activities; and then an assessment of obligations, dues, and boundaries (again, traversed) between cultivator, soldier, nomad, and the more permanent governing strata of military men *cum* administrative custodians (*'askeri*).[90] Some clear differences from Bayezid's *kanunname* indicate that, despite a similarity in content, change was afoot in the domain of imperial law. Raised prices, alternative regional emphases, and heightened focus on both social and territorial boundaries, as well as on market prices and vagaries of land administration, together brought the *kanunname* more prominently into the expanding terrain of the empire. These more expansive concerns also entailed an amplified role for the legislative authority of the sultan, as several innovations clearly indicate. First, unlike any previous renditions, the versions compiled during his reign listed in stunning detail market prices of everyday items such as soap, oil, honey, varieties of meat, vegetables, spices, yogurt, butter, flour, and some forty more products.[91] Furthermore, it explicitly labeled almost fifty commercial and artisanal crafts in a section devoted to the circulation of market goods and input and output taxes that were only briefly referenced in either Mehmed II or Bayezid II's *kanunname.*[92] Reading through this final section of the *kanunname* is like walking through an urban neighborhood and passing the fishmonger, the butcher, barber, baker, pastry chef, apothecary, and grocer, while grazing on grapes, cheese, watermelon, börek, olives, and halva. Prices were set by the market inspector, in consultation with the local judge, and created an organized urban economic sphere that paralleled the effort to systematize agrarian taxes.[93]

Second, each copy of Bayezid's *kanunname* employed a vocabulary for fines (*cürm*) and punishment (*cinayet*) distinct from the shar'ia designation (*ta'zīr bi'l-māl*). Bayezid's criminal edicts had also clearly distinguished between crimes such as adultery, which was customarily adjudicated according to the *shar'ia*, and the "*siyaset* only" crimes assessed by the state.[94] Selim's *kanunname*, however, divided the two categories into some twenty statutes or measures and, in the copy presented by Pulaha and Yücel, indicated this with the title *Cürmü cināyet ve siyāset.* Furthermore, both versions of the *kanunname* explored here put a twist on the relationship between *shar'ia* and *siyaset* in the first statute of the criminal section. This statute fines a married (male) adulterer four hundred *akçe* if the adultery was definitively proven. As noted above, however, proof of adultery according to the shar'ia (*şer'ile sabit olsa*) required four witnesses, a notoriously difficult thing to achieve.

Uniquely, in one copy of the *kanunname* the requirement for proof was only partially invoked, and only *sabit* was used.[95] In the copy contained in Akgündüz the phrase *şer'ile sabit olsa* did indeed appear; however, the statute also called for punishing the crime according to *siyaset* provisions and thus, in a significant move, folded adultery into the ambit of political governance.[96] One other notable point within the criminal statutes attributed to Selim I is that Bayezid's fine distinctions between Muslim and non-Muslim disappear; these measures, if not now deemed standard for all *kanun*, at least suggested the possibility that the arm of the sultan extended indiscriminately over the inhabitants of the realm.

However, this sultanic reach was configured slightly differently here. The third point of note is that Selim I's *kanunname*, unlike those of Bayezid, did not incorporate substantial portions of regional *kanunname*s, nor did it reference the paramilitary groups (*eflak*) from the regions surrounding the principality of Wallachia or other provinces north of Istanbul. Provincial references remained grounded in Anatolia, or regions around Bursa, which paralleled the military campaigns Selim I famously conducted. During his reign, the two major Türkmen states, the Akkoyunlu sultanate that controlled eastern Anatolia from western Iran and the Dulkadir principality that encompassed central and southeastern Anatolia and parts of northern Syria, were both conquered. Both had consistently challenged Ottoman consolidation. Absorbing these principalities, however, also intensified Ottoman encounters with the strong legal traditions of these regional states, a point Ömer Lüdfi Barkan emphasized in his work on regional *kanunname*.[97] Leslie Peirce also called attention to the significant impact that the Dulkadir *kanunname* may have had on Selim's criminal code, as well as on the evolving Ottoman legal system more generally.[98] She further underscored, as had Barkan before her, that the Dulkadır *kanunname* was not replaced by Ottoman provincial regulations until the 1560s. The legislation passed by the Akkoyunlu sultan Uzun Hasan (r. 1453–78) also shaped Ottoman customary practices, yet it was replaced slightly earlier, between 1518 and 1540.[99] Part of the inheritance of Anatolian principalities seems to have been a legal system that attentively regulated social and economic relations. Territorial gains inflected the *kanunname* with an even more heightened concern with description and with the "emplacement" of personages and regions into the appropriate register, administrative category, and location in the sociopolitical language of the realm. As the final feature of note, Selim's *kanunname* consistently referred to previous *defter*s and registered statutes, especially the statutes that concerned agrarian taxes, such as the *resm-i çift*, and the measures intended to police the mobility of the rural population. Significantly, these references deliberately insert a comparative measure across provinces and between past records and present conditions. For example, as the *kanunname* shifts from criminal concerns to questions of agrarian administration, the first statute indicates that while in some provinces the complete *çift* tax was recorded as thirty *akçe* and *nim çift* as half that, in the province of Hamid, the tax was fixed at forty-two and twenty, in Menteşe at thirty and fifteen, and the same for the territory of Hüdavendigar. Formerly part of a strong regional principality, the interior territory of Germiyan was assessed "according to custom" at thirty-two *akçe* indicating the gradual incorporation of local into imperial practices.[100] This comparative principle also functioned for changes in status that required consultation with previous records or with provincial measures recorded in the cadastral surveys. One marginal note simply indicates that tax amounts should follow those recorded for each province.[101] The *kanunname*'s statutes thus expended an immense amount of energy tracking these changes: cultivators not previously registered in the cadastral surveys, but who were now active producers of local agriculture; former bachelors who were now married; deceased personages now represented by another; cultivators from outside the territory now functioning within it, or who had fled but now returned, or who had now reached their maturity and could claim cultivation rights, or those who enriched their status by acquiring more cultivation rights, or had become impoverished and could no longer pay their previously assigned taxes. Arguably, every statute concerning taxation and the status of the *re'aya* policed distinctions between "what was written" and present realities. The statutes further tracked the cultivators' relationships to administrators or religious representatives and mapped their daily activities as they moved among towns and villages, mosques and markets. Compilers of the *kanunname* thus persistently attempted to define a set of categories capable of rendering the diverse regions, demographics, and sociopolitical structures intelligible, veritable, and actionable.[102]

Süleyman I: Principles of Order

As I noted earlier, the best-known manuscript copies of general *kanunname* compiled during the early years of Süleyman I's reign (most likely between 1523 and 1540) can be attributed to two successive *nişancıs*: Seydi Bey and Celalzade Mustafa. Seydi Bey's *kanunname* closely resembled copies attributed to Selim I: its organizational structure is more streamlined and did not devote a section to the *eflak*. It also includes almost direct copies of diverse market goods and prices and avoids distinctions concerning Muslim and non-Muslim in the opening criminal code. The *kanunname* compiled through the efforts of Celalzade Mustafa, in contrast, more closely resembles that of Bayezid II. The text contains a coherent organizational précis as part of its *mukaddime*, and the criminal code clearly notes confessional identities and concludes with a separate section on *siyaset* punishments. The *kanunname* further includes a separate section for the *eflak* paramilitary group but does not display the same focus on market goods and taxes as Seydi Bey's manuscript. It distinguishes potentially divisive regional and customary taxes and obligations in a section titled "*bād-ı havāyı*" and concludes with duties and obligations owed to the palace kitchens and statutes delivered in response to complaints about various forms of oppression and excessive taxation. Despite these respective similarities with past iterations, however, several features either illustrate extensions of previous legislation or a shift in the discursive intent of the *kanunname*.

Seydi Bey's copy has two strikingly unique innovations. The first, also following the shifts in Selim's *kanunname*, explicitly forbids stoning as a punishment for adultery, even if the crime was proved according to the *shari'a*, and then simply repeats the variable monetary fines set by economic status during Selim's reign (450 *akçe*).[103] As Akgündüz noted, this inserted clause indicates a clear preference for monetary as opposed to criminal punishment, at least for adultery, and a widening of the sovereign's discretionary power to stabilize sociosexual behavior. This same copy illustrates one other signature feature of the *kanunname*s issued during Süleyman's reign: they record the imperial council's efforts to supervise and direct the implementation of these regulatory edicts by both administrators and judges across the realm. Chapters 16 and 17 of Seydi Bey's text clarify provisions concerning various auxiliary units such as the *müsellem* and *yaya*. Chapter 16 inserts a typical assortment of land measures and tax exemptions in exchange for service. Statutes laid out mechanisms for inheritance of usufruct rights and property transfers, designated to whom dues and taxes should be remitted, and set criminal procedures for when an individual reneges on his military service obligation.[104] Chapter 17, however, breaks form and includes an imperial order (*hükm-i şerif-i sultani*) that evokes the authority of the imperial seal and *tuğra* of the sultan and concludes with the typical closing and signature date of an imperial command (*ferman*): so let it be known, and trust in the imperial sign (of this order).[105] The *ferman* states explicitly that this text of sultanic laws and governance was delivered to Aydın's provincial district commander of *yaya* units to ensure that the statutes of the Exalted Porte were appropriately followed.[106] Dated May 1523, this inserted copy of an imperial command may indicate the continued importance of military defense and order in a notoriously intractable region of southwestern Anatolia. But it also presents a more general emphasis in manuscript copies of Süleyman's *kanunname* on lawmaking practices and the implementation of sultanic command. While previous *kanunname* generated the formulae for administrative order, Süleyman's moved beyond the grammar of rule to the techniques and strategies of governance.

This point is also made clear in the opening structure of Seydi Bey's copy: the *ferman* recorded in the preamble notes that the reason for this record is that "my late father and grandfather" had observed that the inhabitants of the land (*re'aya*) were in great distress as they were "tyrannized by oppressors." The *ferman* then notes that his ancestors' response, after investigating these oppressive conditions, was to "implement the Ottoman *kanun*." Therefore, "I also have commanded that the governor-generals, provincial governors, district military commanders, police officers, and *sipahi* should demand their privileges and taxes from the population (*re'aya*) in accordance with the Ottoman *kanun*." The *ferman* closes, in typical fashion, with a threat, stating that if oppression increases, then these administers of the realm will find themselves on the receiving end of their sultan's grievous rebuke.[107] Here, for the first time in the *kanunname* reviewed thus far, is a direct statement of principle behind the statutes outlined in the regulations. The content of each mapped, often in minute detail, the human and material resources of the realm. They further included the basic provisions for public order and marked a passageway for the insertion of the *kanun* into everyday life. But principles of justice and relief from oppression pointedly find their way into the *kanunname* when rapid expansion necessitated a bold statement of sultanic legitimacy for the assertion of imperial control.

Although Celalzade's copy does not explicitly mention justice, it presents the import of the bound defter (*mücelled defter*) in a detailed preamble that adheres to the basic rubrics adopted in Bayezid's *kanunname*. Its opening prayer repeats the same wording as the one found in Bayezid's, wherein God places the sultan as the fundamental cause and reason of the world and makes all follow the sultan's edicts. The preamble, however, continues to rationalize the significance of the register and claims that the world's sound purity and the order of society have been held in suspension by the Ottoman imperial laws and dynastic statutes.[108] This register was bound, the preamble continues, to ensure compliance to the destined imperial commands and fated edicts. It then summarizes the three sections and eighteen chapters that constitute this copy of the *kanunname* and that, in large part, follow the structure of Bayezid's, albeit with slightly more detailed and elaborate explanations for certain statutes. The preamble thus quite definitively binds world order to the presence of a divinely sanctioned ruler and to the proper articulation of sovereign laws. The *kanunname* of Süleyman's reign bound together canonical *shari'a* precepts, discretionary punishments (*ta'zir*) determined now by judges and regional administrative officials, and local practices along with standard measures and categories. The end product was a sovereign, authoritative, and textual assertion of imperial order that proclaimed the rightness and sanctity of a sultan's legislative role. Moreover, this role sustained the empire. It was the fulcrum on which order was suspended and the measure of imperial greatness.

The Kanunname *in Action: Dialectics of General and Provincial Measures of Order*

Both the offices of the head chancery and the finance ministry maintained copies of the *kanunname*, indicating the persistent link between imperial and fiscal order and the increased focus on a written archive of past regulations. These copies were consulted when administers of the imperial council sent out directives and led to marginal notes cautioning that the content was "contrary to the *kanun*."[109] A range of imperial commands and the *kanunname* copies themselves demanded that practitioners of order in the provinces, the *shari'a* judges and the governors and their subordinates, adhere to the statutes bound together in the *kanun*. Uriel Heyd identified an *'adaletname* sent to the governor-general of Anatolia in the first months of Mehmed III's reign (May of 1595) that stated, "In the days of justice of his majesty the late Sultan Süleyman Han, *kanunname*s were written (copied) and a bound *kanunname* [copy] was deposited in the *kadı*'s court of law in every town."[110] When Celalzade Mustafa prepared the provincial *kanunname* for Egypt in 1525, he ordered that a copy of the current *kanunname* in force in the territories of Rum be kept in the *divan* of Egypt and that one copy should also be entered into the registers of each judge in the province as well, and that they should publicly proclaim its contents.[111] The increasingly sophisticated circulation of knowledge among graduates of the imperial *medrese*s, and the more general awareness of the role played by the imperial council in setting the standards for lawmaking, led judges along with provincial governors to request copies of Süleyman's "new *kanun*." These requests also appeared in the preambles of various manuscript copies of the *kanunname* as the reason for writing and compiling bound regulations. Registers of the *shari'a* courts contained copies of imperial commands and amply demonstrate that judges applied the *siyaset* measures of the *kanun* and rendered them part of local interpretations of sociopolitical order.[112] The registers reveal that administrators demanded that fines be assessed "in accordance with the imperial *kanun*," that judges cited the *kanun* to legitimize sentences, and that plaintiffs referenced the *kanun* in their accusations.[113] Later sources indicate that provincial *kanunname* were "read out" to their respective publics, and copies could be purchased for 120 *akçe*s, as could specific *'adaletname* for the purpose of safeguarding rights.[114]

Thus, while circulated in textual form, even general *kanunname* served as a living, mobile tradition, as variations among multiple copies indicated an evolving corpus of laws, attentive to regional taxation schemas and historical variables. Regional diversity was intentionally addressed, however, within individual provincial *kanunname*, as these mediated between the rubrics specified in general regulations and the practices of governance in the expanding empire. Yet there were also hybrids, such as comprehensive provincial *kanunname*, dedicated to the hierarchy of provincial administration and the meticulous organization of relationships among governing officials, land, cultivators, and agricultural surplus. These *kanunname* set categories of taxation, policed distinctions between custodians of the land, military units, and agriculturalists, and thus set the standards for the basic fiscal and social principles that governed the realm. One example, issued between 1522 and 1523, captures the various agendas achieved by the *kanunname*. It both delineated salaried officials and the bundles of tax-collection privileges assigned to various members of the *'askeri* group, and circulated a full "*kānūnnāme-i 'Os̱mānī*" complete with criminal code to the territories of Egypt, Aleppo, İnebahtı, Modon, and Koron (the latter three in contemporary Greece), and Kara Boğdan (principality of Moldovia).[115] It thus inscribed copies of imperial certificates (*berat*s) for officeholders as Süleyman I renewed contracted relationships after assuming the sultanate, including those for judges and other religious functionaries. It further specified land-grant recipients and monitored the uneasy relationships between elite privilege and the military service required as a part of *'askeri* status. These *kanunname* transformed imperial territory into transactional service arrangements and served as précis and, increasingly, as substitute references for regional cadastral surveys.[116]

A total of 506 territorial divisions necessitated an elaborate set of mechanisms for documenting the peoples and resources of the realm. During the expansionary reign of Süleyman I, *kanunname*s proliferated in part because they were needed as a mechanism to identify, categorize, and order provincial divisions and regional headquarters. The populace, and their various assigned burdens and obligations, were sorted into either provincial seats (*kanunname-i vilayet* or *liva*), districts (*sancak*), dependent territories (*tab'ileri*), or as designated segments of a district, such as for a port or harbor (*iskele*). Specialized *kanunname*s also existed for mobile groups seeking pasturage (*kanunname-i yörükan*), particular ethnic divisions (say for Kurds, Gypsies, Tatars, etc.), auxiliary military categories, workers in imperial mints or in the rice fields, or for tracking particular activities, such as market regulations (*bac-i bazar kanunname*). *Kanunname* produced after the latter part of Selim I's reign also increasingly served as preambles to cadastral surveys. These preambles intentionally emphasized the direct relationship between the sultanic justice embodied by *kanun* and the inhabitants of the realm, and they thereby suggested that the Ottoman taxation system served to ameliorate conditions of oppression.[117] They thus enabled the gradual incorporation of regional diversity into a set of Ottoman legal and administrative norms. While these norms still varied from province to province, they were intentionally inscribed into the textual terrain of the empire and constituted a new form of standard measurement that knitted human and material resources into a preserved record of imperial governance. This record also proclaimed dynastic authority and indicated an emerging hegemonic voice for the Ottoman establishment.

The Territories of Erzurum: Supplanting Past Customs with Ottoman Norms

This process of measurement and its link to imperial authority are vividly illustrated in the preambles to *kanunname* issued to territories in Anatolia, Greater Syria, and southeastern Europe that each exemplified major processes of incorporation between 1516 and 1540. Anatolia particularly dramatizes these transformations, as *kanunname* dated across that time frame shift from old to new practices, from old to new *defter*s, and from regional customs to a normative legal framework. Once a significant part of the Akkoyunlu sultanate, southwestern Anatolia had been governed according to the "customary" legal regulations issued by Uzun Hasan. Centered in Erzurum, the city and its hinterland underwent several major administrative reorganizations. Initially conquered by Selim I, this region was first attached to either Diyarbekir or Erzincan, but after Süleyman's major military campaign against the Safavids and conquest of Baghdad in 1534, Erzurum became its own regional seat. The *kanunname* for Erzurum dated 1540 was thus intended to address the administrative confusion stemming from warfare, consistent earthquakes, and, most importantly, the gradual sublimation of past customs into Ottoman dynastic law.[118] The first *kanunname* to begin assimilating this territory was for one of its dependent districts, the *sancak* of Bayburt. Issued in 1516, it generally incorporated into the "new *defter*" the statutes outlined by Uzun Hasan.[119] But the preamble to a *kanunname* contained in the 1520 cadastral survey issued to Bayburd, as well as Kemah, states that it was compiled in response to a petition submitted to the Exalted Porte by the tribal contingents of the *re'aya*, the merchants, and other inhabitants of the protected domains of the empire. This petition painted the laws of Uzun Hasan as overly oppressive and requested that the Ottoman (*Rūmi*) law be applied instead. The sultan thus responded duly with compassion and justice by applying the *kanunname* of *Rum* to them as well.[120] The *kanunname* for Bayburt dated 1530 references this petition once again and declares that the transition from the old *defter* under Uzun Hasan to the new had still not been achieved. This instantiation also references an inherent confusion about the relationship among *shari'a* practices, customary taxes, and the regulations in the Ottoman *defter*s (*defatir-i Osmaniyye*). Thus, the sultan commands that for the continuation of the state (*devam-ı devlet*) and for the order of the realm (*nıẓām-ı memleket*) the old laws be repealed and some of the measures lightened.[121]

When, in 1540, the *sancak*s of Erzurum and nearby Pasin were reorganized in a new cadastral survey, a *kanunname* positioned in the middle of the register outlined this history of petitions and imperial edicts regarding the substitution of Ottoman for Akkoyunlu laws.[122] A record of earlier efforts to impose a new standard, this *kanunname* also illustrates the particular challenges that administrators faced in managing the inherent complexity of an agrarian system with overlapping categories. It is thus in large part devoted to distinguishing among land that was tithed (*öşür*), imperial land that was taxed (*harac*), the rates assessed on the latter through divisions of *çift*, the acquisition and transfer of usufruct rights, and a widened scope for dues grouped under the *bad-ı hava* designation.[123] The *kanunname* also blamed general confusion in the region on warfare, the agitation of nomadic groups semiattached to the Safavids (identified with the derogatory term *kızılbaş*), and the resulting population displacements. It was therefore necessary both to reinscribe the *re'aya* into a new *defter* and to distinguish between loyal and disloyal segments of the mobile population.[124] Finally, the statutes of the criminal code included at the end of the text explicitly substitute *siyaset* punishments for crimes of transgression, assault, and murder. This, the *kanun* states, may have been distinct from the old law (referencing the laws of Uzun Hasan), but was necessary to sustain the order of the realm.[125]

Trablus-ı Şam in Greater Syria: Replacing Tyranny with Justice

Supplanting old laws and *defter*s with new ones was also a troubled affair in the former Mamluk provinces conquered by Selim I. This was particularly the case since Selim had been forced to broker a rationale for attacking a fellow Muslim polity, one that also embraced Sunni practices of ritual and governance as a legitimating basis for rule. The sharply angled tone adopted in postconquest *kanunname* circulated to provinces in Greater Syria implied an awareness of the potential for future conflicts with regional scholars and interpreters of the law. Rifa'at Abou-El-Haj analyzed one striking example of this process in a *kanunname* for the province of Trablus-ı Şam, dating to 1519 (a mere two years after the region's conquest by Selim I). The preamble addressed the communities of the region in their own language, Arabic, and was intended to be read out as a performative proclamation of Ottoman suzerainty.[126] It states that the objective of the proclamation, issued on the return of Selim's campaign against the Mamluks, was to raise the banner of the empire by looking carefully into the affairs of the locale and aligning the norms of the land with the organizational rubrics of agrarian administration gradually defined within the *kanunname* genre. The text launches a range of ad hominem attacks against the "Circassians," the derogatory name for the Mamluk dynasty; they were cunning (*khubth*), criminals (*mukhalifin*), and dominated by wickedness and tyranny (*tughyan*). The *kanunname* and cadastral register are characterized not as an imposition of perverse exploitation but rather as a proclamation of justice. Justice is achieved by "reconciling" the inhabitants of the land to the ruler "through the right (*salah*) and proper (*sadad*) action and by ascertaining what is canonically permissible (for these domains) to give (pay) in the form of *jizye, 'ushr and kharaj*."[127] Its potential oral nature addressed the inhabitants directly and documented a rubric for administrative governance that imperial representatives, newly recognized indigenous leaders, and future petitioners could reference. It also provided the space necessary to rationalize, if not excuse, the Ottomans' invasions against other Muslim rulers. Attacking the prior system of rule as tyrannous, manipulative, and evil, the proclamation highlighted the legality of this new sovereign authority and equated justice with the "right" and "proper" ordering of socioeconomic relations. Most compellingly, the *kanunname* identified a key principle of governance: "reconciling" the cultivator to the sultan, the very embodiment of justice.

Tyranny, then, is here understood as the imposition of unjust taxation systems by coercive governments and is countered by a contract based on the "right" rather than the "criminal" hierarchy of financial and social obligations. The sultan's authority, as configured in the preamble, resided in his ability to embody and proclaim the ideals of a just ruler. This authority was positioned in the text after an invocation of the power of God to define victory and grant authority to the rightful sovereign and of the role played by the Prophet Muhammad as God's caliph. The Prophet's role, as caliph, is explicitly linked to issuing laws: he is thus a caliph "in the assignment (*wad'*) of *jizya* and *kharaj* on the Arabs, Turks and Daylam . . . who conveyed the laws (*kawanin*) of Islam for all mankind, in the most accurate and complete fashion."[128] Prophet Muhammad is thereby characterized as the first arbiter of a taxation system presumed just by virtue of his status as God's representative on Earth. The preamble then clearly defines Sultan Selim I's position as caliph and protector of the two holy cities of Islam. Furthermore, as Abou-El-Haj noted, attributes attached to God such as "eminent, arbiter, lofty, avenger, conqueror, yet merciful and clement" are also accorded to the sultan. He is thus a victorious sovereign and a law-making caliph, firmly situated within a powerful religious rationale for both the conquest of the region and the promulgation of statutes.[129] The sultan's legislative role, and his sanctioned position as conqueror and sovereign, prefaced the statutes that instituted the appropriate mechanisms for extracting human resources from the region. The preamble suggests that rendering laws concerning taxation was thus rendering justice, and the sultan possessed the ultimate right to do so.

Buda and the Occupied Hungarian Territories: Defining New Standards

Twenty-one years later, the Ottoman campaign and administrative apparatus had shifted its attention northward, toward the protracted conquest of Hungarian domains, continued rivalry with the Habsburgs, and negotiations with regional principalities and kingdoms. The Buda preamble was composed immediately following the full occupation of the city in 1541 and its establishment as the administrative headquarters of territories now under Ottoman suzerainty. Much like the *kanunname* preambles crafted for Anatolian and Greater Syrian territories, it indicates shifts in the practice and principles of law and justice formulated under the auspices of Sultan Süleyman.[130] His *tuğra* emblazons the preamble, and the text both triumphantly states his power and provides the skeletal structure of a land system recrafted under the aegis of Ebu's-su'ud. Then acting as the head judge of Rumelia, Ebu's-su'ud assumed the position of head jurisconsult, or *şeyhülislam*, in 1545. With his comrade in reforms, the *nişancı* Celalzade Mustafa, he would consolidate formerly mixed land practices into a systematic set of legal strategies informed by both the Hanafi school of *shari'a* jurisprudence and the by then substantial record of lawmaking in Ottoman domains. The brief text of this *kanunname*, however, gave a preview of what would later become hallmarks of his role in defining a newly envisioned Ottoman law:

> All praise belongs to God. King of the heavens and earth, and of that which lies between. The Almighty, Magnificent, Mover of the earth, Caliph and successor to the Prophet of God. Arranger of the precepts of religious law, strengthener of the religion of God, raiser of the world of believers into the farthest reaches, extender of the protection of God's shadow to all peoples. Through God's mercy, victorious conqueror of East and West. Holder of the position of greatest leader of the faith. Accomplished sultan; sharer in the great heritage of the Caliphs, promulgator of the laws of the sultans, inheritor of the house of Osman. Victor of the downtrodden, sultan of the Arabs, Persians, and of Rum, assumer of the protectorship of the two holy cities, holder of the illustrious, august station of Sultan, born of sultans-Sultan Süleyman, son of Sultan Selim Han. May nothing discontinue this chain and may it extend into eternity. May no diversity befall these laws, which flow into the four corners of the occupied world.[131]

Intended to assert sultanic power in a fiercely competitive period, the statements in this preamble include performative declarations of universal sovereignty and practical explanations of sultanic achievements. Designated as the rightful successor to the Prophet, the sultan possesses authority that extends to the "heavens and the earth" and "from the east to the west throughout all time." The sultan acts as the representative or "extender of the protections of God's shadow" over both the Muslim *umma* and populations, as in the Hungarian territories, which did not espouse Islam. He further claims overlapping inheritances of a caliphal tradition extending from the Prophet Muhammad, of the *kanun*s of the sultans, or sovereign authorities, that preceded him, and of the Ottoman dynasty itself. He commits to raising the downtrodden and acting as the impartial dispenser of justice. The extension of justice, conceived here as the rationale for military campaigns, was further amplified by a characterization of the sultan as the giver of law. His jurisdictional authority included the Arab, Persian, and former Byzantine worlds and was signified most decisively in his ability to assume the role of preeminent negotiator in defining a system of tax collection and of acting as the ultimate protector of the *re'aya*, the holy cities of Islam, and thus of the realm's stability.[132] This role extended even to the *shari'a*, as the text asserts that the sultan acted as the "arranger of the precepts of religious law."

As a crafted part of the *kanunname*, these opening references to the glory and justice of sultanic rule worked to demonstrate the "naturalness" of the sultan's authority and to position him as the purveyor of a disciplined order to his subjects. Addressed to the various power brokers in each region and to the subject populations who produced the empire's wealth, these preambles attest to subtle shifts in the discourse used to assert administrative control. The *kanunname* for territories attached to Erzurum emphasized the abrogation of the laws of Uzun Hasan and suggested that Ottoman laws relieved an overburdened population. A slightly different agenda shaped the contents for Trablus-ı Şam; thus, the preamble characterized former Mamluk rule as tyrannous and the imposition of Ottoman law as relief from wickedness and evil. For Buda the preamble emphasizes the various genealogies of authority embodied in the rule of Süleyman and then explains in précis to the region's inhabitants the agrarian system of taxation. Cultivatable lands were *miri*, and rights of ownership (*rakabe-i arz*) belonged to the sultan, although here Ebu's-su'ud uses the Hanafi distinction "treasury of the believers" (*beyt-ü'l mal-ı Müslimin*).[133] It also specifies that *miri* land was originally *harac* land, land that had been acquired through war, but left in the hands of non-Muslim proprietors, and that all transactional taxes should be assessed accordingly. Personal property (*mülk*) consisted of the built environment of towns and villages such as domiciles and shops, along with vineyards and gardens, and these could be deposed of at will. These short statements constituted the opening declaration of a new administrative framework for the region, although later instantiations would specify these principles in greater detail. Although typically portrayed as an "Islamization" of the Ottoman tax system, this can also be viewed as a standardization of conflicting typologies for the land tax, assessed within the embrace of imperial *kanun* traditions, and applied in order to enhance agricultural revenues.[134]

Taxing Consent and Performing Justice: A Framework for Shares and Principles

These distinct preambles demonstrate how the *kanunname*, both in their more comprehensive forms and as directives to individual regions, simultaneously functioned within, and helped to disseminate, a set of organizational principles. They created a discursive space for the legislation of administrative affairs, assigned shares to participants in the administration of the realm, and inserted taxation schemas into a framework of just governance and relief from oppression. As such, one of the primary objects of the *kanunname* was the continued productivity of the land. An overwhelming number of statutes worked against the possibility that land would lay fallow, and, as stated by Ebu's-su'ud in a copy of the Buda preamble included in the *kanunname-i cedid*, the larger intent was to "make the land flourish."[135] While cultivators held the usufruct of the land, and thus possessed the right to use it (*tasarruf*) rather than outright ownership, he linked this right directly to productivity: "By means of a loan [from the imperial treasury] they use it, planting and harvesting and exploiting it in all such ways . . . as long as they do not leave it barren, but in the ways identified make it flourish and pay for its rights no one may interfere or protest."[136] Thus, one of the primary targets of these regulations was the cultivator, on whom the viability of the imperial agrarian system depended.[137] Yet if the ideal of the just ruler implied a direct relationship between the sultan and the *re'aya*, in actuality there were multiple mediating parties that complicated and diverted this relationship. Some of these mediating parties were part of the state apparatus, dispatched as governors, surveyors, judges, or tax collectors, and so functioned as direct representatives of his authority; others were indigenous power brokers with the social capital necessary to assay their own claims on provincial surplus. Thus, the language of duty and obligation deployed in the *kanunname*s ensured the loyalty of the former, and the language of exploitation and disorder constrained the latter. Both, however, were apt to disrupt the collection of resources; thus, the *kanunname* followed in the traditions of rescripts of justice, which aimed to relieve oppression. Acting on complaints and petitions for redress, these rescripts threatened governors, members of the *'askeri*, and various collectors of revenue with punishment and insisted that the sultan's primary desire was to maintain the *re'aya* in peace and comfort and the country in prosperity.[138] The *kanunname*s built on these traditions of petition and complaint, in that the legal formulations provided to those they governed options for redress and an administrative vocabulary that ensured rectification of wrongs if social harmony was disrupted or oppression rampant. Infractions were penalized, and grievances could be aired to either regional *shari'a* courts, provincial representatives such as the *beylerbey*, or in direct petitions to the suzerainty of the sultan.

The *kanunname* therefore placed both administrators and provincial elites accustomed to acting in their own interest within three overarching categories: loyal servants fulfilling their duties, local leaders assisting them in this process, and recalcitrant individuals who provoked havoc, caused disruption, and deserved punishment. Herein lies the essential paradox of the *kanunname* and the sustaining tension of early modern Ottoman governing strategies: the impulse to create a framework for the extraction of resources, while also limiting coercive and exploitative measures to ensure the mutual participation of the empire's inhabitants and thus the reproduction of its legitimacy. The *kanunname* crafted an addresser and addressee and reified the relationship between sultan and agricultural producer as the foundation of imperial stability and order. Regional particularities resisted universal application of a single socioeconomic structure, but a shared vocabulary of governance ensured stable relations between agricultural producers and collections agents and diminished the likelihood of social upheavals that might challenge the legitimacy of the sultanate. The organizational rubrics of the *kanunname* were thus framed with references to custom and ideological principles of justice. The *kanunname*s consistently indicted the seemingly pervasive exploitation of cultivators and censured actions that were "against law and *shari'a*" (*bi-vech-i şer' ü kanun*). This enabled the sultan, through the proclamation of law, to intimate that the imposition of an imperial standard actually represented the restoration of previously defined principles of social organization and thereby a return to the proper order of things. "Injustice" was qualified as the disruption of this preserved record and thus precipitated the intervention by other groups in the government's direct relationship with the *re'aya*. Justice, then, consisted of a balancing act on the part of the sultan (as the embodiment of the state) between procuring the means necessary to reproduce his authority in the midst of multiple claimants to resources and guaranteeing that the burdens laid on his subjects were not *too* exploitative or "unjust."

The practice of issuing laws in bound *kanunname* registers was therefore simultaneously a performative act aimed at declaring the justness of Ottoman military achievements and an assertion of textual authority and thus centralized control over the empire's productive wealth. This assertion of textual authority was informed by earlier imperial traditions of lawgiving and by the particular socioeconomic features and personages of the territories conquered. While the *kanunname*s attempted to adapt to geographic and agricultural distinctions, as well as to different elite constituencies or power brokers with varying relationships to the local population, they most often represented a face-off between imperial ideals and the recalibrations necessary to ensure a consistent revenue supply. Regional variation in the codes marks the remnants of these negotiations, when an imperial map was forced to shift and give ground to traditions claimed by its inhabitants. The result was a map that aimed to centralize but was forced to negotiate, yet one that steadfastly proclaimed the right of the sultan to define territorial law and thereby to provide the rubric through which divine law must be interpreted.

Laying Claim to the Past and a New Ottoman "Custom"

The interpretive reading of the *kanunname* provided thus far presumes a positive, productive role for a classificatory vocabulary through which the Ottoman state environment was imagined and then rendered actionable as a legal standard for negotiation. Regional specificities were ordered according to this imagination by an administrative apparatus that depended on the meaningfulness of its categories to secure revenue and reproduce the continued stability of the empire. Yet this reading is only partial since the state environment, while perhaps defined by terms set within the sultan's imperial council, also evolved in relation to practical and historical transformations in the conditions of life. Represented through everyday resistance to oppressive norms by cultivators, the simple heterogeneity of the empire, the issuing of later sultanic writs to address changes or reevaluate priorities, and the manipulation of categories by local power brokers to service their own interests were all fluid conditions that constantly tested the definitive categorizations of the state. Although the intent of the regulatory framework was to locate individuals and communities in a vocabulary of power meant to stabilize the empire's population and, thus, its revenue supply, these outcomes were never assured. The heightened emphasis on boundaries between social groups, types of land, and peculiarities of ownership rights evidenced in the *kanunname* renders visible a certain anxiety about the effect this diversity might have on the sultan's claim to absolute authority. Even as it engendered categories and registers of proper order, the coercive arm of the sultanate could not fully apprehend the discursive and material mobility of its subjects across such vast distances. Its solution, and one that was quite deft indeed, was to render "custom" into an imperial category, a framework for legal interpolation, and even a law unto itself.

As a salient feature of each legal proclamation, the constant reference to former tax registers (*tahrir defterler*) and to customary tax practices (*rüsum-ı örfiye*) located the current sultanic proclamation within an archival legacy. These references to "what went before" (*min ba'd*) appeared in moments when regional knowledge formed a necessary depository for the efficient operation of the imperial apparatus. Visible in the various iterations of *kanunname* to the territories of Erzurum, however, local customs were gradually subsumed into imperial registers and thus into an imperial custom of lawmaking. The multiple valences of phrases such as *kadimü'l-eyyamdan* (from the old days), *üslub-ı sabık üzere* (according to formerly established methods), or even the listing of previously designated villages and farms (*liva-ı mezburda vaki' olan kur ve mezari'i*) mark the authority carried by practices established as part of Ottoman legal tradition prior to the laws and decrees of a present *kanunname* or survey. These phrases invoked a past record or practice in order to sanction the imposition of an Ottoman regulatory framework. The past itself became a tool to legitimize the sultanate's claim to resources and to curtail the rights of any competitors. Still, the effectiveness of the *kanunname* required the formation and education of an elite cadre composed of imperial agents and regional power brokers to serve variously as bureaucrats, military campaigners, judges, police authorities, and tax collectors in an interlocking system of dependency created between the Ottoman establishment in Istanbul and regional administrative hubs. *Kanunname* issued from the imperial council proclaimed, and in that proclamation created, the new vocabulary of order and reeducated the participants into this organizing language. "Scattered" (*perakende*) practices were organized into a "new" defter (*defter-i cedid*) that superseded previous norms and acted as a baseline for future negotiations over resources.

The sultanate thus lay claim to the past through an elaborate system of measurement and legal proclamations, and it worked to override remnants of earlier archival precedents with its own. It asserted a new "custom" and bent a jurisprudential literature on the nature of *örf* to an administrative compulsion for regularity. While ostensibly serving to adapt regional practices into an administrative rubric designed by lawmakers and statesmen at the court, it resulted in a new legal history of imperial intent. The *kanunname* proclaimed a new legal order and inserted a new imperial history of territorial control over the landscape. The next chapter traces how the scribal traditions of the Ottoman establishment and a new impetus for lawmaking together transformed this Ottoman custom into an Ottoman way, one with its own set of linguistic, legal, and political expectations for participants in the imperial apparatus.

CHAPTER THREE

THE BUREAUCRATIC STATE

Reforming Documentary Practices

> Those procedures of the previous sultans that do not hurt the subject will remain. Those that are mere innovations and pure fabrications, and that the weak and poor complain of and are distressed by, will be removed. This [evaluation of past procedures] will be ordered, arranged, designated, recorded and registered by imperial command. . . . These just laws should become engraved in the seals of legal procedure and forever remain on the pages of government regulations.
>
> —Preamble to Egyptian *kanunname* (1525)[1]

The forms of textual and legislative authority inscribed in the *kanunnames* reveal a particular craft, or art of government, that depended increasingly on a widening corpus of record-keeping practices used to assert and perform imperial power. Sovereignty came to be measured by the ability to dictate a specific organization of norms, values, and categories, and *kanunnames* constituted a key discursive terrain in which this process of dictation occurred. This record-dependent aspect of sovereignty, and the distinct genres that inscribed a vision of sultanic legitimacy and proper order, crystallized within the context of Sultan Süleyman's court when the pressures of expansion necessitated the elaboration of a systematized grammar and structure of rule.[2] During the varied expansionary agendas from Selim I (r. 1512–20) to Mehmed III (r. 1595–1603), new literary agendas interwove the paradox of composite rule with enunciations of imperial universalism. This paradox can be traced through the roles played by the men who wrote, organized, legislated, and translated sultanic edicts. In the early years of Süleyman's reign the conjunction between redefined, newly realized, or extended roles for the *şeyhülislam* (head *müfti* or jurisconsult for the realm), the *nişancı* (head chancellor), and scribes or registrars (*el yazıcılar*) drove a process that formalized the bureaucratic management and textual authority visible in the *kanunname* issued during this period.[3]

Increasingly complex regional realities faced by the expanding empire transformed military campaigns into projects of administrative reorganization led by Sultan Süleyman's interventionist court. New career paths, compilations of documents, and strategies of governance directly linked the management of records to that of the realm as a whole. This link between records and the realm can be characterized as a unique conjunction: the archiving state. Conquered territories, as illustrated in the previous chapter, were managed by their insertion into a series of notebooks, a "defterization" that systematized text and tamed diversity within a "world of records."[4] This chapter nuances the discursive and historical evolution of the *kanunname* addressed previously by reflecting on the emergence of key court interlocutors who reshaped the record-keeping practices of the empire. These interlocutors worked explicitly to redefine the scope of the *kanun* and then formalized the archiving of sultanic orders into a new category of registers, the *umur-ı mühimme defter*.[5] These registers gave the Ottoman establishment the capacity to manage imperial diversity from within a referential record of statutory interventions.

The relationship between new bureaucratic agendas, presented in the first part of this chapter, and new registration impulses, explored in the second, reveals significant links among documentary production, legislative reform, and a centralizing state. The chapter thus demonstrates how these links emerged as a particular vision of Ottoman dynastic rule in the sixteenth century. Documentary production and statecraft were mutually constitutive projects that yielded new textual and scribal forms. Recording and interpreting legal acts, evaluating the relationship of overlapping legal traditions (religious, dynastic, regional, customary), formulating a standardized framework for assessing petitions and collecting revenue, and maintaining a just vision for the application of law and the distribution of resources became the primary activities of the members of the imperial council and various chanceries. Thus, a remarkable slippage occurred between administrative practitioners, legal scholars, and intellectuals that ultimately contributed to the analytic interventions written by scholars *cum* bureaucrats.[6] These combined activities lent themselves toward a language of court practice, one that symbolically expressed the empire's grand claims and quite literally enabled its administrative agendas. This chapter thus focuses on the means by which literary and legal acumen crafted territorial sovereignty and solidified the overlapping terrains of administrative and textual practices. It was precisely these spheres of overlapping order that were reexamined by the men of the pen (*kalemiye*)—those who wielded the text as a mode of agency and power distinct from that of the sword (*sefiye*) and of knowledge construed in religious terms (*'ilmiye*).

Strangers into Scribes: The Formalization of Registry Practice

The gradual elaboration of a complex chancery system, new techniques of registration, and the scribes and clerks who made all of this possible fitted the dynamics of conquest and the province into the very heart of the sultanate's daily activities. As a sign of these changes, from 1529 onward, the central bureaucracy mushroomed in size.[7] Scribal cohorts working on behalf of the sultanate furthered its supervision into the legal, religious, and diplomatic aspects of daily governance. Changes in the career paths and recruitment patterns for secretaries and religious functionaries underpinned this process. Instead of relying on scholars gathered from newly acquired lands, the empire's hiring focus shifted to those trained within established imperial education systems, paving a clearer path of recruitment and appointment in a hierarchy of officialdom for religious and administrative posts.[8] Systematizing scribal appointments and chancery protocols was necessary for centralized administration and a defense against imperialist rivals such as the Habsburgs, Safavids, Portuguese, Mughals, French, and Venetians who were intent on similar paths. Efforts to control new territories, co-opt elites, and create mechanisms for the extraction of revenue relied on record-keeping methods to manage such demands. Centralization thus focused on the ecology of land management and administrative coherence. Sam White has termed this the evolution of a unique "imperial ecology," fashioned to control material and human resources in order to maintain the court and sustain expansionary warfare: "Goods had to keep pouring from the peripheries into the core; and settlement had to reach as far as possible for agriculture, extraction, and transportation. Resources had to be harvested, requisitioned, and managed to secure supply. The peasantry had to be taxed, cajoled, coerced, and sometimes moved about for imperial ends, and yet at the same time protected, secured, and held loyal to the imperial dynasty."[9]

As we saw in the previous chapter, the *kanunname* both enacted and recorded the Ottoman dynasty's paradoxical efforts to coerce, cajole, protect, and demand loyalty from its subjects. Yet as the harvesting of resources depended on record-keeping practices, the scribal cadres, too, were subjected to increasingly heavy-handed management. The early Osmanlı confederacy, as Joel Shinder described it, "pursued an articulated policy which employed all human resources at hand without any kind of ideological orientation."[10] This meant the incorporation of *medrese*-trained, Turkic-speaking men from former Seljuk and Ilkhanid principalities, scholars from the established centers of Islamicate learning deploying Arabic and Persian jurisprudential and literary mentalities, as well as Grecophone secretaries commandeered or converted from the Byzantines, or Slavic speakers from the war frontiers across the straits between Edirne and Belgrade. These men helped facilitate the shift from *feth etmek* (to conquer) to *kaleme etmek* (to record) and were frequently criticized by those who abhorred the move from a presumably frontier-minded ethos to the settled court policies of centralized administration.[11] Fifteenth-century chroniclers traced the "evils of bureaucracy" in the reigns of Bayezid I (r. 1389–1402), Murad II (r. 1421–44, 1446–51), and Mehmed II (r. 1444–46, 1451–81) and framed the accumulation of wealth and expansion of the official household as signs of corruption and oppressive taxation resulting from interventionist governments.[12] One malefactor of these trends even called Bayezid the "son of a Mongol, totally lacking knowledge and grace," in reference to the strong influence of Ilkhanid governance patterns on early Ottoman administration.[13]

Early scribal cohorts were thus either religious scholars, servants of contemporaneous or lapsed principalities and empires, or simply natives of conquered regions co-opted as record keepers of Ottoman imperial expansions. The mix of traditions and impulses that gradually coalesced into the textual authority of the *kanun* derived from this multiethnic, multiconfessional cohort. These early scribes forged the record-keeping practices that produced registers of taxation and certification from their own experiential backgrounds. The oldest preserved Ottoman chancery collection (*inşa'* or *münşe'at*, a "guidebook" of official protocols and documentation practices) is the *Teressül* of the poet Ahmed-i Da'ī (d. circa 1421), a former client of the Germiyan prince Ya'kub Beğ II (1387–90, 1402–29), who entered the service of the Ottoman commander sultans Süleyman and Murad II.[14] Umur Beğ, the official responsible for the production of what is believed to be the earliest cadastral register, dated 1431, was a foot soldier in the service of both Murad I and Bayezid I.[15] A scribe of Serbian origin managed Murad II's correspondence in Turkish, Slavic, and Greek, and Mehmed II inducted Akkoyunlu scribes into his secretarial cohort after his defeat of the principality at Otlukbeli in 1473.[16] The registers and the authority they ultimately inscribed carried the imprint of these earlier influences and led to the gradual emergence of a formal system of Ottoman clerks, the *yazıcılar*, as a contemporary observer described them.[17]

While links between Ottoman and Seljuk chancellery practices are difficult to trace, Ilkhanid registers directly overlap with Ottoman practice. Journals for daily transactions and appointments, a register of ordinary payments, and one for tabulating the current fisc (*ruznamçe*, *tevcihat*, and *tahvilat*) are all derived from a large known corpus of Ilkhanid registry genres.[18] The Ottoman extraordinary tax (*'avariz*) and remand for the quartering of campaign armies (*'ulufe*) were Ilkhanid practices, as were the basic divisions of land systems into state (*miri*), royal domain (*has*), religious institutions or pious endowments (*vakıf*), or private lands (*mülk*), although these were also composed from canonical *shari'a* categories. Successor principalities to the Ilkhanids, such as the Akkoyunlu, left explicit citational trails in the *kanunname*. As addressed in the previous chapter, comparative references to the prominent role of lawmaking under the Akkoyunlu sultan Uzun Hasan (d. 1478) served at times to legitimize the insertion of an Ottoman extraction regime, while at other times marked a past that the Ottoman regulations abrogated. *Kanunname* dispersed to provinces established in former Akkoyunlu territory, such as Çermin, Çüngüş, Hisaran, Harput, Mardin, and Urfa, often asserted that they stood "in accordance with the *kanun* of Hasan Padişah [Uzun Hasan]."[19] But they also clearly marked a distinction between Ottoman and Akkoyunlu *kanun* practices and mediated the concerns of local inhabitants and officials, the governor and judge, in a process that ultimately replaced past customs with Ottoman principles.[20]

Such was also the case with a contemporary of Uzun Hasan, the Mamluk sultan Qaytbay (r. 1468–96), to whom customs and regulations were attributed (*Kayıtbay kanunu*) in regulations ranging from Selim I's initial conquest of Egypt to Süleyman I's entrenchment in former Mamluk territories across Greater Syria.[21] More striking, however, than the valences of these attributions to prior lawgiving rulers were specific actors explicitly co-opted into the emerging systematization of an Ottoman land regime and thus into the production and circulation of legal registers that secured the textual authority of the dynasty. Wakako Kumakura has demonstrated that two families, the Jiʿans and the Malakis, were instrumental in both the gradual physical transfer of Mamluk land registers to the Ottoman storehouse of documents and the initial administration of land governance in the newly conquered Egyptian province.[22] The bookkeeping skills and computational facility of doyens from these families led to postconquest affirmations of their positions as *katib al-sirr* (literally, scribe of secrets, the highest position possible within the provincial scribal bureaucracy), *daftardar*s, or *mustawfis*, designations that also migrated into Ottoman parlance.[23] These affirmations of local scribes and keepers of the books also led to the deep irony of conquered subjects who enabled, in their scribal practice or direct transference of registers, the efficient management practices of their conquerors.

This transfer of documents and loyalties also represented a shift from household-dependent scribal traditions, to court-centric attachments, and to the emergence of a particular rationale and systematicity at the heart of the Süleyman regime. While the Mamluk records that were reprinted in Ottoman land registers remained a reference point into the seventeenth century, the local, family-based managements of the Jiʿans and Malakis did not. Kumakura asserts that "while in the Mamluk period, management depended on the households of specific families, the Ottomans tried to manage land records systematically within a government institution."[24] Ahmad ibn al-Jiʿan's supervisory role as *katib al-sirr* spanned the Mamluk to Ottoman transition, yet the inherent vulnerabilities of his position as a local figure led to accusations of illegality and conspiracy that ultimately culminated in his execution.[25] The fate of the Ji'an family mirrors broader transformations within Süleyman's court. The subsidence of captive converts *cum* scribal secretaries and the ascent of a unique cohort distinct from both the military (*'askeri*)—although often also recruited from the sons of this social strata—and the religious scholars (*'ulema*) leveraged these "new men" into positions that reinforced the consolidation of power at the center.[26]

A Language for the Realm: Registering Insiders and Outsiders

Newly reshaped scribal services within the palace also waged a linguistic and aesthetic campaign of Ottomanization that accompanied military feats of conquest. As the court of Süleyman made "Ottoman Turkish" the language of the realm and began utilizing it in diplomatic correspondence, the scripts of its rivals such as Italian, Polish, Greek, Slavic, and Persian were increasingly eclipsed.[27] This led to a new appreciation of translation (*tercüme*), wherein the fortunes of intermediaries able to traverse linguistic thresholds shaped the broader centralization efforts of the mid- to late sixteenth century.[28] While the language of state was suffused with borrowings from Arabic and Persian, *lisan-ı Türki* or *lisan-ı Rum* was ultimately grounded in West Turkish and Çagatay and came to embody the distinct linguistic identity of the empire's new political elite.[29] Multilingualism remained key, especially in translation projects from Arabic and Persian, but the separation of a cosmopolitan elite through the aegis of Ottoman Turkish meant that these projects framed legacies of Islamicate learning within the language of the dynasty. This linguistic framing, alternating between the terms *lisan-ı Türki* and *lisan-ı Rum*, was distinct from either the ethnic or regional connotations these terms respectively evoke. Even the term for ethnic Türks (*etrak*) was used pejoratively, in distinct contrast with urbane, court-attached elites. And the shorthand designations for *Rum* (Rome, territories once ruled by the Byzantines in Anatolia and southeastern Europe and thus current occupants of those regions now under Ottoman rule) do not adequately capture how the term as a linguistic register came to define precisely those "servants" of the realm who worked within the bureaucracy or acted as evangelists for its power. Thus, the bureaucrat and scholar Mustafa Ali (d. 1600) commented on the "astonishing language current in the state of Rūm," distinguished by its heterogeneous mix of Arabic and Persian, and drew attention to this new distinctiveness by charging that "in the view of those eloquent in Turkish [*lisān-ı Türkī*], the use of simple Turkish should be forbidden."[30]

Ottoman Turkish was thus a heteroglossic linguistic register, one that blended the complex worldviews of Arabo-Persianate literary cultures; the traditions of interpretation, commentary, and discursive argumentation fostered by Islam; and the Chinggisid and Türkmen cultures of the steppe. It created a complex unity from these hybrid utterances, and the writers of policy, poetry, prose, and history together cocreated a new cultural reality.[31] Despite this heteroglossia, users highlighted its uniqueness and asserted the necessity for new translations of this past heritage. Hence, the doyen of diplomatic arts Celalzade Mustafa Çelebi (d. 1567) ascribed his motivation for translating a Persian history and biography of the prophets (*sira*) to the desire to "make its benefit general" to the "people of Rūm [who] are not familiar with this language [Persian]."[32] And Ta'likizade Mehmed was forced to translate his Persian verse account of the 1593–94 Ottoman Hungarian campaign into Ottoman Turkish prose on the explicit instruction of Sultan Mehmed III. Ta'likizade substantiated this order by claiming that "*lisān-ı Rūm* has gathered the best and most beautiful elements" of the languages spoken by the conquered, and anything else should be "relegated to a corner in the house of neglect and obscurity."[33]

Because *lisan-ı Rum* remained deeply inflected by mixed linguistic codes, however, *translation* came to mean resituating the past within the Ottoman present, and multilingualism was constrained within an Ottomanism that defined both an identity and a language of courtly production.[34] *Lisan-ı Rum* or *Türki* became the language of the Ottoman inheritors of the Roman legacy (*memalik-i Rum*), now conceived more broadly as an urbane, professional, educated Muslim strata tied to the fortunes of an Ottoman polity.[35] Elite literary identities were defined by this Ottomanized rubric, with poets (*şu'ara'-yi Rum*), belletristes (*udeba'-yi Rum*), religious scholars (*'ulema'-yı Rum*), and the elite public (*zurefa'-yi Rum*) all bearing this designation.[36] These were contrasted with broad references to groups "foreign" (*ecnebi*) to this evolving urbane imperial consciousness: the uncultivated Turk (*el-etrak*), the Arab (with a shifting meaning from nomad to Arabic-speakers in former Mamluk territories), and the Acem (Persian speakers or, increasingly, allies with the Safavids). Distinctions among these groups were carried into designations of imperial sovereignty, as found in the inscription on a fountain in Jerusalem that refers to Süleyman as the "sultan al-Rūm wa'l-'Arab wa'l-'Ajām."[37] Definitions of outsiders to the Ottoman establishment gained resiliency as notions of an ordered realm increasingly preoccupied the diplomatics of the court.

Drawing lines between insiders and outsiders was the means by which an emergent "bureaucratic consciousness" linked to a "Rumi way" came to define the operations of Ottoman dynastic governance.[38] A significant part of this process was the reorganization of the learned hierarchies of law and religious education under the rubric of the sultan.[39] Just as early malcontents decried centralization efforts beginning in the fourteenth century, so too did sixteenth-century regional religious scholars who resented the empowerment of the *şeyhülislam* under Süleyman I. The *şeyhülislam*, appointed by the sultan and acting to preserve the semblance of conformity between state stability and religious ordinance, had increasingly intervened in religious appointments across the imperial domains.[40] But Ebu's-su'ud Efendi (d. 1574) formalized the use of distinct registers for these appointments, and these registers further tracked the matriculation of *medrese* students and directed their patronage and placement across the learned institutions of the empire.[41] Part of the "defterization" of the sixteenth century, then, was the affirmation of a particular legal school, the Hanafi, and at least the *assertion* of an Ottoman legal hegemony. The legal pluralism of the state subsided along with multilingualism, though the consistent, and often volatile, resistance to this hegemony became a prominent subject in administrative and intellectual debates of the period.[42] The imposition of new fees on marriage or trade partnerships in the *shari'a* courts in Damascus and Aleppo antagonized judges who were forced to comply with imperial decrees, and literary salons pitted "Rumi" and "Arab" definitions of culture and learning against each other.[43]

Conflicts over the Ottoman dynasty's relationship to learned cultural heritage also played a role in the short-lived appearance of an official court historian, the *şehnameci*, in 1555.[44] Emine Fetvacı has averred that "the illustrated manuscripts produced by the office of the Ottoman court historian during the last quarter of the sixteenth century were instrumental in negotiating the changing social hierarchies of the Ottoman court during the same period."[45] While court historians produced panegyrics and eulogies of the sultan, they also invented novel techniques for both supplanting past rivals with the Ottoman present and asserting the dynasty's new claims to imperial universalism.[46] Of the five men who held this "office" from approximately 1555 to 1605, Seyyid Lokman's lengthy tenure from 1569 to 1596–97 virtually defined both the position and the stakes involved in definitions of history and historical legacies. He oversaw the production of the *Quintessence of Histories* (*Zübdetü't-tevārīḫ*), a "copy" of sorts, consisting of three codices produced from a scroll, the *Ṭomār-ı hümāyūn* (the *Imperial Scroll*) completed under the tenure of 'Arif and Eflatun during the reign of Süleyman.[47] The scroll and the codices positioned the Ottoman dynasty within a genealogical history that began with a cosmological chart of the world's origins and then drew parallel connections to prophets and kings in ancient Persian and pre-Islamic dynasties emanating from the first humans, Adam and Eve.

But this formalized definition of Süleyman's universal sovereignty was as much a product of the scribe as it was of the royal historian. The stylized ornamentation of an imperial script became the frontispiece of sultanic commands, as well as the marker of the literary producers' aesthetic performance. The tightly rhymed prose was decorated with Persian and Arabic and elliptically composed through alliteration, wordplay, and metaphor.[48] Compositions of these carefully stylized texts came to be known by a distinct term, *inşa'*, which means "constructed" or "creatively composed," and embodied an imperial idiom found in both the chancery and the literary salon. The next two sections of this chapter chart how two interventions within the domain of *kanun* regulation elaborated this imperial idiom. First, in the Egyptian *kanunname* he composed in 1525, Celalzade Mustafa forged a new idiom that embodied a carefully constructed vision of universal sovereignty for Sultan Süleyman. This imperial literary image became a template for future linkages between textual and territorial authority and an emerging Ottoman legal hegemony. Second, the preamble drafted by Ebu's-su'ud Efendi for the Buda *kanunname*, along with his other legal manipulations concerning land registration, rendered these assertions part of a newly canonized agrarian administration.[49]

Thus, "Ottoman Turkish"—both as an imperial script and a language that symbolized a loose collectivity across a vast terrain—enclosed scribal duties, legislative reforms, and dynastic history into a coherent imperial project with multiple domains of action.[50] Centralization processes were architecturally and sociopolitically performed within early modern court ceremonials and idealized in chancery proclamations; they also constituted an effort to shape multiple interests within the domain of the court.[51] This Ottomanized visual and legal landscape came to be symbolized, in part, through the architectural forms of Mimar Sinan, the legal manipulations of Ebu's-su'ud Efendi, the record-keeping and chancery reforms introduced by Celalzade Mustafa, and the new role played by Hanafi Sunnism both in confessional displays and in reassessing administrative practice within the Ottoman court.[52] In each, combinatory tactics yielded a new imperial vision. The wedding of Timurid, Seljuk, Roman, Byzantine, and Islamicate forms into the multiple domes and minarets of the Selimiye and Süleymaniye complexes created by Mimar Sinan in Edirne and Istanbul became the touchstone for design models that sought to incorporate past forms while yet surpassing them and proclaiming a distinctly Ottoman aesthetic.[53] The welding of *kanun* and *fiqh* in the interventions of Ebu's-su'ud rendered divine law into a forum for imperial action. In addition, the use of refined Hanafi laws with regard to usufruct and the cultivator reterritorialized Ottoman rule in regions resistant to centralization schemas.[54] And, finally, the melding of stylized invocations of imperial glory with land registers and tax cadasters in the *kanunname* under the auspices of Celalzade Mustafa epitomized these processes. The chancery, revenue collecting agencies, and imperial council met at the crucible of efforts to promulgate sultanic authority. Each sphere of practice, the varied agents, and the new scope of activities defined therein throw into sharp relief the combinatory and composite nature of the early modern court addressed in Chapter 1 and suggests that military, linguistic, legal, fiscal, and visual reforms were of a piece and thus part of a broad centralizing effort common across Eurasia in the sixteenth and seventeenth centuries.

A Collaboration in Governance: The Nişancı *and the* Şeyhülislam

The long tenures of Celalzade Mustafa Bey—first as head secretary (*re'isülküttab*, 1525–34), then as chancellor (*nişancı*) in the secretariat of the *divan-ı hümayun* (1534–57)—and Ebu's-su'ud Efendi—as regional judge of

Rumeli (*kadı'asker*, 1541–45) or head jurisconsult (*şeyhülislam*) (1545–74)—profoundly influenced the directions of these reforms. In distinct ways, each man reinforced the link between a particular order, based on justice and prosperity, and an administrative practice that displaced rival claimants to revenue collection or territorial authority. They further ensured that administrative efforts of the imperial council were appropriately dispersed, via legal proclamation and their own literary productions, both to inhabitants within the realm and to competitors outside of it. The foremost administrative preoccupation was with land, its registration, and the notions of sovereignty linked to just supervision and stewardship. The outcome was that the law became a medium for Ottoman imperial action, and the archived records of these increasingly systematized actions sustained through text the territorial extent of the empire. And, as illustrated here and in the following chapters, efforts to enforce an occupation regime in Hungarian territories, and to reassert sovereignty in Egypt and Greater Syria, became a crucible for the new deployments of imperial law, of textual authority, and of the power necessary to bend the realm to the will of the sultanate.

Thus, a strikingly collaborative project emerged between Celalzade Mustafa's reformation of the *kanunname* in the chancery and Ebu's-su'ud's recanonization of a land-based revenue system via the *müftülük*. Both men shaped the *kanun* issued during the reign of Süleyman, and Ebu's-su'ud continued to refine his vision during the reign of Selim II (r. 1566–74), as well. At stake was not merely the method for the distribution of land but also how overlapping ownership rights in contested territories, acquired during expansionary campaigns, should be assessed, categorized, and written into legal frameworks adopted for the extraction of revenue. The consequence of these assertions was a new formalization of Ottoman sovereignty and claims to universal legitimacy within increasingly competitive arenas of inter- and intrastate diplomacy. These frameworks, and resulting claims, structured the increasingly systematized registers from the 1520s to the 1650s—principally the *cizye*, *ahkam*, *mühimme*, and *şikayet defterleri* (with each representing a further specialization of the former), but they also shaped the titulature ascribed to the sultans, diplomas of investiture, and deeds of land transfer. Amid conquests in Hungary, wars with the Safavids, and insurrections in former-Mamluk provinces, two major transformations decisively linked land-management strategies with imperial claims to legitimate rule: (1) the elaboration of a unique form of universal sovereignty under Süleyman in order to legitimize conquest and occupation over territories in Egypt, Greater Syria, parts of Iraq, western Anatolia, and southeastern Europe; (2) the effort to assert (or reassert) imperial control via the commodification of land and the extension of sultanic rights to taxation.[55] These transformations in the textual record then became the touchstones for diplomatic negotiations, the descriptive content in treatises produced by foreign observers of the Ottoman governing apparatus, and the baseline for internal imperial analysts of the Ottoman political order and its practice.

Celalzade Mustafa and Ebu's-su'ud Efendi linked the textual and territorial authority of the sultantate through the emergent power of the chancery and the *şeyhülislam* office. Each confronted the troubled incorporation of territories, Mamluk and Hungarian respectively, with the pen and with a vision of textual coherence that etched a coherent land-management regime out of diverse customs and claims to property rights. The *nişancı*, Celalzade Mustafa, equipped with the *tuğra* of the sultan and acting as head secretary (*reisülküttab*) in 1525, faced down the insurrectionary governor of Egypt with a new vision of dynastic law. This vision would also improve perceptions of the sultan's spiritual authority in order to quell the disquieting pro-Safavid rebellions that swept Anatolia in the 1520s and 1530s. Meanwhile, the judge and jurisconsult, Ebu's-su'ud Efendi, equipped with certified legal opinions (*fetva*s, issuing judgments), redefined conquered territories as imperial property belonging to the sultan. When assuming the newly fortified office of the *şeyhülislam*, he supplanted the tenuous intercessions of chief jurisconsults who had previously shaped the notion of empire in the new expansive domains of the early sixteenth century. The ad hoc land categorizations developed by Zenbilli 'Ali Efendi (serving from 1503 to 1526), Kemalpaşazade (from 1526 to 1534), and Çivizade Muhyiddin Mehmed Efendi (from 1539 to 1542) were rationalized during the long tenure of Ebu's-su'ud Efendi into a clear pattern of textual order.[56]

For both Celalzade Mustafa and Ebu's-su'ud, tensions between Muslim and non-Muslim territories and between Ottomanized notions of subjecthood and those elaborated within the *shari'a*, or within regional customary law, had become more pressing for the expanding empire. Thus, notions of sovereignty (*hükumet*) also expanded to encompass the conduct of state (*siyer*) within contexts where subject populations were mixed, with protected peoples (*zimmi*), foreigners (*müste'min*), and cultivators (*re'aya*) that increasingly included both Muslim and non-Muslim groups and persons. As the sultanate sought new mechanisms for asserting control, the chancery joined with more traditional legal actors to assert newly defined Hanafi notions of sovereignty: performing the Friday prayer in the sultan's name; collecting the poll tax and tribute from non-Muslims; obtaining one-fifth of all plunder taken in a holy war; and executing the fixed (*hadd*) penalties.[57] Hence, taxation and land administration became central to definitions of sovereign authority.[58] Deliberations over how to allocate the poll tax (*cizye*), to assess the status of tribute as its own form of coercive revenue (*harac*), to survey and measure arable land (*çift*), and to determine the transferable rights to this land, affixed through the purchase of a title (*tapu*) that ensured rights of use (*tasarruf*) and of transfer (*tefviz*), preoccupied both chancery and judicial offices. Concerns escalated over both registration tactics and categorical stability as official representatives struggled to record cultivated lands, the grantees or landholders who collected dues and watched over (*sipahi*, *sahib-i 'arz*, or *zemin*) these lands, and the relatively mobile population that had yet to be fitted into the categories of tax assessment. Hence, refrains to ensure that the *re'aya* were appropriately recorded in the "new" defter; that they should be recorded in the place where they were found, even if they had moved from another locale; and that they should not have to pay taxes or owe duties to more than one overlord, all played a considerable role in the legal proclamations issued during the period.

From Dynastic to Imperial Law in the Egyptian Kanunname

Celalzade Mustafa's actions within the chancery office brought land registration and sovereignty into direct correspondence with each other. He inscribed a new ideological supremacy for the sultan that repositioned Ottoman imperial legitimacy within escalating debate and rivalry. After the major campaigns against the Safavids to the east and Mamluks to the west, Selim I's dramatic conquests of Çaldiran in 1514 and Cairo in 1517 permanently altered the fabric of Ottoman imperial territories. For the first time the population of the empire now contained a majority of Muslims, although internal cultural and religious controversies and animosities would continue to fester over the duration of Ottoman control. With Selim's death in 1520, rebellions on the borderlands of western and southeastern Anatolia broke out even as his heir, Süleyman I, staked his own claim to an expansionary ethos and universal state via campaigns in Hungary. He was forced to return after the seemingly decisive victory at Mohács in 1526 to address these rebellions and did not successfully develop Ottoman suzerainty over Hungarian territories until the conquest of Buda in 1541. And, while Ottoman-appointed governors presumably submitted to imperial control in Egypt and Greater Syria, resistance to authority escalated to the point that the governor of Egypt, Hain Ahmed Paşa, declared independence in 1524.

Süleyman met this rebellion with a combination of sword and pen and with an organizational structure that reinforced the relationship between sovereignty and discourse. The newly appointed grand vizier, İbrahim, and Chancellor Celalzade Mustafa undertook a campaign of reterritorialization that amounted to a manifesto of Süleyman's claim to universal emperor.[59] This manifesto emerged first in the lengthy, treatise-like preamble to the *kanunname* for Egypt (Mısır, 1525) and articulated a program of sultanic oversight led by the sultan, his grand vizier, and his head secretary.[60] The preamble narrates the history of the region's conquest as a triumph of order over disorder, and it is one of the clearest statements of textual and territorial authority from the sixteenth century. The text reflects the heteroglossia of *lisan-ı Rum*, with invocations of divine scripture and legislative history composed in Arabic, poetic commentaries and parables of statecraft in Persian, and a contrapuntal syntactical structure that weds competing strands of authority into a vision of Ottoman glory. It further outlines an ideological structure for legitimate governance, one that asserts *kanun* as a mechanism for universal legislation, the sultan as the arbiter of proper order, and history as the proof of the supremacy of an Ottoman custom of rule. This narrative of order and authority employed new ideological conjunctions and discursive formulae that would migrate across documentary genres, diplomatic negotiations, and literary acclimations of proper governance for the next two centuries. The preamble itself concludes with instructions that "this imperial *kanunname*," since it was composed with precise methods and "loaded with justice" and was accepted by the sultanate and by the preservers of divine law, should "become engraved in the seals of legal procedure and forever remain on the pages of government regulations."[61]

The preamble opens with an invocation in Arabic that cements sultanic power, as it was God "who made sultans the means of obtaining the good order of the world, and who made their laws effective on all tent dwellers and city-dwellers." This order was achieved through God's grace and by imperial commands, which were bound "to the tongues of my well-tempered swords and to the pens of my felicitous deputies."[62] This sword and pen girded the dynasty's lineage, which "from ancient times . . . until the end of time . . . formulated statutes of justice" that came to provide a set of "ancient rules and upright (just) regulations" that might be used as a standard of judgment for all social strata and a reference for future lawmakers.[63] But over the course of his declamation, Celalzade Mustafa subtly outlines a significant shift from dynastic fortunes to universal empire. The dynasty was charged with "arranging the affairs of the dominions and putting in order the constructions, fortifications and roads, improving the conditions of the realm and people, making binding decisions concerning the affairs of the dominion, administering the properties of the sultanate, carrying out the important affairs of the caliphate, and removing oppression and corruption."[64]

The sultan, in order to ensure social and moral equilibrium, joined his dominions to the "currents of commands" and to the "discourse and law" that together constituted a just order and thus proper sovereignty.[65] This just order was a necessary corrective to deceit and disorder, which could not be addressed by the *shari'a* alone but required the use of *siyaset* to strengthen commands and administer punishment.[66] It was the *kanun* that guided the practice of the *shari'a* and righted the tyranny and oppression resulting from interpretations that had strayed from divine sanction. This ensured that the "structure of religion has remained firm, welded with the lead of *kanun*s marked by justice."[67] The dynasty thus composed a just and imperial law, loosely following the traditions of the Prophet and of his noble successors, a *kanun* intended as a "just method" for "easing the conditions of mankind and satisfying the hopes of widows and orphans."[68] This imperial law was also universal in scope, as it applied to everyone who "supports the flourishing of the *shari'a* and is accepted by the whole world." All of its decrees reinforce the *shari'a* like a "loyal friend."[69] Celalzade Mustafa deftly plays with the relations between these traditions of lawmaking, but he also insists that imperial statutes guide, implement, and preserve the *shari'a* and thus a balanced sociopolitical order.

This conception of the Ottoman establishment as one that joined a preexisting "current of laws," which it then sought to support and extend, shifts with the role of Selim. With highly figurative language, Celalzade Mustafa positions Selim's triumphant conquests in Egypt, Greater Syria, Yemen, and the Safavid frontiers in a chessboard of regional and heresiological opponents. He "played a game" that relieved the inhabitants of the Mamluk realms from the oppression of greed and vanity, restored tranquility to the Safavid borderlands, and "annihilated [the Abyssinian governor's Yemeni army] as if they were children's toys." Selim "played swift and fair by the rule aimed at breaking" other regional powers and thus asserted a more universal vision of territorial sovereignty.[70] The "high-flying falcon of his ambition" led him to resolve that this could only be achieved through specific policies of textual organization. He therefore charged, according to Celalzade Mustafa, that "the *kanun*s that had been instituted in the progression of the years be organized and arranged." Organizing the *kanun*s would cleanse "his inherited dominion from the dung of oppression and tyranny with the broom of justice and equity." The "broom" of imperial order erased the harms done by "followers of innovations and vanity who had overwhelmed the countries of Islam on all sides."[71] This suggestion, that Selim's conquests corrected the errant innovations of legal scholars under Mamluk and Safavid authority, reconfigures the *kanun* as an imperial, rather than a dynastic, act—an imperial act that supersedes, through an organizational strategy, the regional, local, and customary definitions of proper order.

Selim's death occurred at the height of his "intention in taking over and regulating the affairs of both the inherited and the acquired dominions," and this task then fell to his son, Süleyman.[72] The sultan's death and Süleyman's resulting scramble to consolidate authority mark a transition in the text. Whereas Selim personified the state, in the remaining sections of the preamble the triumphant feats of Süleyman are brokered through the actions of his newly appointed vizier, İbrahim, who dominates the latter part of the text in first-person commentary. While Süleyman is the "world conquering and world-bestowing emperor," one who adorns himself with the "attributes of earlier kings" and attends to the nourishing of his subjects and the dispersion of justice, it is the appointed servant İbrahim who ultimately acts as physician "for the reform of the state of the world" after the death of Selim. Süleyman "took up residence in the hearts of the troops like the sacred spirit which rules the regions of the body," but his ultimate wisdom lay in appointing a councilor to carry out the affairs of state.[73] Süleyman's *devlet* was thus not in his person but in his administration.

The task of that administration was to divine and remedy "the sickly humor of the dominion" and to restore the "natural disposition" of the body politic. This natural disposition, conceived as a state of tranquility for the inhabitants, free from the corrupting influence of local tyrants, was achieved through the harmony of law. To treat local tyranny, Süleyman instituted a process whereby "all the *kanun* and interpretation of the [past] centuries of the dominion were narrated in [a] summarized way."[74] And it was İbrahim who was dispatched to ensure the thoroughness and probity of this empire-sustaining process. İbrahim is lauded in the preamble at a length even slightly greater than that devoted to eulogizing Süleyman and dominates the preamble's scenes of dramatic action. Praised for his wisdom, right opinion, and unwavering devotion to Süleyman, he is entrusted with "the secret coffers and the most confidential affairs of the state" and guards the treasury of information with his whole being.[75] This "information" was gathered and preserved to better the conditions of the poor and weak and lift the oppression of the realm. Again, this was achieved through the imprint of law. As the preamble insists "while the regulations of the laws of the sultans of Rum had been erased from the page of time, they were recorded again with the ink of his assistance." The disorder of the realm, the lapsed administrative continuity in Egypt and the "Arab lands," derived from the lack of an empire-wide information database encoded with legal principles of taxation, retribution, and distribution. Earlier officials had "returned home without putting together and ascertaining the appropriate conditions and desirable order that would create the necessity of perseverance and orderliness appropriate for that region." Thus, the inhabitants of the realm remained in a state of oppression, and Süleyman's reign remained clouded "with the dust of anxiety and annoyance."[76]

In İbrahim's hands, however, and in the campaign of order and registration that forms the impetus for the *kanunname* itself, the fortunes of the province were carefully investigated, immoral officials expelled, and loyal servants rewarded. While duplicitous officials and rebels carry some weight here, the true "safety and security, peace and repose" of the region devolves on the "annihilation" of the "traces of evil pharaonic custom, and the practices of corrupt innovation of the tyrants."[77] General references to "pharaonic" or "Circassian" customs, pejorative indicators of Mamluk traditions, become explicit in the final pages of the preamble. Here, the cause of disunity, as divined by İbrahim, was that the land tax (*harac-i erazi*) "had become removed from the circle of justice." The preamble concludes not with a testament to the Ottoman dynasty but with a kind of proof text for the proper management of the realm. It delineates the methods whereby "control" of a province might be achieved: first, via the army and aligning the interests of the regional governor and other dignitaries of the official hierarchy; second, by writing down the regulations for its cavalry and thus the dispersal of land grants; third, by judging the actions of local administrators and intermediaries by the "established order and *kanun*"; and, finally, by meticulously investigating past and present legal custom: "then the fees, obligations, penalties and other innovations and inventions that everybody among the peasant groups became accustomed to from the time of the previous sultans, will be examined in detail and commented upon."[78]

This process of investigation resulted in a new *kanunname*, and the preamble presents a history of proper imperial order. The subjects of the realm, and the edict of justice, reign supreme: "Those procedures of the previous sultans that do not hurt the subject will remain. Those that are mere innovations and pure fabrications, and that the weak and poor complain of and are distressed by, will be removed." But the true innovation was the legal imposition of a management strategy, executed by a delegate of the sultan. The sovereignty of the sultan lay in his imperial command, in the instruction to arrange, and in the authority that derived from the text itself: "This [evaluation of past procedures] will be ordered, arranged, designated, recorded and registered by imperial command."[79] These instructions for order, arrangement, and registration reveal a sultanate intent on archiving past customs and present actions. The might of the sultan, at least partially, was now configured in his ability to perceive the necessity for this order and to delegate officials capable of fulfilling the expectations for proper registration.

Registration and record keeping, in Celalzade Mustafa's preamble, constituted the basis, and the basic framework, for the successful integration of newly conquered territories. The practices of record keeping and systematic registration became the very ground of universal sovereignty.

Imperial Domain and Sovereign Land

The preamble to the Mısır *kanunname* invoked the title of *halife* (caliph) and combined it with *sahib-i kıran* (ruler/conqueror born under an auspicious astrological conjunction). Celalzade Mustafa thus executed a different kind of conjunction—that of temporal and spiritual power, with an astrological and messianic destiny of becoming world conqueror.[80] He thereby clearly enunciated the emergent tension between local, regionally specific definitions of power (Islam and the jurisprudential definition of limited sultanic authority) and global designations (world conqueror and universal ruler), now conjoined in an assertion of ownership over a lucrative provincial territory (Mısır) that would be extended as a possessive construction of sultanic ownership across the domain. This possessive construct would later be echoed in Ebu's-su'ud's sleight of hand—literally using the Ottoman Turkish possessive genitive, which is also legally nonspecific—whereby landownership was commuted into an equity held by the *beytü'l mal-ı Müslimin* (treasury of the Muslims), and the sultan, as administrator of the Muslims (*imamü'l-Müslimin*), engaged as its proprietor.[81] This definitional shift for both sultanic authority and the treasury (and corresponding to larger structural changes in finance administration) reinforced the connections among land; the legal stipulations for its cultivation, productive yield, taxation, and transfer; and the authority necessary to manage these governing practices.

It would fall on Ebu's-su'ud Efendi to orchestrate the necessary legal manipulations that might extend the impulses of the Egyptian *kanunname* to the exigencies of continual expansion and incorporation.[82] Ordering and registering the realm could take place only within a coherent policy for the extraction of revenue. And Ebu's-su'ud faced a seemingly insurmountable challenge: how to incorporate territories acquired during the fiercely expansionary regimes of Selim I and his son Süleyman into a systematic legal rubric consonant with both imperial and jurisprudential norms. The primary problem he sought to address, and one raised in the Egyptian *kanunname* as well, was to identify the standard of measurement for proper legislative action. The "current of laws" that the Ottoman dynasty embraced now gave way to a balancing act between the canons of divine law (*shari'a*), the regional approximations to this law that had become customized (*örf*), and imperial interventions that combined the two as *kanun*. With the incorporation of territories north of Belgrade, and finally of Buda itself, this also entailed sifting through accretions of Byzantine and Hungarian structures that did not fit into land and taxation categories derived from the *shari'a*. Although scholars have primarily focused on the relationship between *kanun* and *shari'a* within both Celalzade Mustafa and Ebu's-su'ud's work on the *kanunname*, Ebu's-su'ud also paid attention to a different opposition: the slippage between *miri* and *mülk* land. His effort to refine the relationship between the two, and thus to systematize registration and taxation strategies, resituated the *shari'a* within the ambit of imperial legislation.

Over the course of his career as a jurisconsult, he consistently, if not obsessively, addressed the possibility that various loopholes in the overlapping legal structures, deployed across conquered territories, might enable the assertion of outright ownership claims to land and thereby thwart new taxation regimes. The historian and bureaucrat Mustafa 'Ali noted his attention to these matters: "in particular, he [Ebu's-su'ud] gave *fetva*s pertaining to land. None amongst those who had held the office of *şeyhülislam* had paid such attention [to this issue] or elucidated it [so thoroughly]."[83] The preambles written for the provincial *kanunname*s of Buda, and of Üsküp (Skopje) and Selanik (Salonica), clearly evince Ebu's-su'ud's efforts to extend sultanic jurisdiction into domains of tithe and taxation customarily governed by divine law. The preamble for Buda was probably written by Ebu's-su'ud in his capacity as superintendent (*emin*) of Buda's registration into the Ottoman record while serving as the head judge of Rumeli from 1537 to 1545, and thus before he assumed the post of *şeyhülislam*. The date of the preamble for Üsküp and Selanik is recorded as *hijri* 976 (1568–69), and he also references Selim II in the introduction. For both towns he acted as the registrar (*il yazicisi*) of the provincial human and material resources, and they therefore embody the consistency and maturation of his ideas across the time span of his career as an Ottoman official and jurisconsult. Yet the ultimate import of these disparate regional interventions becomes clear in that they were incorporated, in expanded form, into the *kanunname-i cedid*, suggesting that they indeed succeeded in establishing a new baseline for land administration.[84] Issued in 1673, this *kanunname* also incorporated *fetvas* (considered opinion) issued by Ebu's-su'ud in relation to agrarian taxes and their appropriate categories and thus enfolded *shari'a* genres of jurisprudential analysis with the *kanun* formulae of imperial command.[85]

The *kanunname-i cedid* also begins with the preamble of Buda, where Ebu's-su'ud asserted that Süleyman conquered the *vilayet* of Budin with "divine guidance and assistance" and undertook to enact "the manifest laws of justice and equity toward all *re'aya*." He went on to state that, by command of the sultan, all people should be registered in their place, and he then listed all movable property such as houses, shops, and other buildings along with the produce of their gardens as canonically belonging to the people, who were free to transfer ownership as they will. But while the fields they customarily cultivated were determined to be in their possession, "they are not in their ownership like their other aforementioned properties." Instead, "like the *arāẓī-i memleket* (state land), which is known as *arẓ-ı mīrī* (imperial domain) in other protected dominions, the *rakabe-i arẓ* (substance, ownership rights) belongs to the *beytü'l māl-ı Müslimīn* (treasury of the community of Muslims), and the *re'āyā* possess it by way of a loan (*i'āra*)."[86] They are to keep the land in a "flourishing condition, and pay their taxes without fail, and no one is to interfere with this." They "possess the land in the manner described" until their death, at which point it should be passed to their sons, or, if no sons remain, to someone outside the family who will then take up the "loaned" possession of the land.[87]

The *kanunname* then proceeds with some eleven questions and answers posed in *fetva* form in order to more fully elaborate on the synthesis outlined in the preamble. In these *fetvas* Ebu's-su'ud directly intervened in the practice of regional judges to ratify the sale and transfer of land through mechanisms that challenged imperial oversight. One question begins:

> According to the time, when *arāẓī-i 'öşrīye* or *ḫarācīye*[88] which was in the hands of the *re'āyā* of Rumeli was purchased, pledged, placed on deposit, loaned, or sold . . . the *ḳadı*s, registering such transactions in their records, customarily had given title deeds into their hands.[89]

The legislative issue hinges on the pointed query that concludes the scenario: "According to the *şer'-ü şerīf*, was what the *kadıs* had done in conformity with sacred law?" Ebu's-su'ud begins his response by explaining, "The aforementioned land is neither *'öşrīye* or *harācīye*, it is *arẓ-ı memleket.* Neither was it divided among the warriors and made *'öşrīye* at the time of conquest, nor was it given to its owners; it was made purely *harācīye* and the *rakabe-i arẓ* pertains to the *beytü'l mal-i Müslimīn.*" He goes on to insist that they "possess" it by way of a rent and then declares the judicial decisions "regarding their loan and deposit" to be illegal. He reiterates this point in a ringing conclusion:

> And for the *ḳadıs* to allow barter in the giving and taking of land among the *re'āyā* merely on their own authority and to give title deeds for them is absolutely contrary to the *şer'-ü şerīf*, and writing deeds to such effect and signing them is entirely null and void.[90]

Ebu's-su'ud provides a more streamlined version of this problem in the 1568 *kanunname* of Üsküp and Selanik, which is also folded into the new *kanun.*[91] Its reiteration testifies to the persistence of overlapping claims to ownership and land management, as well as to Ebu's-su'ud's consistent attention to stabilizing the system. The preamble to the *kanunname* for these provinces states that in former registers "no attempt was made to determine the true nature of various forms of landholding in the well-protected territories of the Ottoman state." This was especially problematic, the preamble adds, because the situation was not properly scrutinized, nor were the inhabitants clearly informed of the difference between lands designated as *'öşri*, which had been in the hands of Muslims since the time of the early Arab conquests and thus individually held and subject to tithe, or *haraci*, which referred to land conquered during war and is thus held by virtue of a *tapu* and taxed. As a result, the cultivators (*re'aya*) bought and sold land as if it was freehold property (*mülk*) and even transformed it into a charitable endowment (*vakıf*) to render it inheritable. As a result, the judges, "unaware of the true status of *miri* land," delivered documents for buying and selling and for *vakıf* deeds "contrary to the sacred *şerı'a*." The preamble then states the rationale for the *kanunname* as a whole:

> Since this situation has caused a substantial deterioration in the orderly functioning of state affairs, and confusion in the transactions made among

> the people, the present sultan [Selim II] ordered that, in the introductions to the imperial survey registers, the true nature of land and the possession rights of their owners in the well-protected territories be thoroughly investigated and specified.

Ebu'su'ud thus follows his sultan's directive and specifies the distinct categories of landholding in the same terms as those in the Buda preamble. Although the terms are the same, the indictment of local judges is sharper, as is the sense, at least to the Ottoman mind, of an administrative process in disarray. Judges were unaware of the "true" status of *miri*, or lands under state jurisdiction. Provincial actors took advantage of this confusion to buy and sell land "as if" they owned it rather than paying the apportioned taxes. Therefore, judges and local inhabitants actively maneuvered around the use of slippery terminology and categories to escape the agrarian-based taxation system. This disorder threatened not only the proper functioning of government but also the very source of sovereign authority since the distribution of revenue rights and mastery over territory remained pivotal to emergent conceptions of sultanic power. Ebu's-su'ud explicitly identified the "deterioration in the orderly functioning of state affairs" as the result of two interdependent issues: the mislabeling of lands as freehold, rather than imperial, and local ignorance of the proper rules and regulations governing land management.

Ebu's-su'ud worked against this disarray through several innovations that would set the tone for later revisions in the *kanunname* and for treatises that analyzed the *kanun* as a template for Ottoman political order. First, Ebu's-su'ud blurred the boundaries between the imperial treasury (*hazine-i 'amire*) and that of the Muslim community as a whole. The meaningfulness of this, for Ebu's-su'ud and the sultanate more generally, was twofold: as the organization of the *hazine-i 'amire* expanded, the direct link between "sultanic lands," held by the sultan himself, and those belonging to the imperial domain, or to the institution of the sultanate, became less rigidly defined. These blurred lines then enabled the assertion that newly conquered territories belonged to the sultan's well-protected domains (*memalik-i mahrusamız*), that the agriculturalists in them were his (*re'ayamız*), as were other inhabitants who acknowledged his sovereignty and became tribute-payers (*kulum ve haracgüzarımdır*), asserted imperial ownership precisely as Ebu's-su'ud attempted to reassess the religious basis for rightful claims to property.[92] He maneuvered within the limits of *shari'a*-minded jurisprudence to ensure that the revenues from these personages and lands filled a general treasury and that this treasury belonged to the Muslim community as a whole, with the sultan acting as steward and shepherd of this community. In so doing, the legal validity of sultanic ownership (*arazi-i memleket*) could be shaped to the canonical precepts of divine law.[93] Furthermore, Ebu's-su'ud singularly collapsed *'öşr* and *haraci* land into *miri*, and thus imperial domain, by declaring that all lands of the Ottoman Empire had been acquired by war and were therefore subject to a higher rate.[94] He thus challenged common distinctions between Muslim and non-Muslim tax-payers in order to augment sultanic oversight over all land-management systems.

Second, in an effort to sustain this oversight amid the gradual commodification of land and the resulting ability of landholders to accumulate territory and disrupt revenue flow, Ebu's-su'ud adopted the canonical juristic term *tefviz* to designate transfer or consignment rather than outright *sale*, which was against the ordinances of the *shari'a*. While he notes that "it is absolutely contrary to the *şer'-ü şerīf* for *ḳadı*s to define the giving and receiving [of land] by the peasants as 'sale' and to issue certificates [accordingly],"[95] he generated a new formula for recording these transfers: "X, with the permission of the fief-holder, received so-and-so many *akçe*s from Y and transferred (*tefviz*) the use of his land to him. The fief-holder also gave the *tapu* to him."[96] This new terminology created a means to render the unabated transfer of lands into a canonically sanctioned revenue for the imperial treasury. It explicitly outlined that it was the *use* of the land, not its soil, that was consigned and reasserted a formula whereby these consignments could be acceptably documented within imperial registers. Moreover, following trends established by preceding *şeyhülislam*s, Ebu's-su'ud extended sultanic jurisdiction over agricultural production by marking a distinction between the substance (*rakaba*) of the land (at the disposal of the sultan) and its usufruct (*tasarruf*), which the subjects have use of by their payment of a tithe (*'ushr* or *'öşr*).[97] While this was a fairly common device, in his additions to the *kanunname* of Buda and in later *fetva*s, Ebu's-su'ud pushed even further in the direction of sultanic power. In canonical juristic treatments of the tithe, a ruler's portion remains limited to one-tenth, and taxes, accordingly, were restricted in theory by this limit. Ebu's-su'ud, however, defined *miri* land (and thus land at the disposal of the sultan) as tributary land. Thus, as he stated in the *kanunname* for Buda, the fields that inhabitants had long cultivated should remain in their possession, but ownership belonged to the *arazi-i memleket* instead. "The substance (*rakabe*) is reserved for the treasury of the Muslims, and the subjects have use of it by way of a loan (*i'āra*). They sow and reap whatever cereals and crops they wish and pay their proportional tribute (*ḫārāc-ı muḳaseme*) under the name tithe (*'öşr*), and benefit from the land however they wish."[98]

This last distinction, that they pay "proportional tribute under the name tithe," marks a masterful move on the part of Ebu's-su'ud. Military campaigns and negotiations with tribute-paying territories necessitated this move and tied conquest to legal manipulation. The distinction ensured that neither the fixed portion of a one-tenth tithe nor the fixed tribute payments (*harac-ı muvazzaf*) negotiated between a Muslim ruler and a conquered population would determine the *miri* tax; rather, the slippery approximation of the proportional tribute would now be the designated framework for taxes due from *miri* land. The proportional tribute became a variable rate, giving the sultan the option of increasing taxation levies and greater leverage in general over agricultural production. Ebu's-su'ud was at pains, despite this ploy, to insist that this was religiously permissible because the taxes were not assessed as a tithe. Thus, he clarified positions outlined in *kanunname* preambles and asserted that "the [Ottoman] tithe is not the [canonical] tithe (*'öşr*). To call it 'tithe' is a gross deception by the common people. *Miri* is tribute land: it cannot possibly be tithe land. The share that is paid is proportional tribute. It is the cavalryman's canonical right."[99]

Referring back to the preamble for Üsküp and Selanik, Ebu's-su'ud had by 1568 clearly outlined the variables in land categories and inserted the rights of the dynasty and its record-keeping practices as the litmus test for all transactions. The "well-protected territories" and the "orderly functioning of state affairs" became the legitimizing rubric for a proper scrutiny of land-management systems. The knowledge of the sultan, mediated by his officiates, trumped that of the local judges, whose interpretations of *miri* status presumably led them astray from an Ottomanized definition of sanctioned divine law. Here, then, knowledge of imperial categories for proper land management constituted a necessary rubric even for the interpretation of divine law. Without the one (proper imperial order), the other is mismanaged (apportionment of property rights according to the *shari'a*). In the Egyptian *kanunname*, Celalzade Mustafa presented the preamble itself, which lays out the rationale behind registration of land, as a textual mechanism for harmonizing the realm into proper order. The *kanunname* indicated the actual state of affairs *by which* the survey registers must be read *and* the actions of *shari'a* judges implemented. And Celalzade Mustafa's preamble situated that practice within a history of sovereignty defined by law and systematized registration. Thus, investigation, careful record-keeping practices, and consistent documentation enshrined a system of order that knit the empire together. Ebu's-su'ud Efendi's use of *fetva*s as a means to clarify the agrarian system enfolded *shari'a* practices within the domain of imperial lawmaking. These became their own preamble to the *kanunname-i cedid* and thus the standard reference for judges, regional administrators, and representatives of the imperial council, as well for the expanding cohort of Ottoman literati. This incorporation of *fetva* into *kanun* solidified a pattern of governance already present in the Ottoman establishment's efforts to create a common language for taxation, petition, and sovereignty in earlier *kanunname*. Yet the explicit link connecting text, order, and empire occurred in the savvy, stylized interventions of Süleyman's chancellor and chief jurist, where pen and document mastered the realm and solidified imperial law.

Laying Claim to the Protected Territories: Sultan as "Administrator of the Muslims" and "Emperor of the World"

Land, law, and sultanic identity all played significant roles in larger debates about the legal basis of the empire and its validity in the face of disparate rivals. Balancing claims to universalism (countering the Habsburgs) and to Sunni purity (in opposition to the Safavids and internal religious reform movements), titles directly attributed to the sultan by Ebu's-su'ud also appeared in proclamations issuing from the chancery. These titles were engraved into the architectural landscape through inscriptions on mosque and medrese complexes and were adopted by treatise writers as part of a linguistic cartography of imperial domains.[100] Thus, Süleyman I (and, by implication, the sultanate more generally) was alternatively characterized as the ruler of Islam (*padişah-ı Islam*) and the ruler who is the refuge of the world (*padişah-ı 'alempena*), or the ruler of the people of Islam (*padişāh-ı ehl-i Islam*) and universal emperor (*hüdavendigar*).[101] The shifting emphases of these titles attest to the sophisticated mechanisms of diplomacy and the carefully leveraged representation of power depending on the historical and textual context. Furthermore, the productive tension between master of the world and master of Islam echoes the dynamic interweaving of divine, dynastic, and imperial law into the foundational precepts of a properly ordered Ottoman state, as well as the heteroglossia necessary to achieve those aims.[102] In this guise Ebu's-su'ud also framed Süleyman as "master of all lands and the shadow of God over all nations, sultan over all the sultans in the lands of Arabs and Persians," and as "the caliph of the whole world," while he was simultaneously "Süleyman in whose name the *ḫutbe* is read in Mecca and Medina."[103]

These titles hint at the larger religio-political battles that emerged as a result of the expanding territorial and legal jurisdiction of the Ottoman dynasty. The proliferating cadres of scribes and scholars, and the emergence of a professional stratum attached solely to the daily apparatus of governance, gradually challenged religious authorities and marginalized voices that were not folded into the state. The apocalypticism of the moment, along with increasingly volatile religious students who jockeyed for positions and protested when they were not provided for, all raised the internal stakes even as Süleyman fought to achieve acclaim on external frontiers.[104] Ebu's-su'ud's conflicts over legal interpretation with contemporaries such as Birgivi and Çivizade Muhiyyiddin Efendi, who was *kadı'asker* (head military judge) of Anatolia and the *şeyhülislam* before Ebu's-su'ud, were part of a new political landscape in which an argument concerning ownership and taxation became a debate concerning the jurisprudential reach of the sultanate.[105] The consequent reinvestment for both legal scholars and political commentators in how (or if) Ottoman governing practice fit into the moral economy of rule, elaborated in jurisprudential literature as *siyaset-i şer'iyye*, indicates that this was indeed a moment for the redefinition of past forms (genre) in order to secure present agency (practice) and project an ideal state (objectification).

Definitions of just (*siyaset-i 'adiliye*) and unjust (*siyaset-i zalimiye*) rule were, via a common trope in the political economy of Muslim rule, reenvisioned in terms of maintaining public order (*masalih-i mursala*).[106] For the sake of public order a Muslim ruler might be granted discretion to create and implement criminal law and act as an administrator of status rights granted by the *shari'a* without laying a blasphemous claim to the ability to interpret divine will. Thus, Süleyman's cadre of supporters sketched out a sanctioned proper order for the realm that pivoted between the sultan as "administrator of the Muslims" (*imamü'l-Müslimin*) and as emperor of the world's refuge (*hüdevendigar-i 'alempenah*). Süleyman laid claim to this sanctioned order, and to his role as protector, preserver, guarantor of justice, the relief of the cultivator, and the principled leader of the Muslim community, in correspondence to an increasingly diffuse imperial cartography. The documents issued from the council, along with the rulings of the *şeyhülislam*, mapped a new imperial dominion and publicized claims to power in an ever-intensifying circuit of diplomatic correspondence and documentary registration. As sultanic correspondence carried more of the burden in this competitive environment of performing imperial power, new formulas marked a shift in status. Characterizations of the sultan morphed according to the ideological and military campaigns of the day, evoking the significance of discursive tropes for the construction of sovereign power. Süleyman transmitted this strategy to stone, as an inscription on the fortress at Bender (modern Tighina) reads: "In Baghdad, I am the shah, in Byzantine realms the Caesar, and in Egypt the Sultan, who sends his fleets to the seas of Europe, the Maghrib and India."[107]

This inscription highlights a core feature of the *kanunname* preamble's declaration of sovereignty: the rhetoric shifted according to the specific historical and discursive environment of its addressees. As compositions in Ottoman and stylized *inşa'* gave standard form to this correspondence, the invocations of authority (*invocatio*) and attributed titles (*intitulatio*) assumed a new intricate shape. Beginning with the Egyptian *kanunname*, Celalzade Mustafa crafted an expanded formula for the opening and the list of titles that decorated the pages of Süleyman's transactions of state and enacted his power from within a framework blessed by divine, dynastic, and imperial lineages.[108] Complete with a linguistic plurality that shifted from an

Arabized invocation to an Ottomanized passage of praise for God's blessings, Muhammad's message, the guidance of the first four successors, and fated constellations, these stylized attributes girded the sultan with the entire apparatus of Islamic sacredness. These preambles, wedded to provincial regulations, became increasingly common and employed multiple mechanisms for configuring sultanic discursive and territorial authority. The Egyptian *kanunname* reasserted the primacy of a religious sanction and met the dual challenges to the sultan's religious preeminence from an established and venerable lineage of Islamicate scholarship in Cairo and from the Shi'i Safavid state. Both catalyzed an emergent Hanafi hegemony within the Ottoman establishment and a push to acclaim both the ideological and the administrative supremacy of its sovereign. It also situated Süleyman's state within an itinerary of power that embraced central Asian traditions of leadership (*khan* and *sultan*), as well as Persian (*padışah*), along with monarchical and imperial power claimed within a patronage of Ottoman greatness. The *kanunname* of Buda, in contrast, was short and to the point. It emphasized territorial supremacy and the sultan's role as a guide for the implementation and promulgation of laws. This role extended from east to west, across all the conquered territories, and prolonged the chain of Ottoman dynastic power from the past into the future. The addressees were officials who would administer a region unaccustomed to an Islamicate discourse of governance.

However, an expanded *intitulatio* pointedly appears in correspondence with Ferdinand I, who is recognized as a regional king dwarfed by the lineage of the sultan. A letter sent in 1554 informed Ferdinand of appointed officials in Buda and dependent territories, and it outlined the basic statutes of Ottoman administrative expectations. The stylized opening frames the sultan's power in direct counterpoint to Ferdinand and within the full cohort of historical legacies. It begins by defining Süleyman as an esteemed warrior for the faith, acting within the embrace of the prophet Muhammad and the first four successors, and then proceeds declaratively:

> I who am Sultan Süleyman, the son of Sultan Selim khan, the sultan of sultans, the proof of emperors, the distributor of crowns to the monarchs of the surface of the earth, the shadow of God on the lands, the sultan and the

> *pādışāh* of the White Sea [Mediterranean], the Black Sea, Rumelia, Anatolia, Karamania, the lands of Rum, of Diyarbakır, of Kurdistan, of the provinces of the Zülkadırs, of Azerbaycan, of 'Acem [Persia], of Şam [Damascus], of Mısır [Egypt], of Haleb [Aleppo], of Mecca and Medina, of Kudüs [Jerusalem], of all the lands of Arabia and Baghdad, the Yemen, San'a, and Aden, Basra and of Cezayir (North Africa) of the many lands conquered by the irresistible power of my noble fathers and illustrious ancestors—may God illuminate their manifestations—and of the many lands which my glorious and august majesty has conquered with a flaming sword.[109]

This territorial mapping moves across land and sea and highlights the jewels of former state and dynastic glory that have now been added to the crown of the sultan's majesty. Süleyman's lineage testifies to the accumulated power of the dynasty, now surpassing regional comparisons to become the "proof of emperors" and "distributor of crowns" to contemporaries who are kings and monarchs, not universal rulers. Conquest girds his power and majesty. Yet the proper order of the realm also depended on circuits of information and on servants loyal to the sultan. The letter therefore references petitions from regional landholders who have recognized Ottoman suzerainty and now act as part of the administrative apparatus in the conquered Hungarian territories. It orders Ferdinand to acknowledge and respect these newly crafted loyalties if he wishes to remain in friendly relations with the sultan. Despite the resplendent material and ideological glory of the text, its contents reflect imperial liabilities in a contentious zone.

Thus, the routines of diplomacy and administration tested the resiliency of claims to universal protector and guardian of the realm, especially in territories that were not fully conquered or occupied. Between 1528 and 1538 Süleyman positioned himself as imperial landlord of the principalities of Wallachia and Moldavia in letters sent to the king of Poland, Sigismund I (r. 1506–48), and set the standard for new alignment practices implemented later within the Hungarian territories. In these diplomatic exchanges Süleyman alone stands as the fount of information, the source of solutions, and the overseer of all affairs. He laid claim to the land, subjects, and diplomatic circuits necessary for the management of provincial affairs. In a letter sent in April or May of 1531 he counters the unruly behavior of the current *voivode* of Moldavia, Petru Rareş, with the assertion that "the voivode of Moldavia as well as that of Wallachia are my servants and tribute-payers (*kūlum ve ḫarācgüzarımdır*), and their possessions, included among our other well-protected dominions (*memālik-i maḥrūsamız*) like Bosnia and Semendria, are my estate." Süleyman references the treaties in place between Poland and the Ottoman Empire and the apparent agreement as to the sultan's oversight in the Moldavian territories. Süleyman's ire, in this case, was particularly evoked by the suggestion that messengers and envoys were circulating directly between the Polish king and the Moldavian deputy, whose position ostensibly depended on Ottoman favor. Süleyman stridently queries, "Who is he [the voivode] to dare and have audacity to send an emissary to you? He and the voivode of Wallachia are my tribute-payers and servants." In response to this disruption in the circuit of authority and knowledge, Süleyman issued "severe orders" that no envoy should be dispatched independent of those sent by the sultanate, "no matter to whom." He states further that "if somebody has a question with them, he must appeal to our powerful Porte, which is opened all times, and acknowledge what he needs."[110]

Affronted by a regional leader, recognized by the sultanate and yet subservient to its demands, who had the audacity to conduct his own affairs of state, Süleyman's letter clearly enunciates his rights to the "servants" of his realm. He suggests further that, as the imperial council is always accessible, there is no excuse to direct questions or concerns elsewhere—the apparatus of the state is ever vigilant. Also clear in Süleyman's outrage, however, is that regional players possessed their own agendas, circuits of information, and the presumed authority to act on them. Key to interfering with, and disrupting, potential challenges from these overlapping claims and jurisdictions was the ability for sultanic discourse to pivot in order to meet, and directly address, multiple audiences and thus to assert variable forms of authority. In this case Süleyman claims the inhabitants of Wallachia and Moldavia as servants and tribute payers of the protected domains. But the exigencies of administration still disrupted pure forms of state control, despite the frameworks for it that the chancery and the *müftülük* promulgated through epigraphic declarations, *kanunname* legislation, and epistolary exchanges. These were but idealized maps and projected expectations; their proliferation could connote vulnerability as much as supremacy.

An undercurrent of vulnerability appeared even in the later work of Celalzade Mustafa, whose textual paeans to Selim and Süleyman offer up an ideological conundrum that would shape Ottoman historiographic representations in the late sixteenth and early seventeenth centuries. This conundrum returns to the significance of the pen, both as an occupation and as an inscription of power. Between his retirement in 1557 and the death of Süleyman in 1566, Celalzade Mustafa dedicated his time to two manuscripts. One, left incomplete, was intended as a map of the imperial dominions culminating in the reign of Süleyman, his *Ṭabaḳatü'l-memālik ve derecātü'l-mesālik* (the Echelons of the Dominions and the Hierarchies of Professional Paths).[111] The other, finalized, but with variant manuscript copies and titles, was a tribute to the reign of Selim I, a *Selimnāme*.[112] Therein he described his position of *nişancı* as "the greatest among all offices and the noblest among all services . . . [because] all great sultans . . . need two types of servants to rule over vast lands: men of pen and men of sword (*erbāb-ı tiğ ve ḳālem*)." He goes on to say that "as a matter of fact, sword and pen are twins, one of them is the soul and the other is the body (*biri ten ve biri can*). But the pen is above the sword because the sword aims to destroy, whereas the pen aims to produce (*biri kāti' biri nābitdir*)." He underscores this point by rephrasing: "the rule of the sword devastates a country whereas the rule of the pen causes prosperity."

Although Celalzade Mustafa had used his position as a man of the pen to institute new paradigms of governance, a paradox emerges between his characterization of power, firmly concentrated within the personhood of Süleyman, and his sense that successful land and population management required persistent care, attention, and oversight. Thus, while crafting an image of omnipotent sultanic power, he also attends to the intricacy of its management in the documentary genres issued by the imperial council. The image of Süleyman in his *Ṭabaḳat* certainly projects a commander with auspicious fortune in a narrative of apocalyptic chaos: he has successfully conquered realms from the east to the west, grants crowns to rivals (*tac-bahş*) instead of sharing his titles, piously bequeaths justice and munificence throughout the realm, and gathers to himself the wealth and the information of the world.[113] He is both the *padişah-ı Islam* and "the abode of kings, the refuge of sultans, the distinguished ruler whose retinue is formed of kings."[114] He has successfully challenged Charles V's claim to universal monarchy by conquering Hungary and thus limited the king's domain to "Christian lands" rather than to the entire inhabited world. But this image of power is still tenuous. The copious notes on official appointments, army inspections, administrative hierarchy, the circulation of diplomatic envoys, and on information gathered from messengers, registers, and reports in an effort to build a bureaucratic fortress remind the reader that even (or, rather, *especially*) amid supremacy, there is the potential for subdual from within and from without.

The voluminous portrait of Süleyman's reign in the *Ṭabaḳat* therefore turns from eulogizing the sultan to enumerating the realm.[115] This textual move, from sultan to system, and from personhood to bureaucracy, masterfully illuminates the dramatic epistemic ruptures of sixteenth- and seventeenth-century Ottoman critical commentaries of dynastic fortunes. More significant, although only the prospective list of section headings remains, the fact that Celalzade Mustafa's projected outline included 30 sections and 375 subsections, and that he believed each was necessary to map the trajectory of the empire, surely reflects the systematization at work both in the palace and in expansionary early modern courts more generally. According to this outline, he was to begin by describing the professional groups that together reproduced the empire as salaried servants of the state, with twenty subjections, or levels (*derece*), on palace personnel, viziers, janissaries, *sipahis*, along with scribes, porters, entertainers, and artisans. He then intended to compose provincial studies of the twenty imperial territories, in addition to the holy cities of Mecca and Medina, focusing on dynamics of the governorships (*beylerbeylik*). The provincial studies were meant to lead into a more specialized section on fortresses across the realm and then to auxiliary troops and the navy. One section in its entirety was reserved for Istanbul, and then he proposed to return for a tour of each of the provinces of the empire with careful notation of their land systems, villages, religious endowments, and demographics. All that remains of this proposed manuscript is the final section (the thirtieth) devoted to Süleyman himself, but the philosophic universe at work within the pages of the *Ṭabaḳat* is still detectable. Although the sultan is central to the project, he is not its center; the categorizations of order outlined by Celalzade Mustafa also compelled him to detach the sultan from the system.

Ironically, the work he *did* complete was the *Selimnāme*, devoted to his patron and master's father, Selim I, and embodying a nostalgic vision for an era that later writers would attribute to Süleyman instead.[116] In both texts Celalzade Mustafa introduced techniques that later analysts would mimic: the use of earlier written *fethname*s and *ruzname*s (campaign narratives and diaries) as historical sources from which information was gathered and assessed and the inclusion of references to documents and registers that he himself had composed or supervised in his tenure as *nişancı*. Even as he draws on his experience as a bureaucrat, however, he yearns for the age of the horseback warrior ideally embodied in Selim's campaigns. Although Süleyman, too, assumed the saddle and the titles of the *gazi* warrior, it would appear that for Celalzade Mustafa, at least, the encumbrance of bureaucracy tainted his image as a protector and savior of the realm.

The Encumbrance of Bureaucracy and Practice in the Mühimme

It was precisely "encumbrance," however, that led to a new register devoted to the affairs of the Ottoman establishment. While the *kanunname* and diplomatic correspondence explored in the preceding sections illustrate general frameworks for the allotment of resources and defined principles of order that legitimated Ottoman governance, the remainder of this chapter turns to record-keeping practices developed for the daily practice of administration. The quotidian affairs of state appear in the varied edicts dispersed to servants of the realm, often in response to petitions or requests to address grievances concerning the implementation of *kanunname* statutes. Although *mühimme* registers would soon "capture" these daily affairs, earlier efforts to preserve a record of decision making can be traced as well. Thus, as the *kanunname* took more coherent form, beginning in the reign of Bayezid II (r. 1481–1512), so did the organized record of the daily operations of the imperial council. This is well illustrated in the earliest extant register of edicts (*hükm*), orders (*emir*), and imperial decrees (*ferman*) issued from the *divan*.[117] Although this register covers only June 8–17 and July 8–17 of 1501, it demonstrates a trend toward systematization in record keeping. The register further demonstrates how a common linguistic formula for dispensing commands and justice was adapted both within decrees promulgated from the center and in the petitionary elocutions sent from inhabitants across the imperial domain. Thus, petitioners adopted discursive strategies that fit their particular grievance into this rubric of proper order.[118] References to oppression (*be-gāyet ẓulümdür* or *ẓulm-ü teʿāddi*), unlawful seizure of land (*elimden alındı*/taken from my hand; *elimden alınıp bir kimesneye virdiler*/taken from my hand and given to another), and disputes over rights (*nizāʿ idüp bana kım virmezler*/disputed that they did not give me my right) were conjoined to notions that these were against customary rights deployed in the past (*atadan dededen*/ancestors' time or *ḳadīm-ül eyyām*/ancient times) or against rights established by law (*ḳānūn*), by divine law/order (*sharīʿa*), or against those defined by registered law (*ḫilāf-ı defter*).[119]

The archiving of sultanic responses to these petitions, and the systematic record keeping of provincial dynamics it entailed, produced an evolving database that could be consulted in case of disagreement over property holdings and taxation. Orders typically called for thorough investigations, either by a local judge, governor, or imperial delegate with knowledge of local conditions. The affairs of the petition were then judged against previous rulings and, especially in conflicts between individuals or groups, the *shariʿa*. Sultanic order came to rest on three mutually reinforcing spheres of authoritative knowledge: local conditions, archived records (*defter*s), and the law, conceived as a combination of *kanun* and *shariʿa*. Anything that went against these authoritative bodies was strongly condemned.[120] Furthermore, judges were explicitly ordered to adhere to the rulings of the sultan and report any signs of resistance to his authority.[121] From the earliest collections of complaints and imperial responses the scribal summaries of petitions reveal that supplicants understood how these principles of government were enacted in daily administrative practice. During the reign of Süleyman these disparate orders were finally compiled into a distinct documentary genre, the *umur-i mühimme defteri*. This genre was at the foreground of efforts to systematize record-keeping practices. Stylized as orders issuing directly from the mouth of the sultan, the *mühimme* were a key step toward creating bound registers for the future consultation and management of administrative activities. It also embodied, in the collaborative projects of the imperial council in which it was used during this period, the travails of bureaucracy and its itineraries of power. Formulated as daily records of affairs presented to the council, the *mühimme* also serve as a transcript of imperial concern. As such, they have typically been assayed as "central" government documents concerning "local" or provincial affairs.[122] Studies deploying them as sources tend to reproduce this opposition and, when their object is a "local" region, address issues of bias and omission resulting from such a state-generated documentary tradition. However, a rigidly oppositional understanding of how these documents were produced belies their structure, the concerns expressed within, and their ability to serve as an alternative framing device for the evolution of sovereignty and textual authority in the early modern Ottoman Empire.

Composed in the form of imperial commands (*hükm*), yet responsive to situational concerns across the realm summarized within each order, the *mühimme* are a hybrid genre. Each command captures a snapshot of an imperial response to concerns sparked by events outside the palace walls. The *mühimme* registers thus have an intermediary presence between legislation and correspondence promulgated from the imperial council, and petitions addressed to the sultan from the provinces.[123] Their foundational grounds were the territories of the empire, the hierarchies of its servants, the vagaries of its population, and the fortunes of its soldiers, defenses, and public works. In other words, the *mühimme* bring into being Celalzade Mustafa's enumeration of layered sovereignty proposed in the *Ṭabaḳat* and exemplify his conviction that systematic textual forms help guard and protect the realm as much as does the use of arms and military stratagems.

They were copied, however, as a chronological record of administrative concern, not a projected outline of the realm. Although the voice of the sultan gave shape to their form, the pressures of the territories dictated their content. Even if these varied copies of administrative orders constituted one of the primary productions of the imperial council, this project was consistently interrupted by counter trends and interests voiced by state and nonstate agents alike. As such, a form of imperial anxiety suffuses the *mühimme*, and the state becomes just one claimant among many. The "work" of the *mühimme* registers was therefore the elaboration of an ethical framework of imperial loyalty and command and the production, from within that framework, of legitimacy. Thus, the formulae used to characterize events and compose responses drew from the vocabulary and grammar of the *kanun* and thus from the multiple genealogies of imperial law outlined in the previous chapter. The bound documents of the *mühimme* thus generated an axis of legitimacy, one that rotated around the sultan and yet increasingly abstracted legitimacy from his person and resituated it within these hybrid legal, ideological, and philosophical inheritances. Imperial commands copied into the registers both embody and construct a grammar of rule, or set of structural norms, grounded in a particular vision of proper order and distributive justice. Consequently, the *mühimme* registers embody a productive slippage between categories of the imperial and the provincial, the ethical and the political, the bureaucratic and the ideological, and thus between discursive and sociohistorical methodologies deployed in the study of early modern dynamics.

The *umur-i mühimme defteri* not only facilitate a more nuanced understanding of discursive authority within the Ottoman bureaucracy, but they also illustrate the importance of careful attention to how documentary registers were produced, circulated, and dispatched. "Reading" the document entails tracing, as far as possible, how they came to be a mechanism for imperial registration. Even using the phrase "the *mühimme*" belies the institutional complexity and documentary plurality of the bound registers. There are a total of 263 registers catalogued as *Mühimme Defterleri* (MD) held in the Başbakanlık Arşıvı, Istanbul. This classification, however, imposed by nineteenth-century reforming projects in the Ottoman archives, assumes a transparency that did not exist. First, only a few of the registers actually contain the self-designation of *mühimme defteri*, even though the tradition of binding directives into notebooks continued until 1905. Thirteen registers classified as MD are actually appointment registers (*ru'üs defterleri*). Furthermore, two registers in the Kāmil Kepeci section of the archival system deployed in the Başbakanlık (addressed in Chapter 1) are also MDs,[124] and two others have been located in the Topkapı Sarayı, one in the archives and one in the library.[125] The two Topkapı registers constitute the oldest in the series, pertaining to 1544/45 and 1552 respectively. They should also be linked to the *şikāyet defteri* (hereafter ŞD), or register of complaints, with bounded entries beginning in 1649, and gradually constituting an entirely separate method of categorization.[126] Thus, the volume that scholars typically point to that does indeed contain a self-designation of *mühimme* (MD 94) appears *after* the emergence of the ŞD registers and was most likely part of an effort to defray confusion among scribes as to the proper placement of a directive's copy once it was issued by the imperial council.[127]

While the most common internal reference to the register was "*aḥkām-i mīrī defteri*," or register of imperial decrees, often an indication as to categorical content is completely absent from a bound register.[128] Date of issuance, or the starting date of a register, is thus the only primary technique for "locating" it within the expanding bureaucratic corpus. While some registers also contain the identity of the head secretary (*re'isülküttab*) or the grand vizier under whose auspices the directives were formulated, even this practice is more haphazard than standard. Thus, even the dates can be misleading, as copies of directives were often misplaced in bound registers, and sections of a presumed *mühimme* register might also include material other than copies of imperial orders.[129] Since it is also unclear what stage of the decision-making process is actually represented in the bound registers of imperial directives, any assessment of bureaucratic action must take into account that these were not full transcriptions of a session of the council. Some were clearly early stages in the registration process, as emendations in the text, unfinished orders, or multiple starts to an individual *hükm* indicate, although for the most part they appear to be finalized copies of directives issued from the sultanate via the auspices of the council.[130]

A further distinction in register entries indicates that, despite these various confusions and limitations, the *mühimme defteri* were deemed indispensable to the workings of government. Some volumes of MD were clearly notations made during imperial campaigns (*sefer-i hümayun*) and accompanied the military impedimenta as a mobile archive. These records, the *ordu mühimmesi*, were often paralleled by entries submitted by the deputy of the grand vizier (*ka'immakam paşa*), who remained in Istanbul when the grand vizier acted as a military commander on campaign. The *ka'immakam paşa* thus attended to matters pertaining to the governance of the domain in the *rikab mühimmesi*, often duplicating dates and agendas across the registers.[131] Whether on campaign or in the daily operations of state, these registers came to embody the art and practice of government. More significant, they did so in the midst of the bureaucratic reorganization projects that attended Süleyman's dual campaigns: expansion and reterritorialization and the enunciation of universal sovereignty through both military might and textual authority. Thus, the first surviving volumes, 1544–45, 1552, then 1559–60 (MD 3), and July 1564–June 1566 (in reverse order, MDs 6 and 5), indicate an initial effort to catalogue and preserve sultanic edicts in sequential notebook form during intense efforts to redefine the administrative scope of the empire. The series then becomes more regular during the reign of Selim II, with fifty-six voluminous registers preserved from the time of his accession, to the end of the sixteenth century.[132]

Contrapuntal Framings of an Imperial Totality

The *mühimme defterleri*'s contents figure as one of the most important indicators of governance in the Ottoman Empire from the mid-sixteenth century onward, not *despite* these irregularities and inconsistencies but rather *on account* of their ability to embody the complexities inherent in framing a bureaucratic enterprise of such depth and extent. They are a record of the Ottoman Empire's records. From the 1550s to 1905, registers of the Ottoman establishment's various administrative affairs traced land-management policies, military operations, diplomatic volatilities, intercommunal relations, apocalyptic fervor, rebellions, trade relations, and the quotidian concerns of the populace mirrored in the *responsa* of the council. The structure of the bound registers and the individual orders further reinforces a sense of the synchronic variables of the imperial enterprise. Arranged chronologically, with no regard to region, subject matter, jurisdictional authorities, or any other apparent consideration, there is something important to be deduced from the "togetherness" of the *mühimme*. Provinces were not assigned distinct registers. Rather, entries move through the quotidian affairs of administrative practice. Thus each copy captures the "affairs of the day," like a news bulletin issued from the sultanate. The territorial expanse of the empire is here not imagined as cleanly compartmentalized by region, topical concern, or administrative bureau but rather as part of a total imperial project, shaped by the legal norms and vocabularies that evolved in the imperial council to direct daily affairs.

Dispatches from the Istanbul-based governing apparatus were intended to be "heard" by the addressees and recipients, but they contain within them their own anxieties concerning whether or not anyone was actually listening. The registers thus also preserve a sense of imperial vulnerability, and individual edicts often assume a tone of exhortation and demand and include threats or, alternatively, even postures of supplication intended to ensure compliance. This documentary variable presents a rather awkward question: if the orders are not implemented, or their process of implementation cannot be tracked, then are they "orders" at all?[133] Here, the framework of legal and discursive history is a useful one, as laws were productive in that they created categories for order and interaction and thus generated a legible grammar across disparate audiences that was later invoked and referenced in petitions addressed to the sultan or diplomatic correspondence delivered via ambassadorial envoys. *Mühimme* registers, therefore, contain their own contrapuntal dynamics, whereby an imperial vision of totality was inflected by the vicissitudes of governance in disparate domains, and the interests of the state were enfolded into the alignment practices necessary for its reproduction.[134] These contrapuntal features were further reflected in the tendency for the *mühimme* directives to contain legal pluralisms; thus, they reveal the multiple fonts of legitimacy deployed by the imperial council to ensure, as far as possible, the extension of territorial sovereignty across the imperial domains. The sultanic orders variously, or at times concurrently, summon references to customary law (*örf*) and thus to traditions from "times of old," even if those traditions are invented ones; to the *shari'a* and the *shar'*, and thereby to the divine law and its obligations of obedience, gradually also meaning "lawful" action in general;[135] and then to the sultan's will as sovereign and to the *kanun*, and thus to statutes, precedents, and records of past imperial actions that scribal and chancery actors wove together in the early to mid-sixteenth century to fashion a vision of imperial grandeur and permanency. As the overlapping codices of legitimacy within the *mühimme*, the registers associate together in one documentary genre the social, jurisprudential, ideological, and political vectors that together constituted a particular imperial ecology of rule during the period.

Mühimme registers thus embody and enact the five key problematics addressed in this book: (1) the record-keeping practices of the court; (2) the production of principles of legitimacy through a focus on textual order; (3) the dispatching of imperial commands that spatialize sovereignty; (4) an imperial totality inflected by, but not divided between, provincial or central concerns; and (5) a grammar of rule that relies on justice as a rationale for sovereign claims. Together these problematics yield a compelling argument for framing the *mühimme* in terms of an imperial practice that invokes a particular vocabulary of governance in an attempt to generate a vision of universalism and tranquility from dissonant regionalisms. The very materiality of the registers personifies these contrapuntal designs. On opening any one of these volumes, a researcher confronts a flood of entries, long and short, in variable handwriting, and with very little to indicate breaks between entries, days, and agendas besides the formulaic preambles and conclusions that characterize the documentary genre itself. It is not hard to imagine that this flood was also part of the experience in the imperial *divan*, where scribes hurriedly transmitted to the page, often summarily, the petitions, reports, and concerns deliberated by the council. There was little time to impose any organizational principle on the process, thus making what does exist—a mediating discourse of rule grounded in notions of proper order and distributive justice—of even more striking interest.

While not exactly "pressure from below," the flood of petitions and requests constitute the hidden backdrop for the majority of the directives issued as responses from the imperial council. This suggests, at the very least, a more involved interaction between imperial and regional concerns than the division between "central" and "local" or "periphery" allows for. In fact, the contrapuntal dynamics of the *mühimme* can be assessed simply from the formulaic structure they rely on, which is as significant to the project of the *mühimme* as the variable details concerning imperial affairs that they also contain. The greater portion of any given directive (*hükm*) consists of an introductory summary: for the majority of directives, this summary provides either details of situations, developments, events, or irregularities in a province (*eyalet* or *beylerbeylik*), administrative region (*sancak*), or district (*nahiye*) from which a petition, complaint, or report originated; reiterates situational concerns that require sultanic instructions to elite representatives of the realm; or delineates diplomatic exchanges or conflicts that necessitated the preparation of a new directive.[136] Opening summary observations are then renarrated from an "official" imperial perspective literally recorded in the first-person voice of the sultan. This first-person narrative, or renarrativization by the sultan, introduces an abbreviated statement intended to form the basis for evaluation, and then judgment, on the situation at hand. These deliberative judgments, and the specific instructions for resolving a given issue or for shaping projected agendas, are rationalized with reference to one or more legitimizing forces: the *şeri'a*, *kanun*, *'adet*, or *'örfiyye*. These hybrid pluralities of legitimacy serve to buttress the authority of the command itself, indicated by the expression *buyurdum ki* (I have commanded).

Variations to this structure certainly occurred, and toward the end of the sixteenth century and especially in the seventeenth, portions often became more abbreviated—either a shortened initial summary or a quick notation sufficing for the final command. Still, the framing structure endured across the diachronic arc of the genre, and situational concerns often ensured that lengthy discussions of the immediate factors that generated a sultanic response remain embedded in the extent of the *mühimme* registers. An order directed to both the governor and the *kadı* of Trablus-ı Şam in 1692 indicates the petitionary process at work.[137] It addresses the case of one Katip 'Umar and reflects the intersection of imperial, provincial, and judicial processes within the documentary genre of the *mühimme*. Katip 'Umar submitted a petition (*arzuhal*) to the exalted threshold (*'atebe-i seniye*) of the sultanate, in which he claimed that he had been imprisoned in the citadel by wicked people despite not having harmed anyone contrary to the *şeri'a*. His case (*da'va*) was brought to the attention of the imperial council (*divan-ı hümāyūn*), and he requested an imperial order (*hükm-i hümayun*) to have justice done and obtain his release from prison. The edict commands the responsible officials to proceed with Katip 'Umar's release. Reference to a *da'va* indicates that the subject of this directive, Katip 'Umar, had most likely already sought redress from the *shari'a* court in Trablus and was now seeking imperial intercession for proper punishment of the accused. Of further interest here, and suggestive of how these orders circulated, is the probability that the petitioner, Katip 'Umar, then kept a copy of the *hükm* on his person as a guarantee that the "wicked people" could not easily submit him to the same injustice in the future. As will become more apparent in the chapters that follow, the overwhelming specificity of the orders, and their direct bearing on issues of contestation, suggests that they probably became part of an evidentiary universe that included resolutions in the *shari'a* court and *fatva*s (judgments made by jurisconsults acting outside of, yet in association with, the court system) and thus part of an actionable legal terrain. Furthermore, while registers of these directives were maintained in the palace archives, copies were also inscribed into the *sijillat* (court records) of whatever administrative seat was included as an addressee and most likely kept among the records of the *beylerbey* as well. This is indicated by admonitions to "preserve this honorable directive in the chest of registers" (*ḥükm-ü şerīfümi defter ṣandūḳında ḥıfẓ idesiz*). There are also references to the *beylerbey* sending "registers of cases" to the imperial *divan*, thereby supporting the idea that a recording system of some sort accompanied the duties of the post.[138] It thus seems unwarranted to simply conclude that the *mühimme* represented the concerns of state, though indeed they did, without also recognizing them as dialogic in nature and as products of a constant, and constantly changing, interchange concerning an administratively strategic language of rule. In other words, the governing structure located in Istanbul couldn't always choose its terms—situations and personalities played a role in defining the daily practice of governance—although it did struggle to situate these singularities within a coherent discursive framework, thereby maintaining order and legitimizing its authority.

While the *mühimme* configure the legality of imperial power, and do so by deploying a language of ethics and proper order within a series of political interventions, they also assume a "natural state" of sultanic supremacy, even as they battle with the ever-multiplying forces and individuals that challenge that supremacy. This chapter has situated the dialectic nature of the process within a reformed bureaucratic vision at the threshold of felicity (*südde-i saʿadet*), one that extended the jurisdictional authority of the sultan, even as it enshrouded and encumbered his personhood by the weight of administrative affairs. The registers of the imperial council "channeled" the voice of the sultan, but the circulated textual edicts, dispatched via messengers of various ranks and status and intended for an oral performance of promulgation, replaced the presence of the sultan by a rhetorical flourish: the sultan commands (*buyuruldum ki*), reports are read in his presence (*hazretlerimizinde*), but the administrative apparatus now stands in for the authority of the sultan. Celalzade Mustafa, like later Ottoman statesmen, bemoaned this fate even as he worked to ensure its prospect.

The next two chapters engage with the terms of the "natural state of order" that the *mühimme* guarded, preserved, and protected. In both, this state of order comes under siege, first in the administrative commotion caused by an extensive campaign of occupation into the territories of Transdanubia, without traditional Ottoman signposts of rule and bearing a distinct dynastic history of its own, and second in the mountainous territory of Greater Syria (Bilad-ı Şam), where the presumption of Ottoman sovereignty required reinforcement and thus the assertion of new forms of legitimacy. Within each venue, efforts to reform territories or personages (*iṣlāḥ* or *iṣlāḥ-ı nefs*)[139] for the "sake of the order of the country" (*nıẓām-ı memleket içün*),[140] or "to ensure the safety of the people and to cleanse the country" (*te'mīn-i 'ibād ve taṭhīr-i bilād*)[141] epitomize an imperial agenda intent on ensuring order in the midst of flux. Thus, the *mühimme* as a guide to territorial disturbances in the mid-to-late sixteenth century exemplify how the ideal of social harmony and justice elaborated in the *kanunname* became a logic of practice.

PART II
Performing Practices

CHAPTER FOUR

THE BROKERED STATE

"The Past Is No Longer the Present" in the "Land Between the Rivers"

> If there should be any necessity for a service at the border of our empire, when it is announced by the *paşa*s and *bey*s, the *voyvode* and the dignitaries of the country should—according to their enduring subservience—show their readiness personally or through sending soldiers, equipment or victuals in the necessary extent.
>
> —Clause from the 1575 imperial confirmation and treaty (*'ahdnāme-i hümāyūn*) issued to István Báthory after Murad III assumed the sultanate[1]

In 1547 the Ottoman text of a treaty negotiated between Sultan Süleyman I (r. 1520–66), Charles V (Holy Roman emperor from 1519–56), and his brother Ferdinand I, then archduke of Austria and king of the Habsburg territories of Hungary and Bohemia, presented a vision of Ottoman hegemony within the competitive claims to universal rulership that dominated fifteenth- and sixteenth-century Eurasian courts.[2] The treaty finalized Süleyman's triumphant, if protracted, conquest of the "land between the rivers," or Hungarian occupied territories between the Sava, Drava, and Danube, and launched Süleyman into a position of supremacy over the Habsburg monarchs. Throughout his forty-six-year reign, Süleyman was preoccupied with rivaling the dynastic splendor and military might of the Habsburgs, and the textual politics of the treaty reveled in the Ottoman victory. A new baseline was set for future diplomacy that granted peace on the condition of annual payments, virtually transforming former rivals into an Ottoman

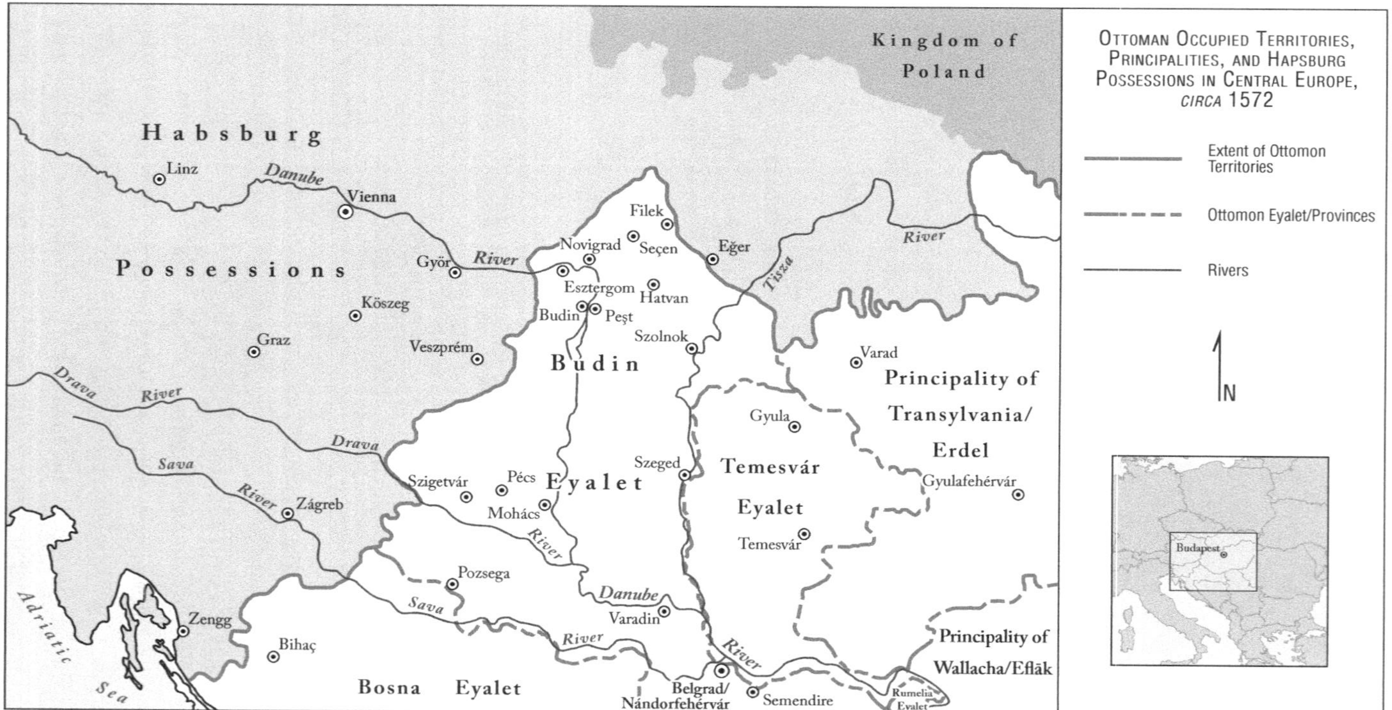

Map 1. Ottoman-occupied territories, principalities, and Habsburg possessions in Central Europe, circa 1572. *Source*: Wikimedia Commons.

revenue stream.[3] The titles used for the key signatories further diminished Charles V's imperial claims, both as the political head of Christendom and as the inheritor of Roman glory, by labeling him merely "King of Spain" and his brother as "King of Germany." These discursive slights relegated the monarchs to a lineage of regional kingship, not universal sovereignty.

By contrast, Süleyman's head jurisconsult, the *şeyhülislam* Ebu's-su'ud Efendi, marked the triumph of 1547 by adding "Caesar of Caesars," "breaker of Caesars," and the "one who casts dust in the faces of Chosroes and Caesar" to Süleyman's list of titles.[4] Alluding to the capture of Baghdad in 1534 and Buda in 1541, the last one laid claim to both Roman and Persianate rubrics of sovereignty. The affirmation of an Ottoman claim to Roman imperial grandeur, asserted first under Mehmed II after his conquest of Constantinople, was now definitively confirmed within the new intensive rivalries of the sixteenth century.[5]

Süleyman commemorated this new position by redefining the skyline of Istanbul.[6] The grand mosque complex of the Süleymaniye, built to counter Emperor Justinian's Hagia Sophia, included the domed majesty of the mosque itself, along with a hospital, primary school, public bath, caravansary, four *medreses*, a specialized institute for the science of *hadith* (collected traditions and sayings of the Prophet Muhammad), a medical college, and a public kitchen (*'imaret*). Ebu's-su'ud, in a now familiar sequence of titles and attributes trumpeting the legislative universality of Ottoman power, composed the inscription that was etched into the mosque's portal:

> [Sultan Süleyman] has drawn near to [God], the lord of majesty and omnipotence, the creator of the world of dominion and sovereignty, [Sultan Süleyman] who is His slave, made might with divine power, the caliph, resplendent with divine glory, who performs the command of the hidden book and executes its decrees in [all] regions of the inhabited quarter. Conqueror of the lands of the east and the west with the help of almighty God and his victorious army, possessor of the kingdoms of the world, shadow of god over all peoples, sultan of the sultans of the Arabs and the Persians, promulgator of sultanic *qanun*s, tenth of the Ottoman *khaqan*s, sultan son of the sultan, Sultan Süleyman Khan . . . may the line of his sultanate endure until the end of the line of the ages.[7]

This conveyed the larger efforts of Ebu's-su'ud and Celalzade Mustafa to redefine the legal jurisdiction of the sultan. As I argued in Chapters 2 and 3, the shifts in activities of the imperial council had created a new textual habitus that enfolded the divine order of the *shari'a* and the temporal order of empire into the mediating rubric of sultanic law. Furthermore, as we saw in Chapter 1, the sultan's power was increasingly configured in universal, rather than regional, terms, and textual feints along with monumental constructions and spatial protocols were as significant in this process as military conquests and territorial expansion. Yet declarative efforts by the Ottoman establishment to redefine the jurisdiction of the sultan—be they spatial, architectural, legal, or textual—could not alone ensure the alignment of men and resources in newly conquered territories with the agendas of the administrative apparatus in Istanbul. The intensified campaigns of conquest during the reign of Süleyman therefore reinforced the need for two aggressive administrative practices: information gathering in regions with multiple political factions and shifting regional alliances, and systematic techniques for registering this information and storing it in an archival base for future actions. These two critical practices, acquiring information and creating a legible database, also focused attention on language, both as a tool of communication and as an arena of political contest between rival interest groups. Scholars attentive to the significant role that linguistic negotiation played in the fortunes of "interimperial" agents tend to focus on the Mediterranean and on the interstitial challenge it poses to historical narratives of monolithic empires. This chapter, by contrast, traces the entangled networks of diplomacy, mediation, and information gathering in what arguably emerged as a *land-based* brokered zone between the fortunes of Hungarian, Habsburg, and Ottoman empires and kingdoms from the 1500s onward.[8] By the mid-sixteenth century this zone extended for more than several hundred kilometers and formed an arc of fortifications that, although consistently challenged from 1541 onward, were not substantially moved until the end of the seventeenth century.[9]

The relationship between conquest and establishing administrative norms is strikingly clear within the protracted military campaigns in the "land between the rivers." These began with fourteenth- and fifteenth-century skirmishes and intensified into full-scale advances between 1521 and

1552.[10] The siege of Belgrade in 1521 and the Battle of Mohács in 1526 ultimately led to the capture of Buda in 1541 and its establishment as the central node of Ottoman territorial authority in the region. The Ottomans administered this region as a zone of military occupation until war with the Holy League in 1683 ended almost a century and a half of Ottoman rule. Yet even after the establishment of an Ottoman "seat" at Buda in 1541 and of a relatively stable boundary line at the River Ilova in 1591, the Ottoman occupation remained a contested historical process.[11] The sultanate's appointed governors (*beylerbeys*) of Buda were forced to balance Habsburg, Ottoman, and regional demands and interests. The 1591 boundary was itself immediately tested by the so-called long war from 1591–92 to 1606. During this extended war the system of rule initially imposed by the Ottomans in the Hungarian territories came under duress, and the concluding truce of Zsitvatorok reset the terms of Ottoman-Habsburg relations.[12] These extended engagements combined with the centralizing agendas of Süleyman's court transformed Buda, and the lands between the rivers more generally, into the proving ground of Ottoman administrative ideologies, expectations, and practices. The emergence of new documentary systems and scribal cultures, such as the bound registers of the *mühimme* and a formalized translation office for interimperial communication, all took place within the travails of territorial control in the region of Hungary.

Given the immensity of this brokered zone, it should not be surprising that richly layered intersovereign exchanges, experiences, and fortunes would evolve from continued contact and proximity.[13] Thus, the following sections demonstrate how the occupation of Hungarian territories over the course of Sultan Süleyman's reign became the inspiration and the testing ground for administrative strategies that would guide imperial intervention in the century that followed. Official appointments; the garrisoning of various fortresses; the distribution of taxes, privileges, and collection rights; and the continuing need to secure the interests of inhabitants of the realm required unremitting management. Cadastral surveys and accompanying *kanunname* functioned as one mechanism to fit provincial dynamics into the rubric of Ottoman administrative regulation, and the sequence of surveys mirrors moments in which the Ottoman territories in the region were redefined through war, treaty, or efforts to reassert control.[14] Yet the emergence of formalized *defter*s of the *umur-ı mühimme* in 1545, coincident with the early years of Ottoman entrenchment in the Transdanubian territories, marked a singular effort to systematically record the circulation of imperial commands, resulting in a textual web that preserved and maintained territorial sovereignty. The scattered fortress defense system on which Ottoman occupation depended was held in place by these documentary circuits. This combined system of fortress and archive also relied on the continuous exchange of knowledge and information. Intermediaries, serving either as diplomats, translators, dispatchers, governors, or soldiers, actively sent field reports and monitored the local populations. Their dispatches formed an archival web of intelligence on a hotly contested region on which the sultanate increasingly depended. Given the multiple factions and rival parties in the region, however, this information was never secure. "The Brokered State" argues that securing the realm therefore also entailed securing trustworthy information, a difficult task that exposed the vulnerabilities of the Ottoman establishment even at the zenith of its power. Here, the fortunes of Buda and its governors capture a moment in which Ottoman imperial genres of political action were in flux, with diplomatic, textual, and linguistic practices working in tandem and across different forms to extend sovereignty over conquered territory. Finally, the chapter shows how persistent contact with rival empires shaped conceptions of regional and universal sovereignty, of the nature of governance, and of just and proper rule.

Campaigns of Conquest and Contested Sovereignty in the Brokered Zone

The history of Ottoman incursions into Hungarian territories itself showcases the ambiguous and uneven nature of imperial conquest and, later, of administrative control. It is therefore meaningful to spend some time in this section illuminating the capricious nature of this process. Beginning in 1512, even before Sultan Süleyman organized a series of full-scale military campaigns into Hungarian territory, Ottoman forays carved out new zones of control and overcame the Hungarian fortresses that had defended the region since 1464.[15] Similarly, prior to the seizure of Belgrade in 1521, Ottoman commanders were pillaging the southern regions of Hungarian domains, even if the military's focus on other regions during the first decades of the sixteenth century spared Hungary from any major assault. This period of relative peace was further reinforced by negotiated truces between Buda and Istanbul that were repeatedly renewed, until the envoy that Sultan Süleyman sent to reinstate the truce on the death of his father, Selim I, in 1520 was rebuffed.[16] Süleyman responded by orchestrating a major military campaign, through which he also cemented his claim to the Ottoman establishment by acting as a commanding hero on the battlefield. When the Ottoman imperial army besieged Belgrade a year after Selim I's death, they met no matching Hungarian royal force, and the castle fell on August 29, 1521, along with the fortresses of Šabac and Zimony (Zemun). The army further laid waste to much of the Syrmium (Sirem) region before the customary conclusion of the Ottoman campaign season.[17] Southern Hungary was now practically defenseless, and successive local Ottoman commanders did their part to weaken defenses further, and so gradually push toward Buda. Five years after the fall of Belgrade, the Hungarian army couldn't even intercept the Ottomans at the fords of the Drava, and when they met at Mohács on August 28, 1526, the Hungarian troops were annihilated by hidden Ottoman artillery within two hours. King Lajos II died fleeing the battlefield, and most of the leading families and elite of the country, ecclesiastical or laypersons, lost their lives as well.[18]

Although Sultan Süleyman's forces won a decisive victory at Mohács and marched triumphantly into Buda castle on September 11, 1526, he soon retreated back across the Danube to keep ahead of the traditional conclusion of the Ottoman campaign season in October and did nothing to gain permanent control over the city.[19] Still, before they retreated, the initial advance of the Ottoman armies during the campaign season of 1526 had wiped clean the defensive fortresses and castles lying north of the Danube-Drava line and left Titel, a fortress heavily garrisoned by the Ottomans, to guard the convergence of the Danube and Tisza Rivers.[20] Furthermore, although Buda was not occupied, many fortresses in the Sirem region certainly were, and Ottoman garrisons left in castles such as Pétervárad, Újlak, Bánmonostor, Szávaszentdemeter, Atya, Cserög, Racsa, Barica, Redned, and others acted as radial points from which the unfolding conflict with Habsburg and Hungarian forces was surveyed or directed.[21] The ultimate result was a tripartite division of the region. The great plains between the

Danube and Tisza Rivers, along with large areas to the east and west, remained in Ottoman hands for more than 150 years. The populations west of these Ottoman lands threw their support to Ferdinand, of the Habsburg line, and elected him king of Hungary in the hopes that he would be able to prevent further losses of life or territory to the Ottomans. This began the era of Habsburg rule that would continue until 1918, when the closing treaties of World War I finally dissolved the large, territorial, composite empires. Last, the population living east of Ottoman-occupied territories elected János Zápolyai, who attempted to reunify the realm and failed. His successors ceded the royal title to Ferdinand, and after Sultan Süleyman assigned the region east of the Tisza River to Zápolyai's wife, Isabella, and infant son, János II, in 1541, a new semiautonomous vassal state, the Principality of Transylvania, emerged.[22]

Yet it took the Ottoman establishment almost twenty years to solidify the gains made during the battle of Mohács. Although Buda would become the linchpin of Ottoman administrative control of the occupied territories of Hungary, Süleyman's campaigns in 1528 and 1532 focused on Vienna instead of consolidating his hold on the former seat of the Hungarian kingdom. As a result, Süleyman initially handed Buda to János Zápolyai in exchange for nominal recognition of Ottoman suzerainty, and he then recognized Zápolyai in the 1528 Treaty of Istanbul as the legitimate king of Hungary and withdrew. Still, he counted on continued disunity in the realm and the invading pressures of Ferdinand's troops to forestall any real resistance to Ottoman control of power alliances in the region.[23] Habsburg forces, commanded by Archduke Ferdinand I (r. 1556–64), brother of Emperor Charles V and allied through marriage to Hungarian royalty, followed in the trail of Süleyman's departure in 1526 to proclaim himself king in December 1527. The antagonism between these two kings extended to their respective envoys. When Ferdinand himself sued for peace at the Ottoman court in June of 1527, his representative, the voyvoda Radu, tried to have Zápolyai's envoy captured and thereby disrupt the channels of communication with the sultan at a crucial time of potential negotiation. This effort was to no avail, as the sultan coldly turned away the luxurious, gift-giving assembly sent by Ferdinand. A letter reporting the events said that the sultan announced to the diplomatic mission, "Your lord has not yet experienced our friendship. He will do so in the future. I will come with all my might and force to personally give him back the castles he demands. Advise him to prepare everything so that he will be able to give us a suitable reception"—a neatly dressed declaration of war.[24] Persistent attacks by auxiliary Ottoman forces or militias of local deputies further destabilized the region and generated the necessary friction to undermine any attempt at alliance between Zápolyai and Ferdinand I. Archbishop András Csézi, an ally and former diplomat of Zápolyai who managed to maintain his position at Esztergom, wrote to a friend in Zagreb on January 18, 1528: "Our public affairs in the strife between the two hostile rulers [Zápolyai and Ferdinand] are most severely endangered, and there is good reason to fear that the third will attain his goals in between the two antagonists, and ousting both of them, will seize power."[25] And when Zengg, one of the strongest fortresses in the defensive line, reached an agreement with the Ottomans on April 9, 1528, letters from Zápolyai to the Doge of Venice, the German Reichstag, and the Tudor court of King Henry VIII unequivocally blamed his rival for the loss of both Jajca and Zengg, deepening the rift between the two Christian claimants to the Hungarian kingdom. Each king struggled to maintain a loyal cohort, and Zápolyai barely mustered the requisite men and resources to return from Poland and combat Süleyman's campaign party on the territory he claimed to represent in late August and early September of 1529. An explicit order was given to the *çavuş* accompanying Zápolyai's envoy, Hieronym Laski, to determine whether he indeed had the necessary support to "represent" Hungary.[26]

The constant fighting dramatically impacted the countryside and its inhabitants; when an Ottoman line advanced up to Szeged and sacked the town in early April of 1528, the misery of the region was noted by the new ambassador to the Porte, Tomà Contarini, who was shocked by the disaster of captive men and ransacked territories as far as Sarajevo.[27] Süleyman returned to Buda for a second time on September 7, 1529, and again passed control of the city to Zápolyai while he continued his quest for Vienna.[28] After this failed siege, he retraced his steps and on October 25 erected his intricate tented campaign headquarters in Óbuda, on the outskirts of the city walls and "with great pageantry" accepted the allegiance of Zápolyai, now crowned King János of Hungary. The sultan then virtually ignored

Buda for the next decade, relying on reports that the strength of Zápolyai's forces and rebuilt fortifications would be sufficient to repel any concerted advance by the Habsburgs.[29] It was only Zápolyai's death, the uncertain prospect of a future ruler capable of acting simultaneously as a local leader and as a servant of the sultan, and the quick mobilization of Ferdinand's army to seize the gap, that prompted Süleyman to permanently occupy the city in 1541.[30] However, only with the seizure of the fortresses of Valpó, Siklós, Székesfehérvár, and Esztergom in 1543, were Ottoman forces able to secure a military and diplomatic thoroughfare from Buda to Esztergom on the right bank of the Danube.[31] Yet clearing a path for sovereign rights would not be as simple as conquering fortresses. Thus, the travails of the governors of Buda illustrate persistent problems faced by Ottoman administrators who worked from within islands of fortressed cities to extend territorial control over the occupied Hungarian zone.

The Fortunes of Imperial Order: Buda and the Rubric of Military Rule

The fortress remained the primary center of Ottoman-occupied Hungary, and large-scale settlement projects that often accompanied conquest in other parts of the empire were never adopted there. Garrisoned fortresses thus served as guardians of Ottoman authority.[32] These forts ran for almost four hundred miles and had six or seven lead commanders who organized linkages between them, ensured the strength of the line, and participated in the border skirmishes that were a daily part of defending the realm.[33] The lead commanders (*beys*) were the heads of *sancak*s (districts) responsible for the mix of military, administrative, and legal issues entailed in maintaining order and collecting revenue.[34] The commander of the castle (*dızdar*), his deputy (*kethüda*), and scribe (*katib*) organized the castle guard (*müstahfize*) and further facilitated the implementation of imperial commands. Fiscal concerns centered on defense and on the remuneration for men devoted to its success.[35] Most of these forces were local agriculturalists or regional notables co-opted into the Ottoman imperial administration through grants of land and title. This policy of incorporation was essential for regional stability because of the uneasy relationship Buda had with its hinterland after the city's full conquest in 1541. Serving as the major *vilayet* (provincial seat) of these territories, it possessed variable and sometimes tenuous relationships with towns and villages placed under its jurisdiction by the Ottomans.[36] The hinterland, furthermore, was scattered rather than contiguous, as Süleyman's army had only fully conquered a small strip between the Danube and the Tisza Rivers. The *has* territories (sequestered lands assigned as revenue base) of the first appointed governor of Buda, Süleyman Paşa, came from as far away as two hundred kilometers from the city itself.[37] This territory was also ambiguous. Cadastral surveys from 1543 and 1545 included variant lists of the *sancak*s attached to Buda: the first list includes Alacahisar, Erdel (Transylvania), İzvornik, the *liva* of Perini Petri, Pojega, Segedin, Semendre, Temeşvar, and Vulçitrin; the second list included Alacahisar, İstolni Belgrad, the *liva* of Eğri, İzvornik, Mohács, Ösek, Segedin, Semendre, and Vulçitrin.[38] Until the full conquest of Temeşvar in 1552, Buda was the sole seat of Ottoman rule and continued to carry the weight of the Ottoman provincial map even after the so-called long war added Eğri (Eger) in 1596 and Kanica (Nagykanizsa) in 1600, to form a total of four administrative seats in the region.[39] Two more were added toward the last decades of Ottoman rule: Várad in 1660 and Uyvar (Érsekújvár) in 1663. But these reorganizations in the late sixteenth and mid-seventeenth centuries never fully challenged the privilege of Buda as ringmaster in the Ottoman Hungarian domain.[40]

The seemingly scattered and noncontiguous nature of the Ottoman territories in 1541 was replaced by coherent administrative seats within a decade—a strikingly swift reorganization emblematic of the growing strength of Süleyman's bureaucratic apparatus. Buda and its associated territories were fully incorporated into the registration and recording mechanisms of the Ottoman establishment by 1546. The one million *akçe* annual income of the first two *beylerbey*s serving between 1541 and 1543, Süleyman Paşa and Bali Paşa, was gathered from more than 450 scattered *sancaks* and villages.[41] By contrast, the income of Yahyapaşazade Muhammed Paşa, who served from 1543 to 1548, was carefully recorded in a summary register (*icmal*) of *timar* holdings and derived from a majority of territories within the actual environs of Buda.[42] The tenure of his service was longer than any other *beylerbey* of the sixteenth century, with the exception of Sokullu Mustafa Paşa, who served as the *beylerbey* of Buda from 1566 to 1578.[43] These durations far surpassed that of the majority of governors in Buda, who typically served two to three years, not to mention that of the nineteen different men who cycled out of the position over the fifteen-year period of the long war. The possible link between a prolonged stay in office and the evolution of more regular forms of registration and imperial oversight may explain the intensification of records concerning the affairs of Buda in the *mühimme* during the longer occupancies of both these men. Together, they oversaw the systematization of governance and the assertion of textual order in occupied Hungarian territories.

"Correct" Knowledge and Tenuous Networks

So factious and unruly were the contested territories of the brokered zone, it appeared the Ottoman conceptual frameworks of imperial order had perhaps met their match. Responding to this grave challenge, the statesmen of Süleyman's court doubled their efforts to write, organize, and legislate administrative norms. Thus, there emerged more systematic mechanisms to record and register petitions, notifications, and imperial commands.[44] Critically, they linked territorial control with an evolving, yet actionable, archival corpus. This corpus then served to sublimate anxieties of fragmentary control to assertions of imperial universalism. The *mühimme defterleri*, in particular, became the lens and the analytic framework through which the court "read" and interpreted provincial affairs and through which it sought to exert managerial oversight. Most notably, the directives issued to the governors of Buda provide a striking account of the obsessions and apprehensions that afflicted the Ottoman establishment. From the earliest extant register (1544–45) to the outbreak of the long war in 1591–92, four concerns were consistently invoked in the gradual defterization of imperial command preserved in the *mühimme*: the acquisition of information and the development of mechanisms to ensure correct record-keeping practices; troop movement between the various occupied fortresses from Belgrade to Buda, along with negotiations concerning remuneration for military service; the establishment of a coherent system for the collection of revenue; and, after the Edirne treaty in 1547, the payment of thirty thousand Hungarian ducats to the sultan in addition to control over the limited territories still in the Habsburg emperor's hands. The primary addressees of the directives issued to the Ottoman occupied territories of Hungary, and thus the mediators for these imperial anxieties, were overwhelmingly the *beylerbeys* of Buda, although the treasurer (*defterdar*), or the district supervisor (*sancakbey*), also figured as a significant arbiter. The registers thus demonstrate an overwhelming dependency on the sultanate's representatives in Buda and link the fortunes of peace and war to the tranquility of Buda's castle. The registers further reveal a military occupation that depended on fortresses, limited government, and a politics of translation, as the hybrid political and linguistic transactions in the brokered zone challenged the production and assimilation of acquired knowledge.

Although the *beylerbey* (with "*paşa*" as an added distinguishing marker for the *beylerbey* of Buda), the *defterdar* (finance minister), and the *hazinedar* (treasury official), along with their subordinates, were the primary recipients of sultanic correspondence, *sancakbeys* (district commanders), and *kadıs* (judges) also appeared in later registers. The *beylerbey*, however, played a uniquely powerful role in the occupied Hungarian territories.[45] In other parts of the empire with long histories of Muslim-based rule, Ottoman administrative tactics worked cooperatively with established court systems, blending the edicts of political rulers with the legal and moral codes interpreted by religious authorities and implemented as *siyaset-i şer'iyye*. As we have seen, administrators such as Ebu's-Su'ud carefully navigated the intersection between imperial command and religious obligation to maneuver the sultan into a position of legislative authority. This was not the case in the Ottoman-controlled territories of Hungary. Here, rival kingdoms rather than rival legists stood in the way of administrators. Here, too, they faced a distinct demographic reality. Until a slight change after the 1568 Edirne treaty, there was no consistent policy to transplant Muslim populations from core Ottoman provinces into the occupied territories.[46] Thus, outside of meeting the needs of garrisoned soldiers (approximately eighteen thousand across the territories), the moral and political roles of the shar'ia court that were so important in former Mamluk and Seljuk territories were of limited function in Transdanubia.[47] As a result, less priority was granted to the *bab-ı mahkeme* as an institutional mechanism for ensuring general order and conformity to imperial law, or to the *kadı* as a quasi-Ottoman official.[48] The governor and the finance minister, rather than the judge, were the focal points for implementing sultanic command.

Located in the Topkapı Palace Archives, the earliest collection of *mühimme* contains 557 imperial edicts and decrees from the years 1544–45, a mere three years after Buda became the fulcrum for internal bureaucratic reform, imperial negotiations, and administrative control of the occupied territories.[49] From that total, eighty-two directives address issues or concerns linked either directly to the affairs of the provincial seat in Buda or to alliances and negotiations orchestrated by its officiates.[50] Seventy-eight were sent to recipients in Buda, and eight designate Buda as a hub and gathering point for materials or information circuits in commands sent to other locales in Transdanubia.[51] Of the seventy-eight directed to Buda's officials, fifty-three were sent to the *beylerbey* of Buda during that period, Mehmed Paşa;[52] fifteen indicated the *defterdar*, Ahmed Çelebi,[53] as the recipient; and ten combined the two as addressees.[54] Only one directive named a *sancakbey*, and there was no record of an exchange sent explicitly to a *kadı* within this collection of orders.[55] This register thus supports the claim that the *beylerbey* of Buda bore the brunt of imperial command and negotiated the hybrid institutional and linguistic terrain of the occupied territories.

Directives to the *beylerbey* overwhelmingly addressed the movement of soldiers, by boat or over land, as they reinforced fortresses against potential threats from regional Hungarian nobility or the Habsburg Empire. The earliest *mühimme* register firmly situates Buda as a way station for both goods and monies from occupied fortresses to the imperial treasury. Thus, five directives referenced the storehouses of Buda and various machinations to replenish them in support of military ventures;[56] two directly appoint Buda's treasury as a way station in revenue streams either redirected across the occupied territories or delivered to Istanbul; and four focus attention on Buda's fortress, its necessary armament and support, or to the upkeep of the bridge across the Danube between Buda and Peşt.[57] Along with provisions, defense, and the circulation of monies, the directives in this register also insisted on the necessity for surveying and gathering the "correct" information concerning the inhabitants of towns and villages now under Ottoman sovereignty. This knowledge ensured that tax demographics could be properly recorded in financial registers, without which the revenue needed to defend the realm might be compromised. Often, the orders concerning revenue streams were addressed to both the *beylerbey* and the *defterdar* of Buda, and insisted on the consolidation of knowledge from outlying districts into a register that would then be copied and sent to the imperial council for consideration and future action. This knowledge circuit constituted one of the most significant job duties of the governor and the treasurer: the acquisition of such information laid the basis for revenue extraction and the proper management of the occupied territories.

This task was all the more important given the fluid fiscal status of the occupied territories, as military men, provisions, and monies circulated among the fortified castles in support of current campaign needs. The gaps between sultanic order and regional implementation can often be discovered in breaches of protocol. Small acts of malfeasance—such as a delayed response or the feigned ignorance of previous edicts by envoys and provincial representatives—were persistently bemoaned in imperial commands. For example, in December 1544 an order that decried the misdirection of bushels of barley from Erdel (Transylvania) to Buda was reiterated to Buda's *beylerbey*, Mehmed Paşa. The barley was intended to be commuted into cash and used to support military endeavors in the region, and the order concerning it produced a textual map of lapsed obligations on the journey from Erdel.[58] The revenue was presumed lost in transition between Seged, Semendre, Toygun, and Sirem, hinting at the difficulties involved in collecting financial resources from newly conquered domains. Despite the fact that these fortresses and intervening territories were all part of "his" sultanic lands (*has-ı hümayunum*), the sultan was forced to plead that the *beylerbey* use any means necessary to acquire the funds, to brook no excuse when doing so, and to make all haste in delivering it to "my threshold of felicity." Three more *hükm*, sent between December and mid-January, continued to trail the disappearance addressed in the original directive and bemoaned inaccurate information and the general lack of knowledge concerning the whereabouts of the funds from Erdel. Based on information acquired from the governor Mehmed Paşa's authorized deputy (*kethüda*) Davud, the imperial council directed suspicion toward the *sancak* of Brata. Thus, orders dispersed to the *beylerbey* of Buda, as well as to the province's *defterdar*, Ahmed Çelebi, and Brata (with no specified addressee) all commanded that these official representatives ensure the safe and timely passage of revenue from Erdel.[59]

Clearly, circuits of money and provisions also required dependable circuits of information and a centralized method of archiving the various duties and obligations assigned to the new territories. An order sent to Mehmed Paşa commands him to find trusted servants to conduct the sale of barley from the areas of Semendre and Sirem, intended for the support of the fortresses of Belgrad, İslankamen, Varadin, and İlok.[60] These servants were entrusted with the actual conversion of barley to currency, but Mehmed Paşa was further instructed to find men of the pen (*ehl-i kalem*) to record this transaction and, thereby, to assure its success. This suggestion, that a record of the transaction was necessary for the ultimate implementation of a sultanic command, explicitly linked archival practices with sovereign claims. Without an immediately clear hierarchy of official control in the territories, and thus lacking dependable networks that traditionally ensured the effective interweaving of knowledge and imperial power, the commands issued from the imperial council were overburdened: they were forced to generate the very networks they depended on. While orders in bound *mühimme* registers recorded rather haphazardly the names of officiating scribes, and of the messengers, it is worth noting that forty-five orders dispersed to various *sancaks* and addressees in the conquered Hungarian territories contained some notation concerning their mode of dispatch. Twenty-three of these messengers were specified by name, eleven possess an official designation such as "envoy" or "servant," and nine simply indicate "a man," whose name is unknown (*ismi ne idüği bilinmedi*).[61] This insistence on recording names, or at least the titles of dispatchers, underscores both the early efforts to trace emergent pathways for dispatching sultanic commands and the flimsiness of imperial control in the immediate aftermath of the Ottoman conquest of Buda.

Conflicted ownership over information and resources was further compounded by vulnerable assertions of sovereignty over the populations of the newly conquered territories. As Ferdinand (Ferandoş) continued to orchestrate disruptions, and the inhabitants of villages and towns were caught between overlapping imperial claims, the *beylerbey* of Buda was called on to address conditions of chaos and disorder (*fitne ve fesad*). This disorder was both conceptual and practical. One order insists that the *beylerbey* make known to the inhabitants, both the agricultural cultivators and the elite (*beğler ve reʿāyā*), that they are servants of the sultan like other servants of the realm (*sāir ḳūllarum gibi ḳūllarumdur*) and are thus bound to his threshold of felicity (*āsitāne-i saʿādetime*).[62] As such, the *beylerbey* was called on to show them justice (*ʿadālet gösteresin*). This demonstration of justice served as a reminder that the inhabitants of the region lived within the sultan's protected domain (*memalik-i mahruse* or *vilayetim*). As protected subjects, they relied on the sultan's oath to maintain order, and the *beylerbey* was charged with ensuring that rebellious elements (*ʿisyan*) would not hold sway in the region and that conditions of oppression (*zarar*) would be relieved rather than aggravated. Directly linking the assertion of just governance with proprietorship and stability, these early orders sought to enfold the conquered populations into the vocabulary and grammar of rule elaborated by lawmakers within the imperial council.

Yet, as the language of sovereignty gradually incorporated the inhabitants of the occupied territory into the sultanic domain, this too became a mechanism for leverage that local elites could exploit, as provincial confusion created a space for dissembling identities. This was especially the case in the border zones between Habsburg and Ottoman domains, as regional lords aligned themselves with one side or the other, depending on perceived advantages. Intriguingly, one mode of doing so was to deny any past connection with Ferdinand and to claim instead a position within the registered cadastral surveys for the region. Thus, the same edict concerning provincial stability references information reported by a Hungarian lord, İşpan İmre, revealing that regional notables in areas between Habsburg- and Ottoman-controlled territories, the majority of whom had once been connected to Ferdinand, now were claiming to be day laborers.[63] As day laborers tended to represent a fairly mobile group that was hard to track in cadastral registers, the summarized information contained in this edict suggests that local inhabitants had a sophisticated knowledge of Ottoman imperial strategies. Furthermore, the imperial council was made aware of this situation not by its own delegates but by a report from a local notable. This clear manipulation of categories suggests that a confusion of personages plagued the efforts of the administrative apparatus in Istanbul to manage Transdanubian affairs without reliable circuits of information.

Thus, even if the ideal categories of just rule had been made clear in the *kanunname* and cadastral surveys, the proper application of these categories was not. Furthermore, the oral and textual transmission of sovereign claims and rubrics of rule was not certain. As the imperial council sought to distinguish between agents aligned with Ferdinand and those now in a contractual relationship with the sultan, the problem of translation rose to the fore. The already difficult quest for information regarding provincial affairs was compounded by linguistic hybridity. Proper action could only be defined through proper knowledge, and the *beylerbey* of Buda was directed to provide internal translations of reports about Ferdinand's military operations and the movement of other dissident factions.[64] The command explicitly states that some reports and news were transmitted in an inappropriate language (presumably in Hungarian or, perhaps, Latin) and therefore led to misinformation and could not be used to coordinate diplomatic or military tactics. The *beylerbey* is therefore instructed to at least include a summary (*mufassal*) of any further reports in a "useful/advantageous language" (*yarār diller*) such that full comprehension and "correct" news (*ṣaḥīḥ haberler*) concerning Ferdinand and his allies might be transmitted to the imperial council in an accessible fashion.[65] This command emphasized the need for an operable language and proper knowledge precisely because unreliable circuits of information from the newly occupied territories posed such a great threat to imperial governance.[66]

By 1545, sultanic commands increasingly specified the names of whoever was charged with executing the imperial affairs in question. This move indicates an effort to more precisely control channels and modes of communication between the occupied territories and the sultanate in Istanbul. The persistent and seemingly intractable problem with the missing provisions from Erdel provides a case in point. In yet another order to Brata, one Oruc Çavuş is named as the envoy responsible for finally carrying out the sultanate's demands. He was tasked with clearing up the confusion to ensure that the storehouses of Buda might be replenished and so continue to function as the distribution center of provisions for the imperial army.[67] The edict specifies the goods involved in more detail, as he was directed to ensure that the tax in kind on barley, sheep, cattle, flour, honey, cheese, and any other necessary supplies be transmuted into cash and then directed to Buda in a consistent fashion. Furthermore, he was informed that these requirements were not extraordinary impositions, nor oppressive mechanisms of any kind, but were rather necessary for the protection and stability of the realm. A note at the bottom of the order records that the *hüküm* was indeed given to Oruc (*Oruc Çavuş'a virildi*), thus affirming the proper transmission of the command itself. Yet two further directives concerning the role of Brata in transmitting provisions from Erdel to Buda suggest that an easy transition to more streamlined communications was never assured. One order states that a man by the name of Baland, connected to Brata, was given an order to deliver to ʿAli Çavuş, now named as the responsible party in the collection of revenues.[68] The directive that immediately follows, with a generic addressee of "Brata," yet again summarizes this information but also contains a series of notes concerning the uneven fortune of the two commands.[69] The note records that the order was given to Baland,[70] but an amendment then indicates that a second directive had been dispatched to one Mehmed Çelebi, who later returned and affirmed that the previous *hükm* had indeed already been delivered. The amendment concludes by announcing that the second directive was therefore now rendered defunct. Implied in this seemingly trivial layering of amendments is that the imperial council, worried that the commands were not successfully transmitted to the occupied territories, had resorted to sending multiple copies of orders with different dispatchers.

Diplomatic Anxieties and Troubled Loyalties

Concerns over the language and mode of transmission were particularly significant in the relationship to Ferdinand and, after 1568, his compliance with the negotiated terms of the treaty. Although later bound *mühimme* registers increasingly criticize the protracted delays in Ferdinand's payment of the annual lump sum, the primary concerns that suffuse this earliest register simply lay in divining the movements and intentions of Ferdinand and his regional allies. An order delivered to the Buda *beylerbey* by his *kethüda*, Davud, asks for any internal knowledge about Ferdinand's activities, those of his allies, possible troop movements, amassing of resources, and possible coordinated efforts with his brother in Spain (Charles V).[71] The security of diplomatic envoys was of special import, and the provisioning of envoys sent to the Ottoman palace by Ferdinand was also recorded in the register.[72] Six of the directives addressed possible joint military campaign strategies between Charles V and Ferdinand and fostered fears of undetected enemy movements.[73] Although the language of these directives never elevated either man to the same level as the Ottoman sovereign, referencing Ferdinand either simply by name or as king of Vienna (*Beç kralı*) and Charles V only as his brother (*karındāşı*), it was clear that both stood as rivals and imminent challengers to Ottoman imperial security.[74]

This sense of an imminent threat pervades the orders directed toward Buda in 1544–45. It may also explain why in 1545 the imperial council put in place elaborate mechanisms to commandeer human and material resources from across the Ottoman domains for a potential naval and land campaign into the region. Nine orders from late January to the first of February simultaneously track Süleyman's departure from Istanbul for Edirne, and a season of hunting in the surrounding areas, and crisscross the provinces in a textual roll call of *timar* holders, *sancakbey*s, or other regional power brokers with obligations to the sultanate during military ventures.[75] The series includes detailed orders to Hayrüddin Paşa, *beylerbey* of Cezayir (Algiers) and now admiral of the sultan's navy, to gather more than a hundred ships, along with the necessary arms, provisions, and men at the imperial shipyards on the shores of the Golden Horn and to ensure that the winter months are spent wisely in preparation for a campaign season.[76] Orders were then dispersed to the *sancakbey*s under the auspices of the *mirmiran*s (commander of commanders, alternative name for the *beylerbey*) of Rumeli, Cezayir, Buda, and Anadolu, as well as to the provincial seats of Karaman, Rum, Zülkadriyye, Erzurum, Şam, Diyarbekir, Baghdad, and the *sancak* of Konya. These *hükm*s demanded that each provincial and district official ready men from their jurisdictions and individually equip them with food, bedding, and weapons for a future gathering at the bridge crossing to the Belgrade fortress. The various lists of provincial seats and connected districts were repeated in several different forms, with special attention paid to the officials responsible for appearing, with all the necessary men and impedimenta, before the fortress of Belgrade. There were notations on the reported receipt of these orders, and portions where names were crossed out and reentered, indicating a gradual process of registering the activated officials and ensuring tactics for information gathering. In the case of Buda, Mehmed Paşa is listed as *mirmiran*, and the *sancakbey*s of Semendre, İzvornik, Alacahisar, Vülçitrin, Travnik, Segedin, Mohács, İstolnibelgrad, and the fortress Eger were all delineated as part of his jurisdiction. The possibility of future military conflicts with the Habsburgs or with the Holy Roman emperor himself set into motion an empire-wide accounting system.

Clearly, something was afoot in 1545 that can be traced across reported rumors and the records of the *mühimme* concerning the potential mobilization of forces in both Habsburg and Ottoman domains, despite the fact that no organized imperial overland military campaign ever materialized during that year.[77] The Ottoman mobilization techniques then alarmed the courts of Charles V and Ferdinand and perhaps hastened their decision to rely on French intermediaries to negotiate another truce with the sultanate in June of the following year. This they did despite knowing it might result in a realignment of French and Ottoman interests (broken by the treaty of Crépy negotiated between Charles V and Francis I), which would not only undermine future joint efforts against the Ottomans but also enable the French to reinvigorate their position as trading partners with the Ottomans rather than crusading soldiers against them.[78] Thus, on June 19, 1547, envoys of Emperor Charles V negotiated the Edirne treaty that opened this chapter. It was a five-year armistice that forced Ferdinand to pay thirty thousand gold florins yearly to the sultan as "taxes" for the right to remain in the territories he controlled. These terms would form the baseline for treaties that concluded episodes of open warfare in 1562 and 1568 and were renewed successfully in 1574, 1583, and 1590 before the outbreak of the fifteen-year war. The solidification of Ottoman authority in the region was now clear, and the annual payment was meant to dissuade the Ottoman army from advancing further into Habsburg-held Hungarian territories.[79] It stood as recompense for the Ottomans' potential loss of income from conquered territories, and it further subordinated Ferdinand's power to that of his brother Charles V, now Holy Roman emperor. The records of the Ottoman chancery, quite appropriately, sometimes labeled this sum as a "tribute" (*haraç*) rather than a tax (*vergi*), and its delayed payment became one of the most common complaints and repetitive refrains throughout diplomatic correspondence with the *beylerbeys* of Buda.[80] Yet the Habsburgs, embarrassed by the imposition of this payment but unable to remove the stipulation, attempted for the remainder of the century to disguise the precise nature of this annual duty.[81] Thus, terms for honor-gift, honorarium, and present were substituted instead, and when cash was scarce, they sent their envoys with ever richer dress, silver goblets, or, after 1562, ever more elaborate mechanized clocks to reinforce the notion that this was a ceremonial gift rather than an admission of inferiority.[82]

Although these "taxes" were duly paid until the end of the century, peace lasted for only four years. Between the occupation of Buda in 1541 and the ultimate Ottoman retreat from the city in 1686 there were five more territorial shifts that shaped Ottoman rule in the region. These were the campaigns of 1551–52, 1566, the "long war" of 1591–1606, and the final fortress captures engineered by the Köprülü grand viziers in 1660 and 1663.[83] Territorial gains were made under the leadership of Sokullu Mehmed Paşa in 1551 (then *beylerbey* of Rumeli but soon to climb the hierarchy and ultimately serve as grand vizier from 1565 to 1579). The following year, under the command of Kara Ahmed, the Ottomans captured Temesvár on July 27, 1552, finally acquiring one of the most important fortresses in the region. The capture of Szigetvár during Süleyman's last military march in 1566, along with key forts along the Drava, ensured that they now held suzerainty over southeast Transdanubia and added Kanizsa as a provincial seat. At this point there was a coherent Ottoman zone in the center of the country that extended from Lake Balat north to the Danube and east to the Tisza and the Transylvanian border.[84] The second peace of Edirne on February 17, 1568 concluded more than a decade of constant war, and for the next twenty-three years Ottoman armies did not fight in the Hungarian territories. Episodic military engagements thus alternated with efforts to maintain control over the occupied territories. Ventures in both war and peace reinforced Ottoman investment of men and monies in the region and committed the empire to a belabored effort to enfold the occupied territories into an evolving sense of administrative order in the sixteenth and seventeenth centuries.[85]

What Transdanubia lacked in full-scale military campaigns, it made up for in localized conflicts. Governors of the major provincial seats, along with commanders of local garrisons, organized their own defense and often pursued new acquisitions, captured prisoners who did not carry assurances of diplomatic safety, and generally assured that "peace" did not mean "quietude."[86] Occupation was thus costly, not only in terms of monetary outlay but also in the human and textual reserves necessary to ensure loyalty to the realm. This was not an easy task because the governing structures of *beylerbey* and *kanunname* imposed on the region lay only superficially over a fractious elite who then used the distance and diffusion of imperial power to their own advantage. References to the *beylerbeys*' role as spies, and as captains of a surveillance system, intensified in the 1560s. The territorial gains since 1552, and the establishment of a new negotiated treaty in 1568, could only be secured through the circulation of textual reports that sought to fit unwieldy dynamics into a systematized record of provincial affairs.[87] Hence, surveillance mechanisms sifted through the imperial commands to border territories, such as in Transylvania, Wallachia, and Moldavia, where commanders and *voyvoda*s were instructed to gather precise intelligence concerning Habsburg military operations or to report on rivals within their own provinces.[88] The registers also reflected an increasing anxiety over concerns that Transylvanian princes would negotiate their own terms with the Habsburgs or not wait for orders from the sultanate concerning troop deployments and reinforcements.[89] Loyalty was never assured, yet regional elites were essential both for defense and for monitoring conditions in a porous zone.[90]

Relinquishing information to the sultanate served to cement professions of loyalty, such as when Zápolyai's allegiance after the Battle of Mohács was confirmed when he seized papers from a Viennese messenger and submitted them to the Ottomans.[91] Yet former Hungarian notables who claimed to report on clandestine operations in the region were often treated with suspicion. This was especially the case if they straddled the borderlands between Habsburg and Ottoman territories. For example, a landowner in the north, János Balassa, was at times trusted as a conduit for information concerning Habsburg movement yet treated dexterously by an imperial council quite cautious with the sources for its information.[92] An edict composed in response to a petition from a former Hungarian notable, Plaj Yanoş, to become allied along with his dependents to the Ottoman state highlighted strategies adopted for wooing potential partners while simultaneously upholding the stipulations of treaties with the Habsburgs.[93] The edict referenced a desire not to disrupt the status quo, which ensured the continued payment of the yearly tribute. Yet, as Plaj Yanoş had repeatedly insisted on his intended obedience to the Ottoman realm, the edict stipulated that the protection and grace of the sultanate would indeed be extended to him and to his sons in perpetuity. Still, as he personally had not been harmed by the king, and thus had no legitimate reason to cross sides, this new relationship should not be disclosed publicly.

As a result of hybrid structures and loyalties in the region, it fell primarily on the *beylerbeys* of Buda not only to secure the financial and political fortunes of the realm, but also to validate the information passed on to the Ottoman establishment. This meant investigating whether co-opted participants into the *'askeri* status continued to abide by their obligations and were properly recorded in the salary lists for the provinces (*ruznamçe*).[94] It also meant that the governorate of Buda was called on to ensure those who contributed to disorder were punished, despite general confusion in the borderlands, according to measures outlined within the *kanunname*.[95] The *beylerbeys* perfected a policy of dissimulation, maintaining equanimity while informing on the various agents operating across the Hungarian territories. The *mühimme* registers captured the dependent nature of Ottoman sovereignty: the sultan's commands relied on sometimes corruptible intermediaries—conflicted dispatchers, reported knowledge, and provincial governors—to secure borders between rival empires, boundaries between loyal and disloyal servants of the realm, and the resources necessary for continued occupation.

Travails of the Pen: Translating Rivalry and Securing Knowledge

Occupation and the demand for knowledge transformed the Hungarian brokered zone into a fulcrum for a new cultural politics of translation. As we saw in Chapter 3, scribal cohorts and record-keeping practices fixed affairs of the province at the center of the sultanate's concerns. Furthermore, provincial affairs and frontier campaigns also shaped linguistic orthodoxies that replaced rival scripts with an imperial language. Securing knowledge from occupied towns and fortresses in the trans-Hungarian territories, however, also required translation and coincided with the appearance of an organized translation office within the Ottoman court. Hungarian speakers in the newly reshaped translation services at Süleyman's court demonstrated the significant role these territories played in defining new diplomatic relations, administrative strategies, and the shape of Ottoman imperial authority.[96]

As the Ottoman dynasts expanded their surveillance networks, they increasingly drew themselves into inter-European rivalries and honed the skills necessary to become independent interlocutors. Their savvy in continental politics led to a more prominent role within the stratagems and struggles of other established courts. Hence, envoys were sent to the Ottoman court from France beginning in the 1480s, from the Grand Duke of Muscovy in 1495, and Holy Roman Emperor Maximilian in 1496–97, firmly establishing an Ottoman role in the great game of early modern courtly rivalries.[97] Although Sultan Süleyman and his representatives engineered the final Ottoman occupation of Hungarian territories, Selim I took the first step toward an independent assertion of Ottoman diplomatic sovereignty in the region. During his reign the Ottoman court opened bilateral negotiations with other states rather than relying on more local proxies (Italian city states in the Mediterranean or Hungary and Poland in central Europe) to do the negotiating for them.[98] Previous accords between the Hungarian kingdom and the Ottoman court since the peace negotiated in 1483 between King Matthias (r. 1458–90) and Sultan Bayezid II made Hungary a key mediator with powers as various as the Papacy, French, Spanish, English, Polish, and Portuguese kings, as well as Venice, the whole of Italy, Naples, Sicily, the grand master of the knights of Rhodes, and the Genovese of Chios.[99] However, when a new "friendship letter" (*muḥabbet-name*) was negotiated between 1512 and 1514 between the Ottoman court and the king of Hungary and Croatia, Vladislaus II (r. 1490–1516), former signatories such as the Polish king Sigismund I (r. 1506–48) and Holy Roman Emperor Maximilian I (r. 1493–1519) were informed that they should petition the Ottomans directly for their own treaties and letters of peaceful agreement.[100] Selim insisted unequivocally on the singularity of his role as arbiter without intermediaries and on his ability to grant or deny peace at will to the surrounding countries and their proxies:

> Now, in response to the request your royal highness has laid before us via his envoy—notably, the Christian rulers should now be included in the peace accord as they were included in the peace in the time of our father—we wish to inform your royal highness that that used to be so, but those times have passed, the present is not identical with the past, and therefore

> the mentioned Christian rulers shall by no means be included in the peace. For the court or Porte of our imperial majesty is glorious, and is not closed against the Christian princes at all. If they would like to have peace and alliance with our imperial majesty, they should send their envoys to our Porte, and when they arrive, we shall do as we see fit.[101]

This moment further marked a new diplomatic clarity as well as the expansion of Ottoman imperial ambition into the region more broadly. The claim that "the present is not identical with the past" is a pithy allusion to Selim's intention to break with past protocol and construct an alternative hierarchy of political order in Eurasia. Indeed, this new mapping of power had become common knowledge within diplomatic circles: "the Grand Seigneur alone had the power to grant peace, so every ruler inferior to him should solicit this gift with deference, under conditions approved by the Sultan."[102] The "gift" of peace did not come cheap, as the escalating expenses of ambassadorial visits surely suggest. Gift exchanges between rival courts fueled the exchange of objects across territories and reified hierarchies of power through the symbolic hierarchies of artifacts and their preservation in the palace treasuries of the Ottomans, as well as Emperor Maximilian II, King Henri II of France, Emperor Charles V, and Prince Constantine of Russia, where "Turkish objects" came to hold pride of place.[103] These "gifts" contributed to an emergent discourse of exoticism and exclusion, but they also ratified positions of superiority and gradually molded a language of imperial competition, with specific tactics of entreatment, exchange, reprimand, and acceptance. Selim I's interactions with transregional rivals also told a story of language, as the surviving letters of key engagements in the sortie (Vladislaus's to Selim's envoy, Maximilian to Sultan Selim, and Selim's to Vladislaus) were all preserved "in the language of the enemy": Vladislaus's and Maximilian's letters in Turkish translation and Selim's in Latin.[104] As such, they serve as reminders that the enterprise of translation was key to the territorial ambitions of early modern centralizing courts.

As exercises in translation, both technical and ideological, came to shape interimperial correspondence, the translator himself became a herald of sovereign claims.[105] Translation projects within the Habsburg and Ottoman courts took on increasingly formal structures. The prisoners or captive converts who had acted as mediators in the negotiations between Ferdinand and Süleyman might have sufficed when Süleyman only vaguely recognized the significance of Ferdinand's position—calling him "king" and obsessing instead over the image and universalist claims of Charles V—but after the 1529 siege of Vienna it became clear to both that stable diplomatic channels would be necessary. Ferdinand at first was forced to admit that he had no translator capable of reading Süleyman's letters, which reinforced the inferiority of his position—linguistic proficiency marked imperial grandeur and power. But Ferdinand tended to avoid drafting traditional mediators, such as Jewish or Venetian merchants, into a translation corps because he believed these savvy Mediterraneanists had proved slippery in their loyalties.[106] Language as a possible vehicle of contamination became a prominent concern during the anti-Turk rhetoric of the reformation. Heightened anxiety about spiritual and physical attack also encompassed anti-Jewish and antimerchant sentiments, again, as a result of their perceived easy and early alliances with the Ottoman dynasty. Yet gradually, and by necessity, a specialized position for translation became a key component in Ferdinand's court. A document from 1531 specifically lists knights capable of translating Ottoman Turkish documents in Ferdinand's retinue, and by 1541 this ability was formalized into the new court position of a resident Ottoman Turkish translator. These translators followed a typical career path, noted in their title of investiture: long captivity among the Ottomans, release and service in the armies of the Habsburgs, a patent of nobility in return for this service, and, finally, the transformation of captivity into a useful tool and marker of allegiance to the Habsburg court as conditions for their rank as court translator. The first chief translator, Hans or Johann Spiegel, granted this patent of nobility and position in 1544, became the model for his successors. As Carina Johnson's work on imperial exchange has suggested, this pathway distinguished them both from merchants, with commercial ties to the Ottomans, and from converts who relinquished their loyalty and were thus suspect for their fluency in the language of "Christianity's hereditary enemy." Instead, the "patents of nobility observed that once survival no longer demanded it, the translators' continued use of Turkish and Persian demonstrated particular devotion to Ferdinand and the empire."[107]

The fear of contagion was less prominent in Ottoman political and discursive practices, where conversion was assumed, institutionalized through the *devşirme*, and formed the very foundation of the empire. As the empire's frontiers encompassed ever more multilingual populations, the translators of the Ottoman court and their chiefs (*baş tercumanlar*) were typically captives and converts beforehand. Then, as part of the reformist enterprise under Süleyman and the professionalization of the chancery, they became a distinct cadre supervised by the *reisülküttab* and his undersecretaries and clerks.[108] Hungarian preoccupations set the stage for this evolving sense of linguistic diplomacy. Four chief translators in the early formation of the diplomatic corps were either Hungarian speakers or intensively engaged in diplomatic exchanges with the Ottomans, Habsburgs, and other claimants to power in the region such as those in Transylvania, Bosnia, and beyond: Yunus Bey, chief translator from approximately 1525 to 1542 or beyond; Mahmud Bey, from 1573 until his death in 1575; Murad Bey, who seems to have served in the corps since 1553 and then as chief dragoman after Mahmud's death until perhaps 1578; and, finally, Zülfikar Bey in the first decade of the seventeenth century.[109] These men helped to broker the form and content of treaty negotiations, the scripted events of ambassadorial visits, and the larger translation projects that signified the degree of administrative and intellectual commitment to the fortunes of imperial order in the occupied territories of Hungary. They were converts both to Islam and to Ottoman Turkish and, as such, revealed in their writings an apprehension of other lands and other philosophies and languages. With their own hybrid backgrounds, imperial translators thus helped shape the hybrid grammatical structures that conjoined political and linguistic power into a new cultural hierarchy, one that rendered Ottoman Turkish hegemonic, at least within the documentary productions of the sultanate. The translators, in effect, reproduced their own experiences of conversation and co-optation within the empire's discursive projections. Rather than mere transmitters of information, they helped shape the textual arc of the Ottoman establishment's past and its potential future. Tijana Krstić has argued that these "men were true Renaissance go-betweens, whose written works were informed by intellectual developments in Europe and synthesized a classical cultural and historical heritage of both Muslim and non-Muslim provenances into unique visions of Ottoman imperial identity."[110]

Renaissance go-betweens played a critical role in responding to the anti-Ottoman sentiments promoted by pamphleteers of the empire's rivals amid

Ottoman advancements during the early sixteenth century. After the siege of Vienna in October 1529, the simultaneous escalation of military conflicts with the Ottomans and religio-political turmoil across Europe led reformation leaders such as Luther and Erasmus to emphasize the "Turkish peril" as a symptom of the crisis within Christendom.[111] Woodcuts depicting atrocities against Christian captives by Ottoman soldiers abounded, as did the equation of Ottoman invasions with apocalyptic horrors. Ottoman military ventures therefore redefined the politics of the reformation: Luther and his followers equated papal licentiousness with Ottoman Muslim deviance, yet Ferdinand I desperately sought to define the Ottomans as the enemy of all Christendom in order to garner support for defensive maneuvers.[112] While the fiction of Christian unity against a common Muslim foe could not quell internal divisions, it did foment a discourse of judgment in which the "Grand Turk" became the perfect other against which a unified and humane political order might be imagined. As anti-Ottoman pamphlets proliferated, diplomats and translators-turned-littérateurs conveyed the grandeur and might of the dynasty's administrative and military regime to their rivals abroad. One of the early chief translators, Yunus Bey, coauthored a pamphlet with Alvise Gritti between 1533 and 1537 that painstakingly translated the intimacies of court life and the technicalities of governance to Venetian audiences.[113] They assiduously described the major provincial domains of the empires, the officials who acted as representatives of the sultan across the imperial expanse, and the varied stipends each received for his service. These lists quite literally introduced the Ottoman grammar of rule to Venetian audiences, inserting the Italianized variants of positions from head cook to financial and legal counselors into the vocabulary of European diplomacy.[114] Thus, rigid oppositions between "Muslim" and "Christian" belied the entangled networks of diplomacy, mediation, and exchange even as Habsburgs and Ottomans competed for claims to universal sovereign authority during the sixteenth century.

The Paşas, the Porte, and Thirty Thousand Gold Coins

Issues of linguistic competency and translation were also central to the successful governance of the Transdanubian brokered zone. The significance of the *beylerbey* in Buda, both in efforts to stabilize the region and as a clearinghouse for the information and resources necessary for future military campaigns, reverberates throughout the registers of the *mühimme*. They addressed persistent upheaval in the borderlands and policed the slave market, captive exchanges, duels, fortification building, dual taxation rights in contested territories, and the safe passage of diplomatic envoys. The *beylerbeys* thus oversaw the circulation of imperial command for all these concerns and, in so doing, perfected a mechanism for governing in a brokered zone. Although appointed by the sultan, they were also dependent on the sanction from the emperors and archdukes in Prague or Vienna and, after its establishment in 1556, the president of the Imperial War Council (*Hofkriegsrat*). Without the ability to placate Habsburg rivals, they would not have been capable of safeguarding the circuit of information on which the Ottoman establishment depended. The *beylerbeys* therefore were in direct correspondence with the sultanate and the authoritative bodies of the Habsburg dynasty, working to ensure that treaties were upheld and infractions kept to a minimum. The *beylerbeys* thus eked out the security of the realm while jostling among these conflicting authoritative bodies. This was a tremulous position indeed, and one that required proficient multilingualism. The evolution of a Buda-based chancery and administration, capable of functioning simultaneously in Ottoman, Hungarian, and Latin, meant that the *beylerbeys* stood at a military and linguistic crossroads.

Observable in the *beylerbeys*' letters to Habsburg authorities, and in directives issued by the Ottoman chancery, was their most pressing task: to ensure the payment of the thirty thousand gulden "present" or tribute, which seemed even to supersede their charge to maintain order by aligning the flux of the occupied territories to the organizational and administrative categories outlined in the *kanun*. As the crucible of Hungarian-Habsburg-Ottoman diplomacy, the payment and the ceremonial delivery of the annual tribute came to symbolize the success or failure of Ottoman authority in the occupied territories.[115] The bound *mühimme* registers and the letters circulated by the *beylerbeys* of Buda to the Habsburg establishment describe the same tactics to entice payment and punish delays. And the *beylerbeys* of Buda, as the brokers of this agreement, sent letter after letter to Vienna alternately pleading, demanding, and threatening the Habsburgs for a payment that was consistently in arrears.[116] The tribute became a wedge, easily manipulated by the Viennese-based court to its own diplomatic advantage, in a war of attrition against the position of the *beylerbeys* and, by extension, the sultanate. Thus, the letters concerning the tribute reveal the tenuous ability of the governor and the Ottoman court to implement the various aspects of the treaty agreements, whether it be the treatment of prisoners, the payment of agricultural taxes, the adherence to border agreements, or even the normalcy of diplomatic correspondence itself.

The correspondence of the *beylerbeys* also offers a rare glimpse into the machinations necessary to actually implement the dictates of imperial orders. In the years leading up to the long war, the office of the *beylerbeys* translated sultanic commands recorded in the *mühimme* into cajoling letters of entreaty to the Habsburg court.[117] There were 107 letters issued by the *beylerbeys* to Hungarian authorities between 1590 and 1593, when the outbreak of war changed the tone and fortunes of Ottoman rule. Of these letters, seventy-one reference the tribute explicitly and the various elements of its delivery. These elements include timeliness; letters of safe conduct for messengers crisscrossing the landscape between Istanbul, Buda, and Vienna; the route of the tribute caravan; and a rationale submitted for delays. These basic requests, however, and the letters dispatched to monitor whether they were met, were anything but routine. Instead, the volatile relations between the parties can be easily assayed in both *mühimme* registers and in letters dispatched by the *beylerbeys* themselves concerning the tribute, which quickly became a barometer of Ottoman imperial authority in the region. On occasion within the *mühimme*, the imperial council fully admitted internal problems and the depredations of officials in its correspondence with the Habsburgs, as when the *beylerbey* of Bosnia was dismissed in 1586.[118] But this was rare, and references to internal infractions were customarily soothed by assertions that peace and amity would be assured in the future.[119] Outright denial of border infractions was more often the case, with imperial orders averring that the Habsburgs themselves had been misled and thereby insinuating that the sultanate possessed greater knowledge, or more reliable informants, concerning regional activities.[120] Another tactic for defraying Habsburg accusations that the terms of the treaty had been transgressed was to assert that Ottoman agents were justified in their actions against Habsburg dissidents, often blaming Habsburg allies for any unrest.[121] Lists of Habsburg infractions were often compiled, and one letter issued by

Murad III stated that "if [your trespasses] were written down one by one, they would come to 3–4 times more than your documents of complaint."[122]

Letters issued by the *beylerbeys* in the lead-up to the full-scale Ottoman military assault in 1593 express an intensifying dismay over the persistent delay of tribute payments. Attempting to tack between Ottoman demand and Habsburg compliance, the *beylerbeys*' letters demonstrate the vicissitudes of their position as a buffer between rival imperial claimants. These letters frame the tribute not in terms of financial reward but rather as a marker of amicable relations and future expectations for peace. Thus, Hasan Paşa, the governor who held the position during the outbreak of full-fledged war, insisted up until the last moment that the sultan was far from dependent on the monies of the tribute but rather that its payment served as demonstration of continued peaceful relations between the rival powers.[123] He further indicated that only rapid payment might defer the outbreak of war.[124] And in his final letter to Archduke Matthias on August 20, 1593, he insisted that if Matthias delayed sending the tributes by even an hour, there would no longer be any need for future communication.[125]

Thus, across these epistolary records, the tribute guaranteed diplomacy, and its lapse led to war. Peaceful relations between the Habsburgs and occupants of the Hungarian territories were also a condition for the annual payment, so many of the *beylerbeys*' remonstrances for payment were met with various quibbles by the archdukes concerning border skirmishes and incursions into Habsburg lands by regional *sipahi*s or by the bordering *beys* of Bosnia and Transylvania. In November of 1592, Archduke Matthias accused then governor Mehmed III of simultaneously demanding payment of the tribute and assembling an army for offensive action. He assured Mehmed that there would obviously be no payment of the tribute if the Ottoman establishment was preparing for war.[126] The *beylerbeys*' response, in the face of such accusations, usually proffered a range of elliptical excuses of their own. They claimed that troops had been dispatched only for defense, or had simply gathered for official duties, or perhaps for the protection of convoys.[127] They also resorted to professing a lack of jurisdictional authority and claimed that only the sultan could rein in unruly soldiers.[128] Also common was the implication that troops were reacting to aggression, not instigating it,[129] or that incursions into Habsburg territory were reprisals for inhumane treatment of prisoners or other depredations by Christians that were far more serious than possible infractions by Ottoman-allied military units.[130] Quite often, the governors argued that violence was warranted as punishment for villagers who were not paying their taxes and that this was an administrative, rather than a military, issue.[131]

Occasionally, however, the possibility of destruction was deployed not as a dodge but as a threat, like the one Ferhad Paşa issued to Archduke Ernest on February 1, 1590. He indicated that unless Ernest provided information concerning the annual tribute and local notables who had been captured by Habsburg forces, the rural inhabitants of the territories would be attacked, and the resulting disorder would undermine the authority of both powers. Thus, to ensure stability, messengers from the sultanate and from the Habsburg ambassador in Istanbul should be dispatched back to their respective sovereigns with timely news.[132] But entreaty played a greater role in these letters than threat, as lapses in communication could also jeopardize the *beylerbey*'s career. If peace and order devolved on the tribute payment, then the *beylerbey*'s reputation and standing arose from his ability to shepherd its timely movement from the Habsburg to the Ottoman courts. Or, if the tribute itself was outstanding, which it always was, then he was tasked with at least ensuring the timely circulation of information about Habsburg activities or intentions. Thus, the *beylerbeys* often expressed anxiety over the amount of time imperial messengers were forced to wait for information and even begged for a brief note from Vienna in order to avoid the outbreak of war.[133] Silence implied war, and the longer messengers waited for news in Buda, the less power the *beylerbeys* held to maintain peace and the more likely the devastation of human and material resources across the lands became.[134]

This querulous correspondence linked the *beylerbey* with the Hungarian ambassador in Istanbul, whose fate was ever dependent on the efficient circulation of reports and responsive commentary from the Habsburg court. For example, Sinan Paşa warned Archduke Ernest on October 24, 1591, that if the *çavuş* Perviz, who had carried an imperial decree demanding the cessation of raids by garrisoned troops, was not released from captivity (he was held by a German count, clearly working under the auspices of Habsburg authority), then it was possible the Habsburg ambassador in Istanbul would be held responsible.[135] Indeed, Grand Vizier Sinan Paşa's first step as he mustered campaign forces to invade Hungary in the summer of 1593 was to imprison the Habsburg ambassador Krekwitz, who died within three months of his capture.[136] The correspondence thus reveals the immense pressure each *beylerbey* faced in the midst of these negotiations, from ensuring proper decorum to assuming the correct posture of humility, cooperation, haughtiness, or grandeur, depending on the circumstances. Decorum was an essential component of the exchange of information between the rival courts, and the governors insisted that information passed to the sultan should be both timely and delivered with the appropriate propriety and etiquette. They should be delivered not by miscreants but by royal courtiers expressly designated for this purpose, and if high-ranking men were not used as messengers, then the *beylerbey* would not feel compelled to grant a letter of safe conduct.[137] The governors further instructed the Habsburg court in the appropriate formulae for communications with the Ottoman establishment: correspondence should be addressed to the sultan, *not* to the grand vizier, even if seemingly only the grand vizier responds, as the grand vizier has the authority to render sultanic intent.[138] If these conditions were met, then the Habsburgs might avoid war, the inhabitants wretchedness, and the *beylerbey* recrimination from the sultanate.[139]

Yet the *beylerbey* was often harassed, caught between two seemingly always-angry sovereigns and their various representatives. The *beylerbey* feared reporting conditions that might upset or infuriate the sultan[140] but also freely passed on to the sultan haughty actions or tones in the correspondence of the archdukes or of the president of the imperial war council so as to deflect responsibility or to incite censure.[141] In turn, he blamed the ferocity of the sultan's anger, and that of his messengers, for hostile tones presumably forced on him in correspondence that he otherwise would have foresworn, as friendship was his primary goal and achievement.[142] *Beylerbey*s even sought alliances with the archdukes in political machinations of their own,[143] or to ensure peace against a perceived common enemy, such as the inroads made by the Bosnian regional leader Hasan Paşa into borderland territories.[144] In the latter case Mehmed Paşa also suggested to the archduke that he avoid any reference to the delayed tribute when attempting to officially report the heinous actions of Hasan, as this would only serve to undermine the veracity of his claims. Held in such a tight balance among multiple parties, time between messages and the travails of distance were often enemies in their own right. Ferhad Paşa was forced to explain to Archduke Ernest that he had *indeed* sent letters in a timely fashion but that a messenger was ill, and he was forced to wait for another in order to pass the letters onward.[145] The *beylerbeys* also contrived to forward letters of request to the sultanate only when tidings of the tribute's arrival might also be shared, so delays were intentionally staged to curry favor with the sultan.[146] The question of just who would carry correspondence also weighed on the letters: would a courier from Vienna be sent,[147] or one from Buda,[148] and should messengers personally deliver the sultan's renewal of treaty and safe conduct directly to Vienna, or should they deliver it instead to fortress commanders responsible for ensuring the safe passage of dispatchers? Furthermore, as mentioned above, determinations about whether the courier was of proper standing to carry correspondence to the Ottoman court were also of utmost importance. Several letters referenced the etiquette involved in transmitting papers embossed with the sultan's seal and signature. Thus, both the handling of material inscribed with sultanic commands and the personnel drafted to transmit them must adhere to standards of magnificence and grandeur deemed appropriate for imperial correspondence.

Explanations for delayed correspondence often reveal details about the daily operations of Buda as an administrative center. Mehmed Paşa informed Archduke Matthias on August 4, 1592, that he made a courier wait for a report that needed to be forwarded to the grand vizier, hence the short delay in Matthias's correspondence with the Ottoman court.[149] Archduke Ernest delayed issuing a letter of safe conduct for one of Sinan Paşa's messengers, as he first demanded to know the purpose of the mission. When Sinan informed Ernest that the *çavuş* was charged with reporting on tensions along the frontier, he also warned Ernest that if he wished to maintain harmony in the region, then he should issue the safe conduct with no further delay.[150] Threats of detainment of envoys and messengers were also a part of the *beylerbey*'s arsenal to render Habsburg officials compliant: Sinan Paşa warned Archduke Ernest on December 29, 1591, that if a kidnapped toll-house officer and a group of merchants were not released, he himself would obstruct the safe return of a delegation from Istanbul.[151] Expedience (bundling multiple letters together) and surveillance (acquiring information about purpose) were also typical explanations for delay, but at times the whole panoply of politics in the border zone appeared in a simple exchange. At one point Ferhad Paşa called Archduke Ernest's bluff when the latter had used delays in the courier system as an excuse for deferred tribute payment. In a letter dated June 10, 1590, Ferhad noted that while the archduke claimed the delegation was waiting in Komarom for letters of safe conduct from the sultanate, he himself had enclosed a certificate for travel, and thus there was no need to delay the progression of the tribute to Istanbul. He further suggested that if hostilities occurred, only the archduke's procrastination might be blamed.[152] In yet another revealing episode, Sinan Paşa complained to the imperial council that, in order to fulfill an explicit imperial command, he had tried everything to engage Archduke Matthias in correspondence concerning the release of two captive *beys*. He submitted that Matthias had been listening to the regional notables, who required ransom payments and generally agitated against the dictates of the treaty. Since the sultan personally requested the captives' release, ransom was deemed impossible. Furthermore, Matthias should avoid the advice of Hungarian notables because their ignorance had lost them Buda and their kingdom.[153] The significant role played by the Hungarian elite or military captains in these interimperial rivalries was salutary if it helped the Ottoman cause and reprehensible if it did not.

While the tribute placed these representatives of sultanic authority in the midst of brokered relationships between elites and rival courts, *beylerbeys* were also entrusted with the economic vitality of the occupied territories and thus straddled yet another multisided administrative problem: tax collection and submission of cultivators in the occupied zone to the duties and obligations enumerated in the *kanun*. They were tasked with reproducing in the province the cycle of just rule and prosperity idealized by the Ottoman establishment yet were dependent on the acquiescence of land-grant recipients, cultivators, and auxiliary and garrisoned Ottoman soldiers, Hungarian notables in the areas of overlapping jurisdiction, and marauding *beys* and *beylerbeys* from Bosnia and Buğday to do so. The letters, like the *mühimme*, make manifest the links between defense of the realm, agricultural productivity, limits to oppression, and the maintenance of sultanic power. Ottoman sovereignty was balanced in the hands of the cultivator and was consistently jeopardized by various actors in the hinterland. A language of proper custodianship thus also suffuses this correspondence, as do references to the wretched and poor common people dependent on conditions of peace for their livelihood, but trapped in a zone of protracted warfare. At times the *beylerbey*s characterize the common people as hostages, wretchedly awaiting the fulfillment of treaty requirements that would ensure the sanctity of their lives and homes.[154] More often, however, the cultivator provokes punishment and reprimand for not fulfilling duties or obligations, and the *beylerbey*s often use this failure to excuse violent reprisals. Thus, these epistolary exchanges commonly place full responsibility on the cultivator for ensuring the continuation of peace and allocates to their refusal of Ottoman suzerainty blame for the upheavals across the hinterland.

Descriptive passages on conditions in the hinterland, outside of the garrisoned cities or fortresses, further dramatize the tenuous Ottoman hold on the territory and the multiple dependencies required for even approximate collections of taxes and dues. Complaints from the archdukes concerning kidnapped villagers and peasants were often met by the *beylerbey*s with equivocation: each incident would be investigated, and if the actors were indeed culpable for crimes against the treaty, they would be punished. But in every reference to violence against the population, the *beylerbey*s also hazard the likelihood that the cultivators had refused to remit taxes to the *sipahis* and thus to the sultan. This is true for cultivators from the vineyards of Leva, Michina, and Kett Seőther, villages in the vicinity of Kis Komar, Galmboch, and Kanizsa, and in Szeioleos Ardo, Farkasfalva, Kis Noh, and other villages that were not specified.[155] Mehmed Paşa's letter to Archduke Ernest on May 19, 1592, succinctly enumerates the conditions necessary for him to uphold the treaty and ensure relative peace in the borderlands. His conditions are twofold: Habsburg and Hungarian militias should not provoke a violent response from garrisoned Ottoman soldiers, and the villages must fulfill their obligations to the *sipahi*s.[156] The letter suggests that disorder results *not* from the Ottoman administrative system itself but rather from external challenges to its proper functioning. Order, that is, the web of tax obligations and duties that inscribe a standard for local compliance, was preserved in the registers, and these were duly consulted to adjudicate complaints. But even the compilation of these registers required cooperation and negotiation. Sinan Paşa requested that Ernest order his captains to send village representatives to the registrar, who was dispatched to record new assessments of the local population and their various tax burdens. These representatives in the borderlands between rival authorities helped create an accurate record of the inhabitants and therefore ensure their continued protection under the auspices of the Ottoman establishment. Yet Sinan goes on to note that a total of sixty-eight villages in the *sancak* of Esztergom alone had refused to engage with the registrar.[157] This refusal captures the plight of a population caught between two (or rather, three, as the Hungarian captains and landholders acted as their own agents as well, outside the control of the archduke, just as intruding warriors from the borderlands tested the jurisdictional authority of the *beylerbeys*) fiercely combative sides. Habsburg captains went so far as to threaten cultivators with impalement if they complied with their *sipahis*, and the Ottoman-allied *beys* ransacked villages, burned them to the ground, and often sold the inhabitants into slavery if they refused.[158]

Still, in between the terror experienced by the inhabitants and the frustrated attempts of the *beylerbeys* to fit the province of Buda and the occupied territories more generally into the territorial map of the Ottoman Empire, the letters afford a glimpse of the rhetorical tropes common to both *kanun* and *mühimme*: the wretchedness of the population deployed as a talisman of maligned governance strategies; the assumption that peace can only be attained through the systematized deployment of surveillance and archiving campaigns and that disorder results from negligence; the conviction that coercive taxation is "just" if the lands have been conquered and registered by the Ottoman state and that punishment is due those who refuse to conform; and, perhaps most stridently, that the *sipahis*, and, by extension, the sultanate, depended on the fulfillment of these obligations and thus on the reproduction of the agrarian taxation system as a whole. The sultan was invoked via threat, admonishment, and reward and was presented via written word and dispatched messengers. Each carried the weight of his imperial majesty, and the messenger was expected to evince the might of the empire in his upright personage and decorum. Correspondence passed to and fro, but it fell to the *beylerbeys* and the officers of the Buda treasury to assess the landscape and strike an appropriate course of action amid the manifold rival interest groups and their claims to territory, revenue, and reward. These officials often sought help even from the Hungarian captains, who were simultaneously blamed for marauding territories and provoking animosities. Sinan urged the captains to force villagers recorded in the registers to act according to the treaty and thereby aid in the cessation of violent reprisals against them,[159] and he assured the archduke that the movement across the land by the imperial notary and his entourage should not be interpreted as preparations for war.[160] Instead, registration forestalled warfare almost as much as the tribute did, and the loss of control over villages was a significant factor in the eventual outbreak of full-scale hostilities.[161] Up until the Ottoman imperial troops crossed into Hungarian-occupied territories, Hasan worked to recreate an opportunity for peace, but the unevenness of imperial control over the region meant that the rubric of order, the successful collection of revenue with terms brokered through law and treaty, had slipped, and war was required for its recalibration.

Transformative Encounters: Enumerating the Realm in the Midst of Conflict

Letters written by the governors to the archdukes of Austria and to the minister of war demonstrate the inherent difficulties in bending the productive capacity of the brokered zone to Ottoman terms. The outbreak of full-scale war between the Habsburgs and Ottomans in 1593 can be linked to the combination of factors outlined in the governors' pleas for order: the inability of the two sovereign forces to control their frontier; disagreements concerning the exchange of prisoners or populations trapped in the frontier zone; and, most important, an overarching refusal on the part of the Habsburgs to ensure the consistent transmission of the thirty thousand gold coins. The war lasted until 1606, but little territory actually changed hands. The territories continued to be unsettled; rebellions and border skirmishes prevented definitive Ottoman advancements and ultimately led to the truce of Zsitvatorok in 1606.[162] The truce recognized a stalemate, but it favorably redefined the position of the current Habsburg ruler of the Austrian territories, Rudolf II (r. as Holy Roman emperor from 1576–1612). The text addressed him as emperor rather than "king of Vienna," as the terms of the 1547 treaty had dictated. It further abolished the annual payment of thirty thousand *ducats* and thereby released the Habsburgs from a position of nominal subordination to the Ottoman dynasty.[163] These features suggested an admission of equality, rather than supremacy, between the rival courts and thereby marked a new basis for future diplomatic relations.[164]

One of the more significant treatises of the opening events of this campaign, Ta'likizade's (d. 1599) *Şehnāme-i hümāyūn*, placed these military encounters within a broader commentary on the vicissitudes of Ottoman imperial power.[165] His treatise, stylized as a campaign history (*gazname*), showcases the glory of the empire, both through the literary virtuosity of its statesmen and in the narrative of its dynasts' challenges and accomplishments. Ta'likizade was first a court scribe and then the fourth *şehnameci* (serving from 1591 to 1600), the position of court historian established by Süleyman I as part of his broader administrative reforms, although by the end of the century the post would lapse. He had also served as a census registrar (*tahrir katibi*) and campaign clerk (*sefer katibi*) before becoming a fixture in the imperial *divan*, first simply as a copyist for daily transactions of the council and then as a stylist for the court itself.[166] His interaction with the textual habitus of the Ottoman establishment thus traversed forms intended to record and preserve administrative practice and those intended to transform those practices into a literary declamation of imperial might.

Ta'likizade's *Şehnāme* tracks the opening years of the long war and concentrates on the 1594 siege of Yanık (Győr). At three critical points in the text—in the panegyric opening, in reports concerning the council of war with Sinan Paşa as the campaign commenced, and on news of the accession of Mehmed III (r. 1595–1603)—Ta'likizade reflected on the fundamental structure of the Ottoman state and the sultanate. In these moments the campaign treatise breaks to enumerate the organizational structures of the empire, comment on its history, and thereby transform the larger imperial project into an object of political criticism and inquiry.

The narrative he constructed suggests that although the military campaign might secure the borders and reassert territorial control, the larger questions of allegiance could only be resolved with a full commitment to proper governing strategies. His list of attributes for successful rule emphasized the connection of law, the personal comportment of the sultan, and a solvent treasury.[167] This framework for imperial vitality then formed an implicit critique of conditions reported to the current grand vizier, Sinan Paşa, concerning the state of Ottoman administration in the Hungarian occupied territories. Local complaints concerning the Ottoman establishment's neglect of fortress defense, the increased numbers of soldiers too inexperienced to adequately police borders, lapsed attention to securing just rule over the population that had increased the likelihood of complaint and rebellion, in combination meant that the loyalty of the region as a whole to the Ottoman sovereign was fragile and must be restored.[168] His episodic narrative of the campaign transformed historical events into a clear itinerary of imperial vulnerabilities and indicated that even the stylized grandeur of the Ottoman court depended on loyal service.

On the accession of Mehmed III, Ta'likizade's 382-verse tribute consecrating the new sultan also included a reckoning of contemporary woes that plagued the dynasty.[169] He enumerated potential crises in order to reassert the importance of the proper ordering of society and the sultan's role in bringing harmony to the disparate elements of the realm.[170] Ta'likizade's treatise ends not in triumphant expectation of future sultanic glory but rather in the chaos accompanying Sinan Paşa's dismissal from office and the failures of his successor, Ferhad Paşa, to deal with a revolt in Wallachia and Moldavia or to prohibit the loss of the key fortress of Esztergom. The reappointment of Sinan Paşa and plans for a new campaign season led by the sultan himself in 1596 referenced in the final folios of the treatise ultimately bore fruit in Mehmed III's conquest of Eger. However, the mixed success of Ottoman efforts to control invaded territories, and to assert continuous rule over a region with independent political forces and ideological narratives, ultimately led not to universalism but, in Ta'likizade's estimation, a weakened authority tempered by political infighting, inconsistent management, and improper adherence to the principles of governance. The *beylerbeys* of Buda had strained to uphold these principles, and the edicts recorded in the *mühimme* sought to organize uneven circuits of knowledge and to implement trustworthy surveillance mechanisms. Yet distance, disruptions in communication, and rival interests often prohibited the achievement of these goals, and claims to universal authority remained painfully insecure.

Conquerors of the World

Ottoman and Habsburg claims to universal sovereignty were framed within newly defined centralized courts and were directed as much at internal rivalries as toward external competitors. Each adopted notions of Roman imperial grandeur and projected an image of their empires as the center of the universe over which they ruled. Ottoman claims emerged first in the context of Selim I's military campaigns against two Muslim rivals. The conquest of the Mamluk territories of Egypt and Syria in 1516–17 meant that for the first time the Ottoman sultan was commander of a predominantly Muslim population and of trade routes that connected the eastern Mediterranean to Anatolia and central Asia. These conquests, however, were coincident with the emergence of a Safavid empire to the east, which tested the expansion of Ottoman rule and challenged the legitimacy of the sultan's status as protector of the Muslim community. Thus, chronicles, royal histories, and policy makers began to emphasize not only the role of the sultan as servant of the two holy cities of Mecca and Medina but also as a messianic renewer of temporal order and Alexandrine traditions of world conqueror.[171] During Süleyman's reign the inherited titles of his father were further redefined to represent him as a new world conqueror, one who would unify and revive the Mediterranean and act as the last Roman emperor, a universal ruler capable of uniting the world under a single authority and religion.[172]

Coincident with these developments, Charles V sought to combine Spanish, Austrian, and Germanic dynastic aspirations into a universal monarchy that also defined him in messianic terms as a "Last World Emperor."[173] Charles V, elected Holy Roman emperor in 1519, was faced almost immediately with Süleyman's conquests of Belgrade, the door to the occupation of Hungarian territories, and the island of Rhodes, which undermined his claim of mastery of the Mediterranean. The two "world emperors" would, throughout their reigns, continue to battle for control of both sea and land, and the Ottomans would use their position as inheritors of Constantinople, the New Rome, to buttress their claims to universality. Sultan Süleyman, like Mehmed II before him, embraced these Byzantine legacies, and literary elites presented the city, and the court, as the center of the world. Yet both Süleyman and Charles V faced confessional politics internal to their realms that challenged claims to universality. Reformation politics swept the princely courts of Europe, and the Shi'i Safavids reinvigorated antiestablishment groups that challenged the Ottoman sultan's position as ruler of a community united in faith. By the end of the sixteenth century, Rudolf II and Mehmed III each faced escalations in these crises.

It is therefore not surprising that grand assertions of power did not figure in the text of the treaty forged in 1606. The Habsburgs faced the politicization of religious difference within their Austrian provinces, and the Ottoman establishment was beset by disturbances that would ultimately redefine the nature of sovereign authority within the realm. A coalition of dispossessed Ottoman soldiers, former state agents, and an increasingly mobile and discontented population launched a series of revolts that spread across Anatolia and into the Arabic-speaking provinces of the empire and once again challenged the assertion of universal imperial authority. Regional power brokers in areas such as Greater Syria took advantage of this unrest to form alliances with dissident elements that threatened the overall stability of the realm. And the Safavid Shah 'Abbas (r. 1588–1629) capitalized on these broader disturbances to abandon a truce negotiated in 1590. He recaptured territories formerly lost to the Ottomans and ultimately initiated yet another long-term Ottoman-Safavid military engagement. The Ottomans would then be engaged on two fronts, to the north and to the east, and became embroiled in campaigns that tempered military might and ideological convictions.

The 1547 treaty between Süleyman, Charles V, and Ferdinand had asserted Ottoman hegemony over a field of competitive rivals, which was then consecrated in the architectural grandeur of the Süleymaniye mosque complex. But the tenuous and interdependent nature of provincial administrative practice, the concerns registered in Ta'likizade's treatise, and revived challenges from the east suggest that the empire faced a new set of dynamics at the close of the sixteenth century. Environmental, commercial, and social factors all challenged the Ottoman establishment and its definitions of proper rule. The next chapter identifies these challenges within the context of Greater Syria and suggests that, as was the case for the governors of Buda, the court relied on the *beylerbeys* of Trablus-ı Şam to reassert Ottoman sovereignty in the region. The failures of administrative practices to prevent war in the Hungarian border zone discussed here, and the attempt to reassert territorial control in an "internal" region laden with disruptive local actors in the following chapter, will serve as the foil to redefinitions of "the perfect state" discussed in Chapter 6.

CHAPTER FIVE

A STATE OF REBELLION

The Reterritorialization of Ottoman Sovereignty in Greater Syria

> You are a loyal servant, and as you have submitted to my threshold of felicity, when villains seek refuge with you, capture them, and obediently send them to my threshold of felicity. If you neglect this, you too will become one of the rebels.
>
> —Imperial council of Murad III to Mansur ibn Furaykh, 1585.[1]

Considered a definitive moment in the history of Greater Syria, the 1585 Ottoman military campaign against chronically rebellious chieftains (*muqaddem*) in the mountains southeast of Beirut (the Shuf) also carved out a new space for the articulation of imperial sovereignty.[2] The Ottoman establishment used the events of 1585 to redefine networks of authority in the region, brokering new alliances in the ensuing chaos, and co-opting local chieftains into the administrative hierarchy of the empire as *emirs* or *bey*s assigned to collect taxes and maintain order. The integration of the provincial district of Trablus, or Trablus-ı Şam, was a strategic piece of this process. Its appointed governors became key to the sultanate's continued efforts to restore stability and to preclude the possibility of future open rebellion in either the coastal highlands or the desert areas of the Biqaʿ Valley. Despite aiming for stability, however, the sultanate was forced to content itself only with preventing any single rival from permanently commandeering the region and its resources. The Sayfa family illuminates the volatility of local and imperial alliances in Greater Syria. The family's patriarch, Yusuf Sayfa, served intermittently as governor of Trablus from 1579 to 1625, and other members of the family remained part of the imperial record until 1641. Yusuf Sayfa and his descendants were alternatingly trusted governors, wily tricksters, and open rebels and, as such, illustrate the Ottoman establishment's uneven success in fastening the fortunes of either the governor or the region to its own interests. Furthermore, the Sayfas' origins in the Zulkadır territories of southeastern Anatolia, their passage as auxiliary units (*levend*) into Greater Syria in the 1520s, and their varied alliances with local dissidents spanning the sixteenth and seventeenth centuries placed them in the midst of a rebellious landscape that registered as a persistent imperial anxiety in the *mühimme*.[3] The Sayfa family thus serves as a prism through which to view the tenuous nature of Ottoman "officialdom," as boundaries between official and rebel, loyal servant and dissident, were consistently challenged. These boundaries were managed in the *mühimme* through certificates of privilege and recriminations of wrongdoing. Yet distance, geography, and unceasing resistance to centralized power often stymied the authority of the text to command regional actors and to assert imperial rights.

Whereas the previous chapter explored imperial efforts to consolidate territory in a brokered external zone during the rapid expansion of Süleyman's reign, this chapter turns to the interior province of Trablus and the dynamics of Greater Syria to highlight continued challenges to Ottoman authority through the seventeenth century. As waves of rebellions rocked the provinces, an influx of silver from Spanish conquests imploded monetary systems, and categorical rubrics formerly deployed to assert order on unwieldy populations could no longer contain newly advantaged interest groups, the sultanate's vision of administrative order came under increasing duress. Notable, amid this strain, were a series of rebellions that tested definitions of loyalty and servitude to the mission of the Ottoman state and, in their testing, served to reveal the alignment practices employed by the sultanate to achieve and sustain a structure of proper order. The fortunes of Trablus, as detailed in the *mühimme*, and of the Sayfa family, as a lineage of administrators who traversed the border of rebel and official in this documentary genre from 1579 to 1641, placed the *beylerbey* at the threshold between order and disorder. The governors of Trablus, unlike those of Buda—who dealt with uneven territorial sovereignty but were not the consistent targets of accusation in the *mühimme*—were themselves figured as

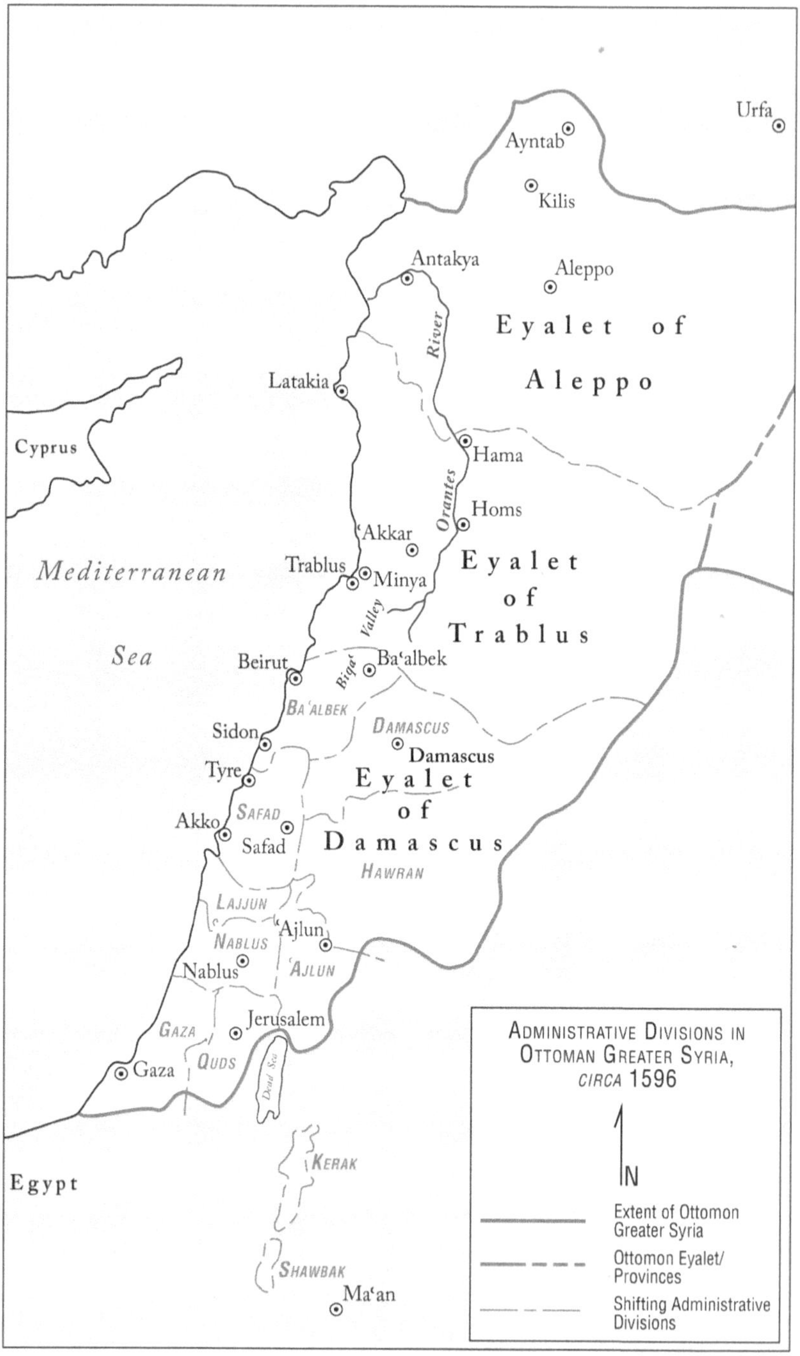

Map 2 Administrative divisions in Ottoman Greater Syria, circa 1596. *Source*: Wolf Dieter Hütteroth and Kamal Abdulfattah, *Historical Geography of Palestine, Transjordan and Southern Syria in the Late 16th Century*. Erlangen: Erlanger Geographische Arbeiten, 1977.

ambivalent fixtures in the Ottoman administrative apparatus. Trablus and the Sayfa family thus illustrate the amount of effort necessary to reorganize provinces into an Ottoman grammar of rule and reveal key moments of contestation over the terms and expectations elaborated through sultanic proclamations.

The Ottoman establishment dispatched proclamations to the governates of Greater Syria and sought to oppress internal rebellions there, while fighting wars with both Habsburgs and Safavids. The examples in this chapter underscore how textual commands wove a tenuous thread for asserting imperial authority, one that remained wholly dependent on provincial compliance. Here, in a constantly shifting textual landscape where "present orders" replace older edicts, and administrators are called on to "pay no attention to previous orders," registers of the *mühimme* record imperial vulnerability more than sovereign command. Thus, both the textual and the physical terrain of Greater Syria remained embattled spaces during the sixteenth and seventeenth centuries. The following sections identify the acts of negotiation necessary to sustain the overarching authority of the Ottoman sultan and emphasize the role that exhortation played in inscribing a structure and grammar of rule deployed by officials and rebels alike.[4] Edicts in the *mühimme* drew on a discourse of duty, obligation, and justice that came to contain and impose standards of administration. These edicts, or "noble orders" to "restore justice," delineated the line between permissible and illegitimate actions, defined as any behavior that disrupted imperial oversight. Furthermore, directives in the *mühimme* quite literally *registered* a history of sultanic command and contributed to the active archive necessary for continued deliberative imperial practice.

An Uneven Terrain: Governors and Rebels

Instability and fraught relationships with the sultanate had typified Greater Syria since its initial conquest in 1516.[5] The Ottoman establishment tried various tactics to incorporate the human and material resources into its imperial fortunes.[6] The territory was left initially in the hands of a former Mamluk governor, Canberdi al-Ghazali, who took advantage of Selim's death in 1520 to form his own independent regional seat. Sultan Süleyman I then sent a military force to restore imperial control and, as part of his massive surveying and lawmaking projects, also initiated provincial divisions and governing structures in hopes of aligning the region to imperial norms.[7] The process for redistricting the province, however, still tended to rely on existing Mamluk territorial divisions. Thus Damascus and Aleppo remained the prominent administrative seats, with Trablus briefly acting as a third, although in 1521 it was folded back into the purview of Damascus.[8] Imperial control remained tenuous at best, and the appointed officials of Damascus and Aleppo were poorly equipped to address the complex internal dynamics of the region.[9] The coastal and desert territories constituted their own frontier zones, populated by increasingly strong regional chieftains. Although they had cooperated peacefully with the Mamluks, and were rewarded for it with grants and privileges, the advent of Ottoman centralizing projects catalyzed unceasing rebellion.[10] This was especially the case in the rugged coastal mountains where the Druze chieftains, the Maʿn, held sway, in the Biqaʿ Valley and extending to Homs, dominated by the Harfush emirs, and the territory extending from Trablus into the Kisrawan controlled by the ʿAssaf clan.[11]

The most rebellious of these clans were the Druze, led by Korkmaz Maʿn, who had made systematic taxation by Ottoman imperial agents virtually impossible.[12] Sultanic edicts sent to the governors of Damascus and Aleppo as early as 1546 further indicate that the Druze clans had muskets and that any effort to disarm them led to open rebellion.[13] These muskets were acquired from Venetian agents in Cyprus, who supported the agitators as part of their own campaigns against the rising power of the Ottomans in the Mediterranean.[14] By 1565 the rebellion had spread to other districts and clans, with members of the Harfush participating in a direct attack on the resident *sipahi* charged with tax collection.[15] The Druze further provided sanctuary for individuals fleeing punishment by state agents for serious crimes such as murder.[16] One edict also cited the presence of more than one thousand muskets in the hands of "evil" men in the region of Matn as a constant threat to the peace and security of the region. Furthermore, the text of the order indicated that firearms acquired from the Venetians outgunned Ottoman muskets of the time: they were longer and capable of firing more rounds. Following the Ottoman conquest of Cyprus in 1570–71, and despite the military resilience of imperial forces on a broader scale, local chieftains from Sidon in the south to the mountainous stronghold of 'Akkar in the north resisted the central authority with increasing temerity. Missionary activity and alliances with the Maronites created a new wedge in the political atmosphere and, more threatening, a new entrée for firearms from Venice despite its loss of Cyprus. Imperial correspondence with the province of Damascus attests to a heightened concern, which by 1574 had turned to desperation, over the region's instability. Other than lump sums occasionally wrested from them, the Druze territories had not paid taxes for more than twenty years. As a result, the *beylerbey* of Damascus was ordered to force the *muqaddem*s of 'Assaf, Ma'n and other chieftains to surrender one to two thousand muskets.[17] But as resistance continued apace, that same year an imperial naval campaign led by Grand Vizier Sinan Paşa brought troop reinforcements to hunt down the dissidents in their mountain retreats.[18]

Two years later, an imperial order addressed to the finance minister, governor, and military commander of Damascus depicted a provincial system gone awry in the Ma'n territories despite military intervention.[19] These officials had reported to the imperial council that constant unrest dissuaded anyone from serving as tax collectors for the districts of Sidon and Beirut, and when appointed delegates were sent to retrieve annual dues, the inhabitants outright refused to remit required payments.[20] Furthermore, residents claimed that they were paying taxes by the old register (*defter-i 'atīḳ*), but in reality they were not even submitting the amount designated therein. And while insisting that the lands assigned to them lay fallow, they were clearly cultivating them but refused to allow the *kadı* to investigate or adjust the schedule of taxes. In addition, villagers were said to treat state delegates with disrespect and harm Muslim residents.[21] The *hükm* instructs the varied provincial officials of Damascus to determine whether state revenue had indeed been disrupted, if the *re'aya* had been harmed, and whether their chieftains were active parties in these rebellious antics. If such conditions were found, then the chieftains should be arrested and punished according to the principles of the *şar'*. The *mühimme* thus record a perception of the region as having descended into anarchy. Disorder was identified with *re'aya* manipulating tax categories, chieftains rousing their followers to pitched battles rather than agricultural labor, and general disrespect for the normative organizational structures used to fit provincial affairs into imperial designs.

This sociopolitical disorder further complicated efforts to standardize tax collection according to categories outlined in the *kanunname*. *Mühimme* edicts likewise labored to identify appropriate representatives and distinctions among taxes, tithes, and dues in the midst of this chaos. In the earliest *mühimme* register from 1545, cultivators petitioned local courts against the misuse of variable fees (*bad-ı hava*) and complained about oppression from imperial delegates appointed to collect revenues from imperial lands.[22] Inhabitants of the region also escaped registration in poll-tax surveys (*cizye defterleri*), and Hasan, the *defterdar* of the 'Arab territories, was instructed to ensure that individuals who were left "outside the *defter*" complied with the law (*kanun*) and were properly recorded.[23] Within the region of Trablus, shifting alliances problematized even the basic assignment of rights to collect taxes from the region. At one point the 'Arab *defterdar* 'Ali Çelebi was charged with investigating a situation in which grants (*berat*s) acknowledging recipients of tax farms (*muḳāṭa'a*) in Trablus were held simultaneously by four people.[24] These included the current supervisor of the *sancak* (*sancāğı beği*), a local *emin*, and two individuals who seem to have shared both the duties and the rights of the contract. From 'Ali Çelebi's seat in Aleppo it seemed increasingly impossible to either disentangle the fraudulent tax claims or, more generally, sort out the affairs of Trablus and surrounding territories.[25]

As a possible solution to this crisis, Trablus was separated in 1579 as a distinct administrative unit from the northwestern territories of Damascus and encompassed the villages, towns, and mountain strongholds deemed most problematic by the sultanate during the preceding decades. The dependent territories of Trablus extended south along the coast past Jubayl, included the rural districts of Futuh, Kisrawan, and Munaytra and continued north into the Lebanon mountains. The venerable tradition of soap manufacturing in Trablus, the wealth of vineyards and gardens surrounding the city, the extensive terrain for cereals and grains in the hinterland, and the mountainous olive farms around it formed a productive and rich agricultural heritage from which the Ottomans sought to benefit the most amid complex regional rivalries. Furthermore, the road from the Trablus coast to the internal trading depot of Homs remained a vital route for commerce and also curbed the rising power of Tuscany as the Venetian Empire's fortunes faltered. This new provincial division also marked a more consistent use of regional intermediaries to register and administer the sultanate's taxation policies. The province thus became the ground for new alignment practices based on a well-tested mode of Ottoman governance: accommodation in return for stabilization, or *istimalat*. As one of the most visible practices in the *mühimme*, co-opting regional elites into the Ottoman establishment became the primary means by which rebellious elements were curtailed or, better yet, transformed into provincial allies.

Legitimacy and Order: The Boundaries of Ottoman Officialdom

The Sayfa family was ideally situated to serve the interests of the Ottoman establishment in the provincial seat of Trablus. Although by 1579 its members were entrenched within the political spheres of mountain and coast, they were not locals themselves and were thus dependent on regional and external alliances to cement and extend their position.[26] The Sayfas arrived in the territory of Trablus in the aftermath of Türkmen revolts in Anatolia, which were sparked by Şeyh Celal's messianic vision of rebellion against the centralizing aims of the Ottoman establishment. Rebellions continued intermittently from 1526 to 1528, when the sultanate restored *timars* to Zulkadır participants in the uprising and thus co-opted potential rebels into the administrative order. These uprisings would shape both the vocabulary and sociopolitical patterns of later acts of resistance and rebellion against Ottoman state order; imperial correspondence and chroniclers tended to identify participants in organized resistance movements as "*celāliler*" and often co-opted other families like the Sayfas to suppress challenges elsewhere to Ottoman sovereignty.[27] The Sayfas appear to have served as *levend* (auxiliary units) during the course of these rebellions and then made their way into the northern territories of Greater Syria by 1528. In 1606 the Sayfa family sided with the Ottoman establishment yet again during the revolt led by the local chieftain, 'Ali Janbulad, and were thus active participants in orchestrated uprisings that spanned the sixteenth and seventeenth centuries and were collectively misnamed the "*celali* rebellions."[28] Their participation as regional brokers in moments critical to the shaping of Ottoman administrative strategy warrants a close look at how their actions were managed in correspondence issued from the sultanate.

The Sayfa family's gradual integration into Greater Syria further illustrates the significance of strategic and variable alliances and would come to play a key role in their relationship with the court in Istanbul. Already experienced in warfare but without local roots in the area, the Sayfas quickly aligned themselves with the 'Assaf *muqaddem* Mansur when settling in the northern mountains of Greater Syria.[29] Mansur 'Assaf then used this support to extend his territorial control from Ghazir, in the Kisrawan, to 'Akkar, in the northern mountain range of the Shuf, and finally even incorporated Beirut and the districts of Homs and Hama into his jurisdiction.[30] The Sayfas settled in 'Akkar, and acted as subordinates to the 'Assaf, although Yusuf Sayfa also worked at times in concert with Korkmaz Ma'n, who vied for control of the region from his stronghold in the south. When he assumed the position of *beylerbey* in the newly reconstituted province of Trablus in 1579, the choice worked to the advantage of both the sultanate and the patriarch. Yusuf Sayfa received recognition from the imperial center, which he used to legitimize authority seized from competitors, and in return the Ottoman establishment relied on him to ensure that remunerative fees from various local tax bases reached their rightful proprietors and to reinstate a system of administrative order in a region that had become a playground for local power brokers. Furthermore, without an extensive local base from which to foment open rebellion, members of the Sayfa family served at the behest of the sultanate. And, if they did rebel, their base was easily accessible, and there was seemingly little consequence to the frequent dismissals that characterized the Sayfa family's volatile history as the region's governors.[31]

Such was the case in 1585, when the continued agitations of local chieftains warranted direct imperial intervention. İbrahim Paşa led a punitive campaign from Egypt to crush these rebellious chieftains (*muqaddem-i 'aṣı*) and attacked the Sayfa fortress of 'Akkar in retribution for their renewed alliance with the Ma'n.[32] The *beylerbey* of Damascus was charged with securing the necessary forces and military provisions as well as solid lines of communication with the sultanate.[33] After the attack, when the heads of hundreds of Druze leaders were sent as a macabre display of power to Istanbul, the *beylerbey* was further charged with facilitating İbrahim's efforts to reassign administrative positions. One entire *mühimme* register was devoted to documenting the rewards distributed to governors, tax collectors, and *timar* holders for their service in the 1585 campaign. This service was identified, fixed, and recorded, thus initiating a new textual and territorial baseline for provincial order.[34] Edicts in the *mühimme* also employed a strategic discourse of loyal service and imperial protection that policed the boundaries between rebel and official and reasserted the primacy of Ottoman territorial authority in a turbulent frontier zone.

The Sayfa family, however, continued to test the validity of the new governing structures set in place after 1585.[35] An edict sent to Ja'far Paşa, the interim governor of Trablus following the military invasion of 1585, set the stage for a chase both geographical and textual as the Ottoman establishment attempted to rein in dissident factions. The edict references a report that the sons of Sayfa, Emirs Sayf and Hasan, were rebels and had joined the Druze leader Korkmaz Ma'n in the unrest that instigated the imperial invasion.[36] The sultan reports that he had been informed "that their rebelliousness has surpassed [all] limits" and that they have committed "acts of aggression and transgression (*ta'adī ve tecāvüz*) against the territory and the people." The acting *beylerbey* was called on to "render justice" by arresting, chaining, and, by any possible means, ensuring their captivity until Grand Vizier İbrahim had the opportunity to attend to the matter.[37] The "acts of aggression" of the sons of Yusuf Sayfa and their flight through Greater Syria map the administrative landscape of the region as, in the documents that follow, current and former governors of Damascus, Safad, and Palmyra were also called on to seize the rebels. The exact nature of their "rebelliousness" is not fully explained, although a discourse of justice and proper service was clearly deployed throughout. As I argued in Chapter 2, reference to "limits" indicates the delicate balance between coercive taxation and sultanic protection and the assumption that only the establishment had the right to distribute shares of the empire's resources. The unsanctioned collection of dues or taxes from local inhabitants or the use of such goods and services to build independent power bases was therefore deemed rebellious. Edicts issued from the imperial council defined rebellion as they responded to it and thereby inscribed how a loyal servant "surpassed the limit" and became a rebel. They assessed the behaviors of provincial actors against an idealized standard, within which volatile circumstances were fitted into a particular grammar of rule and rendered actionable by the Ottoman establishment.

The sultanate called on all possible resources to intercept the fugitive sons of Yusuf, signaling both the import of their actions and the inherent difficulties posed by distance and possible indifference to imperial command. Although the figure of the sultan as an ultimate (in the sense of both final and definitive) authority was an essential feature of these edicts, and his voice imbued the registers of the *mühimme* with expectations that his commands would be fulfilled, the scenario with the Sayfa family reveals a profound sense of imperial anxiety. The *mühimme* invoked the sultanic voice of command, yet the sultan himself rarely generated the documents, and the edicts were forced to use repetition, entreaty, and threat. The persistent rebellion in Greater Syria brought into bold relief the brokered and dependent nature of administrative practice. The tenuous nature of this relationship seems particularly evident when the directives called for coercive measures, as was the case here. The *beylerbey* of Damascus was the next official corralled into the chase of Yusuf's sons. The order first narrates events addressed thus far, informing the *beylerbey* that the two emirs had fled Trablus and had now arrived in the plains of the Biqaʿ and Baʿalbek, where they took refuge with two formerly dismissed *sancakbeys* (district commanders), ʿAli ibn Khuraysh from Palmyra and Mansur ibn Furaykh from Safad.[38] As it did the *beylerbey* of Trablus, the edict orders the Damascus governor to investigate and report back to the imperial council any adverse developments. He is further commanded to arrest the "villains" by any means necessary and deliver them to the imperial representative, now named as Üveys Hüseyn, *kapıcıbaşı* of Grand Vizier İbrahim, who, with his "loyal men," would send them on to "my threshold of felicity." The command closes by insisting that "arresting the said [persons] is your duty. Perform it after making good preparations and show diligence in arresting them."[39]

This concluding note, as well as other emphatically insistent phrases in the edict such as "Do not give them a chance to escape" and "Have them arrested in any way possible," disguise a deep and underlying concern that the order will not be fulfilled. For the *beylerbeys* of Trablus and Damascus, the sultan could employ the language of duty and justice to signal the mode of compliance expected from his administrators. They acted, then, under threat of dismissal. But what of those actors who were no longer sanctioned officeholders within the bureaucracy of empire yet obviously retained authority of their own? These men, too, and even prevailingly, played a role in the story of Yusuf Sayfa's sons. In fact, their role was sufficiently necessary to overburden the question of just who constituted a designated Ottoman representative in a region typified by such flux. Demands for information issued from the sultanate imposed a dichotomy between loyal servant and rebel upstart yet willingly accepted rebels who later returned to the fold of imperial authority, even if it was for their own purposes. This preference for information and order over rigid categories becomes strikingly clear in the next edict concerning the flight of the Sayfas, addressed to Mansur ibn Furaykh, the dismissed *sancakbey* of Safad.[40] Here, the edict summarizes the situation but then states, "In fact, they [the sons of Sayfa], have joined up with you." At this point the sultanic command follows the formulae issued to the *beylerbey*s of Trablus and Damascus: arrest them with due diligence and by any "imaginable" means, and then deliver them to Üveys Hüseyn, who will convey them to his master, the grand vizier. The following lines, however, pointedly mark a threshold moment and a clear departure from the previous commands: "[You,] too, must not become a rebel (*bāğī*)."

The edict then proceeds to tell ibn Furaykh that he is being watched—noting that a copy of the imperial command had also been sent to 'Ali ibn Khuraysh—and reports knowledge of the collusion between the two men, and even of a "sighting" of another of the Sayfa sons, Husayn, in their company.[41] The edict closes with fine-tuned definitions of service and rebellion: "You are a loyal servant. Because you have submitted to my threshold of felicity, when wrongdoers seek refuge with you be obedient, capture them, and send them to my threshold of felicity. If you neglect this, you too will become one of the rebels." This phrase vividly illustrates the fragile threshold between servant and agitator inscribed in the *mühimme*. These varied strategies indicate the available tactics available to the Ottoman establishment when faced with disquieting events outside its immediate control. Furthermore, the basis for any coherent plan of action was knowledge and the power it availed. Mansur ibn Furaykh learns, by reading the "footnote" referencing the copy sent to 'Ali ibn Khuraysh, that the Ottoman establishment possessed surveillance mechanisms capable of observing and reporting not only on suspicious activities but also on the comings and goings of former and acting officials. The imperial council then acted decisively on this knowledge in an attempt to disrupt allegiances counter to its own agenda. It did so by creating a textual and evidentiary web so tight that there was little room to maneuver. The larger umbrella of the two regional seats, Damascus and Trablus, held in place by the presumed loyalty and faithfulness of their respective *beylerbeys*, was still not enough to ensure a swift resolution to the problem. In fact, the edicts concerning the Sayfa sons provide further evidence for previous arguments that the *beylerbeys*' authority was itself quite tenuously held and defined and was in turn dependent on alliances that often ran counter to imperial goals. Surveillance was thus essential for managing regional politics. Yet even the knowledge gained from surveillance networks could only be enacted through the textual universe of the sultanic command itself. The imperial council thus "papered" the terrain with directives and commands, hoping that it could assert its authority via diffusion, if not through a direct assertion of will.

These layers of anxiety and authority were specifically referenced when the directive called on Mansur ibn Furaykh and 'Ali ibn Khuraysh individually, reminding them of their former status as *sancakbeys* and the duties they performed when functioning as officials. The difficulty, of course, was that these were only "remembered" duties, because neither man currently held an official post within the administrative network. Even more problematic, they had been dismissed and, as indicated by their willingness to harbor fugitives, likely held some animosity toward imperial motives. Yet, because they had previously submitted to the "threshold of felicity," the men's continued loyalty remained a possibility. The edict hinges on this possibility, and the whole scenario is held in dramatic tension as its successful resolution depends on the acquiescence and continued participation of these former district commanders in the empire's governance structure. Thus, the sultanic command draws a clear line in the sand, one it assumes that neither 'Ali ibn Khuraysh nor Mansur ibn Furaykh has yet crossed, despite each man's known association with the rebels. Both still have a chance to act as loyal servants if they adhere to the current command to "capture them, be obedient and send them to my threshold of felicity." Mansur ibn Furaykh's execution less than a decade later suggests, however, that this effort to maintain allegiances was also often futile and partially explains why, by

1590, Yusuf Sayfa is back in the position of *beylerbey* in Trablus despite his or his sons' participation in the events of 1585.

Between 1585 and 1590, however, edicts in the *mühimme* attempted to retrieve the privileges and rewards Yusuf Sayfa had acquired during his term as governor. Dismissal from office once an individual rebelled could not guarantee that funds associated with loyal service could be reappropriated or reassigned. Other members of the family, however, seemingly worked to maintain their ties to the Ottoman establishment. In the register that recorded promotions and honors distributed for service against rebels during the 1585 campaign, a son of Yusuf Sayfa paid twenty-four thousand *akçe*s due from his land grant (*ze'amet*) along with other monies owed to the imperial treasury. As a reward for this diligence and service, he was granted the title of *müteferrika* and given a promotion of fifteen hundred *akçe*s.[42] As for Yusuf Sayfa himself, he still controlled a *timar* worth 17,400 *akçes* in the province of Trablus. The current governor, Ja'far Paşa, was ordered to ensure that it was properly assigned to Mahmud, who had obtained an imperial certificate (*berat*) naming him as the rightful supervisor of the *timar*.[43] The edict notes that the sultanate had commanded when he had rebelled that Yusuf Sayfa be found and killed, though it seemed satisfied that he had merely been defeated and compelled to flee. The problem addressed in the edict was that he still pillaged the countryside. Furthermore, the establishment in Istanbul seemed to be working at cross-purposes with İbrahim's efforts to stabilize the region, as Yusuf Sayfa had apparently obtained the right to continue acting as manager of the *timar* from the vizier. The edict absolutely forbids this, as Yusuf Sayfa's "corruption and abomination (*fesād ve şenā'at*)" had increased. Moreover, if Yusuf Sayfa truly intended to supervise the *timar*, then he should have joined the Tabriz campaign as part of his obligations, but the edict reports that he did not and so now "deserves to be killed." The customary summary statement of the order, prefaced by the sultan's direct order of command (*buyurdum ki*), places the various factors involved in the case in direct relationship to each other: based on reports concerning Yusuf Sayfa's rebellion and refusal to perform in the imperial service, the *timar* should be given to Mahmud, who possesses a *berat* to that effect, and Yusuf is not to interfere: "he must deliver what is due from him."

The edict used precise and strong language concerning Yusuf Sayfa's second rebellion—refusing to show up for the ongoing campaign against the Safavids. Once again he deserved to die for his negligence, this time for refusing to adhere to his obligations as supervisor of a *timar*. The 17,400 *akçe*s was no minor sum, so its deviation, through the personal exploits of its previous holder, not unsurprisingly provoked a heated response from the sultanate.[44] The problem, of course, was how to ensure the fulfillment of this command, given the fluid nature of provincial authority. What was now labeled pillage or plunder in the edict had previously been the rightful reward for a governor merely collecting his dues from a *timar*. Yusuf Sayfa's "corruption and abomination" and general references to him as a "mischief-maker" resulted from his refusal to hand over the bundle of rights associated with a privileged status. Further muddying the waters, İbrahim Paşa contradicted the sultanate's judgment that Yusuf Sayfa was a rebel and declined to implement the imperial council's commands. Why this did not constitute an act of rebellion is in itself an interesting question.

Part of the answer may lie in the subtext. Despite strong recriminations, the edict also used a discourse of loyalty and obligation essential to Ottoman provincial administration: "He deserves to be killed," yet "he must deliver what is due from him." These two statements leave open the possibility that rebellion might turn into acquiescence and surrender. They could only coexist within an awareness of the porous and fluid nature of authority. At least within the context of this edict, the fact that İbrahim was not reprimanded for presumably negotiating with Yusuf Sayfa after the events of 1585 further indicates the dependent nature of sultanic command. It could only negotiate across the distance via textual orders, and these negotiations, ongoing and vexed, continued to stitch an otherwise unwieldy empire together and thus were instrumental to its success. İbrahim and Yusuf Sayfa's actions in the field, so to speak, indicated both the tenuousness of sultanic command and the significance of a language of justice and loyalty that situated the actions of co-opted servants within a shared understanding of imperial practice. Reward was owed to a son who met the obligations of his father. Penalty was meted out to Yusuf Sayfa for absconding with revenue, yet he still served as the Ottoman establishment's tenuous link to the region and was thus restored to the position of *beylerbey* in 1590. Shortly thereafter,

Fakhr al-Din ibn Ma'n was awarded the rank of *sancakbeyi* of the district of Sidon-Beirut, which would be constituted as a distinct provincial seat the following year in an ongoing effort to divide the region into manageable units.[45] Both positions enabled the recipients to prevail over their rivals, for the Sayfa family, removing the last 'Assaf emir in 1591, and for Fakhr al-Din, another significant Druze chieftain, 'Alam al-Din. But the two would go on to pass in and out of favor with the establishment and variously ally with or against each other in their own campaigns for regional control.[46]

The Beylerbey *as "Supervisor of Revenue"*

Sultanic commands issued to the governors of Trablus may have varied considerably in whom they addressed, but they rarely wavered from the link between the *beylerbeylik* and imperial revenues. Soon after Yusuf Sayfa was restored to his function as *beylerbey*, one of the first edicts sent his way addressed the monies still due to the treasury from the *iltizam* controlled by the murdered Muhammad 'Assaf.[47] He was further instructed to imprison Muhammad 'Assaf's accountant, Ghumayda, after checking his registers and confiscating any remaining money.[48] In 1595 an edict succinctly stated that "the collection of taxes for the payment of salaries is a particular function of yours."[49] Given that successful remittance of expected revenues all but defined the governor's function, rebellion figured as the refusal to act accordingly, either through negligence, delayed payment, or misallocation of revenue from its proper source. By the late seventeenth century this aspect of the governor's role was explicitly appended to the introduction of a sultanic proclamation: "Order to Arslan, *beylerbeyi* of Trablus and supervisor and treasurer of revenue."[50] Here, the governor's duties were explicitly conflated with those of the *defterdar* and were thus defined through the lens of the imperial treasury. Approbation, praise, dismissals, and appointments were all expressed within this monetary framework, suggesting that remunerating the imperial treasury remained the establishment's primary concern. The governorship was conferred by a contractual agreement similar to that of a tax farm (using the phrase *ber vech-i iltizam*), wherein the *beylerbey* agreed to a once-yearly remission of funds (*irsaliye*) assessed in terms of a lump sum (*maktu'*). The governorship itself functioned as a contractual partnership or business relationship of sorts. Specifying the terms of this contract, an edict from 1605 sets the conditions of governorship as an agreement to collect one hundred thousand *filori* from the *emin*s of Trablus annually.[51] Yusuf Sayfa had sent half that amount already, but an order from the finance department (*maliye*) demanded the remainder for "deserving soldiers" engaged with Sinan Paşa in a military venture against the Safavids.

The Ottoman establishment was engaged in two major military campaigns—one with the Habsburgs, which would not end until 1606, and one with the Safavids, who had wisely attacked when Ottoman forces were engaged elsewhere. The central government needed cash to ensure the viability of these campaigns, and it called on its "man in Trablus" to partially meet the demands of its soldiery. Refusal to remit the second half to the "deserving" salaried soldiers jeopardized a vision of sovereign authority that knitted together revenue production, military defense, and administrative order. But the primary object of this directive was "your undertaking" to collect revenue from the "*emin*s of Trablus." The *emin* was yet another designation for individuals who were recipients of land grants, had established themselves as tax collectors in the region, or were regional power brokers brought into imperial categories. The term literally translates as "the entrusted one," thus conferring on the individual an assumption of loyalty in relationship to the sultan and transforming what was in all likelihood self-interested collection of wealth into the performance of duty. The *emin*s' heritage was varied. Some were indigenous elites recognized by the invading Ottomans after conquest; others rotated in as landholders from assignments throughout the empire but gradually ensconced themselves within the provincial social fabric. All, however, jostled for control over revenue rights and were reluctant to relinquish them. They made the *beylerbey*'s primary task—remittance of provincial revenue to the imperial treasury—an almost immeasurable one.

The *mühimme*, although issued in the form of commands, acknowledged this state of affairs and assumed that the alignment of interests between the Ottoman establishment and the governor was of mutual benefit. As long as Yusuf Sayfa continued to pay into the system (in both a literal and a metaphorical sense), his position vis-à-vis the imperial government was assured. Yet, charged with managing the treasury, Yusuf Sayfa constantly battled other groups vying for a part in the revenue stream. Thus, to fulfill his function as manager of revenues, he had to continually make alliances on the ground, the very activity of which contradicted the imperial ethos. Collecting assigned revenues required delegation, yet this might allow extraimperial agents to gain more control over material resources. Hence, an order sent to the *beylerbey* in 1605 reports that Yusuf Sayfa awarded revenue collection rights to "undeserving people in different capacities that cause harm to the treasury: in collecting the money of the *nahiye*s, in collecting the revenue of the *vakıf* and tax farms (*mukata'at*) in the territory of Trablus." Yusuf was commanded to abolish all "superfluous salaries and awarded positions now" and to "restore all salaries and awarded positions to the treasury, [and] record all of the revenue in a sealed register and report back immediately." The final line of the edict warns him of potential negligence and reiterates a threat against his tendency to protect "undeserving personages."[52] The sultanate required not only a streamlined process of revenue extraction but also a clear record in a sealed register, presumably for future reference. Note also the complexity of Yusuf Sayfa's task: he must guarantee the collection of revenue from three distinct sources (the *nahiye*, *vakıf*, and *mukata'at*), each with his own power field and thus his own code of action. These were, respectively, villages paying rent on rain-fed fields, returns from *vakıf*s whose revenues belonged to the imperial treasury, and taxes from villages and lands paid in lump sums and farmed out to various provincial strongmen. The *beylerbey*'s primary task was to fit these contesting fields of power within an imperial administration grounded in a general assurance of social order and relief from "above the ordinary" oppression. Thus, he must shape tax collection to the will of the sultanate, while, through both political and coercive means, sustaining his own position of regional power. The greatest challenges to his status were, of course, competing families who had much stronger ties to the land and its peoples and thus to any assertions of indigenous authority outside the ambit of an imperial ethos.

Two of these, the Ma'ns and the Janbulads, were of particular consequence for Yusuf Sayfa and his uneven status as a designated imperial official. Both families also played a cat-and-mouse game with sultanic authority—at times currying its favor, at others standing in outright rebellion.[53] In 1606–7, headed by two of their most infamous representatives, Fakhr al-Din ibn Ma'n and 'Ali Janbulad, these lineages joined forces against the Sayfas. Yusuf Sayfa, then appointed by Istanbul as military commander of the troops dispatched to quell the rebellion, was severely beaten, fled by sea from Trablus to Cyprus, and then returned to take refuge in Damascus.[54] Sayfa's alliances with janissaries garrisoned in Damascus, which he had forged by contracting out tax-farm revenues to them, secured his escape from the city at night but not its defense, so Damascus folded to Janbulad's forces as well. Fakhr al-Din Ma'n used the opportunity of Yusuf Sayfa's absence to seize Kisrawan, and 'Ali Janbulad moved toward the seat of the Sayfas in 'Akkar. Yusuf Sayfa stopped this progress by agreeing to relinquish control of all territory save Homs in a compromise with 'Ali Janbulad. Only on the arrival of the grand vizier, Murad Paşa, was Janbulad finally defeated, though by that point the savvy Fakhr al-Din had distanced himself from the rebellion and, as the reappointed district governor of Safad, in 1610 was even called on to facilitate one of Yusuf Sayfa's many dismissals from office.[55] A mere three years later, in 1613, while fallen from imperial favor and deprived of the government of Trablus, Yusuf Sayfa briefly sided with the Ma'ns during yet another one of their skirmishes with imperial troops.[56] This pattern held until the 1630s, when the constant upheaval of such transactional politics was quelled for a time by the strong-armed interventionist policies of Murad IV (r. 1623–40).[57] The fortunes of both the Sayfa family and the imperial treasury were balanced on the tip of a pin, and the line between state and extrastate agent was anything but firm. At times this worked in favor of imperial management, as the sultanate played off interregional rivalries to its advantage. As a result, however, imperial interest became one of many, and short of full-scale military invasion (costly in the extreme), remonstrance was the ultimate weapon.

Manager or Miscreant? The Limits of Authoritative Command

The deep ambivalences of Yusuf Sayfa's position, and of imperial sovereignty itself, suffuse the *mühimme*. Correspondence from the imperial council was abundant in praise when Yusuf Sayfa assured the peaceful collection of revenue—a "loyal" and "courageous" man who exerts himself in "maintaining and guarding" territories under his authority, expending the necessary effort with respect to the imperial treasury. This earned him imperial favor: thus the sultan sends "a sword and a splendid robe of honor (*ḫil'ăt-i fāḫire*)." He was commanded to receive "with every sign of respect and esteem (*ikrām ve ta'ẓīm*)" and to "don the robe of honor and gird the sword for the destruction of the enemy." The governor was also to exert himself "without limit in maintaining and guarding your province, and preserving and increasing the revenue."[58] Management, as figured here, meant that the *beylerbey* was charged with preserving the rights of the imperial treasury over other interest groups.

Yusuf Sayfa became just one more threat to the imperial coffers, however, when he sought to augment his own status. In the aftermath of Janbulad's rebellion, Yusuf Sayfa seized the opportunity to expand his own fortunes and was therefore replaced by his son Husayn in 1610. Once again, however, the transfer of authority and resources was not assured, so an imperial order called on the *beylerbey* in Damascus to prevent Yusuf Sayfa from interfering in any way.[59] This "interference" entailed any disruption in Husayn's ability to assume control of the tax farm assigned to the *eyalet* of Trablus or in the collection of taxes from the province in general. Authorities in Damascus were therefore required to assist in implementing textual commands, which also implied that Yusuf Sayfa remained an imminent threat to administrative order. Copies of this edict were also sent to the *beylerbeyi* of Aleppo and to the *sancakbeyi* of Safad (then Fakhr al-Din), suggesting that imperial appointments depended in part on the collaborative effort of regional officials with a stake in maintaining their own positions vis-à-vis the ruling establishment. It also implied efforts to prioritize imperial over familial ties and to intrude into the intricacies of transactional politics in Trablus. Once again, from the perspective of the sultanate, and in the equivalency made between Trablus as a provincial seat and as a designated unit of tax collection, the *beylerbey*'s primary task was to ensure the consistency of the region's revenue stream. Given the volatility of overlapping alliance strategies, however, relationships brokered in the province often inhibited the fulfillment of this role and frustrated the designs of the council to prioritize the treasury.

A few months after his removal from office Yusuf Sayfa still malingered and asserted his own claims to resources in the region. He even went so far as to allegedly murder a representative from the former vizier, Hafız Ahmad Paşa, sent to collect an annuity of sixty-three "loads" of *akçe*s from "the treasury of Trablus."[60] The sultan's order to Husayn, acting *beylerbey* of Trablus, to its *kadı*, and to a *kapıcıbaşı* (military commander) stationed there weaves a story of intrigue quite daring in its particulars and demonstrative of the liberties Yusuf Sayfa felt capable of taking. According to notes in the *mühimme* registers, Yusuf was accused of killing the representative and his two servants, stealing their possessions, and then sealing the bodies in a sack and throwing them into water under a bridge. When, under investigation, Yusuf Sayfa sought to incriminate the representative by placing some of the servants' effects in his lodgings and thereby avoid paying the customary fine for murder, an edict directed the officiates of justice to investigate the affair and arrest and punish the murderers. The edict notes, however, that this was the second command sent in regard to these events, which indicates that the Ottoman establishment was quite obviously disarmed by distance and its efforts thwarted, in part, by its own dependency on intermediaries, including the Sayfa family members themselves.[61] Thus, although it commands the local officials in Trablus to abide by the order and mete out punishment according to the *shari'a*, the edict specifically charges its imperial representative, the *kapıcıbaşı*, with fulfilling the sultanate's wishes. Although the *kadı* should be the person responsible for officiating in these matters, the *kapıcıbaşı* was singled out instead. Furthermore, the edict notes that he would be questioned on his return to the threshold of the sultanate and should therefore make certain that he fulfilled his responsibilities with the utmost care. Yusuf Sayfa's audacity, and the Ottoman establishment's reliance on an individual directly tied to the sultanate, indicates the persistent challenge to imperial sovereignty despite repeated military interventions. Furthermore, as Yusuf Sayfa seemingly escaped punishment, was later restored to the position of *beylerbey*, and continued to play a role as regional power broker for another fifteen years, the threats contained in the edict were obviously never carried out.

In fact, Yusuf continued to adjudicate matters in the region even when not serving officially as the governor of Trablus. This was particularly the case when the sultanate attempted to stop Husayn from disruptive acts against both the local population and various agents sent from Istanbul to collect revenues assigned as salaries.[62] Husayn at one point went so far as to attack a representative of the finance minister, who barely escaped with his life: "As I have been informed that [your son] has frequently wronged and oppressed [people] in the aforesaid manner, my noble order has been issued that a legal investigation [of the matter] be conducted and justice be done."[63] Compelled to pay an indemnity, Husayn retained his position only to turn around and seize a ship carrying provisions meant to relieve a famine in the territories of Safad.[64] He arrested two *sipahi*s serving as the boat's captains and arrested and killed a janissary and three servants. The edict turns to Damascus and its *kadı* to adjudicate the matter, as clearly there would be little recourse for justice within the provincial headquarters of Trablus. The edict commands that the matter be investigated, copies of relevant documents proving the case (*da'va*) be made and forwarded to Istanbul, and that all should be done according to the noble *shari'a*. Two years later, however, in 1616, Husayn was still the acting *beylerbey*, and yet another order was sent to Yusuf Sayfa to investigate an issue pertaining to the apportionment of tax collection privileges. As an activity that typified the duties of the governor, it would seem that at least from the perspective of the Ottoman establishment, Yusuf rather than Husayn was the guardian of imperial order in the province. Thus, the edict addresses Yusuf Sayfa as the "previous" *beylerbey*, although by now it had been a full six years since he held the post, indicating that he continued to function as the only recourse or hope for proper adjudication of the province's affairs.[65] In it, he is asked to requisition from army general (*bolukbaşı*) Shalhub the fees from a *mukata'at* amounting to fifteen thousand piasters that rightfully belonged to his rival kinsman, Emir Yunus [Harfush], *sancakbey* of Homs.[66]

The problem, however, was that the *bolukbaşı* possessed a legal deed to revenue generated from the cultivation of these lands, attained when he had also been granted control of the Biqa' by the *beylerbey* of Damascus.[67] The internal balance of the region changed dramatically shortly thereafter, as the newly appointed grand vizier, (Öküz) Mehmed Paşa, intervened more directly in the various alliances forged in Greater Syria.[68] While he was barracked in Aleppo on his way to the eastern front, many local chieftains appeared before him to pay homage and vie for favor amid efforts to unseat the Sayfas from dependent territories of Trablus. As one example of this reapportionment of alliances and territories, Yunus Harfush paid off the grand vizier and was restored to his position in the Biqa' and Homs as a result. Yet *bolukbaşı* Shalhub had steadfastly refused to relinquish the funds despite repeated sultanic commands to that effect. Yusuf Sayfa, although disadvantaged by these new imperial alignments, was still called on either to force the delivery of the funds or to extract their equivalent from lands under the jurisdiction of the *bolukbaşı*. Husayn was simply ignored as an imperial recourse in the sultanate's effort to infuse certificates of rights with a modicum of authority.

Shares and Principles: The Definition of Order

The sultanate would continue to accommodate Sayfa's fickle behavior, a source of constant imperial complaint, for the next decade. Even murder or accusations of constant pillage did not warrant the permanent removal of either father or son from the possibility of loyal servitude. Thus, Husayn retained his official seat until 1616 and was accorded, like his father before him, both praise and opprobrium in the correspondence issued from the Ottoman establishment. Early in his appointment as *beylerbey*, an edict enthusiastically acknowledged his service to the sultanate in previous efforts against the Ma'n.[69] He was commended for his courage, service in the army, and trusteeship of the province. The edict enumerates a textual itinerary of imperial expectations for provincial custodianship. These expectations entailed industrious efforts in maintaining the territory, ability in both controlling and protecting the *re'aya*, and diligence in collecting state monies and dispatching them to Istanbul in a timely manner. Word of these loyal services had reached Istanbul, and Husayn Sayfa was deemed worthy of the sultan's exalted attention (*'inayet-i 'aliye*). Consequently, the edict reaffirmed Husayn in his position as *beylerbey* and underscored the connection between provincial governorship and the imperial treasury by commanding his continued support of the imperial treasury. Amid the various duties expected of him, protecting the province and attending to the affairs of its inhabitants, Husayn was especially rewarded for his fiscal responsibilities as manager of imperial resources.

Shortly after this paean, however, the reluctant interdependency of the sultanate on the aegis of a fickle governor becomes visible once again. Subcontracting tax-collection rights was a strategy, both regional and imperial, to broker political support. The sultanate welcomed the practice when it reinforced imperial claims to revenue and chastised the *beylerbey* when it served his own territorial designs. Ideally, the *beylerbey* acted to sustain and extend sovereign territorial claims, yet clearly in practice these claims were severely jeopardized by regional alliances. The Sayfas consistently relied on garrisoned forces in Damascus to augment their own power, and in return for military support, they subcontracted rights to tax collection. This relationship remained a sore point throughout the Sayfa family's claim to the provincial governorship and, under Husayn, the sultanate called on the governor and the finance minister of Damascus to assist once more in curtailing the practice. One edict sought to reclaim rights to imperial lands in the province of Trablus[70] by asserting that monies collected from villages (*kariyeler*) and farms (*mezarʿe*) on imperial lands attached to the tax farms (*mukataʿat*) of Trablus rightfully belonged to the treasury but had been wrongfully rented out instead to regimental commanders and other members of the janissary corps in Damascus. The edict forbade the janissaries to control or interfere with imperial lands in any way. This misappropriation of funds was further qualified as an abuse of justice and was used to legitimize the intervention of the sultanate. The edict was issued "to restore justice" after reports that the janissaries oppressed the *reʿaya* had reached Istanbul. The *beylerbey* and *defterdar* of Damascus were further asked for written documentation of the offending parties' names and details, thus attesting to a secondary effort to constrain the circulation of contrary textual authorities or future claims for rewards and privileges. Subcontracting was reframed as a perversion of justice, and order was restored ostensibly to protect the *reʿaya* from oppression, but implicitly it secured the reassertion of imperial oversight. Restoration of justice further depended on the continued circulation of information, a priceless commodity of its own as the Ottoman establishment sought any means necessary to maintain territorial sovereignty.

Yet subcontracting was also a mechanism deployed by the sultanate to co-opt and control regional power brokers. An edict issued to the *beylerbey* and *defterdar* of Trablus thus demonstrates a moment, in contrast to the previous example, when a janissary was explicitly legitimized by imperial favor. The *hükm* provides an intricate map of the techniques for making official appointments and of the continued role that Damascus and Aleppo played in the *eyalet* of Trablus, once a subdistrict of these urban regimes. The finance minister of Trablus had written a letter to the sultanate explaining that a *serdar* (commanding officer) or *bolukbaşı* (regimental commander) had traditionally been appointed to collect taxes for the treasury of Trablus. In response, the imperial council's order reinforced the authority of the *defterdar* to follow through on his suggested appointee for the collection of revenue. As referenced in the edict, the finance minister had recommended one 'Ali Idris, from among the *bolukbaşı* of the Damascene janissaries, for this position and described his qualifications: energetic and upright service. For these reasons he was appointed *serdar* of the treasury of Trablus. But janissaries from Aleppo, with their own memorandum of appointment (*tezkere*) issued by their commanding officer, had arrived with a counterclaim, stating that "this is contrary to custom and cause for disturbance." The *defterdar* therefore requested the intercession of the imperial council, and the right to appoint 'Ali Idris and forbid any interference from the rival janissary cohort. Thus, the edict commands that if 'Ali *bolukbaşı* was indeed functioning as *serdar* for the treasury, he should be officially appointed in recognition of his upright and perfect service. Furthermore, the *defterdar* should forbid anyone from acting contrary to the customary granting of rights, even those who possess a written memorandum, if there is a "noble order" that contradicts their request.

The convoluted distinctions in this edict—memorandums accompanied by noble orders and those without; janissaries qualified to assume the position of *serdar*/tax collector and impostors; practices functioning from earlier times and those that disrupt the norm—dramatically convey the minute negotiations necessary to ensure the "rightful" appointment of state agents in the field. Janissaries must not control imperial land unless, it would seem, the imperial council itself assigned that right and, in doing so, affirmed its power to define the terms and principles of provincial shares. Furthermore, the edict recognized that such appointments were "customary" and long practiced in the region and so did not forbid them, as such, but rather prohibited the mechanisms by which such positions were granted. Yet conditions on the ground forced the sultanate to compete not only with varying consortiums of men with rival claims to resources but also with varying collections of documents and archives. Free-floating and potentially counterfeit documents were especially troubling because they enacted the Ottoman language of rule without first attaining the authority to do so; thus, they jeopardized the legitimacy of the imperial contract. Authentic documentary evidence was thus increasingly important to an imperial administration ever reliant on written orders. References to previous orders sent, letters and petitions received by the imperial council, legitimate certificates and memorandums, and those distributed by dismissed imperial agents, as well as to registers of cases concerning provincial affairs, all testify to the vibrancy and ambiguity of circulated texts.[71] Many edicts in the *mühimme* appear to be "shouting" for attention among the bustle of paper; thus, they tend also to contain a repetitive insistence in the various directives that "my present noble order" is the right and true one. A command sent to the *beylerbey* of Trablus concerning tax evasion from the Druze instructs him to collect old and new revenue "according to my present order."[72] He is further told to "pay no attention to any orders sent earlier" and that he is "bound by my present order." Sent in May of 1595, amid the various upheavals and redistricting efforts in the region of Trablus outlined earlier, this edict suggests that even the commands issued by the sultanate may contradict each other, given the shifting ground of its authority in the province. As a result, at times, recent edicts trumped past ones, and at other times, their repetition reinforced previous instructions.

The Kadı *of Last Resort: Laying Claim to the* Shari'a

It is not surprising that the heavy burden of managing imperial interest was often shared with the local judge (*kadı*), who, after the *beylerbey*, was the second most common addressee of sultanic proclamations sent to Trablus. The crucial presence of the *kadı* in directives to the province suggests that the *shari'a* courts in the former heartlands of Muslim dynastic systems became increasingly intertwined with the imperial administrative apparatus, unlike the strategies deployed in the occupied Transdanubian territories.[73] Corresponding to overlapping functions between *kanun* and *shari'a*, as well as between *din* (religion) and *devlet* (sultan or state), edicts addressed to the *kadı* indicate a fundamental ambiguity in the role played by religious precepts and legal traditions in an imperial ethos that embraced Islam as one of its legitimizing principles.[74] Links between imperial strength and religious purity also inflected edicts addressed solely to the *beylerbey*, where defense and protection of the inhabitants were also framed as strengthening "the true religion" and the sultan's "imperial majesty."[75] No easy line distinguishes *kadı* from *beylerbey* or *shari'a* from *kanun* in the expanding territorial and textual reach of the sultanate, and the edicts explored here indicate two primary arenas in which a *kadı* was called on to adjudicate matters of administrative concern. The first entails the transfer of property, a key function of the *shari'a* courts as they managed issues of inheritance, contractual law, and commercial transactions. When shifts in ownership or management of properties also entailed tax collection privileges, *kadı* and *beylerbey* acted in concert to secure imperial resources, especially in cases that addressed the proper supervision and collection of remuneration from *vakıf*s.[76] The second area of overlap occurred in moments of social, fiscal, or criminal disorder, when the *kadı* and the *beylerbey* were instructed to act in concert to carry out imperial orders. These entailed a range of diverse issues, from the anxieties pursuant to rebellious elements in the province to illegal activities concerning commodities such as soap or counterfeiting or to the more obvious penalties assigned for murder, treachery, and vigilante actions.[77]

One edict, although from a slightly later period (1663), testifies to the almost naturalized presence of the *kadı* within a list of imperial representatives and officeholders tasked with ensuring the safe delivery of the treasury, or rather the chest containing collected revenues, from Trablus to Istanbul.[78] It addressed *kadı*s, *mütesellim*s, *kethüda*s, *serdar*s of janissaries, and all *dızdar*s (wardens) along the road from Trablus to the threshold of the sultanate. They were collectively required to keep watch, appoint soldiers to guard it, and to pass it on from one to the other until it arrived safely in Istanbul. Collective action was also required in moments of potential chaos, when the *kadı* became an imperial resource. In the context of Trablus, where trade with Venice and Tuscany and coastal access provided an entrée for multiple currencies, imperial control over currency also notably required the attention of multiple authorities. Monetary fluctuations and monetization of resources had increased empire-wide, and Trablus became a test case for the consequences.[79] The *beylerbey*, *kadı*, and *defterdar* of Trablus were all called on, for example, when forgeries and adulteration of the *akçe* destabilized the value of revenue remittances in the early seventeenth century. Stating clear knowledge that forgeries had occurred, and that the *akçe* was then circulated at neither the correct measure nor the full weight, the edict holds each trustee of imperial order "responsible and subject to reprimand (*mes'ūl* *ve mu'āteb*)" for this state of affairs. The representatives were then ordered to abide by the command and to punish anyone who acts contrary to the purposes of the sultanate.[80] The edict suggests the sultanate relied on regional administrators to stamp out financial crimes.

Anxieties over revenue remission were consistently relayed to both the *kadı* and the *beylerbey*, and the edicts doing so linked imperial rights to the jurisdiction of the *shari'a* court. The ordering principles of the *shari'a* are conspicuously present in commands that include the *kadı* as one of the addressees. In such cases, "abide by the noble *şar'*" rather than the "noble command" may operate as the concluding formula for the text. Still, it would be dangerous to divide the two forms, as they often worked in tandem, which purposely suggested that sultanic and divine order were codependent. This symbiotic relationship became particularly pronounced in cases where edicts from the imperial council sought to manage revenues once apportioned as *vakıf* to deceased servants of the sultanate.[81] In these situations, the imperial council was absolutely dependent on reports issued from the provinces concerning the dereliction of duties with regard to *vakıf* remittances. Thus, when Muhammad—the supervisor of the *vakıf*s in Trablus and Aleppo bequeathed by Mehmed Paşa[82]—sent a letter reporting that for the ten years since Mehmed Paşa's death the rent from two shops, a mill, and the fixed tax sum (*maktu'*) from the village Kufur, all part of the designated *vakıf* revenue, had not been paid, the council acted promptly.[83] The order reviews the allegations reported by Muhammad that local *emin*s confiscated two shops near the port of Trablus, which rented for forty-eight piasters a year, and turned them into a large salt storehouse without paying the set rent, and that the people of the village of Kufur have also not paid taxes for the last ten years. The edict commands that "the rent of the two shops and the fixed (*maktu'*) revenue of the said village, and of the *vakıf*, be brought under control on behalf of its supervisor." Furthermore, the *kadı* and *beylerbey* were directed, on arrival of the order, to collect the unpaid rent from the *emin*s and the revenue from Kufur. They should do so "according to the *şar'*," restore the rightful fees to the *vakıf*, and ensure that the supervisor retains control of the revenues and is not thwarted by the *emin*s or by workers in the commercial properties. The command exhorts the *kadı* and the *beylerbey* not to waste "a single *akçe*" and to exert themselves in order to render the "*vakıf*s productive" now in the interest of the imperial treasury. The treasury therefore places its management and fiscal supervision within the normative practices of imperial administration in the provinces.

When the *beylerbey* himself becomes one of the parties willing to abscond with *vakıf* revenues, then the *kadı*, as the sole representative of sultanic interests, must act alone to ensure the brokering of responsible administration. In 1610, during the period that Yusuf Sayfa was removed from the position in favor of his son, the former governor's illegal control of *vakıf* revenues became yet another part of the troublesome transition from one *beylerbey* to the next.[84] Again, knowledge of these matters derived from the reports of official and unofficial sources. In this case an appointed messenger (*çavuş*), Safar, was entrusted with the supervision of the *vakıf* fees for the late grand vizier, İbrahim Paşa.[85] He sent a letter on his arrival in Trablus reporting that when he sought to take control of a commercial building (*han*) from the deceased's *vakıf*, it was brought to his attention that it had been illegally controlled by the former *beylerbey* for several years without paying rent. On arrival of the order, the *kadı* was directed to determine whether the building had indeed been under the custodianship of Yusuf Sayfa and, if so, then to "act according to the *şār*ʿ." In other words, he was to prove that this was indeed the case and return the *han* to the *vakıf*. The *kadı* should further "collect all the rent due to the *vakıf* until now, according to the *şār*ʿ" and "not do anything contrary to the noble *şār*ʿ."

Both the circumstances of this edict and the language deployed in it highlight the intricate relationship between illegality, authority, and the discourse of legitimacy that suffuse the *mühimme*. What was illegal in the eyes of the imperial council was not precisely Yusuf Sayfa's continued control of revenues derived from the *han*; instead, the council was concerned about the back rent he owed and whether it could be collected by Çavuş Safar. Although ostensibly the *kadı*'s directive was to investigate the matter according to guidelines of the *shariʿa*, the order treated it as a foregone conclusion ("after the matter is proven") that Yusuf Sayfa owed rent. The final statement, however, "do not do anything contrary to the noble *şār*ʿ," unlike others that concluded with adaptations of "act only in accordance with this present order," couched imperial interest within legalese derived from the *shariʿa*. Calling on the *shariʿa*, like calling on the *kadı* himself, represented both a practical strategy and a moral tradition and wove a web of legitimacy around demands for the proper management of revenue streams. The subtle interweaving of these codes of authority and legitimacy, imperial and divine, belies any easy disengagement of the two and suggests, at least within the context of the *mühimme*, that they worked together to secure sultanic interest.

The two records pertaining to *vakıf* discussed here touch not only on overlapping fields of authority between the *beylerbey* and the *kadı*, and the interweaving of divine and imperial law, but also on the heterogeneous nature of *vakıf* administration. Here, instead of a strict set of rules and definitions, we see a combination of commercial properties and rural taxes into a single *vakıf*; transformation from one market usage (shops) to another (a *han*); transition from an endowment assigned to public servants (Mehmed or İbrahim Paşa) to one held in private hands; and generally the continued difficulty in amassing expected revenues from a potentially unwilling tax base of villagers, cultivators, urban laborers, and local merchants *cum* strongmen. The recalcitrant *emin*s, whether empowered as governor or not, were unwilling to relinquish personal control to imperial agents, even though the governor was himself intended to carry out the interests of the sultanate. Often, the *kadı* stood as the Ottoman "official" of last resort, demonstrating the critical importance of the judicial system to the administrative management of the empire.

The Space Between: Imperial Expectation and Regional Implementation

The expectations and limits of sultanic authority are immediately palpable in the orders directed to the province of Trablus and contained in the *mühimme* registers. The vastness of the Ottomans' rule was an acknowledged part of the brokered alignment practices used by the administrative apparatus and was in some ways advantageous to the men of power in the provinces: space and time together confabulated against direct oversight of regional affairs. Thus, the edicts embody an art of persuasion. Intent on bringing its addressees into a shared universe of ruling authority and in enticing their acquiescence, the language of command was tempered by awareness of the space that existed, both literal and metaphorical, between the order and its implementation. Hence, the expectations set in these commands also reveal the gap between imperial goals and outcomes wherein lies the real, albeit curtailed, agency afforded to the *beylerbey*. The edicts' formal construction clearly manifests this space as a rhetorical distinction between the two key phrases "*ḥükm ki*" and "*buldurum ki*." The first, "as it is ordered," precedes the specific content of each set of instructions, and the latter, "as I have commanded," concludes this process and marks the start of another brief declarative summary of the order as issued directly from the mouth of the sultan. Implementation could only be phrased in the conditional, such as "upon receipt of my noble command, you will . . . ," and was typically accompanied by a thinly veiled threat: "beware of carelessness and negligence," "punish anyone who acts contrary" to this order, "beware of not complying with this order," or "do not delay in complying with this order."[86] Many of the orders also allude to instances of past cooperation as a way of highlighting a previously agreed on performance of obligation and service. They remark on the reputation of the *beylerbey* as one known to uphold the standards of rule in the province and to dutifully follow the imperatives sent his way. The repetitious language of the edict, the attempt at coercion through the power of the pen and word of the sultan, and, finally, the reference to previous examples of compliance or complicity, all point toward the exhortative and dependent nature of sultanic power: command structures could only be implemented by proxy.

Also clear in the examples provided throughout this chapter is a hierarchy of sultanic concerns that structured the decrees and regulated their dispersion. In brief, these were the receipt of monies from the province writ large; the appointment of "deserving" men to ensure that this occurred; preservation of a regional status quo, where no one individual or group gained primacy or threatened imperial claims; a normalized system of tax collection acceptable to the agricultural producers so as not to provoke flight or abandonment; quick action on the part of its agents when any of these were disrupted; and thus the maintenance of order and harmony in which each received his or her due. The repeated insistence on these overarching concerns served to translate the idealized norms of justice and proper order into an imperial standard of administration. Disturbances over the efficient transport of revenue to the imperial city, "unlawful" appropriations of funds, restless *re'aya* complaining about oppression, and unpaid rents evoked a definitive sultanic response as much as outright armed rebellion. Both daily disruptions and planned uprisings challenged expectations of authority and leadership, at once enshrining principles of imperial order even as they disrupted divisions of shares.

The *beylerbey*, along with the *defterdar* and the *kadı*, was indispensable to the achievement of imperial expectations. This dependency explains the imperial hesitation to follow through on threats issued in response to myriad disruptions, from "plunder" to delayed revenue streams to criminal ventures. The antics of Yusuf Sayfa were reprimanded, but also ameliorated, because of the interdependent nature of imperial power. For it was the imperial treasury—synecdoche of Ottoman power itself—and the imperial city—symbol of its glory—that reign supreme throughout the *mühimme*, "because the provisioning of Istanbul is an important matter."[87] So prominent is this treasury that it appears almost as a living character, hungry and demanding, petulant and ill-tempered, and emerging as the ultimate concern in the language of administration.[88] Successful stewardship of the provincial revenue was consistently equated with the relative calm and security of the populace at large. We can see this in the links between prosperity and the preservation of the peace that pervade the individual edicts, as well as in the specific praises offered to the *beylerbey* by the sultanic voice. As manager of the provincial treasury, the *beylerbey* was charged with the prosperity and comfort of the province, the protection of its assets, and the continuity of its human and natural resources.

Herein lay the key to successful provincial administration: direct collection of agricultural revenue through imperial agents of a volatile territory was abandoned in favor of contractual agreements with regional power holders with the material and political means necessary to accumulate capital. The goal was to strike a proper balance between collecting enough from the agricultural and human resources of the province to replenish the treasury, without provoking undue dissatisfaction that might lead to flight or the permanent abandonment of cultivatable lands. This "balance" equaled "justice" within the rationale of the state. In the case of Yusuf Sayfa's appointment to ensure the "equitable" collection of Trablus's fortunes, the imperial government assumed his outsider status within this fraught local power structure would be a catalyst for loyal adherence to commands from the imperial council. But this instead forced Yusuf Sayfa to engage all the more exhaustively in his own alliance strategies. The distribution of tax-collection duties (and thus the potential for personal gain) was an effective strategy for Yusuf to appease competing regional leaders and bolster support among janissaries in Damascus, who could thus prolong his ability to "represent" the province to the sultanate. Viewed from the administrative apparatus in Istanbul, however, these recipients were "undeserving" in that they did not participate directly in any contractual relationship with the sultanate. In other words, revenue was siphoned away from the imperial treasury yet was not used to cement ties of duty and obligation through the imperial circulation of privilege. Furthermore, this regional allocation of tax collection drained capital from an empire desperate for cash to maintain its frontiers. Such turmoil had its limits when the quietude of the population at large was threatened and escalating complaints concerning injustice and oppression jeopardized the legitimacy of Ottoman sovereignty.

As a result, concern for the populace emerged as a priority only in moments of distress, and the Ottoman establishment identified this distress as unsanctioned interference in the circle of textual command and provincial obedience. Registers of the *mühimme* characterize provincial actors primarily in the negative, as they emerge as potential threats to stability or as recalcitrant participants in the administrative cycle. The "undeserving persons" are rarely elaborated on, but their label becomes meaningful when fitted into the imperial expectations of balance and justice. They were "undeserving" because they did not abide by the categories of supervision inscribed through imperial command and so emerged as outsiders and foreigners to its proper functioning: property-owning janissaries not directly appointed through channels certified by the imperial council, officials withholding money from the imperial treasury, "bandits" pilfering wealth from the populace, regional families assuming power without imperial sanction, and previously sanctioned authorities amassing personal power past their deadline of appointment—all drained resources from the treasury and thus from the ability of the sultan to ensure the reproduction of justice. Subcontracting tax collection, from the perspective of the sultanate, led to the oppression of the *re'aya*, and imperial commands were issued to "restore justice" and reset the balance of the province.[89] As such, alliances also enfeebled sultanic authority and threatened territorial power, serving as insidious threads of rebellion from within an administrative system constructed to guard imperial order. The interplay of sovereign authority, administrative strategy, and textual anxiety invoked in these edicts illustrates the fragility of social stability and thus of imperial legitimacy premised on its preservation.

Yet the repetition of threats and insults directed at interfering provincial actors, and the strenuous effort displayed in the *mühimme* registers to reassert imperial oversight, should not overshadow the art of rhetorical persuasion that they also enact. Along with recitations of honor and praise, constant refrains of "guarding," "preserving," "promoting," and "protecting" exhort the *beylerbey* to play a positive role in reproducing the cycle. When the system worked, commands and rewards together crafted a symbiotic relationship between regional representative and imperial expectation. In a moment of imperial exuberance, Yusuf Sayfa was lauded for upholding the principles of provincial administration.[90] Reports of his diligence had reached the sultanate, and the accolades enumerate a list of imperial expectations. He protected and guarded the province but also promoted the prosperity and general well-being of the people (*re'aya ve beraya*). This well-being was secured by maintaining order in the territory and by the sultan's imperial justice ensuring "the serenity of the poor," a phrase that captures the internal tensions of proper order and stability. This was not a system of full equality and had no pretense as such. The *re'aya*'s "serenity" should be assured, but their impoverished condition was an expected, and even an essential, agent in its reproduction. "Undeserving" participants threatened to overburden cultivators with increased extortions of taxes, provisions, and labor, thereby encroaching on imperial profit and authority. The edict thus calls for God's protection on Yusuf Sayfa because he has "done what was expected" of him by weeding out potential profiteers. He was then commanded to continue to act with zealous commitment, as befits his temperament, and to preserve the province "in a manner that is compatible with religion and with the honor and dignity of my state." The *beylerbey* was further urged to exert himself "without limit" in these endeavors in order to preserve the province and to prohibit outlaws from doing harm.

Accolades in the edict served as both a commendation and a petition for the *beylerbey*'s continued participation in preserving stability. Furthermore, the rhetorical reference to God's protection signaled that loyal service preserved both the sanctity of the Muslim community and the authority of the sultanate. Consequently, the sultan's "command" that Yusuf Sayfa should continue to comport himself in a deserving manner suborns the willing participation of the *beylerbey* in a system maintained by both divine and imperial power. That this participation, if not voluntary, could not easily be forced is clearly indicated throughout the edicts directed toward the Sayfa family. Gifts of swords and robes of honor, requests for outstanding payments to the finance department, prayers for Yusuf and Husayn Sayfa's welfare, and accusations of pillage, murder, theft, and dubious alignments follow each other in quick succession. What remains constant, however, is a discursive and administrative strategy intent on yoking the interests of the *beylerbey* to that of the Ottoman establishment in order to preserve stability and the fiscal viability of the empire. The *beylerbey* was entrusted with the "prosperity and comfort of the people" and thus with the foundational materials of imperial triumph.

The End of an Alliance

The key power brokers for Greater Syria who had been put in place after the imperial military invasion in 1585 had vanished by 1641.[91] Husayn Sayfa, in an attempt to curry favor with the grand vizier who had dismissed him from office in 1616, accompanied Mehmed Paşa on his campaign against the Safavids. His plans went awry, however, when the *beylerbey* of Aleppo, Karakaş Mehmed Paşa, captured him on his return from the eastern front and executed him in March of that same year.[92] Yusuf Sayfa gradually lost allies, both within his extended family and across the territories that he had once ruled through strong-armed policies and deals with other local chieftains. He fought to retain his governorship after Fakhr al-Din Ma'n returned from Tuscany in 1617 and was once again restored as *beylerbey* of Safad. Between 1618 and 1625 Yusuf Sayfa variously collaborated with and fought the Ma'ns for control of the province and for support from officials and janissaries in Damascus, Aleppo, and Homs. His inability to secure the resources necessary to maintain regional allies, however, or to sustain his contractual relations with the sultanate meant that when he died in 1625, his territorial reach was limited to the city of Trablus and to his original fortress of Akrad.[93] By 1627 the position of *beylerbey* of Trablus, and by 1633 the Akrad fortress as well, were in the hands of Fakhr al-Din. Yet this success was short-lived, as the strength of the Ma'n in the region transgressed yet another limit from the perspective of the Ottoman establishment, which feared that his power might even enable the capture of Damascus. Murad IV thus appointed Küçük Ahmed Paşa, a provincial statesman experienced in quelling revolts in Anatolia, to the position of *beylerbey* of Damascus with the express purpose of eliminating Fakhr al-Din and the territorial reach of the Ma'n. Küçük Ahmed Paşa captured him in 1633, and he was subsequently imprisoned in Istanbul at the fort of Yediküle and beheaded by imperial order in 1635.[94]

Still, from 1579 to 1625 Trablus and the Sayfa family served as a prism for the administrative concerns of the Ottoman establishment. The fortunes of each were linked, and this alignment worked to cement the Sayfa family's territorial control even as they ostensibly served as proxies for the sultanate. In moments after major military campaigns, or when passing viziers and governors directed their attention to the affairs of the coast and its hinterland, direct imperial intervention seemed capable of resetting the terms of these alignments. Punitive military campaigns, however, were too costly during a period when both eastern and northern fronts were embroiled in constant wars, so textual commands sought to maintain order when the army could not. The *mühimme* focused on security, stability, and the rights of the sultanate to the resources of the province. Yet these textual commands could only approximate absolutist control through rhetorical formulae that asserted the territorial sovereignty of the Ottoman dynast and the justness of his rule. Imperial edicts may have defined expectations, yet they were conflicted by geographic and sociopolitical obstacles and dependent on playing regional factions off of each other. Still, the copies of these commands in the registers of the imperial council did serve as guidelines for appointment, standards for recognizing deserving personages, and as a database for reviewing the apportionment of revenue. The registers thereby created the threads of authority the edicts were meant to embody and shaped a discourse of provincial order that encompassed regional and imperial actors alike.

The Sayfa family and the *mühimme* illuminate the intricate transactions undertaken between 1585 and 1641 to police the threshold between official and rebel, governor and villain. During this same period definitions of order, rebellion, and loyal service became part of a contested political discourse concerning the nature of Ottoman imperial power. Produced in part to navigate shifts in military technologies, the increased commodification of the land regime, and the emergence of new interest groups as a consequence, this discourse gradually objectified the Ottoman past and perceived the present as a corruption from an ideal. As I argue in my final chapter, the textual genres and administrative practices deployed to assert Ottoman territorial sovereignty in the fifteenth and sixteenth centuries became idealized categories of order and judgment in the seventeenth.

PART III

Objectifying Generic Politics and Practices

CHAPTER SIX

ON THE PERFECT STATE

An Ottoman Vision of Order

> The laws of the Ottoman sultanate violated . . . the treasury possessing a deficit; the governors torn apart by infighting; the judges receptive to bribery; the opportunity to tackle the enemy [missed]; among those close to the [sultan] treason; among the theologians a lust for gold and inanity; among the *re'āya* futile labor and fear; in brief: innovations and all sorts of grievance everywhere.
>
> —*Kitāb-i müstetāb*[1]

Monitoring expansive imperial domains, as the examples of Buda and Trablus illustrate, entailed an elaborate textual apparatus defined more by its vulnerabilities than by its ability to command order. Potential rebellions cast an ever-present shadow over imperial authority and generated a discursive anxiety over the border between rebel and servant. This border, as much as the empire's more tangible frontiers, preoccupied Ottoman elites from the 1580s to the 1650s. They perceived the manifold transgressions against it as a collapse in the natural order of Ottoman imperial strength. Scholarly elites during this period revived philosophic, juristic, and legal genealogies of proper government within a new political project: objectifying the Ottoman past in order to create practical guides for navigating future crises. In the process, they reenergized intellectual debates about the nature of proper governance and developed a more abstract conception of the state as a distinct political body. The formal characteristics of these guides combined the highly literary traditions of both *adab* (the polite arts) and *nasihatname* (advice to rulers) into more comprehensive exercises in historical analysis. Intellectuals produced tracts and memoranda, or *risaleler*, that sought to intervene in and redefine the fundamentals of Ottoman dynastic power.[2] The "Perfect State" presents a number of these treatises, composed mostly by former administrators and bureaucrats, and argues that they often deployed administrative genres such as the *kanunname*, the cadastral survey, the memorandum (*telhis*), or the sultanic edict (*hükm*) in an effort to outline a new model for assessing governance. Authors placed a new emphasis on administrative history in order to redefine how the Ottoman establishment "remembered" past policies.[3] Whereas the textual edicts discussed in previous chapters functioned to extend the territorial reach of sovereign control, the treatises explored here respond to the potential collapse of this textual order and seek alternative strategies to renew the life cycle of the Ottoman Empire. The following sections thus return to the narrative arc traced through the work of Katip Çelebi in my introduction and situate reform-minded tracts within both regional and global crises of the late sixteenth and early seventeenth centuries.

Manuals of advice framed as *nasihat al-muluk* (Arabic, "counsel for kings"), *pandnameh*, and *andarznameh* (Persian, "book of advice") were part of a Eurasian "mirrors for princes" genre that accompanied the establishment of centralized courts and dynasties from the eleventh century to the fourteenth.[4] Within the Arabo-Persian tradition this practice of counseling the court helped to legitimize, even as it critiqued, the emergence of temporal states in a postcaliphal world. After the collapse of the 'Umayyad dynasty in 750, the Muslim community was no longer led by God's vice regent and Muhammad's successor, and questions of rightful leadership and sovereignty became the major preoccupation of an emergent scholarly cohort. Beginning in the fifteenth century, these scholars reacted to the extension of sovereign power and the universalist and absolutist claims that buttressed it with increasing caution.[5] They emphasized just government and divine sanction as key organizing principles for proper governance, and scholar-bureaucrats drew from mixed jurisprudential, philosophical, and historical conventions to devise a textual mechanism for dispensing their ideas.

Traditional advice writers folded their critique into a literary genre of counsel that typically interwove multiple authorial perspectives. Quotations from figures of authority, often from the remote past, and stories set in a distant time and place provided a channel for political commentary in the historical present. The authors' dependence on the continued patronage of rulers put them in a precarious position, in which proffering suggestions for royal improvement involved a real risk of offense and the possibility of punishment. Thus, in their treatises they strove to balance elements of praise with those of counsel and critique. The genre thus functioned as a form of camouflage, as adhering to its conventions offered the author protection and spared its recipient from the obligation of censuring him. These techniques of leveraging multiple layers of authority and speaking through other writers allowed the author to put critical distance between himself and the advice he was conveying.

Books of counsel were therefore hybrid literary forms, combining traditions of political philosophy and ethics (*akhlaq*) with the assembled literary treatise (*adab*) composed of maxims, proverbs, verse, and anecdotes and organizing them according to a particular theme or topic. Both were often presented.[6] The genre was sufficiently flexible for authors to take up a wide range of topics, not all of which were directly or obviously related to governance or governed by literary convention.[7] Advice literature was also amenable to multiple purposes: the combined aims of moral instruction and aesthetic enjoyment so prevalent in other forms of *adab* are often unmistakable, and the authorial stance of offering counsel frequently concealed more personal objectives, such as the consolidation of ties between the writer and the addressee or professional advancement.[8] But these individual treatments and arrangements still played an active role in shaping political discourse. They most often emerged during periods of crisis and came to form a bulwark against perceived sociopolitical chaos. Their role deepened, however, amid a period of global transformation and internal turmoil in the late sixteenth and early seventeenth centuries, as a sense of impending collapse prompted intellectuals to more seriously interrogate the political philosophy of the empire.

A Disordered Realm and New Managerial Tactics

Ottoman advice treatises proliferated among the environmental, social, economic, and political turbulence that characterized Eurasia in the seventeenth century and have consistently been studied against this backdrop.[9] Jan de Vries, in his now classic assessment of the seventeenth-century economic crisis, pointed to a corresponding literary phenomenon wherein "a whole school of economic reformers, the *arbitristas*, wrote mountains of tracts pleading for new measures."[10] This boom in reformist manuals tracked shifts in the ideals of statecraft and created an idealized vision of past imperial foundations in order to critique dependencies in the present. As a result, contemporary commentators identified the past as a golden age, the present as a period of decline, and the future as potential catastrophe if reform measures were not implemented. They further moralized this state of crisis by blaming natural and fiscal transformations on human corruptibility. This was especially true for writers whose privileged status was also tied to a stable agrarian economy increasingly jeopardized by the emergence of a market economy and new intermediary interest groups.[11] Rather than being peculiar to the Ottomans, courts across Eurasia shared the concern that governance had been declining since the Renaissance.[12] Authors from the two continents made similar ethical, philosophical, and medical interpretations of the body politic and articulated an imperial life cycle in order to assess current woes.

Within the Ottoman context these reform-minded writers joined a lineage of chroniclers who had long ruminated on questions of proper governance and the nature of just rule. The emergence of a stable, expansionary imperial ethos in the fifteenth and sixteenth centuries begat literary commentary on centralized power that also sought to temper strength and authority by virtuous rule. Royal counselors defined kingly attributes and prescribed actions to guard against the potentially exploitative extension of sovereign rights.[13] Beginning in the late sixteenth century, however, and coincident with a series of global and regional crises, Ottoman pamphleteers sought instead to rearticulate the fundamentals of social and political order.[14] Authors criticized the emergence of powerful interest groups both in the provinces and within the court itself, labeling these phenomena "innovations" that jeopardized the Ottoman establishment. In so doing, they transformed crisis into a novel form of political analysis that objectified the state as a phenomenon distinct from the personhood of the sultan, which set a new baseline for the assessment of sovereignty.

This vision of Ottoman imperial order emerged precisely at a moment when sovereign power, territorial control, and provincial stability were coming under particular duress, especially for Sultans Murad III (r. 1574–95),

Mehmed III (r. 1595–1603), and Ahmed I (r. 1603–17). The combination of environmental, social, and fiscal upheavals forced their courts to redefine the textual and territorial habitus of the empire. First, efforts to reterritorialize regions at the margins of imperial control after initial waves of conquest in the fifteenth and sixteenth centuries led to shifts in land-management strategies, as we saw in the previous chapter.[15] Fertile lands and their cultivation remained essential to the efficient provisioning of both the Ottoman court in Istanbul and its forces on imperial military campaigns.[16] Agricultural lands also served as the basis of a system of appeasement and co-option for both custodians and cultivators of the land.[17] Initially, this was achieved through grants of freehold tracts (*temlik*) to semialigned elites in areas of strategic concern.[18] This practice then shifted toward sultanic grants of *timar*s, which retained the lands as part of royal domain but also mandated the presence of a manager with ties of obligation to the sultanate.[19] Reassessment of *timar*s occurred after major battles and upheavals, such as for regions around Baghdad, Mosul, southwestern and northeastern Anatolia in the 1560s, Cyprus and coastal regions of the Mediterranean in the 1570s, and Greater Syria in the 1580s.[20] These administrative tactics corresponded with the privileging of the *beylerbey* as administrator of regional affairs and as a conduit for imperial control over both dispersed territories and an increasingly mobile population. But volatile monetary fluctuations from the 1550s onward, combined with escalating wars of conquest and defense, turned the Ottoman establishment increasingly toward farming out the remission of revenues to designated agents for a fixed price.[21] Already fairly standard in areas such as Greater Syria, this practice spread across the empire as demands for cash to compensate the salaried men of both the bureaucracy and the military escalated in tandem with their size.[22] This led to a commodification of the land and the ties of loyalty between servants and the sultan. Power devolved to local notables, and the sultan became one claimant among many, forced to negotiate for control over resources.[23] Such measures reinforced the empire's links with an already fluid fiscal environment and bolstered new regional markets designed to accommodate the commutation of the agricultural surplus into cash.[24] Institutions and practices such as guilds, money lending, regional and international trade, and tax farms dedicated to mints, mines, customs, and market dues all made for an extensive money economy.[25] This new financial landscape either benefited new intermediary groups or buttressed regional associational ties already tending toward independence from imperial management.

As these transformative processes continued apace, they coincided with major cultural and environmental phenomena beginning in the 1590s. The last decade of the sixteenth century corresponded to the dawn of a new millennium in the Muslim world, with the passage of 1591 to 1592 marking the transition to year 1000 in a calendrical reckoning based on the flight of the prophet Muhammad from Mecca to Yathrib (Medina) in 622. Millenarianism inspired apocalyptic visions and fueled concerns that the fabric of order would unravel and collapse.[26] The generalized sense of foreboding was then seemingly confirmed by an unprecedented drought lasting from 1591 to 1596, which was itself compounded by a miniature ice age in the first decades of the seventeenth century that trapped the inhabitants of Eurasia between arid land and freezing temperatures.[27] These dreadful environmental and cultural conditions across the imperial domains precipitated a third sociopolitical crisis, as consistent acts of banditry, hoarding resources, and exploiting cultivators triggered a massive flight from the land (*büyük kaçgun*). Widespread agricultural devastation and desperation spurred on a wave of rebellions that spanned the two decades from 1590 to 1610 and then flared up again in the 1620s and beyond. These constituted a fourth major upheaval, anachronistically labeled the "*celali* rebellions," but generally referring to mobile bands that challenged imperial control over resources or ties of loyalty. These swept the provinces from Anatolia to Greater Syria in a cycle of upheaval and revolt referenced in the previous chapter. These layers of crises further enveloped a fifth major concern: provisioning long-lasting military campaigns in the midst of drought, agricultural disarray, banditry, and famine. As we saw in Chapter 4, Ottoman military forces encountered a resurgent, more centralized Habsburg fortress defense system in a protracted engagement from 1591–92 to 1606 that concentrated on pushing the frontier boundaries around Esztergom and invading the city of Peşat as an entrée to Buda. Although neither side made notable permanent gains, the exhaustion of the war, and the resulting treaty that recognized an entente between the two powers, dampened Ottoman universalist aspirations. Furthermore, the long war in Hungarian territories overlapped with intermittent military engagements with the Safavids from 1603 to 1618, which pressed Ottoman mechanisms of provision and mobilization to their greatest extent.[28]

In combination, these pressures led to an imperial population on the move and therefore strained previous techniques for fitting provincial realities into imperial categories. The Ottoman establishment increasingly supplied cultivators with weapons to arm themselves against elements labeled *ehl-i fesad*, or criminals, by the sultanate, because they interfered with the prosperity of the realm. In actuality, the *ehl-i fesad* consisted of new interest groups capable of taking personal advantage from crisis. These included regional power brokers, bands of religious students (*suhte*) spreading from Amasya to the northern reaches of Syria, various auxiliary militias, and even designated fiscal agents in the provinces. The latter included men co-opted as district or provincial governors but also increasingly encompassed the janissary corps, which, as seen in the environs of Greater Syria, had become a hereditary privileged class and political interest group of their own. Their ranks had swelled to almost forty thousand men, their threats of mutiny taxed the imperial treasury, and their participation as subcontractors in the provinces turned *timar*s and *mukata'at* into financial investments.[29] Efforts to exert broader administrative control over revenue collection in the face of these crises led to new campaigns of centralization and a move toward imperial policies suited better to the dispersive tendencies of war, agricultural devastation, population movement, and the market. These policies can be detected in the gradual privileging of provincial (*beylerbey*) over district (*sancakbey*) governors; the creation of new internal (*enderun*) palace officials, such as the chief back eunuch (*darusa'ade agası* or *kızlar agası*), or the empowerment of older posts such as the chief gardener (*bostancıbaşaı*), as protection against the growing strength of vizier and pasha households; the stronger linkage between the sultan and the religious establishment through the position of the head jurisconsult (*şeyhülislam*); the expansion of the palace household via marriage alliances between statesmen and princesses; and the retention of potential princes in the harem instead of their dispersion across the provinces.[30] As a consequence of the latter, political factions emerged internal to the palace itself, and mothers and wives of potential or acting sultans brokered their own alliances.[31]

Fiscal registration strategies and mechanisms for extracting resources from this fluid territorial landscape also changed. The *re'aya* were increasingly kept off-record, outside the register (*defter haraci re'aya*), and thus outside of traditional textual mechanisms of control. As power in the imperial council became increasingly diffuse, and custodianship of land a commoditized practice, the systematic recording strategies of either the cadastral survey or the *mühimme* were gradually either specialized or compartmentalized. Bureaucratic records tracked provincial revenue, its collection by various tax farmers, office holders, and subcontractors, and the number of household heads in towns and villages in registers produced by the ministry of finance, the *maliyyeden müdevver.*[32] These recorded the increasingly normative imposition of extraordinary taxes (*'avarız-ı divaniye*), once used as a mechanism of provision during war and famine but now assessed as a head tax on the households of villagers and townsmen.[33] The sultanate relied on detailed (*mufassal*) *avarızhane defter*s, along with a similar investment in poll tax (*cizye*) and salary (*ruznamçe*), to implement new management procedures within a fluid imperial environment.[34] These were accompanied by forced resettlement campaigns (*sürgün*), long a strategy to deal with nomadic elements but now used to reclaim fallow lands and subvert alliances with roving populist bands.[35] Furthermore, taxes that had formerly been assessed in kind, or were collected in cash and kind in alternating years, were by the 1660s annually demanded in cash.[36] The circulation of sultanic rescripts that identified justice as the preserve of imperial order (*'adaletname*s) also intensified during this period and laid the basis for the ultimate codification of the *kanunname-i cedid.*[37] Although formally circulated in 1573–74, it contained *ferman*s, *fetva*s, and *'adaletname*s issued from the 1570s to the 1640s, thereby suggesting that it emerged as a means to rearticulate imperial control and establish a new baseline for jurisprudential action after the various upheavals outlined above. Thus, by the end of the seventeenth century, a quiet revolution in imperial management strategies was officially recognized by two major reforms: an effort to overhaul the poll tax (*cizye*) on non-Muslims (1691), and the granting of lifetime leases on tax farms (1695).[38] The imperial council used the *malikane*, or life-term revenue tax farm, to reassert control over the widespread proliferation of tax farming, which had always challenged the idealized rubric of the *timar* as the primary mechanism for collecting agricultural revenue.[39] These reforms embodied a new approach to population management, eventually finding their way into manuscript copies of the *kanunname-i cedid* intended for empire-wide distribution and application. In combination these measures suggest that the Ottoman establishment was forced to reconfigure its understanding of imperial resource acquisition and thus its ideology of authority and legitimacy.

As illustrated in the pages that follow, in response to these varied crises and administrative transformations, authors of advice manuals and memorandums generated a number of assumptions about the nature of Ottoman imperial authority and linked the fortunes of the dynast to its foundation in a system of land management dependent on the loyalty of servitors to the sultan and to the realm. They characterized the Ottoman Empire as a patrimonial system where the revenue interests of the sultanate, as expressed in the *kanunname*, were achieved by categorizing and stabilizing the social organization of productive labor. Commentators assumed that the categories deployed in the *kanunname* maintained control over the empire's vital resources and identified the *kanun-ı kadim* as the basis of sovereign power. At the heart of this sense of the rule of law was the land grant (*timar*) offered under the rubric of Ottoman authority to the *sipahi* in return for military and administrative service. The core of this agrarian system in the establishment's perception was also the family farm (*çiftlik*), a fiscal and social unit that aimed to fit diverse territories into a standard taxation rubric. They viewed the disruption of the *timar* system and the commodification of imperial service and tax-collection duties as developments that jeopardized the foundational division between an administrative and military elite (*'askeri*) and the population at large (*re'aya*). Although it was a textual assertion rather than a consistent reality, this division functioned as the discursive touchstone for the ideological productions of Ottoman elite. We have seen how this compartmentalized social order constituted an idealized paradigm of imperial expansion and territorial control that was inherently unstable, with administrative practice constantly adapting to regional demand. Even efforts to assert a generalizable textual authority and grammar of rule ran into overlapping systems of land-tenure, allowing those who were able to best manipulate categories articulated in the legal activities of the Ottoman establishment to exploit the system for personal gain. Moreover, the land grant was never implemented universally, and even at the provincial level, it still competed with regional power brokers and cultivators who moved around too much to provide a steady imperial revenue flow. In Trablus, sultanic edicts revealed how even the office of regional governorship resembled that of a tax-farm contract, thereby linking provincial administration directly to the empire's fiscal viability. Still, general and provincial *kanunname*s and directives in the *mühimme* continued to equate loyalty to the Ottoman establishment with conscientious management of the land and delineated proper behavior only when individual agents provoked systemic disorder.

The combined factors of the late sixteenth and early seventeenth centuries precipitated a crisis in the ideology of the imperial establishment writ large as it faced the disruptive consequences of drought, famine, banditry, and the market. It was precisely these crises that reform-minded Ottoman observers confronted and reinterpreted as a decline in the ability of the sultanic establishment in Istanbul to (1) assert the primacy of its revenue rights and (2) thus legitimately continue to act as a dispenser of justice and order. "Decline" thus became a discourse of reform, concentrated on elucidating, sometimes remedying, and often bemoaning, turbulent transformations that challenged the very structure of order. Statesmen and Ottoman literati thus idealized past glories, policies, and virtues. They decried the dispersion of sultanic authority, the infiltration of the *re'aya* into the elites, the sale of offices, women's political influence increasingly exerted from the harem, the diversion of *timar* resources to support those other than cavalry officers, and the immiseration of cultivators through oppressive taxation. Even though these developments were generally assessed as "practical" responses to immediate problems and ad hoc resolutions with little significant philosophical meaning, commentators significantly invoked a past intellectual genealogy and instantiated a new archival history that gradually redefined Ottoman political culture.

Gardening: A Genealogy of Order in the Midst of Crisis and Rebellion

We have seen how various chieftains and governors in Greater Syria teetered on the threshold between rebel and loyal official. The textual commotion surrounding their antics, and the events more generally associated with the year 1585 in Greater Syria, serves as a synecdoche for the fraught linkages between rebellion and the reproduction of imperial sovereignty in the late sixteenth and early seventeenth centuries. The intellectual genealogy of the rebel, specifically in relation to one of the customary terms for disruptive agents, *bağı*, illustrates how the threshold between rebel and official crystallized into a unique vision of Ottoman political consciousness and governance. This political consciousness rested on the relationships drawn between the empire as a garden of proper order, the categories that generated this order, and the new forms of social mobility that threatened the perceived foundations of the state. *Bağı*, as the dialectic against which this consciousness was constructed, enables therefore an imaginative interpretation of Ottoman political theory. The term *bāghī* (active participle of *bagha*, plural *bughāt*) hinges on the tripartite root system of Arabic grammar and, like Ottoman as a hybrid discursive register more generally, acquired meanings and moods from Persian and Turkic contexts. The word thus contains at least three interpretive levels, all linked to notions of excess, abuse, or hubris. These entail the technical language of jurisprudence concerning the usurpation of authority in early Islam, the characteristics of a tyrannous ruler or the possession of a rebellious nature more generally, and the debauched perversions related to sexual trespass, disorder, or unrestrained wickedness.

In addition to these layered meanings are the symbolic homologies drawn among paradisiacal perfection, earthly gardens, and the space of the empire present in both imperial correspondence and Islamicate literary cultures more generally. The garden conveyed properly managed imperial order, blooming under the jurisdiction of the sultan, organized via a balanced dispensation of justice, and thus representing the opposite of an excess or improper usurpation of power. Representing an effort to create an earthly paradise, elaborate gardens quickly came to symbolize royal munificence and the notion of the *padişah* as the shadow of God on Earth. The sovereign cultivated an earthly garden homologous to the paradisiacal one. Royal gardens thus constituted an important historical art form, cultivated throughout various invasions, empires, and cultural influences.[40] Characterized by a protective wall, fountains, and archways separating interior and exterior spaces, the garden became an important physical and metaphorical image of intimacy throughout the region. Walter Andrews's work on

Ottoman lyric poetry traced the textual journey of this garden imagery into the Ottoman context.[41] He argued that the primary setting for both poetic performance and the symbolism of its verses was the garden—an ordered and exclusive space that was internally organized by the vertical relationship between patron and beloved. Andrews drew quite compellingly on the theories of Gilles Deleuze and Félix Guattari to suggest that this tableau constituted a well-known metaphor for the empire at large, wherein the garden symbolized a striated, state-dominated, hierarchically organized and ritualized space of decorum and order, and the "wilderness" outside its walls signified the rough, unconstructed frontier resistant to the imposition of a functioning royal ideal.[42]

These oppositions between interior and exterior, royal/civilized and frontier/uncivilized, rule-bound and chaotic, protected and unprotected were essential to medieval and early modern conceptions of just rule. Jurists such as Abu al-Hasan al-Mawardi (d. 1058) generated foundational texts concerning proper state authority within an ideological universe shaped by Islam. He worked to interpret the connections between divine law and political rule and sought to identify a proper religio-political system during another period of radical turmoil. As the 'Abbasid caliphate in Baghdad was beset by challengers from without (the emergent Fatimid caliphate in Egypt) and within (the powerful Buyids, who asserted political and military command for most of al-Mawardi's lifetime), his interpretations were also shaped by apprehensions of crisis and potential decline. His treatment of the relationship between political sovereignty and religious norms became a standard manual in theories of governance within Muslim-ruled dynasties.[43] Significantly, he elaborated in an administrative rather than a philosophic mode on the links between knowledge (*'ilm*), power (*sultaniyya*), and justice (*'adala*). For al-Mawardi the *bāghī* was an internal lawbreaker, a violator of legal, social, religious, or moral standards. He popularized *bughāt* (pl.) as the primary term for rebels in his careful analysis of legal problems related to political upheaval, such as techniques of warfare against insurgents, their rights as such or as prisoners, their unlawful collection of taxes and dues, and the validity of law formalized under their authority.[44] These rebels were seen as Muslims who abided even in their insurrection by the norms of the *dar-al Islam* (abode of Islam). What constituted their rebellion, then, was withholding obedience from the ruler (in this case the caliph). This version of rebellion hinged on a threat to withdraw, and to establish an independent authority that rivaled that of the sovereign. Hence, al-Mawardi stated, "If the insurgents (*bughāt*) refuse to obey the ruler, withhold their taxes, and undertake to collect money and enforce judgments imposed by themselves without, however, nominating a ruler or leader of their own, the money collected is in the nature of extortion that does not absolve anyone of what is owed, and the judgments enforced are null and void and establish no right."[45]

Al-Mawardi's concern here was not only with the disruption of revenue but also with the legitimacy of power. He proceeds to note that if rebels performed these acts in the name of a ruler, then their judgments could not be reversed nor their levies requisitioned. In other words, their authority must be recognized, although they should also be fought, following the Qur'anic injunction that if two parties of believers fight, peace should be made between them, but if one wrongs the other, then it is incumbent to do battle in order to bring the group back to the ordinance of God. If the group returns to the appropriate path, "then make peace between them justly and act equitably, for God loves the equitable."[46] Al-Mawardi, desperately concerned to regularize a severe challenge to caliphal power during a period of Buyid domination, argued that "certain concessions might be made to the governors of outlying regions, without prejudice to the rights of the caliph as effective ruler of the central province," provided the governor demonstrated respect and eschewed insubordination.[47] As such, the *bughat*, as Muslim rebels who, in principle at least, upheld shared notions of order and law prescribed by Islam, could indeed be brought back into the fold; they only definitively became an enemy when they reneged on their oath to the sovereign. The threshold between loyal servant and rebel within al-Mawardi's conception of authority was thus always ambiguous and easily tipped from one to the other.

Al-Mawardi's conviction that peace could be made with potential rebels evolved into a medieval philosophy of justice that further inflected Ottoman notions of sovereignty and the establishment's approach to potential upheavals. While al-Mawardi defined justice as the attainment of moral and religious perfection through the auspices of the caliph who possessed right knowledge (*'ilm*), later scholars and administrators such as Nizam al-Mulk (d. 1092),

Abu Hamid al-Ghazali (d. 1111), Nasir al-Din Tusi (d. 1274), and ibn Khaldun (d. 1406), as well as Ottoman and Safavid scholar-bureaucrats Tursun Bey (d. after 1490), Husayn Va'iz Kashifi (d. 1504–5), and Kınalızade 'Ali Çelebi (d. 1573), gradually translated conceptions of justice from "right religion" to "righteous government."[48] The remaining pages of this section thus show how authors conscientiously referenced and adapted paradigms of previous scholars into new formulations of the relationship between temporal power and justice. The primacy of Greek and Islamicate philosophical traditions in the interpretive frameworks of these authors also placed them within an intellectual tradition that addressed homologies between cosmos and state, divine order and temporal order. The sections that follow use this conceptual genealogy of proper rule and legitimate governance as the framework for assessing how reform writers of the early seventeenth century reimagined Ottoman sovereign power.[49]

Nizam al-Mulk's *Siyāsatnāma* (manual of governance) blended administrative protocol with the genre of mirrors for princes to create an etiquette manual for rulers that linked right religion with stability. His position as vizier within the emerging Seljuk dynasty shaped his use of religious authority to buttress the power of a vulnerable state. He removed kingship from the jurisprudential theories of the caliphate and proposed that divine light (*nur-i zade*) and knowledge (*'ilm*) united the temporal and the spiritual world into proper conditions of sovereignty, the aim of which was to ensure justice on Earth.[50] Divine light indicated God's election of an individual in possession of the kingly virtues (combinations of temperance, probity, courage, and wisdom) "so that people may pass their days under [the shadow of] his justice, enjoy security, and desire the continuance of his rule."[51] While he alleged that disorder in religion resulted in disorder in the kingdom, he still asserted that justice, not religion, was the basis of proper statecraft, writing an oft-referenced formulation: "Kingship remains with the unbeliever but not with injustice."[52] He insisted that the sovereign must constantly supervise not only his own disposition but also the actions of his officials, whom he must restrain in their efforts to collect taxes and in all their financial dealings. This restraint was not simply altruistic, for the intent was to ensure that all such wealth and treasure was amassed for the support of the kingdom. Furthermore, in addressing land management, he suggested that the security and prosperity of the realm could only be assured through proper custodianship that curtailed potentially rebellious regional governors. He thus refined and revised the practice of *iqta'*, introduced into 'Abbasid parlance by the Buyids, which had established the link between military service and tax-collection rights adopted by both Ottoman and Safavid administrators. In response to oppressive taxation, Nizam al-Mulk stated that the recipients of land grants had no authority over the cultivators beyond collecting taxes because the country and the subjects (*re'ayyat*) belonged to the Seljuk sultan.[53] His attention to these practices suggests that justice, according to the *Siyāsatnāme*, should be used as a standard for managing agrarian relations, thus rendering land itself a measure of sultanic legitimacy.

In his famous advice manual *Naṣīhāt al-mulūk*, Abu Hamid al-Ghazali conceived justice and sovereignty in much the same way as Nizam al-Mulk did, while introducing a number of innovations. He was the first to assert that the ruler is like a shepherd, which provided the basis for later Ottoman notions of the *re'aya* as flock and the sultan as shepherd.[54] Al-Ghazali also implied that the personal justice of the ruler was not enough and must be augmented by the just appointment of officials and servants whose loyalty to the ruler should dissuade them from tyrannous acts.[55] This distinguishing note, that loyalty to a ruler (assuming that this ruler is just) served as a barrier to tyranny, marks a significant transition in the shift from divine to temporal sovereignty and administration. But it was his emphasis on the link between justice and prosperity that truly marked him as an important synthetic figure in the intellectual heritage of Islamicate thought: "The efforts of these [the Persian] kings to make the world prosperous," he argued, "were because they knew that the greater the material prosperity the more extensive their dominions and the more numerous their subjects. They knew the sages had rightly said 'religion depends upon kingship, kingship upon the army, the army on wealth, wealth on material prosperity, and material prosperity on justice.'"[56] He thus weaves justice, sovereignty, and the welfare of the people together in a new conceptualization of a kingdom's ability to ensure the loyalty of its subjects.[57] He furthermore invokes the circle of equity—the reproductive wheel of beneficent power—to represent the interdependencies of the system as a whole.

Nasir al-Din Tusi wrote his *Muqaddimah-yi qadīm-i akhlāq-i Nāṣirī* scant moments before the fall of the ʿAbbasid caliphate to the Mongol invaders and then functioned as court adviser to Hulagu until his death.[58] He was instrumental in transmitting the theory of the philosopher-king into Persian and Ottoman thought, and he quoted extensively from al-Farabi and ibn Sina, and thus from the traditions of Plato and Aristotle. His manual followed the threefold Aristotelian division of practical philosophy adopted by many philosophers and statesmen who wrote in Arabic and Persian, or in Latin and other Eurasian vernacular languages: governance of the self, the household, and the polity. Nasir al-Din Tusi's conception of order and political philosophy became the conduit for Ottoman conceptions of the body politic and ethics elaborated by bureaucrats and scholars such as Tursun Bey and Kınalızade ʿAli Çelebi.[59] In his conception justice consisted of equity and was less a pure state of being than an act of distribution or correction undertaken by an ethical leader.[60] He believed that individuals were compelled to live together, that livelihood was only assured through cooperation, and that this cooperation required three things: a divine foundation (conceived as the *shariʿa*), a supreme ruler, and monetary currency.[61] Like others before him, he argued that the basis of the kingdom is justice, that the ruler should care attentively for his subjects, and that people should enjoy equality in the division of good things. The ruler must be beneficent, accessible, preserve security, attend to infrastructure, restrain desire, and associate with the learned. But none of this, equity and equanimity between individuals, and between the ruler and his subjects, would be possible without a balance and proper order of groups, divided into four classes: the people of the pen, the people of the sword, merchants, and cultivators.[62] This four-part division (*erkān-i erbāʿa*) suffused the cultural and literary productions of the Ottoman elite and thus served as one of the most significant conceptual tools deployed by critics of Ottoman governance, as well as the basic foundation of the provisional reforms they proposed as solutions.

These divisions, however, served only as a synopsis of the more comprehensive framework defined by al-Farabi (d. 950) as the "virtuous city" or "the perfect state" outlined in numerous forms throughout his work.[63] Al-Farabi's virtuous city embodied his more general effort to articulate a framework for political analysis and philosophical inquiry within the ambit of Islam. He harmonized classical political philosophy with the divine dictates of revelation by positing the philosopher-king as the ultimate lawgiver.[64] The ruler, acting as both the font of wisdom and the leader in war, ensured the virtue of the realm by aligning all social groups with their specialized duties and regulations, and thus putting them in their proper order. The qualities of the ruler were thus assessed in terms of his proficiency in the art of jurisprudence, that is, in knowledge of the laws and customs of his predecessors and the wisdom to meet new circumstances with new adaptations of these laws. The virtue of the world was guaranteed by the virtue of the ruler, who set his state and its cities in alignment with each other and sought, through this alignment, the contentment of all.[65]

Thus, Nasir al-Din Tusi, following al-Farabi, defined the virtuous city (*al-madīnāt al-fāḍila*) as containing five social strata. These were the "distinguished" ones (*afāḍil*), who rule and guide the city by their superior knowledge of custom and ability to apply its meaning; the orators and rhetoricians (*dhu' al-alsina*), who instruct and guide the masses with literary arts of pen and word; the accountants and administrators (*muqaddirūn*), who control price measures and supervise weights; the warriors (*mujāḥidūn*), who protect the community against external enemies and internal apostates; and the economic producers (*māliyūn*), who generate the consumer goods circulated in society.[66] Justice, configured as proper governance, depended not only on each individual remaining in his proper strata but also on the power of the sovereign to maintain sociopolitical distinctions and categories of service and revenue production. The blurring of boundaries, in this articulation of just sovereignty, led down a path toward domination, injustice, and tyranny.[67]

Husayn Va'iz Kashifi's *Aḫlāḳ-i muḥsinī*, dedicated to a Timurid ruler of Herat in 1494–95, was translated into Persian and then by Mustafa Celalzade into Ottoman.[68] Mustafa Celalzade's translation indicates the appeal that philosophic traditions of the Islamicate world had for sixteenth-century bureaucrats and how these traditions helped shape an ideological framework for the administrative expansionism of Süleyman's court. Like his predecessors, Kashifi envisioned that the world flourished through justice, that balance must be preserved, and that this was achieved by assigning each group its place according to the categories outlined by Tusi. He insisted that the ruler listen to petitioners and redress wrongs, and that "if his intention is justice, the result will be blessing and [the country] will become populous; but if, God forbid, the contrary is the case, blessing will depart, the crops will not give their increase, and the population will be scattered."[69] If justice was secured, then the kingdom endured. Furthermore, sovereignty was dependent on four pillars: an *emir* who commands defense; a *wazir* who secures finances; a *qadi* (judge) who will ensure the protection of the weak and the punishment of the wicked; and, a *sahib khabr*, or "possessor of news," who will report on the affairs of the realm and of its peoples.[70] Links between defense, fiscal viability, the protection of the weak, and actionable surveillance mechanisms were all dominant features of the *mühimme*. They were deployed as standards from which to judge inappropriate action, as attributes of loyal servants to reward, and as goals and imperial expectations dictated by the various commands. Together, these principles and standards wove a peculiar rationality of sovereignty through administrative practice and illustrated the nexus between intellectual inquiry and territorial management.

The Circle of Equity as a Principle of Order

Sovereignty, justice, and a compartmentalized social order together defined the *nızām-ı alem*, or the "well-founded world order," which the Ottomans inherited. The foundations of this order were closely aligned with a vision of distributive justice, inscribed as the circle of equity.[71] One of the more outstanding theorists of this circle, and the political ethos it embodied, was ibn Khaldun. His *Muqaddima*, or prolegomena to a philosophical work of universal history, departed from normative theological or juristic works, from advice manuals, whose authors often deployed obsequious devotion to their patrons, and from abstract philosophic formulations. His insistence on history as an analytic intervention fundamentally reshaped later treatises concerning governance, as ibn Khaldun outlined the techniques through which a scholar might map, analyze, and interrogate the political dynamics of dynastic rule.[72] His formulations are particularly important to the Ottoman experience because his work, along with the paradigms synthesized by Nasir al-Din Tusi and Husayn Va'iz Kashifi, framed the conversations and publications of critical formulations of world order and sovereignty by Ottoman treatise writers.

Ibn Khaldun combines three sources for descriptive references of the circle of equity to create a framework for his own interpretation of proper rule, thereby demonstrating the variegated inheritance of this idiom: Mobedhan (a Zoroastrian priest), Anushiran (a Sassanian king, r. 531–79), and Aristotle.[73] The saying that ibn Khaldun attributes to the Zoroastrian priest has already been Islamized, as the insertion of the *shari'a* for legal institutes and the Arabic use of the term *mülk*, with its connotations of worldly possession for secular authority, clearly demonstrate. These "quotations" have thus been inflected by the genealogy of order and justice outlined above. Here, ibn Khaldun emphasized the legal basis of the circle:

> Oh King! Secular authority (*mülk*) cannot maintain its glory without *sharī'a* (Islamic law), obedience to God and behaving under his command and his prohibitions. And there is no support for the *sharī'a* without kingship; And there is no glory for kingship without men; And there is no support for men without property; and the only way to property is through cultivation, and the only way to cultivation is through justice, and justice is a balance erected among God's creatures, belonging to the lord (*rabb*). And the lord chose a caretaker and he is the king.[74]

His reference to the formulation espoused by Anushiran inscribes the circle within the roles definitively played by the king, who ensures the reproduction of power through attentiveness and discipline:

> The king rules by the army; The army by money; Money comes from taxes (*kharāj*); Taxes come from cultivation; And cultivation comes from justice; Justice comes from righteous governing officials, honest ministers; And the king is to check up on the condition of his subjects himself and to discipline them so that he governs them and they do not govern him.[75]

Thus both of these attributions begin and end with the ruler and depict justice as a right ordering of social groups. The first saying emphasizes the importance of the *shari'a* and its connection with the king's rule, and the second focuses on the role that a king's authority plays in maintaining authority and discipline. They therefore integrate medieval theories of kingship with a moral conception of rule and suggest that only in combination is justice, conceived as proper order, realized. Yet it is in the version attributed to Aristotle that ibn Khaldun invokes the imagery of the garden as the metaphoric space of a well-maintained regime. He further argues that tradition, or customary laws, establishes the ruler's authority and ensures the sociopolitical divisions that reproduce the system as a whole:

> The world is a garden enclosed by the dynasty; the dynasty is an authority which is kept alive by tradition; tradition is a system which the ruler establishes; the ruler embodies the system of rule, which is supported by the soldiers; the soldiers are aids, money supports them; money is sustenance which the subjects gather; the subjects are slaves, justice protects them; justice is familiar, and by it the world is set into place; the world is a garden.[76]

For ibn Khaldun a society is just when its inhabitants possess *'aṣabīya*—the feeling of group solidarity he associates with nomadic relations of kinship and patronage.[77] Ibn Khaldun maps his cyclical understanding of dynasties onto the life phases of the human body and argues that in the period of senility, when the necessity of collective action is abandoned in favor of personal gain, injustice predominates, dynasties decline, and ruin results for all.[78] Injustice (*zulm*) represents not just a state of material depredation but is also, and most consequentially, a wicked and corrupt act (*fesad*), one that jeopardizes both the sanctity and prosperity of a community based on the laws of Islam.[79] In his analysis of the prophet Muhammad's prohibition of injustice, ibn Khaldun integrates moral, philosophical, and Islamic definitions of the concept.[80] He thus argues that the aims of divine law (the preservation of religion, the intellect, the soul, the species, and his property), and the rightly guided rules of political authority (*ahkam al-siyasa*) are to rescue society from both the condition and the historical instance of injustice and thus to preclude its demise.[81] One primary example of injustice contained in the *Muqaddima* reads like the complaints of corruption so oft-repeated in seventeenth-century reform manuals:

> You, O King, went after the farms and took them away from their owners and cultivators. They are the people who pay the land tax and from whom one gets money. You gave their farms as fiefs to your entourage and servants and to sluggards. They did not look for the things that would be good for the farms. They were leniently treated with regard to the land tax (and

> were not asked to pay it), because they were close to the king. The remaining landowners who did pay the land tax and cultivated their farms had to carry an unjust burden. Therefore, they left their farms and abandoned their settlements. They took refuge in farms that were far away or difficult (of access), and lived on them. Thus, cultivation slackened, and the farms were ruined. There was little money, and soldiers and subjects perished. Neighboring rulers coveted the Persian realm, because they were aware of the fact that the basic materials that alone maintain the foundation of a realm had been cut off.[82]

Clearly stated here is that land and agricultural production ensure not only the wealth of the realm but also the foundation of the sovereign's authority and thus his ability to preserve its integrity in the eyes of envious outsiders. The "unjust burden" placed on the cultivators, as a result of sultanic favoritism and self-aggrandizement led to widespread flight, crop failure, and destitution. Servants had become disloyal and greedy usurpers, jeopardizing the sanctity of the realm as a whole.

Early Ottoman Adaptations of Proper Order and Political Ethics

These gradual accretions of a conceptual framework that affixed the order of the world to the righteous rule of a sovereign appear within the earliest characterizations of Ottoman sovereignty. The *kanunname* attributed to Mehmed II opens with the following invocation (in Arabic): "Praised be the true king [God], who commands justice and good deeds, and forbids the vile and the wrongful, and who made the rulers the cause for the world order [*nıẓām-ı 'alem*] and made their rulings valid over all the tent-dwellers and city-dwellers."[83] *Kanunname*s, chancery manuals, and chronicles used *nıẓām-ı 'alem* both as a title granted to sultans or grand viziers and as a principle of natural order held in place by the legislative dictates of the sultan and his imperial council.[84] This conception of world order and political ethics crystalized into a key organizing principle in Tursun Bey's *Tārīḫ-i ebū'l-fetḥ*.[85] Tursun Bey wrote this work after he retired from the imperial chancery sometime after 1488, and in it crafted a historical genealogy for the Ottoman Empire suited to the triumphs of Mehmed II and his newly reconstituted capital, Istanbul. Tursun Bey had been a *timar* holder, a participant in major military campaigns, and a scribe within the imperial council.[86] Tursun Bey was, therefore, like other scholar-bureaucrats, attentive to the intersection between ideological principles and administrative shares. He attributed to the sultan the cause "for the duration of the order of the world" (*baqā-yi nıẓām-ı 'ālem içūn*), and he combined medieval conceptions of statecraft with the philosophical universe constructed by al-Farabi and ibn Sina.[87] He therefore assumed a universalist conception of natural order, one that recognized the innate social nature of humanity, the mutual cooperation necessary for the attainment of happiness, and the potential for social disorder if proper relationships were not managed. In his formulation, a ruler prevented social chaos by aligning each individual with a particular role, thereby preserving the outlines of divine grace in the social fabric of a state. He specifically referenced Nasir al-Din Tusi and assessed rightful sovereignty in terms of the cardinal virtues (wisdom, courage, gentleness, and justice) of wise rule.[88] But he also suggested that the ruler brings order to the world with "his lightning sword, and by the auspices of granting lands," thereby also associating virtuous order with stewardship of the land.[89] These actions bring about a state (*devlet*) of happiness for this world and the next, which can only be obtained through the mechanism of proper sultanic governance. It is worth noting that the link between virtuous rule and good fortune in both this world and the next also inflects the term *devlet* with the multiple valences of fortune, state power, and a ruler capable of forging a "state" of stability through administrative action. These valences were incorporated into Ottoman chronicling traditions as sultans Bayezid I (r. 1389–1402) and Murad II (r. 1421–44, 1446–51) began incorporating Anatolian principalities and embraced the traditions of frontier warfare as a means to assert legitimacy in a competitive milieu. Such parallelisms between the ruler, the fortune of the realm, and appropriate uses of power were then incorporated into the expanding aims of chroniclers under the reigns of Mehmed II (r. 1451–81) and Bayezid II (r. 1481–1512).[90]

Kınalızade 'Ali Çelebi's (d. 1572) *Aḫlāk-ı alāī* also addressed happiness and fortune in the foundation of the state and more directly translated the hierarchies of order outlined by al-Farabi, Nasir al-Din Tusi, and Jalal al-Din Davani into an Ottoman context. His work, which he composed while serving as judge of Damascus between 1563 and 1565, embodied the jurisprudential and philosophical traditions that circulated through the imperial *medreses* of the sixteenth century. Caught up in internal rivalries of the religious establishment, he ultimately came under the patronage of Ebu's-su'ud Efendi. His career highlights the institutionalization of a hierarchy in religious appointments, as he served first as the head of *medreses* in Edirne, Bursa, Kütahya, and Istanbul, then as judge in Damascus, Cairo, Burse, Edirne, and Istanbul, before finally becoming head judge of Anatolia in 1571.[91] Although the manuscript carries the title of *Sublime Ethics*, Baki Tezcan argued that "far from being a work on ethics, [it] lays down the theoretical foundations of the compartmentalized social order used by the Ottoman *nasihatname* authors."[92] His threefold division, following Aristotle, affirmed the importance of social hierarchy and thus outlined the paradox of social harmony preserved through social inequity so readily apparent in the *mühimme* registers. Order was achieved precisely through the distinction of ruler and servant and thus in the "four pillars" (*erkān-i erbā'a*) and five social strata elaborated in al-Farabi's "virtuous city." Kınalızade further associated these divisions with a combination of humoral harmony and the four natural elements. The pen was associated with blood and water; the sword with phlegm and fire, productive commerce with yellow bile and air, and agricultural production with black bile and earth. He therefore inscribed social order within the individual body, the state, and the primordial order of the world. In this way homologies between universal, political, social, and natural order became, in combination, the perfect state.

Kınalızade's perfect state was also metaphorically linked to the garden present within ibn Khaldun's formulation of order. He, too, invoked an Aristotelian conception of equity and its relation to the cultivation of social order. The empire, in his formulation, inhabits a botanical metaphor of guardianship and custodianship. The sultan was a gardener-king, who supervised a flourishing realm, with each product in its respective place and guarded by the thorny hedge of military defense.[93] Kınalızade's circle of equity, presented as advice given by Aristotle to Alexander the Great, brings all of these associations together:

> I have written the connections between the causes for the order of the world in a circle . . . which contains the essence of this book and the synopsis of

> its topics . . . : Justice leads to rightness of the world; the world is a garden, its walls are the state; the state is ordered by the *shari'a*; the *shari'a* is not guarded except by the ruler; the ruler cannot rule except through an army; the army is summoned only by wealth; wealth is accumulated by the subjects; the subjects are made servants of the ruler by justice."[94]

Here, al-Farabi's effort to bring divine and philosophical principles of order into harmony within one another take a uniquely Ottoman form. This form, hybrid in both influence and formulation, suggests that divine law can only be realized through the auspices of a ruler. The state may be ordered by the *shari'a*, but justice was the means for ensuring right order, and justice was implemented through the auspices of sultanic governance.[95] Justice, in the famous formulation of Idris Bitlisi (d. 1520), lay in putting things in their proper order under the supervision of the sultanate.[96] The threat to leave one's place was hence one of the most effective sources of leverage available to a subject or servant of the realm. Thus, threats of rebellion either against the state or against the mechanisms of imperial surveys and registration were rejoined by a call to justice. As illustrated in previous chapters, justice was both a strategy of the petitioner and an assertion of imperial authority. It was therefore not merely a theoretical or philosophical principle but an administrative and political strategy that inscribed a grammar of rule shared between the Ottoman establishment and the diverse inhabitants of the realm.

Disturbance in the Well-Ordered Realm: Genre Convention as a Literary Disguise

The relationship between justice and a well-ordered realm also dominated the literary genre of advice-giving. Political crisis and social upheaval turned Ottoman scholar-bureaucrats toward a genre of counsel, used to create manuals for statecraft and, ultimately, a craft for the state. The mirror form had migrated into Ottoman literary circles quite early; copies of the *Kābūsnāme* of Ka'i Kabus ibn Iskandar, the *Siyār al-mulūk* of Nizam al-Mulk, and the *Naṣīḥāt al-mulūk* of al-Ghazali were all available in Ottoman translations.[97] But the genre expanded most profusely in the late sixteenth and early seventeenth centuries, as the Ottoman literary elite attempted to intervene against what they perceived as an unraveling of the natural order of things. These texts thus accompanied the major transformations in the polity outlined previously. But these authors did not merely register concern over the state of imperial fortunes.[98] Instead, Ottoman bureaucrats *cum* treatise writers redefined the very notion of proper order via references to natural law and universal faith. They further objectified the theoretical foundations of a past imperial order as they bemoaned its collapse in the present. Within the advice manual's posture of humility, they managed to conceal a critique of the sultanate and a move toward a more abstract political analysis of the state.

It is not without irony that one of the key harbingers of crisis was Lütfi Paşa, a former grand vizier of Süleyman who wrote the *Asafnāme* from retirement, sometime between 1541 and 1563: "The kingdom of this mortal world is fleet in its passing and full of death. It is better to find leisure but not unmindful repose in the enjoyment of gardens and meadows. May God, from whom we seek aid, and in whom we trust, secure the laws and foundations of the house of 'O̱smān from the fear and peril of fate and the evil eye of the enemy."[99] In a text primarily devoted to articulating the duties and qualities incumbent on a grand vizier is a critical appraisal of reality and the listing of various corruptions of an ideal that would become standard in later compositions: the spread of bribery, excessive swelling of a mercenary army, infiltration of the *re'aya* into the military class, vacant *timar*s, and the sultan's retreat from the daily administration of affairs. The "laws and foundations," according to the vision inscribed in the *Asafnāme*, were ensconced in the circle of equity: "The sultanate stands on its treasury. The treasury stands by good management. By injustice (*ẓulm*) it falls."[100] Lütfi Paşa characterized injustice as the disordering of social relations, which must be restored to their rightful place for the state to regain its healthy balance. Thus, even within the era of Süleyman, concerns for the fortune of the empire created a paradigmatic treatment to which later treatise writers adhered.

The reign of Sultan Süleyman (1520–66) constituted a watershed, representing in turn both the embodiment and the inversion of an ideal moment in Ottoman imperial glory. The period of his reign functioned on two levels: first, as a trope of perfection, of the old days, when the order of the world fit intelligible paradigms of just and proper rule; and second, as the pinnacle of achievement, which, in true ibn Khaldunian fashion, contained the signs, and symptoms, of its degeneration. Once a specific idealization of past "foundations and laws" emerged, any departure or innovation from it became cause for fear and was blamed for the rampant disorder surrounding them. Thus, shifts in land-tenure management and challenges to territorial control challenged the proper order of the empire by corrupting boundaries between social groups. Lütfi Paşaa clearly enunciated the concern over boundary transgression: "we must insist that none from the *re'āya* be made *sipāhīs*, that none be made *sipāhīs* except those who are sons of *sipāhīs*, whose fathers and ancestors were *sipāhīs*."[101] For Lütfi Paşa and others, problems emerged when the basis of transactions became money rather than land; the intended domain of the *sipahi* was *miri*, or state-held land, granted to the individual in return for loyal service, who was then entrusted with the economic, social, and political functions of protecting and administering his assigned territories. While certainly not a system of outright ownership (he collected revenue in the form of taxes and services), his function within the imperial governing apparatus was firmly grounded in the land itself. Increasing demands for cash to support elite privilege, along with the more rapid and diverse circulation of currency, escalated trends toward tax farming and the transformation of *miri* lands into mobile property.

Acquiring the position of a *sipahi* and gaining control of a *timar* became a profit-generating venture instead of a bond of loyalty. In the eyes of the treatise writers, this constituted the grievous root of corruption, as *intisab* (personal favor and influence) became more pronounced in the granting of official positions. Mustafa 'Ali claimed that *timars* were "all reserved for the mercenaries (*levend*) and for the slaves of the great (*ekābir ķūlları*),"[102] and Lütfi Paşa summarized the state of affairs: "For officers of the state, corruption is a disease without remedy. . . . Beware, beware of corruption; O God, save us from it."[103] This "corruption" from earlier imperial moments represented a fear that change or departure from established traditions necessarily meant a departure from the legal foundations of the state (*kanun-ı mukarrer*). These foundations, also deemed "customary" in the *kanunname* and *mühimme*, located virtuous order within the bond between sultan and servant. If this bond of loyalty could not be assured, then neither could the fate of the Ottoman Empire. Veysi Efendi (d. 1628), for instance, in his *Habnāme* or *Vāki'anāme* (Book of Sleep/Vision or Dream-Book),[104] written sometime after 1610, has Sultan Ahmed I ask: "If the *ķūl*, my *ķūl*, refuses to obey me, how am I to protect the *reʿāya* with the sword of justice and equity, and lead and govern the country?"[105]

Disorder, according to the anonymous author of the *Kitāb-ı müstetāb* (The approved/agreeable book)[106] written during the tumultuous reign of Osman II (1618–22) and perhaps presented directly to him, looked like the following: "The laws of the Ottoman sultanate violated; . . . the treasury possessing a deficit; the governors torn apart by infighting; the judges receptive to bribery; the opportunity to tackle the enemy [missed]; among those close to the [sultan] treason; among the theologians a lust for gold and inanity; among the *reʿāya* futile labor and fear; in brief: innovations and all sorts of grievance everywhere."[107] At stake were the very foundations of the house of Osman: the supposed weakening of sultanic authority, governors incapable of serving as managers, judges intent on greed rather than the law, and the deleterious effects of these on the treasury and thus on the ability of the empire to outfit itself for campaigns of offense or defense. The writers made a direct link between "corruption" in the realm of appointments and the exorbitant taxation and oppression of the *reʿaya*, who occasionally emerge as feeble victims in need of protection. As the author of the *Kitāb-i müstetāb* phrased it: "*Timār*s have become the prerogative of the viziers, that when using a ten-*akçe* scribe, they name the slave girls in their households, their beardless youths and slave boys, even their cats and dogs, every one of them being designated by a separate name, and they are awarded a diploma for a *ziʿāmet* or *timār*."[108] With the accumulation of wealth an end in itself, and the use of trickery to attain status (naming cats and dogs as able-bodied *timar* holders), the true and rightful *timar* holder was eclipsed by money-grabbers inattentive to the needs of the cultivator. Corruption jeopardized the social harmony inscribed in the circle of equity and could lead to the fiscal and moral bankruptcy of the empire. Thus, an increasingly fatalistic vision of affairs dominated the literature.

This fatalistic vision also shaped early seventeenth-century imperial commands, which momentarily eclipsed the *kanunname* as the primary mechanism for adjudicating the realm. A decree issued by Sultan Ahmed I (r. 1603–17) addressed the disorder in the realm left in the wake of the violent waves of rebellion that had spread across the Anatolian and Arabic-speaking provinces. Recorded in a *mühimme* register dated from March

1609 to February 1610, this *hükm* sought to restore order by reasserting the links joining justice, social harmony, and proper governance. It echoes the conceptual universe of order and disorder developed in past chronicles and reform treatises and illustrates the synchronicity between intellectual and administrative projects. Addressing governors, bailiffs, commanders, local supervisors, and members of the janissary, the sultan accuses them of unwarranted pilfering from the population and of acting for personal gain rather than for the replenishment of the collective treasury and the sanctity of the realm. The decree provides an intricate list of reported abuses that amount to "tyrannizing and injustice." The sultan accuses his representatives of "not making the rounds of your provinces doing your duties"; instead, they "are going around taking money from the *re'āya* unlawfully." During "so-called patrols," and accompanied by armed militias threatening force, they upend lists of fines, punishments, and property laws sanctioned by the *kanunname* into exercises in profiteering. They turn accidental deaths into murder in order to harass villagers into paying blood money "by putting them in irons and beating them." In the specific case that precipitated the imperial edict, corrupt officials had invented a story about someone falling out of a tree. Demanding a long investigation into it, they then required villagers to support them during the process, unlawfully requisitioning "horses, mules, slaves, barley, straw, wood, hay, sheep, lambs, chickens, oil, honey and other things to eat."[109]

The imperial decree also captured the problem posed by subcontracting tax-collection privileges to regional interest groups: "You lease out your incomes to collectors at excessive rates. They on their part go out to collect with far too many horsemen and, instead of satisfying themselves with collecting your incomes according to law and as is prescribed in the record, try to get as much money as they please." Furthermore, these delegates went beyond the properties assigned to their tax farm to encroach on imperial domains exempted from collection or transfer. They did so "under the pretense of following criminals" and once again accompanied by an armed guard "demand thirty or forty extra gold or silver pieces per month." In this guise, false accusations of criminal behavior provided leverage for exploitative demands. Still further, officials took bribes from bandits and brigands they had been commanded to punish, enabling the spread of their influence and further contributing to regional distress: "brigands have been gaining ground and descend upon the *reʿāya* in bands."[110]

Remarkable in its specificity (a fall from a tree disguised as murder), and referring to the presence of informants and attempted surveillance ("that I have been hearing about"), the sultanic voice castigates his administrators for crossing territorial, jurisdictional, and moral boundaries. Instead of collecting income "according to law" and "as is prescribed in the record," they have acquired the means of intimidation and coercion ("they go out to collect with far too many horsemen"), used subterfuge to take what is not rightfully theirs, and accepted bribes from the very brigands they were meant to seize. Despite being representatives of the sultan, their deeds were barely distinguishable from those of the bandits and rebels. Further, the indictment that these men "try to get as much money as they please" provides a clear example of the overlap between injustice (*zulm*) and corruption (*fesad*), wherein the selfish pursuit of money worked against the common good and thus against the proper maintenance of a just society. Any act that jeopardized the continuity of this proper order was an act against the sultan, and, as he personified the state, against the well-being of the whole. Put simply, it constituted an act of ideological rebellion.

Distressed Bonds of Obligation: Loyalty and Rebellion Reconfigured

In 1622, potential ideological rebellion became actual, and the murder of a sultan sparked a new frenzy of pens intent on alleviating dismay and reinstituting a vision of proper order. The men behind these pens, however, began to shift away from a genre of advice toward a mode of critique, thus opening up a distinct space for political analysis within the world of Ottoman letters. Ahmed I's efforts to reconfigure the realm faltered after his death in 1617. In 1623 the eleven-year-old Murad IV (r. 1623–40) would ascend to the sultanate, gradually seize power from a cohort of advisers led by his mother, Kösem Sultan, and initiate new campaigns of conquest against the Safavids. He recaptured Baghdad in 1638 and gained territory in the Crimea that would not be lost until the wars with Russia and the Concert of Europe in the 1850s. Between 1617 and 1623, however, a cycle of events that would ultimately assume tragic proportions rocked the foundations of the state even further.[111] Sultan Osman II attempted to gain control over the disorder of the realm and address the cycles of disloyal servants revealed in administrative records of the period. He sought to reinvigorate the image of a warrior sultan, shift recruitment patterns for the military away from the burgeoning power of the janissaries, and reassess the relationship between privilege and service as the key mechanism for acquiring loyalty.[112] These proposed policies culminated in his supposed intention to perform the *hajj* to Mecca, something no sultan had ever hazarded to do before, which instigated a janissary rebellion and the shocking regicide of the sultan on May 20, 1622. Osman II's uncle Mustafa I was brought back to the throne even though he had been deposed for mental instability in 1618.[113] His tenure would lapse after only one year, when an elite cadre opted for the youth of Murad IV over the escalating mental imbalance of Mustafa.

By way of explanation, chroniclers and treatise writers linked these dramatic events to Osman II's failure at the Battle of Hotin (in Poland) in 1621 and to the deteriorating bonds between the sultan and the military that ultimately transpired in a shocking tale of murder. Hüseyin bin Sefer, writing under the pen name Tuği Çelebi, and İbrahim Peçevi (d. 1650) both placed these events within the broader crises narrated in reform treatises.[114] Both focused on the collapse of social boundaries—in this case the lapsed ties between sultan and servant—and placed rebellion at the heart of the empire. He hearkened from the institution of the *devşirme*, was a clear partisan for an idealized system of loyalty between the janissary and the sultan, and decried the monetarization of a once virtuous bond. Born in Belgrade to a janissary father, and following this career path through several campaigns in Anatolia and Persia, Tuği was seemingly quite dexterous at networking and became one of the sultan's elite bodyguards (*solak*).[115] Presumably retired when he wrote his history of Osman II's deposition, Tuği suffered the consequences of this sultan's attempts to streamline the army and cut extraneous costs by denying pensions to veterans. He directly links the curtailing of such customary privileges to sultanic injustice, and thus to a decline in the empire's moral order.

İbrahim Peçevi, in contrast, came from a family of landholding military commanders in the Bosnian region and was himself a product of the Ottoman mechanism of incorporating and accommodating local elites through the granting of income rights via the *timar*. After participating in the notorious Hungarian campaign of Sinan Paşa described in Chapter 4, Peçevi spent much of the remainder of his career in various provincial and administrative posts in Anatolia and Rumelia. Significantly, he served as the *defterdar* (financial scribe) for a staunch supporter of sultanic authority, Hafız Paşa, the *beylerbeyi* of Diyarbekir, and was a known acquaintance of Abaza Mehmed Paşa, the *beylerbeyi* of Erzurum, whose rebellious antics all but defined the 1620s. While certainly also a part of Istanbul's sphere of influence and the clear product of a centralizing bureaucracy, his military and provincial experience constitutes a noteworthy component of his history writing. Peçevi's texts exhibit a virtual compendium of terms devoted to the technical and strategic aspects of siege warfare, along with descriptive tales of the intricate patron-client networks dominating administrative practices; thus, in their ethnographic feel these texts serve to insert the province within this period's politics.

Tuği blames the loss of Hotin on the bricolage of forces Osman II gathered together. He labels these forces *sekban*, essentially mercenaries, and rhetorically asks the sultan whether it was "with *sekbān* that your forefathers conquered provinces?" He suggests that they were a lackluster replacement for the janissaries and transgressed the boundary between rebel and servant of the realm. He argues that it was through their disobedience and "*sekbān* brigandage" that famous rebels and bandits such as Kalenderoğlu (Anatolia) and Janbulad (northern Syria) not only caused the loss of territories but "brought desolation to the world" despite sharing "with your father, Sultan Ahmed, his *ḫutbe ve sikke* [sermon and coinage]."[116] Here Tuği, in fine oratorical style, references the pivotal point of contention between soldiers and administrators whose power was predicated on, even if in actuality no longer directly tied to, an agrarian system of rule and the *sekban*. The *sekban* are judged as bandits because they are unattached to the land-granting *timar* system and the *devşirme* system of recruitment. These two institutions, constructed in the historiography of the period and idealized as the empire's foundation, come to represent for Tuği the former glory and success of an empire now in disarray.

The key tension in Tuği's synopsis of events lay between the reality of a salaried military force and the mythic ideal of service motivated by loyalty rather than financial reward. Recognizing that the sultan's servants had always depended on monetary remuneration, Tuği distinguishes between the customary bonus the sultan would distribute as an act of gratitude following victorious battles (*bahşiş*) and money exchanged as the sole motivation for participating in military campaigns. The intrusion of the latter into the bond between sultan and servant led to an increasingly arbitrary relationship between service and reward. Servants who were formerly willing to "sacrifice their lives for him and bring heads of the foes of religion and state" have now "turned war and combat into a child's game." Instead of seeking to "conquer the camp of trifling infidels," they shirked their duties and sued for peace.[117] Willingness to sacrifice their lives for the sultan, formerly motivation enough, was now attenuated through a cash relation, the value of which determined the quality of the soldiers' efforts. With the empire's liquidity increasingly dependent on currency flows, it became almost impossible to ensure constant reward for services rendered.

Tuği rationalized the defeat at Hotin without reprimanding the janissary force itself and laid blame instead at the feet of the sultan. In his view the institutionalized military force that had ensured the breathtaking conquests of the early warrior-sultans now stood on the brink of collapse. The problem was not the exchange of money but rather the collapse of a system of order that produced its own rewards. Currency had become a commodity exchanged in return for military duties that had formerly been assumed out of bonds of loyalty. Implicit in his analysis of this commodification is a critique: the sultan's abandonment of his own role in the system as a custodian who ensured the proper distribution of resources. The sultan, in Tuği's eyes, broke the reproductive basis of the system as a whole and thus broke the constitutive contract between defense and the prosperity of the realm. The collapse of this contract, and of the customary *bahşiş*, or largesse of the sultan, alienated the soldier from the sultan and thus from a system based on loyalty, service, and honor.

Peçevi, in contrast, directly accused the *kul* for the humiliation of Hotin. As the ranks of the army swelled, its effectiveness diminished—a paradox that diagnostic treatises from the period labored to explain, making it a key pillar in the decline metanarrative. "Last year at the Hotin campaign, they were unable to defeat a small infidel force. Incompetent and useless, is this lot of salary-drawers, the *ḳūl*."[118] Tuği explained the disaster at Hotin as a break between sultan and soldier, with monetary reward serving as the wedge; Peçevi explains that break as a consequence of the soldiers' indifference to their part of the contract—they didn't even show up to the battlefield.[119] According to Peçevi the few soldiers who did appear refused, or became irritated by, the imposition of a *yoklama*, or formal inspection.[120] Here Peçevi alleges a common complaint recorded by treatise writers: the purchase or sale of office or title that ultimately falsified the salary lists for *timar* holders or other members of the *'askeri* social strata. A formal inspection would necessarily reveal the gap between *timar* registers and the men who were actually soldiers, capable of routing the enemy. Peçevi conveniently forgets that the Ottoman establishment was complicit, using the sale of offices to support the salaries of a large infantry-based army. Both Tuği and Peçevi perceive the disruption in social order in terms of the categories reified in an ethos of distributive justice and the circle of equity. They differ not in the categories deployed but in the object of their accusations. Tuği held the sultan responsible, and Peçevi the *kul*, but both chroniclers assumed that social disorder emerged from a lapsed state of perfection. The perfect state inhered in the sustaining bond between sultan and servant and thus between a virtuous moral order and a triumphant body politic. But the perceived corruption of this moral order, and the explanations thereof, opened up an avenue for critique that would become central to treatises written during and after the reign of Murad IV.

From Ideals of Governance to a System of Management

Treatises intent on reform opted for a moralizing vocabulary to describe what their authors considered a retreat from perfection. Yet the final two sections of this chapter explore how, after the events of 1622, the implied fatalism in the descriptions of rot masked significant innovations in the genre's form of critique. During the reign of Murad IV (r. 1625–40) these writers shifted away from simply characterizing the ideals of governance and toward enumerating its system instead. Increasingly, the authors' intentional reference to the corruptibility of an ideal signified an effort to interpret and analyze administrative practice and, as such, to compose actionable memoranda. This is particularly true for Koçu Bey (d. circa 1650).[121] A product of the *devşirme* trained in the palace school, and intimate adviser to sultans Murad IV and İbrahim (r. 1640–48), he was assigned to various scribal posts and then, under Murad IV, to the personal retinue of the sultan (*has odası*). He presumably accompanied the sultan on his eastern campaigns against the Safavids but also produced a memorandum and commentary on the state of the empire prior to these experiences, presented in 1632. This *risale* embodies both the stylized features of the mirror tradition and the invention of a new kind of policy-oriented writing.[122] On the surface he captures the fatalism of the period well: "It is a long time since the many-chambered household of the high sultanate (may it remain always under the protection of eternal grace) was served by solicitous, well-intentioned, worthy *'ulema'* and by obedient, humble, willing servants. Today, considering the state of affairs has changed, and evil, disorder, agitation and discord have passed all bounds, I have sought the means to observe the causes and reasons of these transformations, and to bring them to the imperial and august ear."[123]

Koçu Bey thus produces the idealized state in the negative. He cautions that disorder prevails because of the broken bond between the sultan and his servants, yet he communicates a purpose, a reform-minded agenda. His *risale* raises perceived problems to suggest solutions. He therefore constructed his treatise in the form of vizierial memoranda (*telhisat*), a mode of communication between the grand vizier and the sultan that suggests the possibility of immediate action on the measures suggested therein.[124] Koçu Bey composed a list of serious, even ominous, problems in the institutional and financial structure of Ottoman administration and closed most of the twenty-two sections submitted to Murad IV with the typical formulaic phrasing: "the rest remains for the imperial order of the sultan." Koçu Bey thus drew on textual constructs generated within the imperial council to present possible solutions for the future. This innovative use of memoranda removes the treatise from the stylized literary tropes of the mirror-for-princes genre. Still, while formally innovative, his overarching vision of the state of affairs was conservative. He invoked the circle of equity as an idealized image of perfection—"The treasure of rulers is their subjects (*re'āya*); the need of the subjects is for care and protection (*ri'āyet*) and safeguarding from injustice"[125]—and therefore locates the legitimacy of the sultan in his role as guardian of perfect order. He further summons the plight of the *re'aya* to serve as a clarion call for addressing empire-wide disorder: "The like of the present oppression and maltreatment burdening the *re'āya* has never happened in any time, clime, or ruler's domain before. If, in any of the lands of Islam one iota of injustice is done to any one individual, then on the day of judgment not ministers, but rulers will be asked for a reckoning, and it will be poor excuse for them to say to the Lord of the Worlds, 'I delegated this duty.'"[126]

The prophetic nature of this moment, one of "reckoning" on the "day of judgment," underscores the continued symbolic role that oppression and injustice play in his evaluation of disorder. Yet Koçu Bey shifts from a specific time and condition ("present oppression") to a general statement of principle ("in any of the lands of Islam one iota of injustice"). Rulers could not shirk their duties, their task of preserving just order, without divine recompense. Koçu Bey furthermore refuses to accept the delegation of authority as an excuse and instead assumes that it is the sultan's personal responsibility to remedy the situation. Even then, however, Koçu Bey turns his attention from the personhood of the ruler to the system itself.

This can be seen both thematically and methodologically in his assessment of the *re'aya* and of the administrative affairs of the realm. For the thematic focus his comments on the *re'aya* first characterize them as victims of oppression and objects of the sultan's grace and then as instigators of disorder themselves, falling outside the purview of sultanic redress. Their distress, formerly a cause for recrimination against profligate officials, now becomes a troublesome indicator of general social disarray and as such, a target for pejorative commentary. For example, Koçu Bey lamented that while in previous times the link between *timar*s and members of the military was assured, and that "outsiders and persons of ignoble origin did not enter their ranks," currently the ranks were filled by "those who were upstarts, those who said 'there is profit here,' who could not distinguish between good and evil, those who had no legitimate connection, those who by origin or status were not possessors of *dirlik*s [certificates of livelihood from land grants], some of them city boys and some of them *re'āya*, a bunch of commoners, not useful for anything."[127]

As in former treatises, the innovation of utmost concern was the monetization of relations—in particular the marketing of official posts and the entrenchment of tax farming—and the slackening of social boundaries that occurred as a consequence. These interlopers had appeared because of corruption that started at the very top—withdrawal of the sultan from direct management, appointment of personal favorites even to the highest post of grand vizier, and the resulting "contamination" of administrative, military, and religious domains by interlopers and outsiders. The imperial household was overrun by "Turks, Gypsies, Jews, people without religion or faith, cutpurses and city riff-raff" and the janissary core with interlopers such as "townsmen, Turks, Gypsies, Tats, Lazes, muleteers and camel-drivers, porters, footpads, and cutpurses."[128] Koçu Bey's pejoratives also reflect the increased diversity of Istanbul's urban milieu. Loosening of hierarchies meant that rural to urban migration intensified, as former cultivators became "city riff-raff" and "camel-drivers" and shared the same space as "cutpurses." Boundaries of all sorts were challenged, giving rise to strong fears of social contamination and imperial disease.

As a consequence, "if the world were ruined, they took no notice, and, God protect us, if the enemy overran the world, they would not even know what the war was about . . . [because] concern for the faith has never entered their thoughts."[129] In this passage Koçu Bey strikingly expresses the bundle of issues associated with a climate of change: the insertion of money into bonds of loyalty; the confusion of social boundaries that resulted, allowing city dwellers and cultivators to compete with traditional authorities; the disarray this caused to the foundations of state, threatening the ruination of the world as they knew it; and the moralization of these changes with accusations that the "upstarts" were ignorant and could not defend "the faith" because they "could not distinguish between good and evil." While drawing on religious morals, "good and evil" and "the faith" function here as social commentary and indicate a concern that ignorance of the foundational principles of the state threatened the integrity of the community as a whole. The implicit interposition of "the faith" with "the state" is an important shift in Koçu Bey's *risale*. Süleyman's court was the first to transform the link between religion and governance (*din ve devlet*) into an armature for imperial legislation. In the *mühimme* of that time the sultan consistently called for his officials to adhere to his commands and therein abide by the *shari'a*. The two, *hükm* and *shari'a*, reinforced each other in the context of an authoritative proclamation. But in Koçu Bey's formulation for maintaining order, faith as a universal replaces the sultan as an individual arbiter of justice. In other words, by privileging faith as a *mode* of governance, he suggests that a properly ordered realm is a moralized system, one that binds all within its armature. The proclivity of the *re'aya* to act of their own accord and transgress social boundaries therefore also results in a lapse of "morality." Thus, even as Koçu Bey sought to reinscribe the imperial hierarchy and the sultan as an active agent, he also tended to act as a social analyst, aware of the independent agency of the *re'aya*, who could only be restored to proper behavior through moral principles.

In consequence, and in keeping with a moralizing response to social upheaval and, specifically in this case, to urban migration, a hint of condemnation emerges concerning the *re'aya*s' tendency toward ignorance, commonness, and self-interest. According to Koçu Bey, they became "upstarts" when they began to climb out from their rightful place as a "flock" safely enclosed within a garden hedge and tended by the shepherd *cum* sultan of the realm. Instead, they now appear as nuisances, "city riff-raff" contributing to the disarray of both the urban sphere and the realm as a whole. Furthermore, the accusation of ignorance commutes a value on literacy. This literacy entailed knowledge of foundational laws, even if it did not emphasize textual fluency. These accusations echo the characterizations included in Veysi's *Hābnāme*. Veysi used historical references to create a general vision of the *re'aya* as profligate members of society, consistently working against social order: "all the woes and disaster described in these pages were made inevitable by the wicked intentions of the *re'āya* throughout time; the kings have had nothing whatsoever to do with it."[130] Veysi presented this vision in order to quell his sense that he had been plunged in a "sea of melancholy" by the continued disturbances of the realm, and he fashioned a dream sequence that seated the Ottoman sultans next to Alexander the Great in paradise. There, Alexander accuses Ahmed I of not following the dictates of philosophical wisdom, wherein the ruler acts as the heart of the world's body. If the ruler does not adhere to the virtues of justice and mercy, Alexander cautions, then oppression and injustice will ruin the subjects. Ahmed I then blames the current state of the empire on the disordered reigns of his predecessors, specifically on the *celali* rebellions, which caused unending unrest and dissonance in the realm. He further defends his efforts to stay the course and restore principles of order to the empire. Alexander's thirty-four stories of corruption, evil, murder, and tyranny, from Adam and Eve to the Mongol invasions, were intended to illustrate that the problem was not the state but its subjects and servants. Although Veysi's position is idiosyncratic, it does portend a general movement toward judgment rather than approbation more fully embodied in Koçu Bey's *risale*. Veysi removes sole blame from the sultan, due in large part to his apprehension of reality as a social organism, interdependent in nature and thus subject to its own laws. As an organic whole, with the state part of a cosmological unity, he repositions the *shari'a* as a universal: "If the foundations of the exalted threshold are the sacred *sharī'a*, it will suffer no shortage or imperfection until the day of judgment."[131] Evil could only be countered by universal good, and the *shari'a* replaced the sultan in his estimation of the state's foundations. Yet this was not precisely an Islamization of the natural order since Veysi presented a universalist vision to identify the limits of sovereignty and critique the present affairs of the sultanate. God and Islam served as acceptable and convenient modes for fashioning this critique and may also have indicated a recognition that this move could be seen as a kind of double blasphemy—using God to define limits for the state and thus overstepping the boundaries of each.

Activating an Ottoman Archive

Even as Koçu Bey relied on the form of the *telhis*, he disparaged its necessity as a medium for policing the affairs of the realm. The essence of his methodological innovation lies here, in that the treatise stood as a stark criticism of the imperial council's dereliction of its duties to register, manage, and produce a textual accounting of imperial domains. In this, Koçu Bey faults the retreat of the sultan from officiating as the heart of the council and thus also suggests that Selim I, not Süleyman, should stand as the model for proper governance. He suggested that during Selim's time the sultan maintained direct relationships with all the premier delegates of authority, both within the walls of the palace and across the provinces. Selim officiated at the imperial council; thus, the servants of the realm were truly his loyal delegates.[132] By performing this role as a supervising sovereign, the sultan ensured that all members of the administrative apparatus abided by the honorable *shari'a* and the veritable Ottoman *kanun*. As a result, taxes were assessed appropriately and placed directly in the hands of custodians who ensured that revenue reached the treasury. But the proliferating numbers of palace bureaucrats and claimants to provincial positions now precluded direct management of affairs. Koçu Bey prepared a comparative list of scribes and administrative officiates, along with divisions of the military establishment, to demonstrate the overweening pace of bureaucratic expansion. In the time of Murad III these numbers totaled 36,153.[133] As he prepared his manuscript, they had reached 92,206.[134]

Although Koçu Bey faulted the rising influence first of the vizier and then of palace factions for displacing the circle of authority that had long sustained the empire, his solution pivoted less on the person of the sultan than on the textual apparatus of the empire. Koçu Bey saw the mechanisms for registering lands and privilege as essential tools in identifying subjects of the realm who were exploiting lapses in the empire's textual authority. Thus, he both consulted and called for the production of new registers, such as the cadastral surveys, the daily account books (*ruznamçe*) that appended changes to surveys and budgetary adjustments, as well as registers variously designated for *vakıf*, *cizye*, and *'avarız* that had previously functioned to define and constrain, in meticulous detail, the territory and fisc of the empire. In a lapsed system of accurate registration, however, men who claimed *timar*s or *ziamet*s now exceeded one hundred thousand, and villages and properties assigned as pensions had defaulted into the hands of profiteers rather than being restored to the imperial treasury, as had *vakıf* lands, which had essentially become freehold estates.[135] In Koçu Bey's estimation the imperial council, acting with the finance minister and in consultation with previous registers, should establish a new accounting of assigned privileges. He urged that, by sultanic order, all provincial governors should call a roll of land grant recipients and judge whether they held these positions rightfully. Furthermore, Koçu Bey suggested that discovering distinctions in taxes due annually, or redeemed from imperial domain, tax farms, or through various mechanisms of a poll tax (*'avarız*, *cizye*, or *haraç*), was the only means by which the disordered realm might be rightfully restored. Disorder was thus rectified not through justice but through precise measures of accounting and registration.

Delivered to Sultan Murad IV in 1632, Aziz Efendi's *Kānūnnāme-i Sulṭānī* encapsulates the gradual shift from advice-giving to an analysis of the state that emerged during the course of the 1630s.[136] While he assumed the now customary vision of imperial corruption and called for the restoration of fundamental institutions and principles, Aziz Efendi, like Koçu Bey, activated the textual authority of the state to present a formula for reform. He included draft versions and outlines of royal proclamations for the sultan's approval that could be immediately released and circulated. These imperial rescripts constituted the basis of the *mühimme* collections and attempted to negotiate tensions between the governing apparatus and regional agents of various sorts. Aziz Efendi removed these imperial commands from their existence as daily records of state operations and inserted them, instead, into an analytic framework of reform. He therefore put the rubric of the *kanunname* and the *mühimme* in a new guise: as a prescription for change rather than a principle of stability.

Yet he still cloaked the *Kānūnnāme-i sulṭānī* within the mode of the mirror genre and adopted a view of reform that emphasized restoring the fundamentals of the past. He humbly cast himself at the feet of the sultan and embraced retirement as protection against the ambiguous outcome of speaking candidly: "I would rather sacrifice my own life than compromise the ideas in my head. I am an old and loyally devoted veteran, the stock of whose life has now reached its limit and who is no longer capable of useful service. . . . In sum, I am an aged servant who has shown his readiness to give not only a dram of his blood, but his whole body and soul for the protection of the reputation and good name of the Sultanate, and for the safeguarding of religion and the state."[137]

He played on the issue of "concealment" throughout the text, employing the typical "may it not be hidden or concealed from the world-adorning knowledge of your prosperous and great majesty, shadow of God on earth that . . . " in order to legitimize the temerity of his project.[138] And ultimately, he entrusted these "secrets concerning the origin of our distress" to the sultan and advised concealment of the rationale behind reform measures so that they might "be brought into being and quickly realized without any interference," thus referencing the tradition of consultation and privileging tradition as a guide to present action.[139] As an aged and devoted servant willing to sacrifice his own life for the sake of the realm, he inserted remedies that counter even his own concerns about greed and corruption within Ottoman officialdom. Aziz Efendi perceived the state to be encumbered by an unwieldy military, incapable of responding to urgent frontier disturbances with the Safavids. He urged the sultan to provide Kurdish *beys* in the border areas with material incentives in order to garner their support against future Safavid incursions. He specifically recommended the policy of *istimalat*, enticing the cooperation of regional power brokers: "documents of inducement (*istimālātnāme*) should be sent to all the Kurdish chiefs accompanied by ceremonial robes of honor, and to their relatives' land grants and benefices."[140] Aziz Efendi advocated this targeted use of financial reward despite lamenting the increasing greediness of traditional military units of the Ottoman army.

Mixing elements of innovation and convention, Aziz Efendi's text captures dramatically the ideological crisis at the heart of late sixteenth- and early seventeenth-century Ottoman advice manuals. The authors feared decline, sought redemption in the fundamentals of the *kanun-ı kadim*, and made restoration of the past the primary vehicle of reform. There was, however, an escalating tension between the writers' stated desire to restore "established laws" (*ḳānūn-ı muḳarrer*) and their strict appraisal of reality that seemingly rendered such a return impractical if not impossible. One of the main products of this tendency to idealize the past in response to a dysfunctional present was the agrarian system of the *timar*, where, in the nostalgic vision of it, custodians and producers held their proper place, functioned according to the dictates of a compartmentalized social order, and benefited from a prosperous treasury. Thus the *timar* emerged in its systematized and hallowed shape particularly within the sixteenth- and seventeenth-century reform-minded treatises, which presumed its collapse. It came to embody a social universe based on land and loyalty that no longer existed, and, indeed, may never have, at least in the form imagined by either early modern Ottomans or present-day Ottomanists.

As a result, treatise writers constructed the system in the negative, regretting what was supposedly lost, and through this regret constructing something that wasn't ever fully there. Yet in producing this ideal vision, they systematized workings of the state, and objectified former practices as institutional foundations. Their literary style partly embraced the mirror genre's art of reflection and concealment, yet it also charged in a new direction with a reform-minded language intent on provoking regulatory actions.

Forming the bridge between these two positions, return to the past versus reformative action in the present, were Ottoman documentary productions and administrative genres that provided treatise writers with new stylistic tools. Past techniques for categorizing the resources of the realm were wielded as persuasive tools to rectify present realities. The writers elaborated a proper order of things that drew on the language of customary practice, even as they created a new baseline for state policy. Although Koçu Bey and Aziz Efendi are the most obvious examples of this departure from mirror conventions, it is possible to detect a general movement toward a new mode of literary intervention based on a narrative structure of *before* and *after*. Authors during the period were intent on discovering what had worked before, what happened, the state of affairs now, and what needed to be done to redeem the empire's fortunes.[141] They juxtaposed lists of delegated officials and custodians of the land with memoranda, cadastral reports, sample *ferman*s, and references to the *kanunname* and in so doing shifted from a paradigm of advice to one of analysis. This shift also entailed a move away from premising statecraft on the character and actions of the sultan and toward an abstracted and bureaucratized vision of governance. In the process the genres of imperial registration were transformed into documentary evidence and fashioned into an archive of the state.

CONCLUSION

The Archiving State

> It took a long time to search for this information in varied and scattered registers.
>
> —'Ayn-ı 'Ali Efendi, *Ḳavānīn-i āl-i 'Os̱mān*[1]

Katip Çelebi's conception of the body politic identified the state as a collectivity and attributed its perfection to the proper regulation of a sociopolitical order. In the penultimate section of his *Düstūrü'l-'amel li-ıṣlāhı 'l-ḥalel*, he outlined the "final consequences" (*netīcetü a'netīcede*) of the various tribulations addressed in the pamphlet: the diminishment of the treasury, the proliferation of the privileged military strata (*'askeri*), the escalation of expenditures, and the weakening of the cultivators.[2] His solution was to entrust the treasury to a reliable servant who could guarantee an annual fiscal reserve. This was critical in his evaluation, as "the presence of a year's revenues in the treasury is the greatest strength of the heart." The "heart," in Katip Çelebi's corporeal metaphors of the state, was less the sultan than the sultanate, the regulatory system that ensured the prosperity of the empire. His prescriptions for reform centered on the "enhanced regulation" deemed necessary to bring harmony among the constituent groups that in turn reproduced imperial power. Enhanced regulation required "dependable, experienced, and honorable servants," the "mature, religious, and moral men of the pen who are the pillar of the treasury"; only this trained professional cadre, upright in bearing and loyal in service, could restore balance to the realm. They would achieve this by weeding out unlawful claimants to revenue and prohibiting the sale of administrative positions, thereby ending the oppression of the cultivator by greedy, profit-seeking trustees.

Texts and Categories: Preserving Order

The greatest strength of the state, in Katip Çelebi's estimation, was the treasury, and the heart of the treasury was a regulatory system operated by loyal servants. These servants were instrumental to extending the reach of the sultanate into the daily practice of governance. They did so by policing the categories of administrative order defined in the various registers, independent judgments, and certificates circulated by the imperial council.[3] This work of assessing the provincial and fiscal affairs of the empire could only be done, however, if the council also managed the systematic production and promulgation of what might be termed "texts of account": authoritative textual edicts, statements of status, and registers of human and material resources that measured the wealth of the empire in a complicated calculus of moral responsibility and productive yield. The system could not be managed without a preserved textual terrain that legislated and accounted for the dispersal and accumulation of resources. A lapse in this management system opened the door for rival claimants to revenue and status and thus planted the seeds of disorder. Focus on registration, and the need for a systematic textual index, indicated by Katip Çelebi, is even more salient in the manual of 'Ayn-ı 'Ali Efendi, to which Katip Çelebi's pamphlet was appended in several manuscript copies. 'Ayn-ı 'Ali Efendi's *Ḳavānīn-i āl-i 'Os̱mān der ḫülāsa-ı mezāmīn-i defter-i dīvān* (Rules of the house of 'Osman summarizing the contents of the registry of the Imperial Council) served as a register in itself—an administrative manual that collected the scattered accounts of the sultanate into one comprehensive index of the fiscal and administrative units of the empire. 'Ayn-ı 'Ali, the former master of imperial record keeping, claimed that "it took a long time to search for this information in varied and scattered registers"; thus, he presented his text as an alternative guide and map of imperial order.[4] In seven chapters he addressed not only the divisions of the empire but also the assigned ranks and current numbers of its official delegates and various military groups, and he focused specifically on how administrative duties and military defense combined to form the *timar* system. Furthermore, he proffered solutions to the demise of this system in a concluding section, thus placing his manual within the stylized innovations discussed in the previous chapter.

As the former supervisor of imperial registers, cadastral surveys in both detailed (*mufassal*) and summary (*icmal*) form, as well as the amended lists (*defter-i derdests*) and shifts in assignments (*defter-i rüznameçes*) recorded by the financial bureau, 'Ayn-ı 'Ali Efendi reinforced the categories of lands, personages, and responsibilities produced in the *kanunname* and reiterated in *mühimme* copies and various sultanic rescripts of justice and order. He differentiated between imperial and freehold domains, kinds of land grants, the officials assigned to each, rules that guided their bestowal, and the obligations required of each rank of administrative, financial, and military officials. He also identified lapsed loyalty and faulty mechanisms of registration as leading causes of the crisis facing the empire, as *timar* holders delegated campaign responsibilities and faulty inspections meant no accurate register existed from which to address flawed accounting procedures.[5] Preserving the order of the realm, 'Ayn-ı 'Ali Efendi intimated, entailed an ordered system of preserved registers indexing its resources. His manual, in both its organizational structure and pointed commentary, suggestively linked imperial power to an archive and to the various textual forms that testified to sovereign authority or the sultanate's right to survey, supervise, and manage its territories. In this he dramatically illustrates a conceit of imperial governance: that the "well protected domains" were a monolithic entity, embraced within the legal apparatus of the Ottoman establishment.

Texts and Documents: Circulating Legitimacy

As this book has demonstrated, 'Ayn-ı 'Ali Efendi's conceit of imperial governance assumed a transparent structure of sultanic command and regional implementation that was actually a fabrication of the very governing practices it enabled. The administration of empire depended on the exercise of delegated authority, and this catalyzed contests over the entitlements of its officials and generated a pervasive anxiety over the boundary between rebel and loyal servant. Forced to incite cooperation from both imperial delegates and regional power brokers, the lawmaking efforts of the Ottoman establishment spawned protest over categories and over the terminology of dues and obligations, and they further provoked rival interest groups that worked against imperial rights to property, persons, and provincial profit. Thus, registration mechanisms, sultanic commands, and legal statutes also catalogued frictions in the territorial regime that worked against imperial claims. They assumed stability, ascribed this stability to an ethical framework of just rule, and fixed the legitimacy of the sultanate to the reproduction of imperial order. Yet assuming stability, they registered mutation, instead, and an uneven extension of legal authority. Thus, the rubrics of rule outlined, for example, in general and provincial *kanunname* also reveal the effort to stabilize a constantly shifting imperial world. They thus inscribed the transparencies of power relations and thereby revealed the intricate technologies of rule adopted by the sultanate.

These dynamics position the Ottoman Empire within a growing scholarly conversation concerning the meaning of archives, archival practice, and state power in the fields especially of history, anthropology, and law. Michel Foucault inspired an interdisciplinary dialogue about the significance of the archive in the early 1960s. In *The Archaeology of Knowledge* he claimed that the archive *is* "the system that establishes statements as events and things."[6] He thus provoked a shift from what Ann Laura Stoler has termed the "archive-as-source" to the "archive as subject," especially as this pertained to the relationship between colonial projects and state archives.[7] Stoler further identifies this as a methodological shift "away from treating the archives as an *extractive* exercise to an ethnographic one."[8] This shift is also part of what Certeau termed "the condition of a new history," when archival activity itself becomes the basis of an analytic reading of historical processes.[9] Distinct from reading against the grain, or turning the archive into an ethnographic field, as in the work of Natalie Zemon Davis or Carlo Ginzburg, such an approach to the archive attends instead to record-keeping practices, documentary production, and the rubrics of order contained in categories of preservation.[10] In this mode the emergence of state archives indicates an effort to consolidate knowledge and to produce "social facts" that then operate as principles of governance. Historians thus particularly attend to the link between modern archiving systems and imperial projects of surveillance, which in turn reinforced the emergent power of a nation-state system.[11]

Yet, as this book has illustrated, the documents produced by an administrative apparatus are also distinct from its repository. The document and the archive represent two, interdependent yet differentiated, facets of governance. Varied documentary forms, fashioned by scribes in a complex chancery, produced categories of order dispersed across a varied terrain. These documents had fixed formats, as well as specialized scripts and notation devices, and were attentive to palace protocols, appointments, patents, conferment of grants and privileges, and the differentiation of revenue sources from individuals, land, charitable endowments, commercial production, and customs and market dues. Yet the ordinariness of these documentary forms—their repetitive formulae, techniques of persuasion, and categories of classification—belied their power as indices of an empire, iconic rubrics that shaped the textual habitus of sultanate and subject alike. Provincial and district governors, as well as judges, preserved these documents in regional registers and storehouses; they were also carried by individuals as proof of privilege, of safe passage, or dispute settlement and thus moved along routes of trade, travel, pilgrimage, and war, as well as through circuits of diplomacy and entreaty. These mobile circuits and regional storehouses were also part of an imperial archive, understood as a technique of registration or "defterization" that transformed an unwieldy terrain into a fixed and formal vocabulary of sociopolitical order. Copies of dispersed documents and commands were preserved on the grounds of the Topkapı Palace until their removal to a newly erected archive on the premises of the grand vizier's palace in 1785. Bound with a seal, they were also carried in wagonloads on military campaigns in order to maintain control over provisioning lines, to record acquired resources, and to account for the diligent participation of *timar* holders in the defense of the realm.

Texts and Space: Projecting Cohesion

Documents dispersed across the provincial terrain of the empire and stored within registers and enclosed cases in the palace embodied an effort to create a coherent system of administrative order. They assumed mastery, even if they lacked comprehensive knowledge, and provided overviews of regions, targeted populations, and reported problems. In this sense documents also embody the elusive nature of sovereignty itself and the troubled relationship between legal claims and a diffuse imperial territory. Lauren A. Benton has characterized the presumption of a unified political space that was in reality persistently "disrupted by irregularities" as a conceit, and she suggests that early modern empires actually consisted of "anomalous legal zones"[12] and that the *cartography* of sovereignty was as much a part of the textual edifice as the document itself. Documents, in her account, follow a "snaking pattern" with "corridors and enclaves" that created "islands" of legal sovereignty rather than a monolithic imperial space.[13] These islands of legal sovereignty and anomalous zones generated competing claims to resources and privilege, leading to the creation of new categories, constructed to rearrange knowledge and reassert power. The efforts to create supervisory oversight in occupied Hungary in the midst of competing linguistic, institutional, and imperial projects illustrates the disruptive nature of provincial governance well. Governors of Buda pivoted between regional power brokers, Habsburg and Ottoman sovereign demands, and foreign subject populations in their effort to secure resources. Fortresses and castles served as "islands" of territorial sovereignty amid a fractured provincial domain. Knowledge of regional activities was primarily partial, often inadequate, and always decried in sultanic edicts issued to provincial governors. Still, the *kanunname*s issued after the conquest of Buda became a standardized rubric incorporated into the *kanunname-i cedid* more than a century later; thus, a fantasy of unity became an actual repository of knowledge and part of a coded archive of administrative order.

The variegated fortunes of the Sayfa as provincial governors of Trablus, and the chaotic terrain of Greater Syria from 1585 to 1641 as a whole, also indicate the fractured nature of territorial sovereignty within the Ottoman Empire. Efforts to entice cooperative engagement with the Ottoman establishment, and negotiated settlements that transgressed the boundaries between officials and rebels, gesture toward a "layered sovereignty."[14] These negotiations further highlight that borders were not just configured as frontiers between rival empires but were also leveraged in internally fractious regions of coastal highlands and desert, and between state and nonstate agents. Dispatched in sultanic commands, delegated legal authority competed with indigenous alliances for claims to resources and access to revenue sources. Imperial efforts to create and shape a vision of imperial order in this competitive environment were intimately linked to, and mutually defined by, the ability to wield influence through legal commands circulated in textual form. The circulation of documents served to both define and supplement imperial authority. Ruling from an established palatial court meant that distance served as the key variable for maintaining sovereignty. While military forces were obviously key to both expansionary campaigns and regional control, internal rebellions and external rivals were also managed through an elaborate reliance on textual edicts of sultanic authority and registered maps of provincial resources; thus, the creation of textual authority accompanied and legitimized the use of force. The web of a documentary corpus first created and then imposed a legal and social order, placed the diffuse inhabitants of the realm within intelligible categories used as the basis for both taxation and redress, and sublimated anxieties of fragmented power to assertions of imperial universalism. Records generated by the establishment thus inscribed a set of institutional expectations and serve as a record of sociopolitical practice.

Texts into Archives: Constituting the State

The Ottoman establishment's devotion to record keeping also entailed the creation of a hegemonic imperial voice and, gradually, more attention to the record as a conduit of power in itself. Attention to record-keeping formulae as objects themselves thus became part of sixteenth-century efforts to systematize administrative protocol and scribal techniques. Thus, at the end of his tenure as head chancellor in 1573, Feridun Ahmed Bey compiled his *Mecmūʿa-ı Münşeʾāt-i Ferīdūn Bey* (Correspondence of the sultans), and Ebu's-suʿud's *fetva* were collected during the same period and became a primer for legislative governance both in Istanbul and in regional *shariʿa* courts.[15] Feridun Ahmed Bey's masterful compendium of stylized imperial correspondence also constituted a critical remapping of both the history and the political geography of the Ottoman sultanate. His introduction enumerated a genealogy of imperial power and a typology of imperial order situated within a manual intended as a shorthand guide for scribes. Feridun Bey's manual was prefaced by a clear itemization of the administrative elite and a competitive map of contemporary Muslim and non-Muslim sovereigns. This ordered presentation of the political geography of the early modern period legitimized the Ottoman dynasts by situating them within both a history of imperial sovereignty and a corpus of textual forms. Yet organizing the flow of paper took a different turn in the seventeenth century, as scholar-bureaucrats asserted the necessity for a systematic archiving method to preserve the vitality of the empire.

In the sixteenth century, the varied administrative, cadastral, and financial registers (*defatir*), as well as the loose-leaf (*evrak*) copies of assorted rulings, notations, individual legal judgments (*hüccet*), memoranda, and certificates, had been part of an ongoing process of documentary production and practice.[16] For example, the *mühimme* "captured" the activities of several major administrative divisions into a running tabulation copied into notations for the imperial council and served as a record of shifting priorities and concerns of governance across the imperial landscape. Additionally, the constant adjustments to *kanunname* regulations reflected the changing tactics deployed by the Ottoman establishment to establish clear sociopolitical and agrarian categories, which were then used to align regional realities with imperial expectations. The "archive" was therefore part of an ongoing practice, shaped by the exigencies of rule and an effort to extend legislative and territorial authority across vast imperial distances. In this sense the archive was constantly renewed, amended, in flux, and interdependent with variable historical circumstances. Disorder, within this sense of the archive as ongoing practice, was abetted by shifting the terms of alignment and cooperation among various stake-holders in the empire and reasserting the sovereign rights of the sultan. Beginning in the late sixteenth to the mid-seventeenth centuries, however, scholar-bureaucrats linked to the Ottoman establishment reified the meaning of the archive and rendered it into a second-order accounting of imperial affairs. In this guise they judged disorder not merely as reflective of shifting circumstances but also as the corruption of an ideal format of order, a *kanun-ı kadim* that established the boundaries of governance and set the terms of its practice. In this moment a paper trail became an objectified archive, as did the state, which it preserved and affirmed.

Consequently, men like 'Ayn-ı 'Ali Efendi, Koçu Bey, and Aziz Efendi, as well as later figures such as Hezarfen Hüseyin Efendi, presented encyclopedic summaries of old and new registers, documents, and *kanunname* in their effort to guard the borders of proper order.[17] Even as they reified a past practice, they instituted a baseline for a new one, as archival activity became increasingly more specialized from the mid-seventeenth century onward. Registers dedicated to adjudicating petitions and grievances, the *şikayet defterleri*, became a separate documentary entity beginning in 1649, whereas previously they had featured as part of the varied contents of the *mühimme*. Efforts to manage an increasingly mobile population, as well as to track the constant exchange of property, land grants, and tax collection rights shifted attention increasingly toward registers of individual account, the *avarız* (extraordinary taxes now normalized), and the *cizye* (poll tax on non-Muslims), as well as to daily account registers (*ruznamçe*) that attended especially to financial transactions concerning imperial lands, official salaries, and apportionments, along with palace expenditures. Once the imperial council's primary object of focus, even the index of provincial affairs (*mühimmeler*), was gradually transferred between 1707 and 1742 into a separate series of registers identified according to provincial units. This is also true for records of treaties, correspondence between rival governments and their envoys, and reports from Ottoman delegates traveling or living abroad, which were accorded separate *defter* series for each country or region of concern. Registers for Hungarian territories had already been set aside in the late 1560s and registers for Dubrovnik/Ragusa established in 1604, Poland in 1607, France in 1634, and continuing in order to incorporate correspondence with key global actors. These procedural reforms in methods of organizing administrative practice indicated increased focus on archiving a history of imperial intent. This accumulated archive supported the Ottoman establishment's effort to extend authority both within its domains and across its borders in an increasingly competitive interstate environment.

Although methods of preservation may have shifted, to some degree the conceptual framework and grammar of rule remained remarkably stable. Under the grand viziership of Merzifonlu Kara Mustafa Paşa (1676–83) and the sultanate of Mehmed IV (r. 1648–87), the basic protocols and administrative mores of the empire were revisited and revised. Although often referenced as a break with the past, and a reassessment after the multiple challenges faced in the early seventeenth century, the principles encoded by Leyszade during Mehmed II's reign were expanded but not necessarily reorganized. *Kanunnames* continued to itemize the personnel, territories, and inhabitants of the empire by invoking the pillars (*erkan*) of sultanic justice and equitable distribution inscribed in the late fifteenth century.[18] Issued in 1839 and 1856, even the presumably transformative edicts of the "new order," or Tanzimat, functioned as a proclamation of justice from the sultan (*'adaletname*).[19] Although the dynast now granted rights to subjects rather than outlining obligations, the textual "voice" of the empire remained the sultan. These edicts may have configured shifts in methods of conscription, punishment, taxation, and communal organization, yet the order of the realm still remained in the hands of the sultan.

And yet, as we have seen, the *kanunname*, *mühimme*, and *nasihatname* each revealed moments in which rival interest groups, socioeconomic transformations, and changing dynamics of interstate competition attenuated textual claims to absolutism. These claims, embodied and legitimated by the sultan as arbiter of order, were thus qualified by mechanisms employed to align provincial communities and power holders with the interests of the Ottoman establishment. Although sultanic edicts asserted a hegemonic textual authority across the empire's dominions, exhaustive negotiations and adaptations also left their residue in its written records. Thus the ideal of the sultan as the pinnacle of order lay in tension with administrative practices dependent on brokering alliances. *Nasihatname* authors then transformed this ideal into an idealization of the sultan and thereby transposed the dynast from absolute arbiter to euphemistic representative of the state. Still, while scholar-bureaucrats lamented a disordered realm and drew attention to its archived history, those who drafted edicts that were intended to reinstate the foundational pillars of the empire ultimately placed the commanding voice back within the ambit of the sultan.

In 1808, however, a gathering of regional notables from regions in Rumelia (modern-day Balkans) and Anatolia, along with key dignitaries of the imperial establishment, produced and signed a deed of alliance (*sened-i ittifâḳ*) that dramatically challenged the sultan and the Topkapı Palace as the source of a textual vision of order.[20] In an assembly at Sa'adabat Palace in Kağıthane along the shores of the Golden Horn, the assembly produced a text that figured as a new baseline for an integrated empire.[21] Composed to quell the chaos of preceding years resulting from dramatic provincial uprisings, a janissary-led popular revolt, the outbreak of war with Russia, and a coup d'état that enthroned the new sultan, Mahmud II (r. 1808–39), this deed placed hope for the restoration of imperial order in the consultative deliberation of regional power brokers rather than in the hands or the voice of the sultan.[22] The seven articles addressed standard facets of imperial administration, such as the collection of taxes, mechanisms for investigation and punishment, appointment of office holders, and army recruitment. Yet architects of the deed invoked a political vocabulary of trust and alliance, a "circle" of surety intended for the maintenance of imperial order. This circle of trust simultaneously echoed the conceptual framework of the circle of justice and transposed its elements to create a new principle of order. Mutual cooperation and a hierarchy of regional dynasts now served as the chief authorities of provincial order.[23] Although the sultan remained the symbolic pinnacle of this order and acted as the ultimate assurance of imperial continuity, his position was now clearly differentiated from the body politic of the state, and he stretched out his hand as a signatory, rather than as the originator, of imperial authority.

In the deed's text the "exalted state" stood as both the ultimate object of reconfigured power and the rationale for the deed itself. Signatories deemed the protection of the sultan's person and the strengthening of the sultanate as two distinct, if interconnected, facets of imperial power.[24] They created the deed as a written surety of both, and Sultan Mahmud II visited the assemblage gathered in Saʿadabat Palace to append his signature to the text and to pledge that he would "undertake the execution and implementation of the letter of promises and recognized conditions written in this deed of agreement."[25] Startling in clarity, this statement figures the sultan as participant in a broad assemblage of power brokers working in tandem to sustain the empire. While the deed's vision of alliance and stability was short-lived, and its principles fell along with Mustafa Bayraktar in a janissary revolt a mere three months after the unique gathering along the Golden Horn, its participatory ethos arguably shaped Ottoman political movements in the last century of the empire.[26] More significant than the deed's defaulted promise, however, is its insistent reference to a grammar and discourse of rule that interweaves textual and legal authority as the ultimate guarantee of imperial stability. The final article invokes this grammar in an ultimate declaration of the deed's intent:

> Since it is essential to protect and support the poor and tax-paying subjects, it is necessary that the local notable houses and chief men in the provinces pay attention to public order in the districts under their administration, and that they be moderate in levying taxes on the poor and tax-paying subjects. Therefore, let everyone give serious attention to the continuous implementation of any decision taken by ministers and local notable houses after discussion [between them], with regard to the prevention of oppression and the adjustment of taxes, and let everyone give serious attention to pre-

> venting oppression and transgression from taking place in contravention of these decisions. Let local notable houses scrutinize each other and inform the Exalted state if one such house commits oppression and transgression in violation of orders and the sacred *shari'a*, and let all local notable houses work unanimously toward the prevention of such actions.[27]

Links among provincial harmony, fair taxation policies, the prevention of oppression, and the legislative guidelines of *qanun* and *shari'a* clearly reiterate justice and distributive order as foundational principles of the Ottoman state. Here, however, they are embraced as the tools and strategies of a provincial and bureaucratic elite rather than as an imperial construct embodied in the personage of the sultan. The "Exalted State" acts only as mediator between elites who manage the affairs of the realm by scrutinizing each other, discussing necessary policy decisions, scrupulously implementing them, and acting in concert to sustain a "unanimous" practice. Although the principles of order remained, the basis of distributing shares had shifted. Administrative practice shifted authoritative command from sultan to delegate and unseated the dynast from his role as progenitor of textual, and by extension, territorial order. This "unseating" was also presaged by the vulnerabilities of textual command revealed throughout this book. Reform-minded authors of the late sixteenth century and the early seventeenth crafted these vulnerabilities into an alternate quest for a well-preserved imperial record of administrative practice. Arguably, then, efforts by scholar-bureaucrats in the seventeenth century to define and preserve a lost, idealized order, and thereby save the empire from "decline," unwittingly launched a new one and became part of the fabric of imperial endurance and reform that sustained the empire into the twentieth century.

NOTES

Introduction

1. Tursun Bey (d. after 1490) served as a high-ranking bureaucrat in the Ottoman chancery. His history, *Tārīḫ-i ebū'l-fetḥ*, is a key indicator of the evolving political understanding under Mehmed II and was written after the author's retirement to Bursa in 1488. For a facsimile with English translation see Tursun Bey, *The History of Mehmed the Conqueror*; for a close analysis of the historical context and rhetorical features see İnan, "A Summary and Analysis of the Tārīh-i Ebü'l-Feth." Tursun Bey's extended discussion concerning the appropriate use of sovereign power and the varied lineages adopted by the Ottoman dynasts will be addressed later in this chapter, as well as in Chapters 2 and 6.

2. Biographical sketches of Tarhuncu Ahmed Paşa's career as a palace administrator, governor, and ultimately grand vizier can be found in: Özvar, *İslam ansiklopedisi*, 20–22; Na'ima, *Tārāḫ-i Na'īmā*, 1284–1475; Danişmend, *İzahlı Osmanlı tarihi kronolojisi*, 418. The head finance minister involved in the project was Zurnazen Mustafa Paşa.

3. I use *Eurasia* here to reference a broad interconnected geographical zone that avoids imposing continental language on the period or the region. *Eurasia* also has the advantage of sidestepping culturalist biases or anachronistic labels that divide Europe from Asia, the Middle East, or the Near East. For a pointed critique of the continental approach to global history and the problem of "Europe" as a designation, see Lewis and Wigen, *The Myth of Continents*, 35–37. Abu-Lughod presents an argument for interconnected world systems during the period in *Before European Hegemony*.

4. The classic text on the "seventeenth-century crisis" is Aston, *Crisis in Europe*. Geoffrey Parker addressed criticisms from global historians and incorporated environmental approaches to sociopolitical upheaval in *Global Crisis*. For comparative adaptations of the overall thesis see Goldstone, "East and West"; and Goldstone, *Revolution and Rebellion*. Participants of an *American Historical Review* forum explored the usefulness of the concept for comparative studies of the early modern period; see Parker, "The General Crisis," 1029–99. Even the *AHR* debate failed to address the Eurocentric bias of comparative models, however; see Murphey, "Continuity and Discontinuity," 424; and Darling, *Revenue-Raising and Legitimacy*, 9–16.

5. The crisis appears within Ottoman historiography as a debate over the so-called price revolution of the late sixteenth and early seventeenth centuries; see Barkan, "The Price Revolution," 3–28; Ortaylı, "Osmanlı impartorluğu'nda iktisadi ve sosyal değişim"; Pamuk, "The Price Revolution," 69–89; and White, *The Climate of Rebellion.*

6. Setton, *The Papacy and the Levant*, 149–57.

7. Peirce, *The Imperial Harem*, 246–55; Börekçi, "İbrahim I"; Gökbilgin, "İbrāhīm," 983.

8. Brummett, "Classifying Ottoman Mutiny," 91–107.

9. Tarhuncu Ahmed proposed raising taxes on basic foodstuffs such as meat and bread within the environs of Istanbul, as well as other measures that demanded a rigorous accounting of tax-exempt statuses throughout the empire. These tax increases were meant to address a reported deficit of 175,393,885 *akçes*: MAD: 15675, 1–8; and D.BSM, 147: 59, 62, 71, 91.

10. There are several preserved manuscripts of this pamphlet. The Süleymaniye Library contains four: Esad Efendi, no. 2067-1; Hıdıv İsmail Paşa, no. 142; Hamidiye, no. 1469; and Lala İsmail, no. 343. There is also one held in the Nurosmaniye Library, no. 4075. A printed copy of the pamphlet was also appended to two works of 'Ayn-ı 'Ali Efendi: *Ḳavānīn-i āl-i 'Os̱mān der ḫülāsa-ı mezāmīn-i defter-i dīvān* [The laws of the Ottoman dynasty, comprising a summary of the contents of the council registers]; and *Risāle-i vazīfe-ḫorān ve merātib-i bendegān-ı āl-i 'Os̱mān* [Treatise on the salaried personnel and the ranks of the servants of the Ottoman dynasty]: Süleymaniye Library, İzmirli İsmail Hakkı, no. 2472. This printed manuscript copy was also published in the late nineteenth century as *Ḳavānīn-i āl-i 'Os̱mān der ḫülāsa-ı mezāmīn-i defter-i dīvān* (Istanbul: Tasvir-i Efkar Gazetehanesi, 1863), 119–40. Quotes from Katip Çelebi's *Düstūrü'l-'amel* are translated from the latter printed copy. On 'Ayn-ı 'Ali's assessment of the administrative and bureaucratic structure of the empire see Gökbilgin, "Ayn-ı Ali risalesi."

11. In "Mirrors for Princes" Linda T. Darling addresses the transregional nature of this phenomenon; however, she ultimately emphasizes the "incommensurability" rather than the connected nature of the trend. For examples from early Timurid, Mughal, and Ottoman contexts see Subtelny, "A Late Medieval Persian *Summa*"; Alvi, *Advice on the Art of Governance*; and Tietze, *Mustafā Ali's Counsel for Sultans.* Neguin Yavari has explored the evolution of political thought from medieval to modern periods and across the various linguistic registers of advice manuals in *Advice for the Sultan.*

12. Howard, "Genre and Myth"; Ferguson, "Genres of Power."

13. The intellectual vitality of the period, once questioned as part of a persistent decline paradigm, has now been soundly criticized in El-Rouayheb, *Islamic Intellectual History*; and Shefer-Mossensohn, *Science Among the Ottomans.*

14. For a succinct overview of the vibrant philosophic dialogues of the medieval period see Gutas, *Greek Thought, Arabic Culture*; Elizabeth and Garth Fowden

provide a closer reading in *Contextualizing Late Greek Philosophy*; and for an analysis of the impact of the archetypal text of the mirror tradition see Fowden, "Pseudo-Aristotelian Politics and Theology in Islam."

15. I would like to thank Glen Cooper for sharing his paper "Medicine and the Political Body" with me. On ibn Khaldun's dynastic cycles within the Ottoman context see Fleischer, "Royal Authority, Dynastic Cyclism." Galen's theories made their way into the Ottoman sphere by way of the work of Jalal al-Din al-Dawani (d. 1502), who incorporated classical and Arabo-Persianate theories of ethical harmony into his famous ethical treatise *Akhlāq al-Jalāli*: A. J. Newman, "*Davani, Jalal al-Din Mohammad,*" *Encyclopedia Iranica*. See also, Pfeiffer, "Teaching the Learned."

16. *Kavānīn-i Āl-i 'Osmān*, 119–20.

17. Ibid., 122.

18. The etymological link between disease, crisis, and the body politic exemplifies a Eurasian dispersion of medical knowledge and political analysis. For examples of this link in English, French, and Italian see J. B. Shank's summary in "Crisis: A Useful Category," 1091–92. Reinhart Koselleck and Michaela Richter explored the Greek origins and gradual dispersion of the term in "Crisis"; and Randolph Starn evaluated the historiographic ambiguity of the term *crisis* itself in "Historians and 'Crisis.'"

19. Appended to 'Ayn-ı 'Ali Efendi, *Ḳavānīn-i āl-i 'Os̱mān*, 124. Adapted from Aristotle or pseudo-Aristotelian traditions, and invoked in various forms across Eurasian contexts, Ottoman litterateurs had embraced it quite early for their own use. Darling has authored the definitive text on this expansive tradition; see Darling, *A History of Social Justice*. For a summary of pseudo-Aristotelian traditions see Manzalaoui, "The Pseudo-Aristotelian *Kitāb al-Asrār*."

20. 'Ayn-ı 'Ali Efendi, *Ḳavānīn-i āl-i 'Os̱mān*, esp. 127–28.

21. Guy Burak has addressed the contested nature of this process in *The Second Formation of Islamic Law*. El-Rouayheb identifies the resurgence of a rationalist mode in *Islamic Intellectual History* (see esp. 60–85).

22. On the evolution of Ottoman political thought concerning the role of the sultan see Sariyannis, "Ruler and State."

23. 'Ayn-ı 'Ali Efendi, *Ḳavānīn-i āl-i 'Os̱mān*, 123–24. On these periods as major Ottoman crises see Kastritsis, *The Sons of Bayezid*; Akdağ, *Celālī İsyanları*; Griswold, *The Great Anatolian Rebellion*; and White, *The Climate of Rebellion*, 164–85.

24. See Heather Ferguson, "Ottomans, Ottomanists, and the State: Redefining an Ethos of Power in the Long Sixteenth Century," forthcoming in *Halcyon Days in Crete 9*, for a historiographic account of these efforts to both define and analyze the nature of the state in the field of Ottoman studies.

25. Certeau, *The Writing of History*, 6. Certeau explicitly linked this moment to Machiavelli and thus to the intrusion of critique into a form devoted to counsel that will be addressed in Chapter 6.

26. Ernst Cassirer also locates a shift in Machiavelli's writing from moral allegory to technical political analysis and links it to the moment when the state became disembodied from its political practice; see Cassirer, *The Myth of the State*, 153.

27. Certeau, *The Writing of History*, 7.

28. Ibid.

29. Murat Dağlı, "The Limits of Ottoman Pragmatism," 194.

30. The following section also draws from Bang and Kołodziejczyk's "'Elephant of India,'" the editorial introduction to their collection of essays on imperial universalism, *Universal Empire*.

31. Timothy M. May has discussed the substantial and diverse impact of the Mongol invasions; see May, *The Mongol Conquests*, 109–256.

32. Bang and Kołodziejczyk, "'Elephant of India,'" 27. This list combines insights from Subrahmanyam and Bang and Kołodziejczyk. Subrahmanyam identified shared features of composite empires in "Written on Water": "(1) as states with an extensive geographical spread, embracing more than one cultural domain and ecozone; (2) as states powered by an ideological motor that claimed extensive, at times even universal, forms of dominance, rather than the mere control of a compact domain; (3) as states where the idea of suzerainty was a crucial component of political articulation, and where the monarch was defined not merely as king, but as 'king over kings,' with an explicit notion of hierarchy in which various levels of sovereignty, both 'from above' and 'from below,' were involved" (43). Bang and Kołodziejczyk emphasized a shared language of imperial universalism, instead, and thus three thematic issues central to the early modern formation: "(1) symbolism, ceremony and diplomatic relations, (2) universal or cosmopolitan literary high-cultures and, finally, (3) the inclination to present universal imperial rule as an expression of cosmic order" (27).

33. Dreyer, *Zheng He*.

34. This exchange of letters was preserved in the sixteenth-century chancery compilation of Feridun Bey, *Mecmū'a-yı münşe'āt-i Ferīdūn Bey*, 382–86. The letters, composed in 1514, were sent in the context of Selim's triumphant march eastward to confront Shah Isma'il. Selim's tone was assertive and emphatic and slandered the Safavid shah throughout the composition. Isma'il's response was more wily than confrontational, and the textual postures of each warrant a careful analysis in their own right.

35. Subrahmanyam, "Aspects of State Formation," 357–77.

36. Johnson, *Cultural Hierarchy*.

37. Necipoğlu, "Süleyman the Magnificent"; Necipoğlu, "Framing the Gaze."

38. Alam, *The Languages of Political Islam*, 122–23, 127; Woodhead, "Ottoman Languages." For the royal ordinances and legal acts that standardized the language of the French, English, and Polish courts see Burke, *Languages and Communities*, 72–76; for a broader discussion of the intersection between chancery organization and standardized language procedures see Chapter 3; and Şahin, *Empire and Power*, 220–28.

39. Tosun Arıcanlı and Mara Thomas foregrounded the relationship between shares and principles in "Sidestepping Capitalism."

40. My approach borrows from Pierre Bourdieu's heuristic categories of habitus (embodied inclination of agents to evaluate and act on the world in particular ways) and field (historical conditions of practice and the resulting tension between change and continuity) and Bakhtin's characterization of dialogism (communicative practices that naturalize the objects and social relations they mediate) to wed literary genre with sociopolitical practice. Despite important differences between these two thinkers, they have in common the concept that agents bring to action an immense stock of sedimented social knowledge that is partially unreflective but in their repetition generative of particular schemes or systems of practice. See especially Bakhtin, "The Problem of Speech Genres" and "The Problem of the Text"; and Bourdieu, *Outline of a Theory of Practice*, 64–89.

41. Arıcanlı and Thomas, "Sidestepping Capitalism," 39. A "shares not principles" approach, however, focuses analysis on the scrabble for resources and leaves unattended the principle that purportedly gives shape to the game as a whole. See Boğaç A. Ergene's rebuttal of Arıcanlı and Thomas in Ergene, "On Ottoman Justice," 70–71.

42. The Ottoman section of the Prime Minister's Archive published a comprehensive guide to the collection: Sarınay, *Başbakanlık Osmanlı arşivi rehberi*; see Uzunçarşılı, *Osmanlı devletinin merkez ve bahriye teşkilâtı* for an early effort to assess and analyze the comprehensive documentary projects of the empire.

43. Categorized as *tahrir defterleri*, these were tax registers that listed provincial social units along with the revenue expectations of the Istanbul government. For the strongest studies based on these registers and critical assessments of their usefulness for historical analysis, see Káldy-Nagy, "The Administration of the Ṣanǰāq Registrations"; Lowry, *Studies in Defterology*; and Darling, *Revenue-Raising and Legitimacy*.

44. Compendia of rulings on cultivation, ownership, rents, and criminal fees, among other concerns, the *kanunname* serve as one of the key sources for this study and the singular focus of Chapter 2. The *kanunname-i cedid*, formalized sometime after 1674, was a compilation of earlier regulations and the reforms primarily introduced by the head jurisconsult of the Ottoman realm, Ebu's-su 'ud Efendi. See Lowry, "The Ottoman Liva Kanunnames"; Greene, "An Islamic Experiment?"; and Burak, "Between the *Ḳānūn* of Qāytbāy and Ottoman *Yasaq*."

45. Labeled as *ruznamçe*, these registers were chronologically organized and listed the names of those who received grants by either regional or central administrators along with the official diplomas issued by the imperial council. Douglas A. Howard addressed the evolution of the office that held these registers in his "The Historical Development of the Ottoman Imperial Registry." Linda Darling upended long-held convictions about the recipients of these bestowals in the early seventeenth century

in her article "Nasihatnameler, İcmal Defterleri, and the Timar-Holding Ottoman Elite."

46. The general *mühimme* (things of import) registers, the complaint registers (*şikayet defterleri*), and the registers for the sultan (*rikab mühimmesi*), military (*ordu mühimmesi*), and representative in the capital (*kaymakam mühimmesi*) were all key to the daily administrative practice of the empire. The first known *mühimme* collection is dated 1544; see Sahillioğlu, *E-12321 numaralı mühimme defteri*. There are a total of 263 registers catalogued as *mühimme defterleri* (MD) held in the Başbakanlık Arşivi, Istanbul, and the series continues until 1905. The first complete *şikayet defterleri* (ŞD), fully distinguished from the *mühimme* registers, appeared in 1649, and the series continued until 1813; however, an intermixture and slow disentanglement of the two collections is also detectable until 1656; see Gümrükçüoğlu, "Şikāyet defterlerine göre Osmanlı teb'asının şikāyetleri," 178. For an overview of these categories and their evolution see Emecen, "Osmanlı divanının ana defter serileri." On "traveling archives" that moved according to the dictates of campaign seasons, see Emecen, "Sefere götürülen defterlerin defteri."

47. The best-known example, referenced previously, is Feridun Ahmed Bey's *Mecmū'a-yı münşe'āt-i Ferīdūn Bey*. It contained more than 528 documents presumably collected from the time of the Prophet Muhammad to the completion of the original work (1574–75). Feridun Ahmed Bey's (d. 1583) manual primarily served the interests of Sokullu Mehmed Paşa, who had a long career in military and provincial governance before serving as grand vizier from 1565 to 1579.

48. For seventeenth-century critiques from this perspective see Aksüt, *Koçi Bey Risalesi*; the anonymous chronicles *Kitāb-ı müstetāb* and *Ḥırzü'l-Mülūk*; and Ipşirli, "Hasan Kafi el-Akhisare ve devlet düzenine ait eseri."

49. Most of the literature on this rhetorical trope links it directly to provincial unrest and to the *celali* rebellions that have come to typify it. Unfortunately, this masks the link between *fitne* and corruption and ignores evidence of "improper orderings" within the imperial administration itself.

50. From a facsimile of his *Ḳānūn-i şehinşahi* published in Akgündüz, *Osmanlı kanunnameleri*, 3:57. Christopher Markiewicz analyzed Idris Bitlisi's emergence within rival chanceries of the period—the Akkoyunlu, Mamluk, and Ottoman—and his contribution to forging an ideology of Ottoman sovereignty in "The Crisis of Rule."

51. Mottahedeh, *Loyalty and Leadership*, 179; Ergene, "On Ottoman Justice," 75n67.

52. Although this designation for the registers is now commonplace in scholarship on the Ottoman Empire, the bound registers in which a wide variety of sultanic decrees were archived did not bear this specific designation until much later, at least until the 1640s, and perhaps after the decision to bind registers of complaint and

their *responsa* in a category of their own, the *şikâyet defteri*. See Temelkuran, "Dīvān-ı hümāyūn mühimme kalemi," 158; Kütükoğlu, "Mühimme defterlerinde muâmele kayıdları üzerine," 95–97; Dávid, "The Mühimme Defteri as a Source," 167–68.

53. "Intermediary" does not suggest that these documentary sets represent distinct positions but rather that they participate in a shared discourse of administrative justice and concern for stable organizational principles.

54. This phrase is adapted from Stefan Winter's brief reference to Ottoman efforts in Bilad-ı Şam to "territorialize" their claims to sovereignty in *The Shiites of Lebanon*, 37.

55. "Scholar-bureaucrat" is Cemal Kafadar's term, taken from *Between Two Worlds*, 18. It has now become quite standard as a reference to the entangled bureaucratic and intellectual horizons of the early modern period. See Atçıl, *Scholars and Sultans*, 83–118.

56. This point builds on Michel Foucault's belief that language is coded and structured by historical processes and Pierre Bourdieu's description of discourse as a field of power "structured and restructured" by the practices and strategies of its participants; see Foucault, *The Order of Things*, 157–62; and Bourdieu, *Outline of a Theory of Practice*, 78–87.

57. Karen Barkey's book *Bandits and Bureaucrats* moved the field toward widespread acceptance of "negotiation" as a historiographic explanation for Ottoman empire building, although the approach still invokes a center-periphery paradigm and reinforces static interpretations of the state. This book follows Huricihan İslamoğlu's argument that the law itself embodies a negotiated process; see İslamoğlu, "An Agenda for Comparative History." It also suggests that "alignment," rather than "negotiation" or "accommodation," best captures Ottoman administrative tactics.

58. See part 1 of Barkey and von Hagen, *After Empire*; and Barkey, *Empire of Difference*.

59. See Barkey, *Empire of Difference*, 10. Incidentally, this is also a significant historiographical debate for scholars of Tokugawa Japan as they work to define the nature of the relationship between the Shogun and regionally based Daimyo lords; see Totman, *The Green Archipelago*; and Hall, "The Muromachi Bakufu." Mary Elizabeth Berry, by contrast, argued in *Japan in Print* for an early modern concept of "Japan" as a clear object of identification and challenged sharp divisions between imperial and national projects.

60. See Ágoston, "Information, Ideology, and Limits of Imperial Policy."

61. Roderick Cavaliero has provided a synoptic overview of Ottomania in the nineteenth-century European imagination; see Cavaliero, *Ottomania*. Elena Furlanetto has explored utopian nostalgias in contemporary Turkish literature in Furlanetto, "'Imagine a Country Where We Are All Equal.'" And Elif Batuman addresses the broader cultural phenomena of this trend in "Ottomania."

62. See Said, *Orientalism*. Originally published in 1978, the 2003 edition includes an afterword from 1994 and a new introduction in which Said attempts to clarify his

theoretical points and to update his political commentary. Still, Said failed to acknowledge previous assessments of Orientalism as a discursive construction and drew only haphazardly on the theoretical language of both Michel Foucault and Jacques Derrida. See Aijaz Ahmad, "*Orientalism* and After," as well as his concluding comments in *In Theory* (333–37). Gerald MacLean summarized concerns about the applicability of his thesis to the early modern period in *Looking East*, 1–27; and Zachary Lockman reflects on "orientalism" as a publishing industry in *Contending Visions of the Middle East*.

63. See Rohde, "The Islamic World's Culture War"; Kraidy and al-Ghazzi, "Neo-Ottoman Cool"; and Rousselin, "Turkish Soap Power."

64. See Shehadeh, *A Rift in Time*; and, for a brief synopsis of his points, see "In Pursuit of My Ottoman Uncle," 82–93.

65. These practices balance myths of unity with exclusionary tactics, as Bülent Batuman argued in the context of the protests that engulfed Turkey in 2013, "'Everywhere Is Taksim.'"

Chapter 1. The Sovereign State

Portions of this chapter were previously published as "From Hyperbole to Bureaucracy: Ottoman and Habsburg Courtly Rivalries," In *Iacobus: Revista de Estudios Jacobeos Y Medievales*, memorial issue for Louis Cardaillac (Issue 33–34, 2015), 265–90.

1. From one of the earliest *kanunname* attributed to the last years of Mehmed II's reign (r. 1444–46, 1451–81). Chapter 2 addresses the derivation and form of this *kanunname* in more detail.

2. Leyszade Mehmed Efendi was chief of the nascent Ottoman chancellery from 1477 to 1480. Only two seventeenth-century manuscripts of these legal regulations exist: the copy from Vienna published in Arif, "Kanunname-yi Al-i Osman"; and a copy found in Leningrad compiled by Bosnalı Hüseyin Efendi, edited by Tveritinova and Petrosjan and published as *Badā'i' al-waḳā'i'*. A critical edition that compares and combines the two is the one referenced here: Özcan, "Fatih'in teşkilat kanunnamesi," 7–56. The title of this edition refers to the infamous rationale for fratricide that places order and social harmony above prohibitions of murder. For various assessments of the authenticity of this *kanun* see Özcan, *Fatih Sultan Mehmed*, xxxv; Tezcan, "The 'Kānūnnāme of Mehmed II,'" 657–65; and Tezcan, *The Second Ottoman Empire*, 58.

3. Necipoğlu, *Architecture, Ceremonial, and Power*, 19.

4. The oath of allegiance, like many Ottoman court rituals, derived from a mix of Islamicate, Byzantine, and Anatolian practices. For a discussion of the oath within the legal traditions and practices of sovereignty in Islam see Tyan, "Bay'a." Palmira Brummett discusses these ceremonial rituals of submission as developed within the Ottoman diplomatic context in "A Kiss Is Just a Kiss." For a broader medieval discussion see Petkov, *The Kiss of Peace*.

5. See Duindam, *Vienna and Versailles*, 181–97.

6. Representative examples of these trends include Rothman, *Brokering Empire*; Kołodziejczyk, *Ottoman-Polish Diplomatic Relations*; Dávid and Fodor, *Ottomans, Hungarians, and Habsburgs*; Peacock, *The Frontiers of the Ottoman World*; and Dávid and Fodor, *Ransom Slavery Along the Ottoman Borders.*

7. Commensurability focuses on a shared ecology of rule across centralizing states and departs either from border analyses or from simple comparisons. Sanjay Subrahmanyam pioneered this trend, which has increasingly framed a burgeoning scholarship on both transregional and global historical processes; see Subrahmanyam, "Connected Histories," 735–62; and Subrahmanyam, *Courtly Encounters.* Two significant recent examples that follow an analytic emphasis on commensurability are Şahin, *Empire and Power*; and Krstić, *Contested Conversions.*

8. Suraiya Faroqhi assesses this interconnected landscape in *The Ottoman Empire and the World*; for another example of entangled diplomatic histories see Goffman, *The Ottoman Empire and Early Modern Europe.* Ariel C. Salzmann critiqued patronage as a rubric for assessing ties between the center and its provinces and proffered instead a "corporate model"; see Salzmann, *Tocqueville in the Ottoman Empire.*

9. This analysis builds on research that links writing, power, and archives in the formulations of imperial and state bureaucracies; see Messick, *The Calligraphic State*; Connery, *The Empire of the Text*; Burns, *Into the Archive*; Raman, *Document Raj*; and Sellers-García, *Distance and Documents.*

10. These tales may date to the ninth century but were only transcribed in the fourteenth; see Sümer, Uysal, and Walker, *The Book of Dede Korkut.*

11. Brummett, "A Kiss Is Just a Kiss," 111–15.

12. Ibid., 112.

13. Brummett traces the image of supplication in manuscript traditions as well. She describes, for example, the set of illustrations in Lokman ibn Seyyid Husayn's (d. 1601–2) *Hünernâme* [The book of accomplishments] as a "set of repeated acts of submission—one kiss after another" and argues that "these images, showing the enthroned sultans receiving the obeisance of their officers, reinforce the notion that kissing the hand of the sultan is what men have always done" (117–18). The significance of supplication and obeisance to Ottoman dynastic power is also visible in Orbay, *The Sultan's Portrait*; and Fetvacı, "From Print to Trace."

14. Tietze, *Mustafa 'Ali's Counsel for Sultans*, 38.

15. I refer here to the copy, dated to the sixteenth century, in Akgündüz, *Osmanlı kanunnameleri*, 1:318–27.

16. See Avcioğlu, "Istanbul"; and Necipoğlu, "From Byzantine Constantinople to Ottoman Kostantiniyye."

17. Necipoğlu, "From Byzantine Constantinople to Ottoman Kostantiniyye," 263; Kritoboulos Imbriōtēs, *History of Mehmed the Conqueror*, 142.

18. Tursun Bey, *Tārīḫ-i ebū'l-fetḥ*, 34.

19. Kritoboulos Imbriōtēs, *History of Mehmed the Conqueror*, 141.

20. Domenico, Domenico's Istanbul, 87.

21. Fleet, "Tax-Farming in the Early Ottoman State."

22. Yücel, *Anadolu beylikleri hakkında araştırmalar.*

23. Demetriades, "The Tomb of Ghazi Evrenos Bey"; Ocak, "Heterodoks Şeyh ve Dervişlerin Rolü"; Karamustafa, *God's Unruly Friends*; Kastritsis, "The Revolt of Şeyh Bedreddin."

24. Zachariadou, "Les notables laïques et le patriarcat œcuménique"; Köprülü, "Bizans Müessesselerinin Osmanlı Müessesselerine."

25. Necipoğlu, "The Life of an Imperial Monument."

26. İnalcık, "The Policy of Mehmed II."

27. See, e.g., Kafescioğlu, *Constantinopolis/Istanbul.* For a provocative reading of early Ottoman identity manipulation see Zirinski, "How Did the Ottomans Become Ottoman?"

28. Neumann, "Devletin adı yok—bir amblemin okunması"; Wigen, "Ottoman Concepts of Empire"; Wigen, Gratien, and Hammon, "Empire in Question."

29. As Sellers-García phrases it, "Spatial history matters to the social history of knowledge. . . . Knowledge was created along routes, and it was gathered radially, resulting in a hierarchical structure that favored the accumulation of knowledge at the empire's center" (*Distance and Documents*, 19).

30. Veena Das addressed the "illegibility" of state documents and suggested that when the state "institutes forms of governance through technologies of writing, it simultaneously institutes the possibility of forgery, imitation, and the mimetic performances of its power" (*Life and Words*, 163). This illegibility does not fully destabilize the state; rather, it precisely enables its ability to penetrate deeper into communal lives. Although Das's analysis focuses on modern India, her argument that forgeries actually extend, rather than fully challenge, the state places even "inauthentic" documents within an environment controlled by centralized power.

31. As I noted in my introduction, Brinkley Messick adapted Pierre Bourdieu's methodology defined in *Outline of a Theory of Practice* to analyze the intersection between authority and text. Messick argued that particular forms of "textual domination" conveyed messages of "ruling ideas" and of the state: "A textual habitus, a set of acquired dispositions concerning writing and the spoken word, and the authoritative conveyance of meaning in texts was reproduced in homologous structures and practices across different genres and institutions. It was the resulting, partly implicit, experience of coherence amid diversity, the reaffirming of basic orientations with multiple forms and sites of expression that enhanced the natural qualities of the dispositions themselves. From domain to domain, the quiet redundancies of discursive routines were mutually confirming." Messick, *The Calligraphic State*, 251–52.

32. This approach to the intersections of space, text, and power adapts Henri

Lefebvre's argument that power relations occur in space, and every society, or mode of production, produces its own space. See Lefebvre, *The Production of Space*, 33, 36–38, 164–66.

33. Evans, "The Court."

34. Key examples of this literature include Adamson, *The Princely Courts*; Chandra, *Parties and Politics*; Duindam, Artan, and Kunt, *Royal Courts*; and Subrahmanyam, *Courtly Encounters*.

35. I have adopted this phrase from notes on the manuscript by my colleagues in the History Department at Claremont McKenna College.

36. Salzmann, *Tocqueville in the Ottoman Empire*, 45.

37. Barkey's *Bandits and Bureaucrats* remains the strongest assertion of brokered relationships across social boundaries.

38. See Peirce, *The Imperial Harem*.

39. Faroqhi, Güven, and Türesay, *Osmanlı dünyasında üretmek, pazarlamak, yaşamak*.

40. Boyar and Fleet, *A Social History of Ottoman Istanbul*; Singer, *Constructing Ottoman Beneficence*.

41. Adamson, *The Princely Courts of Europe*, 14.

42. Ibid., 10.

43. Necipoğlu, *Architecture, Ceremonial, and Power*.

44. See Kamen, *Philip of Spain*, 31.

45. Adamson, 315n27.

46. See Necipoğlu, "From Byzantine Constantinople to Ottoman Kostantiniyye"; and Murphey, "Ottoman Sovereignty in Motion," 207–51.

47. Atasoy, "Ottoman Garden Pavilions and Tents."

48. Necipoğlu, *Architecture, Ceremonial, and Power*, 31.

49. Ahmed Refik edited and published two sources that reveal an emergent Ottoman palace bureaucracy: an early expense account from the imperial kitchens (the month of July 1473) and that of a pay register detailing the categories and allotments for palace personnel a mere decade after the completion of the Topkapı Palace (from May to July 1478). See Refik, "Matbah-i amire [harc] defteri (şaban 878)"; and Refik, "Defter-i mevacib."

50. Barkan, "933–4/1527–8 mali yılına ait bir bütçe örneği," 315. Barkan's collected treasury accounts for 1527 and 1528 contain key examples of early palace expenditures. Murphey, *Exploring Ottoman Sovereignty*, 159.

51. For the initial formulation of the *gazi* thesis see Wittek, *The Rise of the Ottoman Empire*. Rudi Paul Lindner qualified yet maintained its key principles in *Nomads and Ottomans*. Kafadar formed the strongest critique of these formulations in *Between Two Worlds*.

52. Köprülü, "Anadolu Selçukları tarihinin yerli kaynakları." On links among historical consolidation, architecture, and legacy see Cahen, *The Formation of Turkey*;

Hillenbrand, *Turkish Myth and Muslim Symbol*; Peacock, *Early Seljūq History*; Turan, *Selçuklular zamanında Türkiye*; and Blessing, "Introduction."

53. Dimitri Korobeinikov reminds us that the Seljukid court aristocracy was "Turkic by origin and Turkish titles were used together with Arab and Persian ones. But the ruling dynasty adopted Iranian names such as 'Kay-Kāwūs,' 'Kay-Qubād,' and 'Kay-Khusraw,' which were derived from the names of the legendary shāhs of the Kayanid dynasty in Īrān, the founders of the Persian Empire." See Korobeinikov, "How 'Byzantine' Were the Early Ottomans?" 4. For a compendium of this interlinguistic frontier see Halasi-Kun and Golden, *The King's Dictionary*.

54. Konyalı, *Söğüt' de Ertuğrul Gazi türbesi*.

55. Korobeinikov, "How 'Byzantine' Were the Early Ottomans?" 13–14. Kafadar argues that this vision of early frontier consolidation and warfare was produced by early fifteenth-century Ottoman chroniclers themselves to disrupt the claims of their rivals; see Kafadar, *Between Two Worlds*.

56. Fortress-centric state building would continue to play a significant role in Ottoman expansion and was the foundation of its program of occupation in the Hungarian territories I will discuss in Chapter 4. For early fortress movements see Korobeinikov, *Byzantium and the Turks*, 284–85. The historians he cites, followed here to track the significance of fortresses in the period, are Aşıkpaşazade, *Āşıkpaşazāde tarihi*, 18–29; Neşri, *Kitāb-ı cihān-nümā*, 96–105. Zachariadou also clearly mapped frontier politics of the early Osmanlı confederation in *The Ottoman Emirate (1300–1389)*, esp.138–46.

57. Uzunçarşılı, *Anadolu beylikleri ve Akkoyunlu, Karakoyunlu devletleri*.

58. Setton, *A History of the Crusades*, 6:248–49.

59. Murphey, *Exploring Ottoman Sovereignty*, 51.

60. Significantly, internal to each court culture the meaning of "the state" changed over time. In England *state* was once a synonym for the canopy that stood over the monarch's throne. In Habsburg Spain *state* also came to reference the canopy in El Escorial that occluded the king and queen from view in the chapel during liturgical services. The variegated meanings assigned to *devlet* in the Ottoman context, and the complex ways in which the meanings of good fortune, divine favor, and state power evolved in relationship to alternative terms for sovereignty such as *memleket*, *kut*, and *saltanat*, will be addressed further in Chapter 6. Recent scholarship on these issues has deftly addressed the problems associated with a simplistic use of the word *state*; see, e.g., Sigalas, "Devlet et Etat," 385–415; and Sariyannis, "Ruler and State," 83–117.

61. For alternative interpretations of the significance of these shifts see Fleischer, *Bureaucrat and Intellectual*, 253–72; and Neumann, "Devletin adı yok."

62. Necipoğlu, "A Kanun for the State."

63. Lewis, *The Political Language of Islam*, 22.

64. For a comparable example see Baillie, "Etiquette and the Planning of the State Apartments."

65. This new spatialization of power can also be traced at Whitehall, the adopted Tudor palace. A new Privy Council was given formal existence in 1540, with a meeting room located in the heart of the monarch's private apartments (the Privy Lodgings) only steps from the king's bedchamber; see Starkey, "Court, Council and Nobility," 200. The appointment of ministers with rights to attend the king's private apartments also occurred in the Castile-Aragon court of the Spanish Habsburgs; see Elliott, "The Court of the Spanish Habsburgs."

66. Scholars have frequently identified the retreat of the ruler and the strategies deployed to mask this absence with a general decline in Ottoman imperial power. One classical illustration can be found in Lewis, "Some Reflections on the Decline."

67. Redworth and Checa, "Courts of the Spanish Habsburgs," 57; see also Rodríguez-Salgado, "The Court of Philip II," 241.

68. Lewis, "Some Reflections on the Decline"; Shaw, *Empire of the Gazis.*

69. Redworth and Checa, "Courts of the Spanish Habsburgs," 52; Elliott, "The Court of the Spanish Habsburgs," 144–45.

70. Redworth and Checa, "Courts of the Spanish Habsburgs," 47–49; Boyden, *The Courtier and the King*, 15–17.

71. Between the council hall and the stables a small gate led to the protected realm, or the harem (*ḥarīm*).

72. This schematic description is based on Necipoğlu, *Architecture, Ceremonial, and Power*, 53–88.

73. Lewis, "Dīvān-ı hümāyūn." The imperial council was not a static institution; membership fluctuated according to territorial expansion, shifts in priority toward particular administrative duties, and the various efforts to reorganize the practice of record keeping at the heart of Ottoman imperial governance. Thus, for example, in an era of reconsolidation with a dynasty of viziers, the Köprülüs (1565–1691), the grand vizier held an additional meeting after the afternoon prayer, which marked the traditional conclusion of the *divan* session, in his private residence. Gradually, this *ikindi*, or second meeting, became the substance of decision making, and the regular council meeting became one concerned primarily with the promotion and dismissal of officials or with questions of general comportment and protocol.

74. The Rumeli judge had seniority over the Anatolian, although both oversaw the appointment of judges and other religious functionaries in their respective realms and possessed the authority to issue commands (*buyuruldu*) in legal cases with the sultan's *tuğra* (cipher) appended to them; see Akgündüz, *Osmanlı kanunnameleri*, 1:320; and Fekete, "Tughra."

75. As part of the reorganization and expansion under the court of Süleyman,

additional financial bureau chiefs were added, and the head registrar of Rumelia became known as the chief, or *baş defterdar*; see Lewis, "Defterdār."

76. The *nişancı*'s position evolved continuously throughout the early modern period, as addressed in Chapters 3 and 4.

77. Özcan, "Fatih'in teşkilat kanunnamesi, 12; see also Asch, "Introduction," 7–13.

78. Redworth and Checa argue that "'court' and 'capital' were much the same thing under the Habsburgs"; see Redworth and Checa, "Courts of the Spanish Habsburgs," 43.

79. Adamson, "The Making of the Ancien Régime Court," 12.

80. Refik, "Defter-i mevacib."

81. Özcan, "Fatih'in teşkilat kanunnamesi."

82. Under the grand viziership of Merzifonlu Kara Mustafa Paşa (1676–83) and the sultanate of Mehmed IV, the basic protocols and administrative mores of the empire were revisited and revised. Although often referenced as a break with the past, and a reassessment after the multiple challenges faced in the early seventeenth century, the principles encoded by Leyszade Mehmed were expanded but not necessarily reorganized. The expansion and inclusion of more personnel, territories, and accompanying etiquette matched the expansion of the realm but did not break with the pillars (*erkan*) of the empire inscribed in the late fifteenth century. See 'Abdi (Tevki'i), "Osmanlı kanunnameleri."

83. Although the entertainment palace of Sa'dabad was destroyed in the rebellion that ended the experimentation of the so-called Tulip Age, this turn away from Topkapı-centric protocol continued and reached its ultimate end in Abdülhamid II's retreat to a new structure and a new isolationist mode at Yıldız Palace, across the Golden Horn and up the shoreline from Beşiktaş; see Hamadeh, "Public Spaces"; and Hamadeh, *The City's Pleasures*. Sibel Zandi-Sayek also links discursive and architectural shifts with the definitive move toward consumption and leisure in "Poetry, Pleasure, and Building."

84. For Ottoman treasury accounts for the years 1527–28 and 1567–68 see Barkan, "933–4/1527–8 mali yılına ait bir Osmanlı bütçesi örneği"; and "974–975/1567–1568 mali yılına ait bir Osmanlı bütçesi örneği."

85. Murphey, *Exploring Ottoman Sovereignty*, 57–58.

86. 'Abdi (Tevki'i), "Osmanlı Kanunnameleri."

87. Murphey, *Exploring Ottoman Sovereignty*, 164. Barkan included two lists of *müteferrika* and *evlad-i ümera* in the budget report referenced earlier. These lists both date from Süleyman's reign; Murphey suggested from approximately 1540 and 1555; see Barkan, "933–4/1527–8 mali yılına ait bir Osmanlı bütçesi örneği," 316–20.

88. By the late sixteenth century, Ottoman statesmen perceived the *devşirme* as part of the foundational pillars of the state, and they labeled as "outsiders" those who had not emerged from within its auspices. Key examples of this mentality can be

found in Tietze, *Mustafa 'Ali's Counsel for Sultans*; and Aksüt, *Koçi Bey Risalesi*. In Chapter 6 I will return to this question of "new men" and accusations of "outsiders/*ecnebiler*" that accompanied shifts in recruitment patterns and managerial tactics.

89. Kafadar, *Between Two Worlds*, 62–90.

90. The 'Abbasid rulers relied on captured slaves, *ghulam* or *mamluks*, primarily as a palace guard. Traced to the caliph Ma'mun (r. 813–30), they were mostly Turkic forces, deployed to subvert the increasing power of tribal militias in major garrisoned cities. Together with the use of land grants (*iqta'*) to generate a supportive cavalry, these two administrative tactics were later adopted by both Seljuks and Ottomans. See Kennedy, *The Armies of the Caliphs*; and Ménage, "Some Notes on the 'Devshirme.'"

91. For a sustained assessment of the scribal cohort, and its evolution from the fifteenth to the sixteenth century, see Chapter 3.

92. For editions of this chronicle, written during Bayezid II's reign (1481–1512), see Giese and Azamat, *Anonim tevārīh-i āl-i 'Osman*; and Öztürk, *Anonim Osmanlı kroniği*.

93. Mehmed II executed Çandarlı Halil Paşa soon after the capture of Constantinople and devised a system of palace recruitment that replaced both the marcher lords and the Muslim-born regional elites who had been instrumental during early campaigns yet maneuvered against his youthful drive to power.

94. Öztürk, *Anonim Osmanlı kroniği*, 31, 38.

95. Ibid., 28.

96. Aşıkpaşazade, *Āşıkpaşazāde tārīḫī*, 483–84. For the various political and social influences that shaped this chronicle see İnalcık, "How to Read 'Ashık Pasha-Zade's History."

97. İnalcık provided a broad overview of these issues in "The Re-building of Istanbul"; and Gülru Necipoğlu explored the link between legal and architectural changes in "From Byzantine Constantinople to Ottoman Kostantiniyye."

98. For these references see Özcan, "Fatih'in teşkilat kanunnamesi," 33–34, 42, 44–45. Gülru Necipoğlu argued for a direct link between the withdrawal of the sultan to this new petition chamber and the curtained window in the old council hall; see Necipoğlu, *Architecture, Ceremonial, and Power*, 19–22.

99. The relationships among food, loyalty, and a ruler's generosity are vividly realized by the symbol of the janissaries overturning their cauldrons of soup to indicate displeasure and possible rebellion; see Necipoğlu, *Architecture, Ceremonial, and Power*, 19. Sultanic beneficence reinforced an architectural commitment to public institutions (*imaret*) such as soup kitchens, hospitals, shelters, and educational structures; see Singer, *Constructing Ottoman Beneficence*; and Ergin, Neumann, and Singer, *Feeding People*.

100. İnalcık, "The Policy of Mehmed II," 245–47. Chroniclers of the period, including Tursun Bey and Aşıkpaşazade, praised Bayezid for restoring principles of governance that they deemed more in line with Islamicate theories of state power and thus of a delimited role for the ruler through oversight by religious scholars.

101. This discussion of writing and documentary production sketches the outline of more fine-grained arguments that I will develop in Chapters 2 and 3.

102. On *hümā* see Huart and Massé, "Huma."

103. The idea of divine election and the significance of the *hümā* is best dramatized in Farid al-Din Attar's (d. 1221) allegorical poem *Manṭiq ut-ṭayr* [The conference of the birds]. The hoopoe leads the birds of the world on a quest for the perfect king, Simurgh, the *hüma*-bird. The birds journey through trials and tribulations in seven valleys, which Attar used to illustrate the mystical stages of Sufi illumination. For an example of the use of these metaphors and the *hümā* in Ottoman poetry see Onay and Kurnaz, *Eski Türk edebiyatında mazmunlar ve izahı*, 276.

104. Uzunçarşılı, *Buyruldı*; and Heyd, "Buyuruldu."

105. Fekete "Tughra."

106. Uzunçarşılı, *Osmanli tarihine ait yeni bir vesika.*

107. Pakalın, *Osmanlı tarih deyimleri*, 1:25–27; Akgündüz, *Osmanlı kanunnameleri*, 1:322; İnalcık "Reis-ül-Küttāb," *İA*; Uzunçarşılı, *Osmanlı devleti.*

108. Uzunçarşılı, *Tuğra ve pençeler ile ferman ve buyurdulara dair* (also found in *Belleten* 5 [1941]: 101–57); Babinger, *Die grossherrliche Tughra.*

109. See Fekete, "Tughra."

110. Özcan, "Fatih'in teşkilat kanunnamesi," 16.

111. Chapter 3 explores how bureaucratic recruitment patterns also led to the emergence of a language of the court, and Chapter 4 addresses these developments within the occupation of Hungary when sovereignty, land law, linguistic exchange, and patronage networks were linked in a scramble for territorial control. Here, the basic outlines of an emergent bureaucracy showcase the relationship between textual edicts and the extension of sultanic power. For one of the strongest assessments of this process see Howard, "The Historical Development of the Ottoman Imperial Registry."

112. The Hungarian National Archives are replete with examples of this trend; there are twenty-four in the Turkish Collection (R 315) alone.

113. Murphey, *Exploring Ottoman Sovereignty*, 77.

114. Pere, *Osmanlılarda madeni para*, 48.

115. Ibid., 55 (nos. 16, 17, and 18).

116. The regionalism inherent in the term *sahib-i kiran* is an excellent example of this early phase because it places the Ottoman dynasts within a rich cultural heritage shared by Timurid, Ilkhanid, and later Mughal and Safavid political imagery that linked rulership to messianism in periods of apocalyptic fervor and crisis. See Bashir, "Deciphering the Cosmos"; and Balabanlılar, "Lords of the Auspicious Conjunction."

117. Murphey argues that, despite early examples of the use of *sultan*, it was not a formative ideological term employed by Ottoman rulers until the late fifteenth century (Murphey, *Exploring Ottoman Sovereignty*, 80). He thus dismisses the importance of the inscription on a pious foundation endowed by Murad I at Iznik (Nicea) in

1388, cited in earlier studies: *al-mālik al-mu'aẓam, al-kāqān al-mukarram, al-sulṭān ibn al-sulṭān* [the great king, honored ruler, the sultan, son of the sultan].

118. Melikoff, "Ghazi."

119. Reychman and Zajączkowski, *Handbook of Ottoman-Turkish Diplomatics*; Kołodziejczyk, *Ottoman-Polish Diplomatic Relations*; and for a more extensive discussion of these forms see Murphey, "Dynastic Image," 84–96.

120. Examples include vigorous (*kudretlu*), forceful (*kuvvetlu*), fearsome (*mehabetlu*), courageous (*şehametlu*), and brave or valiant (*şeca'tlu*).

121. Sultan of great renown (*sultan-i 'azim al-şan*), great, august (*'azmetlu*), glorious or esteemed (*'izzetlu*).

122. The following comments are based on İnalcık, "Şikayet hakkı."

123. Reorganization efforts in the chancery form a major part of the arguments outlined in Chapter 3.

124. Ateş, "Fatih Sultan Mehmed tarafından gönderilen mektuplar"; Lugal and Erzi, "Fâtih Sultan Mehmed'in muhtelif seferlerine ait fetih-nāmeleri."

125. Şahin, *Empire and Power*, 223–27; Theunissen, "Ottoman-Venetian Diplomatics," 191, 308; Finlay, "Prophecy and Politics," 1–31; Finlay, "'I Am the Servant.'"

126. Burke, *Languages and Communities*, 72–76.

127. Alam, *The Languages of Political Islam*, 122–23.

128. Goffman, "Negotiating with the Renaissance State."

129. This section builds from Tschudi, *Ein Schreiben Sülejmans I. an Ferdinand I*, 317–28; and Reychman and Zajączkowski, *Handbook of Ottoman-Turkish Diplomatics*, illus. 21–26. Another important source connected to the reorganization efforts of the late seventeenth century is Meniński's thesaurus. Compiled in 1680, and thus coinciding with the vizierate of Kara Mustafa Paşa, his linguistic study of the philosophy and structure of Islamicate bureaucracies illuminates conceptual shifts in the Ottoman context. For examples of imperial *intitulatio* included under the headings *sultan* and *padişah*, see Meniński, *Thesaurus linguarum orientalium Turcicae-Arabicae-Persicae*, 2:632–39.

130. Imber, *Ebu's-su'ud*, 68.

131. *Şeh-i Bağdad ve 'Iraq kayser-i Rum Misra sultanım*, translated in Kołodziejczyk, "Khan, Caliph, Tsar and Imperator."

132. Alam, *The Languages of Political Islam*, 98; Blake, *Time in Early Modern Islam*, 271–73.

133. Notes on composition, structure, and phrasing can also be found in Heyd, *Ottoman Documents on Palestine*, 7–22. For further examples see the earliest collection of orders, distributed during the year 1501 of Bayezid II's reign, in Şahin and Emecen, *II. Bāyezid dönemine ait 906/1501 tarihli ahkām defteri*.

134. "Ḥükm yazıla ki" or "ḥükmi oldūr ki."

135. "Diyū bildūrdi."

136. "Şöyle bilesiz" and "'alāmet-i şerīfe i'timād idesiz."

137. Heyd, *Ottoman Documents on Palestine*, 16–17.

138. The phrase in the earliest record was *al-ḥāletü hāẕihī*, whereas later it was expanded to *tevki'-i refi'-i hümāyūn vāsıl olucak ma'lūm olā ki.*

139. "Bir türlü dahi etmiyesiz."

140. "Lazīm belāya uğrarsız."

141. Murphey, "Formation," 165. The prime example of scribal "textbooks" is, once again, Feridun Ahmed Bey's *Mecmū 'a-yı münşe'āt.*

142. "Telḫīs üzerine ḫatt-ı hümāyūn."

143. Murphey, *Exploring Ottoman Sovereignty*, 145–48.

144. Ibid., 148.

145. Ibid., 149: "kendi kārihe-yi şerifelerinden."

146. Murphey, *Exploring Ottoman Sovereignty*, 153.

147. Ibid., 155.

148. Lambton, *State and Government in Medieval Islam.*

149. Fetvacı, *Picturing History at the Ottoman Court.*

150. The relationship between sight and knowledge within Islamicate traditions bears mentioning here. Rosenthal suggests an etymological connection between *'ilm* (knowledge), sign (Arabic: *ma'lam*; Ottoman Turkish: *'alamet*) and travel, as *ma'lam* served as signposts in the desert, "which guided [the Bedouin] on his travels and in the execution of his daily tasks" and constituted "the kind of knowledge on which his life and well-being principally depended." Rosenthal, *Knowledge Triumphant*, 10.

151. For recent assessments of geographical knowledge and authority within the Ottoman domains see Brummett, *Mapping the Ottomans*; and Emiralioğlu, *Geographical Knowledge and Imperial Culture.* Ariel Salzmann's chapter "On a Map of Eurasia" provocatively addresses the constructed and fragmentary nature of the cartographic enterprise in the eighteenth century and cautions against any notion of coherent Ottoman dominion; see Salzmann, *Tocqueville in the Ottoman Empire*, 31–74.

152. Raman, *Document Raj*, 3. Raman draws in turn from the formulation of David Dery in "'Papereality' and Learning."

Chapter 2. The State of Stability

1. Cited in Kerslake, "A Critical Edition and Translation," 21a–b. Kerslake's thesis draws from six manuscript copies and contains a handwritten copy, accompanying analysis, and translation. The lines quoted here were part of Mustafa Celalzade's (*nişancı* from 1534–57) introductory rationale for the text. He argued that while affairs of state are necessarily secret, to deter enemy advances, the universal import of the Ottoman dynasty must also be proclaimed to the world. Mustafa claimed that his close proximity to power would stand as a corrective to erroneous past depictions of the dynasty as a whole, and Selim I's reign in particular.

2. Emecen, "Sefere Götürülen Defterlerin Defteri."

3. MM 4285, folios 24–25; cited as well in Murphey, *Regional Structure in the Ottoman Economy*, xiv.

4. Murphey, "Book Review." Many registers, manuscripts, and loose folios survived these military expeditions within provincial spaces or even across the border in enemy hands, thus rendering the archival collections of Venice, Vienna, Austria, Bulgaria, Croatia, and others key to any investigation of Ottoman imperial action.

5. İnalcık, "Ottoman Methods of Conquest," 105.

6. "Timar" designates the usufruct from eminent domain lands (*miri arazisi*) assigned, at least in principle, to provincial cavalrymen (*timar sipahisi*), who functioned as regional administrators and mobilized auxiliaries fully equipped for campaign in return for stipends accruing either from their designated *timar* lands or from other, often scattered, agricultural dues. See *kanunname*s issued in 1530 and 1536, as well as an undated register that records the organizational structure, units of measurement, and assignments dispersed across the provinces during the reign of Süleyman I, in Akgündüz, *Osmanlı kanunnameleri*, 4:528–81. A "zi'amet" was a timar apportioned to high-ranking *sipahi*s yielding an annual income of twenty thousand *akçe*s or more. The silver content of the Ottoman *akçe* remained the measure of account even as it was progressively debased over the course of the late seventeenth century and replaced, save for in treasury reports, by other currencies.

7. *Ḫāṣ*, translated as "special," or "highest quality," designated the most productive and lucrative revenue sources reserved for the sultan, for female members of his household (via the *has-ı başmaklık*, or slipper money, used for upkeep and assigned for life, returning to the sultan's eminent domain when the party died), and elite members of the administration.

8. These grants represented rights to revenue accruing from productive activities (agricultural and commercial) but not to ownership of the land or property itself.

9. For the history and development of these registers see İnalcık, "Kanun" and "Kānūnnāme"; Howard, "Historical Scholarship"; and Coşgel, "Ottoman Tax Registers."

10. Darling analyzed these shifts and critiqued assumptions that such shifts in record-keeping practices embodied a decline in bureaucratic efficiency in *Revenue-Raising and Legitimacy*.

11. A massive compendium of published facsimiles and transcriptions of sultanic commands and legal regulations related to the Ottoman administrative system has been published in nine volumes: Akgündüz, *Osmanlı kanunnameleri ve hukukī tahlilleri*; Ömer Barkan also published selections of provincial legal regulations in *XV ve XVI inci asırlarda Osmanlı Imparatorluğunda Ziraī*. For ease of reference, I have cited those contained in Akgündüz while also noting discrepancies across varied copies of *kanunname*.

12. Approximately twelve hundred cadastral surveys survive in various forms. While the greatest wealth of materials related to provincial administration and land registration is now housed in the Ottoman Section of the Prime Minister's Archives (Başbakanlık Osmanlı arşivi, hereafter BOA), other important holdings of sultanic proclamations, tax registers, and addendums preserved as both registers (*defter*) and loose sheets (*evrak*) exist in the Topkapı Sarayı Arşivi and in the Tapu ve Kadastro Umum Müdürlüğü, in Ankara: *Topkapı Sarayı Müzesi Osmanlı Saray arşivi kataloğu*. The entire series of tax registers prepared under Sultan Murad III is housed in the Tapu ve Kadastro archive, along with a large collection of tax and foundation records.

13. For a methodological approach to these defters see Halasi-Kun, "Some Notes." Heath W. Lowry also indicates the diverse way in which these *defter*s might be incorporated into historical analysis in his *Studies in Defterology*.

14. The *icmal* registers combined and condensed information contained in the *mufassal* and *müfredat* (inventory lists of income and expenditures reviewed by the central treasury) registers. For the role these registers played in the Ottoman financial system see Uzunçarşılı, *Osmanlı devletinin merkez ve bahriye teşkilâtı*, 353. Both *icmal* and *mufassal* registers reveal many hands and thus the negotiations necessary to fit regional realities into imperial norms; see İnalcık, *Hicrī 835 tarihli Süret-i defter-i sancak-i Arvanid*.

15. The question of "general codes" will be addressed in more detail later in this chapter. "Provincial law codes" remains the common translation for the *liva kanunnames*; however, *code* implies standardization, or the assumption of universal application, and thus projects a fixed designation on what was in fact a historical process. As this process played a role in bureaucratization, here the focus is on genre creation and on the moments in which issuing legal regulations became a specific, imperial tactic. Furthermore, as the contents of both general and provincial *kanunname* incorporated regional variations, any implication of a universal, unchanging "code" ignores the consistent addendums issued for the *kanunname*s and their existence as part of an active archive. Variability suggests that the *kanunname* were a result of constant negotiation necessary to fit regional realities into an imperial grammar of rule.

16. Scholars often mine registers of financial and military affairs for sociohistorical detail and ignore the significant way in which these proclamations formed a set of political categories deployed to both extend and resist Ottoman sovereignty. Examples of a positivist approach to data can be found in Genç, "A Study of the Feasibility"; and Sahillioğlu, "Bir mültezim zimem defterine göre XV." For uses of financial records with an implicit critique of the objectivist approach see Salzmann, "An Ancien Régime Revisited"; Erim, *İktisadi düşünce tarihi*; and Erim and Nakiboğlu, *Gümrük yıllığı*.

17. Burak discusses a juristic backlash to this process in "Evidentiary Truth Claims."

18. For overviews of this history see İnalcık, "Kānūnnāme"; Akgündüz, *Osmanlı kanunnameleri*, 1:41–77; Barkan, *XV ve XVI inci asırlarda Osmanlı imparatorluğunda zirai*, x–xiv. For the most recent effort to redefine this legacy and to address differences in Ottoman, Ilkhanid, and Mamluk legal traditions, see Burak, "Q̱ānūn." The Mughal and Safavid Empires also adopted comparable administrative practices derived from similar legacies; see Moosvi, *The Economy of the Mughal Empire*; and Floor, *A Fiscal History of Iran.*

19. For other examples of limits to sovereign power see Pagden, *The Burdens of Empire*; Henshall, *The Myth of Absolutism*; and Gross, *Empire and Sovereignty.*

20. *Shari'a* is the structure and practice of canonic law and, depending on the various legal schools of interpretation, is drawn directly from a variety of debated sources, including stipulations in the Qur'an, sayings of the prophet Muhammad (*hadith*), legal analogy (*qiyas*), social welfare (*maslaha*), and the evaluative judgment of a legal scholar (*ijtihad*). For a history of the evolution of *shari'a* as both divine law and social practice see the essential writings of Hallaq: *A History of Islamic Legal Theories*; "What Is Shari'a?"; and *Shari'a Between Past and Present.*

21. Fred Donner and Garth Fowden have each identified new frameworks for thinking about the evolution of this Muslim polity in the late antique world. Attentive to religious, philosophical, and political dynamics, they trace the complex evolution of a new empire and its connections with a range of regional and intellectual influences. See Donner, *Muhammad and the Believers*; and Fowden, *Before and After Muḥammad.*

22. I will address these interactions and their consequence for Ottoman governing practices in more detail in Chapter 6. For the evolving relationship between religious and political ordinances see Calder, "Friday Prayer"; Fakhry, *Ethical Theories in Islam*; Mahdi and Butterworth, *Political Aspects of Islamic Philosophy*; and al-Azmeh, "God's Caravan."

23. Lambton, *State and Government in Medieval Islam; Brown, Religion and State*; Crone, *God's Rule.*

24. al-Mawardi, *The Ordinances of Government*; for the Arabic text see al-Mawardi, *al-Aḥkām*. Although the title of the English translation captures the intent of the text, like many translations it misses the intellectual play that drives the formal structure of titles in Arabic.

25. al-Mawardi, *al-Aḥkām*, 137–60.

26. Roy Mottahedeh developed these ideas in *Loyalty and Leadership*, 175–89.

27. al-Mawardi, *al-Aḥkām*, 148–71.

28. Etymologically, *siyasa* was also linked to equestrian skill and to the nomadic cultures that continued to shape Muslim polities. Thus, the symbolic mobility of horse-backed conquest and the circulation of a sultanic ordinance played a role in delimiting sovereignty; see Crone, *Slaves on Horses.*

29. Ibn Taymiyya (d. 1328) is credited with developing the most extensive assessment of *siyasa shar'iyya* in the wake of Mongol invasions into 'Abbasid domains; see C. E. Bosworth, "Siyāsa"; and, for the Ottoman context, Heyd, *Studies in Old Ottoman Criminal Law*, 198–204.

30. For a classical introduction to *kanun* see Halil İnalcık, "Kanun" and "Kānūnnāme". İnalcık's more extensive commentary can be found in his *The Ottoman Empire*, 70–75. Colin Imber addressed the evolution of *kanun* as well in *Ebu's-su'ud*. More recent efforts to reframe the field of Ottoman legal studies form the basis of this chapter. Linda T. Darling has provided a synopsis of how the *kanunname* figured in the field, both past and present, in "*Kanun* and *Kanunname* in Ottoman History and Historiography," a paper presented during the Toyo Bunko Session, Tokyo, Japan, Feb. 22, 2017. Her paper serves as a resounding call for a new collective effort to assess the varied practices and meanings associated with the *kanunname*.

31. The historical intersection between Mamluk and Ottoman law constitutes a core component in the work of Guy Burak, who has fundamentally transformed the way scholars now think of the dynamic innovations within Ottoman legal developments; see Burak, "Qānūn"; and Burak, "The Second Formation of Islamic Law."

32. Both cited in Burak, "Qānūn," 2.

33. Ibid.

34. Feridun, *Mecmū'a-yı münşe'āt*.

35. Ibn Kannan al-Salihi, *Ḥadā'iq al-yasmīn*. Dana Sajdi has illuminated the dynamics whereby regional authors made a bid for inclusion in an Ottoman courtly elite in Sajdi, "Ibn Kannan"; and Sajdi, "Peripheral Visions."

36. For a printed version of *kanun*s dedicated to janissary protocol, see Toroser, *Kavanin-i Yeniçeriyan*.

37. Burak has investigated the way in which jurists of Arab lands conquered by the Ottomans vehemently resisted these new techniques for using *kanun* as an assertion of dynastic legislative authority. These jurists labeled this intervention as a return to Chinggisid yasa, with the negative connotation that it inscribed actions foreign to the dictates of the *shari'a*; see Burak, "Evidentiary Truth Claims," 235–36, 249–53.

38. See the four-part Chinggisid studies of David Ayalon, "The Great Yāsa of Chingiz Khān," where Ayalon examines the classical treatment of the legal terminology and influence of the Mongol *yasa*. However, Ayalon discounted the continuing controversies regarding the relationship between the *yasa* and the *kanun*-generating activities of the Ottomans. Burak argued that there was a "*yasa* anxiety" in Mamluk authors that shaped a negative accounting of *yasa*-like activities by authors who witnessed the Ottoman conquest of Arab lands; see Burak "Between the Ḳānūn of Qāytbāy," 5–6, 15–18.

39. Burak, "Qānūn," 2.

40. For examples of Turkic and Indo-Persian practices of governance and law-

making, see İnalcık, "*Kutagu Bilig*'de Türk ve İran siyaset nazariye ve gelenekleri," 259–75.

41. Burak, "Between the Ḳānūn of Qāytbāy," 5–6, 16–18. Halil İnalcık consistently emphasized the way in which the rubric of "custom," or *örf*, also indicated the authority of the sultan to decide and to execute his decisions and thus gestured toward the decisive lawmaking ability of the sultan. İnalcık further links this to ancient Persianate state traditions and Seljuk practice; see the following pieces by İnalcık: "Osmanlı Hukukuna Giriş," 319; "Örf," 480; "Şeriat ve Kanun, Din ve Devlet," 40; and "Türk-İslâm Devletlerinde Sivil Kânûn Geleneği," 27. Ömer Barkan also argued that *örf* opened up a space for the sultan's legislative power distinct from the *shari'a*, and in his overview of the *kanunname* he indicated its relationship to *yasa*; see Barkan, "Kānūnnāme," 185. Neşet Çağatay extended the implications of *örf* even further and proposed that it indicated a "national system of law," in the sense that it was distinct from the *shari'a* but also not simply a record of local customary practices; see Çağatay, "An Outline of Islamic Law." Each of these authors built on the preliminary work of Mehmed Fuad Köprülü, who argued for the autonomy and independence of Ottoman law as an institutional development distinct from the *shari'a* and thus also emphasized the emergence of public law even within early Muslim polities: Köprülü, "İslam 'amme hukukundan ayrı bir Türk 'amme hukuku yok mudur," 40, 49, 54, 59.

42. İnalcık, "Kānūn."

43. This *kanunname* will be addressed in detail below. See Akgündüz, *Osmanlı kanunnameleri*, 2:39; and Peirce, "Domesticating Sexuality," 133n20.

44. al-Mawardi described the books of the *divan* (*kitāb al-divān*) in *al-Aḥkām*, 356–61.

45. Lambton, *Landlord and Peasant in Persia*, 92. The Safavids also deployed this meaning of the *qanun*; see Floor, *A Fiscal History of Iran*, 96.

46. Tursun Bey, *Tārīḫ-i ebū'l-fetḥ*, 17: "Ve hīç bir şahs müstahıkk-ı medh ve müsta'idd-i mübāhāt ü müfāharet olmaz, illā bu dört fazīletün cümlesiyle yā ba'ziyle olur. Ve şunlar ki neseb ü kabîle şerefiyle fahr iderler, merci'i budur ki, ābā vü eslāfında bu fezāyil ile mevsūf kimesne var imiş."

47. Ibid., 12–13:

> Ve eğer şöyle ki bu tedbīr bervefk-ı vücub ve ḳāide-i ḥikmet olursa ana ehl-i hikmet siyāset-i İlahi dirler, ve ehl-i şer' ana şerī'at dirler. Ve illā, ya'ni bu tedbir ol mertebede olmazsa, mücerred tavr-ı 'aḳl üzre nıẓām-ı 'ālem-i ẓāhir içün, meselā Cingiz Ḫān gibi olursa, sebebine izāfet iderler, siyāseti sulṭanī ve yasağ-ı pādişāhī dirler ki, 'örfümüzce ana 'örf dirler. Keyfe mekān, anun iḳāmeti elbette bir pādişāh vücuduna mevkūf. Ḥatta şöyledir ki, her rūzgārda vücūd-ı şāri' ḥācet değüldür . . . ; ammā her rūzgārda bir pādişāḥun vücūdı ḥācettir ki anun taşarruf-ı cüz'iyyātta vilāyet-i kāmili vardur. Ve anun tedbīri munkati' olsa, baḳā-yı eşḫās ber-vech-i ekmel süret bulmaz; belki bi'l-küllī fenā bulur. Ve ol nıẓām fevt olur.

Tursun Bey complemented Chinggis Khan, but later chroniclers tended to link Ilkhanid Mongol practice with tyranny and oppression and claimed that Ottoman imperial authority, grounded in the *shari'a*, represented a superior system; see Uzunçarşılı, *Osmanlı tarihi*, 30–31; and Tezcan, "The Memory of the Mongols."

48. Burak, "Q̱ānūn," 2. Buzov, "The Lawgiver and His Lawmakers," 19–45. Celalzade Mustafa (c. 1490–1567) became part of the Ottoman scribal service in 1516, and his career coincided with, and helped manufacture, the administrative reforms of Süleyman's court. He became chief secretary of the imperial council in 1525 and chancellor in 1534, and until his retirement in 1557 (and a brief return from 1566–67) he used this position to develop new techniques and agendas for imperial correspondence. Intent on propagating a specific image of the sultan and of the grandeur of the empire, he produced histories of Selim and Süleyman, along with a treatise addressing the intersection between ethics and politics. For the most comprehensive study of both the man and these new imperial agendas see Şahin, *Empire and Power*.

49. See İnalcık, "Adaletnameler."

50. According to Mehmet Yılmaz, Celalzade Mustafa "never tries to reconcile *siyâset* with basic principles of *şerî'at*, which suggest that he accepts *'urf* as an independent, autonomous field, and not as a concept within *şerî'at*." See M. S. Yılmaz, "Koca Nişancı of Kanuni," 133.

51. Celalzade, *Selimnāme*, 22; Kerslake, "A Critical Edition," 20a–b. This is a highly stylized list of imperial forebears: Darius (d. 486 BC) was the third king of the Persian Achaemenid Empire; Alexander (d. 323 BC) was founder of the ancient Greek kingdom of Macedon; Cyrus (d. 530 BC) founded the Achaemenid Empire; Bahrām Gūr (d. 438 CE) was the Sasanian king of Persia; and Chosroes, or Khosrow I (d. 579 CE), was known as Anushiruwan the Just and "king of kings" of the Sasanian Empire.

52. Celalzade, *Selimnāme*, 22–23; Kerslake, "A Critical Edition," 20a–b.

53. Celalzade, *Selimnāme*, 23; Kerslake, "A Critical Edition," 20a–b.

54. Özcan, *Kānūnnāme-i āl-i 'Os̱mān*, 14: "Bu kadar aḥvāl-ı salṭanata nıẓām verildi. Şimden sonra gelen evlād-ı kirāmım dāḫi islāḥa sa'y itsünler." The infamous rationale for fratricide also appears for the first time here as a means to maintain world order (*nıẓām-ı 'alem*); see ibid., 18.

55. Ibid., 3: "Bu kānūnnāme atam ve dedem ḳānūnudur, benim daḫi ḳānūnumdur, evlād-ı kirāmım neslen bāde neslen bununla 'āmil olalar."

56. Leslie Peirce has traced the evolution of sociosexual discipline within the criminal codes of these *kanunname*s. She illustrates how the *kanunname* evolved from "a handful of basic rules . . . to a complex set of interrelated sanctions" ("Domesticating Sexuality," 129). Her work on various sexual crimes, notions of the household, and the harem served as a significant model for the arguments constructed here. For a complete list of *kanunname* manuscript copies for each of these sultans see Heyd, *Studies in Old Ottoman Criminal Law*, 33–37.

57. There is much debate concerning the existence of general *kanunnames* and whether or not they indicated a systematic process of codification. Halil İnalcık argued that they did and that Mehmed II's *kanunname* "formed the nucleus of the codes of the following sultans" (İnalcık, "Kānūnnāme"); İnalcık, "Osmanlı hukukuna giriş," 327. Ömer Barkan, by contrast, suggested that they were instead compilations of sultanic ordinances and that the provincial *kanunnames* represented the most important source for the law in practice: "Kānūn-nāme." While Uriel Heyd tends to agree with Barkan and points to a potential gap between general *kanunnames* and the actual practice of law, he insists that the regulations produced by Bayezid II and Süleyman I were official codifications, even if they also compiled previous *kanun* activities; see Heyd, *Studies in Old Ottoman Criminal Law*, 19–31, 173. Buzov locates the codification of general *kanunnames* within the period of Süleyman I's rule, arguing that provincial regulations were organized with increasing systematicity and that multiple copies attest to their role in a vibrant intellectual debate concerning the role of sultanic law in governance; see Buzov, "The Lawgiver and His Lawmakers," 7–10, 127–29. Here, the relationship between Bayezid's *kanunname* and that of Süleyman's underscores the earlier emergence of a set of organizational principles that, while in flux, established the parameters for a grammar of rule adopted in both general and provincial regulations, as well as in daily transactions of the imperial council.

58. The dynamics of Mehmed II's court were addressed in the previous chapter. Important here, however, are his confiscations of lands belonging to Muslim elites or representing part of the pasturage of local nomads who resisted the increased centralization of state administration and its lawmaking activities. For examples of resistance to these early reforms and their consequence for the reign of Bayezid II, see İnalcık, "Otman Baba and Fatih Sultan Mehmed"; and Káldy-Nagy, "VI. yüzyılda Osmanlı imparatorluğunda."

59. İnalcık, *Seçme eserleri II, devlet-i aliyye*, 121, 130–31.

60. Peirce, "Domesticating Sexuality," 113.

61. Complete transcriptions and facsimiles are available in Arif, "Kanunname-yi Al-i Osman"; and Akgundüz, *Osmanlı kanunnameleri*, vol. 2. It should be noted that Akgündüz added article numbers that did not exist in the original compilations, although they do provide a more efficient mechanism for identifying individual sections of the *kanunname*. His version of Bayezid's *kanunname* relies on a copy found in the Konya Koyunoğlu Library that includes, unlike other copies, a colophon date of Reb'iülevvel 907, or 1501; see Akgündüz, *Osmanlı kanunnameleri*, 2:34–35.

62. As the Ottoman state emerged, its leaders consistently opposed the division of lands among offspring and favored "unigeniture," in that after a sultan's death, and often in anticipation of the event, princes fought among themselves for the right to become sultan. This practice ensured the integrity of conquered territory but also sanctioned civil war and ultimately led to the law of fratricide as a means to diminish

the potential crisis; see İnalcık, "The Ottoman Succession"; and Kafadar, *Between Two Worlds*, 136–38.

63. Cağatay Uluçay provided an early and extensive account of Selim's rise to power in his tripartite study "Yavuz Sultan Selim nasıl padiaşh oldu." For an updated assessment of current scholarship on his reign see Cipa, "The Centrality of the Periphery."

64. Multiple versions of this *kanunname* exist, yet they were discovered more recently and were previously considered to be copies or amendments to Süleyman's *kanunname*. Thus, Uriel Heyd does not list any manuscripts for Selim I in his accounting of general *kanunname*s. However, Selami Pulaha and Yaşar Yücel published a colophoned manuscript (971/1563–64) found in the Albanian state archives, which they compared with the "Leningrad" transliteration and facsimile published by Tveritinova; see Pulaha and Yücel, *I. Selim kānūnnāmesi*, 12; and Tveritinova, *Qānūnnāme-i Sultān Selīm*. Akgündüz argued that the Albanian manuscript belongs to the reign of Süleyman, rather than to Selim, and relied instead on a comparison between a St. Petersburg manuscript that belongs to the Old Asia Museum and one located in the National Library in Ankara; see Akgündüz, *Osmanlı kanunnameleri*, 3:85–86. Leslie Peirce suggested, like Pulaha and Yücel, that Akgündüz's concerns about attribution are unfounded; see Peirce, "Domesticating Sexuality," 133n17.

65. Peirce, "Domesticating Sexuality," 118–19.

66. The classical treatments of law and state during the reign of Süleyman can be found in İnalcık, "Suleiman the Lawgiver and Ottoman Law"; and Imber, *Ebu's-su'ud*. For more recent assessments and commentary on the link between bureaucratization and the extension of legal power, see H. Yılmaz, "The Sultan and the Sultanate"; and Buzov, "The Lawgiver and His Lawmakers," esp. 116–30 and 161–71

67. Uriel Heyd grouped thirty-eight manuscript copies of *kanunname* attributed to Süleyman I according to their length and basic features (long, short, short with additions, and incomplete) and included a printed version of the Ottoman text and a full English translation of the opening section of the criminal code as well; see Heyd, *Studies in Old Ottoman Criminal Law*, 36–37, 54–131. Ahmed Akgündüz includes two versions of Süleyman's *kanunname* without specific attribution. According to the work of Mehmet Yılmaz, one can be attributed to *nişancı* Seydi Efendi, and was quite probably based on Selim I's *kanunname*, while the second was likely composed by his successor, *nişancı* Celalzade Mustafa, and follows instead the *kanunname* of Bayezid II; see Akgündüz, *Osmanlı kanunnameleri*, 4:293 and 364, respectively; and M. S. Yılmaz, "Koca Nişancı of Kanuni," 30, 45, 200–202. This point will be addressed further below, but both the composition (sections vs. chapters) and the content (style of the preamble, inclusion or omission of *kanun*s on *eflak*s, individual regulations and phrasing) of each *kanunname* suggests this pairing.

68. The most significant development during the reign of Murad III was a compilation designed to address perceived "corruptions" in the religious hierarchy, the

'İlmiye kanunname, dated 1598. This *kanunname* represented the legal intervention of the state in an increasingly vexed sociopolitical environment wherein graduates of the imperial *medrese*s, for lack of clear positions and general frustration with hierarchies defined by the court, continued to participate in cycles of urban and regional rebellions; see Uzunçarşılı, *Osmanlı devletinin 'ilmiye teşkilâtı*, 243–47. On the general upheavals of the period, the classic study is Zilfi, "The Kadizadelis," 251–69.

69. Mustafa Ali, for example, linked the *kanun-ı kadim* to the *kanunname* of Süleyman and characterized deviations as perversions and corruptions of an ideal. For one example, the customary payment of one hundred thousand filori to the grand vizier renewed the submission to Ottoman suzerainty (*tecdid-i devlet*) when the title of *voyvoda* was transferred to an heir in the northern principalities of Wallachia, Erdel, or Boğdan. During the reign of Murad III, however, this amount became a yearly requirement and thus contributed to the abandonment of cultivatable land as a result of excessive oppression of agriculturalists. Mustafa Ali stated that the law of Süleyman was broken (*bozuldı*); see Çerçi, *Gelibolulu Mustafa Âli ve Künhü'l-Ahbârı*. Fleischer's study provides the most comprehensive treatment of the role *kanun* played in definitions of state power and legitimacy; for his assessment of *kanun* as an "Ottoman way" within the context of Mustafa Ali's career and writings, see Fleischer, *Bureaucrat and Intellectual*, 93.

70. Peirce, "Domesticating Sexuality," 118–19.

71. Aspects of the *kanunname-i cedid* and inclusion of key legal reformulations developed under the auspices of Ebu's-su'ud's tenure as *şeyhülislam* (1545–74), and *şeyhülislam* Baha'i Mehmed Efendi (served 1649–51) from the mid-seventeenth century will be addressed in the next chapter. His judgments concerning land and property rights, collected in the *Ẓāhir al-qudāt*, extended the work of Ebu's-su'ud and illuminated the increasing importance of the cultivator and the role of dynastic law in assessing land tenure. Scholars still debate the appropriate dating for the formalization and distribution of this *kanunname*. But given that the "new" *kanunname* contained large portions of text based on various *fetva*s, edicts, and additions to *liva kanunname*s between 1540 and 1655, it clearly embodies the significant reforms to Ottoman legal structures that came to define imperial authority for the next century and a half. Furthermore, a *ferman* regarding this new intervention, specifically in the areas of land tax and agrarian administration dated 1674, clearly distinguishes a founding moment for the circulation of this *kanunname*; see İnalcık, "Kānūnnāme." A published copy of the *Kanunname-i cedid*—Abdi (Tevki'i), "Osmanlı kanunnameleri"—dates the text to 1717 and is incomplete, based on scattered compilations. An alternative copy, dated 1732 but inclusive of the *ferman*, can be found in the Süleymaniye Library, Esad Efendi 854.

72. "Reis-ül-Küttāb." *İA*, 9:681, 2:39, facsimile 79: "ve ce' ale l'l-selāṭīne sebeben li-nıẓām l'l-'ālemi ve neffeze aḥkāmehum alā kāffeti ehl'il ve berri ve 'l-meder."

73. Ibid., 40–41. Later general and regional *kanunname* retain the basic measures outlined in this section but abbreviate the title to *ahval-i re'aya*.

74. Peters, *Crime and Punishment in Islamic Law*, 127–33, 196. Also see Leslie Peirce's chapter "Punishment, Violence, and the Court," in *Morality Tales*, 311–48. For specifications outlining various punishments and their measures established by al-Mawardi see *al-Aḥkām*, 361–91.

75. Akgündüz, *Osmanlı kanunnameleri*, 2:40.

76. Uriel Heyd provided an overview of customary fines and their evolution both within the Ottoman context and in earlier historical periods; see Heyd, *Studies in Old Ottoman Criminal Law*, 275–99. For both a quantitative assessment of this transition and a discussion of the relationship between Ottoman and Byzantine monetary punishments, see Coşgel et al., "Crime and Punishment in Ottoman Times."

77. Peirce, "Domesticating Sexuality," 115. Heyd argued that this section draws from other earlier forms of criminal regulations known as *siyasetname*, which were addressed to officials of the state, such as provincial and district governors, but also instructed local judges to participate in implementing imperial standards of punishment. These were retrospectively added to copies of Mehmed II's *kanunname* and directly incorporated into the 1501 composition of Bayezid's; see Heyd, *Studies in Old Ottoman Criminal Law*,15–18.

78. See articles 79–84 in Akgündüz, *Osmanlı kanunnameleri*, 2:50–51.

79. İnalcık, "The *Çift-Hane* System," in *An Economic and Social History of the Ottoman Empire*, 143–54. On agricultural taxation in general see İnalcık, "Osmanlılarda ra'iyyet rüsūmu"; and, Coşgel, "Efficiency and Continuity in Public Finance."

80. Akgündüz, *Osmanlı kanunnameleri*, 2:53–54, article 99.

81. Ibid., 2:53, article 102.

82. Ibid., 2:55–56, articles 103–6.

83. Ibid., 2:57–59, articles 107–23.

84. Singer, "Marriages and Misdemeanors," 113–52.

85. Akgündüz, *Osmanlı kanunnameleri*, 2:59–60, articles 124–27.

86. Ibid., 2:60–65.

87. See ibid., articles 140, 144, 146, and 161, for examples of these concerns.

88. Ibid., 2:69–70, article 209.

89. Ibid., 2:73, articles 227–29.

90. The version presented by Pulaha and Yücel includes a total of twenty *fasıls*, ten with numbers and ten without (*fasl-ı sānī*, for example), whereas Akgündüz includes divisions (and his standard insertion of articles) that did not otherwise exist in the manuscript copies he used.

91. Akgündüz, *Osmanlı kanunnameleri*, 3:124.

92. Ibid., 3:110–16, articles 153–200.

93. Fixing prices (*narh*) has often been used as an indication of potential eco-

nomic stagnation in the Ottoman Empire. Pamuk challenges this theory in "Prices in the Ottoman Empire."

94. There was an uneasy slippage between *cürm* and *cināyet*, as they appear together in their Persian form as possible synonyms for criminal behavior (*cürm-ü cināyet*). In Selim's code, however, it is possible to see the separation of the two and a clear indication that *cürm* indicates the fine for the criminal act (*cināyet*). Compare article 18 in Bayezid's *kanunname* (Akgündüz, *Osmanlı kanunnameleri*, 2:41) with article 20 in Selim's (Akgündüz, *Osmanlı kanunnameleri*, 3:91). Heyd suggested that ultimately both words came to designate "fine"; see Heyd, *Studies in Old Ottoman Criminal Law*, 276.

95. "Eğer bir kimesne zinā itse dāẖi üzerinde sābit olsā," Pulaha and Yücel, *I. Selim kānūnnāmesi*, 17.

96. "Siyāset olunmadığı taḳdirce 400 akçe cürm ālına": Akgündüz, *Osmanlı kanunnameleri*, 3:81. Leslie Peirce claims that the "terminology and the format employed in Selim's kanunname render political legal authority—siyaset—a stronger force than religious legal authority, at least discursively," and that his *kanunname* also secured for Selim a position "as the architect of the patriarchal household." Peirce, "Domesticating Sexuality," 118. This extension into the household is strikingly apparent in efforts to define boundaries between villages, the inside and outside of households, and between neighborhoods. See Akgündüz, *Osmanlı kanunnameleri*, 3:82, articles 30 and 33, for examples. It was also the case, however, that at times marginal notes indicated that a specific *kanun* was lacking (*kanunı yokdur*) and that the terminology and provisions of the *shari'a* should therefore be followed.

97. Barkan, "Osmanlı devrinde Akkoyunlu hükümdarı," 91–106.

98. Peirce, "Domesticating Sexuality," 121–26.

99. The substitution of Ottoman regulations for those of Uzun Hasan will be addressed in more detail below. See Barkan, *XV ve XVI inci asırlarda Osmanlı imparatorluğunda ziraī*, 145; İnalcık, "Adaletnameler," 108, 132; and Peirce, "Domesticating Sexuality," 121.

100. Akgündüz, *Osmanlı kanunnameleri*, 3:94–95, articles 51 and 54. The phrase for the Germiyan example is "ādet üzerine."

101. "Ve dahi her sancakda defterde ne yazılmış ise, ol mikdārdır": Akgündüz, *Osmanlı kanunnameleri*, 3:95n5, facsimile, 119.

102. Akgündüz, *Osmanlı kanunnameleri*, 3:94–99. Many articles from 51–84 indicate some reference to past records that do not capture present realities (56, 57, 59, 61, 63, 64, 67, 71, 72, 73, 75, 76, 77), or statements of fact that contradict records (70, 71, 74, 82), or include an intricate analysis about how to assess land transfers or taxes in complex situations, such as conflicting documentation (80, 84), or prohibiting female rights to dispose of land (81 and 82), or assessing multiple claimants (75) and thus contains in some way a reference to ensuring a standard application.

103. Akgündüz, *Osmanlı kanunnameleri*, 4:296, facsimile, 331: "Eğer bir kimesne zinā eder görülse, şer'an üzerine sābit olsā, lākin alā vech-i l'l-şer'i recm ḳılmalu olmasa." The Celalzade copy does not include the phrase, but it does contain a similar suggestion that the monetary fine replaces the *hadd* punishment. It also includes a more expansive description of variable economic status, with fines assessed at the rates of three hundred, two hundred, one hundred, fifty, and forty *akçes*, Akgündüz, *Osmanlı kanunnameleri*, 4:366, facsimile, 403.

104. Akgündüz, *Osmanlı kanunnameleri*, 4:318–19, facsimile, 346.

105. Akgündüz, *Osmanlı kanunnameleri*, 4:320–21, facsimile, 348.

106. The pertinent part of the text reads: "Aydın sancağı yayaları ṣāncāğı bey olān 'Ali . . . yayaya mute'allık olan ḳānūn ve siyāsetnāme içün dergāh-ı mu'allamdan ḳānūn ve siyāsetnāme ta'yib ettüği ecilden işbu ḳānūn ve siyāsetnāme verdim ve buyurdum ki, zikr olunur."

107. Akgündüz, *Osmanlı kanunnameleri*, 4:296, facsimile, 331.

108. Akgündüz, *Osmanlı kanunnameleri*, 4:365, facsimile, 403: "Āyīn-i kavā'id-i cihān-bānī ve ḳavānīn-i 'örfiyye-i 'O̱smānī ki, medār-ı salāḥ-ı 'ālem ve menāt-ı nıẓām-ı cumhūr-ı kāffe-i ümemdir."

109. Heyd, *Studies in Old Ottoman Criminal Law*, 172. These comments follow Heyd's observations concerning the probable implementation of *kanunname* across provinces.

110. Ibid., 151.

111. Ibid. The *kanunname* for Egypt will be addressed in more detail in the following chapter.

112. See the meticulous scholarship on sex, social order, and punishment in Peirce, *Morality Tales*; and Semerdjian, *"Off the Straight Path."*

113. Heyd, *Studies in Old Ottoman Criminal Law*, 152. Heyd cited seven cases from Üsküdar and Bursa to support these statements. Peirce and Semerdjian included hundreds of registered *shari'a* cases from 'Aintab and Aleppo that demonstrate the interpenetration of canonical and imperial legal measures and punishments. This interpenetration is also visible in legal regulations imposed on the inhabitants of the capital city; see Sariyannis, "Prostitution in Ottoman Istanbul"; and Zarinebaf, *Crime and Punishment in Istanbul.*

114. Heyd, *Studies in Old Ottoman Criminal Law*, 177.

115. Enver Çakar identified this *kanunname* in the holdings of the Beyazıt Devlet Library, Veliyüddin Efendi, no. 1969. For his analysis of the dates and various administrative divisions of this manuscript see Çakar, "Kanuni Sultan Süleyman kanunnāmesine göre."

116. Akgündüz argued that one of these *kanunname*, although it appeared in a treatise composed by Ömer Efendi in 1641, was most likely composed earlier, from registers held in the imperial *divan*, and then served as the basis for reform treatises

written by Aziz Efendi and Hezarfen Hüseyin Efendi in the seventeenth century; see Akgündüz, *Osmanlı kanunnameleri*, 4:458.

117. There is general disagreement about the import of provincial *kanunname*s. İnalcık argued that they fundamentally concerned the conditions of the *re'aya*; thus, he claimed that "the *Kanunname* of a *sancak* was primarily intended to be used by government or courts to settle differences between the timar-holders and the *re'aya*"; see İnalcık, "Suleiman the Lawgiver and Ottoman Law," 112. Barkan also emphasized the status of the *re'aya* and prioritized sections of *kanunname* that addressed their status in his selective compendium of regulations concerning agrarian administration; see Barkan, *XV ve XVI inci asırlarda Osmanlı imparatorluğunda zirai*. Heath Lowry, however, insisted that they inscribed the dues and obligations of all participants in the agrarian economy; see Lowry, "The Ottoman Liva Kanunnames." This chapter demonstrates, however, that it is possible to trace how the *kanunname*s were instrumental in establishing a compendium of legal regulations, governed by principles of justice and order, which legitimated the extraction of resources and sustained the sovereign claims of the empire.

118. Akgündüz, *Osmanlı kanunnameleri*, 5:503–4, 533–34.

119. Ibid., 3:290–93.

120. BOA, TTD 387; Akgündüz, *Osmanlı kanunnameleri*, 5:506; Barkan also discusses and presents selections: *XV ve XVI inci asırlarda Osmanlı*, 63–73. Leslie Peirce assessed the implication of this process for the inhabitants of Aintab and Maraş in Peirce, *Morality Tales*, 321.

121. BOA, TTD 966; Akgündüz, *Osmanlı kanunnameleri*, 5:507. For many regions these legal regulations represented a reduction of the tax burden and thus also played a key role in manufacturing the consent of the governed. See İnalcık, *Fatih devri üzerinde tetkikler ve vesikalar* for the initial statement of this argument.

122. BOA, TTD 205; Akgündüz, *Osmanlı kanunnameleri*, 5:533. The *kanunname* appears on folio 700 of the cadastral survey.

123. See passages designated as articles 6–19 (facsimile 545) and 35–42 (facsimile 547–48) in Akgündüz, *Osmanlı kanunnameleri*, 5:536–37.

124. Identified as articles 27 (facsimile 546) and 58 (postscript on facsimile 547) in Akgündüz, *Osmanlı kanunnameleri*, 5:538, 543. An imperial anxiety over mobility, referenced in the previous chapter, pervades these regulations and testifies to the significant concern that unsettled populations, or uncategorized members of the population, jeopardized the classificatory order of the regulations. Reşat Kasaba's work has consistently highlighted the pervasive nature of mobility; see Kasaba, *A Moveable Empire*; and Kasaba, "Nomads and Tribes."

125. "*Devām-ı nızām-ı memleket.*" Article 47 (facsimile 548), Akgündüz, *Osmanlı kanunnameleri*, 5:542–43.

126. Abou-El-Haj, "Aspects of the Legitimization of Ottoman Rule." Four of the

eleven *tapu tahrir defterleri* preserved for Trablus-ı Şam contain some form of *kanun* regulations. As part of the initial efforts to incorporate the region, the first defter dated to 1519, and the source for Abou-El-Haj's analysis, contains the initial legal formulations for the district (BOA TTD 68). This was followed by a second survey with clarifications and addendums in 1525 (BOA TTD 998). For the other *defter* with *kanunname* see BOA TTD 372 [undated, but from the reign of Süleyman, 1520–66]; and 513 [1571].

127. Abou-El-Haj, "Aspects of the Legitimization of Ottoman Rule," 376. Abou-El-Haj provided a brief but masterful section-by-section textual analysis of the preamble and also included for comparative purposes a *kanunname* for Aleppo issued in 1584. Consult TTD 610, which was composed in Ottoman Turkish and contained abbreviated statements of dynastic history and legitimacy. Other cadastral surveys for Aleppo with *kanunname* include BOA TTD 93 [dated 1519]; 998 [1525]; 391, 454 [undated, but from the reign of Süleyman, 1520–66]; 493 [1570]; 524 [1572]; 530 [1573]; and 564 [undated]; and the facsimile of the *Tapu ve Kadastro Arşıvı* TK 3 [dated 1536].

128. Abou-El-Haj, "Aspects of the Legitimization of Ottoman Rule," 375. Daylam was a region along the Caspian Sea and the origins of the Buyid dynasty that acted as de facto rulers of the 'Abbasid Empire from the year 950. *Jizya* (*cizye*, in Ottoman Turkish) was a head tax on non-Muslims and *kharāj* (*ḫarāc*, in Ottoman Turkish) was presumably an agricultural tax on cultivatable land, although it was also conceived as a tribute payment from conquered territories. Distinctions between *cizye* and *harac* increasingly collapsed in Ottoman administrative usage and necessitated later clarification. The *ispence* was an equivalent tax on land paid by non-Muslims to custodians or land-grant recipients; see İnalcık, "Kānūnnāme." Local customary taxes and dues, especially in the Hungarian territories, were folded into the *cizye* designation. Thus, the head tax was called *resmi-filori* (using the Hungarian *florin* as the unit of measurement), and *ispençe* was often referenced as the local portal tax, *resmi-kapu*. The slippage between *cizye* and *harac* and the use of *resmi-kapu* were all features of the 1541 *kanunname* for Buda as well; see Akgündüz, *Osmanlı kanunnameleri*, 5:272. Yet these designations were clarified in the 1560s in a *kanunname* issued to Budin, Novigrad, Seçan, Filek, and Hatvan: BOA, TTD 343; Akgündüz, *Osmanlı kanunnameleri*, 5:279–80, facsimile, 284. For comparative purposes with early juristic definitions of *jizya* and *kharaj* see al-Mawardi's specifications in *al-Aḥkām*, 253–73.

129. Abou-El-Haj, "Aspects of the Legitimization of Ottoman Rule," 378–79. Abou-El-Haj emphasized that the descriptions of both the empire as a whole, and the jurisdiction of the sultanate referenced in the preamble, indicate that these lists were carefully crafted to the conditions particular to each administrative region and are thus instrumental for assessing the evolution of legitimacy and sovereignty within the Ottoman context.

130. I will address these reforms in the following chapter, especially as they relate to scribal traditions and new assessments concerning the imperial treasury, the land

tax, and the relationship between legal formulations defined by the *shari'a* and articulated in Ottoman *kanun*. The specific historical dynamics concerning the occupation of Buda and its governance constitute the subject of Chapter 4.

131. Originally issued around 1541, BOA TTD 449. It is incomplete and contains only the opening *ferman*. See also Akgündüz, *Osmanlı kanunnameleri*, 5:265–70, with facsimile on 270. The following copies of *tapu tahrir defterleri* contained an accompanying *kanunname* for Buda: BOA TTD 410 and 449 [without dates, but reference to territories occupied in 1541–45 and beyond]; BOA TTD 343 [dated 1562]; and BOA TTD 611 [dated 1590].

132. The fairly standardized text reads: *sulṭān 'l-'arab ve 'l-'acem ḥāmī himmet 'l-ḥarīmeyn 'l-müḥtermeyn.*

133. I address this sleight of hand in the next chapter; here it should be noted that Süleyman was characterized as the protector of the faith and arranger of the *shari'a*, so this was an assertion, rather than an inhibition, of his power.

134. İnalcık, "Islamization of Ottoman Laws." The relationships between *shari'a* and *kanun* became an obsessive focus of Ottoman jurists, especially as the office of the *şeyhülislam* also became more involved in the administrative governance of the empire. A sharp divide between the two obscures the way in which the *shari'a* itself became part of an imperial provenance; see Burak, *The Second Formation of Islamic Law*. Uriel Heyd also provided an assessment of how these issues shifted during the reign of Süleyman; see Heyd, *Studies in Old Ottoman Criminal Law*, 180–92.

135. "Kanunname-i cedid," *Milli tetebbu'ler mecmu'ası* 1, no. 1 (1913): 51, 58.

136. Ibid., 58.

137. Darling argues that this formed the crux of an Ottoman innovation in statecraft, as authors of political treatises increasingly emphasized the need to ally with the agricultural producer against rival elites capable of challenging dynastic claims either to taxes or to superior authority. She even suggests that earlier dynasties, such as the Akkoyunlu and the Timurids, unable "to balance the demands of nomadic warlords against the welfare of their subjects," were conquered or assimilated into the large agrarian empires of the Ottomans, Safavids, and Mughals; see Darling, "Political Change and Political Discourse," 505. Martha Mundy and Richard Saumarez Smith took this relationship a step further, insisting that the cultivator became enshrined in the legal apparatus of the Ottoman state as a quasi official, with newly specified rights; see Mundy and Smith, *Governing Property*, 16–20.

138. İnalcık, "Adaletnameler," 77–89.

Chapter 3. The Bureaucratic State

1. A phrase from the concluding section of the preamble to the Egyptian *kanunname*, issued in 1525. Translated in Buzov, "The Lawgiver and His Lawmakers," Appendix A, 196–232, quote from 230–31. This *kanunname* was the product of a reg-

istration campaign to reorganize the administrative structure of the province conducted by the finance minister of Rumeli, İskender Çelebi, head of the campaign treasury Hayreddin Ağa, head envoy Sofuoğlu Mehmed, along with Celalzade Mustafa, then acting as chief secretary of the chancery. For a copy of the manuscript held in the Süleymaniye Kütüphanesi, Aya Sofya 4871, folios 118a–57b, and preliminary commentary, see Akgündüz, *Osmanlı kanunnameleri*, 6:86–140, facsimile, 141–76. The quote can be found on pages 100–101 and 150–51.

2. Cornell H. Fleisher's scholarship laid the groundwork for studies in Ottoman bureaucratic formation and new imperial frameworks during the sixteenth century; see his *Bureaucrat and Intellectual*; and "Preliminaries to the Study of Ottoman Bureaucracy". See also Uzunçarşılı, *Osmanlı devletinin merkez ve bahriye teşkilâtı*.

3. For the strongest articulations of the link between legal and bureaucratic reform during Süleyman's reign see İnalcık, "State, Sovereignty and Law"; and Buzov's arguments, in "The Lawgiver and His Lawmakers," concerning the emergence of a discursive field that moved from activities in the chancery into intellectual and religious debates of the period. Three key encyclopedia entries for bureaucratic formation and the role of the *nişancı* are Afyoncu, "Defter emini"; Babinger, "Nishandji"; and Gökbilgin, "Nişâncı." For the development of a religious hierarchy see Uzunçarşılı, *Osmanlı devletinin ʿilmiye teşkilâtı*; Pixley, "The Development and Role of the Şeyhülislam"; Repp, *The Müfti of Istanbul*; Imber, *Ebu's-suʿud*. Madeline Zilfi's work is also instrumental for any assessment of the role piety played in the elaboration of institutional hierarchies and religious affiliations within the Ottoman sultanate and its administration; see Zilfi, *The İlmiye Registers*.

4. This phrase is Buzov's; see "The Lawgiver and His Lawmakers," 1.

5. Although this designation for the registers is now commonplace in scholarship on the Ottoman Empire, the bound registers did not bear this specific designation until much later, at least until the 1640s, and perhaps after the decision to bind registers of complaint and their *responsa* in a category of their own, the *şikayet defteri*. See Temelkuran, "Dīvān-ı hümāyūn mühimme kalemi," 158; Kütükoğlu, "Mühimme defterlerinde muâmele kayıdları üzerine," 95–97; and Dávid, "The Mühimme Defteri," 167–68.

6. Abdurrahman Atçıl's *Scholars and Sultans* is now regarded as the definitive treatment of the relationships among imperial, scribal, and intellectual communities.

7. Josef Matuz's work on the Ottoman chancery remains an indispensable source for the period, particularly in terms of tracing the genealogy of various positions within the expanding institutional heart of the empire; see Matuz, *Das Kanzleiwesen Sultan Süleymāns des Prächtigen*. Two dissertations have set a new standard for research into bureaucratic standardization, chancery practice, and the broader questions of law and language: H. Yılmaz, "The Sultan and the Sultanate"; and M. S. Yılmaz, "Koca Nişancı of Kanuni."

8. Repp, *The Müfti of Istanbul*, 25–32.

9. White, *The Climate of Rebellion*, 17.

10. Shinder, "Early Ottoman Administration," 514–15.

11. Ibid., 502–6. Shinder credited this juxtaposition to personal communication with Rudi Lindner; see also Şahin, *Empire and Power*, 215.

12. Shinder traced this evolution in the earliest chronicles of 'Aşıkpaşazāde, Oruç Beğ, Karamani Mehmed, Şukrullah, Tursun Bey, Ahmedi, and Neşri; see Shinder, "Early Ottoman Administration," 503–6. For key examples of antibureaucracy sentiment see 'Ali Bey, *Tevārīḫ-i āl-i 'Os̱man'dan Aşıkpaşazade tārīḫī*, 19–20; Banarlı, *Dāsitānı tevārīhi mülūki Āl-i Osman*, 83; and Atsız, *Osmanlı tarihleri*, 118, 139, NaN-77. Gottfried Hagen has also addressed the presence of antinomian voices in seventeenth-century heroic hagiographies. He argues that chronicles preserved the voices of those opposed to Ottoman centralization, and he perceives the period as one of loss, chaos, and chronic disorder; see Hagen, "Chaos, Order, Power, Salvation."

13. İnalcık, "Emergence of the Ottomans," 280. Also cited in Shinder, "Early Ottoman Administration," 509.

14. Shinder, "Early Ottoman Administration," 506; see also a facsimile of the manual in Ertaylan, *Ahmed-i Dā'ī*, 325–28.

15. İnalcık, *Hicrī 835 tarihli sūret-i defter-i sancak-i Arvanid*, xii–xv.

16. Şahin, *Empire and Power*, 216.

17. Shinder, "Early Ottoman Administration," 515.

18. Ibid., 509. For a full assessment of Ilkhanid registers see Hinz, "Das Rechnungswesen Orientalischer."

19. The typical phrase reads, *ber mūceb-i ḳānūn-ı Ḥasan Pādişāh*. Akgündüz, *Osmanlı kanunnameleri*, 3:236–38, 259–85. Also cited in Burak, "Between the *Ḳānūn* of Qāytbāy and Ottoman *Yasaq*," 9.

20. Akgündüz, *Osmanlı kanunnameleri*, 3:236–38, 259–85. A typical rendering reads, *bi-iḫtiyār-ı aḥālī-i vilāyet-i mezkūre ve bi-ma'rifet-i mīri mīrān ve be ḳāḍī-i*.

21. Burak, "Between the Ḳānūn of Qāytbāy and Ottoman Yasaq," 9.

22. Kumakura, "Who Handed over Mamluk Land Registers?"

23. Ibid., 292. See also Shinder, "Early Ottoman Administration," 507. It should be noted that Kumakura's research pointedly disproved the assertions in the initial Egyptian *kanunname* concerning the transferal of Mamluk registers and relied on later surveys as well as chronicles to decipher an alternative genealogy of this process. The larger point remains significant, however: scribal actors in former principalities were commandeered into Ottoman land-registration efforts.

24. Kumakura, "Who Handed over Mamluk Land Registers?" 293.

25. Ibid., 292–93.

26. Şahin, *Empire and Power*, 219; Fleischer, "Preliminaries," 135–38. Muhammet Zahit Atçıl argued that this process during the reign of Süleyman represents an "in-

digenization" of the scholarly class and the chancery services in particular; see Atçıl, "State and Government," 213–21.

27. The last letter issued to a foreign dignitary in Greek by Sultan Süleyman's imperial council was sent to Sigismund I, king of Poland, in 1529 and announced the victorious military campaigns that cemented Ottoman control of key Hungarian territories, even though the siege of Vienna itself had failed: Venetian State Archives (Archivio di Stato di Venezia), online: *Miscellanea documenti turchi*, no. 250, www.archiviodistatovenezia.it/divenire/ua.htm?idUa=37803.

28. These issues will be explored in more detail in Chapter 4. Tijana Krstić has provided a succinct summary of these major developments concerning Hungarian intermediaries within the Ottoman chancery; see Krstić, "Of Translation and Empire." For the first study, and perhaps now the model, of the links among language, translation, and legitimacy, see Hagen, "Translations and Translators," 95–134.

29. Fleischer, *Bureaucrat and Intellectual*, 22–23.

30. Ibid., 22.

31. This definition of *heteroglossia* derives from Bakhtin, who attempted to understand the shift from Platonic monologue to Socratic dialogue as "the co-existence of socio-ideological contradictions of both present and past" and thus a shift from single-voiced rhetoric to dissonant discourse; see Bakhtin, *The Dialogic Imagination*, 291.

32. Hagen, "Translations and Translators," 106. Hagen further insisted that references to a public who did not know Persian was more likely a *topos* than a reality and that the individual strategies and practices of translators should be studied as part of a broader effort to investigate Ottoman intellectual culture more thoroughly. Here, Celalzade Mustafa's statements should be read not as motive but rather as indicative of a clear articulation of a distinctly Ottoman practice and public.

33. Woodhead, *Ta'līḳīzāde's Şehnāme-i Hümāyūn*, 134–35.

34. Ibid., 131.

35. Kafadar, "A Rome of One's Own," 10–15; Krstić, *Contested Conversions*, 3–5.

36. Artan, "Questions of Ottoman Identity," 92.

37. Singer, *Palestinian Peasants and Ottoman Officials*, 127, 189.

38. Burak, *The Second Formation of Islamic Law*, 99. Karen Barkey has argued that the Ottoman dynasty's ability to manage difference was a key factor in the durability of the empire; see Barkey, *Empire of Difference*, 9–27; Baki Tezcan presents a more focused account of ethnic and racial markers in "Ethnicity, Race, Religion and Social Class."

39. The traditional account of this process can be found in Repp, *The Müfti of Istanbul*. For a reassessment of the emergence of an Ottoman learned hierarchy see Atçıl, "The Formation of the Ottoman Learned Class."

40. The office of the *şeyhülislam* embodied the increasingly powerful role that the imperial establishment played in orchestrating legal and administrative affairs.

Although charged with ensuring proper adherence to the *shari'a* as part of the bureaucratic hierarchy, the *şeyhülislam* served, like other officials of the realm, at the behest of the sultan. For example, Selim I famously ignored Zenbilli 'Ali Efendi's protests over the execution of 150 treasury officials as "contrary to the *sharī'a*," and they were dismissed and even executed by the sultan's order as well. The first *şeyhülislam* to be forcibly dismissed was Çivizade Muhyiddin Mehmed Efendi, by order of Süleyman I in 1542; see İnalcık, *The Ottoman Empire*, 92–95.

41. İnalcık, "The Ruznamçe Registers," 251–75.

42. For key examples of oppositional voices in the sixteenth and seventeenth centuries see E. Turan, "Voices of Opposition"; and Pfeiffer, "Confessional Polarization."

43. Pfeifer, "Encounter After the Conquest"; Rafeq, "The Syrian *'Ulama*."

44. Christine Woodhead's work on this office brought history and history-writing into the forum of debates concerning sixteenth-century Ottoman dynastic claims. She outlined the careers of each of the five officeholders and identified the manuscripts produced under their tutelage in "An Experiment in Official Historiography." Emine Fetvacı has most recently redefined the multiplicity of voices in the Ottoman court and identified how this position, while ostensibly at the service of the sultan, became increasingly dependent on other patrons and may have contributed to diverse representations of the Ottoman past; see Fetvacı, "Office of the Ottoman Court Historian"; and Fetvacı, *Picturing History*.

45. Fetvacı, "Office of the Ottoman Court Historian," 7.

46. The role played by the historian as critic, rather than panegyrist, appears in chapter six, where Lokman's position is slightly redefined by his administrative roles and internal oppositions emerge concerning the nature of sultanic power and the centralizing reforms of Sultan Süleyman.

47. Fetvacı, "From Print to Trace." Baki Tezcan addressed the manipulation of history as a facet of early modern politics in "The Politics of Early Modern Ottoman Historiography" and explored comparative features between the work of Seyyid Lokman and Mustafa Ali in "Ottoman Historical Writing."

48. For the evolution of Ottoman Turkish see Kerslake, "Ottoman Turkish." On Ottoman epistolography and the creation of *inşa'* collections (*münşe'at*) see Riedlmayer, "Ottoman Copybooks of Correspondence."

49. For an extended treatment of these connections see Buzov, "The Lawgiver and His Lawmakers."

50. There were significant dissident voices to this process, but even dissidents tended to reinforce the triumph of Ottoman history. For example, although Mustafa Ali critiqued sultanic absolutism after the fashion of earlier opponents to Ottoman centralization, he still avidly traced and embraced the evolution of an "Ottoman way" and judged individual sultans against this idealized standard; see Fleischer, *Bureaucrat and Intellectual*, 93–97.

51. For scholarship on the role played by representation, performance, and ritual ceremonies in the production and projection of imperial power see Necipoğlu, "Süleyman the Magnificent"; Murphey, *Exploring Ottoman Sovereignty*, 207–51; and Ertu, "Depiction of Ceremonies."

52. Three publications have traced these significant interactions and inform the arguments presented here: Krstić, *Contested Conversions*; Burak, *The Second Formation of Islamic Law*; and Şahin, *Empire and Power.*

53. See Necipoğlu, "Framing the Gaze"; and Necipoğlu, *The Age of Sinan*. On the relationship between the built environment and an evolving imperial identity see Bozdoğan, Bailey, and Necipoğlu, *History and Ideology*.

54. Heyd, *Studies in Old Ottoman Criminal Law*; Imber, *Studies in Ottoman History and Law*; Imber, *Ebu's-su'ud*; Buzov, "The Lawgiver and His Lawmakers," esp. 172–89; Taylor, "Keeping Usufruct in the Family"; Mundy, "Ethics and Politics in the Law."

55. Imber, "The Law of the Land," 53. This approach builds from scholarship dedicated either to southeastern and central European tributary relations with the Ottoman Empire or to diplomatic negotiations with other regional powers with overlapping claims to, or intensive trade with, these territories (Venetian, Crimean, Muscovite, Habsburg, Bavarian, etc.). Work on these frontier territories consistently explores questions of identification (how territories are identified as either "inside" or "outside" of the Ottoman imperial realm), of authority (what strategies were deployed to assert nominal control over tribute states), or representations of sovereignty (power relations and tactics of subordination); see Kármán and Kunčević, *The European Tributary States.* Dariusz Kołodziejczyk addressed these questions in his work on the Crimean Khanate and the Kingdom of Poland: *Ottoman-Polish Diplomatic Relations*; and *The Crimean Khanate.* See also the work of Panaite: "Power Relationships in the Ottoman Empire"; *The Ottoman Law of War and Peace*; and "The Voivodes of the Danubian Principalities." On Russian relationships Alan Fisher is a good guide; see his *A Precarious Balance* (Istanbul: İsis Press, 1999). For a general reference to the period as a whole see Baramova et al. *Power and Influence in South-Eastern Europe*. The founding voice for this work was, as usual, İnalcık: "Yeni vesikalara gore," 185–229.

56. Buzov, "The Lawgiver and His Lawmakers," 77–80; İnalcık, *The Ottoman Empire*, 94. Çivizade Muhyiddin Mehmed Efendi was the first *şeyhülislam* to be dismissed from his post, in part owing to his opposition to the influence of the mystic philosophies of ibn al-'Arabi and Celaleddin Rumi but perhaps also because of his opposition to the commodification of charitable endowments (cash *vakıf*); see İpşirli, "Çivizade Muhyiddin Mehmed Efendi," 348. Kemalpaşazade famously supported Selim I's military advancement on the Safavid empire with a *fetva*-based pamphlet that accused the Shi'i of apostasy. Kemalpaşazade's *fetva* on *miri* land were also included in the *kanunname-i cedid* along with Ebu's-su'ud's, although the latter standardized, clarified, and extended the commodification of land; see Parmaksızoğlu,

"Kemāl Pāşa-zāde," *TDVİA*, 6:561-66. For details concerning the legal basis for Selim I's military campaigns see Üstün, "Heresy and Legitimacy," 35–59; and for his position as a bridge between classical land definitions and those of Ebu's-su'ud see Ökten, "Ottoman Society and State."

57. Imber, *Ebu's-su'ud*, 73.

58. Panaite, "The *Re'ayas* of the Tributary-Protected Principalities."

59. This phrasing is derived from Snjezana Buzov's treatment of the preamble in chapter 1 of her dissertation, "The Lawgiver and His Lawmakers," 19–45.

60. There are multiple copies of the preamble, suggesting that it was also intended for a readership wider than the province itself. There are three copies in the Süleymaniye Library, one in the Topkapı Saray Library, and one in the Bibliothèque nationale. See also Akgündüz, *Osmanlı kanunnameleri*, 6:82. Buzov provided the first major analysis of this preamble, along with its translation. This section focuses on the relationship between text and sovereignty and cites Buzov's translation (Appendix A of Buzov, "The Lawgiver and His Lawmakers," 197–231), and the edited copy in Akgündüz for reference (6:86–140, facsimile, 141–76).

61. Buzov, "The Lawgiver and His Lawmakers," 230–31; Akgündüz, *Osmanlı kanunnameleri*, 6:100–101, facsimile, 176.

62. Buzov, "The Lawgiver and His Lawmakers," 197–98; Akgündüz, *Osmanlı kanunnameleri*, 6:86, facsimile, 141.

63. Here, Celalzade Mustafa also references, in Arabic, the import of Ottoman collective knowledge concerning *siyaset-i şer'iyye* and explicitly states the equivalence between *'urf* and *shari'a*: *al-ma'rūf 'urfān k'l-maşrū' şa'rān* (what is practiced through customary law is what is permitted by the *shari'a*).

64. Buzov, "The Lawgiver and His Lawmakers," 198; Akgündüz, *Osmanlı kanunnameleri*, 6:86, facsimile, 141.

65. Buzov, "The Lawgiver and His Lawmakers," 201; Akgündüz, *Osmanlı kanunnameleri*, 6:88, facsimile, 142. The phrase for "discourse and law" is *nesk-ü ķānūn*.

66. Buzov, "The Lawgiver and His Lawmakers," 201; Akgündüz, *Osmanlı kanunnameleri*, 6:88, facsimile, 142. Celalzade Mustafa explicitly linked lawmaking with the need to fill in the lacunae left by the various interpretive mechanisms for the *shari'a*.

67. Buzov, "The Lawgiver and His Lawmakers," 202–3; Akgündüz, *Osmanlı kanunnameleri*, 6:88, facsimile, 142–43.

68. Celalzade Mustafa listed as the key figures deserving of emulation "the guidance of the two 'Umars" and insisted that the sultans, or *padişah*s, performed their obligations like Ali and Husayn. The "two 'Umars" refers to two successors who had a hand in designing the administrative and legal structure of the expanding Muslim state after the death of Muhammad. 'Umar (I), was the second designated successor after Abu Bakr, led the *umma* from 634 to 644, and was known for his piety and knowledge of emerging legal strictures in Islam. He divided conquered territories into

provinces; created positions for a chief secretary, treasury official, revenue collector, and judge; and was the first to set up a *mazalim* court for investigating complaints and addressing petitions. See Cook, *Commanding Right*, 97. 'Umar (II) was an 'Umayyad caliph from 717 to 720 known for abolishing taxation divisions between original Arab adherents to Islam and converts to the faith and for generally shifting administrative patterns toward equality. Converts would no longer pay the *jizya*, and their lands would be registered at the *kharaj* rate, as was also assessed on the lands of Muslim cultivators. He, too, emphasized redress for those wronged and was also known for his pious attention to the law and for his efforts to standardize collections of *hadith*. See Kennedy, *The Prophet and the Age of the Caliphates*, 106–7; and Hoyland, *In God's Path*, 195–201. The reference to 'Ali (the fourth caliph, cousin and son-in-law of the Prophet) and his son Husayn folds figures also held as martyrs within the Shi'i tradition into the current of moral code followed by the Ottoman establishment.

69. Buzov, "The Lawgiver and His Lawmakers," 204–5, Akgündüz, *Osmanlı kanunnameleri*, 6:89–90, facsimile, 143.

70. Buzov, "The Lawgiver and His Lawmakers," 206–8; Akgündüz, *Osmanlı kanunnameleri*, 6:90–91, facsimile, 144.

71. Buzov, "The Lawgiver and His Lawmakers," 205–6; Akgündüz, *Osmanlı kanunnameleri*, 6:90, facsimile, 143–44.

72. Buzov, "The Lawgiver and His Lawmakers," 208–9; Akgündüz, *Osmanlı kanunnameleri*, 6:91, facsimile, 144.

73. Buzov, "The Lawgiver and His Lawmakers," 212–14, Akgündüz, *Osmanlı kanunnameleri*, 6:93–94, facsimile, 146.

74. Buzov, "The Lawgiver and His Lawmakers," 214; Akgündüz, *Osmanlı kanunnameleri*, 6:94, facsimile, 146.

75. Buzov, "The Lawgiver and His Lawmakers," 217–18; Akgündüz, *Osmanlı kanunnameleri*, 6:95, facsimile, 147.

76. Buzov, "The Lawgiver and His Lawmakers," 219–20; Akgündüz, *Osmanlı kanunnameleri*, 6:96, facsimile, 148.

77. Buzov, "The Lawgiver and His Lawmakers," 226–28; Akgündüz, *Osmanlı kanunnameleri*, 6:97–99, facsimile, 149–50.

78. Buzov, "The Lawgiver and His Lawmakers," 229–31; Akgündüz, *Osmanlı kanunnameleri*, 6:100–101, facsimile, 150–51.

79. Buzov, "The Lawgiver and His Lawmakers," 230–31; Akgündüz, *Osmanlı kanunnameleri*, 6:100–101, facsimile, 151–52.

80. Şahin, *Empire and Power*, 188–89.

81. Imber, "The Law of the Land," 53.

82. There were also intervening historical and ideological moves that escalated debates concerning the nature of imperial law and its relationship to land registration. Most significantly, and ultimately leading to his execution, Grand Vizier İbrahim

agitated for a more purist, *shari'a*-minded policy of lawmaking and issued *kanunname* to various Rumelian provinces that reinforced this shift against imperial legal sovereignty; see Buzov, "The Lawgiver and His Lawmakers," 46–75.

83. Ālī, "Künhü'l-Aḫbār," f. 476b.

84. For discussion of the *kanunname-i cedid* see Chapter 2. The text of the Buda preamble is contained in the 1541 tax register of Buda held in the Başbakanlık (BOA, TTD, no. 449) and was addressed as well in Chapter 2. Besides the copy contained in Akgündüz, *Osmanlı kanunnameleri*, 5:268–70, it has been transcribed and translated several times: see, e.g., Barkan, *XV ve XVI inci asırlarda*, 296–97; Barnes, *An Introduction to Religious Foundations*, 36–37; İnalcık, "Islamization of Ottoman Laws," 101–2; and Imber, *Ebu's-su'ud*, 122–23. For convenience the references that follow rely on the printed form of the *kanunname-i cedid* in *Milli tetebbu'ler mecmu'ası*, 47–112, esp. 49–50, 54–55, and 56–58, in consultation with the copies held in the Topkapı Palace Library (Revan, 1935, folio 1a), and the Süleymaniye (Cārullah Efendi, 968, folios 3b–6b).

85. These *fetva*s were gathered in manuscripts known as *Ma'ruzat*, with the earliest requested by Selim II of his successor to the position of *şeyhülislam*, Hamid Efendi. The number of manuscript copies (Akgündüz references three in the BOA, two in the Topkapı Library, six in the Süleymaniye, one at Istanbul University, and one at Selçuk University, which he uses as the basis for his facsimile and transcription) attests to the significance of these *fetva*s and their continued role in Ottoman governance; see Akgündüz, *Osmanlı kanunnameleri*, 4:31–75.

86. *Milli tetebbu'ler mecmu'ası*, 49–50; Akgündüz, *Osmanlı kanunnameleri*, 4:79.

87. In the 1548 preamble for Srebrenice and Sas in the district of İzvornik, a dependent territory of Buda, Ebu's-su'ud extends inheritance rights to daughters in an explicit effort to maintain stability and efficiency in the seemingly continuing practice of transferring and selling land outside of the control of the state. This would then become standard and was included in copies of the *Ma'rūżāt*; see Akgündüz, *Osmanlı kanunnameleri*, 4:81 (response to the third *fetva* question), and 302–3 (note articles 31 and 43).

88. *'Öşrı* (from the Arabic "' ashrī" or "ten") refers to lands that had remained in the hands of Muslims since the time of the early Arab conquests and were subject to a lower rate of tithe; *ḫarācī* (from the Arabic "kharājī," with the literal meaning "outside of," gradually transitioned from a tax assayed on non-Muslim agricultural lands conquered during war to a customary land tax. The historic slippage between conquered and customary became all the more troubling during the intensive military campaigns of the sixteenth century.

89. *Milli tetebbu'ler mecmu'ası*, 52; Akgündüz, *Osmanlı kanunnameleri*, 4:80, facsimile, 86.

90. *Milli tetebbu'ler mecmu'ası*, 52; Akgündüz, *Osmanlı kanunnameleri*, 4:80, facsimile, 86.

91. The preamble is held in the archives of the Tapu ve Kadastro Umumi Mudürlüğü, no. 190. See *Milli tetebbu'ler mecmu'ası*, 57–58, and Akgündüz, *Osmanlı kanunnameleri*, 7:663–68. It is also translated in İnalcık, "Islamization of Ottoman Laws," 103–6. Other versions can be found in Barkan, *XV ve XVI inci asırlarda*, 297–99; and, Barnes, *An Introduction to Religious Foundations*, 32–33.

92. Panaite, "Power Relationships in the Ottoman Empire," 50–52.

93. İnalcık, *Essays in Ottoman History*, 156; Mundy and Smith, *Governing Property*, 15.

94. İnalcık and Quataert, *An Economic and Social History*, 113; İnalcık, "Islamization of Ottoman Laws."

95. Akgündüz, *Osmanlı kanunnameleri*, 7:665, facsimile, 667; *Milli tetebbu'ler mecmu'ası*, 51.

96. This formula is outlined by Imber in "The Law of the Land," 49.

97. Hanafi legal theorists were adept at reconfiguring *shari'a* limits in favor of a ruler's discretionary power. Ebu's-su'ud's predecessor, Kemalpaşazade (d. 1534), had laid the groundwork for later revisions by addressing the status of the imperial treasury and the sale of property in terms that granted sultanic jurisdiction over both. It was left to Ebu's-su'ud, however, to finesse these efforts and to create a more tightly crafted argument that fit sixteenth-century realities into the rubric of canonical law.

98. *Milli tetebbu'ler mecmu'ası*, 50; Akgündüz, *Osmanlı kanunnameleri*, 4:79, facsimile, 85.

99. Düzdağ, *Şeyhülislâm Ebussuûd Efendi fetvaları*, 839. Cited and translated in Imber, *Ebu's-su'ud*, 125. This question was also addressed within the collected editions of the *Ma'rūżāt*; see Akgündüz, *Osmanlı kanunnameleri*, 4:80–81.

100. Necipoğlu, "From International Timurid to Ottoman"; Necipoğlu, "Challenging the Past"; Dijkema, *Ottoman Historical Monumental Inscriptions*; Ebel, "Representations of the Frontier."

101. H. Yılmaz, "The Sultan and the Sultanate," 176–91; Şahin, *Empire and Power*, 189; Gerber, *Islamic Law and Culture*, 53–54.

102. Şahin, *Empire and Power*, 192; Krstić, *Contested Conversions*.

103. İnalcık, "State and Ideology," 78; İnalcık, *The Ottoman Empire*, 41.

104. See Cornell Fleischer's work on the emergence of critics of imperial power within the context of messianic movements: "The Lawgiver as Messiah"; "Mahdi and Millennium"; and, "Seer to the Sultan."

105. Mandaville, "Usurious Piety." For a more recent discussion of this debate see Buzov, "Appendix F: While Cognizant of Dissent," in "The Lawgiver and His Lawmakers," 251–58.

106. Heyd, *Studies in Old Ottoman Criminal Law*, 199.

107. İnalcık, *The Ottoman Empire*, 41; Finkel, *Osman's Dream*, 129.

108. Şahin, *Empire and Power*, 224; Ménage, "On the Constituent Elements."

109. Fekete, *Bevezetés a hódoltság török diplomatikájába*, 12–16. This letter was written from Aleppo, during a campaign against the Safavids, and was issued, with the sultan's *tuğra*, as an imperial order that reasserted the terms negotiated after the failed siege of Eger in 1552.

110. Panaite, "Power Relationships in the Ottoman Empire," 48.

111. Şahin has provided the most recent, and definitive, assessment of the *Ṭabaḳāt* and also addresses the variable portraits of Selim I and Süleyman I by Celalzade Mustafa; see *Empire and Power*, 166–78.

112. Kerslake, "A Critical Edition and Translation," 10, 302n1.

113. Şahin, *Empire and Power*, 189–93; Celalzade, *Kanunī'nin tarihçisinden muhteşem çağ*.

114. Şahin, *Empire and Power*, 191; Celalzade, *Kanunī'nin tarihçisinden muhteşem çağ*, 364.

115. Şahin, *Empire and Power*, 171–73.

116. For Şahin's critical exegesis of the *Selimnāme* see Şahin, *Empire and Power*, 178–83. The clearest discussion of how nostalgia figures in Ottoman historical writing can be found in Kafadar, "The Myth of the Golden Age." Also see Tezcan, "Politics of Early Modern Ottoman Historiography."

117. Şahin and Emecen, *II. Bāyezid dönemine ait 906/1501 tarihli ahkām defteri*. The original register can also be found at BOA; see A.DVN 790. Şahin and Emecen describe its contents and physical description in *II. Bāyezid dönemine*, xvii–xxxv.

118. For the intersection between imperial intervention and petitionary subjects see İnalcık, "Şikayet Hakkı," 33–45; Faroqhi, "Political Activity Among Ottoman Taxpayers"; and Ursinus, *Grievance Administration (Şikayet) in an Ottoman Province*. Faroqhi cautioned against overreliance on these documents owing to their summary nature because they are copies of petitions presented to the council. But since my goal here is simply to comment on the emergence of rhetorical devices that place both the petition and sultanic response (*ḥükm*) within a framework of sovereignty defined by the extension of justice and legal order, I have included them as examples of an emergent pattern. See Faroqhi, "Political Activity," 4.

119. For key examples of each of these phrases in turn see Şahin and Emecen, *II. Bāyezid dönemine*, 1, no. 4; 17, facsimile, 58; 40, facsimile, 142; and 83, facsimile, 297.

120. Prohibitionary remarks were indicated with phrases such as *ḫilāf-ı şer'ü ḳānūn* (against *shari'a* and *kanun*); *bī vech-i şer'ü ḳānūn dāḫl iderlerse men'idesiz* (if found to be against the dictates of *shari'a* and *kanun* you should prohibit it); *min b'ad defter mücebiyle 'amel idüp ḫilāfına cevāz vermeyesiz* (from now on you should act according to the register and do not allow anything contrary to the register). See Şahin and Emecen, *II. Bāyezid dönemine*, 65, facsimile, 229; and for reference to the *shari'a* as a standard alone, see 77, facsimile, 275.

121. A previously cited order, 77, facsimile, 275, is a good example of a clear strategy

to reference the authority of the *shari'a* within an order sent to a local judge, in this case İnegol. In other words the reference to the *shari'a* is still rendered as a sultanic act.

122. Uriel Heyd's *Ottoman Documents on Palestine* is the earliest and still the most comprehensive statement on this issue. Heyd is one of three scholars who carved an early path for careful analysis of the *mühimme*; see Heyd, *Studies in Old Ottoman Criminal Law*. See also Abu-Husayn, *The View from Istanbul*; and Dávid, "The Mühimme Defteri."

123. "Intermediary" does not suggest that these documentary sets represent distinct positions but rather places them together within a shared textual habitus of administrative justice and concern.

124. Heyd, *Ottoman Documents on Palestine*, 36.

125. These are, respectively, Sahillioğlu E 12321 and Koğuşlar 888.

126. The broad similarities between these two documentary traditions should not be overlooked, as it substantiates an argument for a common language of administrative concern.

127. Dávid, "The Mühimme Defteri," 167–68.

128. Kütükoğlu, "Mühimme defterlerinde muāmele kayıdları üzerine," 95. Dávid references MD 19 in this regard, with "*mīrī aḥkām ḳaydıdır*," or notation of imperial degrees; or MD 61, "*Ḥamza bey zāmanında vāḳi' olan mīrī aḥkāmın ibtidā' ḳaydıdır*," or initial notations of imperial decrees that "happened" in the time of Ḥamza bey (the incumbent *reisülküttab*). See Dávid, "The Mühimme Defteri," 168.

129. MD 42 (1579–91), as Dávid's careful analysis suggests, represents an ideal example of both problems. The bound register flips back and forth between dates across those two years, contains almost 150 pages of a *ru'us defteri*, then picks up a misplaced fragment from an earlier year; thus, it contains excerpts from three registers (two distinct *mühimme* registers and one *ruūs*). See Dávid, "The Mühimme Defteri," 177.

130. On this point there is some disagreement about whether the registers were entered at some phase of the drafting process or represent copies after an order was sent out from the imperial council. Dávid suggested that, because the registers were composite in structure, both cases are true; see Dávid, "The Mühimme Defteri," 169; see also Peachy, "Register of Copies."

131. The campaign of Szigetvár (1566), which ended in Süleyman's death, for example, left records in 154 pages of MD 5; see Káldy-Nagy, "The First Centuries," 181. Dávid further notes that MD 32 begins with a clear designation of its records as part of the eastern campaigns: "Its content is almost completely *hüküm*s and *name*s written to Mustafa Paşa, appointed as serdar to the eastern campaign and to [officials] of the eastern *vilayets*, in order to make preparations for warfare." He also suggested that MD 44, 12, and 77 contained prominent "leafs," or folios, dedicated to the imperial campaigns; see Dávid, "The Mühimme Defteri," 179.

132. There are actually six more that should be added to the sixteenth-century

notation of *mühimme defteri*s but were classified instead under *mühimme zeyli defterleri* (MZD); see Sarınay, *Başbakanlık Osmanlı arşivi rehberi*, 90–91.

133. It is not exactly true to state that the directives cannot be tracked, as copies of orders were preserved in the various outposts of the *shari'a* courts in the empire, often appended to the back of their own registers of legal affairs (*sijillāt* [Arabic]/*sicilleri* [Ottoman]). Of course, these registers are themselves often scattered, haphazardly preserved, and entail their own complexities for scholarly perusal. Unfortunately for both Buda and Trablus-ı Şam, these legal registers were either entirely lost (in the case of Buda) or only preserved from the 1680s onward (in the case of Trablus-ı Şam). As a result, the chapters in this book seek to construct a study of Ottoman administrative practice without the help of a key set of resources most scholars customarily rely on to understand textual and legal authority. While Ali Yaycioğlu argued that the *shari'a* courts, along with their judges and records, were key "partners" in the project of empire building in chapter 3 of *Partners of the Empire*, here the focus is on imperial decrees, their formulations and strategies, and thus on the emergence of a hegemonic discourse that contained evidence of negotiation between imperial and regional interest groups.

134. A "contrapuntal reading" shares simultaneously in its original definition as alternative melodic strains and in postcolonial notions of alterity framed by Edward Said. First introduced in "Reflections on Exile" and developed further in *Culture and Imperialism*, contrapuntality figured as a key component in Said's response to critics of *Orientalism* who claimed that he focused exclusively on European culture and ignored the resistance and agency of the colonized; see Said, "Reflections on Exile." Said averred that "in the counterpoint of western classical music, various themes play off one another, with only a provisional privilege being given to any particular one; yet in the resulting polyphony there is concert and order, an organized interplay that derives from the themes, not from a rigorous melodic or formal principle outside the work." Said, *Culture and Imperialism*, 59–60. While Said's impact and contrapuntal approach has, for obvious reasons, played a dominant role in cultural theory and postcolonial studies, scholars of other historical periods have also increasingly employed this device to move beyond comparative or interconnected histories; see, e.g., Ingham and Warren, *Postcolonial Moves*.

135. Heyd, *Studies in Old Ottoman Criminal Law*, 167–87.

136. Although a two-part summary section is indeed typical of orders in the bound registers, the format is often linked to directives formed in response to petitions. Diplomatic negotiations do not necessarily follow the same outline, although the formulaic weight of a petitionary apparatus tends to result in the reshaping of most correspondence issued from the imperial council in accordance with this structure.

137. MD 102:79 and 1692.

138. See MD 78:1563 and 1564 for examples of this in the provincial seat of Trablus.

139. MD 6:88.
140. MD 62:228.
141. MD 67:80.

Chapter 4. The Brokered State

1. The *'ahdname* affirmed his position as prince of Transylvania and employed terms common in orders sent to the principality since 1541. The treaties indicated the significant role played by Transylvania in the defense and diplomacy of Hungarian territories, and the unique concerns facing the Ottoman establishment in a region where boundaries between states, and between friend and enemy, were difficult to police. In fact, the formula "be the enemy of my enemy and a friend of my friend" became a common feature of imperial orders (*hükm-i hümayun*) to the region. János B. Szabó provided the translation of this treaty and a fine-grained analysis of cooperation and tension between Transylvania and the Ottoman establishment in "'Splendid Isolation'?" (cited passage on 312). He also stated that these treaties only exist in their Latin translations and that the Ottoman Turkish text was not preserved. A preliminary review of the contents of the Başbakanlık Arşivi in 2012 confirms this point. For the Latin texts of treaties delivered across the last three decades of the sixteenth century, see Papp, *Die Verleihungs-, Bekräftigungs- und Vertragsurkunden der Osmanen*, 214–21.

2. Schaendlinger and Römer, *Die Schreiben Sûleyman des Prächtigen*, 11–18.

3. Necipoğlu, "Süleyman the Magnificent."

4. Imber, *Ebu's-Su'ud*, 75.

5. Rhoads Murphey addressed the gradual transformation in Süleyman's court concerning the significance of Hungary more generally, and emphasized the broader transimperial dynamics in the process, in "Süleyman I and the Conquest of Hungary."

6. Necipoğlu, "Süleyman the Magnificent."

7. Imber, *Ebu's-su'ud*, 75.

8. This phrase, along with the notion of a "brokered empire," derives from Natalie Rothman's reassessment of Venetian-Ottoman relations in *Brokering Empire*. Eric Dursteler also addressed interimperial identity formation in *Venetians in Constantinople*. This scholarship represents a return to the dynamic interactions first envisioned in the work of Fernand Braudel. His comparative methodology broke through previous historiographic tendencies that embraced a paradigm of persistent warfare, tracked specific military engagements, or reflected on the economic vulnerabilities of interimperial warfare; see Braudel, *The Mediterranean and the Mediterranean World*. For key examples of scholarship that tests even as it revisits Braudel's model, see Horden and Purcell, *The Corrupting Sea*; Abulafia, *The Mediterranean in History*; Harris, *Rethinking the Mediterranean*; and Ruiz, Symcox, and Piterberg, *Braudel Revisited*.

9. The frontier extended from the Maros-Temes region in the east, across the northern edge of the Great Plain, central and southwestern Transdanubia, Slavonia,

and Croatia, to the Dalmatian coast in the southwest. See Dávid and Fodor, *Ottomans, Hungarians, and Habsburgs*, xvi. For the dynamics of the fortress defense system see Hegyi, "The Ottoman Network of Fortresses"; and Ágoston, "The Costs of the Ottoman Fortress-System."

10. At a major fourteenth-century battle at Kosovo Polje in 1389, Ottoman forces encountered Sigismund of Luxemburg (1387–1437), the son of Emperor Charles IV, who was married to Mary, the daughter of Louis of Anjou, and thus the last of the Angevine dynasty (1301–89). The Angevines had maintained a semblance of unity against threats from the Venetian Republic, the expanding Ottoman dynasty, and the Byzantine Empire for almost a century. Sigismund was one of three exceptions to foreign rule since the death of the last Árpád (considered to be the founding dynasty of an independent Hungary) in 1301, when rulers from Bohemia, Bavaria, Austria, Poland, Luxemburg, and Naples assumed leadership of the region. Along with Louis I of Anjou (Naples, 1342–82), and the brilliant Renaissance court shepherded by Matthias I Corvinus of the Hunyadi family (1458–90), these three men ensured that the Carpathian Basin would play a key role in Eurasian fortunes. The Jagiello period, with the rulers Vladislaus (r. 1490–1516) and his son Lajos II (r. 1516–26), then placed a Bohemian ancestor of Sigismund on the Hungarian throne. See Engel, *The Realm of St Stephen*; Engel, "The Age of the Angevines"; and Klaniczay, "The Age of Matthias Corvinus."

11. A voluminous literature exists concerning the relationship between Hungarian and Ottoman studies. The most succinct summary of this literature, and of its evolution over the course of the past century and a half, can be found in Dávid and Fodor, "Hungarian Studies in Ottoman History." The terminology for this history is in itself problematic because a coherent, unified "Hungary" was more fiction than fact.

12. Besides a shift in how each of the powers was represented in the texts, the territories of Transylvania, Wallachia, and Moldavia became less tightly controlled by the Ottoman establishment, which upset the diplomatic balance in the region for reasons explored further below.

13. Although most of the literature on this engagement invokes the terminology of the "frontier" and the "border," *brokered zone* captures the porous nature of the territorial markers, the negotiations necessary to maintain a semblance of control, and the language that evolved to contain these negotiations and frame categories for land, taxation, and defense that ensured the proper administration of Ottoman occupied Hungary. For examples of significant studies of border politics in the region see Dávid and Fodor, *Ransom Slavery*; and Fodor, *In Quest of the Golden Apple*.

14. Pay registers for various contingents of soldiers, castle guards, and auxiliary forces for Buda were recorded in BOA, MM 34 for 1543; BOA, MM 17329 for 1574–75; BOA, KK 35 for 1584; BOA, KK 336 for 1589–90; and BOA, KK 344 for Buda, Temeşvar, and Bosnian territories in 1596. References to the contingents and shifts in payment strategies will be addressed below.

15. Major military ventures orchestrated by Süleyman occurred in 1521, 1526, 1529, 1532, 1541, 1543, and 1566. For earlier forays in the region see Szakály, "Phases of Turco-Hungarian Warfare"; and Pálffy, "Origins and Development of the Border Defense System."

16. Bak, "The Late Medieval Period," 81.

17. Dávid and Fodor, *Ottomans, Hungarians, and Habsburgs*, xv.

18. Bak, "The Late Medieval Period," 81.

19. Fekete, *Buda and Pest Under Turkish Rule*, 9.

20. Barta, "A Forgotten Theatre of War," 94.

21. Ibid., 101–5. Fleeing Serb and Croatian peasants and rival local magnates inflamed the southern border regions of the Hungarian territories. Deputized Ottoman officials, such as *bey*s, *sancakbey*s, and *paşa*s in territories previously conquered, occupied, or incorporated by the Ottomans played a dramatic role in carving out the path pursued by future, full-scale military campaigns. Hüsrev Paşa, in Bosnia, as well as Balı and Yahyaoğlu Mehmed, and *bey*s of Szendrő agitated the border along the Drava and Sava Rivers in the immediate aftermath of Mohács.

22. Bak, "The Late Medieval Period," 81.

23. Szakály, "The Early Ottoman Period," 83–84.

24. Ibid., 123.

25. Ibid.

26. Ibid., 105–6, 124, 127.

27. Ibid., 107.

28. Fekete, *Buda and Pest Under Turkish Rule*, 9.

29. Süleyman did, however, work against the alliance proposed between Habsburg and Hungarian royal claims at the Treaty of Várad in 1538.

30. Fekete, *Buda and Pest Under Turkish Rule*, 11.

31. Szakály, "The Early Ottoman Period," 85.

32. Ibid., 89; Hegyi, "The Ottoman Network of Fortresses," 166–72; and Pálffy, "Origins and Development of the Border Defense System," 4–20.

33. Official janissaries within the military defense or administrative system of the occupied Hungarian territories played a relatively minor role. Until 1591 only Buda possessed an attached janissary contingent, which never exceeded one thousand. The localized nature of military defense altered only during major campaign seasons, such as in 1596–97, when a total of 7,581 janissaries supplemented fortress garrisons at Buda (2,676), Győr (370), Temeşvar (1,414), and Egri (3,121) once it was captured during that venture. See Hegyi, "The Ottoman Military Force," 146–47.

34. Despite the entrenched costs of fortress-based occupation, the Ottoman administrative system in the occupied territories seems to have supported itself, at least until the exhaustion of the long war between 1591 and 1606. Caroline Finkel suggested that 70 percent to 90 percent of the province of Buda's revenues were locally derived,

from *cizye* taxes, customs, and dues. Finkel, *The Administration of Warfare*, 290–91. Gábor Ágoston also argued that, unlike the Habsburgs, the Ottoman defense system remained fiscally solvent; see Ágoston, "The Costs of the Ottoman Fortress-System," 220–24. The monies from imperial properties (*hass*) apportioned to the *paşa*s and *bey*s of the occupied territories often derived from larger towns, customs stations, or ferry crossings and amounted to more than thirty thousand *akçe*s yearly; see Káldy-Nagy, "Two Sultanic H̱āṣṣ Estates."

35. Although the *composition* of the military forces assigned to protect these provinces, garrison the key fortresses, and police the surrounding territories changed over the course of the sixteenth century, surprisingly, the *numbers* were rather stable, at least as far as they can be detected in the *timar* and *tapu* defterleri or in the *ruzname* (salary list of *beratli* soldiers with imperial diplomas). Combined lists of military men reached twenty to twenty-two thousand registered in 1543 and closely matches the approximately twenty-five thousand recorded at the end of the century. For the composition of the military and fortress defense costs see Káldy-Nagy, "The First Centuries"; Ágoston, "The Costs of the Ottoman Fortress-System," 197; and Hegyi, "The Ottoman Military Force," 145.

36. Ágoston, "The Costs of the Ottoman Fortress-System," 213.

37. Ibid., 196; Dávid, "Ottoman Administrative Strategies." See also Dávid, "Incomes and Possessions," 113–14.

38. Káldy-Nagy, "The Administration of the Ṣanǰāq Registrations"; Káldy-Nagy, *Macaristan'da 16. yüzyılda*; Ágoston, "The Costs of the Ottoman Fortress-System," 196; Gévay, *A Budai Pasák*.

39. Efforts to reconfigure the terms of Ottoman control over Buda, Peşt, and Temesvár can be traced in documents with mixed characteristics of *ahdname*s and *kanun*s: Hungarian National Archives / Magyar Országos Levéltár (MOL) R 315: 5 (Peşt, 1549); 6 (Buda, 1555); 7 (Temesvár, 1558).

40. Fekete, *Buda and Pest Under Turkish Rule*, 43–47.

41. Dávid, "Administration in Ottoman Europe," 79–80. At the Peace of Edirne, the *akçe* contained 1.7 grams of silver and was considered to be worth fifty Hungarian florins, although its value seems to have declined over the course of the next century owing to fluctuating currency standards. The income of Sokullu Mustafa Paşa, for example, when he assumed his post of *beylerbey* in 1566, was 924,000 *akçe*s; see Dávid, "Incomes and Possessions," 119.

42. Dávid, "Administration in Ottoman Europe," 79–80. These early registers were collected and published in Káldy-Nagy, *Kanuni devri Budin tahrir defteri*.

43. Antal Gévay outlined the biographies and careers of the governors in *A Budai Pasák*. For the governors referenced here see Gévay, *A Budai Pasák*, 6, 11.

44. The standard general assessment of Ottoman administrative systems in the region can be found in Dávid, "Ottoman Administrative Strategies." Other signifi-

cant general works include Fekete, *Buda and Pest Under Turkish Rule*; Káldy-Nagy, *Macaristan'da 16. yüzyılda*; and Dávid, *Osmanlı Macaristan'ında.*

45. Furthermore, although a *kadı* was dispatched to Buda, as well as to other key fortress towns, none of the *mahkeme sicilleri* survived, and scholars can only intuit their practice from within the directives issued from the Ottoman establishment. See MD 6:1148 for an example of an order sent to the *kadı* of Buda and Peşt concerning relations between Ottoman arrivals and indigenous communities.

46. Nenad Moačanin uses the term *re-colonization* for territories along the Middle Danube to indicate the Ottoman administrative effort to revitalize fallow lands with various incentives plied to regional populations who had fled to surrounding territories or into more mountainous zones; see Moačanin, *Town and Country*, 121–46.

47. Ágoston, "Muslim Cultural Enclaves in Hungary." For garrisoned soldiers see Hegyi, "The Ottoman Military Force," 143.

48. Fekete, *Buda and Pest Under Turkish Rule*, 32–35. The *kadı* is still one of the addressees of the *mühimme* registers, however, which suggests precisely the opposite—there was no large Muslim confessional community to serve, *and yet* the *kadı* was appointed and enfolded into the administrative hierarchy of the Hungarian territories.

49. Sahillioğlu, *E-12321*.

50. This is an extraordinary number of commands, considering the extent of imperial territories at this period, with a total of seven major provincial divisions, 506 administrative units, the tributary kingdoms of Wallachia and Moldavia, and the newly crafted principality of Transylvania (Erdel).

51. These orders, with a few explicit examples explored below, generally refer either to the mobilization of revenue for the support of military ventures, salaries, and fortress support or to the registration of inhabitants in financial registers. See Sahillioğlu, *E-12321*, nos. 30, 150, 269, 296, 297, 398, 413, and 491.

52. Eight referenced Mehmed by name, in order numbers 110, 194, 305, 308, 326, 398, 433, and 535.

53. Ahmed Çelebi stands as the sole named addressee in nos. 49, 228, 410, 529, and 535.

54. For directives addressed to the generic titles of the *beylerbey* and *defterdar* of Buda, see nos. 48, 217, 219, 252, 275, 312, 441, 442, 535, and 544.

55. But one order (398) was addressed to the regional *beys* and *kadıs*: "*beylere ve ḳādılara ḥüküm ki*," concerning safe passage of envoys sent from Ferdinand.

56. The story of this effort emerges below, but the order numbers can be found here: 110, 273, 296, 297, and 523.

57. Orders 162 and 163; the bridge appears in 418.

58. This specific order (43) is undated, but it lies between two *hükm* dated December 27 and 29, 1544; Sahillioğlu, *E-12321*, no. 34.

59. MD 38:48; MD 39:49; MD 90:110.

60. Mehmed Paşa was the acting *beylerbey* of Buda but is referenced here as "vezir": MD 35:44.

61. Dávid also noted the prevalence of named dispatchers for *hüküms* addressed to provincial officials in the occupied territories; see Dávid, "The Mühimme Defteri," 174.

62. Sahillioğlu, *E-12321*, 117–18: no. 147.

63. Ibid.: "Amma ol beylerin ekseri Ferandoş cānibine dānışık gider rençberdir deyü dergāh-ı mu'allama irsāl olunan İşpan İmre ḫaber virdi deyü bildirmişsin ma'lūm ve mefḥūm oldu."

64. Sahillioğlu, *E-12321*, order no. 148.

65. This order also contains the first reference in the register to the unpaid tribute due from Ferdinand, a subject addressed in the next section.

66. Although translation was an issue, there were also purposeful efforts to disguise information through the use of a cipher, and cryptography also masked the identity of dispatchers who might just as easily serve as spies. For a meticulous analysis of Ottoman efforts to countermand these ploys, see Gürkan, "The Efficacy of Ottoman Counter-Intelligence."

67. Sahillioğlu, *E-12321*, no. 273.

68. Ibid., no. 296.

69. Ibid., no. 297.

70. Presumably, this is a reference to order no. 296.

71. Ibid., no. 309.

72. See ibid., e.g., order no. 398.

73. This is evident in the following orders: 148, 183, 215, 428, 434, and 456.

74. This situation seems to have changed slightly in a later period. Dávid discusses the insertion of emperor (*imparador*) into bound registers in the periods between 1560 and 1565 and 1590 and 1605, although there was also a tendency to interchange *king* and *emperor* across the registers; see Dávid, "The Mühimme Defteri," 192–93.

75. Sahillioğlu, *E-12321*, nos. 191–200. There is some confusion in the way in which the orders are bound, which may indicate the duplication or late combination of registers carried in the company of the sultan and those left with the vizier's deputy in Istanbul. Thus the initial order (no. 190) indicates the arrival of the "Padişah" in Edirne on January 30; the roll call recorded in order no. 192 contains internal notes concerning the receipt of the information by regional commanders between February 16 and 20; and then order nos. 195–200 track backward, covering dates from January 22 to 30, when the sultan is yet again noted to have arrived in Edirne.

76. Sahillioğlu, *E-12321*, nos. 191, 197, and 199. Incidentally, this would be the last campaign of Hayrüddin Paşa, popularly known as Barbarossa, wherein he continued a prolonged naval encounter with Spanish and French admirals along the Mediterranean coastline. He targeted the Spanish mainland and entered Majorca and Minorca

a final time. In 1540 Charles V had attempted to coerce him to his side, with no success, and Hayrüddin Paşa ultimately retired to his seaside palace on the northwestern shores of the Bosphorus, where he died in 1546, only one year after his final ventures, which transformed the Mediterranean into an "Ottoman sea" during his tenure as commander of naval forces.

77. The Ottoman establishment may have stoked fears of a Habsburg invasion to heighten focus on crafting an official cohort within the occupied territories.

78. The treaty of Crépy, which contained a subtext of aligning interests against the Ottomans, freed Charles V to deal with continued religio-political unrest in his German territories and Francis I to address an impending English invasion; see Setton, *The Papacy and the Levant*, 472–73.

79. Ibid.

80. Bayerle, *Ottoman Tributes in Hungary*; Bayerle, *Hungarian Letters of Ali Pasha.*

81. They were unable to do so, however, until the treaty negotiated to conclude a fifteen-year period of protracted warfare in 1606 allowed them to redefine the relationship between the two imperial claims.

82. Johnson, *Cultural Hierarchy*, 221–26.

83. Hegyi, "The Ottoman Military Force," 134.

84. Szakály, "The Early Ottoman Period," 86–87.

85. Ibid., 147–48. The radical focus of the Ottoman imperial elite on these provinces during the tenure of their reign can be substantiated from a 1613 treasury account from Buda that concludes with a brief record of garrisoned troops in much of the empire, excluding Anatolia, Egypt, the Greek Peninsula, and the European shores of the Marmara. The register records an empire-wide total of 38,196 dispersed troops. In Hegyi's words: "Without attaching too much importance to numbers, astonishing ratios can be detected: out of the 38,196 soldiers, 18,024 occupied Hungary and Bosnia, roughly 10% defended the line of the Drava-Sava-Lower Danube-Black Sea, 1% of the interior of the Balkans, and 16% the Middle East. . . . The territory between the Drava and the Sava and Bosnia were defended by at least twice as many soldiers as the vast eastern part of the Empire."

86. Dávid and Fodor, *Ransom Slavery.*

87. See MD 16:523; MD 19:472 and 581; MD 22:279; and MD 23:19 for imperial commands to the *beylerbey*s of Buda concerning surveillance mechanisms and their responsibility to report regional disturbances to the sultanate in 1572, 1573, and 1574. On information gathering and spy tactics more generally see Ágoston, "Information, Ideology, and Limits of Imperial Policy."

88. For Transylvania see MD 5:58; and MD 48:964. For Wallachia and Moldavia see MD 12:688. János B. Szabó has discussed the broader dynamics of these awkward cooperative alignments in "'Splendid Isolation'?"

89. See MD 6:1009, 1126, 1150, and 1152. See also copies of orders sent by Sultan

Süleyman to Transylvanian princes reasserting terms of the alliance and requesting continued support in border skirmishes: Hungarian National Archives, MOL, E 142: facsimile 12, no. 23; facsimile 26, no. 30; facsimile 20, no. 42.

90. Pál Fodor investigated the significant role played by "volunteer soldiers" (*gönüllü gharīb yiğit*) in the borderlands, who capitalized on consistent frontier skirmishes in order to become salaried participants in Ottoman military defense; see Fodor, "Making a Living on the Frontiers." He explored the transference of another category of auxiliary military units, the *cerehor*, within the occupied territories, as well, in Fodor, "The Way of a Seljuq Institution."

91. MD 7:2759.

92. Dávid traces Balassa's movement through the registers in "The Mühimme Defteri," 200–203.

93. See MD 12:826.

94. MD 7:1531, 1623, and 1627; MD 12:928.

95. MD 12:1067.

96. Tijana Krstić has provided a succinct summary of these major developments and a brief biographical and interpretive assessment of the Hungarian intermediaries within the Ottoman chancery; see Krstić, "Of Translation and Empire."

97. Dávid and Fodor, "Hungarian-Ottoman Peace Negotiations," 13.

98. Remnants of a historiographical insistence on the arbitrary nature of Ottoman diplomacy, and thus on removing the empire from emergent formal negotiating structures between rival renaissance and early modern states, continue to plague comparative assessments of Ottoman diplomacy. Although critiques of Eurocentrism abound, and alternative paradigms for assessing interstate dynamics are by now quite common, even perceptive articles tend to reproduce these assumptions by dismissing pre-eighteenth-century patterns and practices. For a clear example of the latter see Arı, "Early Ottoman Diplomacy." For significant alternative frameworks see Goffman, *The Ottoman Empire and Early Modern Europe*; Brummett, *Ottoman Seapower and Levantine Diplomacy*; Kołodziejczyk, *Ottoman-Polish Diplomatic Relations*; and Goffman, "Negotiating with the Renaissance State."

99. Dávid and Fodor, "Hungarian-Ottoman Peace Negotiations," 14.

100. For a meticulous account of this interchange, and its possible ramifications for Ottoman diplomatic history, see Dávid and Fodor, "Hungarian-Ottoman Peace Negotiations." Kenneth Setton's comprehensive history of European diplomatics pays keen attention to the role played by the Ottomans and provides essential information for these early negotiations; see Setton, *The Papacy and the Levant*, 150–65.

101. Dávid and Fodor, "Hungarian-Ottoman Peace Negotiations," 44–45.

102. Ibid., 40.

103. Carina Johnson presents an excellent analytic framework for assessing the larger symbolic meanings contained in gift-giving within the Hungarian-Ottoman

context and its role in heightening the link between sovereignty and collections of treasure and artifacts; see Johnson, *Cultural Hierarchy*, 235–39.

104. Ibid., 10.

105. For strong recent examples of this work that address intersections between Venetian and Hungarian translation projects see Rothman, "Dragomans and 'Turkish Literature'"; Rothman, "Interpreting Dragomans"; and Krstić, "Of Translation and Empire."

106. Johnson, *Cultural Hierarchy*, 190–91.

107. Ibid., 193.

108. Ibid., 177. Josef Matuz also provided detailed information concerning the backgrounds and linguistic proficiency of the emerging translation corps; see Matuz, "Die Pfortendolmetscher zur Herrschaftszeit Süleymân des Prächtigen," 26–60.

109. Tijana Krstić has presented a clear chronology and exegesis of key literary productions of the first three dragomans listed here in Krstić, "Of Translation and Empire." For a list of the *baş tercumanlar* see Reychman and Zajączkowski, *Handbook of Ottoman-Turkish Diplomatics*, 166–67.

110. Krstić, "Of Translation and Empire," 130. On humanism within Hungary and central Europe more generally, and the Ottomans as active players in this context, see Birnbaum, *The Orb and the Pen*; Almási, *The Uses of Humanism*; and Contadini and Norton, *The Renaissance and the Ottoman World*. On the role of popular opinion, the press, and the humanist tradition in generating stereotypes of East and West see Bisaha, *Creating East and West*; Meserve, "News from Negroponte"; and Morrison, "A Scholarly Intermediary," 32–57.

111. Johnson, *Cultural Hierarchy*, 179–80.

112. Ibid., 181–89.

113. Albert Howe Lyber published the full text of the manuscript in its original Italian in *The Government of the Ottoman Empire*, 314–417. Formerly a Venetian subject, Yunus Bey was captured and transformed first into a cavalryman then into an Ottoman envoy, before becoming chief translator (*baş tercüman*) in 1525. He undertook six missions to Venice, could operate fluently in Italian and Greek as well as Latin, and famously attempted to defray the outbreak of an Ottoman-Venetian war in 1537 by conveying the sultan's request for a joint alliance with the French against Charles V. Although ultimately unsuccessful in this endeavor, the Venetian press eagerly published both his oration before the Senate and the singular pamphlet concerning Ottoman governance, presumably coauthored with Gritti (d. 1534), the illegitimate son of the Venetian doge Andrea Gritti, and a merchant and businessman with complex connections of his own with Süleyman's court. On Yunus Bey and Alvise Gritti's role in supplying tin for Ottoman weapons manufacturing, along with his alliance with Grand Vizier İbrahim, see Krstić, "Of Translation and Empire," 131–34; Ágoston, *Guns for the Sultan*, 187–89; and Setton, *The Papacy and the Levant*, 300–301.

114. Lyber suggested that later pamphleteers, such as the Venetian *bailo* Benedetto Ramberti; Guillaume Postel, who accompanied the embassy of Francis I to the Porte in 1535; and Antoine Geuffroy, the knight of St. John, whose description of "The Order of the Great Turcks Court of Hye Menne of War" was published first in French (1542) and then in English (1546), seem all to have relied on the meticulous financial details contained in the work of Yunus Bey and Alvise Gritti; see Lyber, *The Government of the Ottoman Empire*, 315.

115. This payment takes precedence over almost all other concerns, save perhaps for maintaining control over seized fortresses, in the varied Ottoman documents that traversed the Hungarian domains; see Bayerle, "Ottoman Records."

116. Bayerle suggests that it was not precisely the payment of the tribute itself (which he assessed at 10 percent of Buda's provincial revenues) but rather the costs associated with its ceremonial presentation at the Porte, along with expenses incurred from travel, that led to the Habsburg court's consistent delaying tactics. When Peçevi observed the annual tribute caravan as it passed through Buda in 1590, he compiled a list of the gifts intended for officials along the road: one thousand *kuruş*, two cups, and one goblet to the *bey* of Esztergom; three thousand kuruş, two cups, a goblet, a rifle, and several watches to Ferhad Paşa; watches and cups to the treasurer of Buda and to the *aga* of the janissaries; four thousand to five thousand kuruş to the grand vizier in Istanbul; and assorted other presents to lower-ranking viziers. Peçevi, *Tārīḫ-i Peçevī*, 2:134; cited in Bayerle, "Ottoman Records," 9.

117. The question of implementation is one of the most pressing for future research with *mühimme* registers. In regions with active *shari'a* courts and their own continuous registers, this can be painstakingly tracked. Within the Hungarian territories, however, for reasons already addressed, this is not possible. As a result, these letters are one means of tracking the impact of imperial command. Gustav Bayerle published the collected letters for these dates and includes summaries of each letter originally composed in Hungarian; see Bayerle, *Ottoman Diplomacy in Hungary*. The correspondence between the Ottoman officials of Buda and key Habsburg representatives prior to the outbreak of the so-called long war were carefully preserved and then organized into the *Turcica* collection of the Austrian State Archives. See Austrian State Archives, Haus-, Hof- und Staatsarchiv, *Turcica I*: 72-81.

118. See MD 61:307.

119. See, e.g., MD 7:2766; MD 34:275; MD 21:468.

120. MD 61:307.

121. MD 35:372.

122. MD 35:372; also cited and translated in Dávid, "The Mühimme Defteri," 195.

123. Letter 101, July 14, 1593.

124. Letter 106, August 18, 1593.

125. Letter 107, August 20, 1593.

126. Letter 89, Nov. 12, 1592.

127. Letters 20, May 24, 1590; 89, Nov. 12, 1592; and 103, August 3, 1593.

128. Letters 24, June 26, 1590; 51, August 9, 1591; 53, August 13, 1593; 66, Oct. 24, 1591.

129. Letters 27, July 7, 1590; and 54, August 25, 1591.

130. Letter 41, May 12, 1591.

131. Letters 32, August 27, 1590; 36, Feb. 4, 1591; 39, April 6, 1591; and 66, Oct. 24, 1591.

132. Letter 4, Feb. 1, 1590.

133. Letter 6, Feb. 17, 1590.

134. See, e.g., letters 7, March 3, 1590; 8, March 22, 1590; and 9, April 9, 1590.

135. Letter 66, Oct. 24, 1591.

136. Bayerle, *Ottoman Diplomacy in Hungary*, 10.

137. Letters 28, July 12, 1590; 29, August 6, 1590; and 34, Dec. 4, 1590. As demonstrated in the earliest *mühimme* defter, the *beylerbey* of Buda relied on appointed envoys and messengers for delivering news and correspondence to the two rival powers and across the occupied Hungarian territories. The chief diplomats and envoys from elite Transylvanian, Wallachian, and Moldavian families also played a significant part in negotiating between Ottoman and Habsburg courts, especially in terms of the transit of the annual tribute.

138. Letters 64, Oct. 20, 1591; and 89, Nov. 12, 1592.

139. Letter 8, March 22, 1590.

140. Letters 49, July 29, 1591; and 65, Oct. 22, 1591.

141. Letter 73, Jan. 21, 1592.

142. Letter 89, Nov. 12, 1592.

143. Letter 64, Oct. 20, 1591.

144. Letter 83, August 30, 1592.

145. Letter 24, June 26, 1590.

146. Letters 22, June 4, 1590; and 86, Oct. 16, 1592.

147. Letter 67, Oct. 25, 1591.

148. Letter 28, July 12, 1590.

149. Letter 78, August 4, 1592.

150. Letter 45, July 5, 1591.

151. Letter 71, Dec. 29, 1591.

152. Letter 23, June 10, 1590.

153. Letter 40, May 2, 1591.

154. See, e.g., letters 9, April 5, 1590; and 20, May 24, 1590.

155. See, e.g., letters 24, 30, 32, 36, 39, 42, 59, and 75.

156. Letter 75, May 19, 1592.

157. Letter 68, Oct. 27, 1591.

158. Letters 39, April 6, 1591; and 47, July 21, 1591.

159. Letters 36, Feb. 4, 1591; and 68, August 13, 1590.

160. Letter 51, August 9, 1591.

161. Ibid.

162. Bayerle, "The Compromise at Zsitvatorok." The "compromise" of this treaty is also a linguistic puzzle and a reminder of the difficult hybrid structures at work here. Variant texts in Latin, Hungarian, and Ottoman, signed and unsigned by Habsburg's King Rudolf and Sultan Ahmed I, indicate the political and linguistic complexities. They also demonstrate a slight preference for Hungarian, as translators were easier to find as intermediaries for both powers. For a collection of texts in all three languages see, in the Hungarian National Archives, Esterházy Family Archives, which Bayerle analyzes in detail, following also the work of Lajos Fekete in *Türkische Schriften*, 3–7, 207–13. A copy contained in MOL, R 315:27, contains both signatures for one clause concerning taxes due the Ottoman custodians of the castle at Eger.

163. Two hundred thousand *florins* were presumably owed the Ottoman sultanate, but the annual payment of thirty thousand ceased. This took some time to negotiate, however, and Bayerle suggested that a firm set of terms was not established until 1612 because prior to that point the vast difference between Ottoman and Habsburg resolutions precluded a clear statement of either boundaries or conditions for maintaining peaceful relations; see Bayerle, "The Compromise at Zsitvatorok," 28. Furthermore, Ottoman versions reinforce a sense of Ottoman sovereign benevolence, granting peace because subjects of the territories had asked for the restoration of calm and order: "For the sake of the realm, province, and subjects, the treaty was concluded." Quoted from Feridun Bey's *Mecmū'a-yı münşe'āt* in Bayerle, "The Compromise at Zsitvatorok," 23.

164. The fragility of Ottoman control can also be seen in the alliance the court of Ahmed I forged with István Bocskay of Transylvania, who had used the chaos of the long war to wage his own bid for power. Between 1595 and 1605 he shifted from a Habsburg to an Ottoman ally and was ultimately recognized by both in the Treaty of Zsitvatorok as the prince of Transylvania and of Hungarian territories not under Ottoman suzerainty. Letters and granted privileges issued from Grand Vizier Murad Paşa and Sultan Ahmed I indicate these efforts to both ensure his loyalty and yet avoid reinforcing his power: MOL, R 315: 26 (Dec. 1605); 28, 31, 32 (July 1606).

165. Christine Woodhead provided a critical commentary and edition of this text in her *Ṭa'līḳīzāde's Şehnāme-i Hümāyūn*. She further outlined the larger stakes involved in the position of court historian in "An Experiment in Official Historiography." For a comprehensive study of manuscript production and image management at the Ottoman court during the period see Fetvacı, *Picturing History at the Ottoman Court*; a shorter version of her arguments concerning the significance of patronage in the composition of official historical narratives can be found in Fetvacı, "Office of the Ottoman Court Historian."

166. Woodhead, "Taliqizade Mehmed."

167. Woodhead, *Ṭa'līḳīzāde's Şehnāme-i Hümāyūn*, 18–19 (commentary), 131a–35b (transcription).

168. Ibid., 15b–20a; 143–54 (Ottoman Turkish).

169. Ibid., 62 (commentary), 105a–19a (transcription); 366–411 (Ottoman Turkish).

170. Ibid., 109a–13b (transcription); 380–97 (Ottoman Turkish).

171. Fleischer, "The Lawgiver as Messiah," 160–63.

172. Turan, *The Sultan's Favorite.*

173. Necipoğlu, "Süleyman the Magnificent"; Ágoston, "Information, Ideology, and Limits of Imperial Policy," 96–97.

Chapter 5. A State of Rebellion

1. These lines were contained in a copy of an edict sent to the patriarch of a Bedouin dynasty, Mansur ibn Furaykh, in late March of 1585. Mansur had been dismissed as the governor of the district of Safad but was still called on to implement the sultanate's commands to restore provincial order in the wake of the military campaigns described in this chapter. The specific dynamics and textual strategies of this edict are addressed in significant detail throughout the chapter. See MD 3:824.

2. The events of this campaign, and the regional dynamics that provoked imperial intervention, have been the subject of extensive commentary by both historical and contemporary scholars. Abdul-Rahim Abu-Husayn provided a succinct summary of the events and their varied interpretations in "The Ottoman Invasion of the Shuf in 1585: A Reconsideration." Other significant references can be found throughout his delineation of leadership structures in Greater Syria, as well as in his presentation of key *mühimme* registers: Abu-Husayn, *Provincial Leaderships*; and Abu-Husayn, *The View from Istanbul.* See also Rafeq, *Bilād al-Shām wa-Miṣr*, 194–98; Bakhit, "Aḥdāth Bilād Ṭrāblus al-Shām," 179–91; and Bakhit, *The Ottoman Province of Damascus*, 165–69. The work of a contemporary historian who spanned Mamluk and Ottoman rule, Muhammad ibn Tulun (d. 1546), is also significant for assessing early transitions in governing structures, and later interpreters of these events, such as the Maronite historian Istvan Duwayhi (d. 1704) and the Aleppo-born Ottoman historian Mustafa Naima (d. 1716), draw attention to shifting alliances and their politicization across the sixteenth and seventeenth centuries; see ibn Tulun, *Mufākahāt al-Khillān*; Duwayhi, *Tārīkh al-ʿazmina*; and Naʿima, *Tārīḫ-i Naʿīmā*, vol. 9.

3. See Salibi, "The Sayfās and the *Eyalet* of Tripoli, 1579–1640"; and Abu-Husayn, *Provincial Leaderships*, 11–66.

4. Previous chapters indicated the use of a vocabulary of justice and oppression in petitions, legal regulations, and traditions of chronicling. In the case of edicts directed to the *beylerbeys* of Trablus, reported knowledge of oppression served as the catalyst for commands issued from the sultanate.

5. Both Jane Hathaway and Bruce Masters have produced general overviews of Ottoman imperial control in the region. See Hathaway, *The Arab Lands Under Ottoman Rule*; and Masters, *Arabs of the Ottoman Empire*. For a selective list of scholarship that addresses alignment practices in relation to land tenure, provincial administration, the circulation of commodities, urban dynamics, and regional factionalism, see, respectively, Khalidi, *Land Tenure and Social Transformation*; Johansen, *Islamic Law on Land Tax and Rent*; Singer, *Palestinian Peasants and Ottoman Officials*; Ze'evi, *An Ottoman Century*; Doumani, *Rediscovering Palestine*; Wilkins, *Forging Urban Solidarities*; and Winter, *The Shiites of Lebanon*.

6. The territories of Greater Syria were combined with the financial administration of Anatolia and Rumeli in 1517–18 and were first designated simply as *'Arab* (*'Arab ve 'Acem vilāyetleri defterdārlığı*), with Aleppo as the headquarters for the finance minister of the region; see Uzunçarşılı, *Osmanlı devletinin merkez ve bahriye teşkilātı*, 327. This organizational structure was outlined in the salary registers produced for the province: BOA, Kamil Kepeci (KK), *Ruūs Defteri*, 211:61; 216:1. The territories of the *Vilāyet-i 'Arab* were organized into fifteen *sancak*s; see Topkapı Palace Archives, no. 9772.

7. Ibn Tulun, *I'lām*, 228. Canberdi's initial role in the province is also referenced in Feridun Bey's collection of chancery correspondence and Celalzade Mustafa's history of Selim I's reign; see Feridun, *Mecmū'a-yı Münşe'āt*, 400; and Celalzade, *Selimnāme*, 195.

8. Provincial reorganization continued throughout the following decades, and the governing structure of Greater Syria (*Şam beylerbeyiliğnin*) constituted its own separate unit from 1522–23 onward; see BOA, TD 993: 286–406. This unit included territories that extended between northern Syria and southeastern Anatolia, such as Ayntab, Antakya, Kilis, and Adana; see Çakar, "XVI. yüzyılda şam beylerbeyiliğnin idarī taksimati."

9. This is partially reflected in the constant variation in territorial designations for the region in *defter*s produced by the imperial council and the finance ministry. The first *mühimme* register from 1545, for example, includes a designation for *vilāyet-i Şam* in its effort to corral troops for the campaign into Hungarian territories. This provincial designation included Şam, Aleppo, Trablus, Safed, Quds (Jerusalem), Hama, Homs, Birecik, Ekrad, Salt-'Ajlun, Gazze, Nablus, and Lejjun, all placed under the financial jurisdiction of Aleppo; see Sahillioğlu, *E-12321*, 154, no. 192. See also no. 443 for a copy of a *hükm* sent to the "*defterdār* of 'Arabistan and Aleppo" to oversee the registration of inhabitants and assignment of tax farms for Trablus. Celalzade Mustafa included eight administrative units in his breakdown of provincial administration (Şam, Kudüs, Gazze, Nablus, Safed, Trablus, Salt-'Ajlun, and Lejjun; see Celalzade, *Geschichte Sultan Süleymān Ḳānūnīs*, 13a–13b. *Mühimme* registers from 1565 to 1570 list ten *sancak*s and emphasize the role of the *defterdar* based in Aleppo for managing the fiscal organization of Greater Syria: MD 2:52, 479; MD 6:537, 1165; MD 19:78, 161.

In 1571 Beirut and Sidon were designated as *sancak*s as well: MD 29:125, 307. After 1579, when Trablus was distinguished as a separate provincial seat, it also for a time included Sidon and Beirut: MD 80:141, 363; BOA, Kamil Kepeci (KK), *Ruūs Defteri*, 262:69–71. After the events of 1585, however, administrative designations shifted from appointments of career imperial officials to regional *beys* and *mukaddems*, and the collection of revenue was standardized as annual remittances (*salyane*) and tax farms (*iltizam*).

10. See Abu-Husayn, *The View from Istanbul*, 14–17; and Salibi, "Mount Lebanon Under the Mamluks."

11. Although each of these clans and their chieftains actively campaigned to extend their territorial reach, prior to the events of 1585 the domain of the Ma'n included the coast north of the town of Junieh, to the valley south of Sidon, and the mountain districts of the Shuf, the Gharb, Jurd, and Matn. The Harfushes were centered in Ba'albek, and 'Assaf control extended from Tripoli to the Kisrawan mountain areas northeast of Beirut. These chieftains were also from mixed confessional backgrounds, Druze, Shi'i, and 'Alawi; and, though at times the target of attacks framed in religious terms, they were also consistently co-opted by the Ottoman establishment. For regional designations and alliances see Abu-Husayn, *Provincial Leaderships*. Stefan Winter has provided a groundbreaking critique of simplistic, sectarian-based analysis of these alliances and of the relationship between Shi'i emirs and the sultanate; see Winter, *The Shiites of Lebanon*.

12. They were listed as "forty un-Muslim *beys* in the mountains, a misguided folk where each follows his own cult," who disrupted the activities of registrars and tax collectors in the *kanunname* of Trablus in 1547: Akgündüz, *Osmanlı kanunnameleri*, 4:538; cited and translated in Winter, *The Shiites of Lebanon*, 36–37. For the genealogy and history of the Ma'n see Salibi, "The Secret of the House of Ma'n"; and Abu-Husayn, *Provincial Leaderships*, 67–128.

13. MD 26:101. Significantly, copies of this *hükm* were also sent to the *beylerbeys* of Zulkadır and Diyarbekir, requesting from each armed Kurdish infantry units as well as garrisoned soldiers.

14. See Ashtor, "The Venetian Cotton Trade," 675–715; and Abu-Husayn, *The View from Istanbul*, 16–21.

15. MD 5:565.

16. MD 5:1091.

17. MD 26:448.

18. MD 26:614.

19. MD 29:70.

20. The *hükm* distinguishes between an *iltizām*, a tax farm for collecting *ḫāṣ* revenue, and annual payments (*ṣālyāne*) collected by appointed custodians (*eminler*). Both of these mechanisms, rather than taxes assessed by the combined land and head tax

of the *çift-hane* system, typified the tax structure for the region and for Greater Syria. In return for fixed sums of money paid to the imperial treasury, local chiefs served as *multezim* even for whole *sancak*s or provinces. This was partly due to patterns set by Mamluk administrators and partly to the fractious nature of the territory itself. See MD 67:453; 70:40, 290, 315; and Lewis, "Ottoman Land Tenure."

21. This comment divides the inhabitants of the region between "Muslim," indicating a normative Ottoman Sunni identity, and the Shi'i affiliations of many inhabitants. There were also increasing numbers of Maronites located in the northern section of the Shuf and a mixed population of Sunni, Shi'i, and Maronite in major towns such as Butrun and Jubayl; see Abu-Husayn, *The View from Istanbul*, 91.

22. Sahillioğlu, *E-12321*, no. 484. This edict also names Piri Paşa as the *beylerbey* of Şam.

23. Ibid., nos. 547 and 548. It should be noted that 547 references Şam, Trablus, and Haleb as *vilayet*, which may indicate an earlier move toward defining Trablus as an independent provincial seat.

24. Ibid., no. 483.

25. The two individuals who shared a contract were named Şeyh Yusuf and Şeyh 'Ali, and there is some possibility that this might indicate Yusuf Sayfa and his son, although there is little independent evidence to support this. The *emin* was Ja'fer/Ca'fer and may be an early reference to the Ja'far Paşa, who would play an active role in the 1585 campaign and replace Yusuf Sayfa as the governor of Trablus.

26. Abu-Husayn, *Provincial Leaderships*, 13–17.

27. See Griswold, "Djalālī"; and Danışmend, *Izahlı Osmanlı Tarihi Kronolojisi*, 49–50. There are also critical gaps in the *mühimme* registers between 1597 and 1606, so scholars have turned to alternative sources to track the events of the period, from local chronicles to *shari'a* court registers and intermittent *'adaletname*s. For the latter see the appendix to Mustafa Akdağ's classic study of the rebellions, *Celālī isyanları*.

28. The standard histories generally begin their account of the "*celali* rebellions" with the battle of Mezö-Keresztes in 1596 and Grand Vizier Çağalazade Sinan Pasha's decision to dismiss those *timar* holders who either never enrolled in the campaign or deserted during its course. For a few examples see Cook, *A History of the Ottoman Empire*, 129–30; and Shaw, *Empire of the Gazis*, 185–86. For more fine-tuned analyses see Griswold, *The Great Anatolian Rebellion*; and Akdağ, *Celālī isyanları*. Famous examples of *celali* movements—whether local (such as that of Yusuf Paşa and Üveys Paşa in Aydın and Saruhan), more disparate and widespread (as were the rebellions organized under the leadership of Karayazıcı Abdülhalim in Amasya and Çorum or Deli Hasan in Ankara, Kütahya, and Afyonkarahisar), or capable of rousing Ottoman armies to quell threats of actual secession (such as by the Janbulad family in Kilis and Aleppo or the rebellion by Abaza Mehmed Paşa in Erzurum)—can thus best be understood as the fallout from central campaigns of reorganization within a new nexus of cash

and firearms. The intermittent arming of the cultivators and nomads (*levendler*), and the employment of temporary musket-bearing troops (*sekban*, *sarıca*) to augment the prestigious cavalry-based army, created itinerant groups, disassociated from the land and utterly dependent either on their salaries as mercenaries when employed by the state or depredatory acts against the countryside when not. Sam White has clarified the various dynamics of these rebellions within a larger argument concerning the ecology of Ottoman rule in *The Climate of Rebellion*; and Oktay Özel relies on *avarız* registers to detail a crisis in the agricultural economy in *The Collapse of Rural Order*.

29. See Naima, *Tarih-i Naima*, 2:242; and Duwayhi, *Tarikh al-Azmina*, 244–48.

30. Salibi, "Northern Lebanon Under the Dominance of azir," 156–57; Abu-Husayn, *Provincial Leaderships*, 14–15.

31. Abu-Husayn, *Provincial Leaderships*, 18.

32. This campaign was led by Ja'far Paşa al-Tuwashi, who acted in collaboration with the Ottoman forces led by İbrahim Paşa of Egypt and then replaced Yusuf Sayfa as the governor of Trablus.

33. MD 53:724.

34. MD 50. Abu-Husayn provided copies of grants made to both local and imperial personages who had participated in the campaign; see Abu-Husayn, *The View from Istanbul*, 175–89. Although Yusuf Sayfa was relieved of his post, at least one of his sons was rewarded with a *timar* worth three thousand *akçe*s (MD 50:310). Stefan Winter argued that this process of reapportioning territories also occurred after the conquest of Cyprus, as well as in the desert interior of the Euphrates Valley to soldiers and loyal Bedouin dynasties for similar reasons of administrative reorganization; see Winter, *The Shiites of Lebanon*, 38; and Winter, "The Province of Raqqa." He also linked this to a broader shift from military commands (*timar*) to farmed provincial revenues (*iltizam*) identified as a major transition in administrative tactics at the turn of the seventeenth century by İ. Metin Kunt in Kunt's *The Sultan's Servants*.

35. For comparative purposes, there is no order in the previous three *defter*s directed to Trablus leaders or officials despite its emergence as a *vilayet* six years before, and only one order appears in MD 56 (from March of 1585). Damascus still remained central to the sultanate's efforts to assert control in the region and indicates continuing turmoil. It is not until MD 75 (1603–5), in the midst of yet another internal rebellion, that a consistent stream of commands and imperial correspondence with the province once again highlights its significance administratively to the Ottoman establishment. The gap in attention may also reflect Ottoman military preoccupations in Hungarian territories during the period, on which see the previous chapter.

36. The Sayfa family's alliances crisscrossed confessional distinctions and placed them variously as partners with Druze or Shi'i tribes. They were not, however, Druze themselves.

37. MD 53:622.

38. These were both Bedouin dynasties that, like the Sayfa family, moved in and out of official positions and were variously allied with them. Mansur Furaykh would ultimately be executed in Istanbul in 1593 for continued acts of rebellion despite efforts to co-opt him into the administrative system. But when his son, Korkmaz Furaykh, was killed in escalating conflicts with the Ma'n, the sultanate ordered the *kadı* of Damascus to investigate the affair and punish the evil doers. See MD 72:889; MD 73:1017; Abu-Husayn, "The *Iltizam* of Mansur Furaykh"; Abu-Husayn, *Provincial Leaderships*, 153–61; and Winter, *The Shiites of Lebanon*, 49–50.

39. Order to the *beylerbeyi* of Damascus, MD 53:801.

40. See MD 53:824.

41. Although here identified as a rebel, Husayn ibn Sayfa would in turn become the *beylerbey* of Trablus and vie with his father for the position between 1610 and 1614.

42. MD 50:314, 813.

43. MD 56:74.

44. Halil İnalcık calculated that the average *timar* in the mid-sixteenth century was around two thousand *akçes*; see İnalcık, *The Ottoman Empire*, 161.

45. Later commentators would identify this move as the creation of a Druze emirate, a territorial designation that would play a key role in confessional and nationalist chronicles and histories of Lebanon.

46. See Salibi, "The Sayfās and the *Eyalet* of Tripoli," 46–52; and Abu-Husayn, *Provincial Leaderships*, 22–35.

47. See MD 67:322.

48. When Yusuf Sayfa married Muhammad 'Assaf's widow and began consolidating his control over Beirut and Kisrawan, the territories controlled by his former rivals, it seems his position as governor was threatened and offered to a member of the Janbulad clan in 1592–93. Husayn Janbulad never assumed the governorship, but this threat may have been one of the reasons Yusuf Sayfa later allied with the Ottoman establishment against the Janbulads when they rebelled in 1606; see Abu-Husayn, *Provincial Leaderships*, 22–24.

49. MD 73:453.

50. MD 106:301.

51. See MD 75:538.

52. MD 75:378.

53. As noted earlier, Fakhr al-Din Ma'n was appointed *sancakbey* of Sidon-Beirut in 1590, and of Safad in 1605, and was even able to disentangle himself enough from the events of 1606–7 to avoid any retribution. In addition, his son was awarded the *sancak* of Sidon-Beirut. But he had maintained his status only by forming alliances with the Ottoman grand vizier, Murad Paşa, and when he died in 1611, Nasuh Paşa's vizierate opted to support rivals of the Ma'n. Ultimately Fakhr al-Din escaped to Tuscany (1613–18), but on his return, he consolidated territory against other Druze

chieftains, encroached on the Sayfas' power, and after Yusuf Sayfa's death in 1625 possessed virtual mastery of areas from Kisrawan to Trablus. See Salibi, "The Secret of the House of Ma'n"; and Abu-Husayn, *Provincial Leaderships*, 87–91, 110–12.

54. Abu-Husayn, *Provincial Leaderships*, 23–25, 84–85.

55. Ibid., 31.

56. Ibid., 32.

57. Na'ima, *Tārīḫ-i Na'īmā*, 3:148–59, 240–43. Fakhr al-Din was executed in Istanbul in 1635.

58. MD 75:376.

59. MD 79:490.

60. MD 79:608.

61. Yusuf would, despite these events, become the *beylerbeyi* of Trablus once again in 1616 following a fairly unsatisfactory, from the perspective of the sultanate, period of stewardship under his son, Husayn.

62. For examples see MD 78:1565; 80:871; and 81:41.

63. MD 80:871. Order to the previous *beylerbey* of Trablus, Yusuf, and to the *kadı*.

64. MD 80:890.

65. MD 81:41.

66. The Shi'i Harfush clan held semidominant sway in Baalbek and the Biqa' Valley, and their reach extended to Homs. Like other clans in the region, they depended intermittently on Ottoman support to assert their own territorial claims but were often accused of unflagging banditry in imperial correspondence; see Winter, *The Shiites of Lebanon*, esp. 44–57. The *bolukbaşı* indicated in the edict was likely Shalhub ibn Harfush, a rival kinsman of Yunus and the holder of a title acquired by local commanders through their varied alliances with Ottoman forces sent to intervene in the region.

67. Abu-Husayn, *Provincial Leaderships*, 38–39.

68. Mehmed Paşa was appointed grand vizier for two brief periods, from 1614 to 1616, and then for less than a year in 1619, when he was deposed in the midst of infighting during the turbulent reign of Osman II (r. 1618–22). He was formerly the *beylerbey* of Egypt and was appointed *beylerbey* of Aleppo after his dismissal from the vizierate and died there in 1622; see Naima, *Tārīḫ-i Na'īmā*, 2:723–24; Danişmend, *Izahlı Osmanlı Tarihi Kronolojisi*, 186; and Uzunçarşılı, *Osmanlı Tarihi*, 2:367.

69. MD 78:1532.

70. MD 78:1562.

71. For registers of cases sent by Yusuf Sayfa to the imperial council, see MD 78:1561, 1563a, 1563b, 1564, and 1565. These all address preparations to build a fortress for the protection of the small coastal village of Antartus, which was afflicted by constant plunder from "wicked infidels" from the sea.

72. MD 73:453, 4 Ramadan 1003.

73. The role of the *shari'a* courts in relation to imperial authority remains an important historiographic debate in the field. For key examples of scholarship that also address methodological issues, see Jennings, "Limitations of the Judicial Powers of the Kadi"; Doumani, "Palestinian Islamic Court Records"; al-Qattan, "Textual Differentiation in the Damascus *Sijill*"; and Ze'evi, "The Use of Shari'a Court Records."

74. For an early assessment of this issue see Johansen, "Sacred and Religious Elements in Hanafite Law." Guy Burak redefined these questions and suggested that lawmaking became an imperial enterprise during the sixteenth and seventeenth centuries; see Burak, *The Second Formation of Islamic Law.*

75. MD 78:3011. Sent to Husayn as he assumed the governorship of Trablus in 1610. The phrase reads, *dīn-i mübin ve uğur-u hümāyūn-u 'izzet.*

76. Formally charitable endowments, *vakıf*s (Arabic "*waqf*s") were often used to shelter private accumulation, and imperial *vakıf*s for the construction of mosques, *medrese*s, and soup kitchens also contributed to social relief and urbanization and were thus one mechanism for the performance of sovereign power. In this context they also served as grants of revenues collected from villages, farms, or commercial properties distributed to delegates and representatives of the sultan. These grants guaranteed a salary from the surplus remaining after taxes and fees were collected from the various properties and were customarily remitted to the imperial treasury on the death of the recipient. On private accumulation see Doumani, "Endowing Family." For general histories of *waqf*s and Ottoman administration see Köprülü, "Vakıf müessesesinin hukuki mahiyeti ve tarihi tekamülü"; Çağatay, "İslamda Vakıf Kurumunun Miras Hukukuna Etkisi"; Barkan, "Şer'i Miras Hukuku"; Barkan, *Türkiye'de toprak meselesi*; Hoexter, "Waqf Studies in the Twentieth Century."

77. For examples see MD 70:80; 71:548; 73:437; 78:204, 310; 79:608; 80:871, 890; 81:24; 94:126; 102:274, 275, 708, 739; and 114:65.

78. MD 94:126.

79. Increased market activity and intensified economic links between rural and urban areas, population growth, urbanization, and a greater velocity in circulation of goods during the sixteenth and seventeenth centuries all contributed to this fluctuation. Furthermore, shifts in military technologies from cavalry to infantry-based armies, along with strategies like tax farming and annual payments adapted from provinces such as Trablus for other territories across the empire, contributed to shifts in the fiscal economy of the Ottoman establishment. These facets also challenge arguments that a price revolution occurred during the period due solely to the influx of silver from the Spanish conquest of territories across the Atlantic. See my introduction for more extensive sources on these points; see also Pamuk, *A Monetary History*; and Pamuk, "Institutional Change."

80. MD 78:310, issued in 1609–10.

81. For comparative examples of *vakıf* management see Jennings, "Pious Foundations"; Hathaway, "Wealth and Influence"; and Çizakça, "Cash Waqfs of Bursa."

82. As there are no further identifications in the text as to the identity of "Mehmed," it is likely that the edict refers to Sokulluzade Lala Mehmed Paşa, who served as grand vizier from 1604 until his death in 1606. He famously captured the fortress of Esztergom in 1605 while serving as *beylerbey* of Rumeli toward the end of the long war between Ottoman and Habsburg forces in the Hungarian territories. As the text of the edict also notes that payments due to the supervisor of the *vakıf* had lapsed for ten years, and the edict was issued between 1615 and 1616, this would be the correct time frame for his service as grand vizier and death. See Danişmend, *Izahlı Osmanlı tarihi kronolojisi*, 3:361–63.

83. MD 81:24.

84. MD 78:204.

85. A reference to the grand vizier responsible for the 1585 military invasion of Greater Syria.

86. MD 67:145; MD 70:80; MD 78:310; MD 79:608.

87. MD 70:80.

88. Robert Mantran identified Istanbul as a "stomach capital" and traced the compulsive focus on provisioning the sultanate and the city in *Istanbul dans la seconde moitié du XVIIe siècle*; see especially chapter 1 of part 2. Rhoads Murphey also called attention to this dynamic in "Provisioning Istanbul."

89. MD 78:1562.

90. MD 75:380.

91. Abu-Husayn, *Provincial Leaderships*, 41. Abu-Husayn cited local historians for the declining fortunes of the Sayfas in relation to the Ottoman establishment, because very few records produced by the imperial council attend to them, or to Trablus, between 1616 and 1670: the biographical dictionary held in the British Museum, *Maʿādin al-dhahab fi al-rijāl al-musharrafa bihim Ḥalab*, of Aleppine Abu al-Wafa al-ʿUrdi (d. 1661); and the pro-Maʿn historians Ahmad al-Khalidi of Safad (d. 1625) and Istvan Duwayhi (d. 1704), see al-Khalidi, *Lubnān fī ʿahd al-Amīr Fakhr al-Dīn al-Maʿnī al-Thānī*; and Duwayhi, *Tārīkh al-Aʿẓmina*. This indicates a shift in the *mühimme* registers toward other regional brokers (the Harfush and Hamada) and toward other administrative units (Damascus, Aleppo, Sidon-Beirut) as key to imperial concerns in the region.

92. Karakaş Mehmed Paşa was a son-in-law (*damad*) of Ahmed I, married to Ayşe and part of marriage alliances *cum* governorships that played a central role in reconfiguring sovereign authority both in Istanbul itself and across the provinces during the seventeenth century; see Peirce, *The Imperial Harem*, 21–25, 58–79.

93. Abu-Husayn, *Provincial Leaderships*, 48–60.

94. Ibid., 121–26.

Chapter 6. On the Perfect State

This chapter reassesses and expands on material originally presented in "Genres of Power: Constructing a Discourse of Decline in Ottoman Nasīhatnāme." In *Osmanlı Araştırmaları Dergisi/The Journal of Ottoman Studies* (Issue 35, 2010), 81–116.

1. From the anonymous author of *Kitāb-i müstetāb*, likely written during the tumultuous reign of Osman II; Yücel, *Osmanlı devlet düzenine ait metinler I*, 33.

2. See my introduction for comparative examples of this literary form along with its political intonations. A good guide to the evolution of advice manuals within the context of an expanding medieval Muslim polity is Yavari, *Advice for the Sultan*. Rifa'at Ali Abou-El-Haj provided an overview of their significance within the Ottoman context in *The Expression of Ottoman Political Culture*.

3. For significant studies that address these genres see Fodor, "The Grand Vizieral Telhis"; Howard, "Genre and Myth"; and Howard, "From Manual to Literature."

4. Other designations that appear both in titles and as generic descriptions include *adab al-muluk* (the manners of kings) and *siyar al-muluk* (conduct of kings), categories that constituted variants of *nasihat al-muluk*.

5. Al-Azmeh, *Muslim Kingship*. On European mirrors for princes see Weber, "What a Good Ruler Should Not Do."

6. Fleischer, *Bureaucrat and Intellectual*, 99–100; and Alam, *The Languages of Political Islam*, 11.

7. Mirror-hybrids abound: Julie Scott Meisami explored the intersection of advisory and moralizing literature with other established genres, including historiography, panegyric poetry, and epic; and Geert Jan van Gelder explored hybridity and the popularization of the advice genre. See, respectively, Meisami, "Dynastic History and Ideals"; Meisami, "The Shāh-nāme as Mirror for Princes"; and Van Gelder, "Mirror for Princes."

8. As an example, an early fourteenth-century Arabic work chose a well-established literary form and shaped it to promote the author's professional relationship with the vizier to whom the book was dedicated; see Marlow, "The Way of Viziers."

9. Sam White and Oktay Özel provide the most succinct and revised assessment of these dynamics, both globally and within the specific ecology of the Ottoman Empire. See White, *The Climate of Rebellion*; and Özel, *The Collapse of Rural Order*.

10. Vries, *The Economy of Europe*, 28.

11. Pocock, *Virtue, Commerce, and History*; and Pocock, *The Machiavellian Moment*.

12. Linda T. Darling has addressed the proliferation of advice manuals across Eurasia during the establishment of strong, centralized courts from the fifteenth century to the seventeenth. Significantly, she places Ottoman dynamics within this broader comparative history, although she also emphasizes the incommensurability of their intent; see Darling, "Political Change and Political Discourse"; and Darling, "Mirrors for Princes."

13. Sariyannis, "The Princely Virtues."

14. Several scholars have critically assessed the relationship of literary productions, historical development, and discursive genres as they relate to Ottoman state formation. Rifa'at Abou-El-Haj constructed his narrative of the early modern state around this premise in *Formation of the Modern State*. See also Fodor, "State and Society"; Abou-El-Haj, "The Ottoman Nasihatname"; Douglas, "Ottoman Historiography"; and Howard, "Genre and Myth." Cornell Fleischer also argued cogently for the evolution of *nasihatname* as a new form of critique in his masterful portrait of Mustafa Ali, *Bureaucrat and Intellectual*, 99–108.

15. Halil İnalcık's discussion of territorial appropriation, "Ottoman Methods of Conquest," remains the standard treatment in the field.

16. Rhoads Murphey addressed the massive imperial effort expended in managing grain supplies, primarily from Egypt but also from Greater Syria, Anatolia, and the occupied Hungarian territories. He estimated that more than one thousand tons of grain were sent to Istanbul annually from Egypt alone; see Murphey, "Provisioning Istanbul." Alan Mikhail has provided a comprehensive account of the interdependencies among the Nile, the Egyptian cultivator, and the Ottoman Empire in Mikhail, *Nature and Empire*. For the logistics of transport involved in the consistent circulation of foodstuffs and other provisions, see Faroqhi, "Camels, Wagons, and the Ottoman State." And for expectations of regional subsistence and imperial requisitions see Güçer, *Osmanlı imparatorluğunda hububat meselesi*. Sam White's thesis for the seventeenth-century crisis rests on the combined factors that undermined the Ottoman establishment's ability to sustain an economic and ideological system grounded in an ethos of provisionism; see White, *The Climate of Rebellion*, 28–51 for specific resources.

17. For a comprehensive study of rural management in the sixteenth century see İslamoğlu, *State and Peasant*. Suraiya Faroqhi also addressed the evolving patterns of loyalty and rebellion in "Political Activity Among Ottoman Taxpayers."

18. Ömer Barkan described this as a process of colonization that also included the use of *vakıfs* to transfer conquered territory into imperial domain; see Barkan's "Osmanlı imparatorluğunda" and his *Türkiye'de toprak meselesi* for a broader discussion of agricultural settlement and land tenure.

19. For an overview consult İnalcık and Quataert, *An Economic and Social History*, chap. 6.

20. This practice is clearly illustrated in *mühimme* registers; see, respectively, MD 6:282; MD 7:462 and 2166; and the entire register of MD 50.

21. Venzke, "The Ottoman Tahrir Defterleri."

22. Grant, "Rethinking the Ottoman 'Decline.'"

23. The rise of regional notables has constituted a major historiographic concern in Ottoman studies. For key examples and historiographic analysis of this issue see Akdağ, "Genel çizgilerle XVII"; Khoury, "The Ottoman Centre"; along with Çevikel, "The Rise of the Ottoman Ayans." A definitive redefinition of the problem is in Ali

Yaycioğlu's *Partners of the Empire*, where Yaycioğlu argues that partnerships between key regional actors, especially governors and judges, itself constituted state governance and thus overturns studies that presume center-periphery divides.

24. On trade, regional distribution, and the emergence of consumer power in towns and villages see Goffman, *Izmir and the Levantine World*; Faroqhi, *Making a Living*; Quataert, *Consumption Studies*; and Faroqhi, "Trade and Revenue Collection."

25. Şevket Pamuk has argued that despite the Islamic prohibition on interest, the development of credit institutions throughout the empire was remarkably developed by the mid-seventeenth century; see Pamuk, *A Monetary History*; and Pamuk, "Institutional Change." Studies using court records further demonstrate networks of credit, lender, and borrower in many towns of the empire as foreign and indigenous merchants, state officials, and rural provisioners followed the lucrative path of resources and contributed to the expansion of trade and the unification of currency zones; see Jennings, "Loans and Credit"; Faroqhi, *Men of Modest Substance*; and Barkey and Rossem, "Networks of Contention."

26. For key assessments of millennial movements and their social and political implications see Griswold, *The Great Anatolian Rebellion*, 13–14; and Fleischer, "Mahdi and Millennium," 42–54.

27. White, *The Climate of Rebellion*, 140–55.

28. For assessments of the relationship between the materiél necessary for war and Ottoman strategies to mobilize and distribute resources, see Finkel, "The Administration of Warfare"; Veinstein, "Some Views on Provisioning"; Murphey, *Ottoman Warfare*; and Ágoston, *Guns for the Sultan*.

29. There were six major uprisings by the end of Ahmed I's reign, motivated by deficit or inflation that impacted military payrolls and donatives. However, the power of the janissaries to pressure the sultan and sway political movements was a consistent facet of their presence in the capital city, in provincial garrisons, and increasingly in commercial and agricultural activities of the empire. Cemal Kafadar foregrounds these paradoxes in "On the Purity and Corruption of the Janissaries"; and "Janissaries and Other Riffraff." For shifts in the ethos and mechanisms of rebellion see Hathaway, *Mutiny and Rebellion*.

30. Baki Tezcan identified these as harbingers of change in *The Second Ottoman Empire*.

31. On these dynamics see Peirce, *The Imperial Harem*, esp. 219–86.

32. See the introduction to Murphey, *Regional Structure in the Ottoman Economy*. Darling, *Revenue-Raising and Legitimacy*, 103–17, addresses the larger trends involved; see also Tezcan, "The Ottoman Monetary Crisis."

33. These taxes have become the basis of scholarship on Ottoman demography, population management, and shifts in fiscal policy. For a review of the registers and their implications see Özel, "17. yüzyıl osmanlı demografi"; Özel, "Avarız ve cizye defterleri"; and Demirci, *The Functioning of Ottoman Avarız Taxation*.

34. For population studies that chart these changes, see Oktay Özel's work: "Population Changes in Ottoman Anatolia"; "Nüfus baskısından 16.-17."; and *The Collapse of Rural Order.*

35. Barkan, "Bir iskān ve kolonizasyon metodu olarak sürgünler."

36. Faroqhi, "Crisis and Change."

37. İnalcık, "Adaletnameler."

38. Cezar, *Osmanlı maliyesinde bunalım ve değişim dönemi*, 32.

39. For a review of controversies concerning whether the *malikane* indicated patterns of decentralization or, by contrast, the reassertion of imperial control, see Genç, "Osmanlı maliyesinde *malikane* sistemi"; and Salzmann, "Measures of Empire." Halil İnalcık traced the gradual accumulation of land and resources in the hands of regional landlords in "Emergence of the Big Farms." Stefan Winter argues that local custodianship actually increased imperial revenues and assisted the government in reestablishing firm fiscal control in Winter, *The Shiites of Lebanon*, 108.

40. Khonsari, Moghtader, and Yavari, *The Persian Garden.*

41. Andrews, *Poetry's Voice, Society's Song*, esp. 143–74; and Andrews and Markoff, "Poetry, the Arts, and Group Ethos," esp. 34–38.

42. Andrews, "Singing the Alienated 'I.'" These oppositions also formed the basis of Cemal Kafadar's and Gabi Piterberg's arguments concerning, respectively, the creation of an Ottoman myth of origins in early historiographic traditions and discursive responses to the regicide of 1622, described later in this chapter; see Kafadar, *Between Two Worlds*; and Piterberg, *An Ottoman Tragedy.*

43. See Chapter 2 for his role in defining *qanun* as a mode of temporal governance.

44. Al-Mawardi, *al-Aḥkām*, 21, 64–67, 69, 120, 153, 183.

45. Ibid., 73. Translation according to al-Mawardi, *The Ordinances of Government*, 65.

46. Qur'an 49:9, cited in al-Mawardi, *The Ordinances of Government*, 65.

47. Gibb, "al-Māwardi's Theory of the Caliphate," 163.

48. Ann K. S. Lambton characterized the shift from justice to good governance and provided an expanded analysis of the figures explored here in *Theory and Practice*, 119. See also E. I. J. Rosenthal, *Political Thought in Medieval Islam*; and Patricia Crone, *Medieval Islamic Political Thought.*

49. What follows is an abbreviated analysis of major figures and trends influential for Ottoman *nasihatname* authors. For an expanded treatment of these figures and the question of rulership and sovereignty in the Ottoman context, see especially the work of Marinos Sariyannis: "The Princely Virtues"; "Ruler and State"; and *Ottoman Political Thought.*

50. Lambton, "Justice in the Medieval Persian Theory of Kingship," 101.

51. Ibid., 102.

52. Ibid., 104.

53. Lambton, "The Internal Structure of the Saljuq Empire," 233–35.

54. al-Ghazali, *Book of Counsel for Kings*, 11–12.

55. Ibid., 18.

56. Ibid., 48.

57. Ibid., 61.

58. Although much has been made of the various confessional sympathies of the intellectuals invoked in this section, these labels are potentially problematic because they assume reified boundaries that were in flux during the late medieval period. Without a clear discussion of historical context, labeling Nasir al-Din Tusi "Shi'i" or al-Ghazali "Sunni" ignores the complexity of the medieval intellectual heritage and willfully imposes a divide established by modernist proclivities. For an application of this argument within the realm of material culture see Mulder, *The Shrines of the 'Alids*.

59. See Hagen, "Legitimacy and World Order"; and Tezcan, "The Definition of Sultanic Legitimacy."

60. Nasir al-Din Tusi, *Muqaddimah-yi qadīm-i akhlāq-i Nāṣirī*, 95.

61. Ibid., 98.

62. Ibid., 261–62.

63. al-Farabi, *Al-Farabi on the Perfect State.*

64. Mahdi, *Alfarabi and the Foundation*, 125–44.

65. al-Farabi, *Kitāb ārā' ahl al-madīna al-fāḍila*, 54, 81–90.

66. Nasir al-Din Tusi, *The Nasirean Ethics*, 213–15.

67. Ibid., 217–18.

68. See Kashifi, *Aḫlāḳ-i muḥsinī*. On the significance of his position within the broader intellectual and political culture of the Timurids see Mitchell, "To Preserve and Protect."

69. Kashifi, *Aḫlāḳ-i muḥsinī*, 57.

70. Ibid., 256–57.

71. Gottfried Hagen has outlined these relationships in "Legitimacy and World Order."

72. There is a large body of secondary literature on this text and its relevance for political theory that spans multiple languages. Many scholars have treated the subjects of the theoretical contributions of this work (M. Mahdi's *Ibn Khaldūn's Philosophy of History*); its originality as a framework for statecraft (E. I. J. Rosenthal's chapter "The Theory of the Power-State" in his *Political Thought in Medieval Islam*); its link to Ottoman political culture (Fleischer, "Royal Authority, Dynastic Cyclism, and 'Ibn Khaldûnism'"); its relation to existing contemporary debates in jurisprudence (Gibb, "The Islamic Background of Ibn Khaldūn's Political Theory"); and its relevance for modern scholarship (e.g., al-Azmeh, *Ibn Khaldūn in Modern Scholarship*). My aim here is not to evaluate ibn Khaldun's work as a whole but rather to explore how he develops

a theoretical framework for understanding the circle of equity and proper order and what role historical and political criticism plays in that framework.

73. Ibn Khaldun, *Muqaddima* (2005), 58; ibn Khaldun, *Muqaddima* (1958), 40. Darling published a meticulously researched, rich survey of this intellectual heritage in *A History of Social Justice*.

74. Ibn Khaldun, *Muqaddima* (2005), 58; ibn Khaldun, *Muqaddima* (1958), 40.

75. Ibn Khaldun, *Muqaddima* (2005), 58; ibn Khaldun, *Muqaddima* (1958), 40.

76. Ibn Khaldun, *Muqaddima* (2005), 58; ibn Khaldun, *Muqaddima* (1958), 41.

77. F. Gabrieli discusses how ibn Khaldun develops the concept of *'aṣabiyya* in his theory of history. See Gabrieli, "'Aṣabiyya." Gabrieli explained that "whether it is based on blood ties or on some other social grouping, *'aṣabiyya* is, for ibn Khaldun, the force which impels groups of human beings to assert themselves, to struggle for primacy, to establish hegemonies, dynasties and empires."

78. Ibn Khaldun, *Muqaddima* (2005), 346; ibn Khaldun, *Muqaddima* (1958), 160.

79. Ibn Khaldun, *Muqaddima* (2005), 80; ibn Khaldun, *Muqaddima* (1958), 238.

80. Ibn Khaldun, *Muqaddima* (2005), 82; ibn Khaldun, *Muqaddima* (1958), 240.

81. Ibn Khaldun, *Muqaddima* (2005), 82; ibn Khaldun, *Muqaddima* (1958), 240.

82. Ibn Khaldun, *Muqaddima* (2005), 239; ibn Khaldun, *Muqaddima* (1958), 81. This is a Persian parable in which a dignitary uses the circle of equity to criticize and advise the king, Bahrām ibn Bahrām.

83. BOA, *Hümayun'dan kanunnamesi*, folio 81, sheet 62. Cited in Hagen, "Legitimacy and World Order," 59. Hagen provides a meticulous analysis of the evolution of *nıẓām-ı 'alem*. We saw in Chapter 2 how the phrase was deployed in relation to sovereign law, and here it serves as a standard of measurement for authors attentive to a perceived crisis in the natural order of things.

84. See Chapters 2 and 3 for a careful analysis of how "order" and sociopolitical categories shifted from the lawmaking activities of Mehmed II to those of Süleyman I.

85. His conception of *siyasa* as a form of sovereign power was addressed in more detail in Chapter 2.

86. Tulum, "Dursun Bey," *TDVİA*, 10:7; Woodhead, "Ṭursun Beg."

87. Tursun Bey, *Tārīḫ-i ebū'l-fetḥ*, 12–13.

88. Ibid., 17.

89. Ibid., 16: *tīğ-ı berk-dırahş ve ḥimmet-i mülk bahşı*.

90. Bayezid I was defeated and captured by Timur in the battle of Ankara in 1402, and Murad II finally consolidated the dynasty after an interregnum that lasted almost two decades. These events, and the consolidation of the dynasty after 1422, generated themes and motifs that remained significant throughout the chronicling traditions of the Ottoman court. Thus, Ahmedi's (d. 1413) tribute to Alexander contained a small section on the history of the Ottoman kings; see Silay, *Dasitān-i tevārīh*. Even though it was dedicated to a Germiyan *emir*, he was later incorporated into the

court of Bayezid I, and the lyrical verse he created concerning Ottoman power influenced numerous anonymous chronicles from the period, as well as the grandees of an emergent Ottoman historiographical tradition who created historical narratives from previous compilations: Aşıkpaşazade (*Āşıkpaşazāde tārīḫī*, c. 1484–1502), Tursun Bey (*Tārīḫ-i ebū'l-fetḥ*, c. 1488), and Neşri (*Cihānnümā*, c. 1493). See 'Ali Bey, *Tevarih-i Āl-i Osman'dan Aşıkpaşazade tarihi*; İnalcık, "How to Read 'Ashık Pasha-Zade's History"; İnalcık, "The Rise of Ottoman Historiography"; Taeschner, "Neşri tarihi el yazıları üzerine araştırmalar"; and Kastritsis, *Ottoman Anonymous Chronicles*.

91. Sariyannis, *Ottoman Political Thought*, 37–39.

92. Tezcan, "The Definition of Sultanic Legitimacy," 110.

93. Hagen, "Legitimacy and World Order."

94. Kınalızade, *Aḫlāḳ-ı ālā'i*, 3:49.

95. The move toward subordinating the *shari'a* to the *kanun* of the state also provoked controversy and mobilized opposition movements to administrative reforms spearheaded by Ebu's-su'ud Efendi as outlined in Chapters 2 and 3. Çivizade Efendi, *şeyhülislam* from 1539 to 1542, and the scholar Birgivi Mehmed Efendi (d. 1573) both challenged Ebu's-su'ud's efforts to extend imperial control over *shari'i* provisions concerning land tenure and taxation, especially in relationship to the management of *vakıf.* Both decried these efforts as "innovations," and suggested that the depravation of the countryside was due not to crisis but to these political interventions into the postulates of divine order. Such criticisms, along with aspersions of Sufi-inspired ceremonial practices and rising social consumer habits of coffee drinking and tobacco smoking, also fueled to the revivalist movement of Kadızade Mehmed (d. 1635) and agitants who acted in his name through the 1680s, the Kadızadelis. The classic text on this remains Zilfi, "The Kadizadelis." For an excellent recent analysis of what Ekin Tuşalp Atiyas terms "sunna-minded" responses to seventeenth-century crises, see her chapter "The 'Sunna-Minded' Trend," in Sariyannis, *Ottoman Political Thought*, 98–122.

96. Idris Bitlisi, like Ahmedi before him, initially served in an Ottoman rival's court, in this case that of the Akkoyunlu. He was part of the legal bureaucracy created by Uzun Hasan between 1452 and 1457, before becoming aligned with Bayezid I in c. 1500. Sariyannis characterized him as part of an "international class," defined by agile movement between various courts as well as between Persianate and Islamicate traditions of thought; see Sariyannis, *Ottoman Political Thought*, 35. For a significant recent study of his participation in diplomatic efforts to create allegiances between Kurdish and Ottoman polities and his role in developing Ottoman claims to legitimacy by subordinating Sunni Islam to the interests of the state, see Sönmez, *Idris-i Bidlisi*. He draws on Nizam al-Mulk's *Siyāsetnāme*, as well as Jalal al-Din Davvani's (d. 1502) *Akhlāq-i Jalālī*, which was an expansion on the work of Nasir al-Din Tusi and helped bridge the ethico-political universes of Persian and Ottoman. For analysis

concerning the importance of Kurdish intellectual circles during the early seventeenth century as well, see El-Rouayheb, *Islamic Intellectual History*.

97. See Robert Dankoff's introduction to Yusuf Khass Hajib, *Wisdom of Royal Glory*, 3–9, for Dankoff's assessment of the integration of Persianate and Türkmen forms in the *Kābūsnāme*, which he dates to approximately 1082. Eleazar Birnbaum published a facsimile edition of the earliest extant Ottoman translation, dated approximately to the fourth quarter of the fourteenth century; see Birnbaum, *The Book of Advice*. A manuscript of an Ottoman translation of the *Siyāru'l-mulūk* of Nizam al-Mulk is preserved in the Istanbul University Library, no. T6952; see Levend, "Siyāsetnāmeler," 176n47. An Ottoman translation of al-Ghazali's *Naṣīḥāt 'l-mulūk* dating from the reign of Mehmed II is in the Topkapı Sarayı Library, Istanbul, Hazine no. 368; see Levend's "Ümmet Çağında Ahlāk Kitaplarımız" for full references.

98. Cemal Kafadar presents a critical summary of twentieth-century reflections on the literature of decline; see Kafadar, "The Question of Ottoman Decline."

99. Lütfi Paşa, *Aṣafnāme*, 6. The best early critical edition of this work remains the one prepared by Rudolf Tschudi from extant manuscripts in Vienna, Dresden, Munich, and the library of the Beyazıt Mosque in Istanbul, *Das Asafnāme des Lutfi Pascha*, although there is now a more recent edition.

100. Lütfi Paşa, *Aṣafnāme*, 35.

101. Ibid., 24.

102. Tietze, *Mustafa Ali's Counsel for Sultans*, 85. Mustafa Ali's *Nasīḥatu's-ṣelāṭīn* stands as the preeminent representative of an Ottoman mirror tradition. Cornell Fleischer's work illuminated the significance of his emphasis on *kanun* as an "Ottoman way" and his "counsel," which served to judge the current state of the empire but did not yet incorporate the sense of crisis that would evolve from the 1590s onward. Lütfi Paşa's themes and concerns would also be reflected in Mustafa Ali's compositions, although the latter paid more attention to the practices of land management and procedures of registration. See Fleischer, *Bureaucrat and Intellectual*, 93–103.

103. Lütfi Paşa, *Aṣafnāme*, 12–13.

104. Veysi was a scholar, judge, and minor bureaucrat, as well as a prolific writer of prose, poems, and stylized letters (*münşe'at*). Ahmet Şen argued that the *Habnāme* was presented not to Sultan Ahmed I but rather to his grand vizier, Nasuh Paşa, who served from 1611 until his death in 1614. A colophon copy includes a date of 1613–14. On the literary characteristics of the text and its distinctions from other *nasihat* treatises see Şen, "A Mirror for Princes."

105. Mehmed, *Habnāme-i Veysi*, 24.

106. Fodor, "State and Society," 230–31; Gökbilgin, "XVII. asrıda osmanlı devletinde islāhat ihtiyaç ve temayülleri ve Kātip Çelebi," 206–9; Sariyannis, *Ottoman Political Thought*, 83.

107. Yücel, *Osmanlı devlet düzenine ait metinler I*, 33.

108. Ibid., 26.

109. *'Adaletname* of Ahmet I, BOA, MD 78:4012. Also translated and cited in full in İnalcık, "The Ottoman Decline," 344.

110. Ibid.

111. See Baki Tezcan's careful reconstructive history of these events in "Searching for Osman." Gabi Piterberg identified the regicide of Osman II as "an Ottoman tragedy," and Tezcan and Piterberg both serve as guides here, although the focus remains on how these events came to be understood in terms of the distressed bonds of loyalty between sultan and servant. Sam White noted that the little ice age also played a significant role in the chaos for this period and should shift historiographic interpretations toward a crisis in provisioning, as famine and lack of supplies rendered military servicemen and elites mutinous; see White, *The Climate of Rebellion*, 192–98.

112. White, *The Climate of Rebellion*, 193.

113. Mustafa's enthronement was a major shift in Ottoman succession policies, which gradually placed seniority ahead of patrilineality; see Peirce, *The Imperial Harem*, 20–23.

114. The dates of Hüseyin bin Sefer's birth and death are not fully known, though his references throughout the short text dedicated to the events of 1622 suggest that he was most likely alive until 1640, if not beyond.

115. Tezcan, "II. Osman örneğinde 'ilerlemeci' tarih"; and, Tezcan, "The History of a 'Primary Source.'"

116. Sertoğlu, "Tarih-i Tuği," 493.

117. Ibid., 494.

118. Peçevi, *Tārīḫ-i Peçevī*, 2:379.

119. Ibid., 380–81.

120. Ibid.

121. The variant spellings of his name reflect a long-standing debate among Ottoman linguists concerning the best phonetic transcription for a language containing such a diverse heritage (Turkish, Persian, Arabic, Uyghur, etc.) and little indication about its enunciatory practice in daily life. There is also some confusion over whether a second treatise dedicated to Sultan İbrahim in 1640 should be attributed to Koçu Bey or represents instead yet another anonymous contribution to the debate. This was decisively settled by Cağatay Uluçay, who argued that the first, in twenty-two sections, was submitted to Murad IV, and the second, shorter version, to İbrahim. See Uluçay, "Koçi Beyin Sultan İbrahime takdim ettiği risale ve arzları." The debate concerning authorship extends to the twelve fragments of reform memoranda (*telhis*) in a copybook (*mecmu'a*) in the Veliyuddin Library. These may have served as possible drafts for the *Risale*, as explored by Rhoads Murphey in "The Veliyuddin Telhis." Howard Douglas believes this to be speculative at best; see Douglas, "Ottoman Historiography," 65–68. More than twenty manuscript copies exist; the three primary are

held at the Millet Kütüphanesi (no. 474), the Nurosmaniye Library (no. 4950), and, as speculated by Uluçay, the Revan 1323 (Mükerrer) manuscript in the Topkapı Sarayı Library, which may be an early copy made by the author himself. For further references, manuscripts, publications, biographical details, and reception see Uluçay, "Koçi Beyin"; and Akün, *TDVİA*.

122. Rifa'at Abou-El-Haj provided a detailed outline of the first treatise and its idealized portrait of a golden era in *Formation of the Modern State*, 101–11.

123. Edited with the original text, its transcription into the Latin alphabet, and a modern Turkish translation in Koçu Bey, *Koçi Bey Risālesi*, 18–75, 18.

124. Pál Fodor used the *telhis* as a means to assess the rising power of palace factions and the displacement of the sultan from the system; see Fodor, "The Grand Vizieral Telhis."

125. This is Koçu Bey's concise reformulation of the circle of justice; Koçu Bey, *Koçi Bey Risālesi*, 105.

126. Ibid., 48.

127. Ibid., 12.

128. Ibid., 32, 45.

129. Ibid., 45.

130. Mehmed, *Habnāme-i Veysi*, 38.

131. Ibid., 46.

132. Koçu Bey, *Koçi Bey Risālesi*, 82–83.

133. Ibid., 29–30.

134. Ibid., 51–52. Possible sources for this accounting from the period of Murad III can be found in a collection of *kanun* concerning the administrative structure of the empire in the Süleymaniye Library, Esad Efendi, no. 2363, folios 75b–84a. And for Murad IV and Ibrahim I, the memorandum (*lāyiḥa*) prepared under the auspices of the grand vizier Kemankeş Kara Mustafa Paşa (served 1638 to his death in 1644). It contains an accounting of military salaries and privileges, those of the palace administration and imperial council, along with provincial divisions, appointments, and custodians of the land. It is presented as a *kanun* composed by Kara Mustafa Paşa for Sultan İbrahim contained in the Nurosmaniye Library, no. 4950.

135. Possible internal documents used for Koçu Bey's analysis, and his accounting of key participants in the imperial council, registered holders of estates, salaried military officials, and administrators, can be detected in a detailed *kanunname* outlining the administrative system of Sultan Süleyman, held in the Süleymaniye Library, Yahya Tevfik Bölümü, no. 278.

136. Commentary, notes, translation, and a facsimile edition published by Murphey; see Aziz Efendi, *Kānūnnāme-i Sultānī li 'Azīz Efendi*.

137. Ibid., 24.

138. Ibid., 4.

139. Ibid., 24.

140. Ibid., 16.

141. Authors such as Ayn-ı Ali Efendi (d. circa 1613) and Hezarfen Hüseyin Efendi (d. circa 1692) should also be referenced in this guise, and will be addressed in my conclusion.

Conclusion

1. There are more than forty manuscript copies of this administrative manual, though the published version used here derives from the copy in the Süleymaniye Library, İzmirli İsmail Hakkı, no. 2472. The manual was dedicated to Sultan Ahmed I (r. 1603–17) and his grand vizier, Kuyucu Murad Paşa, so it was likely composed during the tenure of the latter between 1606 and 1611. Ayn-ı Ali also defines himself as the ex-*defter-i hakani emini*, or superintendent of the "imperial register," a position he held until 1607. For the details of his biography see the introduction to Mustafa T. Gökbilgin's edition of the manuscript: Gökbilgin, *Kavānıīn-i Āl-i Osman*, 3–40.

2. *Düstūrü'l- 'amel* is contained as an appendix in a combined manuscript that includes 'Ayn-ı 'Ali Efendi's *Ḳavānīn-i āl-i 'Os̱mān*. It was published in 1863 from the manuscript copy in the Süleymaniye Library referenced in the previous note. For this section of his pamphlet and the passages translated here, see pages 137–40.

3. The role of the imperial council was central to the circulation of edicts, decrees, and certificates of privilege and travel, as well as for the production of treaties and correspondence to internal inhabitants and external agents. But, as the *mühimme* indicate, the *mühimme* contained threads of other administrative activities generated from the land registry office or from the office dedicated to appointments and bestowals These were gradually recorded in distinct registers beginning in the mid-seventeenth century.

4. 'Ayn-ı 'Ali Efendi, *Ḳavānīn-i āl-i 'Os̱mān*, 4.

5. Ibid., 75–79.

6. Michel Foucault, *The Archaeology of Knowledge*, 81–133; see also Foucault, *The Essential Works of Foucault*, 2:289–90, 309–10.

7. Ann Laura Stoler, *Along the Archival Grain*, 44.

8. Ibid., 47.

9. Certeau, *The Writing of History*, 75.

10. See Davis, *Fiction in the Archives*; and Ginzburg, *The Cheese and the Worms*.

11. See Bayly, *Empire and Information*; and Dirks, "Colonial Histories and Native Informants." Or, following an alternative track, scholars also employ the archive as a means to assess the interaction between history and memory, between a place of origin yet also of perpetuation, of stated order yet repressed disorders; see Le Goff, *History and Memory*, 87–89; and Steedman, "The Space of Memory." This move is propelled especially by the work of Jacques Derrida, who addressed both the ordinariness of

the archive and its subterranean shadows in *Archive Fever.* For an excellent analysis of Derrida's reach and impact see Carolyn Steedman, *Dust.*

12. Benton, *A Search for Sovereignty*, 29–30.

13. Ibid., 10, 36–39, 279.

14. Ibid., 31.

15. Feridun's collection remains indispensable for reviewing early modern Ottoman diplomatic forms, styles, and agendas; see Feridun Bey, *Mecmūʿa-yı Münşeʾāt.* There are many manuscript copies of Ebu's-suʿud Efendi's *fetva*s concerning the land regime, *Maʿrūżāt.* The Süleymaniye Library alone contains six. For one of the more comprehensive versions see Esʿad Efendi, no. 587, folios 105–24. For a printed collection of various *fetva* see Düzdağ, *Şeyhülislām Ebussuūd Efendi fetvaları.* Research on record-keeping practices during the foundational years of the empire continues to be a pressing concern. The influences of Mongol, Mamluk, Seljuk, Indian, and Timurid techniques were significant, especially in the genre of the *mecmuʿa-i inşaʾ* (anthologies), which typically contained copies of correspondence between kings (*sultaniyat*) or between friends (*ikhwaniyat*). While the latter proliferated as a more general device for the demonstration of literary competence and elite status among scholar-bureaucrats and literati in the late fifteenth and early sixteenth century, Feridun Bey's focus on courtly protocol and documentary production indicates shifts in the bureaucracy during the period as well. For scholarship on the *mecmuʿa-i inşaʾ* see Tekin, *Menāhicü'l-inşa*; and Tekin, "Fatih devrine ait bir inşaʾ mecumʿası."

16. There are approximately three hundred thousand bound notebooks, of which the *mühimme* and the cadastral surveys constitute the largest collection, although salary registers and expense accounts also represent a sizable proportion. The approximately 150 million loose papers occupied early cataloguers such as Ali Emire, who sorted 180,361 of them chronologically according to the reigning sultan (designated by the code "A.E."). The comprehensive guide for the BOA contains an exhaustive list of the collections and flow charts indicating the path individual documents might take through the Ottoman administrative apparatus; see Sarınay, *Başbakanlık Osmanlı arşivi rehberi.*

17. Hezarfen Hüseyin Efendi's work "Summary of the Laws of the Ottoman Dynasty," completed in 1675–76, follows similar compulsions and concerns as his predecessors. He identified a past ideal during the reign of Süleyman and explicitly referenced the use of varied administrative documentary genres, along with chronicles, as part of his effort to compile a comprehensive account of Ottoman governance; see Hezarfen Hüseyin Efendi, *Telḫīsü'l-beyān fī ḳavānīn-i āl-i ʿOs̱mān*, 38. For a general introduction to the text see Anhegger, "Hezarfen Hüseyin Efendi."

18. See Abdi (Tevkiʿi), "Osmanlı kanunnameleri"; and Ahmed Cevdet Paşa, *Mecelle-yi aḥkām-ı ʿadliye.*

19. Kili and Gözübüyük, *Türk anayasa metinleri*, 11–73; Kubalı, *Türk esas tşkilat hukuku dersleri*; İnalcık, "Sened-i İttifak ve Gülhane Hatt-ı Hümâyûnu."

20. A copy of the imperial writ can be found in BOA, Hatt-ı Hümayun: 35242. Akyıldız published a full edition of this text in "Sened-i İttifak'ın ilk tam metni"; it was translated into English in Akyıldız and Hanioğlu, "Negotiating the Power of the Sultan." Yaycioğlu's adapted translation and section-by-section analysis now stands as the most expansive treatment of this document; see Yaycioğlu, *Partners of the Empire*, 203–23. Two late nineteenth-century Ottoman historians, Şanizade and Ahmed Cevdet Paşa, also included versions of the document in their descriptions of the varied crises and reforms of the period; see Şanizade Mehmed Ataullah Efendi, *Şānīzāde tārīḫī*; and Ahmed Cevdet Paşa, *Tārīh-i Cevdet*.

21. The deed contained seven articles, an introduction and epilogue, and a writ of agreement composed by Mahmud II.

22. Grand Vizier Mustafa Bayraktar, a onetime military commander in Danubian Bulgaria, also led a coup against the janissary-led resistance to the reformist government of Selim II (r. 1789–1807) and drafted the Deed of Alliance as a short-lived grand vizier; see Yaycioğlu, *Partners of the Empire*, 163, 178–82, 219–22, 237.

23. These alliances "established an empire-wide web of trust, from the center to regional dynasties, and from regional dynasties to subordinate local notables"; see Yaycioğlu, *Partners of the Empire*, 212–14. I am indebted to Yaycioğlu's insightful analysis of the deed's import for the following comments.

24. Ibid., 207.

25. Ibid.

26. Ibid., 204, 239–48.

27. Adapted translation from Hatt-ı Hümayun: 35242; and Yaycioğlu, *Partners of the Empire*, 215.

BIBLIOGRAPHY

Abbreviations

ARCHIVES

A.DVN	Divan (Beylikçi) Kalemi Defterleri
BOA	Başbakanlık Osmanlı Arşivi [Prime Ministry Ottoman Archives]
D.BSM	Başmuhasebe Kalemi Defterleri
KK	Kamil Kepeci
MM	Maliyyeden Müdevver
MD	Mühimme Defterleri
MOL	Magyar Országos Levéltár [Hungarian National Archives]
TTD	Tapu Tahrir Defterleri

JOURNALS AND INSTITUTIONS

AOASH	*Acta Orientalia Academiae Scientiarum Hungaricae* (Budapest)
AO	*Archivum Ottomanicum*
BSOAS	*Bulletin of the School of Oriental and African Studies*
EI2	*Encyclopaedia of Islam* (electronic edition), 2nd ed., edited by P. Bearman et al. (Leiden: Brill, 1954–2009)
İA	*İslam ansiklopedisi: İslām alemi coğrafya, etnografya ve biyografya lūgati.* 13 vols. (Istanbul: Milli Eğitim Bakanlığı, 1940–88)
İFM	*İktisat Fakültesi mecmuası*
IJMES	*International Journal of Middle East Studies*
IJTS	*International Journal of Turkish Studies*
JTS	*Journal of Turkish Studies*
SI	*Studia Islamica*
TDVİA	*Türkiye Diyanet Vakfı İslam ansiklopedisi.* 44 vols. (Istanbul: Türkiye Diyanet Vakfı, 1988–2013)
TOEM	*Tarih-i Osmanı encümeni mecmuası*
VD	*Vakıflar dergisi*

Archival Materials and Manuscripts

ANKARA

Tapu ve Kadastro Umumi Mudürlüğü, 3, 117, 190.
National Library, Koçu Bey's *Risāle*, no. 474.

BUDAPEST

Hungarian National Archives / Magyar Országos Levéltár (MOL).
Collection of Turkish Records. R 315: 5, 6, 7, 26, 27, 31, 32; E 142: facsimile 12, no. 23; facsimile 26, no. 30; facsimile 20, no. 42.
Esterházy Family Archives. P 108:71, facsimile 26a.

ISTANBUL

Başbakanlık Osmanlı Arşivi (BOA)

Başmuhasebe Kalemi Defterleri (D.BSM): 147.
Divan (Beylikçi) Kalemi Defterleri (A.DVN): 790.
Hatt-ı Hümayun: 35242.
Maliyyeden Müdevver (MM): 842, 2787, 2993, 4285.
Mühimme Defterleri (MD): 1–90 (and published *defter*s listed below).
Tapu Tahrir Defterleri (TTD): 68, 93, 200, 205, 343, 345, 372, 388, 391, 410, 421, 449, 454, 493, 513, 524, 530, 548, 564, 610, 611, 965, 998, 1017, 1044, 1107.

Beyazıt Devlet Library

General *kanunname*, Sultan Süleyman, Veliyüddin Efendi, no. 1969.

Istanbul University Library

Mustafa 'Ali. *Künhü'l-aḫbār,* nos. 1320, 2359, 2400, 5959.
———. *Nasīḥatu's-ṣelāṭīn*, (in Turkish, titled *Nasīhatül 'l-mülūk*), no. 4098.
Nizam al-Mulk's *Siyāru'l-mulūk*, no. T6952.

Nurosmaniye Library

'Ayn-ı 'Ali Efendi's *Ḳavānīn-i āl-i 'Os̱mān der ḫülāsa-ı mezāmīn-i defter-i dīvān*, no. 4950.
Koçu Bey's *Risāle*, no. 4950.
Memorandum of Kemankeş Kara Mustafa Paşa, no. 4950.
Mustafa 'Ali's *Künhü'l-aḫbār,* nos. 3406, 3407, 3408, 3409.

Süleymaniye Library

Aya Sofya, no. 4871, folios 118a–57b.
'Ayn-ı 'Ali Efendi's *Ḳavānīn-i āl-i 'Os̱mān der ḫülāsa-ı mezāmīn-i defter-i dīvān.*
Cārullah Efendi, no. 968, folios 3b–6b.

Celalzade Mustafa's *Mısır eyāleti kānūnnāmeler.*
Ebu's-su'ud Efendi's *Ma'rūẓāt.*
Es'ad Efendi, nos. 587, 852, 854, 2067-1, 2063.
Hamidiye, no. 1469.
Hekimoğlu 'Ali Paşa, no. 558, folios 33b–71a.
Hıdıv İsmail Paşa, no. 142.
Hüsrev Paşa, no. 311.
İzmirli İsmail Hakkı, no. 2472.
Kānūnnāme-i cedid.
Katip Çelebi's *Düstūrü'l-'amel li ıṣlāhi 'l-halel.*
Lala İsmail, nos. 106, 343.
Mustafa 'Ali's *Nasīḥātu's-ṣelāṭīn.*
Pir Mehmed Efendi's *Ẓāhir al-Quḍāt.*
Yahya Tevfik Bölümü, no. 278 (general *kanunname*, Sultan Süleyman).

Topkapı Palace Archives

Provincial *kanunname*, no. 9772.

Topkapı Palace Library

al-Ghazali's *Nasīḥātül 'l-mülūk*, Ottoman-Turkish translation, Hazine, no. 368.
Kānūnnāme-i cedid, Revan, 1935.
Koçu Bey's *Risāle*, early copy, Revan, no. 1323.

VIENNA

Austrian State Archives / Österreichisches Staatsarchiv. Haus-, Hof- und Staatsarchiv, *Turcica I*: 72–81.
Venetian State Archives / Archivio di Stato di Venezia (online). *Miscellanea documenti turchi*, no. 250.

Published Archival Sources

6 numaralı mühimme defteri (972/1564–65). 3 vols. Ankara: T. C. Başbakanlık, Develt Arşivleri Genel Müdürlüğü, 1995.
'Abdi (Tevki'i), Abdurrahman. "Osmanlı kanunnameleri." *Milli Tetebbu'ler Mecmu'ası* 1, no. 3 (1912): 497–544.
Ahmed Cevdet Paşa. *Mecelle-i aḥkām-ı 'adliye.* Istanbul: Matbaa-yı Osmaniye, 1300 [1883].
———. *Tārīḫ-i Cevdet: tertīb-i cedīt.* 12 vols. Istanbul: Matbaa-yı Osmaniye, 1309 [1893].
Akgündüz, Ahmed. *Osmanlı kanunnameleri ve hukukī tahlilleri.* Vols. 1–9. Istanbul: FEY Vakfı, 1990–94.

Akyıldız, Ali. "Sened-i ittifak'ın ilk tam metni." *İslam araştırmaları dergisi* 2 (1998): 209–22.

Akyıldız, Ali, and Şükrü Hanioğlu. "Negotiating the Power of the Sultan: The Ottoman Sened-i İttifak (Deed of Agreement), 1808." In *The Modern Middle East: A Sourcebook for History*, edited by C. M. Amin, B. C. Fortna, and E. B. Frierson, 22–30. Oxford: Oxford University Press, 2006.

Arif, Mehmed, ed. "Kanunname-yi Al-i Osman: Suret-i hatt-i hümayun-i Mehmed Han." *TOEM* 3, nos. 13–19 (1912).

Ateş, Ahmet. "İstanbul'un fethine dair Fatih Sultan Mehmed tarafından gönderilen mektuplar ve bunlara gelen cevablar." *Tarih dergisi* 4, no. 7 (1953): 11–50.

Banarlı, Nihad Sami, ed. *Dāsitānı tevārīhi mülūki Āl-i Osman ve Cemşit ve Hurşīd mesnevisi XIVüncü asır Anadolu şairlerinden Ahmedīnin Osmanlı tarihi*. İstanbul: n.p., 1939.

Barkan, Ömer Lutfi. "Osmanlı devrinde Akkoyunlu hükümdarı Uzun Hasan Beye ait kanunlar." *Tarih vesikaları* 1–2 (1941): 91–106; 3 (1941): 184–96.

———. *XV ve XVI inci asırlarda Osmanlı imparatorluğunda zira'ī ekonominin hukukī ve malī esasları: kanunlar*. Istanbul: Bürhaneddin Matbaası, 1943.

———. "933–4/1527–8 Mali yılına ait bir Osmanlı bütçesi örneği." *İFM* 15 (1953–4): 251–329.

———. "974–975/1567–1568 mali yılına ait bir Osmanlı bütçesi örneği." *İFM* 19 (August 1957): 276–332.

Bayerle, Gustav. *The Hungarian Letters of Ali Pasha of Buda, 1604–1616*. Budapest: Akadémiai Kiadó, 1991.

———. *Ottoman Diplomacy in Hungary: Letters from the Pashas of Buda, 1590–1593*. Bloomington: Indiana University Press, 1972.

Binark, İsmet, ed. *3 numaralı mühimme defteri* (966–68/1558–60). 2 vols. Ankara: T. C. Başbakanlık, Develt Arşivleri Genel Müdürlüğü, 1993.

———, ed. *7 numaralı mühimme defteri* (975–76/1567–69). 2 vols. Ankara: T. C. Başbakanlık, Develt Arşivleri Genel Müdürlüğü, 1999.

———, ed. *12 numaralı mühimme defteri* (978–79/1570–72). 3 vols. Ankara: T. C. Başbakanlık, Develt Arşivleri Genel Müdürlüğü, 1996.

Binark, İsmet, and G. Necati, eds. *5 numaralı mühimme defteri* (973/1565–66). 2 vols. Ankara: T. C. Başbakanlık, Develt Arşivleri Genel Müdürlüğü, 1994.

Çerçi, Faris, ed. *Gelibolulu Mustafa Āli ve Künhü'l-Aḫbārı*. Vol. 2. Kayseri: Erciyes Üniversitesi Yayınları, 2000.

Düzdağ, Mehmet Ertuğrul. *Şeyhülislām Ebussuūd Efendi fetvaları işiğinda 16*. Istanbul: Enderun Kitabevi, 1972.

Erim, Neşe, and Aslıhan Nakiboğlu. *Gümrük yıllığı: Rüsūmāt salnāmesi*. Ankara: Gümrük ve Ticaret Bakanlığı, 2014.

Fekete, Lajos. *Bevezetés a hódoltság török diplomatikájába*. Budapest: n.p., 1926.

———. *Türkische Schriften aus dem Archive des Palatins Nikolous Esterházy, 1606–1649.* Budapest: n.p., 1932.

Gévay, Antal. *A Budai Pasák.* Bécs (Wein): Strauss, 1841.

Gökbilgin, Mustafa Tayyib. *Kavānīn-i Āl-i 'Os̱mān der ḫülāsa-i mezāmin-i defter-i dīvān.* İstanbul: Enderun Kitabevi, 1979.

———. "Venedik devlet arşıvlarındakı vesika külliyatında Kanunī Süleyman devri belgeler," *Belgeler* I (1964) 1–2: 234.

Güçer, Lütfi. "XVI. yüzyıl sonlarında Osmanlı imparatorluğu dahilinde hububat ticaretinin tabi olduğu kayıtlar." *İFM* 13, no. 1–4 (1952): 79–98.

İnalcık, Halil. "Adaletnameler." *Belgeler* 2, no. 3–4 (1965): 49–145.

———. *Fatih devri üzerinde tetkikler ve vesikalar.* Ankara: Türk Tarih Kurumu Basımevi, 1954.

———. *Hicrī 835 tarihli Sūret-i defter-i sancak-i Arvanid.* Ankara: Türk Tarih Kurumu Basımevi, 1954.

———. "Osmanlı hukukuna giriş: Örf-i sultani hukuk ve fatih'in kanunları." In *Osmanlı imparatorluğu: Toplum ve ekonomi üzerinde arşiv çalışmaları,* 319–43. Istanbul: Eren Yayınevi, 1996.

Káldy-Nagy, Gyula. *Kanuni devri Budin tahrir defteri (1546–1562).* Ankara: Ankara Üniversitesi Basımevi, 1971.

"Kanunname-i cedid." *Milli tetebbu'ler mecmu'ası* 1, no. 1 (1913): 47–112.

Kołodziejczyk, Dariusz. *The Crimean Khanate and Poland-Lithuania International Diplomacy on the European Periphery (15th–18th Century): A Study of Peace Treaties Followed by Annotated Documents.* Leiden: Brill, 2011.

———. *Ottoman-Polish Diplomatic Relations (15th–18th Century): An Annotated Edition of 'ahdnames and Other Documents.* Leiden: Brill, 2000.

Kütükoğlu, Mübahat. *Osmanlılarda narh müessesesi ve 1640 tarihli narh defteri.* Istanbul: Enderun Kitabevi, 1983.

Özcan, Abdülkadir. "Fatih'in teşkilat kanunnamesi ve nıẓām-ı alem için kardeş katlı meselesi." *Tarih dergisi* 33 (1982): 7–56.

———. *Fatih Sultan Mehmed: Kānunnāme-i Āl-i Osman (tahlil ve karşılaştırmalı metin),* xxxv. Istanbul: Kitabevi, 2003.

———, ed. *Kānūnnāme-i Āl-i Osman (tahlil ve karşılaştırmalı metin).* Istanbul: Kitabevi, 2007.

Özel, Oktay. "Avarız ve cizye defterleri." In *Osmanlı devleti'nde bilgi ve istatik,* edited by Şevket Pamuk and Halil İnalcık, 33–50. Ankara: T. C. Başbakanlık Devlet Arşivleri Genel Müdürlüğü, 2000.

Pulaha, Selami, and Yaşar Yücel, eds. *I. Selim kānūnnāmesi (1512–1520) ve XVI. yüzyılın ikinci yarısının kimi kānūnnāmeleri.* Ankara: Türk Tarih Kurumu Yayınları, 1988.

Refik, Ahmed, ed. "Defter-i mevacib-i mülazimin-i Dergah-i Ali, min gürre-i safer ila gayet rebi' al-ahir, sene 883." *TOEM* 8, no. 62 (1335/1916): 5–23.

———, ed. "Matbah-ı Amire [Harc] Defteri (Şaban 878)." *TOEM* 8, no. 62 (1335/1916): 24–58.

Sahillioğlu, Halil. "Bir mültezim zimem defterine göre XV. yüzyıl sonunda Osmanlı darphane mukataaları." *Istanbul Üniversitesi İktisat Fakültesi mecmuası* 23, no. 1–2 (1962): 145–218.

———, ed. *Topkapı Sarayı Arşivi H. 951–952 tarihli ve E-12321 numaralı mühimme defteri.* Istanbul: İslam Tarihi, Sanat ve Kültür Araştırma Merkezi (İRCICA), 2002.

Şahin, İlhan, and Feridun Emecen. *II. Bāyezid dönemine ait 906/1501 tarihli ahkām defteri: Osmanlılarda Dīvān, bürokrasi, ahkām.* Istanbul: Türk Dünyası Araştırmaları Vakfı, 1994.

Şanizade Mehmed Ataullah Efendi. *Şānīzāde tārīhī: 1223–1237/1808–1821.* Edited by Ziya Yılmazer. 2 vols. Istanbul: Çamlıca, 2008.

Sarınay, Yusuf, ed. *82 numaralı mühimme defteri (1026–27/1617–18): özet, transkripsiyon, indeks ve tıpkıbasım.* Ankara: T. C. Başbakanlık, Develt Arşivleri Genel Müdürlüğü, 2000.

———, ed. *83 numaralı mühimme defteri (1036–37/1626–28): özet, transkripsiyon, indeks ve tıpkıbasım.* Ankara: T. C. Başbakanlık, Develt Arşivleri Genel Müdürlüğü, 2002.

———, ed. *85 numaralı mühimme defteri (1040–41/1630–31): özet, transkripsiyon, indeks ve tıpkıbasım.* Ankara: T. C. Başbakanlık, Develt Arşivleri Genel Müdürlüğü, 2001.

Theunissen, Hans. "Ottoman-Venetian Diplomatics: The 'Ahd-names. The Historical Background and the Development of a Category of Political-Commercial Instruments Together with an Annotated Edition of a Corpus of Relevant Documents." *Electronic Journal of Oriental Studies* 1, no. 2 (1988): 1–698.

Topkapı sarayı müzesi Osmanlı saray arşivi kataloğu: fermânlar. Edited by İsmail Hakkı Uzunçarşılı, İbrahim Kemâl Baybura, and Ülkü Altindağ. Ankara: Türk Tarih Kurumu Basımevi, 1985.

Tschudi, Rudolf. *Ein Schreiben Sülejmans I. an Ferdinand I.* Leipzig: Harrassowitz, 1932.

Tveritinova, Anna S. *Qānūnnāme-i Sultān Selīm: Kniga Zakonov Sultana Selima I.* Moscow: Russian Academy of Sciences, 1969.

Tveritinova, Anna S., and Jurij A. Petrosjan, eds. *Badā'i' Al-Waḳā'i'.* Vol. 2. Moscow: Russian Academy of Sciences, 1961.

Yıldırım, Osman. *85 numaralı mühimme defteri (1040–41/1630–32).* Ankara: T. C. Başbakanlık, Develt Arşivleri Genel Müdürlüğü, 2002.

Published Narrative Sources

Ali Bey, ed. *Tevarih-i Āl-i Osman'dan Aşıkpaşazade tarihi.* Istanbul: Matbaa-yi Āmire, 1914.

Anonymous. *Ḥırzü'l-Mülūk.* In *Osmanlı devlet teşkilātına dair kaynaklar.* Edited by Yaşar Yücel. Ankara: Türk Tarih Kurumu, 1988.

———. *Kitāb-ı müstetāb.* In *Osmanlı devlet düzenine ait metinler I,* edited by Yaşar Yücel. Ankara: Ankara Üniversitesi, 1974.

'Arif, Mehmed. "Kanunname-i Al-i Osman." *TOEM,* supp. (1911–12).

Aşıkpaşazade. *Āşıkpaşazāde tārīḫī.* Edited by Necdet Öztürk. Istanbul: Bilgi Kültür Sanat, 2013.

Atsız, Hüseyin Nihal, ed. *Osmanlı tarihleri: Osmanlı tarihinin anakaynakları olan eserlerin, mütehassıslar tarafından hazırlanan metin, tercüme veya sadeleştirilmiş şekilleri külliyatı.* Vol. 1. Istanbul: Türkiye Yayınevi, 1949.

'Ayn-ı 'Ali Efendi. *Ḳavānīn-i āl-i 'Os̱mān der ḫülāsa-ı mezāmīn-i defter-i dīvān.* 1280. Istanbul: Tasvir-Efkar Gazetehanesi, 1863.

Aziz Efendi. *Kānūnnāme-i Sultānī li 'Azīz Efendi: Aziz Efendi's Book of Sultanic Laws and Regulations: An Agenda for Reform by a Seventeenth-Century Ottoman Statesman.* Edited by Rhoads Murphey. Cambridge, MA: Harvard University Press, 1985.

Birnbaum, Eleazar. *The Book of Advice by King Kay Ka'us ibn Iskander: The Earliest Old Ottoman Turkish Version of His Kabusname.* Cambridge, MA: MIT Press, 1981.

Celalzade Mustafa. *Geschichte Sultan Süleymān Ḳānūnīs von 1520 bis 1557, oder, Ṭabaḳāt ül-Memālik ve Derecāt ül-Mesālik.* Edited by Petra Kappert. Wiesbaden: Steiner, 1981.

———. *Kanunī'nin tarihçisinden muhteşem çağ: Kanunī Sultān Süleymān: Ṭabaḳāt ül-memālik ve derecāt ül-mesālik.* Edited by Ayhan Yılmaz. Istanbul: Kariyer Yayıncılık İletişim, 2011.

———. *Selimnāme.* Edited by Ahmet Uğur and Mustafa Çuhadar. Istanbul: Millī Eğitim Bakanlığı Yayınları, 1997.

Domenico Hierosolimitano. *Domenico's Istanbul.* Edited by Michael Austin and Geoffrey Lewis. Warminster, Wiltshire: Printed and published for the E.J.W. Gibb Memorial Trust by Aris and Phillips, 2001.

Duwayhi, Istfan. *Tārīkh al-'zmina 1095–1782.* Edited by Fardinan Tawtal. Beirut: Catholic Press, 1951.

Ertaylan, İsmail Hikmet. *Ahmed-i Dā'ī: Hayatı ve eserleri.* Istanbul: Üçler Basımevi, 1952.

Farabi, Abu Nasr al-. *al-Farabi on the Perfect State: Abū Naṣr al Fārābī's Mabādi' Ārā' Ahl al-Madīna al-Fāḍila: A Revised Text with Introduction, Translation, and Commentary.* Translated by Richard Walzer. Oxford: Oxford University Press, 1985.

———. *Kitāb ārā' ahl al-madīna al-fāḍila.* Edited by Albert Nasri Nadir. Beirut: Catholic Press, 1959.

Feridun Ahmed Bey. *Mecmū'a-yı münşe'āt-ı Ferīdūn Bey.* 2 vols. Istanbul: Daru't-tıba'ati'l Āmire, 1848.

Giese, Frederich, and Nihat Azamat, eds. *Anonim Tevārīh-i Āl-i 'Osman.* Istanbul: Edebiyat Fakültesi Basımevi, 1992.

Hezarfen Hüseyin Efendi. *Telḫīsü'l-beyān fī ḳavānīn-i āl-i 'Os̱mān.* Edited by Sevim İlgürel. Ankara: Türk Tarih Kurumu Basımevi, 1998.

Husayn Va'iz Kashifi. *Ahlāk-i muhsinī*. Translated by Henry George Keene. Hertford: Stephen Austin, 1850.

Hüseyin Tuği. "Vak'a-i Sultan Osman Han." Edited by Midhat Sertoğlu as "Tarih-i Tuği." *Belleten* 43 (1947): 489–514.

Ibn Kannan al-Salihi. *Ḥadā'iq al-yasmīn fī dikr qawānīn al-ḫulafā' wa-'s-salāṭīn*. Edited by 'Abbas Sabbag. Beirut: Dar an-Nafa'is, 1991.

Ibn Khaldun. *Muqaddima*. Edited by 'Abd al-Salam al-Shaddadi. Beirut: Dar al-Bayda', 2005.

———. *The Muqaddima: An Introduction to History*. Translated by Franz Rosenthal. New York: Pantheon Books, 1958.

Ibn Tulun. *'Ilām al-warā bi-man wulliya' nā'iban min al-atrāk bi-Dimashq as-Shām al-kubrā*. Edited by Muhammad Duhman. Damascus: Wazirat al-Thaqafa, 1964.

———. *Mufākahāt al-Khillān fī ḥawādith al-zamān*. Edited by Khalil al-Mansur. Beirut: Dar al-Kutub al-'Ilmiyya, 1998.

Ipşirli, Mehmet. "Hasan Kafi el-Akhisare ve devlet düzenine ait eseri *usulü'l-hikem fi nızām-ı'l-'alem*." *Istanbul Üniversitesi Edebiyat Fakültesi Tarih dergisi*, no. 10–12 (1979–80): 247–78.

Kastritsis, Dimitris. *Ottoman Anonymous Chronicles*. Leiden: Brill, 2012.

Katip Çelebi. *The Balance of Truth (Mizan ül-Hakk)*. Translated and edited by Geoffrey L. Lewis. London: Allen and Unwin, 1957.

———. *Düstürü'l-'amel li ıṣlāhı 'l-ḥalel*. In *Ḳavānīn-i āl-i 'Os̱mān der hulāsa-ı mezāmin-i defter-i dīvān*. 1280. Istanbul: Tasvir-Efvar, 1863.

Kemalpaşazade Ahmed. *Tevārīḫ-i Āl-i 'Osmān. X Defter.* Edited by Şerafettin Severcan. Ankara: Türk Tarih Kurumu, 1996.

Kınalızade 'Ali Çelebi. *Ahlāk-ı ālā'i*. Cairo: Bulak Matbaası, 1832.

———. *Ahlāk-ı ālā'i*. Edited by Mustafa Koç. Istanbul: Türkiye Yazma Eserler Kurumu Başkanlığı, 2014.

Koçu Bey. *Risāle-i Koçi Bey*. Istanbul: Ahmet Vefik Paşa, 1863.

———. *Koçi Bey Risālesi*. Edited by 'Ali Kemalı Aksüt. Istanbul: Vakit Matbaası, 1939.

Kritoboulos Imbriotes. *History of Mehmed the Conqueror*. Edited by Charles T. Riggs. Westport, CT: Greenwood, 1970.

Lameer, Joep, ed. *The Arabic Version of Tusi's Nasirean Ethics: With an Introduction and Explanatory Notes*. Leiden: Brill, 2015.

Lütfi Paşa. *Aṣafnāme*. Edited by Rudolf Tschudi. Berlin: n.p., 1910.

———. *Tevārīḫ-i āl-i 'Os̱mān*. Edited by Ālī Bey. Istanbul: Matbaa-yı Āmire, 1922–23.

al-Mawardi, 'Ali ibn Muhammad. *al-Aḥkām al-sulṭānīyya w'al-wilāyāt al-dīnīyya*. Beirut: Dar al-Kutub al-'Arabi, 1994.

———. *The Ordinances of Government: A Translation of al-Aḥkām al-Sulṭāniyya W' al-Wilāyāt al-Dīniyya*. Translated by Wafaa H. Wahba. London: Center for Muslim Contribution to Civilization; Reading, UK: Garnet, 1996.

Meniński, Franciszek. *Thesaurus linguarum orientalium Turcicae-Arabicae-Persicae*. Edited by Bernhard Freiherr von Jenisch, Franz von Klezl, Stanisław Stachowski, and Mehmet Ölmez. 6 vols. Istanbul: Simurg, 2000.

Mustafa 'Ali. *Künhü'l-aḫbār*. Istanbul: Istanbul Üniversitesi, n.d.

———. *Künhü'l-aḫbārın tezkire kısmı*. Edited by Mustafa İsen. Ankara: Atatürk Kültür, Dil ve Tarih Yüksek Kurumu, 1994.

Na'ima, Mustafa. *Tārīḫ-i Na'īmā*. 9 vols. 1280. Istanbul: Tabhane-i Āmire, 1863.

———. *Tārīḫ-i Na'īmā*. Vol. 3, *1284–1475*. Edited by Mehmed İpşirli. Ankara: Türk Tarih Kurumu, 2007.

Nasir al-Din Tusi. *Muqaddimah-yi qadīm-i akhlāq-i Nāṣirī*. Edited by Jalal al-Din Huma'i. Tehran: Tehran University, 1956.

———. *The Nasirean Ethics*. Translated by G. M. Wickens. London: Allen and Unwin, 1964.

Neşri, Mevlana Mehmed. *Cihānnümā: Osmanlı tarihi (687–890/1288–1485)*. Edited by Necdet Öztürk and Franz Taeschner. Istanbul: Çamlıca, 2008.

———. *Kitāb-ı cihān-nümā: Neşri tarihi*. Edited by Faik Reşit Unat and Mehmed A. Köymen. Ankara: Atatürk Kültür, Dil ve Tarih Yüksek Kurumu, 1996.

Öztürk, Necdet, ed. *Anonim Osmanlı kroniği, 1299–1512*. Istanbul: Türk Dünyası Araştırmaları Vakfı, 2000.

Pakalın, Mehmed Zeki. *Osmanli tarih deyimleri ve terimleri sözlüğü*. 3 vols. Istanbul: Millî Eğitim Basimevi, 1946.

Peçevi İbrahim Efendi. *Tārīḫ-i Peçevī*. 2 vols. Istanbul: Matbaa-yı Amire, 1863–64.

Silay, Kemal, ed. *Dasitān-i tevārīh-i mülūk-i Āl-i Osman*. Cambridge, MA: Harvard University Press, 2004.

Tekin, Şinasi. "Fatih devrine ait bir inşa' mecum'ası." *JTS* 20 (1996): 267–311.

———. *Menāhicü'l-inşa': Yaḥya bin Meḥmed el-kātib'in 15. yy'dan kalma en eski Osmanlıca inşā' el-kitabi*. Cambridge, MA: Orient, 1971.

Tietze, Andreas, ed. *Mustafa 'Ali's Counsel for Sultans of 1581*. 2 vols. Vienna: Österreichischen Akademi der Wissenschaften, 1979.

Toroser, Tayfun, ed. *Kavanin-i yeniçeriyan. (Yeniçeri kanunları)*. Istanbul: Türkiye İş Bankası Kültür Yayınları, 2011.

Tursun Bey. *The History of Mehmed the Conqueror*. Edited by Halil İnalcık and Rhoads Murphey. Minneapolis: Bibliotheca Islamica, 1978.

———. *Tārīḫ-i ebü'l-fetḥ*. Edited by Mertol Tulum. Istanbul: Baha Matbaası, 1977.

Üveys ibn Mehmed Veysi. *Habnāme-i Veysi*. Istanbul: Şeyh Yahya Efendi Matbaası, 1876.

Woodhead, Christine. *Ta'līḳīzāde's Şehnāme-i Hümāyūn: A History of the Ottoman Campaign into Hungary, 1593–94*. Berlin: Klaus Schwarz, 1983.

Yusuf Khass Hajib. *Wisdom of Royal Glory (Kutadgu Bilig): A Turko-Islamic Mirror for Princes*. Translated by Robert Dankoff. Chicago: University of Chicago Press, 1983.

Secondary Studies

Abou-El-Haj, Rifa'at Ali. "Aspects of the Legitimization of Ottoman Rule as Reflected in the Preambles of Two Early Liva Kanunnameler." *Turcica* 23 (1991): 371–83.

———. *The Expression of Ottoman Political Culture in the Literature of Advice to Princes (Nasihatnameler) Sixteenth to Twentieth Centuries.* Calcutta: Anthropological Survey of India, 1995.

———. *Formation of the Modern State: The Ottoman Empire, Sixteenth to Eighteenth Centuries.* Albany: State University of New York Press, 1991.

———. "The Ottoman Nasihatname as a Discourse over Morality." In *Mélanges Professeur Robert Mantran*, edited by A. Temini, 17–30. Zaghouan, Tunis: Centre d'Etudes et de Recherches Ottomanes, Morisques, de Documentation et d'Information, 1988.

Abu-Husayn, Abdul Rahim. "The *Iltizam* of Mansur Furaykh: A Case Study of *Iltizam* in Sixteenth Century Syria." In *Land Tenure and Social Transformation in the Middle East*, edited by Tarif Khalidi, 249–56. Beirut: American University of Beirut, 1984.

———. "The Ottoman Invasion of the Shuf in 1585: A Reconsideration." *al-Abhath* 32 (1985): 13–21.

———. *Provincial Leaderships in Syria, 1575–1650.* Beirut: American University of Beirut, 1985.

———. *The View from Istanbul: Ottoman Lebanon and the Druze Emirate.* New York: Centre for Lebanese Studies in association with I. B. Tauris, 2004.

Abulafia, David. *The Mediterranean in History.* Los Angeles: J. Paul Getty Museum. 2003.

Abu-Lughod, Janet L. *Before European Hegemony: The World System A.D., 1250–1350.* New York: Oxford University Press, 1989.

Adamson, John. "The Making of the Ancien Régime Court, 1600–1700." In Adamson, *The Princely Courts of Europe*, 7–41.

Adamson, John, ed. *The Princely Courts of Europe: Ritual, Politics and Culture Under the Ancien Régime 1500–1750.* London: Weidenfeld and Nicolson, 1999.

Ágoston, Gábor. "The Costs of the Ottoman Fortress-System in Hungary in the Sixteenth and Seventeenth Centuries." In Dávid and Fodor, *Ottomans, Hungarians, and Habsburgs in Central Europe*, 195–228.

———. *Guns for the Sultan: Military Power and the Weapons Industry in the Ottoman Empire.* New York: Cambridge University Press, 2004.

———. "Information, Ideology, and Limits of Imperial Policy: Ottoman Grand Strategy in the Context of Ottoman-Habsburg Rivalry." In Aksan and Goffman, *The Early Modern Ottomans*, 75–103.

———. "Muslim Cultural Enclaves in Hungary Under Ottoman Rule." *AOASH* 45, no. 2–3 (1991): 181–204.

Ahmad, Aijaz. "*Orientalism* and After: Ambivalence and Metropolitan Location in the

Work of Edward Said." In *In Theory: Classes, Nations, Literatures*, 159–219, 333–37. London: Verso, 1992.

Akdağ, Mustafa. *Celālī İsyanları*. Ankara: Üniversitesi Basımevi, 1963.

———. "Genel çizgilerle XVII: Yüzyıl Türkiye Tarihi." *Tarih araştırmaları dergisi* 4 (1966): 201–47.

Aksan, Virginia H. "Locating the Ottomans Among Early Modern Empires." *Journal of Early Modern History* 3, no. 2 (1999): 103–34.

Aksan, Virginia H., and Daniel Goffman, eds. *The Early Modern Ottomans: Remapping the Empire*. Cambridge: Cambridge University Press, 2007.

Akün, Ömer Faruk. "Koçi Bey." *TDVİA*. Vol. 26, 143–48.

Alam, Muzaffar. *The Languages of Political Islam: India, 1200–1800*. Chicago: University of Chicago Press, 2004.

Al-Azmeh, Aziz. "God's Caravan: Topoi and Schemata in the History of Muslim Political Thought." In *Mirror for the Muslim Prince: Islam and the Theory of Statecraft*, edited by Mehrzad Boroujerdi, 326–97. Syracuse, NY: Syracuse University Press, 2013.

———. *Ibn Khaldūn in Modern Scholarship: A Study in Orientalism*. London: Third World Center, 1981.

———. *Muslim Kingship: Power and the Sacred in Muslim, Christian, and Pagan Polities*. London: I. B. Tauris, 1997.

Almási, Gábor. *The Uses of Humanism: Johannes Sambucus (1531–1584), Andreas Dudith (1533–1589), and the Republic of Letters in East Central Europe*. Leiden: Brill, 2009.

Alvi, Sajida S. *Advice on the Art of Governance: An Indo-Islamic Mirror for Princes: Mau'iẓah-i Jahāngīrī of Muḥammad Bāqir Najm-i Sānī*. Albany: State University of New York Press, 1989.

Anderson, Perry. *Lineages of the Absolutist State*. London: Verso, 1979.

Andrews, Walter G. *Poetry's Voice, Society's Song: Ottoman Lyric Poetry*. Seattle: University of Washington Press, 1985.

———. "Singing the Alienated 'I': Guttari, Deleuze, and Lyrical Decodings of the Subject in Ottoman *Divan* Poetry." *Yale Journal of Criticism* 6 (1993): 191–219.

Andrews, Walter G., and Irene Markoff. "Poetry, the Arts, and Group Ethos in the Ideology of the Ottoman Empire." *Edebiyat*, n.s., 1 (1987): 28–70.

Anhegger, Robert. "Hezarfen Hüseyin Efendi'nin Osmanlı Devlet Teşkilatına Dair Mülahazaları." *Türkiyat mecmuası* 10 (1953): 365–93.

Arı, Bülent. "Early Ottoman Diplomacy: Ad Hoc Period." In *Ottoman Diplomacy: Conventional or Unconventional?* edited by A. Nuri Yurdusev, 36–65. Basingstoke, Hampshire: Palgrave Macmillan, 2004.

Arıcanlı, Tosun, and Mara Thomas. "Sidestepping Capitalism: On the Ottoman Road to Elsewhere." *Journal of Historical Sociology* 7, no. 1 (1994): 25–48.

Artan, Tülay. "Questions of Ottoman Identity and Architectural History." In *Rethinking*

Architectural Historiography, edited by Dana Arnold, Elvan Altan Ergut, and Belgin Turan Özkaya, 86–109. London: Routledge, 2006.

Asch, Ronald G. "Introduction: Court and Household from the Fifteenth to the Seventeenth Centuries." In Asch and Birke, *Princes, Patronage, and the Nobility*, 7–41.

Asch, Ronald G., and Adolf M. Birke, eds. *Princes, Patronage, and the Nobility: The Court at the Beginning of the Modern Age, c. 1450–1650*. Oxford: Oxford University Press, 1991.

Ashtor, Eliyahu. "The Venetian Cotton Trade in Syria in the Later Middle Ages." *Studia Medievali* 17 (1973): 675–715.

Aston, Trevor. *Crisis in Europe: The General Crisis of the Seventeenth Century*, edited by Geoffrey Parker and Lesley M. Smith. London: Routledge, 1978.

Atasoy, Nurhan. "Ottoman Garden Pavilions and Tents." *Muqarnas* 21 (Jan. 2004): 15–19.

Atçıl, Abdurrahman. "The Formation of the Ottoman Learned Class and Legal Scholarship." PhD diss., University of Chicago, 2010.

———. *Scholars and Sultans in the Early Modern Ottoman Empire*. Cambridge: Cambridge University Press, 2017.

Atçıl, Muhammet Zahit. "State and Government in the Mid-Sixteenth Century Ottoman Empire: The Grand Vizierates of Rüstem Pasha (1541–1561)." PhD diss., University of Chicago, 2015.

Atiyas, Ekin Tuşalp. "The 'Sunna-Minded' Trend." In Sariyannis, *Ottoman Political Thought*, 98–122.

Atwell, William S. "Some Observations on the 'Seventeenth-Century Crisis' in China and Japan." *Journal of Asian Studies* 45, no.2 (1986): 223–44.

Ayalon, David. "The Great Yāsa of Chingiz Khān. A Reexamination (Part A)." *SI*, no. 33 (Jan. 1971): 97–140.

———. "The Great Yāsa of Chingiz Khān. A Reexamination (Part B)." *SI*, no. 34 (Jan. 1971): 151–80.

———. "The Great Yāsa of Chingiz Khān. A Reexamination (Part C1)." *SI*, no. 36 (Jan. 1972): 113–58.

———. "The Great Yāsa of Chingiz Khān: A Reexamination (Part C2). Al-Maqrīzī's Passage on the Yāsa Under the Mamluks." *SI*, no. 38 (Jan. 1973): 107–56.

Avcioğlu, Nebahat. "Istanbul: The Palimpsest City in Search of Its Architext." *RES: Anthropology and Aesthetics*, no. 53/54 (April 2008): 190–210.

Babinger, Franz. *Die grossherrliche Tughra: Ein Beitag zur Geschichte des Osmanishen Urkundenwessens*. Leipzig: Verlag, 1925.

———. "Nishandji." *EI2*.

Baillie, Hugh Murray. "Etiquette and the Planning of the State Apartments in Baroque Palaces." *Archaeologia (2nd series)* 101 (January 1967): 169–99.

Bak, János. "The Late Medieval Period, 1382–1526." In *A History of Hungary*, edited by Peter F Sugar, Péter Hanák, and Tibor Frank, 54–82. Bloomington: Indiana University Press, 1990.

Bakhit, Adnan. "Aḥdāth Bilād Ṭrāblus al-Shām." *Majallat majma' al-lugha al-'arabiyya al-Urdunī* 1 (1978): 179–91.

———. *The Ottoman Province of Damascus in the Sixteenth Century.* Beirut: Librairie du Liban, 1982.

Bakhtin, M. M. *The Dialogic Imagination: Four Essays.* Edited by Michael Holquist. Austin: University of Texas Press, 1981.

———. "The Problem of Speech Genres." In *Speech Genres and Other Late Essays.* Edited by Caryl Emerson and Michael Holquist. Translated by Vern W. McGee, 60–102. Austin: University of Texas Press, 1986.

———. "The Problem of the Text in Linguistics, Philology, and the Human Sciences: An Experiment in Philosophical Analysis." In *Speech Genres and Other Late Essays.* Edited by Caryl Emerson and Michael Holquist. Translated by Vern W. McGee, 103–31. Austin: University of Texas Press, 1986.

Balabanlilar, Lisa. "Lords of the Auspicious Conjunction: Turco-Mongol Imperial Identity on the Subcontinent." *Journal of World History* 18, no. 1 (2007): 1–39.

Bang, Peter Fibiger, and Dariusz Kołodziejczyk. "'Elephant of India': Universal Empire Through Time and Across Cultures." In Bang and Kołodziejczyk, *Universal Empire,* 1–40.

———, eds. *Universal Empire: A Comparative Approach to Imperial Culture and Representation in Eurasian History.* Cambridge: Cambridge University Press, 2012.

Baramova, Maria, Plamen Mitev, Ivan Parvev, and Vania Racheva, eds. *Power and Influence in South-Eastern Europe, 16th–19th Century.* Berlin: Lit Verlag, 2013.

Barkan, Ömer Lütfi. "Bir iskān ve kolonizasyon metodu olarak sürgünler." *İktisat Fakültesi mecmuası* 11–15 (1949–54): 523–69.

———. "Feodal düzen ve osmanlı timarı." *Hacettepe Üniversitesi Türkiye İktisat Tarihi semineri.* Ankara, 8–10 Hazıran, 1973. 1–32.

———. "Osmanlı imparatorluğunda bir iskān ve kolonizasyon metodu olarak vakıflar ve temlikler." *VD* 2 (1942): 279–387.

———. "The Price Revolution of the Sixteenth Century: A Turning Point in the Economic History of the Near East." *IJMES* 6 (1975) : 3–28.

———. "Şer'i miras hukuku ve evlatlık vakıflar." *Toplu eserler,* 209–30, 249–80. İstanbul: Gözlem Yayınları, 1980.

———. *Türkiye'de toprak meselesi.* Istanbul: Gözlem Yayınları, 1980.

Barker, Rodney. *Legitimating Identities: The Self-Presentations of Rulers and Subjects.* Cambridge: Cambridge University Press, 2001.

———. *Political Legitimacy and the State.* Oxford: Clarendon, 1990.

Barkey, Karen, and Roman van Rossem. "Networks of Contention: Villages and Regional Structure in the Seventeenth Century Ottoman Empire." *American Journal of Sociology* 102 (1997): 1345–82.

Barkey, Karen, and Mark von Hagen, eds. *After Empire: Multiethnic Societies and*

Nation-Building, the Soviet Union and the Russian, Ottoman, and Habsburg Empires. Colorado: Westview, 1997.

———. *Bandits and Bureaucrats: The Ottoman Route to State Centralization.* Ithaca, NY: Cornell University Press, 1994.

———. *Empire of Difference: The Ottomans in Comparative Perspective.* Cambridge: Cambridge University Press, 2008.

Barnes, John Robert. *An Introduction to Religious Foundations in the Ottoman Empire.* Leiden: Brill, 1986.

Barta, Gábor. "A Forgotten Theatre of War, 1526–1528 (Historical Events Preceding the Ottoman-Hungarian Alliance of 1528)." In Dávid and Fodor, *Hungarian-Ottoman Military and Diplomatic Relations*, 93–130.

Bashir, Shahzad. "Deciphering the Cosmos from Creation to Apocalypse: The Hurufiyya Movement and Medieval Islamic Esotericism." In *Imagining the End Visions of Apocalypse from the Ancient Middle East to Modern America*, edited by Abbas Amanat and Magnus Thorkell Bernhardsson, 168–84. London: I. B. Tauris, 2002.

Batuman, Bülent. "'Everywhere Is Taksim' The Politics of Public Space from Nation-Building to Neoliberal Islamism and Beyond." *Journal of Urban History* 41, no. 5 (2015): 881–907.

Batuman, Elif. "Ottomania: A Hit TV Show Reimagines Turkey's Imperial Past." *New Yorker*, Feb. 17 and 24, 2017.

Bayerle, Gustav. "The Compromise at Zsitvatorok." *AO* 6 (1980): 5–53.

———. "Ottoman Records in the Hungarian Archives." *AO* 4 (1972): 5–22.

———. *Ottoman Tributes in Hungary According to Sixteenth Century Tapu Registers of Novigrad.* Berlin: De Gruyter Mouton, 1973.

Bayly, Christopher A. *Empire and Information: Intelligence Gathering and Social Communication in India, 1780–1870.* Cambridge: Cambridge University Press, 1996.

Benton, Lauren A. *A Search for Sovereignty: Law and Geography in European Empires, 1400–1900.* Cambridge: Cambridge University Press, 2010.

Berry, Mary Elizabeth. *Japan in Print: Information and Nation in the Early Modern Period.* Berkeley: University of California Press, 2006.

Birnbaum, Marianna D. *The Orb and the Pen: Janus Pannonius, Matthias Corvinus and the Buda Court.* Budapest: Balassi, 1996.

Bisaha, Nancy. *Creating East and West: Renaissance Humanists and the Ottoman Turks.* Philadelphia: University of Pennsylvania Press, 2004.

Black, Antony. *The History of Islamic Political Thought: From the Prophet to the Present.* New York: Routledge, 2001.

Blake, Stephen P. *Time in Early Modern Islam: Calendar, Ceremony, and Chronology in the Safavid, Mughal, and Ottoman Empires.* Cambridge: Cambridge University Press, 2013.

Blessing, Patricia. "Introduction: Reframing the Lands of Rūm." In *Rebuilding Anatolia*

After the Mongol Conquest: Islamic Architecture in the Lands of Rūm, 1240–1330, 1–20. Burlington, VT: Ashgate Variorum, 2014.

Börekçi, Günhan. "Ibrahim I." Edited by Gábor Ágoston and Bruce Masters. *Encyclopedia of the Ottoman Empire*. New York: Facts on File, 2009.

Bourdieu, Pierre. *Outline of a Theory of Practice*. Cambridge: Cambridge University Press, 1977.

Bosworth, C. E. "Siyāsa." *EI2*.

Boyar, Ebru, and Kate Fleet. *A Social History of Ottoman Istanbul*. Cambridge: Cambridge University Press, 2010.

Boyden, James M. *The Courtier and the King: Ruy Gómez de Silva, Philip II, and the Court of Spain*. Berkeley: University of California Press, 1995.

Bozdoğan, Sibel, Julia Bailey, and Gülru Necipoğlu. *History and Ideology: Architectural Heritage of the "Lands of Rum."* Leiden: Brill, 2007.

Braudel, Fernand. *The Mediterranean and the Mediterranean World in the Age of Philip II*. New York: Harper and Row, 1976.

Brown, Leon Carl. *Religion and State: The Muslim Approach to Politics*. New York: Columbia University Press, 2000.

Brummett, Palmira. "Classifying Ottoman Mutiny: The Act and Vision of Rebellion." *Turkish Studies Association Bulletin* 22, no. 1 (1998): 91–107.

———. "A Kiss Is Just a Kiss: Rituals of Submission Along the East-West Divide." In *Cultural Encounters Between East and West, 1453–1699*, edited by Matthew Birchwood and Matthew Dimmock, 107–31. Newcastle: Cambridge Scholars, 2005.

———. *Mapping the Ottomans: Sovereignty, Territory, and Identity in the Early Modern Mediterranean*. New York: Cambridge University Press, 2015.

———. *Ottoman Seapower and Levantine Diplomacy in the Age of Discovery*. Albany: State University of New York Press, 1994.

Burak, Guy. "Between the Ḳānūn of Qāytbāy and Ottoman Yasaq: A Note on the Ottomans' Dynastic Law." *Journal of Islamic Studies* 26, no. 1 (2015): 1–23.

———. "Evidentiary Truth Claims, Imperial Registers, and the Ottoman Archive: Contending Legal Views of Archival and Record-Keeping Practices in Ottoman Greater Syria (17th–19th Centuries)." *BSOAS* 70, no. 2 (2016): 233–54.

———. "Qānūn." *Oxford Encyclopedia of Islam and Law*. Forthcoming on Oxford Islamic Studies Online, oxfordislamicstudies.com.

———. *The Second Formation of Islamic Law: The Hanafi School in the Early Modern Ottoman Empire*. New York: Cambridge University Press, 2015.

———. "The Second Formation of Islamic Law: The Post-Mongol Context of the Ottoman Adoption of a School of Law." *Comparative Studies in Society and History* 55, no. 3 (July 2013): 579–602.

Burke, Peter. *Languages and Communities in Early Modern Europe*. Cambridge: Cambridge University Press, 2004.

Burns, Kathryn. *Into the Archive: Writing and Power in Colonial Peru.* Durham, NC: Duke University Press, 2010.

Buzov, Snjezana. "The Lawgiver and His Lawmakers: The Role of Legal Discourse in the Change of Ottoman Imperial Culture." PhD diss., University of Chicago, 2005.

Çağatay, Neşet. "İslamda vakıf kurumunun miras hukukuna etkisi." *VD* 11 (1977): 1–7.

———. "An Outline of Islamic Law and Different Applications of Some of Its Rules by the Ottomans." *Belleten* 51 (1987): 637–49.

Cahen, Claude. *The Formation of Turkey: The Seljukid Sultanate of Rūm: Eleventh to Fourteenth Century.* Translated by P. M. Holt. Harlow, England: Longman, 2001.

Çakar, Enver. "XVI. yüzyılda şam beylerbeyiliğnin idarī taksimati." *Fırat Üniversitesi Sosyal Bilimler dergisi* 13, no. 1 (2003): 351–74.

———. "Kanuni Sultan Süleyman Kanun-Nāmesine göre 1522 yılında osmanlı imparatorluğu'nun idarī taksimati." *Fırat Üniversitesi Sosyal Bilimler dergisi* 12, no. 1 (2002): 261–82.

Calder, Norman. "Friday Prayer and the Juristic Theory of Government: Sarakhsī, Shīrāzī, Māwardī." *BSOAS* 49 (1986): 35–47.

Cassirer, Ernst. *The Myth of the State.* New Haven, CT: Yale University Press, 1974.

Cavaliero, Roderick. *Ottomania: The Romantics and the Myth of the Islamic Orient.* London: I. B. Tauris, 2013.

Certeau, Michel de. *The Writing of History.* New York: Columbia University Press, 1988.

Çevikel, Nuri. "The Rise of the Ottoman Ayans: A Case Study of the Province of Cyprus During the Eighteenth Century." *IJTS* 15 (2009): 83–94.

Cezar, Yavuz. *Osmanlı maliyesinde bunalım ve değişim dönemi.* Istanbul: Alan Yayıncılık, 1986.

Chakrabarty, Dipesh. "The Muddle of Modernity." *American Historical Review* 116, no. 3 (2011): 663–75.

Chandra, Satish. *Parties and Politics at the Mughal Court, 1707–1740.* New Delhi: Oxford University Press, 2002.

Çiçek, Kemal. "Osmanlı tahrir defterlerinin kullanımında görülen bazı problemler ve metod arayışları." *Türk dünya araştırmaları* 97 (1995): 93–111.

Cipa, Hakki Erdem. "The Centrality of the Periphery: The Rise to Power of Selim I, 1487–1512." PhD diss., Harvard University, 2007.

Çizakça, Murat. "Cash Waqfs of Bursa, 1555–1823." *Journal of the Economic and Social History of the Orient* 38, no. 3 (1995): 313–54.

Connery, Christopher Leigh. *The Empire of the Text: Writing and Authority in Early Imperial China.* Lanham, MD: Rowman and Littlefield, 1998.

Contadini, Anna, and Claire Norton, eds. *The Renaissance and the Ottoman World.* Burlington, VT: Ashgate, 2013.

Cook, M. A., ed. *A History of the Ottoman Empire to 1730.* Cambridge: Cambridge University Press, 1976.

Cook, Michael. *Commanding Right and Forbidding Wrong in Islamic Thought.* Cambridge: Cambridge University Press, 2000.

Cooper, Glen. "Medicine and the Political Body: A Metaphor at the Crossroads of Four Civilizations." Paper delivered at Rutgers University, March 8, 2014.

Coşgel, Metin. "Efficiency and Continuity in Public Finance: The Ottoman System of Taxation." *Review of Social Economy* 33, no. 3 (2004): 329–41.

———. "Ottoman Tax Registers (Tahrir Defterleri)." *Historical Methods* 37 (2004): 87–100.

Coşgel, Metin, Boğaç Ergene, Haggay Etkes, and Thomas J. Miceli. "Crime and Punishment in Ottoman Times: Corruption and Fines." *Journal of Interdisciplinary History* 63, no. 3 (2013): 353–76.

Crone, Patricia. *God's Rule: Government and Islam.* New York: Columbia University Press, 2004.

———. *Medieval Islamic Political Thought.* Edinburgh: Edinburgh University Press, 2005.

———. *Slaves on Horses: The Evolution of the Islamic Polity.* Cambridge: Cambridge University Press, 1980.

Dağlı, Murat. "The Limits of Ottoman Pragmatism." *History and Theory* 52, no. 2 (2013): 194–213.

Danişmend, Ismail Hami. *Izahlı Osmanlı tarihi kronolojisi.* 6 vols. Istanbul: Türkiye Yayınevi, 1971.

Dankoff, Robert. *An Ottoman Mentality: The World of Evliya Çelebi.* Leiden: Brill, 2006.

Dankoff, Robert, and Sooyong. Kim, eds. *An Ottoman Traveller: Selections from the Book of Travels of Evliya Çelebi.* London: Eland, 2011.

Darling, Linda T. *A History of Social Justice and Political Power in the Middle East: The Circle of Justice from Mesopotamia to Globalization.* New York: Routledge, 2013.

———. "*Kanun* and *Kanunname* in Ottoman History and Historiography." Presentation. Toyo Bunko [Oriental Library] Session, Tokyo, Japan, Feb. 22, 2017.

———. "Mirrors for Princes in Europe and the Middle East: A Case of Historiographical Incommensurability." In *East Meets West in the Middle Ages and Early Modern Times: Transcultural Experiences in the Premodern World*, edited by Albrecht Classen, 223–42. Berlin: De Gruyter, 2013.

———. "Nasihatnameler, İcmal Defterleri, and the Timar-Holding Ottoman Elite in the Late Sixteenth Century." *Osmanlı araştırmaları* 63 (2014): 193–226.

———. "Political Change and Political Discourse in the Early Modern Mediterranean World." *Journal of Interdisciplinary History* 38, no. 4 (2008): 505–31.

———. *Revenue-Raising and Legitimacy: Tax Collection and Finance Administration in the Ottoman Empire, 1560–1660.* Leiden: Brill, 1996.

———. "Social Cohesion ('Asabiyya) and Justice in the Late Medieval Middle East." *Comparative Studies in Society and History* 49, no. 2 (1997): 329–57.

Das, Veena. *Life and Words: Violence and the Descent into the Ordinary.* Berkeley: University of California Press, 2008.

Dávid, Géza. "Administration in Ottoman Europe." In *Süleyman the Magnificent and His Age: The Ottoman Empire in the Early Modern World*, edited by İ. Metin Kunt and Christine Woodhead, 71–90. London: Longman, 1995.

———. "Incomes and Possessions of the *Beglerbegis* of Buda in the Sixteenth Century." In *Studies in Demographic and Administrative History of Ottoman Hungary*, 113–28. Istanbul: Isis Press, 1997.

———. "The Mühimme Defteri as a Source for Ottoman-Habsburg Rivalry in the Sixteenth Century." *AO* 20 (2002): 167–209.

———. *Osmanlı Macaristan'ında toplum, ekonomi ve yönetim: 16. yüzyılda Simontornya sancağı.* Istanbul: Tarih Vakfı Yurt Yayınları, 1999.

———. "Ottoman Administrative Strategies in Western Hungary." In *Studies in Ottoman History in Honour of Professor V. L. Ménage*, edited by Colin Heywood, and Colin Imber, 31–43. Istanbul: Isis Press, 1994.

Dávid, Géza, and Pál Fodor, eds. *Hungarian-Ottoman Military and Diplomatic Relations in the Age of Süleyman the Magnificent.* Budapest: Loránd Eötvös University, 1994.

———. "Hungarian-Ottoman Peace Negotiations in 1512–1514." In Dávid and Fodor, *Hungarian-Ottoman Military and Diplomatic Relations*, 9–45.

———. "Hungarian Studies in Ottoman History." In *The Ottomans and the Balkans: A Discussion of Historiography*, edited by Fikret Adanır and Suraiya Faroqhi, 305–50. Leiden: Brill, 2002.

———, eds. *Ottomans, Hungarians, and Habsburgs in Central Europe: The Military Confines in the Era of Ottoman Conquest.* Leiden: Brill, 2000.

———, eds. *Ransom Slavery Along the Ottoman Borders: Early Fifteenth–Early Eighteenth Centuries.* Leiden: Brill, 2007.

Davis, Kathleen. *Periodization and Sovereignty: How Ideas of Feudalism and Secularization Govern the Politics of Time.* Philadelphia: University of Pennsylvania Press, 2008.

Davis, Natalie Zemon. *Fiction in the Archives: Pardon Tales and Their Tellers in Sixteenth-Century France.* Stanford: Stanford University Press, 1987.

Demetriades, Vasilis. "The Tomb of Ghazi Evrenos Bey at Yenitsa and Its Inscription." *BSOAS* 39 (1976): 328–32.

Demirci, Süleyman. *The Functioning of Ottoman Avarız Taxation: An Aspect of the Relationship Between Center and Periphery.* Istanbul: Isis Press, 2009.

Derrida, Jacques. *Archive Fever.* Chicago: University of Chicago Press, 1995.

Dery, David. "'Papereality' and Learning in Bureaucratic Organization." *Administration and Society* 29, no. 6 (1998): 677–89.

Dijkema, F. Th. *The Ottoman Historical Monumental Inscriptions in Edirne.* Leiden: Brill, 1977.

Dirks, Nicholas B. "Colonial Histories and Native Informants: Biography of an

Archive." In *Orientalism and the Postcolonial Predicament: Perspectives on South Asia*, edited by Carol A. Breckenridge and Peter van der Veer, 279–313. Philadelphia: University of Pennsylvania Press, 1993.

Donner, Fred McGraw. *Muhammad and the Believers: At the Origins of Islam*. Cambridge, MA: Belknap Press of Harvard University Press, 2010.

Douglas, Howard A. "Ottoman Historiography and the Literature of 'Decline' of the Sixteenth and Seventeenth Centuries." *Journal of Asian History* 22 (1988): 52–77.

Doumani, Beshara. "Endowing Family: Waqf, Property Devolution, and Gender in Greater Syria, 1800 to 1860." *Comparative Studies in Society and History* 40, no. 1 (1998): 3–41.

———. "Palestinian Islamic Court Records: A Source for Socioeconomic History." *Middle Eastern Studies Association Bulletin* 19 (1985): 155–72.

———. *Rediscovering Palestine: Merchants and Peasants in Jabal Nablus, 1700–1900*. Berkeley: University of California Press, 2000.

Dreyer, Edward L. *Zheng He: China and the Oceans in the Early Ming Dynasty, 1405–1433*. New York: Pearson Longman, 2007.

Duindam, Jeroen Frans Jozef. *Myths of Power: Norbert Elias and the Early Modern European Court*. Amsterdam: Amsterdam University Press, 1994.

———. *Vienna and Versailles: The Courts of Europe's Major Dynastic Rivals, 1550–1780*. Cambridge: Cambridge University Press, 2003.

Duindam, Jeroen, Tülay Artan, and Metin Kunt. *Royal Courts in Dynastic States and Empires: A Global Perspective*. Boston: Brill, 2011.

Dursteler, Eric. *Venetians in Constantinople: Nation, Identity, and Coexistence in the Early Modern Mediterranean*. Baltimore: Johns Hopkins University Press, 2006.

"Early Modernities." *Daedalus* 127, no. 3 (1998).

Ebel, Kathryn A. "Representations of the Frontier in Ottoman Town Views of the Sixteenth Century." *Imago Mundi* 60, no. 1 (2008): 1–22.

Elias, Norbert. *The Civilizing Process*. New York: Urizen, 1978.

Elliott, J. H. "The Court of the Spanish Habsburgs: A Peculiar Institution?" In *Politics and Culture in Early Modern Europe: Essays in Honor of H. G. Koenigsberger*, edited by Phyllis Mack, Margaret C. Jacot, and H. G. Koenigsberger, 142–61. Cambridge: Cambridge University Press, 2002.

———. "The General Crisis in Retrospect: A Debate Without End." In *Early Modern Europe: From Crisis to Stability*, edited by Philip Benedict and Myron P. Gutmann, 21–51. Newark: University of Delaware Press, 2005.

———. *Spain and Its World, 1500–1700*. New Haven, CT: Yale University Press, 1989.

El-Rouayheb, Khaled. *Islamic Intellectual History in the Seventeenth Century: Scholarly Currents in the Ottoman Empire and the Maghreb*. Cambridge: Cambridge University Press, 2015.

Emecen, Feridun. "Osmanlı divanının ana defter serileri: Ahkām-ı miri, ahkām-ı kuyūd-ı mühimme ve ahkām-ı şikāyet." *Türkiye araştırmaları literatür dergisi* 3, no. 5 (2005): 197–239.

———. "Sefere Götürülen Defterlerin Defteri." In *Kütükoğlu'na armağan*, 241–68. Istanbul: Edebiyat Fakültesi Basımevi, 1991.

Emiralioğlu, M. Pinar. *Geographical Knowledge and Imperial Culture in the Early Modern Ottoman Empire.* Burlington, VT: Ashgate, 2014.

Engel, Pál. "The Age of the Angevines, 1301–1382." In *A History of Hungary*, edited by Peter F. Sugar, Péter Hanák, and Tibor Frank, 34–53. Bloomington: Indiana University Press, 1990.

———. *The Realm of St Stephen: A History of Medieval Hungary, 895–1526.* London: I. B. Tauris, 2001.

Ergene, Boğaç A. *Local Court, Provincial Society, and Justice in the Ottoman Empire: Legal Practice and Dispute Resolution in Çankırı and Kastamonu (1652–1744).* Leiden: Brill, 2003.

———. "On Ottoman Justice: Interpretations in Conflict (1600–1800)." *Islamic Law and Society* 8, no. 1 (2001): 52–87.

Ergin, Nina, Christoph K Neumann, and Amy Singer, eds. *Feeding People, Feeding Power: Imarets in the Ottoman Empire.* Istanbul: Eren, 2007.

Erhan, Afyoncu. "Defter Emini." *TDVİA.* Vol. 9, 91–93.

Erim, Neşe. *İktisadi düşünce tarihi.* Ankara: Palme Yayıncılık, 2007.

Ertu, Zeynep Tarim. "The Depiction of Ceremonies in Ottoman Miniatures: Historical Record or a Matter of Protocol?" *Muqarnas* 27 (2010): 251–75.

Evans, Robert John Weston. "The Court: A Protean Institution and an Elusive Subject." In Asch and Birke, *Princes, Patronage, and the Nobility*, 481–91.

Fakhry, Majid. *Ethical Theories in Islam.* Leiden: Brill, 1991.

Farah, Caesar E., ed. *Decision Making and Change in the Ottoman Empire.* Kirksville: Thomas Jefferson University Press at Northeast Missouri State University, 1993.

Faroqhi, Suraiya. "Camels, Wagons, and the Ottoman State in the Sixteenth and Seventeenth Centuries." *IJMES* 14, no. 4 (1982): 523–39.

———. "Crisis and Change, 1590–1699." In İnalcık and Quataert, *An Economic and Social History of the Ottoman Empire*, 411–636.

———. *Making a Living in the Ottoman Lands, 1480 to 1820.* Istanbul: Isis Press, 1995.

———. *Men of Modest Substance: House Owners and House Property in Seventeenth-Century Ankara and Kayseri.* Cambridge: Cambridge University Press, 1987.

———. *The Ottoman Empire and the World Around It.* London; New York: I. B. Tauris, 2004.

———. "Political Activity Among Ottoman Taxpayers and the Problem of Sultanic Legitimation (1570–1650)." *Journal of the Economic and Social History of the Orient* 35, no. 1 (1992): 1–39. https://doi.org/10.2307/3632686.

———. "Trade and Revenue Collection in Later Sixteenth-Century Salonica." *Oriente Moderno*, n.s., 20 (81), no. 1 (2001): 97–108.

Faroqhi, Suraiya, Gül Çağalı Güven, and Özgür Türesay. *Osmanlı dünyasında üretmek, pazarlamak, yaşamak*. İstanbul: YKY, 2003.

Fekete, Lajos. *Buda and Pest Under Turkish Rule*. Budapest: n.p., 1976.

———. "Tughra." *EI2*.

Ferguson, Heather. "Genres of Power: Constructing a Discourse of Decline in Ottoman *Nasihatname*." *Osmanlı Araştırmaları* 35 (2010): 81–116.

———. "Ottomans, Ottomanists, and the State: Redefining an Ethos of Power in the Long Sixteenth Century." In *Political Thought and Practice in the Ottoman Empire, Halcyon Days of Crete 9*, edited by Marinos Sariyannis. Crete: Crete University Press, forthcoming (2018).

Fetvacı, Emine. "From Print to Trace: An Ottoman Imperial Portrait Book and Its Western European Models." *Art Bulletin* 95, no. 2 (2013): 243–68.

———. "Office of the Ottoman Court Historian." In *Studies on Istanbul and Beyond*, edited by Robert G. Ousterhout, 7–21. Philadelphia: University of Pennsylvania Press, 2007.

———. *Picturing History at the Ottoman Court*. Bloomington: Indiana University Press, 2013.

Finkel, Caroline. "The Administration of Warfare: The Ottoman Campaigns in Hungary, 1593–1606." PhD diss., University of London, School of Oriental and African Studies, 1986. http://search.proquest.com.ccl.idm.oclc.org/docview/301450960?pq-origsite=summon.

———. *The Administration of Warfare: The Ottoman Military Campaigns in Hungary, 1593–1606*. Wien: VWGÖ, 1988.

———. *Osman's Dream: The Story of the Ottoman Empire, 1300–1923*. New York: Basic Books, 2006.

Finlay, Robert. "'I Am the Servant of the Turkish Sultan': Venice, the Ottoman Empire, and Christendom, 1523–1534." In *Venice Besieged: Politics and Diplomacy During the Italian Wars, 1494–1534*, 1–45. Aldershot: Ashgate Variorum, 2008.

———. "Prophecy and Politics in Istanbul: Charles V, Sultan Suleyman, and the Habsburg Embassy of 1533–1534." *Journal of Early Modern History* 2, no. 1 (1998): 1–31.

Fisher, Alan. *A Precarious Balance: Conflict, Trade, and Diplomacy on the Russian-Ottoman Frontier*. Istanbul: Isis Press, 1999.

Fleet, Kate. "Tax-Farming in the Early Ottoman State." *Medieval History Journal* 6, no. 2 (2003): 249–58.

Fleischer, Cornell H. *Bureaucrat and Intellectual in the Ottoman Empire: The Historian Mustafa Âli (1541–1600)*. Princeton, NJ: Princeton University Press, 1986.

———. "The Lawgiver as Messiah: The Making of the Imperial Image in the Reign of Süleyman." In *Soliman Le Magnifique et Son Temps, Actes Du Colloque de Paris*, edited by Gilles Veinstein, 159–77. Paris: La Documentation Française, 1992.

———. "Mahdi and Millennium: Messianic Dimensions in the Development of Ottoman Imperial Ideology." In *The Great Ottoman-Turkish Civilization*, edited by Kemal Çiçek, 42–54. Ankara: Yeni Türkiye, 2000.

———. "Preliminaries to the Study of Ottoman Bureaucracy." *JTS* 10 (1986): 135–41.

———. "Royal Authority, Dynastic Cyclism, and 'Ibn Khaldûnism' in Sixteenth-Century Ottoman Letters." *Journal of Asian and African Studies* 18, no. 3–4 (1983): 198–220.

———. "Seer to the Sultan: Haydar Remmal and Sultan Süleyman." In *Cultural Horizons: A Festschrift in Honor of Talat S. Halman*, edited by Jayne L. Warner, 290–99. Syracuse, NY: Syracuse University Press, 2001.

Floor, Willem M. *A Fiscal History of Iran in the Safavid and Qajar Periods, 1500–1925*. New York: Bibliotheca Persica Press, 1998.

Fodor, Pál. "The Way of a Seljuq Institution to Hungary: The Cereḫōr." *AOASH* 38, no. 3 (1984): 367–99.

———. "State and Society, Crisis and Reform, in 15th–17th Century Ottoman Mirror for Princes." *AOASH* 40, no. 2/3 (1986): 217–40.

———. "The Grand Vizieral Telhis: A Study in the Ottoman Central Administration, 1566–1656." *AO* 15 (1997): 137–88.

———. *In Quest of the Golden Apple: Imperial Ideology, Politics, and Military Administration in the Ottoman Empire*. Istanbul: Isis Press, 2000.

———. "Making a Living on the Frontiers: Volunteers in the Sixteenth-Century Ottoman Army." In Dávid and Fodor, *Ottomans, Hungarians, and Habsburgs in Central Europe*, 228–63.

Foucault, Michel. *The Archaeology of Knowledge and the Discourse on Language*. New York: Pantheon, 1982.

———. *The Essential Works of Foucault, 1954–1984: Aesthetics, Method, and Epistemology*. Edited by James D. Faubion and Paul Rabinow. 3 vols. New York: New Press, 1998.

———. *The Order of Things: An Archaeology of the Human Sciences*. New York: Vintage, 1994.

Fowden, Elizabeth Key, and Garth Fowden. *Contextualizing Late Greek Philosophy*. Athens: Diffusion de Boccard, 2008.

Fowden, Garth. *Before and After Muḥammad: The First Millennium Refocused*. Princeton, NJ: Princeton University Press. 2014.

———. "Pseudo-Aristotelian Politics and Theology in Islam." In Bang and Kołodziejczyk, *Universal Empire*, 130–48.

Furlanetto, Elena. "'Imagine a Country Where We Are All Equal': Imperial Nostalgia in Turkey and Elif Shafak's Ottoman Utopia." In *Post-Empire Imaginaries?* edited by Barbara Buchenau and Virginia Richter, 159–80. Leiden: Brill, 2015.

Gabrieli, Francesco. "'Aṣabiyya." *EI2*.

Genç, Mehmet. "Osmanlı maliyesinde *malikane* sistemi." In *İktisat tarihi semineri*, edited by Osman Okyar and Ünal Nalbantoğlu, 231–96. Ankara: Hacettepe Üniversitesi Yayınları, 1975.

———. "A Study of the Feasibility of Using Eighteenth-Century Ottoman Financial Records as an Indication of Economic Activity." In *The Ottoman Empire and the World Economy*, edited by Huri Islamoğlu-İnan, 345–73. Cambridge: Cambridge University Press; Paris: Maison des sciences de l'homme, 1987.

Gerber, Haim. *Islamic Law and Culture, 1600–1840*. Leiden: Brill, 1999.

Ghazali, al-. *Book of Counsel for Kings: Naṣīhāt al-mulūk*. Edited by Jalal Huma'i and H. D. Isaacs. Translated by F. R. Bagley. London: Oxford University Press, 1964.

Gibb, H. A. R. "al-Māwardi's Theory of the Caliphate." In *Studies on the Civilization of Islam*, edited by Stanford J. Shaw and William R. Polk, 151–65. Boston: Beacon, 1962.

———. "The Islamic Background of Ibn Khaldūn's Political Theory." *Bulletin of School of Oriental Studies, University of London* 7 (1933): 23–31.

Ginzburg, Carlo. *The Cheese and the Worms: The Cosmos of a Sixteenth-Century Miller*. Baltimore: Johns Hopkins University Press, 1980.

Goffman, Daniel. *Izmir and the Levantine World, 1550–1650*. Seattle: University of Washington Press, 1990.

———. "Negotiating with the Renaissance State: The Ottoman Empire and the New Diplomacy." In Aksan and Goffman, *The Early Modern Ottomans*, 61–74.

———. *The Ottoman Empire and Early Modern Europe*. Cambridge: Cambridge University Press, 2002.

Gökbilgin, M. Tayyib. "XVII. asrıda Osmanlı devletinde islâhat ihtiyaç ve temayülleri ve Kâtip Çelebi." In *Kâtip Çelebi: Hayatı ve eserleri hakkında incelemeler*, 197–218. Ankara: Türk Tarih Kurumu, 1957.

———. *Ayn-ı Ali risalesi ve Osmanlı imparatorluğu teşkilat ve müesseselerini aydınlatmaktadi büyük önemi*. Istanbul: Enderun Kitabevi, 1979.

———. "Ibrāhīm." *EI3*.

———. "Nişancı." *İA*. Vol. 3, 299–302.

Goldstone, Jack A. "East and West in the Seventeenth Century: Political Crises in Stuart England, Ottoman Turkey, and Ming China." *Comparative Studies in Society and History* 30 (1988): 103–42.

———. *Revolution and Rebellion in the Early Modern World*. Berkeley: University of California Press, 1991.

Grant, Jonathan. "Rethinking the Ottoman 'Decline': Military Technology Diffusion in the Ottoman Empire, Fifteenth to Eighteenth Centuries." *Journal of World History* 10, no. 1 (1999): 179–201.

Greene, Molly. "An Islamic Experiment? Ottoman Land Policy on Crete." *Mediterranean Historical Review* 11, no. 1 (1996): 60–78.

Griswold, William. "Djalālī." *EI2*.

———. *The Great Anatolian Rebellion*. Berlin: Klaus Schwarz, 1983.

Gross, Hanns. *Empire and Sovereignty: A History of the Public Law Literature in the Holy Roman Empire, 1599–1804*. Chicago: University of Chicago Press, 1975.

Güçer, Lütfi. *Osmanlı imparatorluğunda hububat meselesi ve hububattan alınan vergiler*. Istanbul: Sermet Matbaası, 1964.

Gümrükçüoğlu, Okur. "Şikāyet defterlerine göre Osmanlı teb'asının şikāyetleri." *Ankara Üniversitesi Hukuk Fakültesi dergisi* 61, no. 1 (2012): 175–206.

Gürkan, Emrah Safa. "The Efficacy of Ottoman Counter-Intelligence in the 16th Century." *AOASH* 65, no. 1 (2012): 1–38.

Gutas, Dimitri. *Greek Thought, Arabic Culture: The Graeco-Arabic Translation Movement in Baghdad and Early Abbasid Society (2nd–4th/8th–10th Centuries)*. London: Routledge, 1999.

Hagen, Gottfried. "Chaos, Order, Power, Salvation: Heroic Hagiography's Response to the Ottoman Fifteenth Century." *Journal of the Ottoman and Turkish Studies Association* 1, no. 1/2 (2014): 91–109.

———. "Legitimacy and World Order." In *Legitimizing the Order: The Ottoman Rhetoric of State Power*, edited by Hakan T. Karateke and Maurus Reinkowski, 55–83. Leiden: Brill, 2005.

———. "Translations and Translators in a Multilingual Society: A Case Study of Persian-Ottoman Translations, Late Fifteenth to Early Seventeenth Century." *Eurasian Studies* 11, no. 1 (2003): 95–134.

Halasi-Kun, Tibor. "Some Notes on Ottoman 'Mufassal Defter' Studies." *JTS* 10 (1986): 163–66.

Halasi-Kun, Tibor, and Peter B. Golden. *The King's Dictionary: The Rasûlid Hexaglot—Fourteenth Century Vocabularies in Arabic, Persian, Turkic, Greek, Armenian, and Mongol*. Leiden: Brill, 2000.

Hall, John Whitney. "The Muromachi Bakufu." In *The Cambridge History of Japan*. Volume 3, *Medieval Japan*, edited by Kozo Yamamura, 175–230. Cambridge: Cambridge University Press, 1990.

Hallaq, Wael B. *A History of Islamic Legal Theories: An Introduction to Sunnī Uṣūl al-Fiqh*. Cambridge: Cambridge University Press, 1997.

———. *Shari'a Between Past and Present: Theory, Practice and Modern Transformations*. Cambridge: Cambridge University Press, 2009.

———. "What Is Shari'a?" *Yearbook of Islamic and Middle Eastern Law* 12 (2008): 151–80.

Hamadeh, Shirine. *The City's Pleasures: Istanbul in the Eighteenth Century*. Seattle: University of Washington Press, 2008.

———. "Public Spaces and the Garden Culture of Istanbul in the Eighteenth Century." In Aksan and Goffman, *The Early Modern Ottomans*, 277–312.

Hankins, James. "Renaissance Crusaders: Humanist Crusade Literature in the Age of Mehmed II." *Dumbarton Oaks Papers* 49 (1995): 111–207.

Harris, William V. *Rethinking the Mediterranean*. Oxford: Oxford University Press, 2005.

Hathaway, Jane. *The Arab Lands Under Ottoman Rule, 1516–1800*. London: Pearson, 2008.

———, ed. *Mutiny and Rebellion in the Ottoman Empire*. Madison: University of Wisconsin-Madison, 2002.

———. "Problems of Periodization in Ottoman History: The Fifteenth Through the Eighteenth Centuries." *Turkish Studies Association Bulletin* 20, no. 2 (1996): 25–31.

———. "Rewriting Eighteenth-Century Ottoman History." *Mediterranean Historical Review* 19 (2004): 29–53.

———. "The Wealth and Influence of an Exiled Ottoman Eunuch in Egypt: The Waqf Inventory of Abbas Agha." *Journal of the Economic and Social History of the Orient* 37 (1994): 293–319.

Hegyi, Klára. "The Ottoman Military Force in Hungary." In Dávid and Fodor, *Hungarian-Ottoman Military and Diplomatic Relations*, 131–48.

———. "The Ottoman Network of Fortresses in Hungary." In Dávid and Fodor, *Ottomans, Hungarians, and Habsburgs in Central Europe*, 163–93.

Henshall, Nicholas. *The Myth of Absolutism: Change and Continuity in Early Modern European Monarchy*. London: Longman, 1992.

Heyd, Uriel. "Buyuruldu." *EI2*.

———. *Ottoman Documents on Palestine, 1552–1615: A Study of The Firman According to the Mühimme Defteri*. Oxford: Clarendon, 1960.

———. *Studies in Old Ottoman Criminal Law*. Edited by V. L. Ménage. Oxford: Clarendon, 1973.

Hillenbrand, Carole. *Turkish Myth and Muslim Symbol: The Battle of Manzikert*. Edinburgh: Edinburgh University Press, 2007.

Hinz, Walther. "Das Rechnungswesen orientalischer Reichsfinanzämter im Mittelalter." *Der Islam* 29, no. 1 (1950): 1–29.

Hobsbawm, E. J. "The Crisis of the 17th Century—II." *Past and Present*, no. 6 (1954): 44–65.

———. "The General Crisis of the European Economy in the 17th Century." *Past and Present*, no. 5 (1954): 33–53.

Hoexter, Miriam. "Waqf Studies in the Twentieth Century: The State of the Art." *Journal of the Economic and Social History of the Orient* 41, no. 4 (1998): 474–95.

Horden, Peregrine, and Nicholas Purcell, eds. *The Corrupting Sea: A Study of Mediterranean History*. Malden, MA: Blackwell, 2000.

Howard, Douglas A. "From Manual to Literature: Two Texts on the Ottoman Timar System." *AOASH* 61, no. 1–2 (2008): 87–99.

———. "Genre and Myth in the Ottoman Advice for Kings Literature." In Aksan and Goffman, *The Early Modern Ottomans*, 137–66.

———. "The Historical Development of the Ottoman Imperial Registry (Defter-I Hakanî): Mid-Fifteenth to Mid-Seventeenth Centuries." *AO* 11 (1986): 213–30.

———. "Historical Scholarship and the Classical Ottoman Kanunnames." *AO* 14 (1995): 79–107.

Hoyland, Robert G. *In God's Path: The Arab Conquests and the Creation of an Islamic Empire*. Oxford: Oxford University Press, 2015.

Huart, Clément, and Henri Massé. "Huma." *EI2*.

Hurvitz, Nimrod, *Competing Texts: The Relationship Between al-Mawardi's and Abu Ya'la's al-Ahkam al-Sultaniyya*. Cambridge, MA: ILSP, Harvard Law School, 2007.

Ilyan, Juzif. *Banū Sayfā, wulāt Ṭarābulus, 1579–1640*. Beirut: Dar Lahd Khatir, 1987.

Imber, Colin. *Ebu's-su'ud: The Islamic Legal Tradition*. Stanford: Stanford University Press, 1997.

———. "The Law of the Land." In Woodhead, *The Ottoman World*, 41–56.

———. *Studies in Ottoman History and Law*. Istanbul: Isis Press, 1996.

İnalcık, Halil. "The Çift-Hane System: The Organization of Ottoman Rural Society." In *An Economic and Social History of the Ottoman Empire, 1300–1914*, edited by Halil İnalcık and Donald Quataert, 143–54. Cambridge: Cambridge University Press, 1994.

———. "The Emergence of the Big Farms, Çiftliks: State, Landlords and Tenants." In *Landholding and Commercial Agriculture in the Middle East*, edited by Çağlar Keyder and Faruk Tabak, 17–35. Albany, NY: State University of New York Press, 1991.

———. "The Emergence of the Ottomans." In *Cambridge History of Islam, 1: The Central Islamic Lands*, edited by P. M. Holt, Ann K. S. Lambton, and Bernard Lewis, 263–91. Cambridge: Cambridge University Press, 1970.

———. *Essays in Ottoman History*. Beyoğlu, Istanbul: Eren, 1998.

———. "How to Read 'Ashık Pasha-Zade's History." In *Studies in Ottoman History in Honour of Professor V. L. Ménage*, edited by Colin Heywood and Colin Imber, 139–56. Istanbul: Isis Press, 1994.

———. "Islamization of Ottoman Laws on Land and Land Tax." In *Festgabe an Josef Matuz*, edited by Christa Fragner and Klaus Schwarz, 101–19. Berlin: Klaus Schwarz, 1992.

———. "Kanun." *EI2*.

———. "Kānūnnāme." *EI2*.

———. "*Kutagu Bilig*'de Türk ve İran siyaset nazariye ve gelenekleri." In *Reşit Rahmeti Arat için*, 259–75. Ankara: Türk Kültürünü Araştırma Enstitüsü, 1966.

———. "Military and Fiscal Transformation in the Ottoman Empire, 1600–1700." *AO* 6 (1980): 283–337.

———. "Örf." *İA*. Vol. 9, 480.

———. "Osmanlılarda ra'iyyet rüsūmu." In *Osmanlı imparatorluğu: Toplum ve ekonomi üzerinde arşiv çalışmaları*, 31–67. Istanbul: Eren Yayınevi, 1996.

———. "Otman Baba and Fatih Sultan Mehmed." In *Doğu batı makaleler I*, 139–63. Ankara: Doğu Batı Yayınları, 2005.

———. *The Ottoman Empire: The Classical Age, 1300–1600*. New York: Praeger, 1973.

———. "Ottoman Methods of Conquest." *SI*, no. 2 (1954): 103–29.

———. "The Ottoman Succession and Its Relation to the Turkish Concept of Sovereignty." In *The Middle East and the Balkans Under the Ottoman Empire: Essays on Economy and Society*, 37–69. Bloomington: Indiana University Press, 1993.

———. "The Policy of Mehmed II Toward the Greek Population of Istanbul and the Byzantine Buildings of the City." *Dumbarton Oaks Papers* 23/24 (Jan. 1969): 229–49.

———. "The Question of the Emergence of the Ottoman State." *IJTS* 4 (1980): 71–79.

———. "The Re-building of Istanbul by Sultan Mehmed the Conqueror." *Cultura Turcica* 4, no. 1–2 (1967): 5–15.

———. "Reis-ül-Küttāb." *İA*. Vol. 9, 681.

———. "The Rise of Ottoman Historiography." In *Historians of the Middle East*, edited by Bernard Lewis and Peter M. Holt, 152–67. London: Oxford University Press, 1962.

———. "The Ruznamçe Registers of the Kadıasker of Rumeli as Preserved in the Istanbul Müftülük Archives." *Turcica* 20 (1988): 251–75.

———. *Seçme eserleri II, devlet-i aliyye: Osmanlı imparatorluğu üzerine araştırmalar II*. Istanbul: İş Bankası Kültür Yayınları, 2009.

———. "Sened-i ittifak ve Gülhane hatt-ı hümāyūnu." *Belleten* 28 (1962): 603–22.

———. "Şeriat ve Kanun, Din ve Devlet." In *Osmanlı'da devlet, hukuk, adalet*, 39–46. Istanbul: Eren Yayınevi, 2005.

———. "Şikayet hakkı: Arz-ı hal ve arz-ı mahzarlar." *Osmanlı araştırmaları* 7–8 (1988): 33–54.

———. "State and Ideology Under Sultan Suleiman I." In *The Middle East and the Balkans Under the Ottoman Empire: Essays on Economy and Society*, 71–94. Bloomington: Indiana University Press, 1993.

———. "State, Sovereignty and Law During the Reign of Süleymân the Second and His Time." In *Süleymān the Second and His Time*, edited by Halil İnalcık and Cemal Kafadar, 229–48. Istanbul: Isis Press, 1993.

———. "Suleiman the Lawgiver and Ottoman Law." *AO* 1 (1969): 105–38.

———. "Türk-İslām devletlerinde sivil kānūn geleneği." In *Osmanlı'da devlet, hukuk, 'adālet*, 27–36. Istanbul: Eren Yayınevi, 2005.

———. *Yeni vesikalara gore Kırım hanlığının Osmanlı tābiliğine girmese ve ahidname meselesi*. Ankara: Türk Tarih Kurumu Basımevi, 1944.

İnalcık, Halil, and Donald Quataert, eds. *An Economic and Social History of the Ottoman Empire, 1300–1914*. Cambridge: Cambridge University Press, 1994.

İnan, Kenan. "A Summary and Analysis of the Tārīh-i Ebü'l-Feth (History of the Conqueror) of Tursun Bey (1488)." PhD diss., University of Manchester, 1993.

Ingham, Patricia Clare, and Michelle R. Warren, eds. *Postcolonial Moves: Medieval Through Modern*. New York: Palgrave Macmillan, 2003.

İpşirli, Mehmet. "Çivizade Muhyiddin Mehmed Efendi." *TDVİA*. Vol. 8, 348–49.

Islamoğlu, Huri, and Çağlar Keyder. "Agenda for Ottoman History." *Review Fernand Braudel Center* 1 (1977): 31–55.

İslamoğlu, Huricihan. "An Agenda for Comparative History: Law and Property as Aspects of State Power." *METU Studies in Development* 19, no. 4 (1992): 607–20

———, ed. *Constituting Modernity: Private Property in the East and West*. London: I. B. Tauris, 2004.

———. *State and Peasant in the Ottoman Empire: Agrarian Power Relations and Regional Economic Development in Ottoman Anatolia During the Sixteenth Century*. Leiden: Brill, 1994.

Isom-Verhaaren, Christine. *Allies with the Infidel: The Ottoman and French Alliance in the Sixteenth Century*. London: I. B. Tauris, 2011.

Jennings, Ronald C. "Limitations of the Judicial Powers of the Kadi in Seventeenth Century Ottoman Kayser." *SI*, no. 50 (1979): 151–84.

———. "Loans and Credit in the Early 17th Century Ottoman Judicial Records: The Sharia Court of Anatolian Kayseri." *Journal of the Economic and Social History of the Orient* 16, no. 2/3 (1973): 168–216.

———. "Pious Foundations in the Society and Economy of Ottoman Trabzon, 1565–1640: A Study Based on the Judicial Registers (Şer'i Mahkeme Sicilleri) of Trabzon." *Journal of the Economic and Social History of the Orient* 33, no. 3 (1990): 271–336.

Johansen, Baber. *The Islamic Law on Land Tax and Rent: The Peasants' Loss of Property Rights as Interpreted in the Hanafite Legal Literature of the Mamluk and Ottoman Periods*. New York: Croom Helm, 1988.

———. "Legal Literature and the Problem of Change: The Case of the Land Rent." In *Islam and Public Law: Classical and Contemporary Studies*, edited by Chibli Mallat, 29–47. London: Graham and Trotman, 1993.

———. "Sacred and Religious Elements in Hanafite Law—Function and Limits of the Absolute Character of Government Authority." In *Islam et politique au Maghreb*, edited by Ernest G. Gellner et al., 281–303. Paris: Centre national de la recherché scientifique, 1981.

Johnson, Carina L. *Cultural Hierarchy in Sixteenth-Century Europe: The Ottomans and Aztecs*. Cambridge: Cambridge University Press, 2011.

Kafadar, Cemal. *Between Two Worlds the Construction of the Ottoman State*. Berkeley: University of California Press, 1995.

———. "Janissaries and Other Riffraff of Ottoman Istanbul: Rebels Without a Cause?" In *Identity and Identity Formation in the Ottoman World: A Volume of Essays in Honor of Norman Itzkowitz*, edited by Baki Tezcan and Karl K Barbir, 113–34. Madison: University of Wisconsin Press, 2007.

———. "The Myth of the Golden Age: Ottoman Historical Consciousness in the Post-Süleymânic Era." In *Süleymân the Second and His Time*, edited by Halil İnalcık and Cemal Kafadar, 45–57. Istanbul: Isis Press, 1993.

———. "On the Purity and Corruption of the Janissaries." *Turkish Studies Association Bulletin* 15, no. 2 (1991): 273–80.

———. "The Question of Ottoman Decline." *Harvard Middle Eastern and Islamic Review*, 4, no. 1–2 (1997–98): 30–75.

———. "A Rome of One's Own: Reflections on Cultural Geography and Identity in the Lands of Rum." *Muqarnas* 24 (2007): 7–26.

Kafescioğlu, Çiğdem. *Constantinopolis/Istanbul: Cultural Encounter, Imperial Vision, and the Construction of the Ottoman Capital.* University Park: University of Pennsylvania Press, 2009.

Káldy-Nagy, Gyula. "VI. yüzyılda Osmanlı ımparatorluğunda merkezi yönetimin başlıca sorunlar." *Ankara Üniversitesi Dil ve Tarih - Coğrafya Fakültesi Tarih Bölümü tarih araştırmalatı dergisi* 12 (1969): 49–55.

———. "The Administration of the Ṣanǰāq Registrations in Hungary." *AOASH* 21, no. 2 (1968): 181–223.

———. "The First Centuries of the Ottoman Military Organization." *AOASH* 31, no. 2 (1977): 147–83.

———. *Macaristan'da 16. yüzyılda Türk yönetimi.* Budapest: Török Tanszék, Eötvös Loránd Tudományegyetem, 1974.

———. "Two Sultanic H̱āṣṣ Estates in Hungary During The XVIth and XVIIth Centuries." *AOASH* 13, no. 1/2 (1961): 31–62.

Kamen, Henry. *Philip of Spain.* New Haven, CT: Yale University Press, 1997.

Karamustafa, Ahmet T. *God's Unruly Friends: Dervish Groups in the Islamic Later Middle Period, 1200–1500.* Salt Lake City: University of Utah Press, 1994.

Karateke, Hakan T., and Maurus Reinkowski, eds. *Legitimizing the Order: The Ottoman Rhetoric of State Power.* Leiden: Brill, 2005.

Kármán, Gábor, and Lovro Kunčević, eds. *The European Tributary States of the Ottoman Empire in the Sixteenth and Seventeenth Centuries.* Leiden: Brill, 2013.

Kasaba, Reşat. *A Moveable Empire: Ottoman Nomads, Migrants, and Refugees.* Seattle: University of Washington Press, 2009.

———. "Nomads and Tribes in the Ottoman Empire." In Woodhead, *The Ottoman World*, 11–24.

Kastritsis, Dimitris J. "Ferīdūn Beg's Münşe'ātü's-Selāṭīn ('Correspondence of Sultans') and Late Sixteenth-Century Ottoman Views of the Political World." In *Imperial Geographies in Byzantine and Ottoman Space*, edited by Sahar Bazzaz, Yota Batsaki, and Dimiter Angelov, 91–110. Washington, DC: Center for Hellenic Studies, 2013.

———. "The Revolt of Şeyh Bedreddin in the Context of the Ottoman Civil War of 1402–13." In *Political Initiatives "From the Bottom Up" in the Ottoman Empire:*

Halcyon Days in Crete 7, edited by Antonis Anastasopoulos, 221–38. Crete: University of Crete Press, 2012.

———. *The Sons of Bayezid: Empire Building and Representation in the Ottoman Civil War of 1402–1413*. Boston: Brill, 2007.

Kennedy, Hugh. *The Armies of the Caliphs: Military and Society in the Early Islamic State*. London: Routledge, 2001.

———. *The Prophet and the Age of the Caliphates: The Islamic Near East from the Sixth to the Eleventh Century*. 2nd ed. Harlow: Pearson Longman, 2004.

Kerslake, Celia J. "A Critical Edition and Translation of the Introductory Sections and the First Thirteen Chapters of the 'Selimname' of Celal Zade Mustafa Celebi." D.Phil., University of Oxford (United Kingdom), 1975.

———. "Ottoman Turkish." In *The Turkic Languages*, edited by Lars Johanson and Éva Ágnes Csató, 179–202. London: Routledge, 1998.

al-Khalidi, Ahmed. *Lubnān fī 'ahd al-Amīr Fakhr al-Dīn al-Ma'nī al-Thānī*. Beirut: al-Maktaba al-Bulusiya, 1936.

Khalidi, Tarif, ed. *Land Tenure and Social Transformation in the Middle East*. Beirut: American University of Beirut, 1984.

Khonsari, Mehdi, M. Reza Moghtader, and Minouch Yavari. *The Persian Garden: Echoes of Paradise*. Odenton, MD: Mage, 1998.

Khoury, Dina. "Administrative Practice Between Religious Law (Shari'a) and State Law (Kanun) on the Eastern Frontiers of the Ottoman Empire." *Journal of Early Modern History* 5, no. 4 (2001): 305–30.

———. "The Ottoman Centre Versus Provincial Power-Holders: An Analysis of the Historiography." In *The Cambridge History of Turkey*, edited by Suraiya Faroqhi, 3:133–56. New York: Cambridge University Press, 2007.

———. *State and Provincial Society in the Ottoman Empire: Mosul, 1540–1834*. Cambridge: Cambridge University Press, 1997.

Kili, Suna, and A. Şeref Gözübüyük. *Türk anayasa metinleri: Tanzimattan bügüne kadar*. Ankara: Ajans-Türk Mabtaası, 1957.

Klaniczay, Tibor. "The Age of Matthias Corvinus." In *The Renaissance in National Context*, by Roy Porter and Mikuláš Teich, 164–79. Cambridge: Cambridge University Press, 1992.

Kołodziejczyk, Dariusz. "Khan, Caliph, Tsar and Imperator: The Multiple Identities of the Ottoman Sultan." In Bang and Kołodziejczyk, *Universal Empire*, 181–83.

Konyalı, İbrahim Hakkı. *Söğüt' de Ertuğrul Gazi türbesi ve ihtifali [yazab] Ibrahim Hakki konyali*. Istanbul: Sinan Matbaasi, 1959.

Köprülü, Mehmed Fuad. "Anadolu Selçukları tarihinin yerli kaynakları." *Belleten* 7 (1943): 379–458.

———. "Bizans müessesselerinin Osmanlı müessesselerine te'siri hakkında bâzı mülâhazalar." *Türk hukuk ve iktisat tarihi mecmuası* 1 (1931): 165–313.

———. "İslam 'amme hukukundan ayrı bir Türk 'amme hukuku yok mudur." *Belleten* 2, no. 5–6 (1938): 39–72.

———. "Vakıf müessesesinin hukuki mahiyeti ve tarihi tekamülü." *VD* 2 (1942): 1–35.

Korobeinikov, Dimitri. *Byzantium and the Turks in the Thirteenth Century*. New York: Oxford University Press, 2014.

———. "How 'Byzantine' Were the Early Ottomans? Bithynia in ca. 1290–1450." Paper delivered at the Oxford Byzantine Seminar, Wolfson College, Oxford, Feb. 3, 2006.

Koselleck, Reinhart, and Michaela Richter. "Crisis." *Journal of the History of Ideas* 67, no. 2 (2006): 357–400.

Kraidy, Marwan M., and Omar al-Ghazzi. "Neo-Ottoman Cool: Turkish Popular Culture in the Arab Public Sphere." *Popular Communication* 11, no. 1 (2013): 17–29.

Krstić, Tijana. *Contested Conversions to Islam: Narratives of Religious Change in the Early Modern Ottoman Empire*. Stanford: Stanford University Press, 2011.

———. "Of Translation and Empire: Sixteenth-Century Ottoman Imperial Interpreters as Renaissance Go-Betweens." In Woodhead, *The Ottoman World*, 130–42.

Kubalı, Hüseyin Nail. *Türk esas tşkilat hukuku dersleri*. Istanbul: Siralar Matbaası, 1960.

Kumakura, Wakako. "Who Handed over Mamluk Land Registers to the Ottomans? A Study on the Administrators of Land Records in the Late Mamluk Period." *Mamluk Studies Review* 18 (2014): 279–98.

Kunt, İ. Metin. *The Sultan's Servants: The Transformation of Ottoman Provincial Government, 1550–1650*. New York: Columbia University Press, 1983.

Kütükoğlu, Mübahat S. "Mühimme defterlerinde muâmele kayıdları üzerine." In *Tarih boyunca paleografya ve diplomatik semineri*, 95–112. Istanbul: Başbakanlık devlet Arşivleri Genel Müdürlüğü, 1988.

Lambton, Ann K. S. "The Internal Structure of the Saljuq Empire." In *Theory and Practice*, 203–82.

———. "Islamic Mirrors for Princes." *La Persia nel Medioevo* (1971): 419–22.

———. "Islamic Political Thought." In *The Legacy of Islam*, edited by J. Schacht and C. E. Bosworth, 404–5. 2nd ed. Oxford: Oxford University Press, 1971.

———. *Landlord and Peasant in Persia: A Study of Land Tenure and Land Revenue Administration*. London: Oxford University Press, 1953.

———. *State and Government in Medieval Islam: An Introduction to the Study of Islamic Political Theory: The Jurists*. Oxford: Oxford University Press, 1981.

———. *Theory and Practice in Medieval Persian Government*. London: Variorum Reprints, 1980.

———. "Justice in the Medieval Persian Theory of Kingship." In *Theory and Practice*, 91–119.

Lefebvre, Henri. *The Production of Space*. Cambridge, MA: Blackwell, 1991.

Le Goff, Jacques. *History and Memory*. New York: Columbia University Press, 1992.

Levend, Agâh Sırrı. "Siyaset-nameler." *Türk dili araştırmaları yıllığı belleten*, 167–94. Ankara: Türk Tarih Kurumu Basımevi, 1962.

———. "Ümmet çağında ahlâk kitaplarımız." *Türk dili araştırmaları yıllığı belleten*, 89–115. Ankara: Türk Tarih Kurumu Basımevi, 1963.

Lewis, Bernard. "Defterdār." *EI2*.

———. "Dīvān-ı hümāyūn." *EI2*.

———. "Ottoman Land Tenure and Taxation in Syria." *SI*, no. 50 (1979): 109–24.

———. "Ottoman Observers of Ottoman Decline." *Islamic Studies* 1 (1962): 71–87.

———. *The Political Language of Islam*. Chicago: University of Chicago Press, 1988.

———. "Some Reflections on the Decline of the Ottoman Empire." *SI*, no. 9 (1958): 111–27.

Lewis, Martin W., and Kären Wigen. *The Myth of Continents: A Critique of Metageography*. Berkeley: University of California Press, 1997.

Lindner, Rudi Paul. *Nomads and Ottomans in Medieval Anatolia*. Indiana University Uralic and Altaic Series; vol. 144. Bloomington: Research Institute for Inner Asian Studies, Indiana University, 1983.

Lockman, Zachary. *Contending Visions of the Middle East: The History and Politics of Orientalism*. Cambridge: Cambridge University Press, 2004.

Lowry, Heath W. "The Ottoman Liva Kanunnames Contained in the Defter-I Hakani." *Osmanlı araştırmaları* 2 (1981): 43–74.

———. *Studies in Defterology: Ottoman Society in the Fifteenth and Sixteenth Centuries*. Istanbul: Isis Press, 1992.

Lugal, Necati, and Adnan Erzi. "Fâtih Sultan Mehmed'in muhtelif seferlerine ait fetihnāmeleri." *Istanbul Enstitüsü dergisi* 1 (1955): 169–84.

Lyber, Albert Howe. *The Government of the Ottoman Empire in the Time of Suleiman the Magnificent*. Cambridge, MA: Harvard University Press, 1913.

MacLean, Gerald M. *Looking East: English Writing and the Ottoman Empire Before 1800*. Basingstoke: Palgrave Macmillan, 2007.

Mahdi, Muhsin. *Alfarabi and the Foundation of Islamic Political Philosophy*. Chicago: University of Chicago Press, 2001.

———. *Ibn Khaldūn's Philosophy of History: A Study in the Philosophic Foundation of the Science of Culture*. Chicago: University of Chicago Press, 1964.

Mahdi, Muhsin, and Charles E. Butterworth. *The Political Aspects of Islamic Philosophy: Essays in Honor of Muhsin S. Mahdi*. Cambridge, MA: Harvard University Press, 1992.

Mandaville, Jon E. "Usurious Piety: The Cash Waqf Controversy in the Ottoman Empire." *IJMES* 10, no. 3 (1979): 289–308.

Mantran, Robert. *Istanbul dans la seconde moitié du XVIIe siècle; essai d'histoire institutionnelle, économique et sociale*. Paris: A. Maisonneuve, 1962.

Manzalaoui, M. "The Pseudo-Aristotelian *Kitāb al-Asrār*: Facts and Problems." *Oriens* 23–24 (1974): 147–257.

Markiewicz, Christopher. "The Crisis of Rule in Late Medieval Islam: A Study of Idrīs Bidlīsī (861–926/1457–1520) and Kingship at the Turn of the Sixteenth Century." PhD diss., University of Chicago, 2015.

Marlow, Louise. "The Way of Viziers and the Lamp of Commanders (*Minhāj al-wuzārā' wa-sirāj al-umarā'*) of Ahmad al-Isfahbadhī and the Literary and Political Culture of Early Fourteenth-Century Iran." In *Writers and Rulers: Perspectives on Their Relationship from Abbasid to Safavid Times*, edited by Beatrice Gruendler and Louise Marlow, 169–93. Wiesbaden: Reichert Verlag, 2004.

Masters, Bruce Alan. *The Arabs of the Ottoman Empire, 1516–1918: A Social and Cultural History*. Cambridge: Cambridge University Press, 2013.

Matuz, Josef. *Das Kanzleiwesen Sultan Süleymāns des Prächtigen*. Wiesbaden: F. Steiner, 1974.

———. "Die Pfortendolmetscher zur Herrschaftszeit Süleymân des Prächtigen." *Südost-Forschungen* 34 (1975): 26–60.

May, Timothy Michael. *The Mongol Conquests in World History*. London: Reaktion, 2012.

Meisami, Julie Scott. "Dynastic History and Ideals of Kingship in Bayhaqi's Tarikh-i Mas'udi." *Edebiyat* 3 (1989): 57–77.

———. "Exemplary Lives, Exemplary Deaths: The Execution of Hasanak." *Actas XVI Congresso UEAI*, edited by C. Vázquez de Benito and M. A. Manzano Rodríguez, 357–64. Salamanca: Union Européene d'Arabisants et d'Islamisants, 1995.

———. "Ghaznavid Panegyrics: Some Political Implications." *Iran* 28 (1990): 31–44.

———. *Persian Historiography to the End of the Twelfth Century*. Edinburgh: Edinburgh University Press, 1999.

———. "Rāvandī's Rāhat al-Ṣudūr: History or Hybrid?" *Edebiyat* 5 (1994): 181–215.

———. *The Sea of Precious Virtues* (Baḥr al-Favā'id). Salt Lake City: University of Utah Press, 1991.

———. "The Shāh-nāme as Mirror for Princes: A Study in Surveying Recent Literature on the Arabic and Persian Mirrors for Princes Genre Reception." In *Pand-o sokhan*, edited by Ch. Balay et al., 265–73. Tehran: Institut français de recherche en Iran, 1995.

Melikoff, Irene. "Ghāzi." *EI2*.

Ménage, Victor L. "On the Constituent Elements of Certain Sixteenth-Century Ottoman Documents." *BSOAS* 48, no. 2 (1985): 283–304.

———. "Some Notes on the 'Devshirme.'" *BSOAS* 29, no. 1 (1966): 64–78.

Meserve, Margaret. "News from Negroponte: Politics, Popular Opinion, and Information Exchange in the First Decade of the Italian Press." *Renaissance Quarterly* 59, no. 2 (2006): 440–80. https://doi.org/10.1353/ren.2008.0312.

Messick, Brinkley M. *The Calligraphic State: Textual Domination and History in a Muslim Society*. Berkeley: University of California Press, 1996.

Mikhail, Alan. *Nature and Empire in Ottoman Egypt: An Environmental History*. Cambridge: Cambridge University Press, 2011.

Mitchell, Colin Paul. "To Preserve and Protect: Husayn Va'iz-i Kashifi and Perso-Islamic Chancellery Culture." *Iranian Studies* 36, no. 4 (2003): 485–507.

Moačanin, Nenad. *Town and Country on the Middle Danube, 1526–1690*. Leiden; Brill, 2006.

Moosvi, Shireen. *The Economy of the Mughal Empire, c. 1595: A Statistical Study*. Delhi: Oxford University Press, 1987.

Morrison, Robert. "A Scholarly Intermediary Between the Ottoman Empire and Renaissance Europe." *Isis* 105, no. 1 (2014): 32–57.

Mottahedeh, Roy P. *Loyalty and Leadership in an Early Islamic Society*. Princeton, NJ: Princeton University Press, 1980.

Mulder, Stephennie F. *The Shrines of the 'Alids in Medieval Syria: Sunnis, Shi'is and the Architecture of Coexistence*. Edinburgh: Edinburgh University Press, 2014.

Mundy, Martha. "Ethics and Politics in the Law: On the Forcible Return of the Cultivator." In *İSAM Konuşmaları: Osmanlı düşüncesi, ahlāk, hukuk, felsefe-kelâm* (*İSAM Papers: Ottoman Thought, Ethics, Law, Philosophy-Kalam*), edited by Seyfi Kenan, 51–76. Istanbul: İslam Araştırmaları Merkezi, 2013.

Mundy, Martha, and Richard Saumarez Smith. *Governing Property: Making the Modern State Law Administration and Production in Ottoman Syria*. London: I. B. Tauris, 2007.

Murphey, Rhoads. "Book Review: Das osmanische 'Registerbuch der Beschwerden' (Şikayet Defteri) vom Jahre 1675. Band I: Einleitung, Reproduktion des Textes, geographische Indices." *Journal of the American Oriental Society* 106, no. 4 (1986): 811–12.

———. "Continuity and Discontinuity in Ottoman Administrative Theory and Practice During the Late Seventeenth Century." *Poetics Today* 14, no. 2 (1993): 419–43.

———. *Exploring Ottoman Sovereignty: Tradition, Image and Practice in the Ottoman Imperial Household, 1400–1800*. London: Continuum, 2008.

———. "Ottoman Sovereignty in Motion." In *Exploring Ottoman Sovereignty*, 207–51.

———. *Ottoman Warfare, 1500–1700*. New Brunswick, NJ: Rutgers University Press, 1999.

———. "Provisioning Istanbul: The State and Subsistence in the Early Modern Middle East." *Food and Foodways* 2, no. 1 (1987): 217–63.

———. *Regional Structure in the Ottoman Economy: A Sultanic Memorandum of 1636 A.D. Concerning the Sources and Uses of the Tax-Farm Revenues of Anatolia and the Coastal and Northern Portions of Syria*. Wiesbaden: Harrassowitz, 1987.

———. "Süleyman I and the Conquest of Hungary: Ottoman Manifest Destiny or a Delayed Reaction to Charles V's Universalist Vision." *Journal of Early Modern History* 5, no. 3 (2001): 197–221.

———. "The Veliyuddin Telhis: Notes on the Sources and Interrelations Between Koçi Bey and Contemporary Writers of Advice to Kings." *Belleten* 43 (1979): 547–71.

Necipoğlu, Gülru. *The Age of Sinan: Architectural Culture in the Ottoman Empire*. Princeton, NJ: Princeton University Press, 2005.

———. *Architecture, Ceremonial, and Power: The Topkapi Palace in the Fifteenth and Sixteenth Centuries*. New York: Architectural History Foundation; Cambridge, MA: MIT Press, 1991.

———. "Challenging the Past: Sinan and the Competitive Discourse of Early Modern Islamic Architecture." *Muqarnas* 10 (1993): 169–80. https://doi.org/10.2307/1523183.

———. "Framing the Gaze in Ottoman, Safavid, and Mughal Palaces." *Ars Orientalis* 23 (1993): 303–42.

———. "From Byzantine Constantinople to Ottoman Kostantiniyye: Creation of a Cosmopolitan Capital and Visual Culture Under Sultan Mehmed II." In *From Byzantion to Istanbul: 8000 Years of a Capital*, 262–78. Exhibition catalogue published in conjunction with an exhibition of the same title organized by and presented at Sakip Sabancı Museum, Sabancı University, Istanbul, June 5–Sept. 4, 2010.

———. "From International Timurid to Ottoman: A Change of Taste in Sixteenth-Century Ceramic Tiles." *Muqarnas* 7 (1990): 136–70. https://doi.org/10.2307/1523126.

———. "A Kanun for the State, a Canon for the Arts: Conceptualizing the Classical Synthesis of Ottoman Art and Architecture." In *Soliman le Magnifique et son temps: Actes du Colloque de Paris. Galeries nationales du Grand Palais, 7–10 Mars 1990*, edited by Gilles Veinstein, 195–216. Paris: La documentation française, 1992.

———. "The Life of an Imperial Monument: Hagia Sophia After Byzantium." In *The Hagia Sophia: From the Age of Justinian to the Present*, edited by Robert Mark and Ahmet S. Çakmak, 195–226. Cambridge: Cambridge University Press, 1992.

———. "Süleyman the Magnificent and the Representation of Power in the Context of Ottoman-Hapsburg-Papal Rivalry." In *Süleymân the Second and His Time*, edited by Halil İnalcık and Cemal Kafadar, 161–94. Istanbul: İsis Press, 1993.

———. "Word and Image: The Serial Portraits of Ottoman Sultans in Comparative Perspective." In *The Sultan's Portrait: Picturing the House of Osman*, edited by Selmin Kangal, 22–61. Istanbul: İş Bankası Kültür Yayınları, 2000.

Neumann, Christoph K. "Devletin adı yok—bir amblemin okunması [The state has no name—the reading of an emblem]." *Cogito* 19 (Summer 1999): 269–83.

Newman, A. J. "Davani, Jalal al-Din Mohammad." In *Encyclopedia Iranica*, vol. 7, 132–33. Costa Mesa, CA: Mazda, 1994.

Ocak, A. Y. "Bazı menâḳıbnâmelere göre xii. ve xv yüzyılllardaki ihtidâlarda heterodoks şeyh ve dervişlerin rolü." *Journal of Oriental Studies* 2 (1981): 31–42.

Ökten, Ertuğrul. "Ottoman Society and State in the Light of the Fetvas of İbn Kemal." MA thesis, Bilkent University, 1996.

Onay, Talat, and Cemal Kurnaz. *Eski Türk edebiyatında mazmunlar ve izahı*. Ankara: Turkiye Diyanet Vakfı, 1992.

Orbay, Ayşe. *The Sultan's Portrait: Picturing the House of Osman*. Istanbul: İşbank, 2000.

Ortaylı, İlber. "Osmanlı impartorluğu'nda iktisadi ve sosyal değişim." *Makaleler* 1. Ankara: Turhan Kitabevi, 2000.

Öz, Mehmet. *Osmanlıda "çözülme" ve gelenekçi yorumcuları*. Istanbul: Dergah Yayınları, 1997.

———. "Tahrir defterlerinin Osmanlı tarihi araştırmalarında kullanılması hakkında bazı düşünceler." *VD* 12 (1991): 429–39.

Özel, Oktay. "17. yüzyıl Osmanlı demografi ve iskan tarihi için önemli bir kaynak: 'mufassal' avārız defterleri." In *XII Türk Tarih kongresi*, 735–43. Ankara: Türk Tarih Kongresi Bildiriler, 1999.

———. *The Collapse of Rural Order in Ottoman Anatolia: Amasya 1576–1643*. Leiden: Brill, 2016.

———. "Nüfus baskısından 16.-17. yüzyıllarda Anadolunun demografı tarihine bir bakış." In *VIII. International Conference on the Economic and Social History of Turkey*, edited by Nurcan Abacı, 219–27. Morrisville, NC: Lulu, 2006.

———. "Population Changes in Ottoman Anatolia During the 16th and 17th Centuries: The 'Demographic Crisis' Reconsidered." *IJMES* 36, no. 2 (2004): 183–205.

Özvar, Erol. "Tarhuncu Ahmed Paşa." *İslam ansiklopedisi*, vol. 40, 20–22.

Pagden, Anthony. *The Burdens of Empire: 1539 to the Present*. New York: Cambridge University Press, 2015.

Pálffy, Géza. "The Origins and Development of the Border Defense System Against the Ottoman Empire in Hungary (Up to the Early Eighteenth Century)." In Dávid and Fodor, *Ottomans, Hungarians, and Habsburgs in Central Europe*, 4–69.

Pamuk, Şevket. "Institutional Change and the Longevity of the Ottoman Empire, 1500–1800." *Journal of Interdisciplinary History* 35, no. 2 (2004): 225–47.

———. *A Monetary History of the Ottoman Empire*. Cambridge: Cambridge University Press, 2004.

———. "The Price Revolution in the Ottoman Empire Reconsidered." *IJMES* 33, no. 1 (2001): 69–89.

———. "Prices in the Ottoman Empire, 1469–1914." *IJMES* 36, no. 3 (2004): 451–68.

Panaite, Viorel. *The Ottoman Law of War and Peace: The Ottoman Empire and Tribute Payers*. Boulder, CO: East European Monographs, 2000.

———. "Power Relationships in the Ottoman Empire: Sultans and the Tribute Paying Princes of Wallachia and Moldavia (16th–18th Centuries)." *Revue des Études Sud-Est Européennes* 37 (1999): 47–78.

———. "The Re'ayas of the Tributary-Protected Principalities: The Sixteenth Through the Eighteenth Centuries." *IJTS* 9 (2003): 79–104.

———. "The Voivodes of the Danubian Principalities as *Hâracgüzarlar* of the Ottoman Sultans." *IJTS* 9 (2003): 59–78.

Papp, Sándor. *Die Verleihungs-, Bekräftigungs- und Vertragsurkunden der Osmanen für Ungarn und Siebenbürgen: Eine quellenkritische Untersuchung*. Wien: Verlag der Österreichischen Akademie der Wissenschaften, 2003.

Parker, Geoffrey. "The General Crisis of the Seventeenth Century Revisited." *American Historical Review* 113, no. 4 (2008): 1029–99.

———. *Global Crisis: War, Climate Change and Catastrophe in the Seventeenth Century*. New Haven, CT: Yale University Press, 2013.

Parmaksızoğlu, İsmet. "Kemāl Pāşa-zāde." *TDVİA*. Vol. 6, 561–66.

Peachy, William S. "Register of Copies or Collection of Drafts? The Case of Four Mühimme Defters from the Archives of the Prime Ministry in Istanbul." *Turkish Studies Association Bulletin* 10, no. 2 (n.d.): 79–85.

Peacock, A. C. S., ed. *The Frontiers of the Ottoman World*. Oxford: Oxford University Press, 2009.

———. *Early Seljūq History: A New Interpretation*. London: Routledge, 2010.

Peirce, Leslie P. "Changing Perceptions of the Ottoman Empire: The Early Centuries." *Mediterranean Historical Review* 19, no. 1 (2004): 6–28.

———. "Domesticating Sexuality: Harem Culture in Ottoman Imperial Law." In *Harem Histories: Envisioning Places and Living Spaces*, edited by Marilyn Booth, 104–35. Durham: Duke University Press, 2010.

———. *The Imperial Harem: Women and Sovereignty in the Ottoman Empire*. New York: Oxford University Press, 1993.

———. *Morality Tales: Law and Gender in the Ottoman Court of Aintab*. Berkeley: University of California Press, 2003.

Pere, Nuri. *Osmanlılarda Madeni Para*. Istanbul: Doğan Kardeş Matbaacılık, 1968.

Peters, Rudolph. *Crime and Punishment in Islamic Law: Theory and Practice from the Sixteenth to the Twenty-First Century*. Cambridge: Cambridge University Press, 2005.

Petkov, Kiril. *The Kiss of Peace: Ritual, Self, and Society in the High and Late Medieval West*. Leiden: Brill, 2003.

Pfeifer, Helen. "Encounter After the Conquest: Scholarly Gatherings in 16th-Century Ottoman Damascus." *IJMES* 47, no. 2 (2015): 219–39.

Pfeiffer, Judith. "Confessional Polarization in the 17th Century Ottoman Empire and Yūsuf ibn Ebī 'Abdü'd-Deyyān's Keşfü'l-Esrār fī Ilzāmi'l-Yehūd ve'l-Aḥbār." In *Contacts and Controversies Between Muslims, Jews and Christians in the Ottoman Empire and Pre-modern Iran*, edited by Camilla Adang and Sabine Schmidtke, 15–55. Würzburg: Ergon, 2010.

———. "Teaching the Learned: Jalāl al-Dīn al-Dawānī's *Ijāza* to Mu'ayyadzāda 'Abd al-Raḥmān Efendi and the Circulation of Knowledge Between Fārs and the Ottoman Empire at the Turn of the Sixteenth Century." In *The Heritage of Arabo-Islamic Learning: Studies Presented to Wadad Kadi*, edited by Maurice A. Pomerantz and Aram Shahin, 284–332. Leiden and Boston: Brill, 2015.

Piterberg, Gabriel. *An Ottoman Tragedy: History and Historiography at Play*. Berkeley: University of California Press, 2003.

Pixley, Michael M. "The Development and Role of the Şeyhülislam in Early Ottoman History." *Journal of the American Oriental Society* 96, no. 1 (1976): 89–96.

Pocock, J. G. A. *The Machiavellian Moment: Florentine Political Thought and the Atlantic Republican Tradition.* 2nd ed. Princeton, NJ: Princeton University Press, 2003.

———. *Virtue, Commerce, and History: Essays on Political Thought and History, Chiefly in the Eighteenth Century.* Cambridge: Cambridge University Press, 1985.

al-Qattan, Najwa. "Textual Differentiation in the Damascus *Sijill*: Religious Discrimination or Politics of Gender?" In *Women, the Family, and Divorce Laws in Islamic History*, edited by Amira El Azhary Sonbol, 191–202. Syracuse, NY: Syracuse University Press, 1996.

Quataert, Donald. *Consumption Studies and the History of the Ottoman Empire, 1550–1922: An Introduction.* Albany: State University of New York Press, 2000.

———. "Ottoman History Writing and Changing Attitudes Towards the Notion of Decline." *History Compass* 1, no. 1 (2003): 1–9.

Raby, Julian. "From Europe to Istanbul." In *The Sultan's Portrait: Picturing the House of Osman*, edited by Selmin Kangal, 136–63. Istanbul: İş Bankası Kültür Yayınları, 1968.

Rafeq, Abdul-Karim. *al'-Arab wa'l-'Uthmaniyun, 1516–1916.* 2nd ed. Damascus: Atlas, 1993.

———. *Bilād al-Shām wa-Miṣr min al-fatḥ al-'Uthmānī ila' ḥamlat Nābilyūn Būnābirt (1516–1798).* Damascus: N.p., 1967.

———. "Mazahir iqtisadiyya wa'ijtima'iyya min liwa' Hamah, 942–3 AH (1535–6)." *Dirasat Tarikhiyya Damascus University* 31–32 (1989): 17–66.

———. *The Province of Damascus: 1723–83.* Beirut: Khayats, 1966.

———. "The Syrian 'Ulama, Ottoman Law and Islamic Sharī'a." *Turcica* 26 (1994): 9–29.

Raman, Bhavani. *Document Raj: Writing and Scribes in Early Colonial South India.* Chicago: University of Chicago Press, 2012.

Redworth, Glyn, and Fernando Checa. "The Courts of the Spanish Habsburgs, 1500–1700." In *The Princely Courts of Europe: Ritual, Politics and Culture Under the Ancien Régime 1500–1750*, edited by John Adamson, 43–65. London: Weidenfeld and Nicolson, 1999.

Repp, R. C. *The Müfti of Istanbul: A Study in the Development of the Ottoman Learned Hierarchy.* London: Ithaca Press, 1986.

Reychman, Jan, and Ananiasz Zajączkowski. *Handbook of Ottoman-Turkish Diplomatics.* Rev. and exp. translation by Andrew S. Ehrenkreutz. Edited by Tibor Halasi-Kun. The Hague: Mouton, 1968.

Rice, Eugene F., and Anthony Grafton. *The Foundations of Early Modern Europe, 1460–1559.* New York: Norton, 1994.

Riedlmayer, Andras. "Ottoman Copybooks of Correspondence and Miscellanies as a Source for Political and Cultural History." *AOASH* 61, no. 1–2 (2008): 201–14.

Rodríguez-Salgado, Mía. "The Court of Philip II of Spain." In Asch and Birke, *Princes, Patronage, and the Nobility*, 205–44.

Rohde, David. "The Islamic World's Culture War, Played Out on TV Soap Operas." *Atlantic*, March 9, 2012. http://www.theatlantic.com/international/archive/2012/03/the-islamic-worlds-culture-war-played-out-on-tv-soap-operas/254247/.

Rosenthal, Erwin Isak Jakob. *Political Thought in Medieval Islam: An Introductory Outline*. Cambridge: Cambridge University Press, 1962.

Rosenthal, Franz. *Knowledge Triumphant: The Concept of Knowledge in Medieval Islam*. Leiden: Brill, 2007.

Rothman, E. Natalie. *Brokering Empire: Trans-imperial Subjects Between Venice and Istanbul*. Ithaca, NY: Cornell University Press, 2012.

———. "Dragomans and 'Turkish Literature': The Making of a Field of Inquiry." *Oriente Moderno* 93, no. 2 (2013): 390–421.

———. "Interpreting Dragomans: Boundaries and Crossings in the Early Modern Mediterranean." *Comparative Studies in Society and History* 51, no. 4 (2009): 771–800.

Rousselin, Mathieu. "Turkish Soap Power: International Perspectives and Domestic Paradoxes." *Euxeinos* 10 (2013): 16–22.

Ruiz, Teofilo F., Geoffrey Symcox, and Gabriel Piterberg, eds. *Braudel Revisited: The Mediterranean World, 1600–1800*. Toronto: University of Toronto Press, 2010.

Şahin, Kaya. *Empire and Power in the Reign of Süleyman: Narrating the Sixteenth-Century Ottoman World*. New York: Cambridge University Press, 2013.

Said, Edward W. *Culture and Imperialism*. New York: Knopf, 1993.

———. *Orientalism*. London: Penguin, 2003.

———. "Reflections on Exile." *Granta* 13 (1984): 159–72.

Sajdi, Dana. *The Barber of Damascus: Nouveau Literacy in the Eighteenth-Century Ottoman Levant*. Stanford: Stanford University Press, 2013.

———. "'Decline' and Its Discontents and Ottoman Cultural History: By Way of Introduction." In *Ottoman Tulips, Ottoman Coffee: Leisure and Lifestyles in the Eighteenth Century*, edited by Dana Sajdi, 1–40. London: I. B. Tauris, 2008.

———. "Ibn Kannan." *Historians of the Ottoman Empire*, edited by Cemal Kafadar, Hakan Karateke, and Cornell Fleischer, University of Chicago Division of the Humanities, 2010. https://ottomanhistorians.uchicago.edu/sites/ottomanhistorians.uchicago.edu/files/ibnkannan_en.pdf.

———. "Muhammad b. Isa Ibn Kannan (d. 1741)." *Historians of the Ottoman Empire*, edited by Cemal Kafadar, Hakan Karateke, and Cornell Fleischer, University of Chicago Division of the Humanities, 2010. https://ottomanhistorians.uchicago.edu/en/historian/ibn-kannan.

———. "Peripheral Visions: The Worlds and Worldviews of Commoner Chroniclers in the 18th Century Ottoman Levant." PhD diss., Columbia University, 2002.

Salibi, Kamal. "Mount Lebanon Under the Mamluks." In *Quest for Understanding: Arabic and Islamic Studies in Memory of Malcolm Kerr*, edited by Samir Seikaly, Ramzi Baalbaki, and Peter Dodd, 15–32. Beirut: American University of Beirut, 1991.

———. "Northern Lebanon Under the Dominance of Ǧazir, 1517–91." *Arabica* 14 (June 1967): 144–66.

———. "The Sayfās and the *Eyalet* of Tripoli, 1579–1640." *Arabica* 20 (Feb. 1973): 25–52.

———. "The Secret of the House of Ma'n." *IJMES* 4, no. 3 (1973): 272–87.

Salzmann, Ariel C. "An Ancien Régime Revisited: 'Privatization' and Political Economy in the Eighteenth-Century Ottoman Empire." *Politics and Society* 21, no. 4 (1993): 393–423.

———. "Measures of Empire: Tax Farmers and the Ottoman Ancien Régime, 1695–1807." PhD diss., Columbia University, 1995.

———. *Tocqueville in the Ottoman Empire: Rival Paths to the Modern State*. Leiden: Brill, 2004

Sarınay, Yusuf, ed. *Başbakanlık Osmanlı arşivi rehberi*. 3rd ed. Istanbul: Başbakanlık Basımevi, 2010.

Sariyannis, Marinos. *Ottoman Political Thought up to the Tanzimat: A Concise History*. Hellas: Institute for Mediterranean Studies, 2015.

———. "The Princely Virtues as Presented in Ottoman Political and Moral Literature." *Turcica* 43 (2011): 121–44.

———. "Prostitution in Ottoman Istanbul, Late Sixteenth–Early Eighteenth Century." *Turcica* 40 (2008): 37–65.

———. "Ruler and State, State and Society in Ottoman Political Thought." *Turkish Historical Review* 4, no. 1 (2013): 83–117. https://doi.org/10.1163/18775462-00401004.

Schaendlinger, Anton C., and Claudia Römer. *Die Schreiben Sûleyman des Prächtigen an Karl V., Ferdinand I und Maximilian II.* Vienna: Verlag der Österreichischen Akademie der Wissenschaften, 1983.

Sellers-García, Sylvia. *Distance and Documents at the Spanish Empire's Periphery*. Stanford: Stanford University Press, 2014.

Semerdjian, Elyse. *"Off the Straight Path": Illicit Sex, Law, and Community in Ottoman Aleppo*. Syracuse, NY: Syracuse University Press, 2008.

Şen, Ahmet Tunç. "A Mirror for Princes, a Fiction for Readers: The Habnāme of Veysī and Dream Narratives in Ottoman Turkish Literature." *Journal of Turkish Literature* 8 (2011): 41–65.

Sertoğlu, Midhat. "Tarih-i Tuği." *Belleten* 11 (1947): 489–514.

Setton, Kenneth M. *A History of the Crusades*. 2nd ed. 6:248–49. Madison: University of Wisconsin Press, 1989.

———. *The Papacy and the Levant, 1204–1571: The Sixteenth Century to the Reign of Julius III*. Vol. 3. Philadelphia: American Philosophical Society, 1976.

Shank, J. B. "Crisis: A Useful Category of Post-Social Scientific Historical Analysis?" *American Historical Review* 13, no. 4 (2008): 1090–99.

Shaw, Stanford J. *Empire of the Gazis: The Rise and Decline of the Ottoman Empire, 1280–1808*. Vol. 1 of *History of the Ottoman Empire and Modern Turkey*. Cambridge: Cambridge University Press, 1976.

Shefer-Mossensohn, Miri. *Science Among the Ottomans: The Cultural Creation and Exchange of Knowledge.* Austin: University of Texas Press, 2015.

Shehadeh, Raja. "In Pursuit of My Ottoman Uncle: Reimagining the Middle East Region as One." *Journal of Palestine Studies* 40, no. 4 (2011): 82–93.

———. *A Rift in Time: Travels with My Ottoman Uncle.* London: Profile, 2010.

Shinder, Joel. "Early Ottoman Administration in the Wilderness: Some Limits on Comparison." *IJMES* 9, no. 4 (1978): 497–517.

Sigalas, Nikos. "Devlet et Etat: Du glissement sémantique d'un ancien concept du pouvoir au début du XVIIIe siècle Ottoman." In *Byzantina et moderna: Mélanges en l'honneur d'Hélène Antoniadis-Bibicou*, edited by Gilles Grivaud and Sokratis Petmezas, 385–415. Athens: Ekdoseis Alexandreia, 2007.

Singer, Amy. *Constructing Ottoman Beneficence: An Imperial Soup Kitchen in Jerusalem.* Albany: State University of New York Press, 2002.

———. "Marriages and Misdemeanors: A Record of Resmi-'arūs ve bād-ı havā." *Princeton Papers in Near Eastern Studies* 4 (1996): 113–52.

———. *Palestinian Peasants and Ottoman Officials: Rural Administration Around Sixteenth-Century Jerusalem.* Cambridge: Cambridge University Press, 1994.

Sönmez, Ebru. *Idris-i Bidlisi: Ottoman Kurdistan and Islamic Legitimacy.* Istanbul: Libra Kitap, 2012.

Starkey, David. "Court, Council and Nobility in Tudor England." In Asch and Birke, *Princes, Patronage, and the Nobility*, 175–203.

Starn, Randolph. "The Early Modern Muddle." *Journal of Early Modern History* 6, no. 3 (2002): 296–307.

———. "Historians and 'Crisis.'" *Past and Present*, no. 52 (1971): 3–22.

Steedman, Carolyn. *Dust: The Archive and Cultural History.* New Brunswick, NJ: Rutgers University Press, 2002.

———. "The Space of Memory: In an Archive." *History of the Human Sciences* 11, no. 4 (1998): 65–83.

Stoler, Ann Laura. *Along the Archival Grain: Epistemic Anxieties and Colonial Common Sense.* Princeton, NJ: Princeton University Press, 2009.

Subrahmanyam, Sanjay. "Aspects of State Formation in South India and Southeast Asia, 1500–1650." *Indian Economic and Social History Review* 23, no. 4 (1986): 357–77.

———. "Connected Histories: Notes Towards a Reconfiguration of Early Modern Eurasia." *Modern Asian Studies* 31 (1997): 735–62.

———. *Courtly Encounters Translating Courtliness and Violence in Early Modern Eurasia.* Cambridge, MA: Harvard University Press, 2012.

———. "Written on Water: Designs and Dynamics in the Portuguese Estada da Índia." In *Empires: Perspectives from Archaeology and History*, edited by Susan E. Alcock, Terence N. D'Altroy, Kathleen D Morrison, and Carla M. Sinopoli, 42–69. Cambridge: Cambridge University Press, 2001.

Subtelny, Maria E. "A Late Medieval Persian *Summa* on Ethics: Kashifi's Akhlāq-i Muhsini." *Iranian Studies* 36, no. 4 (2003): 601–13.

Sümer, Faruk, Ahmet Edip Uysal, and Warren S. Walker, eds. *The Book of Dede Korkut: A Turkish Epic*. Austin: University of Texas Press, 1972.

Szabó, János B. "'Splendid Isolation'? The Military Cooperation of the Principality of Transylvania with the Ottoman Empire (1571–1688) in the Mirror of the Hungarian Historiography's Dilemmas." In *The European Tributary States of the Ottoman Empire in the Sixteenth and Seventeenth Centuries*, edited by Gábor Kármán and Lovro Kunčević, 301–40. Leiden: Brill, 2013.

Szakály, Ferenc. "The Early Ottoman Period, Including Royal Hungary, 1526–1606." In *A History of Hungary*, edited by Peter F. Sugar, Péter Hanák, and Tibor Frank, 83–99. Bloomington: Indiana University Press, 1990.

———. "Phases of Turco-Hungarian Warfare Before the Battle of Mohács (1365–1526)." *AOASH* 33 (1979): 65–111.

Taeschner, Franz. "Neşri tarihi el yazıları üzerine araştırmalar." *Belleten* 15 (1951): 497–505.

Taylor, Malissa. "Keeping Usufruct in the Family: Popular and Juridical Interpretations of Ottoman Land Tenure Law in Damascus." *Bulletin d'études orientales*, no. 61 (Dec. 1, 2012): 429–43.

Temelkuran, Tevfik. "Dīvān-ı hümāyūn mühimme kalemi." *Tarih Enstitüsü Dergisi* 6 (1975): 161–75.

Tezcan, Baki. "II. Osman örneğinde 'ilerlemeci' tarih ve Osmanlı tarih yazıcılığı." In *Osmanlı düşünce*. Vol. 7, edited by Güler Eren, 658–68. Ankara: Yeni Türkiye Yayınları, 1999.

———. "The Definition of Sultanic Legitimacy in the Sixteenth Century Ottoman Empire: The Ahlāk-i Alā'ī of Kınalızâde Alî Çelebi (1510–1572)." Master's thesis, Princeton University, 1996.

———. "Ethnicity, Race, Religion and Social Class: Ottoman Markers of Difference." In Woodhead, *The Ottoman World*, 159–70.

———. "The History of a 'Primary Source': The Making of Tūghī's Chronicle on the Regicide of Osman II." *BSOAS* 72, no. 1 (2009): 41–62.

———. "The 'Kānūnnāme of Mehmed II': A Different Perspective." In *The Great Ottoman-Turkish Civilization*, edited by Kemal Çiçek, 3:657–65. Ankara: Yeni Türkiye, 2000.

———. "The Memory of the Mongols in Early Ottoman Historiography." In *Writing History at the Ottoman Court: Editing the Past, Fashioning the Future*, edited by H. Erdem Cipa and Emine Fetvaci, 23–38. Bloomington: Indiana University Press, 2013.

———. "Ottoman Historical Writing." In *The Oxford History of Historical Writing*, edited by Jose Rabasa, Masayuki Sato, Edoardo Tortarolo, and Daniel Woolf. Reprint. Vol. 3, *1400–1800*, 192–211. Oxford: Oxford University Press, 2015.

———. "The Ottoman Monetary Crisis of 1585 Revisited." *Journal of the Economic and Social History of the Orient* 52, no. 3 (2009): 460–504.

———. "The Politics of Early Modern Ottoman Historiography." In Aksan and Goffman, *The Early Modern Ottomans*, 167–98.

———. "Searching for Osman: A Reassessment of the Deposition of the Ottoman Sultan Osman II, 1618–1622." PhD diss., Princeton University, 2001.

———. *The Second Ottoman Empire: Political and Social Transformation in the Early Modern World.* New York: Cambridge University Press, 2010.

Todorova, Olga. "The Ottoman State and Its Orthodox Christian Subjects: The Legitimistic Discourse in the Seventeenth-Century 'Chronicle of Serres' in a New Perspective." *Turkish Historical Review* 1, no. 1 (2010): 86–110.

Totman, Conrad. *The Green Archipelago.* Berkeley: University of California Press, 1989.

Trevor-Roper, H. R. "The General Crisis of the 17th Century." *Past and Present*, no. 16 (1959): 31–64.

Tulum, Mertol. "Dursun Bey." *TDVİA.* Vol. 10, 6–7.

Turan, Ebru. *The Sultan's Favorite: İbrahim Pasha and the Making of the Ottoman Universal Sovereignty in the Reign of Sultan Süleyman (1516–1526).* Chicago: University of Chicago Press, 2007.

———. "Voices of Opposition in the Reign of Sultan Süleyman: The Case of İbrahim Paşa (1523–36)." In *Studies on Istanbul and Beyond*, edited by Robert G. Ousterhout, 23–35. Philadelphia: University of Pennsylvania Press, 2007.

Turan, Osman. *Selçuklular zamanında Türkiye: siyasî tarih Alp Arslan'dan Osman Gazi'ye, 1071–1318.* 12th ed. Istanbul: Ötüken, 2013.

Tveritinova, Anna S., and Jurij A. Petrosjan, eds. *Badā'i' al-Waḳā'i'.* 2 vols. Moscow: Russian Academy of Sciences, 1961.

Tyan, E. "Bay'a." *EI2.*

Uluçay, Cağatay. "Koçi Beyin Sultan İbrahime takdim ettiği risale ve arzları." In *Zeki Velidi Togan Armağanı*, 177–99. Istanbul: N.p., 1950–55.

———. "Yavuz Sultan Selim nasıl padişah oldu." *Tarih dergisi* 6, no. 9 (1954): 53–90.

———. "Yavuz Sultan Selim nasıl padişah oldu." *Tarih dergisi* 7, no. 10 (1954): 117–42.

———. "Yavuz Sultan Selim nasıl padişah oldu." *Tarih dergisi* 8, no. 11–12 (1955): 185–200.

Ursinus, Michael. *Grievance Administration (Şikayet) in an Ottoman Province: The Kaymakam of Rumelia's "Record Book of Complaints" of 1781–1783.* London: Routledge Curzon, 2005.

Uzunçarşılı, İsmail Hakkı. *Anadolu beylikleri ve Akkoyunlu, Karakoyunlu devletleri.* 4th ed. Ankara: Türk Tarih Kurumu Basımevi, 1988.

———. *Buyruldı.* Istanbul: Maarif Matbaası, 1941.

———. *Osmanlı devletinin ilmiye teşkilâtı.* Ankara: Türk Tarih Kurumu Basımevi, 1965.

———. *Osmanlı devletinin merkez ve bahriye teşkilâtı.* Ankara: Türk Tarih Kurumu Basımevi, 1948.

———. *Osmanlı tarihi*. Ankara: Türk Tarih Kurumu Basımevi, 1947.

———. *Osmanli tarihine ait yeni bir vesikanin ehemmiyeti ve izahi ve bu münasebetle Osmanlılarda ilk vezirlere dair mütalea*. Istanbul: Devlet Basımevi, 1939.

———. *Tuğra ve pençeler ile ferman ve buyurdulara dair*. Istanbul: Maarif Matbaası, 1941.

———. "Tuğra ve pençeler ile ferman ve buyurdulara dair." *Belleten* 5 (1941): 101–57.

Üstün, İsmail Safa. "Heresy and Legitimacy in the Ottoman Empire in the Sixteenth Century." PhD diss., University of Manchester, 1991.

Valensi, Lucette. *The Birth of the Despot: Venice and the Sublime Porte*. Translated by Arthur Denner. Ithaca, NY: Cornell University Press, 1993.

Van Gelder, Geert Jan. "Mirror for Princes or Vizor for Viziers: The Twelfth-Century Arabic Popular Encyclopedia Mufīd al-ʿulūm and Its Relationship with the Anonymous Persian Baḥr al-fawāʾid." *Bulletin of the School of Oriental and African Studies, University of London* 64 (2001): 313–38.

Veinstein, Gilles. "Some Views on Provisioning in the Hungarian Campaigns of Suleyman the Magnificent." In *Osmanistische Studien zur Wirtschafts- und Sozialgeschichte: In memoriam Vančo Boškov*, edited by Vančo Boškov and Hans Georg Majer, 177–85. Wiesbaden: O. Harrassowitz, 1986.

Venzke, Margaret. "The Ottoman Tahrir Defterleri and Agricultural Productivity: The Case for Northern Syria." *Osmanlı araştırmaları* 17 (1997): 1–13.

Vries, Jan de. *The Economy of Europe in an Age of Crisis, 1600–1750*. Cambridge: Cambridge University Press, 1976.

Weber, Wolfgang. "What a Good Ruler Should Not Do: Theoretical Limits of Royal Power in European Theories of Absolutism, 1500–1700." *Sixteenth Century Journal* 26, no. 4 (1995): 897–915.

White, Sam. *The Climate of Rebellion in the Early Modern Ottoman Empire*. New York: Cambridge University Press, 2011.

Wigen, Einar. "Ottoman Concepts of Empire." *Contributions to the History of Concepts* 8, no. 1 (2013): 44–66.

Wigen, Einar, Chris Gratien, and Timur Hammon. "Empire in Question: Did the Ottomans Consider Themselves an Empire?" Ottoman History Podcast, no. 77. Podcast audio, Nov. 5, 2012. www.ottomanhistorypodcast.com/2012/11/ottoman-empire-was-history-name.html.

Wilkins, Charles L. *Forging Urban Solidarities: Ottoman Aleppo, 1640–1700*. Leiden: Brill, 2010.

Winter, Stefan. "The Province of Raqqa Under Ottoman Rule, 1535–1800: A Preliminary Study." *Journal of Near Eastern Studies* 68 (2009): 253–68.

———. *The Shiites of Lebanon Under Ottoman Rule, 1516–1788*. Cambridge: Cambridge University Press, 2012.

Wittek, Paul. *The Rise of the Ottoman Empire*. London: Royal Asiatic Society, 1938.

Wong, Roy Bin. *China Transformed: Historical Change and the Limits of the European Experience.* Ithaca, NY: Cornell University Press, 1997.

Woodhead, Christine. "An Experiment in Official Historiography: The Post of Şehnāmeci in the Ottoman Empire, c. 1555–1605." *Wiener Zeitschrift für die Kunde des Morgenlandes* 75 (1983): 157–82.

———. "Ottoman Languages." In Woodhead, *The Ottoman World*, 143–58.

———, ed. *The Ottoman World.* New York: Routledge, 2012.

———. "Taliqizade Mehmed." *Historians of the Ottoman Empire*, edited by Cemal Kafadar, Hakan Karateke, and Cornell Fleischer, University of Chicago Division of the Humanities, 2010. https://ottomanhistorians.uchicago.edu/en/historian/taliqizade-mehmed.

———. "Ṭursun Beg." *EI2*.

Yavari, Neguin. *Advice for the Sultan: Prophetic Voices and Secular Politics in Medieval Islam.* London: Hurst, 2014.

Yaycıoğlu, Ali. *Partners of the Empire: The Crisis of the Ottoman Order in the Age of Revolutions.* Stanford: Stanford University Press, 2016.

———. "Provincial Power-Holders and the Empire in the Late Ottoman World: Conflict or Partnership?" In Woodhead, *The Ottoman World*, 436–52.

Yılmaz, Hüseyin. "The Sultan and the Sultanate: Envisioning Rulership in the Age of Süleyman the Lawgiver (1520–1566)." PhD diss., Harvard University, 2004.

Yılmaz, Mehmet Şakir. "Koca Nişancı of Kanuni: Celalzade Mustafa Çelebi, Bureaucracy and 'Kanun' in the Reign of Süleyman the Magnificent (1520–1566)." PhD diss., Bilkent University, 2006.

Yücel, Yaşar. *Anadolu beylikleri hakkında araştırmalar I: Çoban-oğulları beyliği candar-oğulları beyliği mesalikü'l-ebsara göre anadolu beylikleri.* 2nd ed. Ankara: Türk Tarih Kurumu Basımevi, 1991.

Zachariadou, Elizabeth. "Les notables laïques et le patriarcat œcuménique après la chute de Constantinople." *Turcica* 30 (1998): 119–34.

———, ed. *The Ottoman Emirate (1300–1389): Halcyon Days in Crete I: A Symposium Held in Rethymnon 11–13 January 1991.* Rethymnon: Crete University Press, 1993.

Zandi-Sayek, Sibel. "Poetry, Pleasure, and Building: Ottoman Architectural Culture in the Eighteenth Century." *Eighteenth-Century Life* 34, no. 3 (2010): 130–34.

Zarinebaf, Fariba. *Crime and Punishment in Istanbul: 1700–1800.* Berkeley: University of California Press, 2010.

Ze'evi, Dror. *An Ottoman Century: The District of Jerusalem in the 1600s.* Albany: State University of New York Press, 1996.

———. "The Use of Shari'a Court Records as a Source for Middle Eastern Social History: A Reappraisal." *Islamic Law and Society* 5 (1998): 35–46.

Zilfi, Madeline C. *The İlmiye Registers and the Ottoman Medrese System Prior to the*

Tanzimat. In *Contributions à l'histoire économique et sociale de l'Empire Ottoman*, edited by J. L. Bacqué-Grammont and P. Dumont, 309–27. Leuven: Editions Peeters, 1983.

———. "The Kadizadelis: Discordant Revivalism in Seventeenth-Century Istanbul." *Journal of Near Eastern Studies* 45, no.4 (1986): 251–69.

———. "A Medrese for the Palace: Ottoman Dynastic Legitimation in the Eighteenth Century." *Journal of the American Oriental Society* 113, no. 2 (1993): 184–91.

———. *The Politics of Piety: The Ottoman Ulema in the Postclassical Age (1600–1800)*. Minneapolis, MN: Bibliotheca Islamica, 1988.

Zirinski, R. "How Did the Ottomans Become Ottoman? The Construction of an Imperial Brand Name in the Time of Cultural Big Bang." *AO* 22 (2004): 125–58.

Ziyada, Khalid. *Al-Sura al-taqlidiyya li-al-mujtama' al-madani: Qira 'a manhajiyya fi sijillat mahkamat Trablus al-shar'iyya fi al-qarn al-sabi' 'ashar wa-bidayat al-qarn al-thamin 'ashar*. Tripoli: Lebanese University, 1983.

INDEX

Page numbers in *italics* refer to illustrations.

Kolibri 360 GmbH
Ferdinand-Jühlke-Straße 7
99095 Erfurt, Deutschland
produktsicherheit@kolibri360.de